AUTOBIOGRAPHY
OF AN
OCTOGENARIAN

BY

ROBERT ENOCH WITHERS, M.D.

COLONEL 18TH REGIMENT VIRGINIA INFANTRY,
C.S.A.; EDITOR *LYNCHBURG DAILY NEWS*;
LIEUTENANT-GOVERNOR OF VIRGINIA; SENATOR OF
THE UNITED STATES; MEMBER OF BOARD OF
REGENTS OF THE SMITHSONIAN INSTITUTE; CONSUL
OF THE UNITED STATES AT HONG-KONG; PAST
GRAND MASTER OF THE KNIGHTS TEMPLAR OF THE
UNITED STATES, ETC., ETC.

HERITAGE BOOKS
2006

HERITAGE BOOKS
AN IMPRINT OF HERITAGE BOOKS, INC.

Books, CDs, and more—Worldwide

For our listing of thousands of titles see our website
at
www.HeritageBooks.com

A Facsimile Reprint
Published 2006 by
HERITAGE BOOKS, INC.
Publishing Division
65 East Main Street
Westminster, Maryland 21157-5026

Copyright © 1907 R. E. Withers
Wytheville, Virginia

— Publisher's Notice —
In reprints such as this, it is often not possible to remove blemishes from the original. We feel the contents of this book warrant its reissue despite these blemishes and hope you will agree and read it with pleasure.

International Standard Book Number: 978-0-7884-2366-5

EPIGRAM BY GEORGE WITHER, THE POET, ON THE WITHER ARMS AND CREST

"To his loving friend and Cousin German Mr. William Wither" (of Manydown), A.D. 1620.

"If that the *Standards* of the House bewray
What *Fortunes* to the owners may betide;
Or if their Destinies, as some men say,
Be in the names of any signified,
'Tis so in thine; for that faire antique Shield
Borne by thy Predecessors long ago,
Depainted with a clear pure *Argent* field,
The innocence of thy line did shew.
Three sable Crescents with a Chevron gul'de
Tells that black *fates* obscured our houses light;
Because the Planet that our fortunes rul'd
Lost her own lustre, and was darkened quite:
    And, as indeed our Adversaries say,
    The very name of Wither shows decay.
And yet despair not, keep thy *White* sustained,
And then it skills not what thy *Crescents* be.
What though the Moon be now increased, now waned?
Learn thence to know thy life's inconstancy;
Be careful as thou hitherto has been,
To shun th' Abuses *Man* is tax't for here:
And then thy soul that's now eclipsed with sin,
When *Moon* and *Sun* are darkened, shall look clear;
And what so'er thy English name may threat,
The *Harvest's son* the *Greeks* entitle thee.
Ere thou shalt want, thy *Hare* will bring thee meat,
And to kill care, herself thy make-sport be:
    Yea, yet (though *Ennui's* mists do make them dull)
    I hope to see the waned *Orbs* at full."

NOTE BY G. W.—For the better understanding of this Epigram, note that his *Arms* are a Field Argent, a Chevron Gules, betwixt three Crescents Sable. His *name* according to the Greeks is υἱθερος (υἱὸς, son; θέρος, summer or harvest). His *Crest* a Hare with three Wheat ears in her mouth.

COL. R. E. WITHERS

AUTOBIOGRAPHY *of an* OCTOGENARIAN

BY

ROBERT ENOCH WITHERS, M. D.

COLONEL 18TH REGIMENT VIRGINIA INFANTRY, C. S. A.; EDITOR LYNCHBURG DAILY NEWS; LIEUTENANT-GOVERNOR OF VIRGINIA; SENATOR OF THE UNITED STATES; MEMBER OF BOARD OF REGENTS OF THE SMITHSONIAN INSTITUTE; CONSUL OF THE UNITED STATES AT HONG-KONG; PAST GRAND MASTER OF THE KNIGHTS TEMPLAR OF THE UNITED STATES, ETC., ETC.

1907

THE STONE PRINTING & MFG. CO. PRESS
ROANOKE, VIRGINIA

COPYRIGHT, 1907,
BY
R. E. WITHERS, WYTHEVILLE, VA.

CONTENTS.

CHAPTER		PAGE
	Introductory...	5
I	Genealogical...	7
II	Biographical and Anecdotal.............................	14
III	Early School Days......................................	26
IV	Sagacity of Dogs and Horses............................	43
V	Temperate Habits.......................................	53
VI	Politics in the Olden Time.............................	57
VII	University Life..	64
VIII	Life in a City Hospital................................	78
IX	Sporting Incidents by Field, Forest, and Stream........	89
X	Country Practice.......................................	101
XI	I Meet My Fate...	105
XII	A Pigeon Roost...	118
XIII	A Change of Base.......................................	122
XIV	War..	128
XV	Reorganization of the Army—Battles of Williamsburg and Seven Pines..	173
XVI	Battles Around Richmond................................	183
XVII	The Prison Post at Danville............................	195
XVIII	Fight at Staunton River Bridge.........................	204
XIX	Danville the Seat of Government........................	214
XX	Chaos..	218
XXI	Danville Under a Provost Marshal.......................	226
XXII	I Turn Over a New Leaf.................................	234
XXIII	Political Life...	245
XXIV	Life on a Farm...	265
XXV	On the Waters of Sandy—Fun on Sandy....................	281
XXVI	A New Rôle	293
XXVII	Coffee and Pistols for Two.............................	307
XXVIII	Elected to the Senate of the United States.............	317
XXIX	Senator of the United States...........................	321
XXX	Pen-and-Ink Sketches...................................	325
XXXI	Impeachment of General W. W. Belknap...................	343
XXXII	The Electoral Commission...............................	350
XXXIII	New Senators in the Forty-fifth Congress	360
XXXIV	Death and Obsequies of Professor Henry—Remonetization of Silver..	372
XXXV	The Rise, Maturity, and Collapse of Readjusters........	377
XXXVI	Lee's Recumbent Statue.................................	390
XXXVII	Democratic Congress....................................	398

CHAPTER		PAGE
XXXVIII	Drifting	411
XXXIX	In Private Life	416
XL	Again an Editor	424
XLI	Crossing the Pacific	434
XLII	Life in Hong-Kong	440
XLIII	A Visit to Canton	450
XLIV	China New Year	460
XLV	Macao	464
XLVI	Caught in a Typhoon	470
XLVII	Revisit Virginia	478
XLVIII	"The King of the Cannibal Islands"	484
XLIX	Life at the Consulate	489
L	Visit from Admiral Chandler	500
LI	Farewell to Hong-Kong	508
LII	"Carry Me Back to Old Virginny"	517
LIII	Relegated to Private Life	525
LIV	Visit to Pittsburg	533
LV	Fifty-fifth Wedding Anniversary	541

INTRODUCTORY.

For some years past I have been urged by personal friends and especially by relatives, to put on record some of the experiences and observations of a long life passed amid the varied and stirring scenes in which my lot has been cast, but have not yielded to these solicitations, partly because I doubted whether a recital of these incidents was of sufficient importance to arrest the attention, or awaken the interest of the public, and partly because I felt unequal to the task of recalling and recording these, in such terms as would satisfy even these partial friends. In addition I rather shrank from the physical labor involved in such an undertaking.

Circumstances, however, have conspired to modify to some extent these considerations. The lonely life to which I was relegated by the death of a dearly loved wife, who for more than half a century had with ready sympathy shared my joys and sorrows, enforced idleness incident to old age, and the absence of congenial occupation, combined to produce a change of sentiment and inclined me to entertain a proposition previously regarded with little favor. Added to this was the flattering request made by two or three publishing houses in New York and Chicago, asking me to furnish a biographical sketch for insertion in cyclopedias or dictionaries in course of preparation. Compliance with these requests necessitating some recall of past events in my life, led me to undertake this autobiography.

Doubtless there will be found in it much that should have been omitted, details of trivial incidents of little interest except to the immediate actors, and possibly criticisms on men and things unwarranted by my position and opportunities of observation; but I can honestly aver that I have narrated as facts no incidents which I did not believe true, criticised nothing that I did not deem worthy of criticism, but have tried not to "set down aught in malice." Of course I must expose myself to the charge of egotism, as a certain degree of that failing is inseparable from any autobiography, but I hope it is not so conspicuous as to be offensive.

Whether this sketch embodies anything of sufficient worth "to point a moral or adorn a tale" the public must judge, but I feel that it will be welcomed and appreciated by those for whose gratification and at whose request it has been recorded. "What is writ is writ, would it were worthier," and with this quotation I leave it.

R. E. WITHERS.

Wytheville, Virginia, February 22d, 1904.

Autobiography of an Octogenarian.

CHAPTER I.

GENEALOGICAL.

[This may be passed over by the public as it will interest only the family connection.]

The first Withers to come to America of whom I have any knowledge was John, and he came from Lancashire, England, about the middle of the seventeenth century, and settled in the northern part of the State, where he died toward the close of the century. He evidently prospered in business, and left a large landed estate, which he disposed of by will, dated the twenty-ninth of August, 1698, and recorded in the Clerk's Office of Fairfax County, Virginia. The following quotation from that testament found in Henning's statutes, will be of interest to his descendants: "An Act, to settle a controversy between William Withers and Augustine Washington," found in Henning's Statutes at Large, Volume "C," Chapter 12, from the 28th of George II, recites as follows:

"Whereas, John Withers, formerly of the County of Stafford, in this Colony, deceased, etc., etc., * * * by his last will and testament bearing date the twenty-ninth of August, 1698, devised 'Chotank,' a parcel of land lying in the Parish of St. Paul and County of Stafford, to his daughter, Sarah Withers, for her life, and after her death to his cousin, William Withers, and heirs male of his body, and for fault of such issue to Thomas Withers, of Lancaster, in great Britain, and his male heirs, and for want of such heirs to any one proving himself to be of the name of Withers as by the said will may more fully appear, and died so seized; and the said William Withers died in this Colony soon after the testator, John Withers, without male issue, having never been married; and the said Thomas Withers in the will aforesaid named afterwards departed this life in England; leaving issue, Edmond

Withers, his oldest son and male heir, who also died in England; leaving his brother, William Withers, another son of the said Thomas Withers, his male heir, and the said William Withers last named also died in England; leaving issue, Thomas Withers, his oldest son and male heir, who also died there; leaving issue William Withers, his oldest son and heir male of his body; and whereas the said Sarah Withers, the daughter and devisee of the said John Withers in the will aforesaid named, after the death of her said father, entered into the said tract or parcel of land called Chotank, and afterwards intermarried with one Christopher Conway; and after the death of her said husband, by her certain indentures of lease and release, bearing date respectively the tenth and thirteenth days of June, one thousand seven hundred and twenty-seven, for the consideration therein mentioned, did sell and convey the said tract or parcel of land called Chotank to Augustine Washington, late of the County of King George, now deceased, and to his heirs and assigns forever; and the said Augustine Washington entered into the said tract or parcel of land called Chotank, and by his last will and testament in writing, bearing date the eleventh day of April, one thousand seven hundred and fifty-three, devised the same to his son, Samuel Washington, now an infant, and his heirs; and by his said will directed that if the said land called Chotank should be recovered from the said Samuel Washington, now an infant, that he should have an equivalent out of the estate by the said will devised to his son, Augustine Washington, as by the said will may more fully appear.

"And whereas several disputes and controversies have arisen between the said William Withers and Augustine Washington concerning their respective rights to the said five hundred and thirty acres of land called Chotank, after the death of the said Conway, who is still living, the said William Withers claiming the same as male heir under the aforesaid will of the said John Withers, and the said Samuel Washington insisting that he had a right to the said land under the aforementioned deeds of the said Sarah Conway and in the said part recited will of Augustine Washington, and the said disputes and controversies concerning the titles to the said lands will be very tedious and expensive as the witnesses to prove the pedigree of the said William Withers are ancient and infirm and most of them live in Great Britian. Wherefore it has been agreed between the said William Withers and the said Augustine Washington, etc."

It is unnecessary to recite further the prolix and verbose preamble or the Act itself. The basis of settlement was an agreement that Washington was to have the land and pay to Withers the sum of five hundred pounds sterling for it.

This William Withers, who had the controversy with Augustine Washington over the ownership of Chotank, had a son named Thomas, who married and left a large family, one of whom, Enoch Keane Withers, was my grandfather. He was the fourth son of Thomas Withers, was born October 14th, 1760; married Jennet Chinn, May 15th, 1786, and died of apoplexy at his home, "Green Meadows," in Fauquier County, July 26th, 1813. The mother of his wife was a Scotch woman named Janet Scott, and was of the same family as Sir Walter, the poet and novelist.

Enoch Keane Withers left six sons and three daughters:

First. Thomas Thornton, born December 11th, 1790; died February 6th, 1855; never married.

Second. Alexander Scott, born October 12th, 1792; married Melinda Fisher; died January 23d, 1865, in Weston, West Virginia.

Third. Robert Walter, born February 22d, 1795; married Susan Dabney Alexander, February 26th, 1819; died October 23d, 1881, in Campbell County.

Fourth. Edward Ball, born January 2d, 1797; married Evelina W. Payne, of Campbell County; died March 10th, 1849.

Fifth. Horatio Chinn, born April 14th, 1799; married Caroline Fitzhugh; died May 20th, 1840.

Sixth. Henry Howard, born October 20th, 1805; died August 7th, 1838; never married.

The daughters were:

First. Eliza Scott, born 1787; married George Lemmon, an Episcopal minister of Baltimore; died June 2d, 1845.

Second. Jane Margaretta, born October 2d, 1788; never married; died 1847.

Third. Mary Enoisa, born January 15th, 1802; married Dr. Samuel B. Fisher; died April 25th, 1867.

My father, Dr. Robert W. Withers, married Susan Dabney Alexander, youngest daughter of Robert Alexander of "Rock Castle," Campbell County, February 26th, 1819. They lived to see the sixty-second anniversary of their marriage, he dying in 1881, and she only lived three months longer. They had a family of eleven children, seven sons and four daughters.

First. Jennet Ann, born April 14th, 1820; died January 27th, 1881; married Dr. Robert Thornton Lemmon, leaving offspring.

Second. Robert Enoch, born September 18th, 1821; still living; married Mary Virginia Royall, of Lynchburg, Virginia, oldest daughter of Joseph Edwin and Elizabeth Royall. They lived to celebrate the fifty-fifth anniversary of their marriage. She died in Evansville, Indiana, while on a visit to her oldest daughter, Mrs. Elizabeth Royall Carter, on the second day of March, 1901, leaving a large family.

Third. Mary Elizabeth, born November 24th, 1823; married George D. Saunders, a lawyer of Buckingham County, Virginia, on the twenty-eighth of December, 1854; still living (1903), has several children.

Fourth. Flora Virginia, born August 28th, 1825; married Philip Thornton Withers (her cousin) November 22d, 1846; still living, has several children.

Fifth. William Alexander, born March 16th, 1827; married Alice Cabell, of Greenbriar County, Virginia, October 14th, 1856; still living; several children.

Sixth. John Thornton, born November 23d, 1828; died in Hospital, June 20th, 1861; was Assistant Surgeon 3d Regiment Virginia Infantry; married Henrietta Alexander, of Pulaski County, Virginia, December 25th, 1857; left one daughter.

Seventh. Edward Horatio, born September 25th, 1830; died December 20th, 1846.

Eighth. Susan Catharine, born November 4th, 1832 (living); married Patrick Massie, of Nelson County, Virginia, June 18th, 1857; has several children.

Ninth. Henry Howard, born July 31st, 1836; died December, 1901; married, first, Mary Y. Anderson of Nelson County, Virginia, November 8th, 1859, and second, Miss Adams, of Campbell County; left issue by each.

Tenth. Walter Lemmon, born January 16th, 1837 (living); married Bettie Hamilton, of Nelson County, Virginia, January 22d, 1868; has issue.

Eleventh. Austin Chinn, born December 21st, 1841; died May 28th, 1883; married Missouri T. Riddick, of Suffolk, Virginia, June 1st, 1871; leaving issue.

All of the six brothers of this family served in the army of the Confederate States.

My grandfather, Robert Alexander, was a native of Rockbridge County, Virginia, his father, Robert Alexander, established the first classical school west of the Blue Ridge, which subsequently became "Liberty Hall Academy," and afterwards Washington College and Washington and Lee University. He was first cousin to Archibald Alexander, of Princeton, New Jersey. The ancestors of the Alexanders came to Pennsylvania from the north of Ireland after the seige of Londonderry and subsequently to the Valley of Virginia. My grandfather was a noted person of some peculiarities. When grown to man's estate he was appointed a Deputy in the Clerk's Office of Bedford County, Virginia, under the noted Clerk of the County, "Jemmy Steptoe," who, as Howe's History of Virginia tells us, was so overcome by the wit and eloquence of Patrick Henry in the trial of the celebrated "Hook Case," that he left his table and ran out into the yard where he rolled on the ground in uncontrollable laughter. When the County of Campbell was formed from Bedford in 1784, Robert Alexander was appointed Clerk and held the office until his death in 1820.

He was married on the tenth day of March, 1774, in the County of Bedford, to Ann Austin, daughter of William Austin, a captain in the British Army. They had ten children.

First. William Alexander, born September 7th, 1776; never married; was murdered by George W. Poindexter, September 12th, 1800, who was condemned and executed for the crime in Pittsylvania County, to which county the trial was moved by Poindexter's counsel on the allegation that he could not receive a fair trial in Campbell County.

Second. Esther, born July 18th, 1778; married Micajah Moorman; moved to Tennessee, where she died about 1840; had issue.

Third. Sally, born October 18th, 1779; married Nathaniel J. Manson, of Bedford County; had a large family; died March, 1861.

Fourth. John, born January 25th, 1782; married Sally Cobbs, of the County of Bedford; succeeded his father as Clerk of Campbell County, and held the office until his death August 13th, 1838.

Fifth. Nancy, born May 8th, 1784; married Adam Clement, of Campbell County; had large family; died November 15th, 1864.

Sixth. Elizabeth, born February 16th, 1787; married Dr. J. T. W. Read, of Bedford County; died January 10th, 1833; leaving issue.

Seventh. Charlotte Austin, born January 15th, 1790; died February 8th, 1809.

Eighth. Mary Glenn, born October 3d, 1793; married William Garland Pendleton, of Richmond; died, leaving issue.

Ninth. Catharine Wilson, born January 17th, 1796; married Dr. Nathaniel W. Payne, of Campbell; died July 26th, 1838, in Mississippi; leaving issue.

Tenth. Susan Dabney, born January 22d, 1799; married Dr. Robert W. Withers, of Fauquier County, Virginia; died February 14th, 1882, at the home of her son-in-law, George D Saunders, in Buckingham County.

I was the second child and oldest son of Robert Walter Withers and Susan Dabney Alexander. Born September 18th, 1821; married February 3d, 1846, Mary Virginia Royall, eldest daughter of Joseph Edwin Royall and Elizabeth Gwatkin, of Lynchburg, Virginia. We had twelve children, viz.:

First. Elizabeth Royall, born November 30th, 1846; married Dr. E. Lewis Carter, of Hanover County, Virginia, August 10th, 1864, in Danville, Virginia. He died in Evansville, Indiana, August 19th, 1894, of apoplexy, leaving three sons and two daughters.

Second. Susan Dabney, born August 4th, 1848; married Henry S. Williams, of Mecklenburg County, Virginia, December 21st, 1865. Have three sons and four daughters. Now living in Martinsville, Henry County, Virginia.

Third. Alice Chinn, born January 10th, 1850; married Edmond Pendleton Goggin, of Lynchburg, Virginia, on June 17th, 1869; died in Bedford County, Virginia, October 31st, 1892, of typhoid fever, leaving one son.

Fourth. Jennett Ann, born December 7th, 1851; married Henry Cook, of Alexandria, January 25th, 1872; was divorced for statutory cause January, 1897, and in August 21st, 1902, married Major Waller Boyd, of Nelson County, Virginia; no children.

Fifth. Mary Virginia, born January 21st, 1853; died July 5th, 1855.

Sixth. Josephine, born December 15th, 1854; married John T. Read, of Henry County, January 13th, 1876, who died in Martinsville, Virginia, leaving two sons.

Seventh. Kate Massie, born October 30th, 1856; married G. Woodville Smith, of Lynchburg, Virginia, February 8th, 1877; has two daughters.

Eighth. Betty Ellison, born March 11th, 1858; married Stephen Putney, of Richmond, Virginia, November 7th, 1877. Has one son and one daughter.

Ninth. Willie Clare, born August 6th, 1859; unmarried.

Tenth. Virginia Secessia, born April 22d, 1861; married John Terry, of Wytheville, Virginia, February 3d, 1896; now living in Seattle; has one son.

Eleventh. Robert Edwin, born March 13th, 1865; married Mary C. Kent, of Wythe County, Virginia, June 2d, 1892. Has one son. Now living near Pittsburg, Pennsylvania.

Twelfth. Mary Thornhill, born September 19th, 1867; died October 21st, 1874.

The tenth daughter, Virginia Secessia, was only eight hours old when her father left home to join the armies of the Confederacy, and she was married on the "Golden Wedding" anniversary of her parents, February 3d, 1896.

CHAPTER II.

BIOGRAPHICAL AND ANECDOTAL.

My earliest recollections cluster around the old "Rock Castle" house, where I was born, and where my grandfather, Robert Alexander, lived and died. He was a man of many peculiarities. From boyhood he was noted for strict integrity and especially for his truthfulness. A family tradition handed down from his early years amusingly illustrates this trait. It is said that on one occasion late in the fall of the year he was sent by his mother to the house of a neighbor who had contracted to weave the cloth required for the children's winter clothes, but who had postponed the completion of her job, until the advent of cold weather had entirely exhausted the patience of her customer. "Robert," said she, "go to the weaver's and tell her to send that cloth home at once, the weather is cold and all the children are naked."

Robert started at once, but on the way reflected on the message with which he had been charged, and came to the conclusion that he could not tell her the children were naked, when he was visibly clothed. So as he passed through a piece of woods, he deliberately undressed, hid his clothes in a hollow tree and then went on to the weaver and delivered his message verbatim. His appearance gave added emphasis to the urgency of the message, and it is said the woman jumped to the loom and made the shuttle fly until the web was completed.

He possessed to an unusual degree that valuable attribute known as "common sense," a fine fund of humor, utterly fearless, of fine business qualifications, an accomplished Clerk, in the days when that office was reckoned the most important in the county organization. He acquired a large property in land and negroes and wielded an immense influence in the community. Added to these attributes he possessed an imposing and striking personality and manners unusually pleasant and prepossessing on all ordinary occasions, but unfortunately, he was at times addicted to an inordinate indulgence in strong drink, a weakness which in those days was regarded very leniently and detracted but little from his influence in the community. When "in his cups," he was perhaps one of the most reckless and fun-loving men who ever lived. Many anecdotes illustrative of this still linger in the minds of the old citizens of Campbell County.

About one hundred yards from the Rock Castle Mansion stood an old Colonial church called "Mollie's Creek Church," in a grove of beautiful oaks between the house and the spring. Of course it was no longer used by the Church of England, of which there was scarcely a representative left in the land. Located on the premises of Robert Alexander, he claimed and exerted a proprietary right over the building, and when Methodist or Baptist preachers asked permission to hold services in the church he always granted the privilege subject to one condition, viz.: that they should conduct themselves in an orderly manner and have no shouting or undue excitement in their exercises. It occasionally happened that "the Captain," as he was called, was on a "spree" when service was held, and then there was a lively time, for as soon as the singing, exhorting and shouting commenced, and the outsiders crowded the windows to look in on the excited congregation, the "old Captain" would appear at the hall window, which looked towards the church, with his long gun, and with stentorian voice would order them to "clear the way." Of course there was an immediate stampede from the end window next to the house, and then "bang!" would go the old gun and the shot would rattle on the weatherboarding like hail, and some of them passing through the open window would so alarm the crowd that the meeting generally was broken up.

When I was a child I heard an old woman who lived near by say, that she had herself been in the congregation on an occasion such as I have described, and in further proof I have often, when a school boy, picked shot from the weatherboarding to make sinkers for my minnow hooks. The old church was blown down during a violent storm about 1830, I think.

He always hated the sound of a cow bell, and the barking of a fice dog, and either being heard, day or night, would arouse him to action and his long gun would be called into instant service to abate the nuisance.

The Clerk's Office building was in his field above the spring and on court days he would take all the books and records he would be likely to need during the term, and with his deputy in his coach and four, drive to the court-house, about ten miles. His deputy was for many years Alexander Austin, a half brother of his wife. The trip to the court-house was usually without any special occurrence of note, but the return trip was often marked by spicy incidents, according to the narrations of my "Uncle Alec." The presiding magistrate of the court was a gentleman named Talbot, who lived a few miles from Rock Castle, and for some time he and his large family connection had control of the bench of magistrates, and did not hesitate to avail themselves of this fact. About the time of the war with Great Britain in 1812, there was great financial trouble in the country and many suits brought to enforce collection of claims. But whenever a judgment of execution was likely to be ordered against any of the special friends or supporters of the presiding magistrate, he would, from the bench, order the sheriff to adjourn the court, and if any objection was raised, the dominant faction would always sustain the motion for adjournment. As this seriously impaired the income of the clerk, it was exceedingly distasteful to him. After dinner and sundry bowls of toddy, the start on the return trip was made. The Clerk and the presiding magistrate with many of his adherents traveled the same road for ten miles or so, and at one place they had to go through a long lane for nearly two miles, the road was both rocky and hilly. The "Old Captain" would so manage as to bring up the rear of the crowd when they reached this lane, from which, when once entered, there was no exit. He would then give orders to his coachman, Luke, to "drive over the d--n rascals," and Luke would put whip to the horses, the Talbot crowd would ply whip and spur to keep out of the way, the "old Captain" occasionally putting his head out of the window and imitating the peculiar squeaking voice of Talbot would mimic his order of adjournment, "Sheriff, adjourn the court until the court in course—" "Drive over the d--n rascals, Luke!" Over the hills and down the dales the race would sweep, the coach lurching first one side and then the other. "Uncle Alec" hurled from back seat to front—now on the seat, now on the floor—deed books, will books, and record books of all sorts flying around; Luke whipping the four horses in full gallop, the Talbot crowd straining to keep ahead of the coach until the mouth of the lane was reached and they could free themselves from their pursuers by turning out into the woods, where it was not possible for the coach to follow. I've enjoyed few laughs more in my early years than while listening to "Uncle Alec" Austin recounting these and similar experiences while deputy clerk.

On one occasion the office building caught fire in some way, and two of the Captain's servants, Luke and Squire, were conspicuous in their efforts to save the books and papers, in which they were so successful that there was little loss of important documents, and their "old master" praised them highly for their zeal, and promised them their freedom when he died, as an additional reward for their efficient service. When he did die, and his will was read, it was found that it contained no provision for the manumission of Luke and Squire, but they both claimed their freedom under this verbal promise of "old master," and no one attempted to interfere; neither executor nor legatee raised a voice in the matter, and they were left in full enjoyment of their freedom. Squire, I think, died before my recollection, but Luke, the old coachman, lived to be a very old man and I have very often seen him when he would come up on his annual visits to his "old mistress." I think he was for some years "overseer" to a planter who lived on Falling River, eight or ten miles from Rock Castle.

I fear that the incident related may produce the impression that my grandfather was a devotee of the bottle and a really hard drinker, but this was not the case. He was thoroughly a gentleman of high tone, a kind-hearted, benevolent man, enjoying the esteem and respect of the whole community, of polished manners, and exerted more influence over the citizens of Campbell than any man in the county. His excesses were only occasional and in those days the drinking habit was universal.

He sometimes, however, met his match when he perpetrated his practical jokes. The sheriff of the county was a man named

Sackville King. He came to Rock Castle on one occasion to attend to some business and found the Captain in the highest state of jocularity. He evidenced this by watching his opportunity to seize the sheriff's hat and throw it behind the roaring fire. Old King made no effort to rescue it, but went into the hall, took the Captain's hat from the rack, put it on his head, mounted his horse and rode off, getting decidedly the best of the trade. No one enjoyed the joke more than my grandfather, and he laughed over it for a long while.

This man King was quite an odd fish himself. He lived to a great age and was twice High Sheriff of the county. When we recall the fact that the High Sheriff of a county was appointed because he had served longer on the bench of magistrates than any other justice, it shows how rarely it fell to the lot of one man to fill the office twice.

I remember him well. He lived in a log cabin, and during the latter years of his life, no white person lived with him. He had his coffin made several years before his death, and kept it under the bed on which he nightly slept. On one occasion he told an enquiring friend that he found the coffin a very useful piece of furniture, as it was "the only safe place to keep his apples, as the little niggers never stole them from that receptacle."

But enough of this—my grandfather Alexander died suddenly in November, 1820, of paralysis.

My grandfather Withers was a staid and dignified country gentleman, devoted to his family, an ardent Federalist, and of course thoroughly detested Thomas Jefferson, the father of Democracy, as was shown in this incident: At his home, "Green Meadows," in Fauquier County, the family were one night aroused by a most unearthly and unaccountable noise apparently proceeding from the dining-room, and my grandmother, in alarm, asked him to see what on earth was the matter. This was before the invention of matches, so without delaying until a light could be procured, as the moon was brightly shining, he entered the dining-room whence the noise continued in unabated volume, and he was able to see something moving over the floor.

"What is it, Mr. Withers?" called my grandmother impatiently.

"My dear," was the reply, "it is either the devil or Tom Jefferson, I can't say which."

When a light was finally procured, the cause of the alarm was seen to be the house cat, which, having been accidentally shut up in the room, found the cream jug, and forcing her head into it to feast on the cream, was unable to draw it out again, and in the effort to free herself both she and the cream jug rolled off the table on the floor, the handle was broken, and she was rolling the jug around on the floor in the vain effort to extricate herself from her dilemma.

My grandfather was in his meadow one hot day in July, 1813, superintending the hay-making, when he fell to the ground in an apoplectic fit, was carried by the negroes to the house, but never recovered consciousness and died in a short time.

During the war with Great Britain in 1812-14, when the British commenced their movement to capture Washington City, the naval forces passed up the Potomac to the city of Alexandria, then a large shipping port, and a place of considerable importance. The American forces, consisting mainly of militia from the adjacent counties, were encamped below Alexandria at the "White House," where the banks were high and it was believed that the British men-of-war could not elevate their guns sufficiently to bear upon the crest of the hill. My father, then a boy of sixteen, had been sent to the army to carry supplies to his elder brothers who were in camp, and happened to be there when the British fleet came up the river and very soon demonstrated the futility of the hope that the guns could not be elevated sufficiently to reach the top of the hill. The "Sea Horse," the largest of the vessels, soon scattered the raw recruits by a few broadsides, causing some casualties. While the British were occupying the city, the Americans, by the aid of glasses, could see the enemy busy rolling barrels of flour, bacon and other commodities along the streets to the wharf to be conveyed to the fleet.

Wishing to conciliate the enemy, as threats had been made to burn the town, some of the leading citizens gave a ball to the officers of the army and navy, at the old "Braddock House." Learning of the proposed festivities, a lot of adventurous officers of the American troops determined to make a raid on the revelers.

They set off on horseback about eleven o'clock, drove in the pickets, and entered the ball room, fully armed, and ordered the surrender of the officers present. Some obeyed the demand, others jumped out of the windows and gave the alarm, the drums soon roused the troops, and the raiding party stood not on the order of their going, but left at once, attempting, however, to carry off their prisoners, but my father said he thought they failed in this, and all the captured escaped before they cleared the city.

The next morning, bright and early, a delegation of the leading citizens of Alexandria were in camp very earnestly remonstrating against the foolish act of the raiders, which, they alleged, very seriously endangered the safety of the city, as the British officers alleged that the citizens of Alexandria had planned and aided the expedition. The burning of the city in retaliation was seriously debated for some time, but better councils eventually prevailed.

These incidents completed my father's experiences in the war of 1812-14.

Not long after this he determined to pursue a mercantile career, and was placed in the counting house of an old Scotch merchant at Falmouth, which at that time was a place of considerable importance. Several Scotch merchants were living there and carrying on a large and profitable importing trade with English and Scotch ports in their own ships. Among these merchants was Mr. Basil Gordon, with whom my grandfather traded a good deal, and to him was my father sent.

Fredericksburg, on the opposite side of the Rappahannock, was a place of less importance than Falmouth, but amongst its mercantile firms was William Knox & Co. Knox married a daughter of Mr. Gordon. Mr. Gordon was an early riser, and it was his custom to walk every morning about sunrise across the long bridge connecting the two towns. During the war of 1812-14, the stock of groceries, particularly of coffee, gradually shrank, and prices, of course, advanced. The stage which brought the mail from Richmond to Washington passed through Fredericksburg and Falmouth and always stopped for breakfast at the first-named town and after half an hour's delay came on to Falmouth.

Mr. Knox on opening his mail found one morning that there had been a great advance in the price of coffee. Remembering the habits of Mr. Gordon, he put off to the bridge and met him on his matutinal walk, and after the usual salutation and some casual conversation, said: "By the way, Mr. Gordon, what are you selling coffee at?" "About so and so, I believe," giving the figure, said Mr. Gordon. "How much have you on hand?" "I do not know exactly, but a pretty good quantity." "Well, Mr. Gordon, I'll take all you have," said Mr. Knox. "Good morning."

When Mr. Gordon got his mail a little later and saw how great had been the rise in price, he simply remarked, "Well, well, Willie Knox could skin a Yankee."

This year the wheat crop at "Green Meadows" was of poor quality, the grain had a great deal of rye in it, which was hard to separate with the defective appliances then in vogue, so when the first wagon-load was sent to Falmouth, it was accompanied by a note to Mr. Gordon from my grandfather to this effect:

"DEAR SIR: I send per wagon a load of wheat, slightly mixed with rye, for which you will allow me as good a price as you can afford, etc."

Mr. Gordon replied as follows:

DEAR SIR: I have received per wagon a load of rye slightly mixed with wheat, for which I can afford to pay, etc."

As I said, Mr. Gordon was very systematic in his habits. He was a temperate man, but was accustomed to take a tumbler of Scotch whiskey grog every day at midday. It was always weak, having a large proportion of water. The porter of the store was an Irishman named Patrick McDougal, who was fond of the "O be joyful," and not infrequently indulged his appetite to such an extent that he was unfitted for work for a day or two at a time, very much to the annoyance of his employer.

On one occasion Patrick had come to the store after one of these sprees very penitent and remorseful. Mr. Gordon was about to take his midday glass and while mixing it was lecturing Pat for his insatiable appetite for whiskey, when Pat spoke up in self-defense, "Why Misther Gordon, you love a drap of whiskey more than I do missilf." "How can you make out that," replied Mr. Gordon, "I take one drink of grog a day, and you never saw me drunk, and you have lost several days from drunkenness." "Well," said Pat, "I've niver seen the day yit when I would dhrink all that water for the little whiskey that's in it." This closed the incident.

I recall one other circumstance connected with my father's sojourn in Falmouth. He was from a boy devoted to field sports, a taste which I inherited to the fullest extent. Hunting and fishing in all the branches of either sport, possessed for him an irresistible attraction.

While living in Falmouth there came a June rise in the Rappahannock, and that meant a probable run of sturgeon. At night my father procured a boat, a rower, and a sturgeon hook and tackle, and anchored in a sluice at the falls of the river, put out his line and anxiously waited for a "rub." Sturgeons do not take a bait, but are caught with three or four large hooks tied together at the end of a strong cord and heavily weighted. This is held in the hand in the strong currents which are the pass ways of the fish running up stream, as they pass this line held by the fisherman, the sensation of something rubbing along the line is felt, the fisherman jerks violently and if lucky, strikes one or more hooks into the body of the fish, and by skilful playing, the game is soon landed. There were several boats out on the night in question, and as a good many logs and drift wood were running down the river, it not unfrequently happened that a rub was followed by burying the hooks into a floating log. My father felt something distinctly rubbing along his line, but felt sure it was a log, but for his fun called to his friends in another boat that he had a "rub," and to carry out the joke made a violent jerk of the line, but the sudden check, the sensation of something solid, but more than all, the dash of the fish, waked him to the full consciousness that he had hooked a large fish. This proved to be the case, as he succeeded, after a long struggle, in landing a sturgeon of 212 pounds weight, the largest of thirteen caught that night by the fishermen. I will not attempt to describe the pride and joy which permeated his being as they could only be understood by one who shared his fondness for sport.

Finding that his tastes did not tend towards a mercantile life, after a year's apprenticeship, my father determined to study medicine and returned to Warrenton and entered the office of his elder brother, Dr. Thomas Thornton Withers.

Conjointly with his professional researches he developed a fondness for more elegant pursuits. Being fond of music he cultivated that taste and became a fine performer on the flute, and also by close attention to the instructions of a French dancing master, an exceptionally graceful and accomplished dancer. He also developed a fondness for histrionic art, and was a member of an amateur company of Thespians, who during the hard winter of 1816, when there was great suffering among the poor, performed a good many plays, the proceeds of which, were devoted to charitable purposes.

My father was six feet three inches in height, well proportioned, active and strong, with fair skin, gray eyes, and decidedly Scotch in his general appearance and physiognomy.

After completing his medical education at the medical department of the University of Pennsylvania, he settled at Lovingston, the County seat of Nelson County, Va., and commenced practice. There he met my mother, then a handsome young girl, while on a visit to relatives, and soon followed her to Rock Castle, and married her shortly afterwards, and carried her to Lovingston where he had located. But my mother was the youngest of her family and much petted by her parents, who were not willing to give her up, so before the first year of their married life was ended, they moved back to Rock Castle, where they continued to reside.

My grandfather died soon afterwards and my grandmother, then advanced in years, gave up the housekeeping to my mother and lived with her until her death in 1846, in the ninety-first year of her age.

She was a remarkable woman, of unusually fine judgment, and certainly the most industrious person I ever saw. Until within a short time of her death, she was never seen to be idle.

Devoted to domestic life, there was nothing about housekeeping of which she was not a perfect mistress. I never saw her lean back in her chair, but she always sat upright, when not moving about the house or yard. A devout christian, a constant reader of her Bible, with a very tenacious memory, she could at once locate almost any passage of scripture mentioned.

I remember on one occasion, Rev. Mr. Osgood had prepared a sermon from a familiar text, which he expected to preach on Sunday, but when he looked for the text, so as to name chapter and verse, he was unable to find it, and not having a concordance, was in quite a dilemma. Coming to Rock Castle Saturday to spend the night, he told of his trouble and appealed to the family to aid him in hunting it up. "What is the text?" said my grandmother. He repeated, "But God forbid that I should glory save in the Cross of our Lord Jesus Christ." "Look in the fifth chapter of Galatians and you will find it," said she.

When my father commenced the practice of medicine in Campbell County, he was confronted by rather an odd condition. Located one and a half miles from him on the east was his brother-in-law Dr. Nathaniel W. Payne, also a practitioner, and four miles to the west, was Dr. John Slaughter, also a practitioner. So the sick in the community had the privilege of patronizing either Dr. Withers, Dr. Payne or Dr. Slaughter as their fancy might dictate. Of course, under the existing conditions, he was not for some time overburdened with practice, but having a good pointer dog, and a double-barreled gun, and game in abundance, he had a pleasant time. By the way, his was at that time the only double-barreled gun in the County and there was no one who could compete with him in wing shooting. Being equally proficient with the rifle, he achieved great reputation as a sportsman. Indeed this fondness for field sports is characteristic of my branch of the Withers family. My father was one of six brothers, all of whom except perhaps one, were devoted to hunting and fishing, fond of fine horses and dogs. There were seven sons in his own family, all of whom were fine wing shots and enjoyed nothing as well as hunting and fishing. My father gave up bird hunting in a measure when I was a small boy, and took to fox hunting with great zest. He had a fine pack of thorough-bred dogs, and was very successful in the pursuit of both red and grey foxes.

have known him to bag two red foxes in a morning's hunt and this occurred more than once.

To catch two greys in a day was nothing unusuual. Occasionally he would vary the sport by going to the Long Mountain or its foot hills, in pursuit of deer and frequently brought back the spoils of the chase in hide, horns and venison. His passion for the chase never waned and for years, after he had secured a large and lucrative practice, he could not or would not give it up.

One of my earliest recollections is of going "possum hunting" at night, riding "pickaback on the shoulders of "Uncle Jack" through the dark woods, lighted by torches and aroused to great excitement when "Old Guilford" would "tree," followed by the cutting down or climbing the tree and the capture of the grinning Marsupial.

I can hardly recall a time when I could not shoot a shot gun, and learned to use the rifle before I was ten years of age.

I generally accompanied my father squirrel hunting, armed with a shot gun, but was not permitted to shoot at a squirrel unless he was running or jumping to reach his hole. When still, they were the legitimate game of the rifle, and were always shot in the head, and, as it was very rarely that a second shot was needed, I usually did but little shooting. I have known him knock off the heads of twenty squirrels at twenty shots in a morning's hunt. He never used a rest, but always fired "off hand." He was just as devoted a disciple of Isaac Walton as of Nimrod, indeed after he became, by advancing years, disqualified for hunting either with hound or gun, he could, and did enjoy fishing in the neighboring mill ponds, for pike, perch, etc., until within a short time of his death.

Reared among such surroundings, and with such an example, it is not surprising that I should have inherited his tastes, and even to a greater degree devoted myself to the pursuit of sport with rod, gun and dog.

CHAPTER III.

EARLY SCHOOL DAYS.

Before commencing a narrative of my early school days, I will mention an anatomical fact, which may have exercised an influence on my whole life. I was born web-footed, that is, the three middle toes on each foot were joined together along their whole length. Had I seen the light of day before the death of my grandfather Alexander, I would doubtless have been a great pet, as he was also twin toed, and was always delighted at the birth of any grandchild possessing the same peculiarity. My mother inherited the same mark, though in less degree.

Now it is a well known fact that all web-footed creatures have a great fondness for water, and take to it from their earliest years, and I proved no exception to the rule. When a small child nothing could keep me out of the branch or creek when accessible. I was started to school with my sister Jennet, older than I, when six years of age. The schoolhouse was more than a mile distant, nearly half the way through woods, and had a branch running near it. I had strict orders from my mother "not to wade in the branch," but the temptation was too great for me to resist, and every day at "playtime" I would roll up my pants and wade, of course often going in over the rolled up garment and wetting my clothes.

My first teacher was a Northern man of course, as at that day the "Yankee School Master" was to be met within every neighborhood, and few teachers of any other nativity were to be found. Mr. Osgood, was however, an excellent teacher, and took great pains in instructing his scholars, who embraced all ages from six to twenty years, both males and females. He was passionately fond of flowers, and managed to get a lot around the building enclosed (the only instance within my experience of which this could be said). He planted the ground with many varieties of flowers and vines and spent his spare time in cultivating them, by the aid of such of the scholars as shared his taste, or could be prevailed on to aid in the work. From the bed of the branch we carried white gravel sufficient to cover the walks, and when the vines covered the arbor in front of the building and the flowers were in bloom it was quite attractive. But he had another peculiarity. He was the only teacher I ever had who required of his pupils that they should keep their clothing neat and clean. This was often a source of trouble and suffering to me, my mother being a stickler for the same virtue of neatness. When after repeated admonitions I neglected her orders about wading in the water, she finally avowed her purpose of switching me whenever I came from school with clothing wet and muddy. I had a hard time of it, for I just could not keep out of the water, and consequently, that summer, I was pretty regularly punished twice a day for wet and dirty clothing.

The teacher after playtime would give it to me, and my mother at night when I came home. I would promise to do better always, and really intended reformation, but the same temptation would assail me the next day, and I would again come to grief. These experiences were never forgotten. After I was the father of several children, on one occasion two of the largest came in one day from the ice pond with their aprons full of frogs, which they had captured by wading in the muddy water, and I suppose no children ever presented a more shocking spectacle to the lover of neatness than did these. Their mother caught sight of them as they entered the yard, and she ordered them to "Bring a switch with them." Said I, "Oh, don't touch the children, they inherited the taste. I was whipped twice a day a whole summer for going in the water and dirtying my clothes, and it never did me any good, so it is useless to punish them, let them go." She laughed and like a sensible woman abandoned her purpose.

Mr. Osgood was a devout churchman and studied for the ministry while teaching school. He was ordained a Deacon, and mainly through his exertions an Episcopal Church was erected near the schoolhouse, though there were few communicants of that church in the immediate neighborhood, but it was a source of great comfort to them and to the other Episcopal families, residing within a radius of twelve or fifteen miles, to have the privilege of enjoying a liturgical service. The consecration of "St. John's" (for it was so called) was a great event in the neighborhood, as few, if any, of the people had ever witnessed such a ceremony. There were several Episcopal ministers from adjoining counties present with Bishop Meade. Among them Rev. Franklin G. Smith of Lynchburg, Rev. Nicholas H. Cobbs of Bedford, Rev. John T. Clark of Halifax, and perhaps others. The congregation not only filled the church to overflowing but the yard as well, and the ceremonial furnished a fruitful topic of conversation for a great while afterwards.

When I started to school I did not know my letters, and my mother, I think, formed a low estimate of my intellectual capacity, as she had faithfully, but in vain, striven to teach them to me. Mr. Osgood made no attempt to teach me the alphabet, but put me to reading in the "New York Reader," then the "horn book" of the schools, and it was not long before I learned to read fairly well, and at the public examination at the close of the session, I read before the assembled congregation of patrons and the public, a piece called "The Butterfly." Commencing, "Butterfly, pretty Butterfly come and rest on the flower I hold in my hand. I will not hurt thee," etc., to the great relief and delectation of my mother particularly.

After Mr. Osgood left, having taken orders and engaged regularly in preaching, I attended the school of Mr. Terrullus Hubby Babcock, a native of New York State, and the author of an arithmetic called by his name, which of course supplanted Pikes' Arithmetic previously used. According to my recollection it was a pretty good treatise, though a good many of the patrons objected to the change, principally I think because of the increased expense involved in the purchase of a new book. I wonder what they would have thought of the present cost of school books, with the frequent changes inflicted on the patrons of the public schools. I think I got on pretty well at school, as I never was punished in my life on account of my lessons. Babcock, I remember particularly from a row we had about the parsing of a word. I was the head of the Grammar class, though the youngest boy, and our lesson contained this sentence, "My dog, the trustiest of his kind," etc. I parsed the word dog and gave the gender as masculine, the teacher said I was wrong and Patrick Henry (grandson of the orator) being next, gave the gender as common and "turned me down." I refused to go down, and contended that I was right, citing the example in the grammar (Murray's) where, under the head of gender, the example was given, masculine dog, feminine bitch. The teacher I am sure saw he was wrong, but insisted that the word was common gender and I must go down. I still demurred and refused to yield, till he got his ferule and threatened to lay it on if I did not obey, so I had to yield, but I never for a long time forgave him, indeed I doubt if I ever have done so. I commenced the study of Latin with him, but soon found that he knew but little about it, indeed, excepting arithmetic and mathematics, he was a poor scholar. He only taught five months. Mr. Phelps followed, who was a fine French scholar, but took little interest in anything else, and the scholars studied or not as it pleased them. He was a very homely man, possessing, however, an inordinate share of personal vanity. He wore glasses, being short sighted, and had a large nose. Having witnessed on some holiday occasion my father's skill with a rifle, he was seized with a strong desire of acquiring similar proficiency, and constantly wished to accompany us on our squirrel hunts, but as he knew nothing about a gun, he made slow progress. I do not remember that he ever killed a squirrel. Indeed it was very difficult to make him see one on a tree, and when he did, my father would cock the gun, set the hair trigger, and hand him the weapon, a flint and steel. On one occasion just as he took hold of the rifle, the lock being opposite his face, he touched the trigger and off she went. The glasses protected his eyes from the powder from the pan, which was however driven into his nose and face with a good deal of force, and doubtless caused him considerable pain. That, however, he did not seem much to regard, but was greatly concerned lest his good looks might be marred, exclaiming frequently, "Oh, Doctor it will spoil my beauty." On our way home we passed Captain Adam Clement's house, whose wife was my sister and a very plain-spoken, sincere woman. As soon as he enterd the house he ran through the hall to her chamber where there was a looking glass on the bureau, which he approached with the exclamation, "Oh, Mrs. Clement, I have spoiled my beauty, spoiled my beauty." "Well," she said, "I didn't think you ever had any to spoil."

My father spent the balance of the day trying to pick the grains of powder from his face, and though it caused him much pain, he constantly said, "Never mind the pain, Doctor, pick them all out." This was impracticable, as he bore the marks of the accident to his dying day no doubt. He also left at the end of his five months session.

The next year we were taught by a tall, raw-boned, pockmarked, native of the Emerald Isle, about the roughest, and most uncouth specimen of that nationality I had ever seen up to that time. His name was Daley. He was a good Latin scholar however, and knew Cæsar by heart, at least all the first portion as it is usually read in schools. He was, of course, a Roman Catholic, and this did not add to his popularity in the neighborhood. Before his session ended most of the patrons of the school took their children home, causing quite a commotion, as he brought suit for the whole session, and I believe recovered it.

When we were taken from school, I was for some months sent to the home of my Uncle, Captain Edward B. Withers of Ivanhoe, to attend school with his children, the teacher being a young man from the North named Joscelyn. He was studying law and was a very nice and gentlemanly man, of culture and refinement, and an excellent teacher, and under his guidance I made satisfactory progress until his time was out, when he left for points further South where he proposed to practice law. I became very fond of him, and in after years endeavored in vain to find out what had become of him, but never knew until 1875, after I entered the Senate, I was told by a cousin of mine, who lived in Houston, Texas, that he knew him well, and that he told him, when the newspapers published the fact of my election to the Senate of the United States, that "I taught him his Latin." He had made a snug fortune by his practice, but never married. Mr. Samuel H. Sadler, a young Virginian from the County of Buckingham, was the next incumbent of the teacher's chair at the old schoolhouse. He was what the boys called "a tight school master," and made free use of the rod which he always kept handy and used on slight provocation and in some cases we thought unmercifully.

There was one boy, particularly, who was severely whipped almost every day, because he did not learn his multiplication table. School children are generally pretty good judges of the laws of equity and justice, and in this case they decided that the teacher was unnecessarily severe, as the boy was so much afraid of him that he could not do himself justice in recitation. This was proven by the fact that he could recite his lesson correctly to another boy, but was sure to miss when he recited to the teacher. So they got up a "round robin" of remonstrance, of which the teacher took no notice whatever, but we observed that afterwards he was not so savage in his discipline of this particular boy. Sadler only taught five months, and left for college.

I was now about thirteen years of age, and was getting to be among the most advanced scholars. Pat Henry and I were classmates all our school days. He was two years my senior and a good scholar. In Latin he was better than I, but in the English branches I excelled him.

About this time the patrons of the school engaged the services of a young man from Vermont, whose name was Ebenezer Taft Allen. He had just graduated at the college of St. Johns, New Brunswick, and was studying law, of course. He was bright and smart and soon had a large school. As the tuition fees were larger for the Latin scholars, he had about half the school, both boys and girls, studying Latin. He was a good teacher too, and we all liked him very well. Patrick Henry and I, under his instructions, made considerable progress in Greek, Latin and Mathematics. He taught a year and then went to Kentucky, married a girl whose acquaintance he formed in Virginia and whose father had removed to Kentucky, and there embarked in the practice of law, in which he succeeded very well, but died a young man. When he first came to my father's and was visiting the people in the neighborhood, soliciting scholars, I accompanied him to the house of my father's overseer, who had a house full of children, to persuade him to send some to school. The overseer's wife asked him "where he come from?" He made no effort to conceal the place of his birth, but replied at once, "Oh, I'm a Yankee." "Well," she said "what is the difference any way between Yankees and white folks?" This of course caused a good laugh.

Allen was a fine shot with the rifle and often hunted with me. One day when we were returing from an unsuccessful hunt, passing through the farm of a neighbor, we saw his flock of geese grazing on a hill more than an hundred yards off and he said, "Now Bob, if those were only wild geese I could knock over one so nicely." I replied, "You could not kill one that distance." "Yes, I could," he replied. We continued the dispute for a while when he said, "Now I'll show you," raised the rifle and fired. To my astonishment, one of the flock gave a squawk and tumbled over. We walked over and examined it and found it shot through the body. "Well," he said, "I'll have to pay Mr. Martin for this old goose when I see him." This was Saturday evening. We saw no one and supposed that no one saw us or had any knowledge of the exploit. But when we went school Monday, Mr. Martin's daughter brought a note from her father saying she would go no more as "He did not wish his daughter instructed in the goose-shooting business." He was much annoyed by this, but would never send any bill or accept any tuition for the time the daughter attended school.

The winter he left, my father spent in Richmond, having been elected in the Spring, a member of the Legislature, after a close contest of which I will speak more at length hereafter.

Being without a teacher at home, I again went to my Uncle Edward's to attend a school taught by an old Scotchman named Thomas Young. He lived at my Uncle's and was an odd fish. He was a good scholar, however, and a good teacher of those to whom he took a fancy, of whom I was fortunately one, but scholars towards whom he imbibed a prejudice had a hard time. He said he "never saw a boy named Thomas who was worth a cent," and Tom Franklin, one of the scholars, never could do anything to please him. I generally studied my lessons in his room at night and he was always ready to give me any help I needed in my Greek. He was devoted to the game of cribbage and he and my uncle played a good deal. He was also fond of reading and had quite a number of books, of which he was very careful, but would let me read them after I got through with my lessons. On the first leaf of every book he had a printed slip pasted, to this effect:

> " This Book Belongs to Thomas Young,
> If thou art borrowed by a friend,
> Right welcome shall he be,
> To read, to study, not to lend,
> But to return to me.

> " Not that imparted knowledge doth
> Diminish learning's store,
> But books I find, if often lent,
> Return to me no more.

Read slowly, pause frequently, reflect seriously, and return duly, with the corners of the leaves not turned down."

I often wondered if these words were original, as I had never seen or heard of them elsewhere, and finally concluded that he must have composed them, and I retained this opinion until the winter of 1900, when I read a book, the scene of which was laid in Scotland in the time of the Covenanters, and one of the characters was said to have posted in each of his books the identical lines above quoted. So the old gentleman brought his book motto from Scotland with him.

In the spring of 1837, I went for three months to a school taught by a crippled and crabbed Presbyterian preacher named Anderson. I was not much benefited by his instructions, as he did not like me, and I had no fondness for him. I never knew where he came from, but he was not a Yankee.

In the fall of that year I was sent to the "Woodburne Classical School," in the county of Pittsylvania, taught by Mr. Samuel T. Miller. This was a large boarding school for boys, of good reputation, and long established. His daughters attended the school and were classed with boys of the same proficiency. Miss Fannie was in our class and a very clever girl; we had to put in our best work to prevent her from out-stripping us, both in classics and mathematics. I remained with Mr. Miller three sessions, studying Latin, Greek, French, and mathematics, and being older, and realizing more fully the importance of diligent application, derived great benefit from his instructions. He had then been teaching more than forty years, he told me, and continued the school several years after I left it.

I had a very good time at Woodburne. One of my classmates was Henry Sydnor, of Halifax County, who was extremely fond of fishing, and he and I spent all our holidays during the spring and fall months on the banks of Staunton River, which is a bold stream and pretty well stocked with fish at that time. We kept several deep holes baited, and caught a great many fish. We were privileged to get corn ash cakes baked at the kitchen to bait with, for the prizes of our skill furnished no inconsiderable amount of toothsome food to the table.

Henry Sydnor was a fine violinist, and one of the other boys played the flute, and on Saturday night after we got over our lessons, we had a frolic of music, dancing, singing, etc., which was never interfered with, as the schoolhouse, in the upper story of which the larger boys slept, was in a corner of the yard, some distance from the dwelling, so no one was disturbed by the noise. In the winter we tracked hares in the snow, caught partridges in traps and coops, and amused ourselves with such games as checkers, backgammon, and chess. I think it creditable to the boys that card-playing and gambling were not known among us.

One fall day when the weather was getting cold and ice beginning to form on the edges of the water, John Craddock, of Halifax County, and I concluded to go to the river and carry an old canoe, that we had gotten hold of, to a point about a mile higher up the river, that we might more conveniently visit our partridge traps, which were located on Long Island. This island contained about seven hundred acres of alluvial and fertile lands, constituting with the adjacent highlands one of the finest farms in that section of the country. As it was never pastured birds and hares were always numerous, hence our selection of it as a good place to set our traps. In order to get the canoe to the point selected we had to pole it through a long boat sluice about the middle of the river, as the stream had been improved by the "Roanoke Navigation Company" so as to furnish batteaux navigation as high up as Salem in Roanoke County. By the way, it is rather a singular geographical fact, that the stream is known as Roanoke River from its source in Montgomery County in Virginia to the point at which it passes through the Blue Ridge, when it becomes Staunton River until it unites with the Dan in the County of Mecklenburg, where it resumes the name of Roanoke. But to return to my story.

Our canoe was a rude specimen, originally a long log trough; one end had become so rotten that it had to be stopped with a pile of dirt to keep the water out. With this we started on our voyage, and got on fairly well until we reached the boat sluice. We had tied a long grape-vine to the bow for a towing line, and our arrangement was that I should take the grape-vine and, walking along the stone wall, built for the purpose, pull the canoe up the sluice, while Craddock was to remain in the canoe, and with the pole aid in pushing the craft through the sluice. But our united strength proved insufficient to force the passage, and when we got fairly into the current, despite my utmost efforts, I was gradually pulled along the wall until the end was reached, and then, rather than be dragged into the water, I let the grape-vine go, when Craddock, finding himself unable to manage the canoe, jumped out into the water and waded to me on the sluice wall, and the canoe drifted some distance down the river and lodged on a rock. Here was a dilemma! The wind was rising and the weather getting colder every minute. After consultation, we determined our best procedure would be to strip off our clothes, leave them on the wall, wade down to the canoe, bring it back to where our clothing had been left, dress and pole to the shore. We made the effort; most of the way to the canoe was comparatively shallow water, but for a short distance we had to swim, and when we reached the canoe we were so benumbed by cold that we became alarmed, and as the shore of the island was nearer than the sluice wall, we poled the canoe to land, jumped out, and naked as we were, and in the face of a strong northwest wind, we raced up the island for several hundred yards and back, to restore our circulation, for when I put my hand on my thigh to climb up the bank, it was so perfectly benumbed that I could scarcely feel the touch of my hand. The tall weeds and occasional briars we encountered in our race served, no doubt, a good purpose in arousing our dormant blood-vessels by the flagellation they inflicted, but at the time we failed to appreciate the blessing. However, we succeeded in bringing on sufficient reaction to enable us to take the canoe back to our clothing, where we dressed and got to our own shore, when we struck a long trot, which we did not break until we reached home. Of course when we told our adventure we were well laughed at and joked, but it was no laughing matter to us. Strangest thing of all was that neither of us was made sick by the exposure. We did not even have a cold.

One Saturday night in the summer of 1838, after going over our lessons, we concluded to have a feast of roasting ears, as we had had none served at the table, much to our dissatisfaction. So we took Henry, the negro man who waited on us, to the corn field and aided him in gathering a lot of roasting ears from the field, which we carried home, and having kindled a fire and put on a dinner pot procured from the kitchen, cooked our corn and ate to repletion, then followed music and dancing until we tired of the fun, and went to bed. Sunday morning Henry came in in great alarm to tell us that "the boss" had been awakened by our noise the night before and had come down to the schoolhouse, looked in at the window and saw what we had been up to and was about to thrash him for getting the corn for us, but he had told him he had nothing to do with it, that the boys had brought the corn home and made him get the iron pot in which it had been cooked, and that was all he did. He begged us not to tell that he had gotten the corn, as he would be thrashed. We promised not to contradict his story. When the breakfast bell rang I was the only one of the party whose turn it was to eat at the first table with the family. I went in boldly and took my seat at the lower end of the table, near Mr. Miller, who after helping me to the dish before him, addressed me in a pleasant way, "Well, Robert, did you boys have as much corn as you wanted last night?" evidently expecting to enjoy the surprise and embarrassment which would follow his inquiry, but forewarned by Henry's morning visit, I replied as coolly as possible, "Oh, yes sir, we had as much as we could eat." He then asked if we got the corn from the field, I replied in the affirmative. To his inquiry why we had taken the corn, I told him we had not been served with any at the table, and we wanted some so badly we concluded to get it and have it cooked. He said he hoped we would not do it again as the negroes would take a dozen ears for every one we took, and lay it on us, and he would see to it that we had it on the table as long as roasting ears lasted. I told him in that case we would not again visit the corn field, and so the affair ended more pleasantly than we had expected.

Another enterprise in which the same John W. Craddock figured, who took part in the canoe adventure, I will narrate.

After the wild geese came south in the fall, large numbers of them frequented Staunton River and the contiguous farms, where they find food in the fields of growing wheat, but they return to the river to roost in the deep eddy water above the "Cornrow Falls, opposite Long Island. John Craddock and I concocted a scheme by which we hoped to bag a goodly number of these beautiful fowls, and add to our reputation as expert hunters. Accordingly, having borrowed a gun apiece, we crossed over to the Island one cold and clear night in December, and getting into a canoe, some half or three-quarters of a mile above the roosting place of the geese, we laid down in the bottom and undertook to float down the river till we got among them, intending then to fire into the flock, expecting great results. There was so little current in the eddy that our motion was almost imperceptible, and lying there without overcoats or any protection from the chill air, we soon began to feel exceedingly uncomfortable. It appeared to me that we would never get to the geese, and some hours really must have elapsed before we were gladdened by a slight note from a goose, and soon after we saw a squad of fifteen or twenty very near us. I touched Craddock with my foot, the signal agreed on, and we fired simultaneously. There was a great flapping and "Konking" from the geese and we shoved the canoe towards the point where we had seen them. One goose, evidently with a broken wing, passed near the canoe and I struck at it with my pole, but it dived and disappeared, one dead one was found, and though we searched long we were not rewarded with another feather.

I learned two things that night, of which I was not before aware, viz: that even in a clear, starlight night you can not see any object flying between you and the sky unless it be very near. A number of geese flew directly over our heads, as evidenced by their cries and the noise of their wings, which was distinct and unmistakable, but they were absolutely invisible. The second point was analogous, that you can not see an object as large as a goose thirty steps away, no matter how brightly the stars may be shining.

In very bad humor we commenced to pole our canoe back to the boat landing where we had procured it, but the water was twelve or fifteen feet deep, and our poles would scarcely reach the bottom, the water was intensely cold, our hands soon became so benumbed that we could hardly hold the poles. We therefore abandoned our purpose, and getting the canoe to the nearest bank, we fastened it to a tree and started on our long walk back, about six miles, with our sole trophy, reaching Mr. Miller's not very long before day. We concluded to give up goose hunting. We heard that two geese with broken wings were caught a few days after in the river, near the scene of our exploit, and always believed they had fallen to our guns that night.

I have narrated these schoolboy adventures, conscious of their trivial character, but thinking they may possess some interest for the boys of the family. I could recall many similar incidents, but these will suffice to bring to a close these reminiscences of my early years and numerous teachers.

Before resuming the story of my subsequent experiences, I will recur briefly to my early rearing and home life at Rock Castle.

The whole work of disciplining and training the large family of children devolved upon my mother, and faithfully and judiciously did she discharge her duty. My father was but little at home in the day time, as the labor of attending to a large country practice kept him constantly busy. I was reared a regular country boy, and as then customary in all respectable families, great attention was paid to the moral and religious training of the children. They were taught to observe the Sabbath day, to read and study the Bible, to tell the truth, to attend religious services when practicable, to be polite and respectful to their elders, and especially to ladies, old or young. Sunday-schools were unknown, at least in the country, but the home Sunday lessons were taught in almost every family and until the Abolitionists of the North commenced their crusade, the black children of the plantation shared the instructions of the white. The mother of the family instructed all until the children were large enough to aid her in these duties. Even after the Legislatures of the Southern States were forced, in self-defense, to make laws making it a penal offence to give ininstruction to blacks, these laws were never, to my knowledge, enforced, and certainly they were violated in almost every household by the children, who would teach the little negroes to read. But it would be idle to deny that the active efforts of the abolitionists caused much apprehension and discomfort to the whites, and suffering and unhappiness to the blacks. Fear of negro insurrections in the eastern section of the State was wide spread, and the source of great anxiety and alarm, especially to the female population. Nat Turner's insurrection in Southampton County, Virginia, in August, 1831, greatly intensified these fears, as fifty-five whites, mainly women and children, were butchered in cold blood by the forty or fifty negroes implicated. Timid persons suffered greatly all over the State for a long time afterwards. In October of the same year there was a false alarm in our neighborhood, which caused the greatest excitement for twenty-four hours. I do not remember that I ever heard any explanation of what ever started the rumor, which originated at Brookneal, a small village on Staunton River, twelve miles south of Rock Castle. The report of a servile uprising was brought into the village early in the morning and of course caused the greatest excitement. Dr. Scott, a young man who was living or visiting in the place, was in a few minutes dispatched on a swift horse to alarm the neighborhood, and performed the duty assigned him in the most effective manner. At full speed he rode to Lynchburg, thirty-five miles distant, calling at every house near the public road, and warning the people to look out for their safety. On the morning in question, after breakfast, my father started out as usual on his professional rounds, and an hour or two afterwards the message was brought to the house by some one, and caused instant commotion. I had gone with George, the dining-room servant, to gather wild grapes from a tree near the house, and while up the tree heard vociferous calls for me to come to the house. Leaving George up the tree I went to the house, by which time my mother had gathered up the gang of children, collected all the guns and ammunition on the place, and with my grandmother, was about starting to my uncle Adam Clement's, a little more than a mile distant. Aunt Eliza, the house woman, was left in charge of the premises, and off we started. Some young lady visitors from Richmond left long before we did, frightened nearly to death, but neither my mother nor my grandmother lost their heads for a moment. We went by a near road through the woods to our destination, which had been selected as being more easily defended than Rock Castle, being a large brick house with no porches, and, consequently, not so readily set on fire. We had not made more than half the distance before we were overtaken by my father, who happened to be with a patient near the main road four miles nearer to Brookneal. This patient was a boy suffering with hip joint abscess, and he was about to open the swelling, when a frightened negro ran in with the appalling news. He never completed the operation, but rushed to his horse, mounted and darted off full gallop, hoping to reach home before the messenger, as he knew no one was at Rock Castle except women and children. He failed, however, in his effort, but was greatly relieved to find that all things possible and proper had been done. He had hardly overtaken us before we saw a negro man coming along the path at double quick, and my mother said, "There is a rascal going to join them now."

"Stop!" called my father, "and give an account of yourself, or I'll blow your brains out."

The negro, greatly frightened, called out, "Marse Adam's Sam, sir. Mistress sent me over for Miss Susan and the children."

"All right then, pick up that child and carry it."

When we reached Captain Clement's, the neighbors were rapidly gathering in. Captain Clement had been in the war of 1812, and my father and he sent runners around, instructed to see the captain of the militia company whose muster ground was about two miles off, with the advice to warn in the men as fast as possible, get what ammunition could be had, and march to meet the enemy. Most of the able-bodied men left on this mission, the old men and women set to work moulding bullets and making cartridges. My mother had brought a bag of number six shot and a few bars of lead, and out of these lots of bullets were cast to fit the rifle and to be used for shotguns in the place of buckshot. These bullets and the patches, greased and ready for use, served as mementos of the panic for several years, as many of the balls contained small shot not fully melted which marred to some extent the spherical outline. As the day wore on, Aunt Nancy Clement had to bestir herself and her domestics to provide food for the assembled multitude, for the house was literally filled with people. I can not recall that I was much frightened at any time, and certainly after a few hours the crowd of boys collected soon made things pretty lively, and we were constantly regaled by the recital of humorous incidents, or odd speeches of those present. Things drifted along all day without further developments. Scouts had been sent out with instructions to go down the road to Brookneal carefully and ascertain the whereabouts and numbers of the insurgents, but none of these had returned at dark. Then sentinels were posted around the house and yard and the countersign given out, and regular routine of military duty observed. Soon after dark the sentinel posted on the spring path was heard challenge, "Halt! who goes there?" Instantly came the reply, "Marse Adam's Sam, missis sent him to spring, lady want drink." This challenge and reply were for a long time by-words with the school boys. About nine o'clock or later, a man named Chapin, a singing-school master, drove up in a buggy seeking quarters for the night, who reported that he had passed Brookneal in the afternoon and everything was quiet, and he had heard nothing of any trouble. This, of course, calmed the fears of the most timid and those who could find a place, tried to get some sleep. Thirteen boys about my age were put in a room with two small beds and told to do the best they could, but what with the pranks of some and noise of others, very little sleeping was done.

The exodus began by daylight in the morning, and every one was soon at home again. Some families, however, in the neighborhood were not so fortunate, as, instead of going to the general rendezvous, they took to the thick woods for concealment, and some of them did not learn of the falsity of the alarm until late the next day. The negroes all behaved well, and to their credit be it said, no incident occurred to indicate a purpose or desire of any of the race to unite their fortunes with the rebellion. Dr. Scott killed his horse, and that was the only fatality as far as I remember.

These reminiscences will suffice to illustrate how sensitive were the people of the slave-owning states to the dangers to which they were constantly exposed, and at the same time show how readily they prepared themselves to meet the threatened evil. The militia companies at Pigeon Run, anl also at Campbell Courthouse, were under arms in a few hours after the alarm was sounded, and two volunteer companies from Lynchburg were also ready to march when the information came that it was all a false alarm.

CHAPTER IV

SAGACITY OF DOGS AND HORSES.

Reared under the influences I have described, I imbibed all the tastes and characteristics common to the country gentleman of that day. An enthusiastic love for the works of nature, a keen enjoyment of life in the open air and out of door sports, and a sincere affection for those animals which are indispensable to the successful pursuit of such pleasures, were developed in me at an early age. This fondness for dogs and horses was a well marked and persistent trait of my character. I can scarcely remember the time when I was not the owner of a dog, and very early attained a skill for managing and training horses, which has always been a source of great comfort and pleasure.

Intimate association with these classes of animals has satisfied me that both possess in no inconsiderable degree the reasoning faculty, and I have never met any one who had cultivated and enjoyed the pleasures of intimate association with them who did not concur in this opinion.

It may perhaps amuse some of my grandchildren, and perhaps others who may read these recollections, to cite a few anecdotes in support of my hypothesis, promising that nothing will be written that is not strictly true, occuring either within my personal experience and observation or sustained by such evidence as would be deemed conclusive in any court of justice.

My father rode for ten years or more a horse he called "Sliding Johnny," from the smoothness and ease of his gait. During all these years he was never known to fall. No effort was made to train him in any way, but his native sagacity taught him many things. When he pleased he could untie himself no matter how intricately the knot might be fastened. When he reached home hungry, he would, when tied, loose the rein, open the gate of the stable lot, undo the door of the stable, which was fastened by a staple over a hasp, with a pin through the staple to keep it in place, then, if the bars of his stall were up he would pull them out and walk in. All these were as you see different fastenings, yet he had learned the trick of each one.

Not long since I saw an account in a newspaper of a horse similarly accomplished, who had been stolen and two years afterwards was found by his owner in a distant County, but the man who had him in possession refused to give him up, and the law was appealed to by his original owner. When the trial of the case came on, the claimant said he was willing to let the horse himself decide the question. "Send him," said he, "by an officer of the Court to my house and hitch him to the rack, if he does not untie himself, unlatch the stable lot gate, unfasten the stable door, and pull out the pin which holds the bar in place that fastens his stall, and go into the second stall on the right, I'll not claim him."

The test was made, and the testimony of the horse was conclusive.

A physican of my acquaintance, in Richmond, drove a horse for some years noted for his sagacity. It was the custom of the hostler to hitch him to the carriage at the stable every morning and tell him to "Go on." He would take the carriage carefully through a narrow alley, turn into the street and stop the carriage before the office door of his owner.

On one occasion a loose horse came into the street pursued by several parties, as soon as the Doctor's horse saw him coming he left his place, at the door of the office, walked to a point ahead of the loose horse and turned himself and the vehicle directly across the street, thus blocking the way until the loose horse was secured. He then took the carriage back to the original position before the office.

Was there not in all this procedure evidence of ratiocination as contradistinguished from instinct or education.

When I was a small boy we had a cart horse named "Snap." He would not unfrequently take it into his head to "balk" when he did not feel like pulling, and when he did, it required a great expenditure of time and patience to overcome his determination. One fall we took him to an orchard of an unoccupied farm belonging to my father a mile or two away, and loaded the cart with apples and children to return home. Snap traveled very cheerfully for more than half the distance, pulling up a long hill and entered upon the big road where it was perfectly smooth and almost level, and without any known cause concluded he would go no further, the boy who drove coaxed, clucked, whipped, and resorted to every device known to him, making us get out of the cart to lighten the load, but all in vain. By chance my father came along and found affairs in this state. He dismounted and with great confidence, real or assumed, took the reins and ordered Snap, in a sharp voice to "get up," but Snap refused positively. He worked with him for sometime, finally losing his own temper, a loss likely to occur to any one under such circumstances, determined that he would make him go or kill him. He took out his pocketknife, entered the woods bordering the road, and cut a stout hickory sappling, and returning with it to the cart commenced to trim off the branches. Snap eyed the proceedings with an appreciative glance, until the last twig was removed and my father shut his knife and put it in his pocket, when, the horse, without a word being spoken to him, started off and took the road home without a pause.

Now it is to my mind clear, that this horse reasoned in this way "That is a formidable looking pole and will cause me great suffering if I do not pull this cart home, but I will not budge until the trimming is completed, but when that is done I must lose no time in starting."

It is unnecessary to multiply examples which might be done indefinitely to establish my premises, and I have not cited any of the extraordinary performances of animals who have been trained, of which there are so many examples, for they are educated, the instances given are certainly not the results of training or instinct.

DOGS.

"Ponto" was a pointer dog of English stock, was a good all around field dog, and a reliable retriever. One day a large hawk was observed by Mr. Dabney, his owner, perched on a tree some quarter of a mile from the house, but near enough to a deep gully which ran across the field, to afford an effective shot. Taking his gun, a flint lock, he walked in a direction away from the proposed quarry, until he reached the gully which he entered, and stooping low crept along, until he gained a point within gun shot, aimed and pulled the trigger, but the gun flashed. The hawk was not alarmed by the slight puff of smoke but Mr. D. had no powder flask, and consequently could not reprime.

He was mentally bewailing this misfortune, when he looked back and saw Ponto crouching on his belly who had crept behind him all the way. Knowing the sagacity of the animal he thought to remove the difficulty by calling Ponto to his aid. He wrote in pencil on the back of a letter, a message to the family to send his powder flask by the dog, handed him the paper and pointed to the house. The dog evidently comprehended the situation fully, and without hesitation crept back towards the house and in a few minutes returned with the flask. The gun was primed anew and the hawk killed.

"Nero" was a large Newfoundland belonging to Sydnor Carter, one of my grandsons, living in Evansville, Indiana, who inherited in full degree the family fondness for dogs and field sports, and enjoyed greatly the conpanionship and training of his dogs. "Nero" displayed most wonderful sagacity and an intellect decidedly human in its characteristics. He speedily learned to do the family marketing, and it was only necessary to hand him the market basket, with a note to the butcher describing the joint or cut wanted, and say, "Go to the butcher and get the meat for dinner." He would walk off in the most business-like way, go to the market house several squares distant and return in due time with the meat. If told to go to the bakers for bread he never made a mistake and went to the butcher, nor vice versa. On one occasion he was not sent to market at all, but meeting in the street a little girl who had a heavy basket of marketing and had set it down on the sidewalk to rest, Nero, who was near, picked it up at once, trotted home with it, and triumphantly placed it on the kitchen table. The little girl soon made her appearance and claimed the basket, saying the dog wouldn't let her have it, and growled at her when she tried to take it from him.

Two daily papers were brought every morning to his home, and were thrown by the carriers into the porch a short distance from the street, one of the papers was for Mrs. Carter whose room was on the first floor, the other, for a lady whose room was on the second floor. It was Nero's delight to carry these papers to their respective owners every morning, and he was never known to make a mistake. How he was able to distinguish between the two, was a puzzle to all. It was not the time of delivery which gave him a clue, for sometimes one paper would come first and sometimes the other, and occasionally the carriers would come together, and both papers would be thrown over at the same time. He had a passion for carrying, and when in company of any of the family walking, insisted on being given something to carry. One afternoon Alice Carter and a friend started out to do some shopping, Nero accompanied them, and as usual begged for something to carry, until Alice who had nothing convenient to give him, handed him her pocketbook with which he trotted along perfectly satisfied. When they reached Main Street, Alice called him up to reclaim her pocketbook, but there was no pocketbook forthcoming. She scolded him sharply, told him he had acted badly and lost her pocketbook and commanded him to go back instantly, find it and bring it to her. He looked ashamed, but trotted back without delay. She followed some distance behind him for more than two squares, when she saw him stop and go to a rock lying near the sidewalk, turn it over and taking the pocketbook in his mouth trotted back, and with wagging tail returned it to the owner. I might fill several pages with similar incidents but forbear.

"Nero" is still living at this present writing, but belongs to another owner. His master "married a wife," and in due time a little girl was added to the family. which was of course greatly petted by all the household, very much to Nero's disgust. This antipathy to the baby steadily increased, until it became so marked that the mother became afraid he would do the baby a mischief, and insisted that he should be sent away and this was done, another example of the pernicious effect of jealousy which thus neutralized the natural instincts of an animal which under ordinary circumstances evinces great fondness for children and soon becomes the efficient guard and protector of all the little folks of the family.

Exhibitions of jealousy are by no means uncommon with animals. Before my marriage I owned an Irish setter named "Io" who always slept on the foot of my bed, to whom I was greatly attached. She lived to the age of sixteen years, and was for twelve years one of the finest field dogs I ever saw. Her father and mother were imported by my uncle Dr. Howard Withers.

When I married and brought my young wife to my father's, "Io" would none of her, but showed such jealousy that every one remarked upon it. If my wife sat by my side she would go around on the other side, but if she laid her hands on me Io's bristles would at once rise and she would growl in the most threatening manner. This hostility continued unabated until my dwelling house was completed and I, with my family, moved into it. She at once recognized the situation and not only ceased her hostile demonstration but became as friendly as possible, and as long as she lived showed the utmost solicitude for the welfare of her mistress and children. When I was at home she usually slept under the porch in a bed prepared for her, but if I failed to return home by bed time, or was called off in the night, Io would at once leave her bed and take her place on the mat at the chamber door, and then no one except the negro boy who made the fires could enter that room until her mistress was up and dressed. She was not fond of strange children and always resented any liberties taken with her by them, but submitted most patiently and uncomplainingly to have her ears and tail pulled or to be rolled over and over by my children. The marked changes in the conduct of this animal which followed my removal to my own residence, were clearly due to the exercise of her reasoning faculties, for they were simultaneous with our occupancy of "Briery," our new residence.

I believe that dogs who are treated by their owners as companions, soon acquire a more or less complete knowledge of language, and have an appreciative understanding of the significence of ordinary conversation. For example, I owned an English pointer named "Hie-a-way," a fairly good bird dog, and without exception, the finest turkey dog I ever saw. Take her into the woods, and if any turkeys had been around she would soon find their trail and at once follow it up, giving mouth as vociferously as a hound. Rushing into the flock when overtaken she would cause them to fly in every direction, and as long as one remained on the ground she would follow it up. When the flock was thoroughly squandered she would return to the huntsman, watch the construction of the blind made for concealment while "yelping," jump into it before it was completed, and remain as still as death until a shot was fired, or if the blind was too small for her accomodation, the hunter could tell her to lie down by a log and cover her head and ears with leaves, and she would never move even if a turkey walked over her, until she was called or heard the report of the hunter's gun. Now this dog might be lying on the rug before the fire apparently asleep and if I would say in an ordinary conversational tone to my wife or any one else, "I believe I will go hunting," she would at once spring up though her name had never been called, rear up and take from the wall where they hung, my bird bag, shot pouch, etc., and bring them to me with every mark of pleasure possible.

Another example: When I left Hong Kong in 1889, I brought home with me a great curiosity in the shape of a Mongolian Pug named "Dot," as he was about the size of your two fists and the only specimen of his kind I ever saw. We had owned him three years, and he was a great pet with the ladies of the family. He displayed more sagacity than any pug dog I have ever known, for dogs of that race are not usually noted for their brightness. I left behind me in Hong Kong a Scotch terrier of the "Dandie Dinmont" breed, noted for his devotion to me and the great care he took of "Dot," with whom he walked out every afternoon and was his self-constituted protector and defender. I called him "Trip." When we returned home, "Trip" was left at the Consulate with my son Robert, who as Vice-Consul, remained in charge of the Consulate. The first letter I had from him, mentioned his fear that "Trip" would grieve himself to death because parted from me. He would not eat, took no notice of him or anyone else, but was constantly roaming around, seeking me at all the places I was accustomed to frequent. This aroused my sympathy, and I wrote instructing Robert to ship "Trip" to me, if still living, by the first vessel sailing for New York and to ask Captain to send him to me by express as soon as he reached port.

"Trip" started from Hong Kong on the 5th of August, on a sailing ship, doubled Cape Horn, and after a voyage of about twenty thousand miles, reached New York in January. The Captain of the vessel wired me announcing his safe arrival, also that he would ship the dog the next day to my address. When I received this telegram, "Dot" was lying in my wife's lap and soon after its contents were made known my wife said, "Dot, Trip is coming." The effect of this announcement was surprising. Dot jumped out of my wife's lap and with every demonstration of joy, rushed to the door barking joyfully, out of doors he ran, looked towards the gate evidently to see and give joyful greeting to his friend. Several times before Trip's arrival the experiment was repeated, and he never failed to respond to the announcement in the same way. After Trip reached home the same words were used, but Dot took not the slightest notice of them. Trip, too, was very clever, and understood every thing I said to him. He was accustomed to follow me every where I went, to church as well as elsewhere, and while in church always behaved with the utmost decorum. He would lay at my feet, or if there was room enough on the seat take his place by my side, and sit up watching the proceedings, but never uttering a sound or moving from his place. Once, however, on communion day, he followed me to the chancel, much to the scandal of my wife, who thereupon issued an edict that he was not to go to church with us on the first Sunday in the month. When that Sunday came and we went to the door to start, followed of course by Trip, she would say, "Trip it is communion Sunday," instantly his ears and tail would fall, and he would shamefacedly return into the house, making no effort to follow us. I taught him Latin, and he soon acquired sufficient knowledge to understand anything, I would say to him, greatly to the astonishment of the children and servants. A visitor to the cook one evening hearing me speak to him in Latin, said, "What dat the Colonel saying?"

I don't know," said she, "but that little yaller dog know every word." You must remember that the language used was not the proverbial "Dog Latin," but the classical Ciceronian dialect. Mr. Richard Baker of Norfolk, a gentleman addicted to field sports and with a weakness for field dogs, narrated to me a circumstance illustrating the point I am discussing. He owned a speckled pointer called "Zero," and regarded him a prodigy of sagacity and canine wisdom. During the hunting season, a friend of Mr. Baker called at his house to arrange for a bird hunt the next day. Owing to some business engagement, Mr. Baker was not sure that he could get off, but it was agreed that if practicable, he would go with his dog to breakfast with his friend at a very early hour next morning, and, if he could not go himself, would leave Zero with his friend, as he had no dog of his own. Mr. Baker overslept himself the next morning and when he awoke found it was about the hour that he fixed to breakfast with his friend, dressing hurriedly, he called Zero, but he was not to be found. He went to his kennel and found his bed still warm, showing he had not long left it. After hunting everywhere for him in vain, he went around to his friend's house and found him in the act of getting into his buggy and Zero with him. The dog was present when the arrangement was made and when the hour came for his master and himself to go to the early breakfast and his master failed to put in an appearance, he went off without him, got his breakfast and was in the act of starting on the hunt without his master. Mr. Baker is satisfied that the dog heard and understood the whole program and was determined to carry out his part of the agreement. He had never gone off in that way before or since, was not accustomed to staying with the gentleman and evidently went on this occasion solely because it had been so agreed.

I will now give an instance of a fox hound which came under my observation. My father and I were fishing in the mill pond a few miles from Rock Castle one afternoon and as the fish were biting pretty well, we did not take in our hooks until nearly dark. My father had brought his gun and several of the hounds were with us. As we were winding up, four or five Mallard ducks came swooping down to roost in a piece of eddy water at the mouth of a small stream emptying into the pond not very far above us. Picking up his gun and telling me to keep the dogs back, my father slipped along, concealed by weeds and bushes and got a shot at the bunch, killing two. I ran up to where he was, accompanied by the dogs, and found him much elated by the successful shot, but utterly at a loss to know how the game could be retrieved, as the slue was about a hundred yards wide though not very deep. He whooped up his dogs and hied them on with cries of encouragement, and we threw stones in the direction of the ducks. Several of the dogs plunged in and two or three swam across the water, passing near the ducks, and one of them, Damon by name, seemed to know what was expected of him as soon as he saw the ducks, and seizing one in his mouth he brought it to the shore, and with a little encouragement swam in again and brought out the other one also. I never saw any one more delighted than was my father at this exploit. Now this dog had never in his life seen game brought in by a dog, and his sagacity alone taught him what he was expected to do. But I have probably consumed too much time and space in these digressions and will resume the thread of my narrative.

CHAPTER V.

TEMPERATE HABITS.

I possessed a fairly good memory, which was trained and improved, no doubt, by memorizing whole chapters of the Bible and nearly, if not quite, all the hymns in the prayer book of those days, which numbered about forty. I memorized the Sermon on the Mount, many Psalms, and the greater portion of St. John's Gospel, before I was twelve years of age. My mother was, I know, proud of my acquirements, though she exhibited it not by words. But when the Rev. Nicholas Cobbs came to our house on his occasional pastoral visits, he had to listen to my recitals, which, as he had baptized me, he appeared to enjoy. I read through the Bible several times and never regretted the time I spent. My mother's rule was that as soon as a child could read he must not come to breakfast until he had read a chapter in the Bible, and I can now recall a practice not infrequent, when I was belated of saving time, by repeating aloud while performing my morning toilet the first chapter of the First Epistle of Paul to the Thessalonians, which, being very short, had been memorized by my older sister and myself for use in such emergencies. Such perfunctory study of the sacred Book was of course an absurdity in a devotional point of view, but the knowledge of the sacred writings thus acquired has often been of great service to me in my checkered life.

I very early developed a taste for reading and have never lost it. At Rock Castle there was a good miscellaneous library, and our neighbor, Captain Alexander S. Henry, a son of Patrick Henry, had also a good library, and from these two sources I could draw *ad libitum*. I was an omnivorous reader. History, biography, poetry and fiction were devoured with equal avidity. By the time I was sixteen I had read Rollin's Ancient History, Plutarch's Lives, Hume, Smollett and Miller's England, Robertson's Scotland, Gillie's Greece, Gibbons'

Rome, Pope's Homer, the English poets from Pope to Byron, Scott's novels and poems, Fielding, Smollett, Cooper, Bulwer, Disraeli, Washington Irving, and odd volumes of many other novels, Shakespeare's and Sheridan's Plays, and various war histories, ancient and modern. But it is useless to say more. I have no doubt that this miscellaneous and, I may say, heterogenious reading, was a mistake on my part, but I had no guide or instruction in the selection of suitable literature, and read just whatever I could lay my hands on. When I was very young, I well remember the pleasure I experienced at listening to the "Lady of the Lake," as read aloud by my father at night, and soon learned to repeat much of it, especially "the combat" between Rhoderick Dhu and Fitz James, which I have never forgotten.

When I was about ten years of age, a traveling menagerie advertised to show at Campbell Courthouse, and my father and mother, with most of our neighbors, took all the children old enough to make the trip of ten miles on horseback, to see the show. I do not believe that I have since ever enjoyed anything of the sort as I did that show. There was a large collection of animals, birds and reptiles, with many performing monkeys, and while there was no circus, the riding of "Captain Jack" and "Dandy Jim," two monkeys, on the beautiful Shetland ponies, and the quips and gibes of the clown left nothing to be desired. I thought it the greatest day of my life.

You must remember that I was the second child of my parents, a sister older than I, and two younger, left me restricted to the society of girls, and as the daughters of the country families were taught all the handicrafts and accomplishments of housekeeping, I, from choice, shared their instruction and employment. Consequently I learned to knit, to sew, to spin, and knet. I never aspired to the loom, however, but with the needle I could hold my own with the girls. In those days the task of clothing all the slaves on the plantation devolved on the mistress of the household. The cotton was grown on the place, picked, spun and woven into cloth, with the wool from the flock of sheep, and flax grown, rotted, hackled, spun and woven on the place. The garments were cut and made, the socks and stockings knit, in short, every portion of clothing was of domestic manufacture. You may therefore imagine something of the cares and responsibilities of the mistress of the family who had to provide for all this, and in addition clothe her own boys in "Virginia cloth," as it was called. My father usually hired an itinerant shoemaker every fall to make shoes for the boys and all the negroes, until he had one of his own negro boys apprenticed to learn the trade. Extra help was also found necessary at the time of making up the winter clothes, all of which had to be completed before Christmas. Whatever the effect of freeing the slaves may have had on them, the emancipation of the mistress of the plantation from the cares and responsibilities I have enumerated, was no small compensation.

My father was very temperate in his habits. I never saw him take a drink of whiskey in my life. He would occasionally take a glass of wine at dinner or on a festive occasion, and a glass of eggnog on Christmas morning, which was about the extent of his potations, and this was given up when I was about twelve years old. At that age I attended a temperance meeting at the court-house where a society was organized, the members of which pledged themselves to drink no ardent spirits, but wine, cider, and beer were not forbidden. I signed the pledge, and consequently when Christmas came and my mother had concocted the annual bowl of eggnog, which was always done before daybreak, I could not take my glass as had been customary. Whether I showed regret at the privation I do not remember, but know that my father, the next Christmas, decreed that there should be no eggnog, evidently with the purpose of offering no temptation to me. So he took his fox hunt as usual on the morning of Christmas, but without the preliminary eggnog. However, he continued the custom of treating all the negroes to a Christmas dram for many years after the eggnog was excluded from the dwelling house.

Up to the age of sixteen years I was rather below the average height of boys of that age, and was rather heavily built, though active, as very few boys at school could beat me running or jumping. About my thirteenth year, my health for a time seemed to fail, and my father feared some affection of the heart, as its action was at times very irregular, and I was subject to fainting spells, became pale and lost my appetite, but this condition did not last very long. After my sixteenth year I shot up rapidly in height, and at nineteen was fully six feet high and weighed a hundred and ninety pounds.

CHAPTER VI.

POLITICS IN THE OLDEN TIME.

In recent years we have witnessed several political contests characterized as exciting, but I recall none which in this respect were to be compared with those when the old Whig Party flourished. Virginia, since the days of Jefferson, has always been Democratic, and the Whigs in their palmiest days were never able to wrest the control of the State from the Democrats, though their struggles to do so were both frequent and enthusiastic. My father belonged to the Whig Party, and I, of course, early imbibed the same principles, and from my boyhood have been intensely partisan.

The County of Campbell was for years a battle-ground, as the people were pretty equally divided in political sentiment, and first one party and then the other would elect its candidates for the Legislature by majorities ranging from twenty to twenty-five. The personal popularity of the candidates was an important factor in the result. In 1836 each party prepared for a bitter fight, as a President was to be elected in the fall, and the Whigs were anxious to defeat Martin Van Buren, who, by General Andrew Jackson's influence, had been nominated as the Democratic candidate to succeed him as President. Each party in Campbell tried to bring out their best men. The Democrats had succeeded in the previous year in electing their candidates and selected for the House of Delegates William Daniel, of Lynchburg, a talented and popular lawyer (the father of John W. Daniel, at present our able and eloquent member of the Senate of the United States), and Colonel James Dearing (father of General James Dearing of Confederate fame), and for the State Senate Dr. Joel W. Flood, of Buckingham County, at that time the incumbent of the place. The Whigs brought out Mr. John Wills, a popular lawyer of Lynchburg, and as his running mate selected my father against his earnest protest, as he had no ambition in that direction, was attending to a very large country practice and my mother was bitterly opposed to his entering political life. His party, however, would take no denial. For State Senator they nominated Colonel Thomas M. Bondurant, of Buckingham, who had given Dr. Flood a very close race in the previous contest. As the canvass progressed, the interest constantly increased until the day of election. There were few precincts in the county and great anxiety was felt by each party in the result at the court-house, where a large vote was cast. The contest was always close, and the party victorious at that precinct usually carried the county. The interest was so great at school that the larger boys petitioned for a holiday on election day that they might attend. Holiday was given and a number of the boys, of whom I was one, made a very early start and walked ten miles to the Court-House, reaching there soon after the polls were opened. Elections in Virginia, at that time, were conducted very differently from what they are now. *Viva voce* voting was the rule, every voter came up to the judge's table, announced his name, and those of the candidates of his choice in an audible voice, all of which was repeated in a still louder tone by the sheriff, who "Cried the votes," which were recorded by two clerks, one of each political party. I believe to this day that this system of voting is greatly preferable to our present method by secret ballot. No charges of fraud or cheating were then heard, no complaint of unfairness uttered by the defeated party, and the result met with general acquiescence as a correct expression of popular sentiment. But this was not the only peculiarity. Each candidate for popular favor was present at the court-house of the county, where he took his seat on the magistrate's bench, and as each vote was announced by the sheriff, the candidates receiving the votes made a low bow and returned thanks to the voter in an audible voice, calling him by name. As our party of boys neared the Court-House we heard at short intervals loud cheers from the building, and on entering, which was a difficult job, we found the room packed with people, and the announcement of each vote was greeted by the most vociferous cheers of the partisans of the candidate preferred. As the parties were nearly equal in numbers the volume of sound on each side differed but little. Now this scene and these cheers continued all day long, and when the polls closed at sunset, the enthusiasm was as great or perhaps greater than in the earlier hours of the morning, for "John Barley Corn" had by evening considerably intensified the interest and added enthusiasm to the cheers. As tallies were kept by many besides the clerks, the result was known as soon as the polls closed, and Wills, Withers and Bondurant beat Daniel, Dearing and Flood by fourteen or fifteen votes at the Court-House precinct, and in accordance with precedent the result in the county did not vary much from that at the Court-House, and the Whigs celebrated their victory with great jollity.

Not long after this time I joined a debating society whose meetings were held at a Methodist Church in the neighborhood. Its membership was at first confined entirely to young men and boys, but before the summer ended many of the older men and staid citizens became members and the debates on all sorts of questions attracted a good share of public interest and our audiences sometimes filled the building. This was especially the case when the subject for discussion was of a political character, for the charge so often made, that the Virginians are born politicians, is in the main correct, and applies as well to the unlearned and illiterate as to the educated and cultivated classes. I suppose I acquired my capacity of expressing my views and maintaining them in the debate mainly from my early experiences in these country clubs. I always had a fondness for investigating and discussing political subjects, though never, until I reached middle age, was I a candidate for political office.

In the spring of 1838, while my father was preparing some prescriptions one morning and I was helping him, he had a sudden attack of vertigo, followed by numbness of the left side which he thought was incipient paralysis. I was very much alarmed, and after assisting him to lie down, called to my mother, who ran from the house, and for a while there was a perfect panic in the family. Old Dr. Read, of New London, was sent for and so was my uncle, Captain Edward B. Withers, of Ivanhoe. They both came promptly that night and remained with him some days. The most threatening symptoms passed off after a short time, but he never after enjoyed the robust health which had previously characterized him. By his instruction I wrote to his nephew, Dr. Robert T. Lemmon, of Warrenton, Virginia, who had not long returned from attending lectures at the Medical Department of the University of Pennsylvania, requesting him to come and aid him in the practice. He promptly answered the call, and was of great assistance in attending to the active work. When I returned from Woodbourne School, my father was anxious for me to study medicine and I commenced to read regularly in the early part of the year 1839, under the instruction of my father, purposing to prepare myself thoroughly for entrance into the Medical Department of the University of Virginia. It soon became necessary, however, for me to modify my plans. No school teacher seemed available for the instruction of the boys in the neighborhood, and I was solicited to undertake this work. I had no special fondness for the proposed role, but as a school was a manifest necessity in the neighborhood, I reluctantly consented to play the part of pedagogue and opened my school in February. My scholars varied in age from seven to twenty years, and in studies from A, B, C's to Virgil and Sallust. I soon found that the theory which prompted my acceptance of the position did not stand the test of experiment, for I had supposed that teaching would interfere but little with my reading. This proved to be a mistake, as interruptions were so frequent that sufficient study on my part was difficult if not impracticable. I persevered, however, through the summer and fall, and completed my ten months' session to the satisfaction, I believe, of both pupils and patrons. I can not now recall any incident of special interest or importance as having transpired during that period.

I think in all candor that I should here narrate briefly the circumstances connected with an episode of my life which occurred about this time, and which was the occasion of much mortification and humiliation to me. Viewed in the light of experience I can not say that I was not excusable to a certain extent, yet I have never ceased to regret my precipitate and ill-advised action. My father was always quick-tempered, and so am I, and in the spring of 1840, while reading medicine I became involved in an altercation with him over some trivial matter, the precise character of which I do not now recall, but my father became very angry and rated me in such offensive and insulting terms that I felt greatly outraged and determined to leave home and endeavor to make my own way in the world. I went at once to my room, packed up my belongings in a pair of saddle-bags which I threw over my shoulder and climbed the back-yard paling unobserved by any one, white or black, "shook the dust of my feet" off against my home, and with only a small amount of money, left it behind me, and traveling through the woods, avoiding all roads until I was several miles from home, set out with no object in view more definite than to "go West" and make my own living. After walking some distance I met a waggoner who would pass, as I knew, by the post-office, and gave him a note I had written to Dr. Lemmon, inclosing some accounts for money due me, requesting him to collect them and pay what debts I owed. Anger sufficed to prevent annoyance from either hunger or fatigue for several hours, and as I met no one I knew, I was perfectly content. I thought when I started that I would be able to reach the home of Dr. Read near New London that night, which was distant about twenty-five miles, but at sunset I found myself some miles short of my destination. Remembering, however, that the residence of Mr. William Payne was near the road, I concluded to go there, as both he and his wife were acquaintances. I was received with much hospitality, but evident surprise, and after a hearty supper was shown to my room and slept as only the young can sleep when thoroughly fatigued. Next morning Mr. Payne asked me where I was journeying, and I told him without hesitation, my reason for leaving home and purpose of making my own way in life. He made no comment, but when after breakfast I commenced my preparations for resuming my journey, he said, "Well, Bob, don't go on this morning, but stay and we will go out and

and kill some squirrels, which are very plentiful now." I could not resist the temptation to hunt, as he well knew, so he soon made his preparations, picked up his rifle, called his dogs, and we started out. We found game abundant and as we were both good riflemen and took shots alternately, we carried home at dinner time as many squirrels as we cared to "tote," as Virginians express it. Mr. Payne complained of being too tired to go out again in the afternoon, but proposed a new route for next day's hunt, and I, suspecting nothing, agreed to share his hunt again, as he said I had no need to hurry and could pursue my journey afterwards. As it turned out, he had, before I got up, started a boy on horseback to my father's, telling him where I was and that he would do his best to keep me until he could send for me. So the next day we started out on our hunt. We had not gone far when I was surprised to see Dr. Lemmon ride up to us, who told me he was hunting for me and urged my return home. I declined to go. He then told me that my father was at Mr. Payne's house and he felt very anxious about his condition and feared if I refused to see him it might have serious results. I told him I would go to see him but I would not go back to his house. We walked on to the house, but before we entered the yard my father came hastily to meet us with every mark of great agitation, his trembling hand extended, his face quivering with emotion, and without a moment's pause commenced a most earnest apology for his hasty words and begged me to forgive him. I can truly say that never in my life, before or since, have I felt so mean and humiliated. It was really painful and I begged him to say no more, and implored his forgiveness for my rash act. All my pride, all my anger, all my wounded feelings vanished, and I felt almost degraded in my own estimation. No word of blame or reproach fell from his lips. He assumed all the blame and only asked that I would forgive him and return home. Never from that day was the subject again mentioned by him or any of the family, a merciful forbearance for which I can never feel sufficiently grateful.

From this time I devoted myself earnestly to my studies

until I had pretty well mastered the text-books on the different branches of the profession and acquired considerable dexterity as a pharmacist, for such knowledge is essential to a country practitioner, which was the role I expected to play. My father planned to take me in as a partner as soon as I passed my examination, which I hoped to accomplish at one session of the University of Virginia. At that date there was no time limit, every student was entitled to his diploma if he could pass the examinations in all the schools of the Medical Department.

Great interest was felt in the Presidential election of 1840, and I was enthusiastic in my support of General Harrison. "Tippecanoe and Tyler, too," was the rallying cry of the "log cabin and hard cider" crowd. The interest in the fight was greatly intensified by the harangues of able and eloquent speakers. At a Convention held in Lynchburg, Virginia, there was an immense crowd in attendance and many fine speeches made, but the palm of oratory was without dissent awarded to General Leslie Combs, of Kentucky, who appeared dressed in a suit of buckskin, hunting shirt and all, and as he had served under "Old Tip," his graphic descriptions of the scenes and incidents of the campaign which culminated in the defeat and death of Tecumseh, his eloquent and rousing appeal in behalf of his old commander met with the most enthusiastic response. General Combs acquired great reputation in that canvass, the most conclusive proof of which was to be found in the large number of boy babies in Lynchburg and vicinity who rejoiced in the name of Leslie Combs.

CHAPTER VII.

UNIVERSITY LIFE.

September came in due time and I took my departure for the University of Virginia, the day before the opening of the session of 1840-41. When I entered the stage coach at Lynchburg, I found as one of my fellow passengers Hunter H. Marshall, of Charlotte County, Virginia, a son of Captain Jack Marshall, a friend of my father and a lawyer of considerable repute. His son was returning to the University to continue his studies and being an old student, was, of course, familiar with student life. As each of us knew who the other was, we soon became acquainted, and I was much indebted to him for information and advice on first entering the University. The friendship thus commenced lasted unbrokenly all our lives, and was cemented and strengthened by mutual kind offices. He became a distinguished lawyer and jurist and enjoyed, up to the time of his death, when quite an old man, the highest reputation for ability and probity throughout the State.

We reached the University, after a fatiguing trip, somewhat behind time, and breakfast was over at the hotels, but Hunter knew the ropes and took me to the house of his old washer-woman, who soon prepared us a nice breakfast of coffee, eggs and ham, to which we did full justice. He then accompanied me to the office of Professor Davis, chairman of the faculty, where I matriculated in due form and then I selected my dormitory, guided by his advice, and by the next morning was ready to go to work.

When I left home, my father gave me a few words of counsel and advice. These were to the effect that my success or failure at the University depended largely upon the character of my associates and friends, and advised me not to select my circle of friends hastily. I determined to follow his advice, but really these matters were determined for me more by chance than by the exercise of my own judgment. For example, when I went to matriculate, Professor Davis introduced me to his son, who happened to be in his office, and I was at once favorably impressed by his bright and intelligent countenance. He told me he was going into the Medical Class but as it turned out he also took Natural Philosophy and expected to graduate in that School also, which would entitle him to A. M., as he had previously graduated in all the other schools required for that degree. This young man was John Staige Davis, and was then only in his seventeenth year. As Hunter Marshall was a member of the Jefferson Society, I concluded to join the same, which I never regretted. By promptly announcing my purpose, I escaped the annoyance of being subjected to the electioneering tactics of partisans of the rival society, "The Washington." My dormitory was on the eastern lawn only a few doors above the office of the chairman of the faculty. The dormitory next to mine on one side was occupied by Dabney H. Maury, of Fredericksburg, and Thomas Michie, of Green County, next to them was John S. Caskie, of Richmond, and Charles H. Barksdale, of Charlotte County; on the other side was first Joseph A. Shanklin, of South Carolina, in a single room, and adjoining him was Powhatan B. Starke, of Petersburg. At first I had no roommate, but in about two weeks James T. Spencer, of Charlotte County, was assigned to the room with my full assent, as he was also a medical student and a young man of high character.

Of the names I have thus enumerated, Marshall took A. M. this session; Davis took A. M. and M. D.; Caskie, A. M.; Barksdale, A. M.; Shanklin, A. M.; Maury, diplomas in three classes; Starke, in three, and Michie in two; and Spencer and myself took M. D. John S. Caskie was, I believe, the brightest and most talented young man I ever knew, and we all predicted for him a brilliant future. Of rather frail physique, he was possessed of wonderful rhetorical gifts, but at the same time had a clear and logical mind, fluent, with wonderful command of language, a ready writer, of bright and amiable disposition, he was beloved by all who knew him. After graduating in law he settled in Richmond, but was pushed forward prematurely by the Democratic party, to which he attached himself, and was elected to Congress when very young, and again re-elected after the close of his first term. But alas! the temptations of Washington society and his own convivial disposition wrecked his brilliant promise, and he passed to an early grave. Barksdale opened a classical school and was a successful instructor. Maury went to West Point, served with distinction in the Mexican war, and was a dintinguished Major-General in the Confederate service. He died very recently. He was one of the most genial and charming men socially, a great favorite with all who knew him, and the author of an excellent school history of Virginia. Michie died young. Spencer, after graduation, settled in Farmville, attained a high position in his profession, and died in middle age. Shanklin' became a minister in the Episcopal Church, commenced a most promising career, but lived only a few years. Stark was a successful business man, an enthusiastic member of the Masonic fraternity, was Grand Master of Masons for Virginia, and died regretted in middle age. James D. Thornton, of Cumberland, whose room was next to Stark's, took A. M., graduated in Law, went out to San Francisco, attained high distinction in his profession, was made a judge in one of the highest courts of California, and is still living. I had the pleasure of meeting him during my last visit to San Francisco in the fall of 1891. Robert L. Dabney, of Louisa County, commenced his university career this year. He was a close student, a rigid Presbyterian, a stern moralist of the Covenanter type, who after taking A. M., studied for the ministry, was ordained, and became one of the most prominent and influential ministers of his denomination, was professor at the Theological Seminary at the breaking out of the war, served as chaplain of my regiment during the first year of the war, was fearless and faithful in the discharge of every duty, and at the request of General Thomas J. Jackson (Stonewall) was transferred to his brigade and served as his Adjutant-General, with zeal and ability. I do not suppose two more congenial spirits were ever thrown together during the war. He wrote the "Life of Jackson," a "Defense of Slavery," and several other works. After the close of the war he was made President of the University of Louisiana. He became blind some years before his death. Matthew Harrison, of Loudoun, entered the University this year. He was quiet, dignified and undemonstrative, and a close student. His roommate was Martin P. Scott, of Fauquier County, and was of precisely the opposite temperament, he was quick, ardent, and impulsive in character and impetuous in manner. These two, of such opposite characteristics, were fast friends. On one occasion, however, they engaged in a game of chess in their room, no other person being present. During the progress of the game a dispute arose and Scott used insulting language to Harrison. In a moment they were clinched in a fight, and no one being present to interfere, they kept up the scrimmage, being pretty equally matched in strength, until both were entirely exhausted and incapable of inflicting further injuries. Finally one said to the other, "Let's quit this foolishness." "Agreed," said the other. They got up from the floor, proceeded to their respective washstands to remove the marks of hostile collision, which having been accomplished, Harrison said to Scott, "Well, Martin, I reckon we had as well finish the game," so they gathered up the scattered pieces, rearranged them, and resumed the game. They told the joke themselves, or it would never have been known. Harrison took A. M. afterwards, graduated in law and settled in his native county, married a daughter of General Walter Jones, of Washington City, generally regarded the ablest lawyer then at the bar of that city. Harrison himself had a deservedly high reputation as a lawyer, served frequently in the Legislature, and was one of the most useful and highly respected citizens of the State. Martin P. Scott, after taking his degree in medicine, was a professor in one of the medical schools of Baltimore and subsequently President of the Agricultural College of Maryland. I formed the acquaintance of J. Randolph Tucker and B. Johnson Barbour while I was a student, though neither of them was then in attendance, but they came to the University not infrequently to visit old friends and associates, with whom both were great favorites. The first named soon entered political life, and was, while quite a young man, nominated and elected by the Democratic party Attorney-General for the State of Virginia, which position he filled with ability and distinction. He served many years in the Congress of the United States, after the war, was popular with men of all parties, as his genial manners, his keen sense of humor and brilliant conversational talents made him a great favorite in the social circle, while his ability as a debater and his thorough knowledge of Constitutional Law, gave him a high stand among his associates in the House. He was for some years Professor of Constitutional Law in Washington and Lee University, a prominent layman in the Presbyterian Church, influential in their Synods and General Assemblies, and charming in his domestic life. He passed away a few years since, honored and regretted by a very large circle of friends and acquaintances. B. Johnson Barbour, as he was generally called, had many of the same characteristics, his wit was sparkling, elocution beautiful, his rhetoric brilliant and attractive. Possessing a handsome competency, he led the pleasant life of a country gentleman on his ancestral farm in Orange County, cultivating and developing to a high degree his literary tastes, and dispensing a genial hospitality to the end of his days. His talent as a popular speaker was of the highest order and was developed at an early age. At the Whig Convention, held in Lynchburg in 1844, he delivered, I think, the happiest, most brilliant, and most successful popular speech I ever heard, which carried his audience by storm, and at once established his reputation as an orator. He served his county and district often as a member of the House of Delegates, and Senate of Virginia, and if I remember aright, was elected to Congress in 1865, but was not allowed to take his seat, as the Republicans were then inaugurating their nefarious policy of Reconstruction. Mr. Barbour was peculiarly sensitive to ridicule, as the following anecdote will attest. When he delivered his celebrated speech to which allusion has been made at the Convention in Lynchburg, the speaker's stand gave way and came down with a crash, just before Barbour commenced speaking. As the meeting was held in a tobacco warehouse, a stand was extemporized by placing planks on some tobacco hogsheads rolled together, and on this platform he stood during the delivery of his speech. Amongst others present was Colonel Robert Whitehead, of Nelson County, an intimate friend of Barbour and a bright, humorous man, who dearly loved a joke. At a social gathering many years after, at which both Barbour and Whitehead were present, in the shank of the evening when the fun grew fast and furious, Whitehead narrated the incident connected with the delivery of that speech something like half a century before, but described Mr. Barbour as standing on the head of an empty tobacco hogshead when he spoke, and he declared while delivering one of his most impressive flights of oratory, the speaker gave emphasis to his utterances by stamping violently on the stage, which suddenly gave way, and Barbour, as if by magic, disappeared from the gaze of his admiring audience. You may imagine the roars of laughter which greeted this narrative told in Whitehead's best style. Barbour, however, was so annoyed by it that he wrote to me conveying the request that I would at once write to him my recollection of the incident, that he might prove to those present at the gathering that Whitehead's version was not correct.

I have given this brief summary of the career in after life of those who were my nearest neighbors and most intimate associates at the University, from which it may be understood that they were good students and honorable gentlemen. Of course, my circle of friends at that Institution embraced many others who attained distinction in after life and adorned the ranks of all professions and callings, but I can not attempt an enumeration of them.

A meeting of the students was called soon after the session opened for the purpose of electing the editors of the *Collegian,* a literary magazine, conducted by the students and at that time quite popular. I attended the meeting, and much to my surprise and gratification, was selected as one of the editorial staff, the others selected were John S. Caskie, of Richmond, Francis S. Rives, of Albemarle County (son of Hon. W. C. Rives, of Castle Hill), J. L. Marye, of Fredericksburg (afterwards Lieutenant-Governor of Virginia and distinguished in law and politics), and L. M. Ayer, of South Carolina. Without any change in the personnel of the editors the *Collegian* was regularly issued during the whole session. The session of 1840-41 was noted for the exceptional steadiness and studious habits of the students, a result due, no doubt, in a large measure to the sober and solemnizing influence of the tragic occurrence which threw a sombre shadow over the whole student body. I allude, of course, to the killing of Professor Davis, chairman of the faculty, by Semmes, a student from Georgia. The circumstances were as follows: Some years previously, the twelfth of November was signalized by a great *emeute* among the students of the University, having its origin, if I remember rightly, in some friction between the faculty and the members of a volunteer company composed of students, the intervention of the civil authorities was invoked, and great excitement and bad feeling aroused among some of the students. For some years after the occurrence its anniversary was made the occasion for disorderly and riotous demonstration on the part of the wildest and most turbulent of the student body, who invaded the campus after dark, shouting, firing pistols, etc. The practice, however, seemed dying out, and no one anticipated any renewal of it that year. Unfortunately, however, it entered the heads of two or three wild young fellows to commemorate the anniversary in the usual way, and early in the night the attention of the faculty and students was attracted by the sound of firearms and the shouts of persons on the lawn. Little attention was paid the disturbance, as the volume of sound indicated that few were engaged in it. Mr. Davis, however, as chairman of the faculty, felt it his duty to put a stop to the disturbance and went out on the arcade in front of his residence to see who were the parties implicated. Some one who saw him, met the parties engaged in the affair and warned them not to go farther in that direction as Professor Davis was on the lookout for them. Instead of profiting by the warning, one of the number, who had been drinking, was aroused to a violent pitch of excitement by the warning and swore he would shoot Professor Davis if he interfered with him, and forthwith put a ball into his pistol and the party continued their walk down the arcade of the Eastern

Lawn, which soon brought them to Professor Davis' pavillion, in front of which he was standing. The three young men had practically masked their faces and when they reached Mr. Davis he reached out to seize and tear off the mask of the nearest, when he was fired on at short range and fell, shot through the pelvis. The party fled precipitately as soon as they realized the mischief done. The alarm was speedily given, a crowd gathered, Professor Davis was carried into his house, remaining cool and collected, but conscious that he had received a mortal wound. The greatest excitement and indignation was aroused by the dastardly crime, much more than sufficient to paralyze the esprit of the student body, and destroy all sympathy for the offender. A meeting of the students was at once convened, resolutions denouncing the outrage and expressing the greatest sympathy for Professor Davis and his family were passed, and a committee of students appointed to ferret out the parties implicated, ascertain who fired the shot, and aid the civil authorities in arresting the offender and bringing him to justice. At that time the three actors in the tragedy were not known to the body of the students and the first efforts of the committee, of whom I was one, was directed to ascertain the identity of those engaged in the disturbance. One of the party was soon identified, arrested and examined by the committee. He was much alarmed and fearing for his own safety, gave the name of the guilty man, who did not reside in the University, but roomed at one of the boarding houses between the University and Charlottesville. A party started immediately to this house, hoping to arrest the offender, but when we reached there, found he had escaped. The search was kept up until long after midnight, and a watch set around the boarding house in expectation of his return during the night, but in this we were disappointed. All these steps were taken by the students themselves, without assistance from the civil authorities, who took no part in it until the next day. Reports as to Professor Davis' condition on the morning of the fourteenth were most discouraging. Nothing definite had transpired as to the whereabouts of the fugitive. Committees were sent to the hotels on the various roads where the stages stopped for meals, in the expectation that the missing man might attempt to escape by boarding these conveyances at these distant points. Warwick N. Miller, of Kentucky, and I rode fifteen miles on horseback in the afternoon to the Stage House on the Staunton turnpike, where supper was taken by the passengers, but when the stage arrived we saw that the man that we sought was not among them and we had our long ride for nothing. We returned to the University, reaching that place between eleven and twelve and were informed of the death of Professor Davis, which occurred about nine o'clock, as I remember it. During that night Semmes was caught by the guard which had been assigned to watch his boarding house. He attempted to get in the building but seeing the approach of the guard, he ran for the woods which had sheltered him the previous night, but was pursued and overtaken by a law student from Halifax County, William Sims. He made no resistance and was consigned to the walls of the jail in Charlottesville. The death of Professor Davis was deeply mourned and cast a gloom over the whole body of students, the shadow of which was scarcely lifted during the session. I will add to the above narrative that the family of the accused, being wealthy people, employed able counsel to defend him, and the Commonwealth's Attorney for Albemarle was aided by the Attorney-General of the State in conducting the prosecution. At the preliminary trial before the bench of magistrates he was sent on, and a strong effort was made before the Circuit Court to have the prisoner admitted to bail, but the Judge denied the motion, and as I remember it, the trial was postponed until the next term. Afterwards it was alleged that the long confinement had wrecked the health of the accused, and on this plea another application was urged, but the Circuit Judge refused to grant it, and an appeal was then taken to the highest Court of the State, which, after hearing argument, granted the plea, and fixed the penalty of the bail bond at twenty thousand dollars, then a sum almost unprecedented. The bail bond was given and the prisoner discharged. In accordance with general expectation, the bond was forfeited, the prisoner never appeared, and the full penalty of the bond was paid into the treasury of the State of Virginia.

I have been told by gentlemen of the legal profession that the action of the highest Court in this case established a precedent in the history of Virginia jurisprudence. The next session of the General Assembly of Virginia purchased from Mrs. Davis the copyright of "Davis on Criminal Law" for twenty thousand dollars. I have thus given the particulars of this sad affair, and though more than sixty years have passed since these occurrences, I think they are stated correctly. I have recently seen accounts of this affair in publications widely disseminated, which are erroneous in many particulars, notably as to the date of the occurrence.

I attended to my studies pretty closely and do not remember that I ever "cut lectures" on more than one occasion. Then Dabney Maury and I concluded we would have one day's hunt; he being as much of an enthusiast as myself in fondness for field sports. We borrowed a gun apiece, procured ammunition, and started about sunrise on a beautiful November day on our hunt. We were unable to secure either a pointer or a setter, but with a half hound and one or two cur dogs, we went to a farm a short distance from the University, belonging to an old gentleman named Garth. The farm was "posted," but we argued that the more carefully the game was protected, the more plentiful it was likely to be, and our theory was verified, for after a good day's sport, in which we were not disturbed by any one, we returned about dark with a fine lot of birds and hares, sufficient to enable us to give the biggest kind of a game supper to our friends, who did full justice to the spread.

My most intimate friend was John Staige Davis. He was very expert at taking notes on the lectures, and I also wrote with great rapidity, and during the whole course we sat side by side, one taking down the first half of the lecture, including the questions asked on the previous lecture, the other taking the last half, and in the afternoon we wrote the notes out in full and found them of great assistance. Indeed, on some of the tickets these notes were highly prized, long after they were taken. My brother, John T. Withers, who attended medical lectures five years afterwards, told me that even then the Davis-Withers notes were much in demand by the medical students.

Staige Davis was appointed demonstrator of Anatomy soon after his graduation and in due time was made full professor and filled the place ably during his short and useful life. Our friendship remained unbroken as long as he lived. He was always a great favorite with both students and professors.

John R. Thompson, of Richmond, who afterwards attained considerable reputation as a poet and litterateur, was in his first year's attendance this session. He was a dapper little fellow and had more speaking acquaintances than any man at the University. He early gave indication of the "Divine afflatus," and the portico of the rotunda the morning after the "English examination" was adorned by a copy of satirical verses descriptive of the farcical procedure, which contained several good hits, of which I can only recall the concluding stanza:

> "Green are the forest trees in Spring,
> In June, green is the clover,
> But far more verdancy you've shown
> Who've read these verses over."

No name was attached to the performance, but the authorship did not long remain a mystery. Thompson was a pretty regular contributor to the *Collegian,* and some of his papers were very creditable productions. This readiness in versification, developed in his earlier years, continued with him through life, and many of his fugitive pieces were marked by a tenderness of sentiment and a delicacy of imagery which proved that he was endowed with the true "poetic fire."

The session of 1840-41 was marked by the death of one of the ablest Professors of the school, Charles Bonnycastle, Professor of Mathematics, died on the thirteenth of October, 1840, after a protracted illness. His loss to the University was almost irreparable. The Board of Visitors made no effort to fill the vacancy permanently, but employed Mr. Pike Powers to complete the course. Mr. Powers came to the University with a fine reputation as a mathematician, and so far as I am informed, fully sustained it. Another vacancy in the corps of professors was caused by the removal of Professor Blattaerman of the School of Modern Languages, who, if I mistake not, was one of the original professors. He was undoubtedly a most accomplished linguist, but his habits became so objectionable as to bring scandal upon the Institution. The Board of Visitors, therefore, removed him and made a temporary selection of two persons to fill his place. One, Dr. Togno, taught French and Italian, and Monsieur Piado taught Spanish and German. They retained their places only until the end of the session. The death of Dr. Bonnycastle and the removal of Dr. Battaerman revived the recollection in the minds of some of the older students of an amusing episode in which each of these dignitaries was said to have borne a part. I do not vouch for the truth of the story, as it was said to have occurred before I was a student. "I tell the tale as 'twas told to me."

Dr. Bonnycastle was at the time chairman of the faculty, and of course the proper discipline of the students devolved on him. Amongst other regulations was one which forbade, under stringent penalties, any student to enter a restaurant. To appreciate the joke it must be remembered that Dr. Bonnycastle, while one of the most learned and able men of his day, was as unsophisticated as a child, knew nothing of dissipation in any form, and always accepted as true any statement made by a gentleman. On one occasion as he was passing along the street in front of a noted restaurant, much frequented by students "on the sly," he almost ran against a student emerging from the forbidden premises. He was of course confused at being thus "taken in the act," and when summoned to meet the Chairman the next morning, repaired to his office with the determination to plead guilty and take the consequences. Accordingly, when the Chairman called his attention to the violation of the law in question, he acknowledged that he had gone into the restaurant, but said he was much fatigued by his walk and concluded "to step in and take some peach and honey."

"Is that all you took?" inquired the Chairman.

"Certainly, sir," replied the culprit.

"Well," was the reply, "if you give me your word that you only had some honey and peaches, I will excuse you, but you must in future keep away from such places."

Astounded by the turn the affair had taken, the offender

left the office in high glee, but the joke was too good to keep and Dr. Blattaerman got hold of it and with the greatest gusto told the story to others of the professors and so worried Dr Bonnycastle that it was said they had a personal collision on the lawn growing out of the incident.

The chair of Law left vacant by the death of Mr. Davis was filled by the appointment of Mr. N. P. Howard, of Richmond, to complete the course. This appointment was generally satisfactory to the press and people of the State and also to the Law Class.

The misfortunes of the session did not end here, for Dr Emmett, the able Professor of Chemistry and Materia Medica died just before the close of the session after a short illness He was a near relative of Robert Emmett, who was executed for high treason in the last century.

Dr. James L. Cabell, Professor of Anatomy and Surgery was a typical Virginia gentleman in every sense of the word Courteous and polished in manner, clear and perspicuous in his lectures, keeping abreast with the progressive march of his profession, he was for many long years an ornament to the University to whose service his life was devoted.

Dr. Henry Howard, Professor of Theory and Practice and Medical Jurisprudence, was an elderly gentleman of amiable disposition, who stuck closely to the text-books, and was consequently a rather dry lecturer. On one occasion, however, he treated his class to a genuine surprise. He was lecturing on Medical Jurisprudence and the particular subject under consideration was "Personal Identity," when without premonition or warning he broke into poetry, thus:

> " Danger, long travel, want and woe,
> Soon change the forms that best we know,
> And blanch at once the hair,
> Hard toil can roughen form and face,
> And want can quench the eye's bright grace,
> Nor does old age a wrinkle trace
> More deeply than despair."

This unexpected excursion into the realms of poetry and the appositeness of the quotation, so astonished the class that he was treated to an enthusiastic round of applause. But what was the astonishment of Staige Davis and myself when engaged in writing out our notes that evening, we found in a foot-note of Beck's Medical Jurisprudence the same lines of Scott *verbatim et literatim*.

I will close the narrative of my life at the University of Virginia with the brief statement that I was successful in all my examinations, and at the annual "Commencement" in July, received from the Chairman of the faculty, with great pride and satisfaction, my diploma as Doctor of Medicine, and with the prize in my possession returned to my home, not having yet reached my twentieth year.

My older sister, Jennet Anne, married Dr. Robert T. Lemmon, who had been associated with my father in the practice, within a short time after my return. The newly married couple located about twelve miles distant from Rock Castle, while I took the place of partner to my father, and commenced the active practice of the profession among the people with whom I had been reared. The embarrassment and timidity with which I was for a while afflicted soon passed away, and I was speedily embarked in the regular routine of the life of a country doctor.

CHAPTER VIII.

LIFE IN A CITY HOSPITAL.

Before I had been practicing a year I was notified of my appointment as one of the "resident physicians" at the Baltimore Alms House Hospital, located about two and a half miles west of the city, and I at once became an inmate of that institution. Two older physicians living in the city were the "Senior Physicians." They were required to visit the Hospital daily, examine and prescribe for the sick and give instructions to the young doctors in the proper discharge of their duties. One of the Senior Physicians had charge of the male, the other of the female wards, and they exchanged duties every half year, the juniors changed every three months. Drs. Annan and Power were the Seniors. The first named was a good practitioner according to the old regime, but slow to accept the advanced views of his colleague, who was an enthusiastic disciple of progress. This gentleman had not long returned from Paris where he had given special attention to Auscultation, a science then in its infancy, but already giving evidence of its wonderful possibilities. Of course he was the favorite of the juniors, and under his careful instruction we soon acquired a useful proficiency in the new science. All the patients in the hospital were divided amongst the juniors in equal numbers, and each had to assume the care and responsibility of attending to their wants and ministering to their necessities, just as they would in regular practice, subject, however, to the supervision of the Senior Physician. Under this system it will be readily seen that most valuable opportunity was given each of us to acquire a knowledge of the practical part of the profession in all its branches and I know the information thus obtained was of incalculable service.

The eight juniors, when I entered the hospital were, on the male side, William P. Palmer, of Richmond, Virginia, James

L. Roper, of Petersburg, William Jenkins, of Kentucky, and Jacob Houck, of Baltimore. On the female side were Rezin H. Worthington, of Maryland, William Wirt, of Baltimore, John S. Gamble, of Florida, and R. E. Withers, of Virginia. Worthington and I were roommates. He was a man of good sense and attended well to his duties, indeed, all of the lot evinced an earnest desire to reap the full benefit of their opportunities. Worthington did not live long after leaving the almshouse. William Wirt was a son of the man of the same name who was Attorney-General of the United States. He was fond of society, a genial, pleasant gentleman, and delightful companion and associate. I do not think he had any special fondness for the profession. Soon after leaving the almshouse he married a lady of fortune, settled on a fine farm in Westmoreland County, Virginia, led the life of a country gentleman, and died a few years since. John Gamble, of Florida, was a descendant of the gentleman who gave the name to "Gamble's Hill," in Richmond. He was very bright and clever, fond of the profession, a good violinist, and would have made a most useful man, but unfortunately, fell in early life a victim to consumption. William P. Palmer, a high-toned gentleman, spent a long life in his native city, Richmond, had a quick sense of humor, was fond of fun and liked by all. He served during the war with the Richmond Howitzers very gallantly and efficiently, and after the struggle was over, lived and died in Richmond. I never heard any one speak of him except in terms of praise. He never married. Roper, after leaving the hospital, returned to Petersburg, but I know little of his future career. Jenkins and Houck soon passed out of my knowledge. The first was not in any way remarkable, and the last was a rollicking and frolicking fellow, fond of fun and was "hail-fellow-well-met," with every one. He possessed few business qualifications but you couldn't help liking him.

The institution was an almshouse as well as a hospital, and the drunk and disorderly, arrested in the city, were sent to the hospital, and when destitute and unable to pay the fines imposed, were required to "work out" these penalties either on the farm attached or in some of the shops on the place. Some of these hard subjects were once men of education and refinement, who had, from too much indulgence in alcoholic drinks, "gone to the dogs." Among this number was Dr. John Loftus, who in early manhood was regarded as of unusual promise, possessing literary talents of a high order, an unusual facility in versification, and was held in high esteem by family and friends. His poetical effusions attracted considerable attention and he received the sobriquet of "The Milford Bard," being a native of the town of Milford in Delaware. When "Tom Moore," the distinguished poet, visited the United States, he met with the "Milford Bard," and being much pleased with the brightness of his fancy, and the sprightliness of his conversation, paid him considerable attention and made flattering mention of him in his reminiscences of his visit. But the convivial tastes which gave a name to "Anacreon Moore" proved too much for the "Milford Bard," and he was now a pretty regular visitor to the cells of the almshouse as the result of his potations. He was absolutely destitute of self-control. After sobering up he would bemoan his fate to the doctor who happened to have him in charge in the most moving terms, and solemnly vow reformation, but the reform never lasted longer than the time required to reach a barroom if he possessed the means of indulgence. He often wrote little fragments of poetry, possessing, however, little merit. I remember a fragment of one of these which he presented to me and which displays some facility in punning. It was a burlesque advertisement of some wonderful quack nostrum warranted to cure everything. I recall thus much:

> " I tried it on a cat dyspeptic,
> The cat was also cataleptic,
> Incapable in every station,
> Of even ratiocination.
> The cat fell sick of grief and grog,
> Her ailments made a catalogue.
> I made her too good cataplasms,
> Which soon relieved her of her spasms.
> But a dogmatical physician
> Was called, who killed her all agree,
> Oh dear! what a catastrophe."

Another inmate of whom I retain pleasant recollections was Tom Rowen, an old, much dilapidated, but most humorous Irishman, who had served the greater portion of his life in the army and navy of Great Britain, but coming afterwards to the United States, had been stranded in Baltimore and now spent the greater portion of his time in the almshouse, where he acceptably filled the place of *"valet de chambre"* to Worthington and myself, when sober. He was never known to return sober from a visit to the city, indeed, he never returned voluntarily at all, but was brought in the "Black Maria" and dumped at the entrance to the workhouse. He made "night hideous," or day either, with his yells and profanity, as he possessed the most unique assortment of oaths of any one I ever knew. His long service "afloat and ashore" furnished him the material. After sobering up in the cell he would send for Worthington or myself to intercede for his release, making the most solemn vows of amendment, and most pathetic appeals to our feelings. the upshot always being that we would go to Mr. Denson, the Superintendent, and secure his release, all hands knowing perfectly well that the whole role would be reenacted the first time he could get to the city. Denson was a good administrative officer and a rigid disciplinarian. Tom was a most excellent servant and perfect *"aufait"* on all the duties of a valet. He knew many recipes for remedies for grease spots, paint, or other damage to clothing, and his services were frequently called into requisition by Mrs. Denson, who, on one occasion gave him a handsome silk dress to treat for a large spot of grease on the skirt. He worked on it all day in our room and not without success, as he restored the fabric to its pristine beauty. A few days after, Tom got a permit to go to town, and was of course brought back in a day or two, crazy from drink, and abused Mr. Denson and all the authorities in such outrageous terms that he was sentenced by Denson to the shower-bath, the usual penalty for insubordination. Some time after this Mrs. Denson met Tom in the hall and, remembering the service he had rendered the gown, asked him if Mr. Denson had ever paid him for the work.

"Oh, yes, ma'am," said Tom, "he paid me well, very well."

"Why, what did he give you?" said she.

"Five buckets of wather, ma'am, from the bottom of the pump, the couldest day in the winther," said Tom.

He claimed to have served under Lord Wellington during the whole of his operations in the Peninsula, and was full of anecdotes and incidents, connected with this celebrated campaign. He also claimed to have served on board Lord Nelson's ship, "The Victory," at Trafalgar. He certainly knew all about the details of duty both in the army and navy, but his claim of service under the immediate eye of these two great warriors may be taken *cum grano salis*. I was very fond of the old fellow and greatly enjoyed his stories. It never required much coaxing to start him, and once started, it was difficult to stop him. Poor old fellow! Peace to his ashes.

I will narrate a circumstance which occurred during my stay at the almshouse and which furnished the juniors much amusement and subsequently very pleasant social intercourse with the other parties concerned. In our visits to the city, usually made on foot, we were accustomed to walk a near way leading through the almshouse farm and others contiguous thereto. Near the path was a fine spring surrounded by a group of maples, and here we were wont to pause for a refreshing drink, but as no drinking cup was obtainable, we had to kneel and pump the water from the fountain in primitive style. A short distance above the spring was a handsome house and yard, presenting every appearance of being the abode of cultivated and aristocratic inmates. One warm afternoon when we paused to drink as usual at the spring, and were regretting the absence of a cup, I took a card and wrote on it, "Please leave a cup at the spring for the benefit of the visitors," and left it on a tree at the head of the spring. The next day, wishing to ascertain the result of the impudent request, we were gratified and rather surprised by finding another card in the place of the one we left. On it was written in a delicate female hand, "We would willingly leave a cup at the spring, but *some* of our visitors carry it away with them." I do not now recall what reply we made to this, but do remember that this spring at once became the terminus of our walk every afternoon, and we christened it the "Naiad's Spring." After the interchange of several cards, we found one afternoon the following, "This correspondence has become too affecting, therefore, who *am you?*"

Only three of our number were originally participants in this pretty game, but after reading the last missive, we called a meeting of the whole crowd, and after due deliberation, decided that the proper thing to do would be to write an acrostic for each of our number, and thus reply to the request conveyed by the last communication. That evening and the next morning were spent in the throes of poetical composition. I only recall at this distant day my own effort, regretting that lapse of memory will not permit me to give each of the acrostics, some of which were very good. My own effusion ran thus:

> "What's this? methinks I hear you say,
> I see those gents were here to-day,
> They've left their cards at last I see,
> Here they are sticking on the tree,
> Enchantress look! These verses scan,
> Read and reread for thus you can
> See who your humble servant am."

The next afternoon we found no response, but the day after we found a scorcher, filling a sheet of letter paper. If I regret my inability to recall the acrostics, the regret is intensified when I can not reproduce the bright, witty, and sparkling repartee. Mention was made of every one of us by name, and the satirical allusions were generally good. I give what I can recall, but, as you will see, there is an *"hiatus maxime deflendus."*

> "At morning noon and other times,
> Are seen acrostics, cards with rhyme,
> Some craving like an Almshouse bard
> The privilege to present his card.

> "This once fair bower whose sombre shade
> Shielded the sporting of the Naiad,
> Now droops its seared leaves and Withers
> Nor moisture from the fount now gathers.

> "No compound philtre can exert
> Its influence to sustain a Wirt,
> The Naiads hearts were never calmer,
> Or more impervious to a Palmer.
>
> "Rezin, may other riddles bring
> To frighten Naiads from the spring,
> But Rezin knows it can't be done,
> Not even by a Worthington."

These will serve to give some idea of the character of the production; it caused quite a stir in our party. It was decided to make a reply in kind, and the best poets of our number were commissioned to prepare the papers and submit them to the consideration of the whole body. About three responses were accordingly presented after supper, but none proved satisfactory. After discussion it was proposed to treat the ladies to a serenade that night, instead of keeping up the correspondence—a virtual admission that we were beaten. About midnight our party started out. Gamble was a good violinist, Wert played and sang to the guitar, several could sing in chorus, and on the whole the serenade passed off satisfactorally. A day or two later Dr. Power, on his regular visit, told us that he had called on the young ladies of the house and been greatly amused by their account of the correspondence, and had very much enjoyed reading the same, and conveyed to us a polite message of thanks for the serenade, with an invitation to call. The young lady of the house had a friend from the city staying with her, who was quite a celebrated belle, and between them they had demonstrated their ability, not only to keep up their end of the correspondence, but to prove how hopeless was the effort on the part of our sex to cope with the ladies in these interchanges of wit. I will not give the names, but bear willing testimony to the pleasant social intercourse to which the escapade led, and which was continued up to the time I left the almshouse.

A NEGRO CAMP-MEETING.

During August of this year, a negro camp-meeting was advertised to be held in the country some six or eight miles from the almshouse, and as I had never been present on such an occasion, and had heard very wonderful accounts of what transpired among the throng of negroes which were in attendance, I felt a strong inclination to visit the meeting. Mentioning my purpose to some of the other young Medicos, two of them agreed to accompany me, and we arranged to procure horses and ride out to the camp when it was in full blast. Accordingly, one afternoon we set out soon after dinner, and after a ride of almost two hours, reached the camp ground. Hitching our horses securely to the trees in the immediate vicinity of the buildings, we entered the grounds, which we found resembled in its general features the usual arrangement, of log huts in a hollow square around the central arbor and pulpit stand. We were greatly disappointed at seeing so few people around. We inquired of some of those who appeared busy with housekeeping cares, "what had become of all the people?" We were told "they were down in Mr. Johnson's field playing Moses and Joshua." This was something new at once, so we asked the way and the distance to Mr. Johnson's field, and having received instructions on both points, walked in the direction indicated. After going rather more than half a mile, we heard loud singing, interspersed with shouts and exclamations, commonly heard when negro worshipers get happy. We soon came in sight of an immense crowd of negroes of both sexes who appeared to be marching around a big pile of stones in the field, singing at the top of their voices, and led by a large mulatto man, who walked in front of the column with a big Bible under his arm and a long tin trumpet in his hand, on which he occasionally blew a resounding blast that made the echoes ring again. There were probably a thousand persons in the procession, and every now and then one, and sometimes several, would commence shouting, clapping their hands, and jumping up and down in the most frantic manner, until exhausted by vocal and muscular exertion they would drop on the ground, limp and apparently insensible, when they would be dragged aside by some of the company and left to recover at their leisure. This continued for some time, when the leader with the trumpet took the road leading back to the camp ground, but still continuing to alternate his singing with loud trumpet blasts. When they reached the grounds, they made a complete circuit of the cabins, and the singing, shouting and jumping up and down, were, if possible, redoubled. We were sitting on the benches intended for the congregation watching the proceedings, when a young woman, who had been unusually vociferous in her cries and active in her saltations, dropped near us and was picked up and laid on one of the benches near by. I spoke to the men who bore her and asked if she were not able to help herself. "Oh! no sir," said he, "she is in a trance and don't know nothing."

"How long will she remain so?" said I.

"There is no telling that," said he, "may be an hour and may be all night."

They left and took their places in the column. We commenced to discuss the condition of the girl from a professional standpoint, some of us contending that it was evidently hysterical, others thought it cataleptic, but one of the party held out that it was all "possuming," and to prove his theory he slipped up near her and without a word stuck a pin in the muscles of her arm lying prone on the bench, expecting her to jump when she felt the pain. But to his surprise, not a quiver of the eyelid or the twitch of a muscle showed consciousness in the slightest degree. We then examined her pulse, which was full but not much quickened considering the violent exercise in which she had been indulging, her respiration abnormally slow, the pupils of her eyes were dilated and appeared to be insensible to light. Our consultation ended in the verdict of catalepsy from nervous exhaustion, and so I suppose it was. We endeavored to ascertain the meaning of the procession and the trumpet sounding, but no one was able or willing to inform us, so we concluded it was designed to commemorate the altar erected by Joshua in the ford of the Jordan when the Children of Israel passed that stream to enter the promised land, and the fall of Jericho's walls at the sound of the trumpets after they had been compassed about seven times. We were satisfied in one thing, and that was that those in a trance, as it was called, were really not at all sensible or cognizant of what was passing around them. We were invited to remain to supper and preaching which would follow that meal, but as the sun was by this time nearing the horizon, we deemed it best to return to the Almshouse.

When I first went to Baltimore I bore a letter of introduction to Mr. Robert Lemmon from my father, and was at once received by his family on terms of familiar intimacy, as my father's oldest sister had married the Rev. George Lemmon, a brother of Robert Lemmon and his three maiden sisters, who composed the family circle. I had a standing invitation to dine with them whenever I came to the city, and as I almost always attended church on Sunday, I usually availed myself of this invitation. Occasionally I visited the homes of two other brothers, Richard and William Lemmon, on Charles Street, the first named being particularly genial in temperament and disposition, with a very pretty daughter, just out. I was much struck and occasionally amused by the dissonant ideas on religious matters prevalent in the Lemmon family. My uncle, Rev. George Lemmon, was an orthodox minister in the Episcopal Church, having charge of the congregations in Warrenton and at the Plains in Fauquier County, the maiden sisters were Baptists of the regular stripe, Mr. William Lemmon and Mr. Richard Lemmon also professed to be Baptists, but each of a different type, and each and all the family were especially severe towards those who did not agree with them in their theological views. I once heard a prominent gentleman in Baltimore characterize Richard Lemmon as the most remarkable man and the greatest enigma of his acquaintance. Said he, "He is one of the most far-sighted, sagacious and enterprising merchants on Change, he is the greatest bon vivant and epicure in the city, the greatest connoisseur in wines, and to crown all is a Baptist preacher, who ventilates his views weekly and whose church is composed of himself alone." He had a large family of sons who came South when the war broke out and served through the whole war with great gallantry and efficiency. One was killed, I think, at Kernstown.

After a pleasant sojourn of nearly a year at the almshouse, I returned to Campbell, availing myself of the opportunity of calling at Warrenton and spending a few days with my relatives in Fauquier County, few of whom I had ever seen before. This visit gave me an opportunity to see my grandfather's family residence, "Green Meadows," then occupied and owned by his son, Horatio Chinn Withers, whose wife was Miss Fitzhugh, of Fairfax County. He was by profession a lawyer, but I do not think he ever practiced.

I came home fully qualified, in my own opinion at least, to practice medicine in all its branches. I brought with me a large box filled with anatomical preparations, showing the bones, muscles, arteries, veins and nerves of the human body, carefully dissected, dried and varnished, with an articulated skeleton and another unarticulated. The various viscera were also shown by good preparations. These sufficed to fill a large press in my office, which from that time was carefully avoided by every negro on the place, whose fears were in turn communicated to others in the neighborhood until it became a difficult matter to induce one of them to enter the door, even when in company with others.

CHAPTER IX.

SPORTING INCIDENTS BY FIELD, FOREST AND STREAM.

While I can not claim that I devoted myself entirely to my duties as a country practitioner, it certainly was my chief occupation. My innate fondness for sport often lured me from my professional duties, and as birds were plentiful in my neighborhood, and fish abundant in Staunton River, I spent considerable time both in spring and fall in their pursuit. The spawning period of the river fish was in the early spring, at which time they frequented the falls of the river and wherever they could find a swift current over a bed of gravel they collected in shoals and deposited their spawn. In these localities we sought them and with a small seine of eighty or a hundred feet in length the fish could be captured in considerable numbers by expert fishermen. It was hard work but lots of fun. The seine was not hauled to the shore, but when the fish were enclosed by running the two staves of the seine together, the "treader" in the center arresting its progress by putting his foot on the lead line, the force of the current brought the two sides of the seine into parallel lines and the fish were then taken out in the middle of the stream. I owned a seine and kept it at the house of Sam Cunningham, who was devoted to the sport, and whose wife had knetted the seine. He lived about half way between my house and the river. Five persons at least are required properly to manage the seine. I always carried a staff, as I was tall and strong and not afraid of the water. When I first began fishing with the seine it was an accepted axiom that whiskey was an indispensable commodity, as in early April the water is very cold and soon gives one a chill, which, in the opinion of experienced fishermen, could be counteracted only by a stiff dram taken after every round. This practice often resulted in the intoxication of one or more of the party with consequent worry and trouble to the others. We were dependent for our supply of whiskey on

"Pannill's Store," located near the fishing grounds, but the liquor he dispensed was of poor quality and by no means a pleasant beverage. One day I asked the old gentleman why he didn't keep some whiskey of better quality, and his reply furnished food for thought.

"Because," said he, "the common whiskey pays the best profit and sells just as well. When it is good they will drink it and bless it, and when it is bad they will drink it and cuss it, but they'll drink it anyhow."

This old gentleman deserves special mention as he was in many respects a noted character. His residence was known as "Green Hill," a lovely place, with beautiful yard and grounds always well kept. He was a man of large wealth, as wealth was then estimated, owned a large merchant mill, the flour from which he shipped by batteaux manned by his own slaves (of which he owned a great number) to the towns of Weldon and Gaston in North Carolina. He was a man of strong intellect, inveterate prejudices, tenacious of his own opinions, and afraid of no man. He was aristocratic in his notions, and consequently not very popular among the common people, though highly respected by all. He ruled his sons and all his employes with a rod of iron, and was as much feared as respected by them. His sons never married, his daughters were all married, and generally to men of prominence in Campbell and adjoining counties. He died at a very advanced age.

But to return to my subject, from which I did not intend to drift so far. Having joined the ranks of the "Sons of Temperance," I had substituted hot coffee for the whiskey as a beverage, and was more than satisfied with the change. It counteracted the effects of the cold water better, was more permanent in its refreshing quality, and was so manifestly an improvement that the strongest advocates of whiskey in time abandoned its use and substituted hot coffee.

The first fish to run in the spring are the salmon, as we call them, which are not, of course, the true salmon, but properly the salmon trout, a very fine food fish. Unless we fished in March we did not often strike a shoal of these. Next to these came the winter or black sucker, followed by the sorrel horse or red fin sucker, the largest of the family. They in turn were followed by the blue fin and they by the May sucker, and the black bass follow these. There are fine game fish, known in that stream as "King William perch." In the spring and fall the mill ponds furnished pretty fair sport with the rod, being generally well stocked with pike or Jack fish, red eyes and silver perch, mill pond and flat-back suckers, and smaller fry.

I always, however, preferred the gun to the rod, and being an expert wing shot, my greatest pleasure was in hunting partridges. For twenty years or more I was the champion wing shot of that section of the country, and as I resided in the midst of the best hunting grounds, always owned good dogs, and kept open house during the hunting season, I had many visits from sportsmen from a distance who sought to win laurels by bagging more birds than I. Gentlemen from Lynchburg, Fredericksburg, Richmond, Petersburg, and Norfolk have at different times visited me with the purpose indicated, but none ever carried off any trophies, though at times some of them came perilously near it. Not unfrequently at the hour for "snack" I would be two or three birds behind, but was always able to make up my lee-way in the "quarter stretch." My friend, Mr. Edmond Taylor, whose home was on the Rappahannock below Fredericksburg, who had married a daughter of Mr. John Blair Dabney, of "Vaucluse," a neighbor of mine, came every fall for years to visit "Vaucluse," bringing his dogs and gun. We hunted a great deal together, and as he was an enthusiastic sportsman and a fine shot, he often pushed me very close, but never succeeded in beating me. He said more than once, "If I can beat you one time I'll never hunt with you again," but we continued to hunt together every fall until I removed to Danville. I recall an occasion when he and I were hunting together we emptied our bird bags at "snack" time, and he had three birds more than I. He was much elated at the fact and boasted that he "had me," and was determined to maintain his lead. There was no one with us except the boy who held our horses, so there was no possibility of outside interference. Soon after we started out again, the dogs came to a stand near the head of a ditch in perfectly open ground. As we walked up to them the covey flew up and I, being on the right, fired both barrels in quick succession, and saw two birds fall to each shot. I was expecting Taylor to claim two of them at least, but he said not a word, and I proceeded to bag my four birds, elated at the prospect of "evening up" so soon. Turning to him as he was storing his own prizes, I said, "How many did you get Taylor ?"

"Two with each barrel," said he. Which proved to be true, the only time I remember to have witnessed such an occurrence in the partridge field. When we counted our birds at night I led him by four birds. When we hunted together we generally bagged from eighty to a hundred birds without counting hares or other game.

A good many wild turkeys were to be found in our neighborhood, and one morning as I walked from my office to the house for breakfast I heard a wild turkey "gobbling" on the "Buzzard Mountain" less than a mile away, and thought I would try and kill him. So returning hastily to my room I found that my double gun was empty, but a small single-barreled gun which I had owned from boyhood was loaded. To save time I picked it up and started for the woods at "double quick." It did not take me very long to reach the neighborhood of the turkey, and I concealed myself behind a log in the woods, took out my "yelper" and gave a soft call. He answered at once and came towards me, but soon stopped and "gobbled" again, awaiting for me to yelp again. As I feared detection, however, I did not repeat the call. Instead I commenced scratching in the leaves, and had hardly done so before I heard him coming in a run. He speedily came up, with head high above the huckleberry bushes, and when I thought him near enough, I aimed at his head and fired, the gun being loaded only with bird shot. At the crack of the gun he tumbled over, and I leisurely walked towards him, but just before I reached him he got on his feet and made an effort to run. I dropped the gun and rushed at him, but he eluded my grasp leaving only a handful of feathers, he waddled off, I grabbing at him every step, he stumbling and falling frequently. I thought a dozen times I had him, but he managed every time to dodge, I could see that one of his eyes was out and his head bleeding from other wounds. I never succeeded in getting hold of that turkey, but I came near running myself to death, for when I finally fell exhausted on the ground, utterly breathless, the game was not five steps distant, apparently almost equally tired, but not quite, as he could walk slowly but I couldn't move. I thought at first that I would never get my breath again, but after gasping and panting a long time I regained sufficient strength to enable me to arise from the ground. I think I have never since during my whole life been so utterly blown. It took me fully half an hour to find my gun, for in the gyrations of the chase I had lost all sense of direction, and hunted long before I recovered it. A few days after while squirrel hunting in the same woods we found the gobbler dead and spoiled not far from where I had to give up the chase. This experience rather disgusted me with turkey hunting, as I never followed this species of game with the zest and enjoyment inseparable from the pursuit of other varieties. Two of my younger brothers, however, were very fond of this sport, and were very skilful and successful.

Though a little out of chronological order I will here detail my first experience in hunting deer. This species of game was almost unknown in Eastern Virginia at the time of which I am writing, though now more plentiful there than in the mountains. My second brother Dr. John Thornton Withers, after graduating at the University of Virginia, located in Southwest Virginia, at Newburn, the County seat of Pulaski County, where he soon succeeded in establishing himself. In his letters and occasional visits home, he talked a great deal about the deer hunting in his county and aroused in me a strong desire to learn something of that sport. The next fall I wrote him that I would pay him a visit on condition that he would guarantee me a shot at a deer. This he readily agreed to do, so one day in November, I started with my gun on the proposed visit. As I passed through the City of Lynchburg, I accidentally met on the street my cousin Dr. Edward D. Withers of Danville, who was in Lynchburg on business. Knowing that he was strongly imbued with the family fondness for field sports, I told him of my proposed visit to Pulaski and urged him to accompany me. He did not require much persuasion, but boarded the train with me and in due time we reached Newburn, and stopped with Mr. Jabin Alexander a distant relative with whom my brother boarded. The next day a hunt was arranged for the day after, and having procured horses and a good gun for Dr. Ned, we rode that night to the house of Mr. David McGavock on Back Creek, a noted huntsman owning a pack of fine deer hounds, and an intimate friend of my brother. I found him a genial gentleman, living on a fine estate, big-hearted and hospitable, a giant in size and a past master of *venery*. He said there would be no trouble in getting up a deer, and he would place me on a stand through which it would be certain to run. "But," said he, "if you have never hunted deer I am not so sure that you will kill it when it comes." He said some gentlemen from Eastern Virginia who were reckoned good shots at birds and small game, he had known to let a deer pass, not only without hurt, but without having a gun fired at it. They had suffered from an attack of "Buck Ague," and forgotten that they had a gun when a big buck dashed by them. I had heard of "Buck Ague," but supposed it to be one of those myths, so often current among mountaineers. I told him I would submit to any amount of chaffing, and willingly undergo the proverbial penalty for missing a deer, to wit: The sacrifice of the extremity of my under-neathest garment, if I failed to shoot one passing within gun shot.

We started out after an early breakfast next morning, passed through the fine farm of Mr. James Cloyd, (where the battle of Cloyd's Farm was subsequently fought during the Civil War) and entered the woods beyond. Mr. McGavock proceeded to post the hunters at their stands, he, himself proposing to drive. He put me on the turnpike road, and pointing to a pine tree on the side of the road told me that if the dogs started a deer on that drive, it would certainly come into the the road within six feet of that pine tree. My brother was placed above about two hundred yards on the same road.

McGavock instructed me that if the deer crossed the road without being killed or seriously wounded, the dogs must be stopped when they reached the road, or they would follow it to the river, and thus prevent us from getting up another. He then entered the drive with the dogs. The day was rather windy and I listened a long time without hearing the note of a hound. Finally my brother, (who was always of an impatient and restless disposition) rode down to my stand, tied his horse and sat down for a chat. I told him I thought it was against the rule for any man to leave his stand, but he only laughed and said it was more fun to talk to me than to stand like a fool waiting for a deer to come to be shot. It was not very long after before I heard the note of a single dog, and he ran back to his stand, leaving his horse, however, standing where he had tied it. In a few minutes a fine doe ran to the edge of the road near the pine tree, but seeing the horse made no attempt to cross, but whirled back into the bushes which were very thick. I made a snap shot, but was pretty confident I had struck her, but in a short time the only dog in pursuit came into the road, and I had some trouble to catch him. Other dogs came in pretty soon, and my brother who had come down when he heard me shoot aided me in stopping them. In performing this duty, we had passed down the road about seventy-five yards, and going to the edge of the woods I sat down on a log to await the appearance of McGavock. Happening to cast my eyes to the ground at my feet, I saw, on the leaves a considerable gout of fresh blood, red and frothy, indicating that it came from the lungs. Knowing that this showed a serious wound we at once put the dogs on the track, and away they went, quickly passing out of hearing. McGavock came up pretty soon, and hearing the facts, thought that the deer would not go on to the river several miles distant, but would probably take to the creek which ran through the adjoining farm. We rode in that direction, and while listening for the dogs heard some of the farm hands hallooing, and riding up to them we found the deer lying on the ground in a dying condition. It had attempted to jump the fence near where the negroes were at work, but had fallen back, and never rose again. So we got our venison.

In butchering it we found that one shot only had struck it in the flank, which having ranged forward passed through the lungs, making of course a mortal wound though she ran a mile or more before falling. I was, of course, pleased with this evidence of markmanship, and at night around the fire, while discussing the events of the day, congratulated myself for having escaped the predicted attack of "Buck Ague." Some of the party thought an explanation might be found in the fact that the sudden and unexpected appearance of the deer, took me by surprise, and I therefore had no time to experience that peculiar sensation. "But," said he, "when you are at a stand, and hear the dogs coming a long way off, and then hear the deer bounding through the bushes a quarter of a mile away the sound constantly growing louder and louder as he nears you, and then see a big buck with branching horns, burst out of cover, then it is that the novice forgets he has a gun."

"All right," said I, "we will try it again tomorrow, and I hope to have a chance to test your theory."

The next day was calm, and pleasant and as before, we started early, reached the same ground, I took the same stand and McGavock carried the dogs into the drive. In less than half an hour I heard them "start," but soon found that they were not coming in my direction as they bore off up the country. I waited patiently expecting them to change their course and in this I was not disappointed. Ere long the pack was heard again in full cry evidently approaching, and listening with all my ears it was no great while before I could distinctly hear the deer bounding through the bushes, every leap becoming more distinctly audible. One barrel of my gun was loaded with a loose charge of buck shot, the other with a wire cartridge, designed for a long shot. When I knew that the deer was coming to me, I recalled the conversation of the night before, and to test the steadiness of my nerves I drew bead on a blaze on a pine tree from which I was distant about twenty-five steps. I was satisfied from this experiment that I was all right, and in half a minute more a magnificent buck burst into the road, and started across. I aimed at the shoulder and fired, but though I knew I had struck him where I had aimed, he gave no sign and made no pause, but kept on his course. He had not taken three leaps however before I fired my left barrel loaded with the cartridge, again aiming at the same point. At the crack of the second barrel he went heels over head, and fell dead in the road the blood spouting from his mouth and nose in a great stream. I walked up to him and saw that the cartridge had gone through him like a bullet. It was so near, the shot had never left the enclosing wire, the whole charge passed through his heart and lungs, and we found on butchering that my first shot had driven seven buck shot through his lungs. "Why," said McGavock, "what was the use of shooting the second time? The first shot was fatal, and he could not have run a hundred yards." "Possibly that may be true," said I, "but I always shoot as long as my game keeps going."

This established my reputation as a sure shot, and all agreed that I was in no danger from an attack of "Buck Ague." The next day we hunted in another direction, and the stands were along a road running on the banks of New River towards the Giles County Line. As soon as McGavock put the dogs into the drive he joined us, and placing me at a point where a small stream entered the river which he thought the best stand, my brother next below me, and two others still farther down. He and Dr. Ned Withers forded the river, which is here wide and shallow, so that if the game escaped those posted on this side the stream they could have a chance at him on the other. A large mountain ran for some distance parallel to the river, down the face of which the deer was expected to run. After some time I heard the dogs top the mountain, and as they were coming directly towards me I expected to see the deer every instant, but was disappointed as no deer came to the water, but the dogs did, passing within a few feet of where I stood, and stopped to lap the water. I was puzzled to account for this, but McGavock from the other side called to me that something had turned the deer from its course, and directed me to take the dogs back up the mountain side and they would find the track. While thus engaged the deer was seen to enter the stream some quarter of a mile below and proceded to swim and wade across the river. McGavock called his dogs, and I urged them to cross, but the deer reached the opposite bank before Dr. Ned or McGavock either could reach that point. There was a cabin not far from where the deer left the water, and our shouts and cries to the dogs attracted the attention of a cur dog at this cabin, and he started towards the river to see what all the noise meant, and met the deer almost face to face. He immediately attempted to seize him, and the hunted animal at once turned back to the river for safety, the dog right behind him, and gaining every jump. Indeed from my point of view it appeared that he could have caught him by the flank, but he seemed to prefer getting a hold farther forward. Before he succeeded in this the deer sprang over a high bank into the water again, and the dog didn't follow. The poor animal recrossed to our side, and we concealed ourselves as well as we could, each hoping to get a shot as he approached the shore. A new actor had by this time made his appearance, in the shape of a gaunt and grizzled mountaineer armed with a flint lock rifle, nearly as long as himself, who was the cause of my missing a shot at first, by turning the deer from his accustomed line of flight, for hearing the pack running he had seized his rifle and knowing the line the deer would take to reach the water he tried to intercept him on the mountain side, but the deer either saw, heard or smelt him and changed his course. This new man now stood ready to take a hand, but the deer approached the shore in front of a Mr. Jones, and he swam towards the bank and came within thirty steps, nothing being visible but his head, this gentleman fired both barrels with no apparent result except to turn him back again towards the other side. The old mountaineer and I both ran to the point nearest the buck and he having a shorter distance to go reached the spot first, and raising his long rifle took aim, and pulled the trigger. A "snap" was the only result and he continued to aim and "snap" until I got there. I sprang on a ledge of rocks a short distance from the banks, ran out to the farthest point, and aiming at the deer's head and neck, the only part visible, fired my left barrel, loaded with the wire cartridge, the distance being about a hundred yards. I did not stop him however, but he shook his head and the old mountaineer said, "You hit him stranger, I seed you jerk the blood."

The persecuted animal struck the further shore at a point nearly midway between McGavock and Dr. Ned Withers, each of whom was making every effort to head him off. When he landed he turned up stream, and nearly ran over Dr. Withers, who fired at him not ten feet away and missed him clear with the first barrel, much to my surprise as I knew him to be a fine shot, but when the deer again took water he fired his second barrel evidently with good effect, but the deer continued up stream, again landed and ran towards a piece of woods a few hundred yards above, but when he tried to jump a low rail fence on the edge of the field, he fell back and only succeeded by a second effort in clearing it. He disappeared in the woods but McGavock having blown his horn and called his dogs prevailed on two or three to swim over to him. He put them on the track at the point where the buck entered the woods, and they did not go far before they "bounced" him, as he had laid down to rest. He was sorely wounded, but made a gallant spurt to reach the water again and ran against McGavock, who finished him by a shot at very short range. We found that my shot "which jerked the blood" had put three buck shot through his nose, but as they passed below the eyes, of course did not produce serious injury. As every feature of the chase I have described passed in open ground, entirely visible to all on each side of the stream, it constituted the most exciting experience I have ever had on a deer hunt.

We returned to McGavock's that night getting in pretty late, but welcomed by our charming hostess to a cheerful fire, and a table loaded with all the substantials and delicacies that form so delightful a finale to a hard days hunt. After doing full justice to these, we passed an hour or two in listening to hunting stories, and amusing incidents connected therewith. McGavock gave an account of a hunt in which he participated the year before when a party of Eastern Virginians, mostly residents of Lynchburg, came to his house to enjoy deer hunting. Among the party who started out was an old and experienced huntsman named Andy Miller, celebrated for his skill with the rifle, and his coolness and deliberation under all circumstances. The visitors were generally young and inexperienced in this species of sport. McGavock's dogs soon found a deer, which after a long chase, took to Big Walker's Creek into a deep eddy where he was presently surrounded by a crowd of dogs and huntmen. From all sides guns began to fire and buck shot to rattle to the great discomforture of Miller and McGavock, each of whom took shelter behind rocks and trees for protection against the flying missiles which threatened death to every one around. At last all the guns being emptied, the deer still unhurt jumped from the water, and started along the mountain side. Andy Miller poked his head out cautiously from his cover, and looking around to assure himself that the fusilade was over, said to McGavock, "Well Dave, I reckon its time somebody was killing of that ar deer," at the same time raising his rifle to his shoulder. He did not at once fire, but turning his head said, "Where shall I hit him Dave?"

"Anywhere you please, just so you kill him," was the reply. "Well I will try his neck," said he, and firing at the next moment tumbled the flying deer over with a broken neck.

I could fill a volume with such stories but think these will suffice as an illustration of the method of hunting deer with hounds. Of "still hunting," the favorite method of the old huntsmen, I have had no experience, from this time I managed almost every Fall to pay a visit to David McGavock, enjoyed his charming hospitality, and even to a greater degree the delights of the chase in his company. He was a man after my own heart, and his untimely death left a void in my circle of friends, which has never been filled. As I have mentioned he was a giant in size and strength, rode a magnificent saddle horse which had won the "blue ribbon" at the State Fair in Richmond. He was well-fitted to bear such a rider, and when McGavock moved through the dense woods carrying a slaughtered buck before him on the saddle, it was a sight to see, for ordinary saplings offered no obstruction to his progress. He would simply turn out his feet, catch and bear down the thick undergrowth and pass along the mountain side like a tornado.

* * * * * * *

CHAPTER X.

COUNTRY PRACTICE.

The years 1843-44 offered little of interest that I can now recall. In 1845, commencing with the early Summer, the County of Campbell was visited by an epidemic of Enteric fever, which will never be forgotten by those who witnessed its ravages. It was confined mainly to the high rolling country where fevers were previously unknown. Few cases occurred on the river plantations where intermittent and billious fevers were apt to appear in the Summer and Fall. The first cases I saw puzzled me a good deal, and I asked my father to visit them as he had been in full practice for twenty-five years. Like myself, however, he could reach no satisfactory conclusion as to its nature. I at first treated the cases tentatively, closely watching the progress of the disease and the effect of remedies. Some of the older practitioners around me treated it as if it were of malarial or billious origin, bleeding at first to relieve the initiatory cerebral symptoms, but it was not long before it was shown that every case so treated ended fatally, as was the case generally with all who submitted to "active treatment," as it was called. My brother William, a boy of nineteen, at the time was living in Lynchburg, with the mercantile firm of Peters and Matthews. He was taken sick and as soon as I was notified I rode to the city to see after him and found him evidently laboring under the same disease. He was under the care of an old time practitioner, who believed in the heroic treatment of all fevers. Dissenting from his views, and desirous of withdrawing my brother from what I regarded a dangerous situation, I determined to take him home though he had much fever, but at that time no delirium. I procured a carriage, put him in it, supported by pillows and accompanied by our cousin, Miss Charlotte Pendleton, we started just before sunset on our journey of twenty-five miles. The horses were kept in a walk, as I thought it would lessen the fatigue of the trip, and I rode behind the carriage all the way, reaching home about daylight. The patient seemed to stand the journey fairly well, but in a day or two he became delirious and for more than a month never regained consciousness. He ultimately recovered, being the only person so fortunate of all who were moved any distance after an invasion of the disease. Almost simultaneously with his attack, several cases occurred in my father's family among blacks and whites, and in a short time there were nearly forty sick on the place. My father ceased to attend any calls, devoting his whole time and attention to the sick at home. Two large tobacco barns near the house were converted into hospitals with manifest advantage to the patients, as contrasted with the dark and ill-ventilated quarters of the negro cabins. My brother-in-law, Dr. Lemmon, whose bounds adjoined mine on the west, was also forced by sickness in his own family to retire almost entirely from practice, thus adding to my labors. Scarcely a family in the whole scope of the country, away from the rivers escaped. I had more work to do than I could properly attend to; it soon took me three days, riding night and day, without rest, to complete my rounds. For nearly five months this condition of affairs was practically unaltered. For more than three months I never took off my clothes to sleep. There was no distinction between night and day. All the sleep I got was on horseback, and the habit thus acquired of enjoying a refreshing nap in the saddle never left me afterwards, and has often stood me in good stead during my subsequent service in the army. I treated between three and four hundred cases of fever in that season. When the epidemic commenced I weighed one hundred and eighty-five pounds, when it ceased, I was reduced to one hundred and forty pounds, but was never sick an hour. My saddle horses were utterly fagged out, but several friends who owned good horses were so kind as to give me the use of their steeds for a few days at a time, thus giving mine some rest, and this enabled me to keep up with my business. I seized every available opportunity to make post-mortem examinations in fatal cases and thus satisfied myself of the true pathology of the disease and this controlled my treatment. I have never been able to give my full assent to the generally accepted theory, that typhoid fever always has its origin in an animal poison taken into the stomach. This was certainly not the case in this, the first and worst epidemic of the disease known in Virginia. I had no cause to complain of any loss of prestige from my experiences in this epidemic. The percentage of mortality in the patients under my charge was notedly less than in the practice of the older physicians around me, and I, of course, did not fail to reap the benefit of this coincident fact. My father never again resumed active practice and thenceforward I was kept professionally busy. In after years I was often called in consultation with physicians in Lynchburg and the adjoining counties having patients ill with this fever, which necessitated long and tiresome rides. Assuming, however, that these professional reminiscences possess little interest for non-professional readers, I will close this branch of the subject.

Having always felt an interest in military achievements, and read with avidity all narratives of battles, campaigns, etc., that I could procure, I generally attended the musters of the militia company in my neighborhood, as well as the regimental musters, and when by special act of the Legislature, authority was given for the organization of a Volunteer Troop of Cavalry at Brookneal, a small village in Campbell County, with membership drawn from the Counties of Campbell, Halifax and Charlotte, contiguous to this place, I enlisted in the troop and was much interested in its success. We drew our arms from the Richmond arsenal after the requisite number were uniformed. At the election of officers I was selected as one of the lieutenants, and at once commenced a careful study of tactics and thus soon acquired a fair knowledge of the subject. As the captain of the company elect soon gave proof of inefficiency, and the first lieutenant was even worse, most of the drilling devolved on me. The captain, after serving a year or two, resigned, and at the election to fill the vacancy, I was chosen by a large majority and for some years served faithfully, enjoying the musters, and especially the "training of the officers," of all the companies in the county, which occurred at the Court-House every spring and was made the occasion of a good deal of fun and gaiety. There were two other cavalry companies in the county, one at the Court-House, and one at the village of Leesville, near the Bedford County line. There were also two companies of volunteers in Lynchburg, and two regiments of militia in the county, all of whose officers were required to drill together. These annual meetings were pretty largely attended, not only by the officers of the military companies, but also by many ladies from Lynchburg and the country adjoining the Court-House, as every night we had music and dancing to satiety. I bore my full part in these festivities and enjoyed them, too.

In those days the Fourth of July was always observed as a holiday and celebrated by a barbecue and dance, which was attended by almost half the county. On one of these festive occasions at Brookneal, I was selected to deliver the oration, and having accepted, prepared a patriotic address in which I lauded the glories of our Union and dilated on the manifest destiny of our country. Mr. John Henry, of "Red Hill," who was the youngest son of Patrick Henry and dwelt in the old residence, read the Declaration of Independence, and read it well. An immense crowd was present, and my effort was very highly lauded and cheered to the echo. This was my first appearance as a speaker after I was grown, and gave me considerable local reputation. A copy was requested for publication, but I wisely declined to furnish it. I have thus mentioned somewhat in detail my connection with the "Brookneal Troop," as it was, in a measure, the cause of my entering the army fifteen years later, as an officer of the line rather than as a surgeon. I will explain this more fully in due time.

CHAPTER XI.

I MEET MY FATE.

In December, 1845, I was invited by Dr. Roy B. Scott to act as one of his attendants at his approaching marriage to Miss Lucy Holcombe, of Lynchburg. He and I had been intimate friends for years, being about the same age, and I, of course, assented to his request. The marriage was to come off a few days before Christmas, and at the time designated I was punctually on hand, and accompanied the bridegroom to the house of Mr. Walter Henderson, on Federal Hill, who was brother-in-law to the bride, and at whose house the ceremony was to take place. It was arranged that I was to "stand up" with an estimable young lady of Lynchburg, a cousin of the bride, with whom I had a slight acquaintance—a service which I performed with due decorum. Among the attendants of the bride was another cousin, Miss Mary V. Royall, with whose appearance, when introduced, I was much struck. She had "stood up" with Mr. Gilbert C. Meem, of Lynchburg, second son of Mr. John G. Meem, one of the leading merchants and most prominent citizens of the place. As soon as an opportunity offered, I sought Miss Royall, at once entered into conversation with her which continued until near supper time, when I remarked, "I must go to find my young lady and escort her to supper, but I had much rather go with you." She said, "Wait a moment, and perhaps we can so arrange it." She called up Gilbert Meems, who was so obliging as to exchange partners with me, and I waited on "Miss Ginnie" to supper, and did not cease to wait on her afterwards during the whole evening. In short, it was a bad case of "love at first sight," a phenomenon of whose existence many are skeptical, but of which I have no more doubt than I have of my own existence. That she was equally impressed may be inferred by this fact which I learned afterwards from her sister. While returning home in the carriage that night Bettie said, "Well, Ginnie, you seem to have caught a new beau. How do you like the country doctor?"

"I like him so well that I tell you now, if he courts me, and I believe he will, I mean to marry him."

"Then," said Bettie, "what will you do with John?" referring to a young gentleman to whom she was engaged at that very time.

"Well, you may have him," was her reply.

I was compelled to return home early the next day, but two days after I came to Lynchburg, proposing to attend a reception given Dr. Scott and his bride at the house of his father, about three miles from town. I called to see Miss Royall, however, at her mother's house (my first visit), and after talking some time, rose to go, telling her I had promised Dr. Scott to go to his reception at his father's.

"Oh, don't go," said she, with an earnestness which impressed me.

"I will stay on one condition," said I.

"What is that condition?" said she.

"That you will agree to marry me right away," said I.

She was evidently startled, for she became very pale, but after a moment's hesitation a roseate blush stole over her face, and a look came into her eyes that told the tale, and "the subsequent proceedings" did not permit the roses to fade. Such was our short courtship, and such the rapid "course of true love." In six weeks thereafter we were man and wife. On my next visit rumors of our love affair had evidently gotten out, as a leading merchant of the city, a friend of mine, but still more intimate with the young gentleman to whom it was said my "lady love" was engaged, took me aside when I met him, and with a serious face said, "Dr. Bob" (for that was my usual sobriquet), "I want to have a serious talk with you."

Suspecting what was to follow, I only replied, "All right, say on."

Said he, "I understand you have come up here to see Miss Ginnie Royall. Now, we've always been friends, and I tell you confidentially that she is only fooling with you, for I *know positively* that she is engaged to marry another man," giving me his name.

I replied very shortly, "I know and care nothing about that, but I do know that I mean to marry her in a month." And so I did.

The gentleman to whom he referred was regarded as the most eligible match in the city, as he was the wealthiest young man in that community, was well educated, and good looking besides. I was a country doctor, of very moderate means, dependent for a living on my own exertions, therefore I see no explanation of her preference possible, except that it was the work of "love, the great conqueror." The young gentleman who thus lost his "lady love" never married, but died an old bachelor many years after, leaving his fortune to nephews and nieces. While I could not help feeling some sympathy for him, I never regretted "cutting him out."

Of course I could think of little else than my charming inamorata, and once a week rode, often through cold and storm, to pay her a visit, always returning the next morning. My father sent her word that he wished she would hurry up the ceremony so that I could attend to my business, little knowing how earnestly I had urged that she should marry me at once and make her preparations afterwards. Of course such a proceeding violated precedent, and she and her friends refused to consider the proposition, but agreed to use all possible diligence in the preparation of the trousseau. So on the third day of February, 1846, the marriage came off. As was customary at that day, each of us was attended by a large number of "waiters," as they were called, twelve on each side, and among the number you may be sure Gilbert S. Meem was one, as it was to his kind offices I was indebted for the opportunity of pushing my suit on the evening of our first meeting. There was a large wedding and the weather was bright, beautiful, and balmy, giving augury of our future happiness, an omen fully verified. We spent the next day with her mother, and the day after started for "Rock Castle," escorted by a large number of friends and relatives. We were to have a reception that evening at the old mansion, where "Dr. Bob's wife" was introduced to a large number of friends gathered for the occasion, to all of whom she was an entire stranger, but her beauty, vivacity, and charming manners made her at once a prime favorite. A succession of entertainments followed, given in our honor, at one of which, at my uncle Edward Withers, at "Ivanhoe," the dancing was kept up all night long. But further description is unnecessary, as it was in the line of those country festivities so often described, the source of much pleasure to the participants, but now have almost passed into desuetude.

Here was a young girl, reared in the city, not yet out of her teens, without any knowledge of country life, a stranger to the community into which she had been suddenly transplanted, ready and willing to give up mother, sister and a host of friends, and entrust her person, happiness, and fortunes to the keeping of a man whom she had seen for the first time only six weeks before. What a marvelous thing is the heart of a woman!

We made our home at "Rock Castle" until I could have a house built, which was completed during the following fall. It was located not far from "Rock Castle" and was an unpretentious cottage of five rooms with the usual outbuildings, furnished in modest style, but in every way a comfortable home, in which we spent many happy years, surrounded by our rapidly increasing family of girls; my wife devoting herself to her household duties, of which she soon acquired a practical knowledge, which placed her in the front ranks of the long celebrated housewives of Virginia.

Our first child was born November 30th, 1846, at Mrs. Royall's, in Lynchburg, Virginia, and was named for her grandmother, Lizzie Royall. We began housekeeping in January, 1847. Few events of sufficient importance to narrate occurred in our lives for some time; I was devoted to my practice and she to her housekeeping and little children. Of course I did not neglect my usual indulgence in field sports in their season, and for the amusement of my readers I will give an account of a day's hunt which came off about this time. I had arranged with Mr. William Payne to meet him on his father's farm on a certain day early in the morning, to hunt partridges.

"Aunt Vicey," my cook, had given me breakfast before day and I started by light and reached the farm about eight miles distant soon after sunrise. As I passed the mill pond, from which the fog was slowly rising, I saw a small flock of wild geese near the dam behind which the road ran. I rode quietly by without pause and when I got out of sight, dismounted and tied my horse and dogs. I searched the pockets of my hunting coat and found about one and a half loads of "double B" shot, drew the charges from my gun and substituted the large shot, walked carefully back and climbed up on the back of the dam, and peeping cautiously over, could not see a goose. The area of the pond was not large, and I was surprised at their disappearance, as I knew they had not flown. After looking some time I spied them at the head of the pond, standing and sitting in the shallow water. The problem now was, how to get to them, as the ground was open, sloping on all sides to the water, and there was no cover except a thin growth of broomsedge and occasionally a small oak bush with leaves on it. After viewing the situation, I concluded to try and crawl within gun-shot, lying flat to the ground and dragging my gun after me. I had to cross a wet, swampy slue, and of course got very muddy, but continued my snake-like progress until I reached a small oak bush, sheltered by which I prepared for action. On inspecting my gun I found the lock caked with mud and perfectly wet. Fearing the caps would not explode, I removed them, and as the powder in the tubes was wet, I took them out with a wrench, poured in some fresh powder, and renewed the caps. This took some little time, as I had to move cautiously, but the geese had never taken alarm and I waited until I got several in a line, when I fired my first barrel and knocked over five, and as the rest rose I downed another with the other barrel. I ran into the water and with one sweep of my arm gathered the five victims of my first shot, the other had a broken wing and swam off across the pond. About this time I heard William Payne halloo, who had reached my horse and dogs. Throwing my five geese over my shoulder, I went down to the dam, but fearing to lose sight of the broken-wing goose, I told Payne to loose the dogs, and as soon as they came to me I threw the dead geese down on the dam and walked back up the pond to retrieve the one with the broken wing. I sent "Io" after her and she soon brought it in. Just then Payne walked across the dam to where the dead geese were lying, and as he reached them I heard a splash in the water, and he exclaimed, "There, be gad!" One of the supposed dead geese had plunged into the water and swam off up the pond and gave us quite a chase before we succeeded in capturing it. Five of the flock escaped. We had a fine day's hunt afterwards, bagging a large number of birds and hares, and I added to these spoils two pheasants which I killed when going home on "Dry Mountain." I believe the results of that day's hunt were more rich and varied than any I had ever gathered in.

In 1850, my health became bad, loss of appetite and impaired digestion pulled me down seriously, and I thought I would try the effect of the waters of the "Rockbridge Alum Springs," to which place I repaired about the first of August, proposing, after a few weeks' visit, to go on to the White Sulphur Springs, in Greenbriar. Finding, however, that I was rapidly improving under the use of the alum water, I thought it best to "let well enough alone," and so spent six weeks at that place of resort, by which time all my ailments had disappeared, and I have had no return of them from that time to this. I met there General Francis H. Smith and family, and became quite intimate with them. He was the Superintendent of the Virginia Military Institute, where his life had been spent and he gave such character and tone to that school that it ranks with the best educational agencies in the United States. The friendship formed at the Rockbridge Alum continued unabated to the time of his death, at a ripe old age. I also met then for the first time Professor Colston, of the same Institution, afterwards a Brigadier-General in the Confederate Army and subsequently a General in the service of the Khedive of Egypt, to which country he had repaired after the fall of the Confederacy. Amongst other visitors was an old gentleman, then well known throughout the State by his political sobriquet, "The Wheel Horse of Democracy." This was Major Charles Yancey, of Buckingham County, a wealthy planter and noted politician, who for many years had represented his county in the Senate and House of Delegates of Virginia, and wielded a powerful influence, not only in the Legislature, but throughout the State. Though the special champion of democracy, he was decidedly aristocratic in his tastes and habits. A high liver, fond of his toddy and even more so of a rubber of whist, he enjoyed the reputation of being one of the best whist players in Virginia. I was one of a party engaged in general conversation on the porch of the hotel one afternoon, when he made some caustic reflections on the characteristics of a public man of some prominence, noted for his agrarian sentiments, when one of the party in reply to the Major's strictures expressed his surprise that so noted a Democrat should object to these traits of character. The Major broke out furiously, "Democracy, sir, is a good thing, a very good thing, but it is made much better by having a spice of aristocracy mixed with it, just as a fine dinner of rich food is improved by due admixture of proper condiments."

An election for delegates to the Constitutional Convention of 1850 was now in progress, and General Smith drove me one day to a public meeting on Kerr's Creek, eight or ten miles from the Springs, where the Hon. Alexander H. H. Stewart, of Staunton, and Major Dorman, of Rockbridge, were to discuss the issues upon which the people were divided, especially the suffrage question. Mr. Stewart opposed the extension of the franchise, and Major Dorman advocated it warmly. The debate was able, and to my mind, Mr. Stewart had the best of the argument, but Major Dorman evidently had a majority of the crowd with him and this proved to be the case throughout the district, as Mr. Stewart was beaten by a decided majority.

My amusements at the Rockbridge Springs were rolling ten pins and playing whist and chess. I met no one of the company who was my superior in the latter game, in my estimation the "game of games." I visited the Natural Bridge for the first time while on this trip, and my first impression on seeing it was one of disappointment, but the longer I gazed upon it the more it impressed me, until ultimately I was as much delighted with this wonderful work of nature as the most enthusiastic of our company.

There were a good many deer in the neighborhood of the Springs, and venison was one of our standing dishes; almost every day a deer would be brought in. I was informed by the huntsmen that most of them were killed at the "Licks," and I made arrangements with one of them to accompany him on a given night and watch for the chance of getting a shot. In due time he called for me and we walked to the "Lick," a mile or two distant, and entered a blind erected on a scaffold near the place frequented by deer, but our long watch was in vain, for none made their appearance. Two nights afterwards, however, a fine buck was killed at the same place.

I returned home about the middle of September, well and hearty, and was happy to rejoin my wife and little ones. I at once resumed my practice, of course, and with the occasional loss of a day or part of a day in the partridge field, stuck to my work pretty closely.

Soon after this my wife's sister, Miss Bettie Royall, of Lynchburg, married Major Andrew Ellison, a civil engineer by profession, but at that time proprietor of the "Piedmont Agricultural Works," for making agricultural and other machinery, in Lynchburg. He had been employed for some years in railroad construction in Virginia. He was a Massachusetts man by birth and education, was a widower without children, and considerably older than his wife. She was a bright and beautiful girl, and a great favorite in Lynchburg society as well as among her kinsfolk and friends. They resided about a year in Lynchburg and he then resumed railroading, having the position of chief engineer on the Covington & Ohio Railroad. They afterwards went to Brazil, South America, where the Major was for some years engaged in building the "Dom Pedro Railroad," under the immediate supervision of the Emperor of Brazil. My wife's youngest brother, Sydnor Royall, then a boy of seventeen, accompanied them to South America, became a sub-contractor, and prospered greatly until his death, which occurred in Rio Janiero before he reached twenty-one years of age.

In the summer of 1855 we experienced our first great sorrow, caused by the death of little Mary Virginia, our fifth daughter, who was taken from us after a short illness when about two and a half years old. My wife was greatly distressed by her death, as she was unusually bright and attractive, and was named for her. This was the first break in our family circle, and though followed by others in after years, the little darling of the "silver tongue" has held her place in our affectionate recollections.

A division of the "Sons of Temperance" was organized in our neighborhood this year, which I joined, and which soon became, and continued for years, an influential power for good in the community, embracing in its ranks almost every man of standing and respectability in the community. I was frequently called on to deliver addresses on the subject of temperance, both in my own and adjoining counties, several times acted as delegate to the State organization, and became so thoroughly identified with the principles of that order, that I have from that time rarely violated its precepts.

There was another organization which about this time attracted a large share of public attention, and wielded, during its ephemeral existence a potent power. This was the "American Party," or "Know Nothings," as they were more commonly called. A lodge of the order was chartered in my neighborhood and quickly absorbed a large portion of the adult males of both political parties. As the principles for which they contended had, in the main, long commended themselves to my judgment, I was among the first to "See Sam," and though the name of "Know Nothing" subsequently became a term of opprobrium and reproach, I have never felt ashamed of my connection with it, or afraid to avow my belief in the soundness of the greater part of the reforms they advocated. I differed with most of the leading members who favored absolute secrecy in regard to all its operations, and it was not long after the aggressive campaign organized against them by Henry A. Wise, the nominee of the Democratic Party for Governor of Virginia, had been entered upon that I took up the gauge of battle tendered by the local Democratic speakers, and appeared in public as the advocate and defender of the "Know Nothing Party."

Colonel Thomas Stanhope Flournoy had been nominated by the "Know Nothings" for the gubernatorial office, being a man of ability, a fine stump speaker, and fully able to sustain himself in debate with Wise or any of his lieutenants. Against his inclination and judgment, a silent campaign policy was decreed in the councils of the party, and Mr. Wise was permitted to traverse the State without interference. As he was beyond all men I have ever known a master of the lexicon of denunciation, vituperation, and invective, the effect of his canvass was very marked. It aroused to frenzy the Democratic leaders and the enthusiasm inspired by their active efforts consolidated not only the avowed members of the party, but eventually secured the withdrawal of a large number of former Democrats from the "Know Nothing" organization. It was generally conceded that had the election taken place two weeks earlier Flournoy would have been elected Governor, but the personal appeals made to former Democrats by organized committees and individuals so wrought on their feelings and fears that before the day of election, the greater part of this class of members had withdrawn. Added to this was the depressing effect of the policy of silence and inaction which had been decreed by the managers, but which did not commend itself either to the judgment or sympathy of the rank and file. The people of Virginia, without respect of party, love a square, stand-up fight, and in their hearts condemn as cowardly the man or the party that evinces either fear or shame in presence of damaging charges publicly made and not resented. I fully shared this feeling, and consequently, the first thing I knew, I was engaged actively in the public defense of my principles. That the people approved of this course I had abundant proof, as I was constantly solicited to attend public gatherings to meet the Democratic speakers on the hustings. I responded to these calls as far as it was possible and I was never conscious that we suffered any detriment at the hands of our adversaries at these public debates. My first encounter was at Leesville, in the northern part of the county, where I had been summoned to meet Mr. Robert Glass, a gentleman of intelligence and reputed to be a fine debater. He was the editor of the *Lynchburg Republican,* and father of the Hon. Carter Glass, at this writing Member of Congress from the Lynchburg district. When I reached Leesville I found Dr. Daniel Tompkins, of Bedford, present and anxious to take part in the discussion. He was an "Old Line Whig" of the straightest sect, an ex-member of the Legislature, a country doctor, and a man of much influence in the community in which he lived. He was violent in his hostility towards the "Know Nothings," which was a fortunate circumstance for me, as it enabled me to spike the most dangerous gun in the Democratic battery, which was the charge that the "Know Nothing Party" was only a Whig device to fool the Democrats and inveigle them into their party under the pretext of opposing foreign immigration and the introduction of Roman Catholics into the country. My role was, therefore, easy, as I had only to point to Dr. Tompkins and his arguments, to prove that the new party had nothing in common with the "Old Line Whigs." This disposed of the most effective part of Mr. Glass' speech, as there was a lurking suspicion in the minds of most "Old Line Whigs" that this charge of the Democracy had some foundation in fact. The discussion at Leesville certainly added strength to our cause if the plaudits of the audience could be regarded as a test.

A few days after this I was invited to attend a larger gathering at Concord Station on the South Side Railroad, where I met Thomas J. Kirkpatrick, a shrewd Lynchburg lawyer, a fine debater, a warm personal friend but a formidable political opponent. General Odin G. Clay, Democratic candidate for the Senate of Virginia was also present and participated to some extent in the debate. Mr. Kirkpatrick and I had it "nip and tuck" for about four hours. That I was enabled to hold my own with him was a matter of surprise both to myself and my friends, but I was able to do this by superior knowledge of general politics, which entered largely into the debate. He was at that time absorbed in the practice of his profession, and had never before participated in a political debate. He afterwards became one of the most influential members of the Senate of Virginia. When Campbell court came on a few days after this, I was pitted against Mr. Trible, of Lynchburg, also a lawyer and a personal friend, who had long represented the Essex district in the Virginia Senate. He was an experienced and adroit debater, but a fair and courteous one, and we had one of the most pleasant but sharp debates in my experience as a public speaker. Presuming on my ignorance of historical events, he denied that the Roman Catholics had ever interfered in political matters in any part of the world. In reply I cited many historical instances where this had been done, even to the extent of deposing monarchs, placing whole kingdoms under "interdict," and subjecting ruling princes to personal humiliation and insult. This took the crowd, and their cheers showed their appreciation of the palpable hit.

I subsequently met at Hat Creek Messrs. Robert Glass and Edmond Irvin, the last a lawyer from Buckingham County, and aided by my friend, Thomas W. Jones, a former Democratic candidate for the Legislature, was enabled so to defend our principles that we suffered no damage in the encounter. I also spoke in Lynchburg and several places in the county.

Henry A. Wise was, however, elected Governor of Virginia, but did not carry the county of Campbell, as we elected our Senator and Members of the House by several hundred majority. I have perhaps entered more into detail of this canvass in Campbell County than I should have done, tempted thereto by my desire of showing by the results in that county the effect of a plucky fight as contrasted with the opposite policy.

About a month after the election, a Convention of the party was held in Lynchburg, where a complimentary banquet was tendered Mr. Flournoy, our candidate for Governor. A very large crowd was in attendance, whom he addressed in eloquent and feeling terms, thanking them for their loyal support, and assuring them of his lasting gratitude. Mr. Imboden, of Staunton, and Judge Staples, of Christiansburg, followed in effective and very eloquent speeches, and when I was called on by the crowd, I was at a loss for something to talk about, as it appeared to me that the previous speeches had exhausted the subject. Fortunately, however, as I rose to respond to the call, an anecdote, both pertinent and amusing, flashed across my mind. I commenced by describing a gentleman who had a passion for devouring raw eggs, seated at his breakfast table one morning, occupied in reading his morning paper, and occasionally bolting a raw egg. As he gulped down one of these, he distinctly heard the chirp of a chicken, without pausing in his occupation he quietly remarked, "I am very sorry for you my friend, but you spoke too late." The application was so patent that the immense crowd in the warehouse greeted it with shouts of laughter and long continued cheers, in the midst of which I sat down satisfied.

CHAPTER XII.

A PIGEON ROOST.

Few persons of the present generation have ever seen a "Pigeon Roost," and I imagine that a brief description of the remarkable scenes there exhibited will not be devoid of interest. During my earlier years almost every fall witnessed the invasion of numerous flocks of wild pigeons, which swept over the forests in every direction, searching for nuts and acorns, which at that season constitute their food supply. When there was a "good mast" the pigeons speedily discovered the food and congregated in the locality in countless thousands. It was a curious and attractive sight to witness their methods. Thousands would settle down in a piece of forest land covering the ground closely and marching in solid mass, with fluttering wings and soft, cooing notes, would closely examine the whole surface. The constant fluttering of their wings would give motion to every leaf, causing them to rise from the ground and thus disclose the hidden treasures of acorns, chestnuts, or other food, not a single one of which would be overlooked. Those in the rear of the flock were constantly taking wing and flying low, pass over and settle down in front of the foragers, and this change of rear to front was going on all the time. The fluttering pinions, the rapid run, the anxious search, the rustling leaves and the monotonous cooing were all together well worth seeing. Towards midday they would pause from their work and, lighting on the nearest trees, would rest there until the afternoon, when they would resume their search for food. To all these scenes I was well accustomed, and often amused myself by shooting into the flocks in the early morning or late afternoon as they were passing to and fro from their roosting places. But during all these years I had never seen a pigeon roost, as they were generally located in the dense forests of the Western States. But about the time of which I am writing, the wild pigeons established their roost in Campbell County, in a densely wooded section known as the "Barrens," which was for miles an unbroken forest covered with a growth of large pines and undergrowth of small oaks and other shrubs. The location of this roost was speedily noised abroad and being only about ten miles from where I lived I paid it several visits. At first the birds roosted in the undergrowth, rarely settling on the tall pines, but in the course of a few weeks they were so worried by hunters that they changed their roosting-place to the pines, but without relief from their persecutors. Hundreds of huntsmen from the contiguous country would throng to the roosts every night in wagons, buggies and vehicles of all sorts, with forage and food for men and beasts, form a regular encampment near some spring, and spend the night traversing the woods in search of the birds, and when found, firing destructive volleys among them and gathering up the game. The birds did not roost in the same locality every night, but often changed their quarters, but always roosted within a certain limited area, extending from four to six miles in width and from ten to fifteen in length. Thus it was not at all certain that a given hunting party would find game, as the birds might be five or six miles from the spot selected by the hunters.

About an hour before sunset the flocks of pigeons, often more than a mile in length, would begin to arrive, and as sunset and dusk approached, they came in constantly increasing numbers. By dark the bushes and trees would be covered with them, each bush bent with the weight of the birds settled on it. When a large number were gathered in one locality, a loud, murmuring sound could always be heard, which on a calm night was audible for a mile or more. It then resembled the roaring of water flowing over the rocky bed of a large stream. The hunters, hearing this noise, would cautiously approach until they reached a point they judged sufficiently near, when all hands would fire in the direction of the sound, this being their only guide. The fusilade would, of course, frighten the birds and they would take flight, but if the night was dark would soon settle down again. As soon as the hunters would fire they would light their torches of split lightwood with which they were generally provided, or with lanterns, and hunt through the woods for the dead and wounded birds which had fallen to their guns, and when all were gathered in would again resume their quest and when the birds were found, repeat the previous procedure. And thus the night would be spent, or so much of it as they deemed necessary or agreeable. In the morning the birds would commence moving off as soon as it was light, and by sunrise the woods would be deserted. The hunters, by searching over the ground in the morning would often gather in as much game as they had collected by aid of the torch light.

The digestive powers of a pigeon are very wonderful. Those killed early in the night have their crops filled with acorns or chestnuts, or both. I have often taken as many as eight or ten large red oak acorns from the crop of one bird. These acorns have a thick, hard shell, yet by morning when the birds leave the roost, no sign of an acorn can be found in their crops. The old stories which I have read of the tameness of these birds, allowing the hunter to approach sufficiently near to thresh them down from their roosts with a stick or pole, I can not verify by my own observation. The nearest approach I ever made to it was one night when there was a moon only a few days old, I had wandered off from my party alone, seeking a roost and listening for the characteristic noise, when I heard the firing of guns some distance away which was speedily followed by a flight of birds, which settled in the bushes all around me. I remained perfectly quiet and soon other flocks were added to the first comers and it was not long before I found myself in the very heart of a pigeon roost. Many settled on the bush by which I stood and finally two alighted on my gun barrel within a foot of my hand. I did not move, indeed scarcely breathed, but the one nearest me, from some cause, became suspicious and turning his beautiful head and neck first on one side and then on the other, peered into my face in the most inquisitive way, and finally concluded it wisest to change his base and hopped off on the bush hard by. By this time they had become so numerous around me that I knew the noise they made would soon attract the hunters, and as I did not relish the idea of being shot for a pigeon, I fired my own gun into the thickest of the flock and proceeded to gather in the game. Now these birds were really sufficiently near to have been killed with a stick, but no one could possibly have approached so near them as they would have taken alarm at the first movement or sound. The pigeons continued to roost until the early spring, but I neither saw nor heard of any effort to breed amongst them before they left for other quarters.

CHAPTER XIII.

A CHANGE OF BASE.

We gave to our residence the name of "Briery," as it was located in a field of forty or fifty acres of worn out and exhausted land which had not been cultivated for years and was overrun with blackberry briers, with scattered oak bushes and broomsedge. The site, however, was a pretty one, accessible and convenient. Wishing to clear up and improve the land near the house, I determined to resort to the use of Peruvian Guano, the wonderful effects of which in restoring fertility to exhausted soil, had just begun to attract the notice of farmers. No one, however, in our neighborhood had ever experimented with it, or had personal knowledge of its efficacy. I procured a ton from Richmond, had ten acres adjoining the house cleared up and plowed, and in October seeded it to wheat, after the application of two hundred pounds of guano to the acre. My two nearest neighbors, my father and Mr. Richard Morgan, old and experienced farmers, came over to witness my start. They examined the fertilizer, and on one point were fully agreed, namely, that "it had an awful bad smell." I sowed every pound myself, broadcast on the plowed land, and both my visitors agreed that if the small dusting I had given the "old brier field" would make it grow a crop of wheat, it would be nothing short of a miracle. By the middle of the following April, however, the guano had given proof of its wonderful power, to the admiration and astonishment of the neighbors. Many persons passing along the public road would ride to the house and ask an explanation of the phenomenon. Being a novice at seeding I managed accidentally to skip a "land" with the fertilizer, but the wheat was sowed on it as on the rest of the field. By the latter part of April the wheat "would hide a rabbit" everywhere except on the land where the fertilizer was missed, and that looked like a road through the field. Indeed, one of my farmer friends who had come over to witness the wonderful effect of the new-fangled manure when I took him to the "skipped land" to show him the contrast in the appearance of the crop, stood for a while in an apparently dazed condition, looking first on one side and then on the other, and at last said, "But, Doctor, I don't see much difference in the wheat on the two sides of the road. One side is about as good as the other." It was hard to convince him that it was not a road on which he was standing or that the same wheat had been sown on that as on the other ground. The result of my experiment at once created a demand for the new commodity in that neighborhood. I continued to clear, plow and fertilize every year ten additional acres until I had gotten the whole field in good condition by the use of wheat and clover. I kept an accurate account of the receipts and expenditures incident to my farming operations and found that the only profit in it was the crop of straw and a moderately good stand of clover on land otherwise incapable of producing it. This was my first experience in practical farming.

In 1856, a vacancy having occurred in the faculty of the Medical College of Virginia by the death of the professor of obstetrics and the diseases of women and children, I determined to offer for the appointment. As I was personally acquainted with several members of the Board of Trustees, upon whom the selection devolved and was backed by strong testimonials from doctors of high repute and influential public men in all sections of the State, I had strong hopes of success. After visiting Richmond, however, and interviewing several members of the faculty, I found they were in fact the appointing power, and had already selected Dr. Conway, of Richmond, for the vacant chair, thus confirming what had always been alleged, that only Richmond doctors had any show for professorships in that college. I was advised to withdraw, but declined to do so, and was, of course, beaten, but I received a very respectable support for the place.

In the summer of 1858 I had a visit from my cousin and former pupil, Dr. Edward D. Withers, of Danville, Virginia, where he had for some years been actively engaged in the practice of medicine. By this time some of our children were large enough to attend school, and as our former rector and teacher, Rev. Samuel D. Tompkins, had moved to Weston, in Lewis County, we were left in a destitute condition, both as to teacher and preacher. Dr. Withers pursuaded us to break up in Campbell and move to Danville, where my old friend, Rev. Dr. Dame, had for several years conducted a large female school of established reputation, which would solve the educational problem. He was also confident that, owing to the recent death of Dr. Craighead, an old practitioner in Danville, there was a fine opening for me professionally. After full consultation we concluded to act on his suggestion, and as I have never long delayed action on a resolution once formed, we sold out at "Briery," and in the month of August moved to Danville. I there purchased a house and lot on Wilson Street, of which immediate possession was given, started the children to school, and commenced practice in partnership with Dr. E. D. Withers under the firm name of R. E. and E. D. Withers. At that time Danville was a town of about eight thousand inhabitants, the center of the tobacco trade for the adjoining counties of Virginia and North Carolina. There were many large tobacco factories in operation and three large female boarding schools, or "Colleges," as they were called, with thriving churches of all leading denominations of Christians, except Roman Catholics. As the society was composed, in the main, of cultured and intelligent people, the country around settled by prosperous planters, many of them owning large numbers of slaves, our prospects of enjoying life and prospering in the world were by no means bad. I at once entered on a remunerative practice, which rapidly increased until I had as much to occupy my time as I desired, and more. My partner was a widower with two children, and thought more of looking out for another wife than of attending sick people, consequently the bulk of the business fell into my hands. As I had left a large country practice and now enjoyed a large town patronage, I was able to estimate the relative advantages and disadvantages of each, but found the question difficult to decide. A country practice involves more physical labor and fatigue, but a city practice much greater loss of sleep. I often did not get any rest the whole night, and nothing is so wearing and exhaustive of the vital forces as loss of sleep. My family soon formed a pleasant circle of friends, and we found our residence in Danville very pleasant, but marked by no events of special interest or importance. Dr. Ned Withers married in 1859 Mrs. Louisa Miller, his first cousin, a daughter of Mr. John Coles, of Pittsylvania, and purchased a residence not far from mine which he occupied with his bride.

This year, 1859, was memorable as the era of the John Brown raid at Harper's Ferry, which produced a tremendous excitement, not only in Virginia but throughout the South. After his capture, trial, and execution, there ensued a wonderful revival of interest in military affairs, resulting in the organization of many volunteer companies throughout the State. In Danville a fine company was raised, called the "Danville Blues," commanded by Captain W. P. Graves, who had served in the Mexican War. Dr. E. D. Withers was one of the lieutenants. Not long afterwards another company was gotten up, called the "Danville Greys," and I was offered the captaincy, as it was known to many that I had some knowledge of military matters, and had served for some years as captain of a volunteer company. I declined the proffered honor, as I had no time to spare from my professional duties. The members of the new company were, however, very persistent in their purpose and begged me to take the place temporarily until I could drill and instruct the officers sufficiently to enable one of them to take command, and with this understanding, I gave a reluctant assent. There was, of course, great rivalry between the two organizations, and this added to my natural fondness for military life, stimulated me to unusual effort to perfect the company in drill and knowledge of military tactics. They soon attained such proficiency that it was a pleasure to turn out with them. A cavalry company was also formed at Whitmel, near Danville, and it was deemed best that a battalion should be formed of these three companies. This was done, and when organized, I was elected and commissioned major. This furnishes an explanation of a circumstance which has been made a frequent subject of remark among my friends, both personal and professional, namely, why I preferred entering the army as an officer of the line, rather than of the Medical Staff. My experience as captain of the "Brookneal Troop" was the cause of my acceptance of the same position in the "Danville Greys," and as I held a commission in the line when the war commenced, I did not think it proper to resign because fighting was imminent. When the Virginia forces were first organized, Dr. C. Bell Gibson, the medical director, wrote, offering me any position on the Surgical Staff that I might prefer, and protested against this abandonment of my profession. I had similar offers from the Medical Department of the Confederate Service also, but for the reasons assigned declined both.

When the Virginia Convention was called after the election of Mr. Lincoln as President, to consider the question of secession, I was asked to become a candidate, but declined to do so. During the canvass, however, I took an active part, made several speeches and participated in two or three discussions with those who advocated the secession policy. The result in my county was the election of the Union candidates by a very large majority. When this fact became known, there was an impromptu celebration of the victory by a large crowd, which, accompanied by a band of music, marched to the residences of prominent Unionists, calling them out for speeches. I was honored by a visit of this kind, and in response to the call gave my views on the situation, declaring my fixed belief that if the policy of secession prevailed, the act would be followed by a war such as the world had never seen, and whatever the result might be, slavery in Virginia would be doomed. I dwelt on the certainty of war as a sequel to secession, because the Hon. Roger A. Pryor, in a speech delivered in Danville a short time before had strongly and eloquently argued that secession was the only means of averting war, and in closing a rhetorical appeal had taken out his pocket handkerchief and, shaking it in the face of his audience, had declared that "he could wipe out with that handkerchief every drop of blood shed in a war caused by the secession of the South."

When the Convention met, the advocates of secession found themselves in a decided minority, and though native and imported orators were called from many localities to advocate that policy, the Convention remained firm in its hostility, until President Lincoln issued his proclamation calling on the State of Virginia to furnish her quota of the seventy-five thousand men called out to coerce the seceded states and force them back into the Union. This precipitated the crisis of course, and the ordinance of secession was speedily passed with few dissenting voices, and the State at once armed for the fray. The ordinance was passed on the seventeenth day of April, 1861, and anticipating the inevitable, the two Danville companies at once tendered their services to Governor Letcher, and made every preparation to go at once into the field. The ladies busied themselves in manufacturing tents, haversacks, etc., for these companies, and when the call came a few days after, we at once responded.

CHAPTER XIV.

WAR.

At no period of my life had I experienced such feelings of anxiety, apprehension and discomfort as oppressed me at this time. The idea of leaving behind me a wife and eight little girls without a protector, was in itself most distressing, but when to this was added the expectation of an addition to the number which might occur at any hour, I was placed in a most embarrassing dilemma. I came to the conclusion that I would not leave home before the expected event occurred, as no consideration of duty or honor demanded such a sacrifice. Providentially, however, my tenth daughter was ushered into a troubled world about midnight of the twenty-second of April. We were under marching orders for eight a. m. on the twenty-third, about eight hours afterwards. My wife, with that unselfish courage which always characterized her, said I must accompany the battalion if I thought it my duty to do so. I continued to balance the conflicting claims of domestic and public duty without reaching a decision, until the beating of the drums and the whistle of the awaiting train forced me to action. I then cheered my wife with the assurance that I would almost surely be able to get leave of absence for a few days before the command would leave Richmond, and would then pay her a visit, and with this promise we parted. I doubt if any other soldier answered the call leaving a wife in bed and a baby eight hours old. Before I started, my wife asked what we should call the baby, I answered that I left it entirely to her. By some means the peculiar circumstances of the case became public, and the *Richmond Whig,* at that time a journal of large influence and circulation suggested as appropriate for the little stranger the name of "Virginia Secessia," and she has been so called from that day to this.

As may be surmised, my feelings at this time were not of

the most jubilant character. In addition to my private anxieties, I did not share the confident anticipation of speedy and glorious victory which seemed to animate a large majority of those around me. I had a pretty correct idea of the odds by which we were confronted, and my hope was that inasmuch as a large number of Northern people of both political parties were opposed to the war and believed it unnecessary, this conservative element might control popular sentiment and compel a recognition of the Southern Confederacy. When such a prominent and influential public leader as Horace Greely, editor of the *New York Tribune,* publicly counselled a pacific policy and urged that the "Erring Sisters should depart in peace," this expectation did not appear so unreasonable as subsequent events proved it to be. Others of our people, I know, shared this feeling and hope, among whom was Colonel John B. Baldwin, of Staunton, who had been, like myself, strongly opposed to the policy of secession and was one of the foremost Union men in the State Convention, until Lincoln made his call for troops, when he at once offered his services to Governor Letcher and was appointed Mustering Officer and Inspector General of the State troops.

My command reached Richmond in the afternoon of the twenty-third of April, and as we marched through the streets to the martial music of drums and fife, the performers being all slaves, we attracted great attention and frequent cheers, as we were amongst the first companies to reach the city. On reporting to the Governor, I found General Francis H. Smith, of the V. M. I., acting as one of his advisory board. The Governor informed me that it had been deemed best to accept no organization larger than a company, but professing himself much pleased with the appearance of my battalion, said he would consult further with the Board as to the advisability of receiving us. We marched out that evening to the old Fair Ground, which had been converted into a Camp of Instruction, creating quite a sensation as we passed through the street, with drums beating and colors flying, for we had been presented with a beautiful State flag of silk by the ladies of Danville. On reaching the camp of instruction, I reported to Colonel

Gilham, of the Virginia Military Institute, who was in command, who assigned us our quarters in the horse stalls of the Fair Grounds, where, with the aid of some straw, we were comfortably housed, until our tents reached us a few days after. I found that the third and fourth classes of cadets from the Virginia Military Institute had been detailed to serve as drill officers for the raw troops, and very efficient instructors they proved themselves to be.

We had orders to report the next day by nine o'clock at the Custom House to be mustered into service. I accompanied them though without any instructions to that effect. Colonel Baldwin, the Mustering Officer, after mustering in the two companies informed me that he had determined to muster me in as Major of the battalion, as the matter had been left to his discretion and he had concluded to do so. I was accordingly so mustered, and returned to the camp of instruction. The organization was as follows: Robert E. Withers, Major of the Battalion; E. C. Edmonds, Adjutant; Musicians—George Price, fifer; Dick Slade, kettle-drummer; Austin Dix, bass drummer.

The *"Danville Blues"*—Captain, W. P. Graves; First Lieutenant, J. M. Smith; Second Lieutenant, Edward D. Withers; rank and file, ninety-five men.

The *"Danville Greys"*—Captain, Thomas C. Claiborne; First Lieutenant, E. N. Sorey; Second Lieutenant, Daniel Turner; ninety-two men, rank and file.

My Adjutant, Mr. E. C. Edmonds, was a distinguished graduate of the Virginia Military Institute, and as I expected did not long retain the position, as he was made Colonel of the 38th Regiment, when organized, a few weeks thereafter. As I had little to employ me while the various companies were being instructed in squad and company drill, I applied for, and obtained, leave of absence for four days to visit my family. I lost not a moment in availing myself of this privilege, and found my wife convalescing more rapidly than I expected, knowing the depressing influences to which she had been exposed. The ladies of the neighborhood were as kind and attentive as possible, and the family seemed to lack nothing. As

I had a large amount due me for medical services, I placed my books in the hands of a collector with instructions to pay over to my wife whatever money he could procure from my patrons. My leave passed all too rapidly, but I was compelled to return to camp, and there found several companies sufficiently advanced to begin my instructions in battalion drill. I commenced with four companies, two others were added within the week, and soon after two others, making a battalion of eight full companies. Everything seemed to work well, and in ten days after my return, the organization of regiments commenced. The first one formed was placed under the command of Colonel Thomas P. August, of Richmond, and was called the 2d Virginia Regiment, and was ordered to Norfolk the next day. The day after, I was surprised by a call from Colonel Gilham, commanding the camp of instruction, who, after some introductory conversation, asked me why I did not apply for a commission as Colonel of the regiment then in process of formation, which embraced most of the companies I had been drilling, authorizing me at the same time to use his name as reference. I acted at once on his suggestion, sent in my application to the Governor, referring him to General Smith for information as to my character and social position, and to Colonel Gilham as to my military qualification. Two days after I was notified that the Governor and his Staff would visit the camp in the afternoon to witness the dress parade of the new regiment. He came accordingly, mounted on a handsome stallion and accompanied by his staff. The dress parade of the regiment went off all right under my command, and when they marched off the field, Governor Letcher rode up and addressed me as Colonel. I corrected him by saying I was only a Major, his reply was "I made no mistake, Colonel, you have been appointed to command this regiment and will receive your commission tomorrow." I, of course, thanked him for the honor conferred and expressed the hope that I might prove myself worthy of the confidence he had reposed in me, and the incident was thus closed. I will not deny that I was much gratified and very proud of the office, as the regiment was an exceptionally fine one, composed entirely of men from the south side of the State. It embraced the two Danville companies, one from Pittsylvania, one from Charlotte, one from Appomattox, two from Nottoway, one from Cumberland, one from Prince Edward, and one from Farmville. This regiment, when organized, was called the Third, and bore upon its rolls a little more than a thousand men. Mr. Henry C. Carrington, of Charlotte County, a graduate of the Virginia Military Institute, was commissioned Lieutenant Colonel, Captain Carter Harrison, of Cumberland, as Major, and Lieutenant E. D. Withers, of Company A, was appointed Adjutant.

I first met Colonel Thomas J. Jackson while at the camp of instruction, soon after my arrival. He was not then the recipient of any special attention, was very quiet and reticent, having little to say to any one. Being without any regular quarters, I invited him one night at bed time to share my blankets, as he appeared to have none of his own, an invitation which he promptly accepted. I spread a blanket on the floor, we took our saddles for pillows, covered with another blanket and passed a rather uncomfortable night, at least I found it so, and since that time I have never willingly slept on a plank floor—I always found the ground much more comfortable. I do not remember that I ever saw him after that night until during the battle of first Manassas.

I received my commission promptly, and at once prepared to take the field. I purchased my accoutrements, and also a pair of pistols for my holsters, but as army and navy revolvers were not obtainable, I substituted a pair of fine dueling pistols, at a cost of seventy-five dollars. These were presented to me by the Adjutant. Our marching orders speedily came. I was ordered to Manassas Junction to report to General Bonham, who commanded the South Carolina Brigade, which had reached there a few days before. We were not assigned to his Brigade, but as Ranking Officer he had command of all the troops at that camp. We left our quarters about three o'clock in the afternoon, and marched through Broad Street, Richmond, in column of companies, presenting, as I thought, a fine appearance, an opinion evidently shared by the people crowded on the sidewalks, who greeted us along the whole route with hearty cheers. We met with a vexatious delay at the station, as our train did not get off until after sunset. We traveled slowly all night with frequent stoppages, and did not reach Manassas Junction until ten o'clock the next day. I at once reported to headquarters, where I met Colonel Thomas Jordan, an old army officer, a Virginian, and a distant relative, who was Adjutant of the Post, whose experience, good sense, and thorough training rendered him very efficient in that position. He assigned my camping ground, which we at once occupied, and those companies provided with tents soon had them pitched, but as the majority were without this protection, they extemporized such shelters as they could construct without the aid of lumber, which the Quartermaster could not furnish. Water was scarce, and I found it necessary to make a detail from each company for the purpose of digging a well to supply us. I found here six companies of the 11th Regiment, commanded by Colonel Samuel Garland, a graduate of the Virginia Military Institute, who had come out as Captain of the Lynchburg "Home Guards," but subsequently promoted. Company C of the 11th Regiment was composed of men from my native county, Campbell, and was commanded by my cousin, Captain Adam Clement. The First Lieutenant was my brother, H. H. Withers, and a younger brother, W. L. Withers, belonged to the same company. General Bonham's South Carolina Brigade was encamped at Fairfax Court-House, some twelve or fifteen miles in advance of our camp at Manassas Junction. Troops were now arriving by almost every train and the organization of regiments and brigades was rapidly effected. Drilling was kept up regularly, picket duty commenced, and it was not long before we were made familiar with the whole routine of military service.

And here I had my first trouble with one of my captains. Company C had no tents and found it impossible to procure lumber from the Quartermaster's department to construct shelters, and while waiting for a supply, several cases of sickness occurred among the men, and the Captain was so exasperated at the delay in delivering lumber that he came to the determination that he would make no detail from his company for any duty, until the Government could furnish shelter for his men. The Adjutant reported his refusal to furnish men either for picket duty, or camp guard. Supposing him to be unaware of the gravity of his offense, and wishing to save him from the consequences of his disobedience, I requested him to come to my tent, and in the kindest spirit I explained the character of the offense and the consequences if persisted in. To all my advice he turned a deaf ear, repeating his determination that his men should perform no duty, until the Government would furnish them shelter for the sick. I tried to convince him that this refusal would not prevent the men from doing duty, for he would certainly be placed under arrest, subject to court martial, with probable loss of his commission, and at any rate the First Lieutenant would succeed him as commanding officer, and the necessary details would be made. He refused to change his views, so after an hour's talk, I placed him under arrest, preferred charges against him, and forwarded them to headquarters. The required details were made by the Lieutenant in command, and the Captain remained in his quarters under arrest for some time, as several weeks elapsed before a Court Martial was convened. A change was made about this time in the numbers of the Regiments, and mine, instead of being the Third, was numbered the 18th Virginia Infantry. The formations of brigades soon followed. My regiment formed part of the 3d Brigade, which was composed in addition, of the 8th Regiment, Colonel Eppa Hunton (which had not yet joined us), the 19th Regiment, under Lieutenant Colonel Strange, a graduate of the Virginia Military Institute, the 28th, Colonel Robert Preston, and the 56th, Colonel Green was subsequently added. General Philip St. George Cocke, of Powhatan County, Virginia, was assigned to the command of this brigade. He was a graduate of West Point, but had, years before, resigned from the army and resided on his beautiful estate on James River. He was possessed of large wealth in land and slaves, owning in addition to his Virginia estates one or more large cotton plantations in Mississippi. He was a high-toned and honorable gentleman, very patriotic and devoted to the Southern cause, but eccentric in many particulars.

He came to Manassas a few days after his assignment, assumed command of the Brigade, and accompanied by his Adjutant and one of his Aides, visited the headquarters of each of his Regiments, became acquainted with its officers, and spent some time in conversation. Though I had long known him by reputation, I had never before met him. When he left my tent the Field officers remained, and Lieutenant Colonel Carrington asked me what I thought of our Brigadier. In reply I spoke of his gentlemanly bearing and evident devotion to the cause, but added that I doubted his proper mental balance. This produced a laugh from the officers present, who supposed I was jesting, but I repeated my impression and asked that they would remember what I said. My opinion was formed from his general manner, which was distraught, he was often abstracted and evidently oblivious of his surroundings, the expression of his eye was not normal and there was an indefinable something in his whole bearing which I thought justified my opinion. This forecast was fully vindicated, as six months thereafter he committed suicide by blowing out his own brains. A more patriotic, gallant, high-toned and honorable gentleman, however, never lived.

About, or perhaps a little before, the time the regiments were brigaded, Gen. G. T. Beauregard, an old West Point man, having been assigned to the command of all the forces in Northern Virginia, assumed command at Manassas Junction. He retained Colonel Jordan as Adjutant, and it soon became manifest that we had a man at the helm whose military knowledge and experience would stand us in good stead. Energy and activity was at once shown in all departments of the service. The improvement was, perhaps, more marked in the administration of the Staff Department than in the line, the Quartermaster and Commissary Department were especially benefitted. Heretofore our commissary stores rarely sufficed to supply food for two days, and although we were in the midst of a fertile country abounding in grain, flour, and bacon, and were sweeping the whole country up to the Potomac of these necessaries, none of the food thus secured could be issued to the troops at Manassas. The Commissary General had issued orders that all food supplies must first be sent to Richmond, then drawn by requisition from his stores there and sent back by rail to the very place from which they had been originally shipped.

In this connection I recall a rather amusing incident which occurred about this time. Colonel Preston of the 28th Regiment had made a regular detail for picket duty, and assigned Captain Spessard, of Craig, to command the picket. He received the usual instruction to take with him three days' rations to supply food during the tour of duty. Now, Captain Spessard was a stalwart six-footer, brave as Julius Cæsar, who above everything else believed in obeying orders. He collected his picket detail, marched them to the Commissary Department to get his three days' rations. He was told by the Commissary that he could not furnish them as the supply on hand would not permit it. Captain Spessard took out his orders, read them over carefully, and handed the paper to the Commissary with the remark, "I want you to read that paper and see what it says." He perused the paper and handed it back, saying, "I see, but you can not get three days' rations for the reason I have already given you."

Spessard said, "You see what my orders read, don't you? They say, 'Captain Spessard will *take* three days' rations and proceed with his command to the picket line, etc.' Now, I propose to obey that order, and if you don't furnish these rations I'll be d--d if I don't *take* them." His determined look and bearing settled the question, and he got what his orders called for.

I mentioned having made a detail of men to dig a well for the regiment. This detail was put in charge of a non-commissioned officer named Yarborough. By my instruction he reported every night the progress made, of which I always made a note. After about two weeks I footed up the sum of these daily reports and found that the well ought to be over an hundred and fifty feet deep. Knowing this depth could not be reached without striking water, I went to inspect the well myself, measured the depth, and found it to be not quite thirty feet. I sent for Yarborough, showed him the daily reports he had been making, and asked an explanation. He broke out in a laugh and confessed that he had "just guessed at it." I gave him a good lecture, and in a day or two more, having reached good water, the well was completed, much to our relief.

The van-guard of the Northern Army, having crossed the Potomac and occupied Alexandria and the adjacent heights without resistance, remained permanently in that city. This invasion was marked by one event of note; namely, the killing of Colonel Elsworth, commanding the New York Zouaves, by a hotel keeper of Alexandria, named Jackson. He was an ardent secessionist and had raised a flag staff on the cupola of his house from which floated a Confederate flag, and he avowed his purpose to kill any man who attempted to pull it down. When the Zouaves under Ellsworth entered the city, Jackson was away from the hotel, and as the column passed up the street Colonel Ellsworth, escorted by a squad of soldiers ran upstairs, and out to the roof and hauled down the obnoxious flag. Jackson, had in the meantime, returned, and hearing that the Yankee officer had gone up to capture his banner, seized his double-barrel gun loaded with buck shot and started up the stairway. He met Ellsworth coming down with the flag draped around him, and without a moment's hesitation fired, and Colonel Ellsworth fell dead, riddled with buck shot. A Sergeant of the squad accompanying him fired at Jackson instantly and shot him through the breast, killing him also. This was the first blood shed during the war on Southern soil. Jackson, however, was not a Confederate soldier, but a private citizen. The death of the first Confederate soldier, however, followed pretty soon, as I will relate.

A company of New York Cavalry was on out-post at Vienna, a few miles from Alexandria, for patrol and vidette duty, and hearing that a company of Confederate soldiers were at Fairfax Court-House, they determined to beat up their quarters and attempt their capture by a night attack. The Confederates consisted of a single company of volunteers from Warrenton, Virginia, commanded by Captain J. Q. Marr, a graduate of the Virginia Military Institute, and esteemed a bright and gallant young soldier of more than usual promise.

They were in camp very near the Court-House, and on the night in question had only the usual camp guard. Soon after midnight the village was aroused by the clatter of horses' hoofs and the shouts and firing of cavalrymen in the streets. The camp was aroused and the company hastily formed to resist the raiders, but after giving orders for the formation of the company, their Captain was no more seen. This, of course, caused delay and confusion, but ex-Governor Smith, who was afterwards Colonel of the 49th Regiment, and subsequently a Brigadier General, happened to be in the village, and going out to aid in repelling the attack, assumed command of the company, by this time, however, the enemy had retreated with as much haste as they advanced. After daylight Captain Marr's body was found lying in a pathway near the camp, having been instantly killed by a random bullet fired by the raiders. His death was greatly mourned by all who knew him. According to my recollection, he was the first Confederate officer or soldier killed in the war.

While in camp at Manassas, on the twentieth of June, I was much shocked and distressed by a telegram announcing the death of my brother, Dr. John T. Withers, at the hospital in Richmond. He was the Assistant Surgeon of Colonel August's Regiment, was taken sick in or near Norfolk, sent to the Hospital at Richmond, and died the next day of heart disease. He came down from Newbern where he resided with the Pulaski Company, then under the command of Captain J. A. Walker, offered his services to the Surgeon General and was commissioned Assistant Surgeon to the first Regiment organized at the camp of Instruction. He left a wife and one child at Newbern. I was greatly distressed at his death as I regarded him the cleverest son of the family, a robust and powerful man physically, six feet three inches high, and weighing two hundred and twenty-five pounds. He was doing a large practice in Pulaski when the war commenced. His body was carried to his old home in Campbell and buried in St. John's Churchyard. It is rather a curious fact that his widow afterwards married a Captain Davidson of the army, who was either killed or died shortly after. She therefore lost two husbands during the war.

Major Robert Wheat reached Manassas in June, commanding a Battalion raised in New Orleans, two companies of which were Zouaves who called themselves the "Louisiana Tigers." These men were a hard lot, and when they reached the camp at Manassas one freight car was pretty nearly full of men under arrest for disorderly conduct, drunkenness, etc., most of whom were bucked and gagged as some of my men reported who were at the station when they arrived. Major Wheat was an adventurous character, descendant of a good Virginia family, and had served with Garibaldi in his Italian campaign. He was a rigid disciplinarian as there was abundant cause to be, two of his men were Court Martialed and shot not long after they reached Manassas for insubordination and resisting their officers. The example had a good effect not only on that particular command, but on the whole army. The first Court Martial convened at Manassas, tried amongst others the Captain of Company C of my Regiment. The volunteer officers composing the court appeared to have very crude ideas of discipline, for while they convicted the Captain under all the charge and specifications, they merely sentenced him to be reprimanded by the Commanding General. In reviewing the sentence of the court, General Beauregard gave them a scathing rebuke for the lenient sentence, declaring that the penalty was so inadequate to the character of the offense that it became ridiculous, and he discharged the accused and directed him to rejoin his command.

In the latter part of the month I was ordered to move my Regiment to Centreville, and was shortly followed by the 19th and 28th Regiments and Latham's Battery. General Cocke moved his Headquarters to the same place which was nearly mid-way between Manassas Junction and Fairfax Court-House. The 28th Regiment was soon stationed about four miles north of Centreville. Nothing of special note occurred while at camp at Centreville, except a night alarm which was generally accredited to Colonel Strange of the 19th Regiment, who wished to see how the command would behave on a sudden emergency. About mid-night the Camp was aroused by picket firing followed by that of the Camp guard of the 19th, at once everything was in commotion. I ordered the "long roll" beaten and in a few minutes the Regiment was under arms and ready for action. I expected every moment to receive orders from Headquarters, but receiving none, I marched the regiment to the camp of the Artillery Company as I wished to be assured of their safety. After waiting here sometime I was ordered back to camp with the information that it was a false alarm.

The first week in July I moved forward to Fairfax Courthouse and camped at a small village called Germantown, where we threw up breast works and rifle pits from that place to a point beyond Fairfax Court-House. In this work we were aided by General Bonham's Brigade of South Carolinians.

The air was now filled with rumors of a speedy advance by the enemy. Not a day passed without information from a "reliable source," that the advance would certainly commence the next day, the pickets were notified to keep a sharp lookout and the Cavalry Videttes cautioned to exercise increased vigilance. It was while thus expecting an attack daily I was waited on by a officer of one of the South Carolina Regiments who asked if I had a pair of duelling pistols, replying in the affirmative, I was requested to lend them for a short time as two of the officers in that command had become involved in a personal difficulty and wished to settle it "under the code." I inquired the cause of the trouble and ascertained that it had its origin in a dispute which arose over a game of chess, when one party having given the other the lie, a challenge promptly followed. I told my visitor, the cause did not, in my judgment, justify a duel, and urged him to return and use every effort to secure a settlement of the trouble, by the withdrawal of the offensive remark, and declined to furnish the weapons. He promised to comply with my request but from his knowledge of the men thought his effort would be useless. I told him that in all probability a few days more would furnish both an opportunity of fighting to their hearts content. The sequel to this was that both the principals passed unscathed through the impending battle, and about a month after met on the field of honor where one of them was wounded.

About the twelfth of July I received a confidential note from Headquarters of the Brigade stating that General Beauregard did not propose fighting on the Fairfax Court-House line, but when the enemy advanced we were expected to fall back to the line of "Bull Run," but to man the trenches and delay the advance as much as practicable, but without actually becoming engaged. In the order for falling back the duty of bringing up the rear was assigned to my Regiment. General Cocke, however, in transmitting the order informed me that he had protested against this arrangement as it would separate my Regiment from the rest of the Brigade, and I replied to him that as the rear was the post of honor on a retreat I didn't wish any change made. It was done; however, in deference to the wishes of General Cocke, and the next day brought a modification of the order directing that my Regiment should be first withdrawn to rejoin General Cocke's Brigade at Centreville. The next morning videttes brought word that the enemy were advancing from "Falls Church." After sending off baggage and getting breakfast, I manned the rifle pits, instructed the pickets to fall back in proper time, and awaited the advance. As I moved the men into the position assigned them, the glitter of the enemy's bayonets was plainly visible and the Colonel of the Regiment on my right, rode up to me and commenting on the novel sensation of expecting to be under fire in a few minutes, asked me how I felt under the circumstances. I answered by quoting a passage of Shakespeare which happened to flash through my mind and said, "My pulse as thine doth temperately keep time." The morning was very sultry with little or no breeze, the advance of the enemy was along the Falls Church road almost parallel with our position and less than a mile away. I remained in the trenches until the column had passed along my whole front and reached a point on my left flank. They appeared apprehensive of being entrapped, as they were moved very cautiously and spent some time in shelling the Redoubt and rifle pits at Germantown, giving us ample time to fall back without a skirmish. We rejoined our Brigade at Centreville, and without halting passed on to Bull Run. We were posted to cover a Ford below a bridge on the stone road, and when shown the position, I was not at all satisfied, as we were placed on the level land on the South of the stream every foot of which was commanded by the bluff on the North side and no troops could prevent the passage across the stream if the bluff were occupied by a Battery of Artillery. I at once rode up to Headquarters and gave General Cocke my views, asking him at the same time to modify my orders and permit me to occupy the hills on the North side of the stream. He concurred in my view of the objectionable features of the position assigned me, but said that as such were the orders from Headquarters, he had no authority to alter them. I then suggested that he should modify them to the extent of directing me to place my command in a position to cover the Ford and the road leading thereto, leaving me to exercise my own discretion in the matter. He finally agreed to this, though very reluctantly; and I placed my command on the North side of the stream, where I felt pretty secure, threw out a strong picket a half mile on front, cautioning the officer in command to be vigilant and watchful. The road ran through a lane debouching into a wood, and I suggested to the officer in command of the picket that if he would have a fence run across the mouth of the lane near the woods and post his men a hundred or two yards in advance, he would probably be able to bag some of the cavalry sent out by the enemy to explore the roads, by permitting them to pass and then close in on them as they could not pass out of the lane. He agreed to try the experiment. A little after midnight I was aroused by the picket firing and, mounting my horse which was already saddled I took a company with me to reenforce the picket, and proceeded at double quick to their post. When I reached them the Lieutenant in command reported that they had fired on a cavalryman who approached them through the field instead of along the road. He was ordered to halt, but as he continued to advance the sentries fired on him, when he retreated in full gallop and they could distinctly hear the rattle of his sabre as he rode off. Censuring the sentinels for being such poor marksmen, I returned to camp and rested quietly the balance of the night. Before the picket was relieved the next day they again heard the tramp of a horse approaching, and presently through the field among the scattered pines, they saw an old blind horse, quietly grazing with a cracked cow-bell on his neck, and this at once explained the visit of the cavalryman the night before. The sentinels and the officer in command of the picket had to stand a good deal of chaffing for several days on account of their mistake.

The next day passed without incident, but early in the morning of the eighteenth of July, we became aware that an attack was about to be made on the troops covering Blackburn's Ford two or three miles below us. As our elevated position gave us a fine view of the valley of the stream, and the road leading to the Ford, we had an opportunity of witnessing the whole affair. We could not only hear, but see the Artillery fight between the Federal Batteries and the Washington Artillery of New Orleans. We could also see the column of the enemy advancing, deploying into line of battle, and charging the troops at the Ford. These were composed of the 1st Virginia Regiment of Richmond, the 11th from Lynchburg, and the contiguous counties, and the Artillery. We could not see our men because of some intervening woods, but the result of the charge was not long in doubt as a mob of disorganized soldiers in blue ran back up the turnpike as fast as their legs could carry them, at which my boys raised a great shout of triumph which might have been heard on the battle-field. The Union General reported this affair as a reconnaissance in force, but to us it seemed very like a battle. Among the killed at that fight was our former Major Carter Harrison, an officer of much promise, a graduate of the Virginia Military Institute, and a gentleman of highest standing and character. He received a mortal wound and died the succeeding day. I omitted to state in its proper place, that George C. Cabell, a private in Company "A" in the 18th Regiment, had been commissioned as Major, and been assigned to the 18th Virginia Regiment, and Major Harrison was transferred to the 11th, and fell as I have stated in his first fight.

The next day was uneventful, the enemy, as was supposed, engaged in reconnoitering to ascertain the best point of attack on our lines. On the night of the twentieth I was requested to attend at Headquarters of General Cocke at eight o'clock, and was of course present. I found that the General had summoned the commanding [officers] of the Regiments under his command to [confer] with them on the state of affairs as the advance of the enemy was imminent. Among others present was Ex-Governor William Smith, who had been commissioned Colonel of the 49th Regiment of Virginia, and had just arrived with five or six companies, after a hard day's march. He was an old friend of my father, and as soon as he was introduced to me asked if I were related to the Fauquier Withers. In reply I told him I was the son of Dr. Robert W. Withers who was born and reared in Fauquier. He expressed great pleasure at meeting me, and at once commenced an animated description to General Cocke of the physical and social characteristics of my father. To which the General listened with manifest impatience. The conversation was very amusing to the other gentlemen present, as well as to myself. General Cocke was full of apprehension and anxiety, not knowing from what quarter the attack would proceed, but whenever he would begin to discuss the probabilities "Extra Billy" would avail himself of the first pause and recur to his youthful reminiscences. The conversation proceeding somewhat in this way:

"General Cocke, the Colonel's father was one of the finest looking men you ever saw, over six feet in height and straight as an arrow."

"Yes, yes," said the General," but don't you think the enemy will probably attempt to force a passage over the Stone Bridge?" "Possibly sir, but as I was saying, the Colonel's father was without a doubt the finest dancer I ever saw on the floor." "Ah! indeed," said the General, "but if they try to turn our left we should be prepared to move promptly to the support of Colonel Evans."

"Well, that would not be difficult I should think, but I am so pleased 'don't you know' at meeting the son of my old friend, I want to ask him if his father plays the flute now, for he was one of the best performers on that instrument you ever heard." "Governor, don't you think you had better move your command to a point nearer the rest of the Brigade?"

"No General, my boys are very tired, and I want them to get a good nights sleep, don't you know, and tomorrow they will be ready for anything." And my father was at last eliminated from the conversation.

Governor Smith or "Extra Billy," as he was commonly called, was a man of note. He gained his soubriquet years before in the old staging days when he was the proprietor of almost every stage line south of Washington City, and of many North of that point. He had contracts for carrying the United States mail over all those routes, but after receiving the contract pay for this service, he always presented claims for "Extra" allowance either for expedited service, increase in number of trips, or something of that sort, and as he generally had the backing of the Post-office Department, succeeded in having these claims allowed, but at the same time secured an "Extra" to his name which stuck to him through life. He was an astute and successful politician, an effective stump speaker, was several times elected to Congress, subsequently elected Governor by the Legislature of Virginia, and after serving his term, removed to California, and when war seemed inevitable returned to Virginia, raised a Regiment, and served with distinction. Though utterly ignorant of military tactics, he was a brave and gallant soldier, was made a Brigadier General, and was for the second time elected Governor to succeed Governor Letcher, and was filling that office when Richmond fell and the war ended. He lived to be ninety years old.

When our conference was over I returned to my camp, but about two o'clock was aroused by a message from Captain Wall of Company D, who was on picket duty, covering an obscure country road leading to the ford I was detailed to defend, stating that the enemy was advancing along the Warrenton Pike. I went at once to the picket, and could plainly hear the rumbling of the artillery and ambulances, and even the words of command as the column passed along the pike not more than a quarter of a mile away. After giving some instructions to the Captain of the picket in case the enemy should send a column down the road he was guarding, I returned to camp and sent a messenger to the General, notifying him of the advance of the enemy. I had the Regiment under arms, and returned myself to the picket post a little after light. When I reached there Captain Wall had just captured a prisoner belonging to an Illinois regiment. He was scouting on the left of the column through the thick woods, and when he turned to regain the road mistook the direction and came up behind our line of pickets and was taken prisoner much to his surprise. He said he thought our company belonged to a Wisconsin regiment, which had grey uniforms, and knew no better until ordered to halt and throw down his gun. I had a short talk with him and then sent him under guard to Headquarters. He was a pretty cool fellow, for as he started off I remarked, "I suppose you all expect to give us Hail Columbia today, don't you?"

He turned, touched his cap, and replied, "Well, Colonel, I think that is the calculation."

I put him in charge of Sergeant Major Buford, a spare, frail-looking man, who had only recently joined us. He was a member of the Legislature from Danville, and a lawyer of reputation, but being patriotic and desirous of serving his country, as soon as the Legislature adjourned, joined us and asked me to give him some place where he could be of service. I told him if he cared to accept the place of Sergeant Major he could have it, as that was the only vacancy. He was entirely ignorant of all military matters but said he would learn the duties of the place as soon as possible. His equipment consisted of a double-barreled shot gun, and an immense sabre which dated back to Revolutionary times, as long, as wide, and more crooked than a scythe blade. The prisoner was a stalwart man of six feet, who looked as if he could swallow Buford, who followed him closely, his double-barreled gun at full cock and ready for action, his long sabre dangling at his heels as it was dragged through the huckleberry bushes. Altogether it was a most ludicrous picture, and one which I can see in my mind's eye at this moment. Colonel Buford, as he is now called, became a prominent railroad man after the war, was for several years President of the Richmond & Danville road, and is still living in Richmond.

Seeing no indications of an advance on my position, I returned to camp, awaiting developments. It was evident that the enemy was advancing in the direction of Sudley Mills for the purpose of turning our left flank. From our elevated position, by looking up the run we could see the glitter of arms some miles to the westward, and about eleven o'clock we witnessed the first collision between the enemy and the command of Colonel Evans, who held the left of our line, and had formed his line of battle at right angles with his original position. Our batteries were well served, and the Infantry held their ground for a time, but were so largely out-numbered and out-flanked that they were obliged to fall back. Then followed the conflict between the brigades of Generals Bee and Bartow and the Federal forces, which lasted longer. They were reinforced by Jackson's Brigade, who prolonged the contest. I did not then know what commands these were, but as I saw them successively borne back by superior numbers, I became anxious about the result and impatiently awaited orders from the General of our Brigade. I conferred with my other field officers, and also with Colonel Preston, of the 28th Regiment, who had visited my position to obtain a view of the field of battle, and we all agreed that it was high time we were moving forward, but having no orders to that effect I did not feel justified in changing my position. Soon, however, one of General Cocke's Aides brought me a note written in pencil on a small slip of paper to this effect, "Colonel, the enemy have turned Evan's flank and are now pressing forward, *prepare* to move to the support of Evans. (Signed) P. St. G. Cocke."

As you will perceive, this was not an order to move, but to *prepare* to move. After conference with my officers I determined to construe it into an order to advance at once, as the necessity was apparent. Colonel Preston followed me with his command. We crossed the stream and advanced in the direction of the McLean house. As soon as we made our appearance on the open ground, we were exposed to the shelling from a heavy piece of artillery posted at the crest of the hill on the turnpike, about a mile distant. The shriek of these large shells as they passed over us was decidedly discomposing. There was no pause in the advance, but many officers and men would involuntarily stoop at the uncanny sound. Nearing the McLean house, the men were ordered to throw off their knapsacks and blankets in readiness for the fray. Just at this time General Cocke and his staff passed us at a gallop and I asked him what direction the column should take as there was now a lull in the firing and I could see no enemy in view. He made no pause but commanded, "Forward, forward!" and passed to our right. We pushed on past the McLean house in the direction of the Henry house, when we met a string of wounded men and stragglers, streaming to the rear. As many of these were unhurt, I urged them to go back with us into the fight, all refused except two "Tigers," who, from their brogue were evidently Irish. They fell into line and we passed through some pines and emerged on the open plateau near the Henry house, where most of the fighting had been done, some skirmishing was going on between a mob of disorganized men on my left and some of the enemy beyond the Sudley road, who were invisible to us. No other troops being in sight, I told the men to lie down until I could ascertain something of my surroundings, expecting each moment to see the other regiments of the brigade emerge from the pines. Just then one of the "Tigers" who had joined us ran up the slope to an orchard occupied by the skirmishers, got behind an apple tree, and fired two or three times, when he was shot through both legs. He squatted down, and turning his head over his shoulder, called to his comrade, "I say, Dennis, come up here and give them hell, for they've got me." Some officers on horseback now approached from the front, one of whom was evidently wounded, as his horse was led by another, who asked me to open my lines to permit them to pass through with a wounded officer. As they were passing, I asked who the wounded officer was, and the reply was, "General Wade Hampton, commanding the Hampton Legion." They passed to the rear and were followed by a captain and a squad of men who came up to me and reported himself as Captain Connor of the Hampton Legion, which had been disorganized and he wished to fall in with the remnant of his company with us. I directed him to form his men on the right of my regiment. Thanking me, he at once took the place assigned him, impressing me very favorably by his coolness and courage. By this time I saw a group of officers on my right and rear, and approaching them, found it to be General Beauregard and his staff. Asking him for orders, he said, "Change your direction to the left oblique and charge across the Sudley road." I at once gave the order to charge and we dashed forward at double-quick. We soon came up to the guns of Ricket's Battery, which had been abandoned, and a short distance beyond encountered a strong line of skirmishers covering the advance of a Massachusetts regiment. A volley scattered these and we engaged the regiment to which they had fallen back. By this time the 28th Regiment had come up on our left, and just at this juncture, the enemy in our front retreated over the hill and we saw no more of them. As the only enemy visible was some distance beyond the turnpike, I called for volunteers to man some guns of the captured Battery, when Captain Claiborne, of Company B of my regiment, a Lieutenant of the Hampton Legion, and a few others placed one of the guns in position, loaded and fired two or three shells into the ranks of the retreating enemy, which perceptably accelerated their movements. I was at a loss to account for the sudden retreat of the Massachusetts Regiment, which evidently had not suffered greatly, but this was soon explained by the appearance of the brigade under the command of Colonel Jubal Early, which was approaching by way of the Chinn house, threatening their flank, when fearing destruction or capture, they precipitately fled. General Beauregard, who was still near, directed me to pursue them along the turnpike road. As I knew the "Long Tom" gun which had shelled us so fiercely on our advance was in a position to command the bridge, I crossed the stream by wading a few hundred yards below. This, of course, caused some delay, and before we had completed the crossing, two South Carolina regiments and the First Maryland crossed on the bridge and we all advanced up the pike. When we reached the top of the slope there was "Long Tom," sure enough, but deserted by the artillerists. We had not proceeded far beyond this point when we were overtaken by a staff officer, sent to recall us, with orders to move as quickly as possible to Union Mills, some miles in front of Manassas Junction, as it was reported that a strong column of the enemy was advancing in that direction. It was now about sunset, and we started in the direction of Manassas, and fortunately met Captain Fitzjames, our Commissary, with wagons loaded with food for the men, who had had nothing but a scant breakfast in the early morning, and gave him a hearty welcome. I halted the regiment, we ate our supper, and resumed our march, passing by Manassas and on to Union Mills, which we reached about midnight, but found no enemy there, as it was all a false alarm. In no very amiable mood the men dropped on the ground, scarcely breaking ranks, and in a few minutes were sound asleep. I took the saddle off my horse, laid down with my head on it with the bridle over my arm, and thus slept until awakened by the rain falling in my face about daylight. We soon resumed the march in the direction of Manassas, but the rain steadily increased and continued to fall all day. At Manassas I was ordered to move back to my old camp, which we reached late in the afternoon.

My regiment was not heavily engaged in this fight, losing only sixteen or eighteen men, killed and wounded. As the command reached the battle-field we were met by Cadet Robert McCulloch, who had drilled some of the companies of my Regiment at the camp of instruction, and recognizing them, fell in with Company B, where he received a warm welcome. He had gone into the fight with the Fourth Regiment, one of the "Stonewall Brigade," which received its baptism that day, and when they were scattered he fell in with the 18th, and remained with us ever after. He was appointed Adjutant of the regiment after Lieutenant Withers' resignation, afterwards elected Captain of Company B, and served with them to the end of the war. Take him all around, I believe he was the best soldier I ever saw. He was absolutely fearless, was always in a fine humor, cool and undaunted in presence of danger, and was one of the few men I have ever seen who really enjoyed a fight. Soon after reaching camp he asked a number of men of Company B to accompany him to the battle-field to find and bury two cadets who had fallen in the fight. They found and buried them with military honors.

Our Chaplain, the Rev. Robert L. Dabney, was a Chaplain

worth having. He was not only faithful in the discharge of his duties as Chaplain, but on the day of battle, followed up the Regiment and with his own hands gathered up the knapsacks and blankets that had been thrown off by my men in their advance, piled them up, covered them with oil cloth, and thus saved to the men of the Regiment all their personal belongings. This was really an important service and was highly appreciated by both officers and men. There were some amusing incidents connected with our first experiences of a battle. Colonel Robert Preston, of the 28th Regiment, was a prime favorite with all who knew him. He was a brother of Colonel James Preston, of the "Stonewall Brigade," but, unlike him, knew absolutely nothing of military drill or tactics. He always spoke of the men and officers under his command as "My people." He made no effort at drilling, but was always ready for a fight. He knew personally, I believe, almost every man under him, and the larger number of those of my Regiment, and always called them by their given names. He rode a large, bobtailed horse called "Bob," and as we were advancing under the shelling, the roar of battle being particularly deafening at this juncture, he rode up to me, remarking, "Colonel Bob Withers, did you ever hear the like?" "I certainly never did," was my reply. "By Gad, sir," said he, "Waterloo was but a skirmish to it." Pretty soon he again remarked, "I see you stuck to your horse." "Oh, yes," said I, "I could be of little use on foot." Right, sir, 'my people' begged me not to ride into the fight as it was much more dangerous, but I told them I would ride old Bob if he was *sixteen feet* high."

A good deal of fun was poked at Fitzjames, our Commissary, who having been delayed at camp did not start with the Regiment when the advance commenced, but followed at a run, overtook us when under fire, and witnessing the stooping and dodging of some of the men at the unearthly shriek of the shells from "Long Tom," he broke out, "What the hell do you mean by dodging so, that's no way to behave. Stand up like men." Just then a well-aimed shell passed just over his head and down he went with several others, raising his head almost instantly and turning towards those he had criticised he said,

"Gentlemen, I take it all back." This raised a laugh and the incident relieved the tension considerably, and afterwards there was less flinching. Fortunately, the gun was aimed too high and overshot us all the time, no one being hurt by it. I saw for the first time President Davis and General Joseph E. Johnson on the battle-field after the close of the fight. They both presented a fine appearance on horseback and General Johnson was a particularly striking figure, looking like the game cock he was.

Why no attempt was made to improve the victory gained at first Manassas is a conundrum I am unable to solve. I know the soldiers generally expected to be led on to Washington City in pursuit of the flying foe, and I certainly expected it myself, until I received the order to counter-march to Union Mills, And I was surprised the next day to hear nothing of orders to advance. Various explanations have been made by different persons, some in high positions, but none were to my mind satisfactory. I once asked Colonel Jordan, Beauregard's Adjutant General the direct question, and his reply was that the army was not prepared for a forward movement, no commissary supplies were on hand, nor ordnance stores sufficient for another battle. Others have said that two divisions of the enemy were held in reserve at Centreville, who could have easily driven back any force attempting to pursue the retreating army. My own conclusion is that a forward movement was not desired by President Davis; he hoped and believed that a strictly defensive policy on our part would strengthen the "Peace Party" at the North, which might possibly suffice to end the war, but there was no "Peace Party" in the North at that time, as was speedily shown. As it was, our army remained in its camps on and around the battle-field with disastrous consequences, as a perfect epidemic of typhoid fever speedily broke out, from the effects of which we suffered greatly. All the streams and springs were contaminated from the putrifying bodies of men and horses, and soon nearly half of our men were in the Hospitals and many died. A few days after we were encamped on the battle-field, I had a visit from my friend and cousin, Captain Alexander, commanding a company of cavalry from Campbell County. He was always full of fun and humor, and in the course of our conversation, I remarked on the folly of quartering the troops in such an infected atmosphere. He replied that matters were much worse where he was camped, and that the drinking water was so strongly tainted by dead Yankees that he could tell by the taste the different states from which they came. About three days after the fight I received a visit from General Cocke, being the first time I had seen him since he passed our front mounted on his beautiful, thorough-bred stallion, armed only with his riding whip as we advanced to the battle-ground on the 21st. After some conversation, I was describing to him the fine view of the battle we had enjoyed from our elevated camp, he said, "You risked a good deal in leaving your position guarding that ford, as it left our right flank entirely uncovered."

"I left it in accordance with your own orders, General."

"My orders," said he, "I never sent you any order!"

I was dumbfounded, but called up Colonel Carrington, the Adjutant, Captain Graves, of Company A, and some other officers to whom I had showed the note, they all remembered the contents distinctly. He seemed much excited, and repeated that if any such order was delivered to me it was a forgery, and asked to see the note. I searched my pockets in vain, it was apparently lost, but I told him it was certainly his hand writing, which was peculiar and easily recognized. He still declared that he had written no order. I again went through my pockets in vain. Remembering finally that on the day of battle I had worn an undress blue jacket and not my uniform, I hunted the jacket up, which had been so saturated with rain that I had taken it off to dry. I went through the pockets a second time without success, but as I was just about to lay it down I felt a hard wad about the size of a walnut in the corner of the breast pocket, and on examination was sure it was the note in question, which had been reduced almost to pulp by the rain and dried in that state. With the greatest care I proceeded to unfold it, and finally succeeded to a degree sufficient to enable me to decipher the greater portion of it.

General Cocke watched the proceeding in silence. I handed it to him, remarking that there was still enough of the writing legible to disclose its contents and the character of the hand writing. He took it in silence, examined it in silence, and finally handed it back to me without a word, nor was the subject ever after alluded to by either of us. The same day the picket stationed on a by-road leading through a dense wood brought in a prisoner dressed in a Zouave uniform, who had been captured near the picket line. At first he was reticent and not disposed to answer questions, but when he was about to be carried off by the guard to the prison pen at Manassas, he hesitated and looked at me as if he wanted to say something and when I asked if he had anything to say, he spoke up and said, "Colonel, I think I ought to tell you that the Colonel of our regiment lies very badly wounded in the woods not far from where I was captured, and unless something is done for him soon, I don't think he can live."

I told him he was perfectly right in disclosing the fact and that I would send for him at once. I got a spring wagon and put some hay in it and sent a squad of men under the guidance of the prisoner, who soon came back with Colonel Wood, of the 12th Brooklyn Zouaves, who had been shot through the hips and so disabled that he could not walk, but when his Regiment gave way after a plucky fight, had been carried by them on their retreat for some distance and finally left with three men to watch over and care for him, which they had done for about three days, but were then out of food and anxious to surrender. He seemed pretty badly hurt, and had high fever. As he bore on his bosom the insignia of high masonic degree, I determined to give him a better chance for life than he was likely to have in the crowded field hospital at Manassas. So I gave up my tent to him and his attendant and sent two others who came in with him to Manassas. I went into Colonel Carrington's tent for a few days, and hearing the next day that the Surgeon of the 12th Brooklyn Regiment was among the prisoners, I sent a note to General Beauregard's Adjutant General, asking that he might be sent over to attend to his wounded Colonel. He came the same day and took charge of the case. After the removal of the ball, the Colonel rallied, and seemed very grateful for the treatment accorded him. He said that in common with the majority of the Northern people he had believed that the people of Virginia favored the Union cause and only needed the presence of United States troops to declare their hostility to the Secession movement. I assured him that the Virginians were perfectly united in their determination to repel the invaders of their soil, that Mr. Lincoln's proclamation had consolidated the whole population, and cited my own case as an example. I had been an outspoken opponent of secession until President Lincoln's call for Virginia's quota of troops to coerce the seceded states. Colonel Wood expressed his surprise at this information and said, "That being the case, he would never again enter the field as an enemy of the South," and he kept the letter of his word, for though promoted to be a Brigadier General, he never again entered the field. He was a cousin of Fernando Wood, long a prominent Democratic representative in Congress from the City of New York. The Adjutant of the 19th Regiment, Charles Wertenbaker by name, took the greatest interest in Colonel Wood's case, and when he had sufficiently recovered to be sent to a hospital, he secured his transfer to Charlottesville, of which town he was a native, and through his friends there was able to secure for Colonel Wood many indulgences, and finally procured his exchange. After reaching his home Colonel Wood wrote me a very nice letter which reached me in some way, I never knew how, but I did not reply to it, as I thought it improper to do so, but I think Lieutenant Wertenbaker exchanged several letters with him. I gave up my tent to him for about three weeks with his Surgeon and orderly, feeding them all from my own mess and yet I was subsequently informed that this same Surgeon, after his exchange, appeared before the Congressional Committee, appointed to inquire into the conduct of the war, and testified that the wounded officers and soldiers of the Northern army were treated with the greatest cruelty after the battle of Manassas. I regret that I can not now recall his name.

About a month after the battle of Manassas I came to the

conclusion that it would be wise to give up my habit of smoking. For many years I had been addicted to the practice, and at times to great excess, cigars or pipe, it mattered little with me. But for some time past I had been annoyed by the irregular action of my heart, and attacks of palpitation were not infrequent. Of one thing the soldiers in camp had an unlimited supply, that was fine smoking tobacco. Mr. John W. Carroll, of Lynchburg, sent me a ten-pound bale of "Lone Jack," the brand of smoking tobacco then recognized as the best, and having little to occupy my time and attention I smoked nearly all the time. The heart symptoms I felt were increasing in violence and very slight exertion sufficed to bring on an attack of palpitation. I began seriously to fear that I was a victim of organic disease of that important organ, and the idea was not particularly cheering. In thinking over the matter, I came to the conclusion that my recent unwonted indulgence in the pipe might be instrumental in causing the increased severity of my cardiac troubles. I determined as an experiment to give up smoking for a time, hoping that entire abstinence might mitigate the severity of my symptoms. This occurred one evening about nine o'clock in my tent, and knocking the ashes from my pipe, I remarked to my Adjutant, "Ned, I mean to stop smoking for a while to see if it will not lessen my heart troubles."

"Yes," was his reply, "I reckon you will stop until tomorrow morning, as it is about bed time now."

This was the end of my smoking. In the course of a month I noticed a marked mitigation of my symptoms, and in six months the irregular action of the heart ceased entirely, and I have never had an attack of palpitation since. About the first of August we moved our camp to the village of Centreville, which we were glad to do, but it was too late. The foul air and fouler water had done their work and typhoid fever cases were developed in constantly increasing numbers throughout the army. Recognizing the dangerous condition of affairs, I made the best arrangements possible for the protection of my men, establishing hospitals in churches, private houses, and tents, to which all sick cases were removed as soon as the disease appeared. Every company had amongst its officers or men physicians of more or less experience and skill, and these were detailed to wait on the sick. The two Danville companies rented a house a short distance in the country, and Lieutenant Smith and Adjutant Withers, both experienced physicians, looked after their welfare. Dr. H. W. Cole, also a practicing physician, came on from Danville to aid in their treatment, and they were furnished with medical and other needed supplies in abundance by the Danville people. Captain Thomas Claiborne, of Company B, was the only captain who suffered a serious attack, and I secured quarters for him at the house of a Mr. Ayres about two miles from camp, where he was well cared for and I visited him daily. His illness, however, lasted several weeks. The number of fatal cases in the Regiment was not large, other commands near us suffered much more. This was particularly the case with Barksdale's Brigade of Mississippians in camp near us, among whom the mortality was distressing. During this invasion of fever we were relieved from all but picket duty. Our pickets had been considerably advanced, and at Masons and Munson's Hill strong outposts were established in sight of Washington City. Skirmishing was going on between the picket lines daily, and now and again a man would be killed or wounded at this foolish fun. My regiment was fortunate enough to escape any casualties. I never rode around the line of pickets, which I did daily, that I was not made the target for one or more sharp shooters, some of whom were good marksmen, too. One day I was at the reserve post of the picket which was established in a stack yard, fully a mile from the enemy's picket line, and the officer in command said, "Colonel, you had better not stand out there exposed to view, for the Yankees will shoot you."

"Oh," I said, "they are too far off."

Just at this time "ping!" went a rifle ball over my head, showing that the warning was not in vain. About half a mile above where we were standing, I heard the crack of a rifle, and enquiring the cause was told that one of our scouts, who had been with us for some time, and who "fought on his own hook," was up there with his Maynard rifle, so I walked up the lane, and found him looking intently across the field towards the woods. And soon as he saw me he said, "Colonel, I am mighty glad to see you have your glasses with you, for I can't make out for my life whether that is a Yankee lying yonder behind the fence or whether it is a stump." I looked and said, "It is a Yankee." "Well, just watch and see where the dust flies when I fire, will you? How far do you think it is?" "About twelve hundred yards," said I. "Well, watch now, and see where the ball strikes."

He fired and I saw a puff of dust rise at least a hundred yards short of the fence and I so informed him. He put up his sight a little and fired a second time. This time the ball struck the ground near the fence and instantly there came a puff of smoke and the whiz of a bullet, which passed through the top of a peach tree under which we were standing.

"Oh, ho!" said he, "I bet I will make it too warm for you to stay there much longer."

Again adjusting his sight he fired and must have cut close to his mark, as not one but two men bolted at once into the woods out of sight. This is a fair sample of the fighting that was going on all day along the picket line.

General J. E. B. Stuart was in command of the Outpost, and I have never seen his equal as an outpost officer. Active, vigilant and untiring; he not only kept his own men constantly on the *qui vive,* but was always planning to annoy and harrass the enemy. One evening he came over to my post, and told me that General Fitz John Porter, who was, I think a class-mate of his at West Point, was in command of the Union Outpost and when the pickets were relieved every morning, was in the habit of accompanying the relief, and seeing that they were properly posted; and he thought he might possibly capture him as well as the relief if I would aid him with a few companies of my command. He, then disclosed his project, which was to take six or eight of the Companies of my Regiment about midnight, and make our way through the picket lines of the enemy, concealing ourselves until the relief came in the morning, then make a rush on them, and capture or stampede the party. I asked if he knew where the pickets were posted. He replied, that a man who did know would guide us, and he had perfect confidence in his reliability. After further discussion of his plan I deemed it feasible, but risky. He thought, however, that there was but little risk attending it, so I consented to aid him. That night I told the Captains of the Companies selected for the expedition what we proposed doing and instructed them to have their men under arms soon after eleven o'clock. The six companies numbered about three hundred and fifty men. It was a clear starlight night with no moon. I left Colonel Carrington and the Adjutant in charge of the Camp, and took command of the Companies selected for the expedition. I carried an Enfield rifle along for I thought it likely that we would have a fight before we got back, and a sword would be of little use. We moved off promptly on time and were soon joined by General Stuart and some of his staff. We had marched about two miles or thereabouts and passed through a body of woodland where it was pretty dark. On emerging into the open field I was struck with the small number of men in some of the companies, and was told by a non-commissioned officer that a great many of the men had turned back in the woods and returned to camp, but said that the officers of the Companies were to blame for it, as they had told their men that the whole expedition was a piece of folly that would land them all in Hell or Washington before night. While I was talking to him I saw two or three men drop out of the ranks, and move off to the rear. I was very angry and running as fast as I could overtook them and ordered them back to their places in rank. One of them demurred, and refused to go. I cocked the rifle and pointing it at his head, told him that unless he obeyed instantly I would blow his brains out. He turned back quick enough then, but I found that the force had been so much reduced that there would not be men enough left to accomplish the object of the expedition, and going forward reported to General Stuart the condition of affairs. He was greatly annoyed, but ordering me to halt the command, inspected it and found as I had told him, that we were not strong enough to carry out our purpose, and ordered a return to camp. He directed me to ascertain the officers chiefly at fault, place them under arrest, and have them Court Martialed. As I had already determined on this action I set to work at once, taking testimony to fix the responsibility on the proper parties. The result of my investigation was to satisfy me as to the guilty ones. I placed them under arrest, preferred charges against them, which I forwarded to General Stuart. He endorsed and forwarded them to General Longstreet's Headquarters. The up shot of the matter was that two Captains and a first Lieutenant commanding a company were tried by a court martial convicted and cashiered. They and their friends of course raised a howl, but my action was approved by the Regiment One of the Captains thus cashiered, and the Lieutenant Commanding disappeared from the army, but the other Captain enlisted as a private in his old company, served as such until the reorgination of the army in the Spring of 1862, when he was re-elected Captain, and though General Pickett at first refused to approve their choice, by my advice he consented as his conduct had been exemplary for several months. This affair was I think the occasion of more worry and annoyance to me than anything which occurred during my whole military service.

My Regiment had been relieved by one from the South Carolina Brigade, and I was amused at an incident which occurred in this connection. Among other Commissary stores brought down for distribution to the Companies of the 18th Regiment were several barrels of rice, the first which had been issued to my command, but the men would not take it away as no one would eat it. The barrels of rice were therefore left where they were unloaded from the Commissary wagon. When the South Carolinians relieved us, they saw the rice left on the ground and enquired the cause. When told that no one would eat it they asked that it might be given to them; assent being given, they raised a shout, fell on the rice and in ten minutes not a pound was left. In those days the army was well fed. The whole country between Fairfax Court-House and the Potomac was cultivated in truck farms, and as the owners were almost all Northern men, when the Southern Troops advanced and covered this section, the inhabitants left their homes in haste, often leaving their furniture, and all their belongings which became the prey of plunderers and bummers, and the crops and gardens were despoiled by the soldiers. With the approach of winter we were ordered back to Centreville for winter quarters, but before we changed our camping ground some wiseacre persuaded our authorities that the issue of whiskey rations would be of great benefit to the health of the army, and though protests were sent up by some of the Officers, myself among the number, who believed this issue would lead to mischief, the order was promulgated. I ordered that in my Regiment the whiskey should be distributed to the men drawn up in line and those who chose could drink it. Many refused to take it in that way, saying it was treating the men like negroes called up by their masters for a Christmas dram. I would not recede from my order, and told those who refused to drink that I was delighted at their action and hoped they would continue their refusal. Now mark the result. In one of my Companies two officers got into a fight, one armed with a revolver, and the other with a Bowie knife. The man shot at was not hurt, but rushed on his adversary with his knife and wounded him so seriously that it was thought he would die. A man came rushing to my tent with the news of the affray, saying that Lieutenant—had been desperately hurt, and was bleeding to death, and that the Surgeon who had been summoned to his relief, had been so overcome by the sight of the blood, that he had fainted. I ran to the tent where the wounded man lay, and found him seriously cut in two places and bleeding freely from a severed artery, which I immediately proceeded to secure, and then dressed his wounds and ordered both parties put under arrest. On investigation I found that the wounded man, being under the influence of liquor was the aggressor, and wholly to blame, so his opponent was relieved from arrest, and the wounded man sent home as soon as he could be safely moved.

Colonel George W. Carr, an old army officer in command of the 19th Regiment had under him a Company composed mainly of Irishmen, most of whom of course became pretty lively under the influence of the whiskey rations, but ere long their jollity lapsed into belligerency, and a half a dozen fights were in progress at once, and a great disturbance arose. The Colonel rushed out of his tent to know the cause of the row, and ordered the combatants to retire at once to their quarters. They paid no attention to his command, which so infuriated him, being a man of quick temper at all times, that he ran to his tent, picked up his sabre and pitched into the crowd, cutting them down right and left as he came to them. Under this heroic treatment the disorder was quickly quelled, but the Surgeon had to treat several incised wounds in this Company.

The whiskey rations were so palpably fraught with mischief that the issue was continued only three days in our Brigade.

When we fell back to Centreville, the General selected his grounds for Headquarters in an open field and had his tents speedily pitched, instructing his regimental officers to encamp near him as it was designed that a line of rifle pits should be at once constructed covering the whole encampment. I looked around and not fancying so exposed a location for winter quarters, I laid out my camp in a near by piece of woodland facing the south and protected on the north and west by a fringe of woods around which I had sentinels placed with orders that no one should be permitted to cut any of those trees. After getting tents up I was much pleased with my location, but had hardly time to congratulate myself on my good fortune when I was summoned by one of the General's staff to Headquarters. I at once proceeded to report and was met by the General who said, "Colonel, you will have to move your camp back into the open ground near my Headquarters. You are too far off."

I was considerably taken aback, but knowing the necessity of a cool and deferential reply I said, "General, I selected that site because it was more suitable for a Camp than any place so exposed as the crest of a hill would be, and I hope, unless there is serious objection, you will permit me to remain where I am."

"Impossible sir, in case of a sudden alarm your men could not get into position with sufficient promptitude. I wish my whole Command concentrated as much as possible."

"General," said I, "my Headquarter tent is not more than two hundred yards from this point, and I will guarantee in case of necessity, I will man the rifle pits in my front as soon as any other Regiment of the Brigade. The crest of the hill is exposed to every wind which blows, and where I am we are entirely protected from the cold winds of the northwest. Please ride up and look at the place I have selected, and I know that your experience and good judgment will recognize the advantage of the location."

He still appeared not satisfied, and I insisted on a visit from him before he determined definitely to require my removal. After considerable pursuasion he agreed to come over the next morning but intimated that his mind was not changed. Fortunately the next day we had a strong and cold wind from the northwest which increased in violence towards evening, and in the night blew a perfect gale. I have rarely seen a more violent blow. The General did not come over and I was satisfied to let the "status quo" remain, but the next morning news was brought that almost all the tents of the 19th Regiment had been blown down and most of those at Headquarters. After I got breakfast I walked over to the General's quarters, and found most of his Staff Officers and his servants holding on to the tent poles and ropes to prevent capsizing and the General himself considerably disturbed by the discomforts of the situation. He asked me how we had fared and when I replied that we had not been seriously incommoded by the storm, he gave a grunt, and said he wished he could say as much. I resisted the temptation to remind him of our discussion two days before as I felt that it would be dangerous, but nothing more was said about changing my Camp. We spent a quiet winter and as most of the men and officers built chimneys to their tents we were fairly comfortable. In December General Stuart took about fifty wagons and started out to bring in forage from the Drainsville neighborhood, and as guard carried the 11th Regiment, and some Cavalry. I don't know whether the Yankees were advised of the movement, but they had made little progress in loading the wagons when they were attacked by a largely superior force of Artillery, Infantry and Cavalry. The 11th Va. held their ground, and kept the enemy in check for some hours, but they suffered heavily. My brother Howard, 1st Lieutenant of Company C, told me that his Company had many killed and wounded, and as this Company was from my old neighborhood in Campbell County, I knew personally almost every one in it. My Regiment was ordered out with several others to their relief, but when we reached the battlefield the enemy had retired and we brought back the wounded and killed.

I was taken sick soon after this affair, had a sharp attack of Catarrhal fever, and was sent home as soon as I could prudently travel. I did not return until after Christmas, and greatly enjoyed my brief visit to my wife and family. I found she had taken as boarders Mrs. Abbott and her three daughters, refugees from Georgetown. One of her sons, Frank, was in the army, the other, William, I think had some clerical position. These ladies, being intelligent and accomplished, were pleasant inmates and remained a long time with us.

When I returned to Camp I found Colonel Rust of Loudon commanding Brigade, as General Cocke had obtained leave of absence and paid a visit to his home in Powhatan, but had committed suicide a few days after, by blowing out his brains with a pistol. A sad ending of an honorable career. I never heard any cause assigned for this rash act except mental aberration. As I was the senior of Colonel Rust, I assumed command of the Brigade much to the joy of Colonel Rust, who was almost crazy to return to his young and beautiful wife in Loudon to whom he had not long been married. I moved my quarters to a house near by where I found Colonel Alexander, Chief of Ordinance, also quartered. He was a graduate of West Point, and an accomplished officer and gentleman. He and I, as well as Captain Asa Rogers of the Loudon Artillery, the Adjutant of the Brigade, messed together the rest of the winter. My duties while commanding the Brigade, were mainly of a routine character and certainly not very onerous. Towards the close of the winter three or four gentlemen drove up to Headquarters and entered my office. They were all strangers to me; one of them stepped forward and introduced himself as Captain Croxton, and turning introduced me to General George E. Pickett, who had been assigned to the command of our Brigade. He handed me a copy of the order of assignment and I saluted him as Brigadier General, and congratulated the Brigade in having as their commander an officer of such distinction, for as Captain Pickett, while in command at the

Island of San Juan, in the bay of Vancouver, he had pluckily refused to surrender the Post to a British detachment of greatly superior force, sent to occupy it during the boundary dispute between Great Britain and the United States. Captain Pickett had only one Company under him, but he paraded them under arms, and notified the officer in command of the British troops that he would fire on them if they attempted to land. His pluck and determination impressed the Officer and though he could have crushed Pickett's small force in a few minutes, he prudently refrained from any aggressive movement, and reported the facts to his Government. Captain Pickett's conduct on this occasion was lauded by the whole country. As soon as news of the Secession of Virginia reached him he sent in his resignation, and started east, but it took him a long time to make the trip, as there was no R. R. in operation west of St. Louis or Omaha. After he reported in Richmond he was appointed a Brigadier, and assigned to Cocke's old Brigade. He was at that time a handsome man, with blue eyes and very black and curling hair worn long. His Adjutant General was Thomas Croxton of Essex County, a lawyer and gentleman of genial and polished manners, who soon became popular with the command. He died July 3d, 1903, in his native County; age 82 years. The order of appointment was read at Dress Parade that evening and he entered at once on his duties. I of course returned to my Camp, and resumed command of my Regiment, and everything proceeded in usual routine. I found however, when I came back evidencs of the presence of more whiskey in camp than ever before, and satisfied myself that the drivers of the wagons were the agents through whom it was introduced. I therefore selected an officer on whom I could rely, and ordered him to take a detail of men, with instructions to make a thorough search through every wagon and every deposit of forage about the Camp, and bring to my tent all the whiskey they could find. It did not require much time to complete the quest; and the result was that I had lying before and in the tent a formidable array of runlets, jugs, and bottles of whiskey, which I ordered to be emptied on the ground, greatly to the surprise and distress of many officers and men.

While in winter quarters I undertook to read again the

whole of the Old Testament and completed the undertaking that winter. The Chaplain of the Regiment was the Rev. Mr. Stoddard, an eccentric old bachelor, nearly related to General Ewell, a half-brother, I think. He dropped into my tent one evening and found me reading the Old Testament, and I remarked, "Mr. Stoddard, it seems to me that many of the old Patriarchs, judged by our standards, were rather a disreputable lot of men."

"Yes Sir," was his prompt response, "if Abraham had lived in the present day he would not have been admitted into decent society, and he was about the best of them."

Mr. Stoddard had with him a little Digger Indian he had brought from the Pacific Coast, who was quite a curiosity. He was not larger than a ten year old boy, but was possessed of uncommon strength and powers of endurance. He could march all day carrying a pack larger than himself, and never evince any fatigue. He was devoted to his master, and served him faithfully.

One of the effects of *ennui* arising from camp life in winter quarters, was the great increase in the number of card players, and some of the parties became so absorbed in their game, that they would sit up the greater part of the night. The tent of Captain Daniel Turner of Company "B," was pretty regularly chosen as the place of meeting for these card parties. Night after night they kept "Uncle Daniel," as they called him, up until the "Wee small hours ayont the twal." As he never played himself, he became very tired of these protracted sittings, but being one of the best natured men in the Regiment, he did not like to give offense to his friends by ordering them out. My tent was not far from Captain Turner's, and in full view. One night as I was about retiring, I was surprised by a visit at that late hour from Captain Turner. Supposing he had some special business I waited a while for him to disclose it, but he only talked of common place matters. I observed that every few moments he would pull back the fly of the tent, and look out with a suppressed smile. Finally I said, "What is it Uncle Daniel that amuses you?" He laughed quietly and said, "I am just waiting to see how long the boys can stand it."

"Stand what?"

"Why, just before I left my tent I made out I was fixing the fire, and put in two or three old shoes, and then placed a board across the top of the chimney so the smoke is bound to fill the tent and drive them out."

I was amused at the dry way he treated the subject, and moved my stool so I could also watch the outcome. I had not very long to wait. In a few minutes the flies of the tent were thrown widely open, and out came the party coughing, sneezing, cursing and calling Uncle Daniel to come to see what was the matter with his chimney. He, however, lay perdu, until the players left, as it was impossible for them to resume their game in that tent. The Captain finally went out, took off the board, and after a short time the smoke cleared away, and he went to his bunk. I think this experiment put an end to the long seances.

With the opening of the Spring, rumors of a speedy advance of McClellan's army became more rife, but it was not until the month of March was considerably advanced that we made any movement. Then it seemed understood that the advance was about to be made; and all preparations on our part were perfected to meet it. Wagon trains and baggage were sent across the Rapidan, which seems to have been selected as the line of defense. By chance or otherwise, I was in command of the picket lines in our front when the advance was made. I received an order to take command of the whole line of pickets, which would constitute the Rear Guards of the Infantry, and General Stuart was in command of the Calvary Rear Guard. I had about half of my Regiment and about the same proportion of the 38th Regiment under command of Lieutenant Colonel Whittle, with some detached Companies, nearly one thousand men in all. I had orders to fall back along the Warrenton pike, stopping at Gainsville to destroy the stores accumulated there, which could not all be carried off. This took us some time and it seemed really a pity to burst open, scatter, and destroy so many thousands barrels of flour, tons of of bacon, and quantities of forage, but it did no good to mourn over the loss as the enemy would have received all the benefit from it, if left behind. General Stuart came up and hurried us off, and we reached a point five miles north of Warrenton, and camped there. I took possession of an old deserted mansion belonging to the Ward family. We expected to be followed by the enemy, and were instructed to delay his advance as long as possible, but no enemy approached our strong pickets during the two days I remained there. On the morning of third day a courier came from General Stuart ordering me to move with my whole command as speedily as practicable to Warrenton Junction, eight miles from Warrenton. We set off at once, passing through the town where we met another courier sent to hurry us up, with the news that the enemy was advancing along the railroad. We pushed on without loss of time, but when within a mile of the Junction had another order to come on at double quick. The command was at once given, and we reached the Junction in short order but the men were pretty thoroughly blown. No one was visible at the Junction, but soon a messenger came, directing us to push on towards Cedar Run, where the enemy was crossing. On going about a mile in that direction, I came upon our Infantry Rear Guard, the column sent along the railroad, which was drawn up in Line of battle near the edge of an open field extending to the Run. We were received with many manifestations of pleasure as we passed along in rear of the Line of battle about half of which was composed of Companies from the 11th Regiment. We prolonged their line and now made a pretty fair show.

General Stuart came up and in reply to my inquiry as to the strength of the enemy's column in front, told me he thought it was composed of Cavalry only, as he could get no intelligence of the presence of Infantry. This relieved me considerably as the Infantry at that time entertained a poor opinion of the fighting quality of the Yankee Cavalry. General Stuart took a Company of Calvary and rode forward to the stream and some distance down it, but was not disturbed. We remained in line of battle however, until after sunset and returned to the Junction.

The whole Command was, with the exception of the pickets, set to work tearing up and destroying the railroad and gathering in all food from the country around us, leaving a little as possible for the enemy. Captain Graves, of Company "A," was detailed on this service, and among other places called at Captain Charles Randolph's, an old friend of my father, who had spent most of his life in the Navy. He was now upwards of eighty years of age. Captain Graves' Company wore the regular uniform of the U. S. Army, and when they filed into Captain Randolph's yard he mistook them, naturally, for Yankee soldiers, whom he was daily expecting. He was seated in his porch, and did not rise or extend any invitation to enter. When Captain Graves explained his mission, the old gentleman was very irate, and informed him that he could get nothing there. Graves demanded the key of the smokehouse that he might examine for himself. The Captain told him that he could not have it. Graves then said, "Well, sir I will have to break it open."

"If you dare do it," said he, "I'll shoot you dead."

"Well, my orders from Colonel Withers compel me to do it, and besides if I leave you with full supplies the Yankees will be along in a few days and they will leave you nothing."

"The Yankees, are you not all Yankees?"

"No sir, we are Confederates."

"Why the h—l didn't you say so at first, you are welcome to any thing I have."

And after getting a good lot of bacon, and some meal and flour the old Captain, asked, "Who did you say was your Colonel?"

"Colonel Withers of the 18th Regiment."

"I wonder if he is kin to the Fauquier Withers?"

"I can't say positively, but I think his father was a native of that County."

"Well, tell him I will be over in the morning to call on him."

Sure enough he came over the next morning, bringing with him a couple of bottles of Champagne to drink our health, and confusion to our enemies. I told him who my father was and he said he remembered him very well as a boy and young man, and professed to be very glad to meet me. The old Captain was a retired Naval officer; a jolly sailor of whom many amusing anecdotes were extant. He it was of whom the story was told that on one occasion when Major Jack Dade, another celebrity, was visiting him and came down rather late for family prayers, which Captain Randolph never under any circumstances omitted; when he opened the door of the sitting room, and found the family on their knees; thinking that he could steal a march on the Captain, he tip-toed to the side-board where the decanters, mint, and sugar, were arrayed in accordance with custom, and undertook to help himself to a drink on the sly. Unfortunately, in his haste he permitted the decantor to "clink" on the edge of the tumbler. At the familiar sound Captain Randolph ceased his prayer, and turning his head towards the side-board remarked, "Hold on there Major, I'll jine you in a minute."

We remained a week or ten days at the Junction, tearing up the railroad and got heartily sick of the job before we were relieved by Seymour's Louisiana Regiment and the 14th Va., then commanded by Colonel James A. Walker. We moved across the Rappahannock and Rapidan, to a point about four miles East of Orange Court-House, around which village, the rest of the Brigade was encamped. Here we remained about a week with nothing transpiring worthy of record, if we except a false alarm stating that the enemy was crossing the river at the U. S. Ford, about eight miles below, and we were sent at double quick on a dark night, to resist the advance. We reached our destination about midnight, and finding no sign of the enemy marched back again.

By this time it was well ascertained that General McClellan was moving his army to the Peninsula in the neighborhood of Yorktown, and our Brigade was ordered to march to Richmond en route to the same place. This was early in April, and the day we commenced this march was about as disagreeable and inclement as if it had been mid winter. Hail and snow, mud and slush combined to make it the most trying and disagreeable march we had yet made. We encamped about a mile short of Louisa C. H. in a skirt of woods, and five minutes after the force was disbanded there was not a rail left on a strong fence enclosing the field, though strict orders had been given forbidding burning rails. General Pickett halted here one day, endeavoring to procure transportation by rail for his

Brigade, but not being successful, we started the next day for Richmond, and two days after, camped on the Chickahominy a few miles from the City. After a days' delay we moved on through Richmond, and embarked for King's Mill Landing, not far from Williamsburg. Steamers and barges crowded almost to suffocation, bore us to our destination by nine o'clock in the morning, and we at once disembarked, and started for Yorktown. We had had no food since the previous morning, but as we passed Lebanon Church, near Williamsburg, the ladies of that City had prepared a sumptious feast to which you may be sure the half-starved soldiers did ample justice. We found General Magruder hard pressed by the overwhelmingly superior forces of General McClellan. He had succeeded in keeping them back only by rapid changes of position, showing strong bodies of troops first at one point, and then at another in their front, compelling the cautious McClellan to move slowly. As soon as we reached Yorktown, we were assigned to a position between that place and dam No. 1. Here we found ourselves in the immediate presence of the enemy, whose sharp shooters occupying points of vantage in trees and other commanding positions, made it dangerous for any man to raise his head above the embankment behind which we were lying. We remained on this picket line three days, one Company being stationed beyond the dam and separated from the rest of the Regiment by the stream. I regarded the position of this advanced picket peculiarly exposed, and so reported to General Pickett, when we came off duty. The reliefs had to reach their posts in the dark, and those relieved moved off in the same way. The 19th Regiment relieved us, and the second night of their tour of duty, Captain Peyton's Company, stationed in the advance position, was gobbled up by the Yankees; almost the whole company being captured about day break.

A few days after this tour of duty in the trenches, I was taken sick with camp dysentary, then becoming quite prevalent and in two days, was very seriously ill. I had only a blanket to lie on, and a shelter tent to keep off the weather. Our Chaplain, Mr. Stoddard, who was well known in Williamsburg, being a half brother of Colonel Ewell, the President of William and Mary College, seemed much concerned at my uncomfortable situation, and went to Williamsburg to try to obtain quarters for me, and when he returned reported that Dr. Coleman would receive me. So I was put into an ambulance and carried there and I think this saved my life, for there I had every comfort and attention possible, and in a short time had sufficiently improved in health to enjoy the bright conversation and sparkling *bon mots* of my charming hostess.

CHAPTER XV.

REORGANIZATION OF THE ARMY—BATTLES OF WILLIAMSBURG AND SEVEN PINES.

Most of the volunteer Companies in our army having been mustered in for a year only, the Government issued orders for their reorganization, providing for elections in all the Companies, and afterwards for the Field officers of the different Regiments. As I had always endeavored to keep up the discipline of my command, I was perfectly aware that a certain element of the organization would make an effort to prevent my re-election. Indeed I was advised by some of the officers that an effort was being made to do this. I paid no attention to the matter, however, and never approached officer or man on the subject. This election came off during my sickness and several changes were made in the company officers. In Company "A" Captain Graves, probably the best Captain in the Regiment, was defeated for re-election, only because he was a good disciplinarian, and kept all his men strictly up to their duties. Lieutenant Smith and Adjutant Withers of the same Company declined a re-election, both being practicing physicians and men of family, and they returned home. In Company "B" Captain Claiborne was re-elected, but shortly afterwards received notice of his election as Lieutenant Colonel in a Cavalry Regiment and resigned, and Lieutenant Daniel Turner was made Captain. McCulloch was elected 1st Lieutenant of Company "B," and I appointed him Adjutant of the Regiment. When the election of field officers came on, rather to my surprise I learned that I had been re-electd without opposition. Lieutenant Colonel Carrington was voted for by the officers of Company "C," but unqualifiedly withdrew his name, declaring that he would not accept the office. He was re-elected Lieutenant Colonel; Major Cabell being re-elected also to his former position. Several changes were made in the other Company officers as well as in the field officers of the Brigade.

On the third of May the sick and wounded of the army were sent to Richmond preparatory to the expected withdrawal of our forces from Yorktown. I was sent in an ambulance to the steamer at King's Mill, and with other invalids was carried to Richmond. Two days afterwards the battle of Williamsburg was fought, when Longstreet in command of the rear had a pretty stiff fight with the advanced forces of McClellan's army. This was mainly to give the wagon trains time to get away. My Regiment was in this fight under command of Lieutenant Colonel Carrington and Major Cabell, and made a good record, losing a good many officers and men killed and wounded. During this fight a brilliant charge was made by the 24th Va., and 5th N. C. Regiments, part of a Brigade commanded by Colonel Jubal Early, which elicited the admiration of both friend and foe; and gave to these commands a high reputation, but they paid dearly for it, having lost very heavily both in men and officers.

On reaching Richmond I applied for sick leave, which having been granted on Surgeon certificate, I proceeded to Danville, where I remained two weeks and then returned to my Regiment, which I found encamped at the Long Bridge on the Chickahominy. A few days after we moved to Richmond, and encamped on the old Fairfield race course near the City.

General Joseph E. Johnson was now in command of all the forces around Richmond. General McClellan advanced on the line of the Chickahominy occupying both sides of the stream and fortifying as he advanced. On the twenty-ninth of May, there was a very heavy rain storm, and another at night. Soon after dark we received orders to prepare to move at daylight to the Williamsburg road, and there await further orders. This of course meant a fight; and it was understood that General Longstreet deemed that a successful attack could be made early in the morning of the thirtieth on that portion of the enemy's line stationed on the Richmond side of the stream, on the hypothesis that the stream would be so high, that the troops on the East side could not cross to reinforce those attacked, and they could thus be destroyed. General Huger's Division, which had just come up from the neighborhood of Norfolk, were ordered to precede us in the line of march down the Williamsburg road, and General Longstreet was to command all the troops on that road. General Johnson, with G. W. Smith's Division was to move down the "Nine Mile" road towards its junction with the Williamsburg road, thus throwing him on the flank of the Federals, who were in front of Longstreet.

Pursuant to orders my Regiment left camp about daybreak, marched in the direction of the Williamsburg road, which we reached about sunrise, and there halted to permit Huger's Division to pass. And there our brigade waited hour after hour, but it was nearly twelve o'clock before we saw anything of Huger's Division. Finally they came along, followed by a long train of wagons. Before they passed us we heard the firing of D. H. Hill's Division, and that portion of Longstreet's which had attacked Casey's Division of the Union Army. The firing was very heavy at times, and indicated stubborn resistance on the part of the Yankee troops. Before reaching the Battle ground, Pickett's Brigade was sent to the left of the Williamsburg road to cover the line of railroad leading to Richmond.

We took our position accordingly, on the edge of a swamp where the bushes were so thick that no one could see five steps ahead, with our left resting on the Railroad. Here we stood all the afternoon listening to the fight on the Williamsburg road and expecting every moment to hear the guns of Johnson's command advancing by the "Nine Mile road." Nothing was heard from them until after three o'clock, when the fighting on the Williamsburg road had practically ceased; the Union forces having been killed, captured or driven back. The advance of Johnson's command was resisted manfully. One Yankee battery of heavy guns seemed to be especially well served, and I had never before heard so heavy a fire of small arms. This continued until dark, and I was satisfied that Johnson's column had not succeeded in effecting a junction with D. H. Hill and Longstreet. Our Brigade was kept in position all night with no food for man or beast. Of course we slept but little. At day break we received orders to advance, and not long after heard of General Johnson's serious wound from a fragment of shell the evening before, and the consequent failure of his attack by the "Nine Mile Road." We soon passed over the ground where the fighting of the day before occurred, and saw abundant evidence of the stubborn character of the fight near Casey's Headquarters where the large number of dead and wounded soldiers of both armies were still lying where they fell. When I saw General Pickett I asked him what was the plan of operations for the day; he replied that he was then on his way to General D. H. Hill's Headquarters, who, being the ranking officer, would direct the operations of the day. He instructed me to move on along the Williamsburg road a short distance, then to halt and await his coming. Saying he would soon rejoin us. We passed down the road for perhaps half a mile, and found General Pryor's Brigade halted in the road near a small house. I also halted, awaiting General Pickett's return. I saw lying in the road a Yankee soldier with a broken thigh, and noting his exposed situation, liable to be run over by any vehicle which passed, I told two of my men to pick him up and carry him through the gate into the yard of the building where he would be comparatively safe. Being grateful, I suppose, for the service rendered, he told the men who moved him, that near by was the Camp of an Artillery Company which had not been visited by any of the Confederates, and where they could find something to eat. They reported this to me, and I ordered the Captain of each Company to detail a squad of men, send them to the place indicated, and bring back such food as they might find for distribution to the command, cautioning them at the same time to keep the other men in line as we knew nothing of our surroundings or the position of the enemy. I then walked into the porch of the building near us where I saw some one lying down, and found it to be General Roger A. Pryor, complaining of being very ill, and suffering from violent headache. I asked if he had any knowledge of the position of the Yankee troops, but he knew no more than I did, and said he was awaiting orders from General Hill. About this time one of my men came up with a bag of shelled oats which he had very thoughtfully brought to me for my horse who had been more than twenty-four hours without food. Thanking him for the favor, I emptied the grain on the ground and calling Colonel Carrington and Major Cabell, invited them to bring their horses to share it. It is needless to say that they "went for the oats" in short order. I noticed that many more men were straggling to the Yankee camp than I had authorized, and I repeated my orders to the Company officers to keep their men in ranks. Just before this I had observed two or more large Regiments of Confederate troops passing diagonally across to my left towards a piece of woods. Recognizing them as part of Huger's Division from their numbers and clean clothes, I said to Colonel Carrington, "Where do you suppose those troops are going in that direction?" He replied, "I have no idea, but don't they look clean and nice?"

Five minutes had scarcely passed after these troops entered the woods, when without a preliminary shot being fired, there was a perfect crash of musketry from the direction in which they had gone as if a whole Brigade had simultaneously fired a volley. In less time than it takes to tell it, a perfect mob of men rushed from that wood without a semblance of organization, each men running for his life. It was "Devil take the hindmost," officers and men mixed in inexplicable confusion, and not only these were running, but not less than a hundred men of our Brigade came rushing from the camp they were pillaging, and I greatly feared they would stampede the rest of the command. Slipping my horse's bridle in his mouth, I mounted and dashed into the road, and pistol in hand ordered them to halt with the threat to shoot the first man who attempted to cross the road. General Pryor came running bare headed from the house where he had been lying down, his long hair flying behind him, and ordering his command to "fall back to the woods." I ordered my men to fall into ranks and not cross the road. Colonel Berkeley of the 8th Regiment ran up to know what I proposed doing. I replied that unless General Pickett came quickly I would order an advance in the direction of that firing. Just then General Pickett came tearing down the road in full gallop accompanied by his Staff, and as soon as he reached us gave the order "Forward," and the Brigade went sweeping through the field into the skirt of woods, and across the "Nine Mile Road." General Pickett ordered me to take my Regiment across a piece of ground covered with felled timber, form them on the crest of hill and hold that position. The 8th

Regiment was formed on my right, thrown back almost at right angles to mine, to protect that flank. The 19th and 28th prolonged my line to the left, through the woods. We drove back a lot of skirmishers from the felled timber as we advanced. When we reached the position assigned, we found the enemy posted in a Railroad cut not more than two hundred yards in our front. We engaged them thus at great disadvantage, the right Companies of the Regiment having little or no protection, but the Yankees were sheltered entirely by the Railroad cut until they would rise up to fire, when we were able to do them some mischief. The three right companies of the Regiment suffered severely, and I anxiously looked for General Pickett to come up and order a charge on the enemy's position, but I saw nothing of him. The commanding officers of the troops with whom we were engaged several times ordered their men to charge us, but they would not come out of the cut, and our men jeered them calling out "Why don't you charge! Why don't you come on." Finally an officer came out carrying the colors, which he stuck in the ground, and ordered his men to form on the colors, but not a man came, and the officer himself being by this time wounded, crawled back into the cut. We remained in this position about two hours, many men killed and wounded. Colonel Carrington was shot through the shoulder and retired from the field. Finally one of General Pickett's Aids came up with orders that we should fall back to the road. We of course obeyed, and as soon as we withdrew the enemy's skirmishers advanced, occupied the ground we had just left and opened fire on us in our new position. Deploying two companies as skirmishers, we soon drove them back, and we remained unmolested in the road for an hour or more when General Pickett rode up and directed us to move back to the Williamsburg road. There was no firing now, and we moved over to the Williamsburg road again. Pryor's Brigade on our right had also been engaged but there was no other collision between the opposing forces all day. I have always thought, and still believe the second day's fight at Seven Pines was the most useless sacrifice of life I have ever known. There seemed to be no plan, no object, no purpose in anything that was done. The 8th Regiment lost their Major, who was mortally wounded and had several other casualties. The left Companies of my Regiment, being in the woods, suffered little, and for the same reason there was little loss in the 19th and 28th Regiments. General Pickett admitted to me that he had received no orders and knew nothing of what was designed except to prevent any advance of the enemy until the captured Artillery, the scattered arms, and the wounded men could be gathered up and carried to Richmond. We encamped that night on the Battle field and next day the whole army was taken back to its former position near Richmond; Pickett's Brigade bringing up the rear, and my Regiment acting as rear guard. We were not molested in any way on our return march, and reached our old camp near the race track about sunset.

I witnessed in this fight a curious example of presentiment. Attached to Company "A," was a gentleman from Danville named Fontaine. He was a most exemplary man, a consistent member of the Episcopal Church, a widower with one daughter, and an officer of the Farmers Bank of Virginia. He was not a member of any military organization, nor had he any fondness for a soldiers life. Some weeks after we went to the field we were surprised one morning by the appearance of Mr. Fontaine dressed in full uniform, armed and accoutered in every particular for service. He said he wished to serve with the Blues as most of his personal friends were in that Company, but he did not propose to enlist. He told some of his friends confidentially that after we left the town, he for the first time gave serious consideration to the question of duty, and had made it the subject of special prayer; the result being that the conviction was forced upon him that it was as much his duty to fight for his country as it was for any of those friends who were then in the field. So he bought him a long range rifle, uniformed himself, came right on and fell in with Company "A." As the Regiment was marching down the road the second day he took his watch out of his vest pocket, remarking to Captain Graves that he felt it would be better to carry his watch, a double case hunting one, in his fob pocket, and proceeded to make the transfer. He had not been ten minutes under fire when a ball struck him as exactly in the center of the watch as if it had been placed there by the fingers and made a complete cup of it, thus unquestionably saving his life.

Another providential escape the same day was that of Captain Morrisett of Company "F." As we were falling back through the felled timber our progress was necessarily slow, owing to the obstruction, we were all the time exposed to a severe enfilading fire by which several were wounded. Captain Morrisett was on my right slightly in advance. I heard the whiz of a bullet just before my face and almost simultaneously the thud caused by striking a person, and Morrisett instantly went down. I immediately said, "Captain, I hope you are not much hurt?" He looked pale as he answered, "Yes, Colonel, I expect I am killed." At the same time putting his hand inside his vest, and I saw as he did so the hole in the breast of his coat made by the ball. It was exactly over his heart, and I thought of course he was right as to the fatal character of the wound, but when he withdrew his hand and saw no blood on it, he appeared considerably relieved, and investigating further found the ball imbedded in a Testament he had carried in the breast pocket of his coat. Beyond a severe bruise he had suffered no injury.

I remember no occurrence worthy of mention, after our return to camp except a pretty extensive reconnaissance on which I was ordered, with my Regiment and a Brigade of Cavalry. We passed down the Charles City road through Darby Town, and some miles below, but neither saw nor heard anything of the Yankees on that line. We did not get back to our camp until long after midnight pretty well broken down.

While lying in Camp near Charles City Road near Richmond, there were a great many applications made to accept substitutes, or for transfers from my Regiment to other commands. In a majority of cases these applications were made for transfer to some battery of heavy Artillery, the ultimate purpose being to get out of the army, and I do not now recall an instance where a substitute was accepted for any soldier, that he remained three days with the command. They *all* deserted, and a regular business of this kind sprang up, and for a while worked successfully. Seeing that if this continued, it would seriously impair the efficiency of my command, I refused to approve the applications for substitute or transfers, thus offending many of my personal friends. The evil soon attained such magnitude that a special order was issued from the war department announcing that no transfers would be granted unless the application had the approval of the commanding officer of the Regiment, and the Brigade. I was gratified by the promulgation of this order as I thought I could control the whole matter by refusing to approve the applications. Two or three sets of papers came in the next day for transfers of some of the best men in the Regiment, but I marked them disapproved, and forwarded them, supposing that was the end. But in less than a week came an order from the War department discharging those very men whose applications I had returned disapproved.

I was very angry, and at once mounted my horse and rode to Richmond, visited the War office and requested to see Colonel Bledsoe, the Assistant Secretary of War, from whose office the order of discharge had emanated. When I was shown into his office I told him that I had that morning received an order over his signature directing the discharge of certain men from my command, and I felt there must be some mistake as I had disapproved the application, and had so endorsed the papers. I asked if I had rightly construed the order requiring my approval before a discharge or transfer would issue.

"Certainly," was his reply.

"Then let me see the papers on which the order for discharge was based."

He directed one of his clerks to bring the papers in the case. He was gone a good while and when he came back held a whispered consultation with Colonel Bledsoe who told me the papers could not be found, but he would have another search made, and if found would let me know. I believed the papers had been found, and that seeing they had not my approval they considered the easiest way out was to say the papers could not be found. I was mad anyway, but at this I blazed out and demanded how it was possible for officers in the field to obey orders emanating from the Department when the Department itself, which issued them, paid no attention to them. I said a good deal more to the same purpose, much to the surprise of the astonished clerks around me, but finally the Assistant Secretary got mad too and said, "Colonel Withers, I will not permit such language to be used in my office."

"How do you propose to prevent it," said I, "I have said nothing but what I can prove if you will produce the papers, and I have no apologies or retractions to make."

The chief clerk, whom I then recognized as Professor Joynes, formerly of Washington College, a charming man and a personal friend, here interposed to assure me he would make every effort to find the papers as he was sure there was some mistake, and he thought it probable that the papers had been sent off with a lot of official documents which had been sent to Lynchburg.

I had perforce to submit, but I have never to this day been able to account for it. I finally suspected that General Pickett must have approved the applications, notwithstanding my disapproval, as the applicants were men of high standing and influence, and I know were able to enlist in their behalf very potent agencies.

This was my first and last visit to the War Department, and I never again saw Colonel Bledsoe until I met him in Alexandria years after the war, when I was in the Senate, and he one of my neighbors. We became quite intimate friends; but the episode I have related was never alluded to by either.

CHAPTER XVI.

BATTLES AROUND RICHMOND.

General Robert E. Lee was assigned to the command of the forces around Richmond immediately after General Johnston received his wound at Seven Pines, and it was not long before he determined to make an effort to break the cordon with which McClellan was gradually encircling the City. His extreme right was now understood to reach almost to the Chesapeake and Ohio Railroad at Meadow Bridge. General Lee instructed Jackson to move with all possible secrecy and celerity from the Valley of Virginia so as to strike McClellan's right wing in the rear simultaneously with an assault by Lee's troops in front and flank. This movement was begun by General Lee's army on the twenty-sixth of June by General A. P. Hill, who crossing the Chickahominy high up, was to turn down that stream driving the enemy before him until the crossing at Mechanicsville was uncovered, when Longstreet's men were to cross, and all sweeping down the stream, would, with the aid of Jackson's column in their rear, destroy McClellan or drive him from Richmond.

Pickett's Brigade was marched out on the road leading to Mechanicsville, and when nearing the stream were halted for A. P. Hill to get in his work. McClellan's balloons were up in the air all the afternoon. I suppose taking observations. About three o'clock the action commenced, and for some time Hill appeared to be driving them all right, as the firing steadily advanced down the stream, but before sunset there appeared to be a heavy engagement and the firing seemed to be almost stationary. This was, however, after the road by which we were to cross was uncovered, and after dark we crossed the stream, but had proceeded only a short distance beyond when we were halted, and stood in the road for a long time. Finally most of us laid down and went to sleep.

Soon after light I was aroused by the sound of Artillery

and the shriek of shells, and found we were the targets for a Yankee Battery, but the shelling had not continued long before some of our Batteries took a hand in the game, and the Yankees were silenced. About sun rise we moved off down the Chickahominy, over the battle ground of the previous day. Evidence of the stubborn fighting was seen in the number of dead bodies of Yankees and Confederates scattered in about equal proportion over the ground. But pretty soon we reached a place where the Confederate dead were greatly in excess. This was at the Junction of Beaver Creek with the Chickahominy, where the Yankees had fortified themselves on the high bluff on the South of the stream. In front there was a considerable stretch of swampy ground which was literally covered with our dead soldiers. A glance at the ground told the tale. Our troops had charged down the line of the Chickahominy until they reached the point where the creek joined the larger stream, and had charged right up to the morass and creek, which they could not cross, and in this angle they were slaughtered by the score. Many of the bodies were within twenty steps of the rifle pits on the bluff. A camp now deserted, was just beyond this point.

We continued our advance, frequently passing deserted camps where little or nothing had been left. What could not be carried off was burned, and every indication showed a well conducted retreat, no sign of haste or panic being visible. While I was examining one of the deserted camps near the line of our march, General Pickett rode up and asked what I thought of the prospects before us. I told him that in my opinion everything indicated a careful falling back of the Yankee army, for the purpose of selecting a strong position where they would await our attack. He said that was precisely his view, and he looked forward to a hard fight before the day passed. This was about one o'clock p. m., and we had not proceeded much farther when firing was heard in front, which speedily increased in volume until it was evident that a big battle was on.

Soon a Staff officer galloped up to Pickett with orders, and he sent us forward. We passed a stream and Gaines Mill, and turned sharply to the right where we saw General Longstreet and his Staff. After a short talk between him and Pickett the last named officer gave orders in person to each of his Colonels directing their movements. The 8th was instructed to follow a ravine, and get under cover of a piece of wood, and then form on the edge of the cleared ground. The 18th was ordered to follow the same route, but as we started, Pickett said, "Colonel, I think you had better march directly to the wood as you would only be exposed to sharp shooters for a short distance, and you would save time which is important." So I made the men double quick, but we had one of our best Sergeants of Company "K" killed outright, two men wounded, and I had a hole shot through my hat slightly wounding the scalp. I sent Company "K" forward as skirmishers, and unfortunately they mistook the advance of an Alabama Regiment, which came meeting them in the woods, for the enemy, and firing on them, wounded two men severely.

We formed line in the edge of the wood ready to advance at the word. I dismounted in obedience to orders issued by General Lee in instructing mounted officers to dismount when going into action to lessen the liability of being picked off by the enemy's sharp shooters. I instructed the captains of each company not to permit the men to fire a gun but to push forward with the bayonet, for I saw a brigade which had halted about half way down the slope suffering greatly under heavy fire in their exposed situation, for when the cover of the woods was left there was an open stubble field all the way to the enemy's line, which was just beyond a gully under cover of a breastwork of felled trees with their batteries on the hill just above them firing over their heads.

The position was a strong one. I knew we had a hard job before us. I was the only field officer with my Regiment, as Colonel Carrington was still suffering from the wound received at Seven Pines and Major Cabell was sick at home. Reflecting on this fact, I was satisfied that it would be impossible for me to command the regiment efficiently on foot. I had not proceeded far when the advance was made. I ran back to my horse, mounted him and moved forward. Just at this juncture the Brigade in our front, finding the fire too hot for them, broke and rushed back in a perfect stampede, attempting to pass through the interval between the 18th and 8th Regiments, but of course overlapping both and creating confusion and disorder. Unfortunately I attempted to rally them, and ordered them to halt in a loud tone. My men, recognizing my voice and naturally supposing the order was addressed to them, halted and commenced firing. The regiments on my right and left followed their example and thus we repeated the error of the troops which had just been driven back.

I saw in an instant the mischief which had been done, and riding down the line, ordered each Captain separately to stop firing and push ahead, but before I reached the left of the line, the companies on the right commenced firing again, as it was not possible for flesh and blood to stand passively under such a fire as we were then receiving. While this was going on I met with Colonel Hunton of the 8th, whom I was surprised to see, as I supposed him sick in Richmond, but hearing that there would be a fight that day, he left his sick bed and rejoined his command. He looked pale and weak, I remember, but was cool and collected as usual. He asked what I thought was best to be done.

"Push forward," said I, "as no troops can live long under such a fire as this."

I concluded there was only one way to relieve the situation, as the men were falling fast, I rode to the Color Guard, and telling the Color Bearer to walk by my side, rode down the slope in front of the line, followed by the Color Guard, as I knew the Regiment would understand what that meant, though they could hear no command. My reasoning was correct, for we had advanced only a short distance before they raised a yell and dashed forward in fine style.

I have seen several accounts of this fight, notably a long description written by General Hunton for the *Confederate Veteran,* a few years since. Almost all have alluded to this halt, and attribute it to the severity of the fire to which we were exposed, but I feel certain that it was occasioned by my attempt to rally the fleeing Brigade which broke through our lines like a flock of sheep, and the men of my Regiment supposing the command to halt was designed for them, obeyed the order as they understood it, and their example was followed by the other regiments of the brigade. Be this as it may, one thing is certain, the line did not move forward until I had carried the colors and their guard so far to the front that my Regiment realized the necessity of resuming their advance.

In taking the step I have described, I was fully impressed with the conviction that I would not survive it, indeed I had gone only a short distance before I was shot through the right arm, but the bone was not broken nor did it cause me much pain or inconvenience. Soon first one and then another of the Color Guard fell, killed or wounded. I remember riding by a small walnut tree and noticing as I passed how the bark was flying from it from the balls of the enemy. We had reached within forty steps or less of the gully and old fence at the foot of the slope when I was shot through the right lung and the force of the ball seemed to knock me from my horse, rather to my surprise. I knew I was shot through the lungs, for my throat and mouth were instantly filled with blood. The litter bearers came up to take me to the rear, but telling them I could walk, I put my arm over the shoulder of one of them and started back, but had not taken three steps before a ball struck me just to the left of the spine, which paralyzed my lower limbs and I sank to the ground.

By this time the Regiment had crossed the little stream and the Yankees were retreating. Captain Wall of Company D, after I fell from my horse, came forward to assume command and was in the act of mounting when the artillery on the hill swept the front with grape, being the last gun fired from their battery. By this discharge, Captain Wall's leg was carried off, and my horse was killed. He had, up to that time, escaped a wound, which I think remarkable. I, of course, did not see any of this, as I was being borne off the field, but knew our Brigade had carried the position we attacked, which was a source of great gratification to me.

I shall not make an effort to describe this or any other fight as a whole, for I am not writing a history. I am merely telling what I saw, and what befell me personally. The deadly fire to which we were exposed at Gaine's Mill may be understood when the following facts are considered. The morning report of my regiment on the 27th showed "present for duty" three hundred and fifty-five men, exclusive of officers. Of this number two hundred and ten men and officers were killed or wounded in about fifteen minutes, and I think the other regiments suffered in almost equal proportion. In addition to the wounds mentioned, I had my clothing pierced by two other balls, my heavy gold watch chain cut in two, and a silver caustic case in my vest pocket also destroyed by another ball which just grazed the skin. General Pickett was shot throug the shoulder and severely wounded. Captain Lysle of Company K, a gallant and promising officer, was shot through the head and instantly killed. Too many officers and privates were killed for me to attempt an enumeration. Of the seven men constituting the Color Guard, only one escaped unhurt, the rest were either killed or wounded.

I was carried to the Field Hospital, but the surgeons did not spend much time on me as they evidently regarded my case hopeless. They gave me a dose of morphia and some whiskey, and sent me to the rear. As I was being taken to the rear I met General Pickett returning from the brigade hospital, where his wound had been dressed. I told him I was no doubt mortally wounded but was very anxious to be sent to Richmond, where I had friends and where my wife could reach me in a shorter time than if I were kept in the Field Hospital. He ordered Sam Price of Company F, who had me in charge, to take the first ambulance he met, put me in it and take me to Richmond at once, but to stop at the Division Hospital, and see if the surgeons there could do anything for me. Before we reached Gaines Mill we met an ambulance returning to the battle-field, and Sam Price seized on it and against the remonstrance of the driver, ordered him to turn around and take me to Richmond. As the ambulance did not belong to our Brigade or Division, the driver remonstrated very earnestly, but it was of no use, he was forced to take me in. We stopped for a few minutes at the Division Hospital, and Price brought out the chief surgeon, who, after a little examination, gave me some more morphia and brandy and gave Price another dose of the same to give me in an hour. We drove slowly in the direction of the city, as the jolting was very painful. I soon felt the effects of the stimulants and morphia very sensibly, and when Price told me it was time to take the other dose, I demurred, saying, "I am so drunk now I scarcely know anything, and I don't propose to die drunk."

We reached Richmond about nine thirty p. m., and drove to the house of Mr. Charles Gwatkin, an uncle of my wife. When I was carried in his wife was greatly shocked, but had a bed put up at once in her back parlor and he himself went for a doctor and also to the telegraph office to send a message for my wife to come at once. My breathing by this time was greatly obstructed from the blood filling the air cells of the lung, and I felt doubtful if I should live long enough to see her. Dr. Conway, of the Richmond Medical College, was the first surgeon who saw me. He did nothing, however, and told Mrs. Gwatkin that I was bound to die in a short time, as either of the wounds through the body was almost necessarily fatal. I slept at intervals under the influence of the morphia which had been so freely administered, and in the morning Dr. William Patterson, an old practitioner, who lived on Broad Street near Mr. Gwatkin, came over to see me and examined my case carefully. The ball which passed through my right lung was lodged under the skin on the other side and was cut out. The shot through the pelvis passed through, but the orifice of the exit in front was much smaller than that of the entrance, which was unusual. He spoke hopefully, however, as up to that time no evidence of injury to any of the pelvic organs was developed. Just after night when the symptoms of suffocation were very urgent and distressing, I was seized with a convulsive paroxysm of coughing and raised a quantity of coagulated blood, by which I felt greatly relieved, and as no active hemorrhage followed this coughing spell, Dr. Patterson felt much encouraged.

I shall always remember with gratitude the many acts of kindness of which I was the recipient. The Superintendent of the Telegraph Company, when the message was sent to my wife, sent instructions to the agent in Danville to take the message himself to my house without delay, and Colonel Talcott, the General Passenger Agent of the Richmond & Danville Railroad, telegraphed the conductor of the train not to leave Danville until Mrs. Withers was aboard. She arrived in Richmond about eight o'clock, and though deeply distressed, bore herself bravely and by her pluck and cheerful bearing did much to inspire me with hope. She was accompanied by Dr. E. D. Withers, my old partner and former adjutant, a skilful physician and surgeon, who remained with me until all danger seemed past.

The weather was very warm and my wounds so numerous, that to lessen the trouble and worry of dressing them, I was kept in bed covered only by a sheet and in other respects entirely naked. Dr. Conway, who passed a death sentence on me the night of my arrival, was Mr. Gwatkin's family physician, and coming in to see me some days after defended himself from Mrs. Gwatkins' criticism by saying, "Well, Madam, there are three great cavities of the human body, and a gun shot wound passing through either is usually regarded fatal, and in the Colonel's case, two out of the three were perforated, so of course, he ought to have died."

In truth, no one has ever been able to account satisfactorily for the fact that none of the pelvic organs were injured by a bullet which manifestly passed directly through that cavity. It certainly was not deflected by the bone which was penetrated by it, which was shown by the many spicula of bone discharged from the wound after suppuration was established. The wound in the lung never suppurated, but healed by the first intention. The only ill effects from it were the formation of several pleuritic bands fastening the lungs to the ribs and restricting to a considerable degree the expansion of the right lung.

On Sunday the battle of Frazier's Farm was fought and the first authentic report was brought to me by Adjutant McCulloch, who was shot through the shoulder and walked into my room Monday with a bright smile on his face and the exclamation, "Well, Colonel, they winged me yesterday but I don't think it will amount to much."

He had leave for three weeks but in less than two weeks was back with the Regiment, his wound not then healed. He told me of the death of Lieutenant Abram Carrington in command of Company D, who was instantly killed by a bullet through the brain. He was a most estimable gentleman and a brave and gallant soldier. He left a large family of little children. I was very fond of him and felt his death to be a great loss to the Regiment.

My wife remained with me a week and was then recalled by the sickness of her baby "Sece," with whom the artificial food she then depended on did not at all agree. She took with her the Minnie ball which had passed through my lung, and kept it treasured as long as she lived. Three weeks after she left, I was permitted to go home. I was put on the train and made the trip with less pain and inconvenience than I expected, being accompanied by my second daughter, Sue Dabney, then a bright and cheerful girl of fourteen years, who had been sent down by her mother as soon as she returned to Danville.

Of course my return was hailed with joy by my family and friends, and I enjoyed being with them, though I could walk only with difficulty and the lameness from the pelvic wound lasted for many years. I was troubled, too, by a painful cough which rendered my family and friends uneasy, but, though painful, I thought it was only the effect of the pleuritic adhesions which I knew existed.

By this time Danville had been made a Prison Post, as the several large tobacco factories located in that town were easily converted into comfortable prisons, which were pretty rapidly filled, as exchanges had then almost entirely ceased. Large Hospitals had also been organized there, as it was regarded the most safe place for such establishments and one least liable to interference from raiding parties of the enemy. The Government had also established an Arsenal there for the manufacture and repair of arms, and storing of ordnance supplies. When in addition, it is known that the town was crowded with refugees from the northern and eastern portions of the State, who filled almost every house to the limit of its capacity, you may judge that it was a pretty busy little place.

Major Wm. T. Sutherlin of the Quartermaster Department, was in command of the Post, and being a thorough business man, got on pretty fairly with his troublesome duties. My wife had shown great business capacity, I thought, in the management of her household affairs. She had sent to the cotton mills in North Carolina and had cloth woven for the children and laid in stores of food and other necessaries for home consumption. Here I wish to bear record to the kindness and friendship of one of our merchants, who was a German Jew, named Lisberger. I had been his family physician for some time and as he was one of the principal dry goods merchants in the place, we dealt with him pretty largely. In the beginning of that summer Mrs. Withers bought a bill of goods from him and he insisted on her buying more. She said, "I have no more money to spend now, and I don't care to go in debt."

He told her in reply that goods of all kinds were advancing in price and would certainly continue to do so as long as the war lasted. "Now," said he, "buy enough of what you know you are obliged to have to last you at least a year and put them away. I'll never ask you for the money. You can pay me when you feel able, and if you never pay it will make no difference, but buy a year's supply and buy it now."

She acted on his advice and ever after regarded him one of the best friends she had.

It was late in the fall before I was able to ride on horseback, and I then returned to the army. I found our brigade in camp near Culpeper Court-House. I traveled with my horses by rail to Gordonsville and thence rode to the camp. The officers and men seemed glad to have me back and I know I greatly enjoyed seeing them. When I joined them I did not see my wife's brother, Holcombe Royall, who was at that time a sergeant in the Quartermaster's department. On enquiring for him I was told that he had gone out that morning with four wagons to gather forage on Hazel River and had not returned, and fears were expressed lest he might have been taken prisoner by the enemy, whose lines were near the point he proposed visiting. This surmise proved correct, for neither sergeant, drivers, nor wagons were again seen in camp. The day after I reached them, General Corse, who had been Colonel of the 17th Regiment, visited us, and gave the first intelligence of his appointment as Brigadier-General and assignment to command Pickett's old brigade, Pickett himself having been promoted to Major General. As General Corse was well known to the brigade as a gallant soldier and genial gentleman, his assignment to that command was cheerfully accepted by all, though the Brigade would have preferred Colonel Hunton of the 8th Regiment. A few days thereafter we were ordered to Fredericksburg to confront Burnside, who was now in supreme command. We reached Fredericksburg without loss of time, and were stationed near the railroad about two miles out from the old town. General Burnside notified the citizens that in two days the town would be bombarded, and warned all non-combatants to withdraw. The roads were speedily filled by a throng of women, children, and old men, black and white, flying from their homes and generally bearing with them portions of their household goods. This was in December, and while we were encamped in a piece of woodland without tents or any other covering, there was quite a heavy fall of snow at night, but as the weather was not cold or stormy, few of us knew that it had been snowing. About daybreak I was awakened by a whoop, and raising my head above my blanket, was made thoroughly wide awake by the snow which fell into my face. Looking around me I could see the grave-like heaps which marked each soldier's resting place, and as the sleepers successively arose it closely resembled a resurrection from the dead. Shouts and laughter spread from camp to camp until every one was aroused. Soon after breakfast snow-balling began, as the snow was soft and wet and there was no trouble in balling it. First there were individual encounters, soon company was pitted against company, and then regiment against regiment, and ere long whole brigades were drawn up in regular battle array with their field officers mounted and leading their men, just as if in regular battle. Charges and countercharges were made, headquarters captured and retaken, and the fun was fast and furious. Never have I witnessed before or since such a magnificent fight with snow-balls. I paid for my share of the fun, however, as the next morning I could neither stand or walk from a severe attack of rheumatism located at the seat of my pelvic wound. The doctors did what they could, but plasters, cupping, and embrocations seemed to have no effect. The next day I was even worse, and as the prospect of a fight was imminent, all the sick were ordered back and I among them. As I was little better after reaching Richmond I was sent home by the Sergeant General and there confined for quite a while. The battle of Fredericksburg was fought two days after I left, but our brigade had but little share in it, being posted about the center of our line they were not under fire. Most of the fighting was done on our left with one pretty sharp encounter on the extreme right, where a strong column of the enemy which had advanced through an interval between two of our divisions, had to be driven back. All this of course I learned afterwards.

This experiment satisfied me that I was no longer fitted for active service in the field, and consequently I declined to apply for promotion as many of my friends wished me to do. I knew that General Lee had recommended it soon after the fights around Richmond, though no notice was taken of it so far as I am advised, but General Bradley Johnson told me since the war that he knew it to be true, for when the papers recommending him for promotion were referred to General Lee, they were returned approved with the added remark that Colonel Withers of the 18th Virginia Regiment had, in his judgment, the best claim for promotion, but he feared that his wounds were of such character that he would be always unfitted for active duty. Not very long after this I was enrolled in the Invalid Corps and assigned to the command of the Prison Post at Danville. I at once entered on the discharge of my duties, which I found neither trivial nor unimportant.

CHAPTER XVII.

THE PRISON POST AT DANVILLE.

We had at that time some six or seven thousand prisoners to guard. The duty was performed by a company of enlisted soldiers detailed for this duty because of injuries or diseases unfitting them for field service, aided by several companies from the contiguous counties, composed of persons between the ages of sixteen and eighteen, and those from forty-five to fifty. These last had to be drilled and instructed in their duties. I had to supervise the construction of redouts and rifle pits for the protection of the post against raiding parties who might attempt to liberate the prisoners. The large hospitals, arsenal, woolen mill, and other Government enterprises, all of which were operated by detailed men, were under my supervision, which, in addition to the regular routine duties of a military post, gave me all the employment I needed. I learned almost by accident that there was at the Methodist Female College, engaged in teaching music, a Prussian, who claimed to be a graduate of one of the best military schools in that kingdom. His name was Charles de Nordendorf. I sent for him, and when he reported and I questioned him as to his antecedents, he told me his family was noble, that he had received a thorough military education, and was fully competent to plan and construct the works necessary to protect the place against any raiding party. I at once assigned him to that duty, and placed him over the hands furnished on my requisition for labor on the fortification. I organized the employes of the arsenal into an artillery company, and the clerks of the Quartermaster and Commissary Departments and the operatives in the woolen mill into a military company for service in any emergency which might arise. It was also my duty to supervise and aid the operations of the various details sent out to arrest deserters, of whom there were many in the mountains of Patrick, Henry, and Franklin. The prisons became very much crowded during this summer, provisions were scarce and I have no doubt that they were often hungry, but do not think there was much actual suffering among them. One large tobacco factory was used as a prison for officers alone. These were of all ranks, from Lieutenants to Generals. Among them was General Neal Dow, of Maine, the father of Prohibition. From time to time I visited and examined the condition of the prisoners, and never performed this duty without having my sympathies painfully aroused. I shall always remember with pleasure that I did all in my power to lessen their suffering, but that was not a great deal.

There were some successfully planned escapes. From one of the factories a tunnel was driven about forty feet to an outhouse under which the outlet was placed so that it was not visible to any one except on careful investigation. Taking advantage of a dark, rainy night, about forty prisoners made their escape through this tunnel, and though a few were arrested and brought back by the people of the neighborhood, most of them escaped beyond our lines. The success of this exploit rendered it necessary to exclude all prisoners from the ground floor of the prisons, which, of course, much increased the crowding and discomfort of the upper rooms.

The officers' prison was the theater of a well-planned effort to escape which nearly proved successful, but eventuated by chance in the death of the officer who planned it. This officer was Colonel Ralston, of the 10th New York Cavalry, a brave and gallant gentleman. Two sentinels were always kept at night on the ground floor of the prison, who had orders not to permit more than two prisoners to come down at a time. Col. Ralston's plan was to get several men on the ground floor under some pretext, who at a given signal were to seize the sentinels just before they were to be relieved, and as soon as the door was opened by the relief, make a rush on the guards, disarm or capture them and liberate all the prisoners. The first part of the plan was successfully accomplished, for five or six men seized the inside guard, disarmed and gagged them, without exciting any alarm. Unfortunately for them, however, the other prisoners were so elated at this initiatory success, and so anxious to be among the first to get out, that instead of creeping down the steps quietly, one or two at a time, they ran down in a crowd, making such a noise that the men on guard on the outside of the prison ran to the window and looked in, and seeing the room filled with excited prisoners, one fired his musket into the crowd and this alarm of course brought out all the guard, and thus brought the scheme to an end. Now, the singular part of it all was that this shot, thus fired at random, through the barred window, struck Colonel Ralston, the ring-leader of the party, passing through his lungs and inflicting a wound of which he died in less than twenty-four hours. He was taken to the hospital and every attention possible shown him, but he recognized the fatal character of the injury and bore himself bravely to the last. He left some of his personal belongings, with the request that I would send them to his family with a statement of the circumstances leading to his death. He expressed no regret at having made the attempt to escape and said he had rather die than remain in prison indefinitely, as his government had positively refused to make any further exchange of prisoners. In this connection I am reminded of the fact that while engaged in the canvass for Governor in 1868, 1 spoke in Petersburg and afterwards was introduced to a goodly number of persons, some of whom were Northern men engaged in business in that city. One of these gentlemen enquired if I were related to the Colonel Withers who commanded the prison post at Danville during the war. I told him I was that man. He appeared pleased to meet me and recalled the death of Colonel Ralston, stating that he was his brother, and spoke in grateful terms of the kind treatment extended him after he was shot and particularly of the return of his effects to his family.

Many applications were made by prisoners for permission to work on the fortifications and I finally agreed to parole squads of twenty at a time to work under guard. One morning the whole batch, by concerted action, seized and disarmed the guards placed over them and made a dash for the nearby woods. Alarm was immediately given and squads sent out in pursuit of the party, but they caught only one, as we had no cavalry and the prisoners could travel as fast as the men sent in pursuit. A few were captured further west but the greater number escaped. So that put an end to the practice of detailing men from the prison to work on the fortifications. To add to their troubles, smallpox broke out in some of the prisons, and though every effort was made to isolate the cases, quite a number occurred with several deaths. There were some cases among the citizens, mostly negroes, however, but the outbreak caused much trouble and apprehension. Before I leave the subject I wish to mention that I was one of the few commandants of prisons who was not arrested and imprisoned after the surrender of General Lee, and I was informed by Colonel Fletcher, of Maine, Provost Marshal at Danville, that I escaped because the officers who were confined in the Danville prisons expressed the belief that I had done everything in my power to lessen their sufferings. I was utterly ignorant of the fact that my conduct was under investigation until some time afterwards when Colonel Fletcher gave me the information.

Not a great while after I assumed command of the post, Captain Welsh, who had for years been the cashier of the Danville branch of the Bank of Virginia, died suddenly of apoplexy, and I received a short time thereafter a visit from the President of the bank, Dr. Thomas P. Atkinson and some of the members of the Board of Directors, who informed me that I had been selected to fill the position made vacant by the death of Captain Welsh and hoped that I would accept the place. I declined because I knew nothing whatever of the methods of conducting banking business, and I was not disposed to accept a position when ignorant of the duties connected with it. For reply they urged that as the teller and bookkeeper were old and experienced officers I would have no trouble on account of the books as these officers would attend to that. They said they wanted me to look after the funds to see that nothing was paid out improperly. There was at that time in the vaults of the bank a large amount of specie, sent there for safe keeping by different branches of the Bank of Virginia and other banks in the eastern and northern portions of the State, and I was loath to assume the responsibility of caring for these large deposits. After discussing the matter, pro and con, for some time, I concluded to take the place, especially as the salary attached to the office would materially aid in supplying the wants of my family, for owing to the rapid depreciation of Confederate money, my army pay now furnished but a meagre support for a family as large as mine. Having decided to accept the place, it became necessary that I should change my residence to the bank building, a very comfortable house on Main Street. I therefore rented out my house on Wilson Street and moved to the bank. On the lower floor in front were two large rooms, separated by a broad hall, one of these rooms was the banking room and I made the other room my office as Commandant of the Post, placing my Adjutant, Lieutenant Royall, in charge, and thus had all my business under one roof and could attend to it without serious inconvenience. For about two weeks affairs at the bank went on very smoothly and the weekly balance of the books easily effected, but the next week the teller, Mr. Denny, was conscripted, and sent to the army, and the week after the bookkeeper was likewise gobbled up by the conscript officers. This left me all the work to do, but as I had been closely studying the complicated system of bookkeeping at the bank, which requires entries in twenty-seven different books, I thought I could get along with an inexperienced assistant. When Saturday came I set to work making out the balance sheet, but in vain did I labor, balance it would not, nor could I for my life detect the error. I worked at it until nearly midnight and then gave it up for the time. On Monday I determined on a new plan of action, which was to balance the books every night while all the transactions were fresh in my memory, and I had little trouble afterwards, but the week's work which had so bothered me still remained unsettled. I called in to my assistance the cashier and bookkeeper of the Farmer's Bank and they went over the whole transactions of the week without finding the error, and I think it was more than a month before I succeeded in tracing it up. But I ultimately found it and, as you may imagine, was greatly gratified thereat. I do not know that any further details of my experience as a bank officer are worth recording as I continued the regular routine work of the bank until some time after the surrender of General Lee. During the summer of 1864 the Surgeon in charge of the Prison Hospital reported a case of what he thought was scurvy, at which I was not surprised, as neither the prisoners or the guard had been able to secure a proper quantity of vegetable food, though vegetables were plentiful in the country. I sent for the purchasing agent of the Government, and directed him to buy a good lot of potatoes, cabbages and turnips for the use of the prisoners and troops on duty, and told Captain Lloyd, Post Commissary, when they came in to issue them at once as the only method of arresting the threatened scourge.

He came back pretty soon asking for further and specific instructions as to the issue of cabbage and turnips, as the potato ration was prescribed in the army regulations, but no provision was made for the issue of any other fresh vegetable. He was a most conscientious officer but exceedingly particular and he called my attention to a table given in the Army Regulations prescribing the quantities of various dessicated vegetables that constituted a ration. I laughed at him saying, "We will not make ourselves ridiculous by issuing a ration of one-fourth of an ounce of fresh cabbage or turnips to men threatened with scurvy."

"Well," he said, "it does look foolish, but if I issue a quantity not prescribed in the Army Regulations the old Commissary General (Northrop) will be certain to haul me over the coals about it unless I first procure authority from his office. Don't you think I had better write for specific instructions from him?"

"You can do as you please about that, but in the meantime continue to issue all fresh vegetables in pound rations."

He would not consent to do this until I closed the discussion by telling him I was in command of the post, and would certainly place him under arrest if he refused to obey my orders. He finally said he would so issue until he heard from the Commissary General. About a week after he brought me his letter to the Department upon which was endorsed, "The Commissary General calls the attention of Captain Lloyd to page —— of the Army Regulations, where he will find the ration prescribed of the various vegetables and will issue them accordingly."

"Well," said I, "I will not permit the issue of fresh vegetables on the basis of dessicated vegetables, and you will continue to issue them as I directed pending a settlement of this matter."

I forwarded the papers to the office of the Commissary General myself as Commandant of the Post. Calling his attention to the fact that the table to which he had referred Captain Lloyd was avowedly to regulate the issue of dessicated vegetables and could not possibly be made to apply to fresh vegetables, as it would be simply absurd to issue a fourth of an ounce of cabbage or turnips at a ration. In due time the papers were returned with the endorsement that the Commissary General admitted absurdity of the issue of one-fourth of an ounce of fresh vegetables, but as the regulations made no provision for the issue of cabbage or turnips except in that table, he must be regulated by that, as he had no authority to alter the regulations, that power being reserved to Congress.

I appealed from his action to the Secretary of War, calling his attention to the endorsements. After two weeks more I received the papers again, and the endorsements showed that the Secretary of War had referred them to the Commissary General calling attention to the endorsement of Colonel Withers, Commandant Post of Danville. The Commissary General returned them to the office of the Secretary of War, again referring to the table of dessicated vegetables as the only provision made by the regulations for the issue of cabbage and turnips. The Secretary of War returned them to Colonel Withers, Commandant Post at Danville, calling his attention to the remarks of the Commissary General. About six weeks had passed since the correspondence began and I seemed to have reached the end of my row, so I gave up letter writing, but told Captain Lloyd that I would take the responsibility and would require him to furnish the food as I had directed. If the Commissary General chose to prefer charges against me he could do it. I never heard anything more of the matter and the scurvy disappeared under the improved diet. I have cited this incident for the purpose of showing the amount of "red tapery" pervading the departments of the Confederate Government and the great lack of common sense apparent in administering its affairs.

During the latter part of the summer of 1863, two ladies accompanied by a handsome young fellow in the uniform of a lieutenant called to see Mrs. Withers and announced themselves as the wife of General John Morgan and her sister, Miss Readey, who, accompanied by Lieutenant Tyler, still lame from a wound, had come to Danville seeking a quiet and safe place to spend the fall and winter. General Morgan, having been captured while on his celebrated raid into Ohio, was then imprisoned with several of the officers of his Brigade in the penitentiary at Cincinnati. They appeared to be nice and refined young ladies, and Mrs. Withers agreed to furnish them rooms and board during the fall and winter. They proved to be very pleasant inmates, and Lieutenant Tyler was quite a toast among the young ladies of the town. In the latter part of the fall Mrs. Morgan gave premature birth to a little girl who only lived a short time. At or about Christmas we were greatly surprised by the appearance of General Morgan himself, his brother, Captain Morgan, and one or two other officers of his staff. He had just effected his escape from the penitentiary and came direct to Danville to meet his family. Of course there was great rejoicing among them, and no wonder, as they knew the Yankees had threatened to hang the whole party.

General Morgan was tall, with black hair and eyes, dark skin, and straight as an Indian. A man of fine appearance and bearing, but not much of a talker, by which I mean he did not talk much. After a few days, however, he entertained us at times with an interesting narrative of the contests of wits between his party and their jailers, each trying to circumvent the other. The prisoners busy in constructing a tunnel, the keepers watching closely to prevent it. They were visited at all hours of the day and night by their guardians, shod in gum elastic to mask the sound of their footsteps, but the prisoners scattered fire coal and cinders through the hall which always warned them of their approach. They finally completed their tunnel, and, escaping from prison, climbed the wall and got off. Only one of the party, as I remember, being captured.

Their adventures were manifold and the narrow escapes they made would read like a romance. The General's brother, Captain Morgan, was a great sportsman and boasted a good deal of his skill as a "wing shot," finally proposing a bird hunt if we could find him a good gun. I told him Dr. Ned Withers had a fine Wesley Richards gun, Number 10 bore, which he thought as good a gun as could be made. He could get that or I would lend him my old Damascus, which had proved its qualities on many a well-fought field. On examination he selected the Wesley Richards, and the Doctor took mine. I told Captain Morgan that I would let him try his hand with Dr. Ned and if he could beat him I would try him myself. They started out one fine day in Christmas week and brought at night a good lot of birds, but the Doctor had killed about two to the Captain's one and he had little to say afterwards about bird shooting. Dr. Ned was about as good a shot as I, and no one in or near Danville could touch either of us.

General Morgan remained in Danville about two weeks, and then with his family returned, I think, to Tennessee or Southwest Virginia, where he was again put in command of a brigade of cavalry. He was finally killed at Greenville, Tennessee, by a party of Federal cavalry, who, by a night march, surprised the General and his staff at a private house where he was staying for the night. The information that General Morgan was in the town was conveyed to the Yankee cavalry by a young lady who rode about fifteen miles at night for the purpose. The detachment reached Greensville about the break of day, surrounded the house, and when the alarm was given, General Morgan attempted to escape in his night clothes through the garden, but as he was climbing the fence was shot and killed by a Federal soldier, his body thrown across a horse and paraded through the streets of the little town in triumph. He left a widow and one daughter, called John for her father.

CHAPTER XVIII.

FIGHT AT STAUNTON RIVER BRIDGE.

In the summer of 1864, General Wilson, of the Federal Army, with two brigades of cavalry, undertook an expedition along the line of the Richmond & Danville Railroad with the purpose of tearing up and destroying that important line of communication, and especially desirous of burning the railroad bridge across Staunton River near Clover Depot. This was a long and well-constructed bridge, and if destroyed it would require some time to replace it. His expedition was to a considerable degree successful, for he tore up and destroyed the greater part of the road from Burkeville to Roanoke. His operations were considerably retarded by the Confederate cavalry who, under Hampton, and I think Fitz Lee also, were hammering at them all the time, requiring the greater part of Wilson's force to repel their attacks.

General Wilson himself, in command of about one thousand five hundred or two thousand men, pushed forward to effect the destruction of the bridge. As soon as it became known that the structure was in danger a very strenuous effort was made to defend it. No regular troops were available for this service, but a promiscuous gathering of wounded and furloughed soldiers, companies of men detailed for duty at Danville in Government work, citizens of Halifax, and others, assembled at the bridge under the command of Captain Farinholt, Colonel Thomas Stanhope Flournoy, and others, and made some preparations to resist the expected column. Captain Farinholt wired to me and I sent down almost every man from Danville, including prison guards, the company of artillery composed of men detailed for duty at the Arsenal and other work, and drew from Charlotte and other points in North Carolina several companies to guard the prisons and form a nucleus for the defense of the post in case the enemy succeeded in passing Staunton River.

Colonel John Withers, Assistant Adjutant General under General Cooper, was among those gathered at the bridge, as he happened to be on a visit to his family then staying in Halifax County. He wrote asking me to come down and take command of the forces gathered there, which of course I could not do, as my presence was constantly required at Danville to look after the safety of the prison and gather in substitutes for the guards sent off to the defense of the bridge. General Wilson did not reach the place as soon as he was expected and the little force gathered in his front had time to complete their preparations for his reception. I think the whole force did not number more than four hundred men, the greater portion of whom had never been under fire. About one half of this number were placed along the north bank of the river next to the water, where the bank gave them pretty fair cover, while the artillery was placed on the hill above the bridge protected by some hastily constructed earthworks, and there they awaited the assault.

After some shelling which did no particular damage, the Yankee force of dismounted cavalry, armed with repeating rifles, moved forward, covered by their skirmish line and were permitted to approach within point blank range, when they were met by such a close and well-directed fire that they broke in disorder and retreated, leaving the ground pretty well covered with their dead and wounded. They were reinforced, again formed and charged the position the second time with great gallantry, but they met with such a steady and sustained fire of artillery and infantry that they were again driven back. General Wilson, knowing that he had little time to spare, as Hampton was pushing back his rear guard pretty rapidly, made preparations for retreat, and soon after nightfall withdrew his troops and took up his line of retreat, closely followed by our cavalry, who kept up a running fight with the rear guard with such effect that the command was almost entirely destroyed and the greater number captured. Our men buried one hundred and thirty-five dead Yankees, their wounded being carried off in their retreat. I think we had only two men killed and half a dozen wounded.

Taking everything into consideration, I regard the fight at Staunton River Bridge one of the most brilliant affairs of the war. A number of repeating rifles and cartridges for the same were picked up on the field and at my request Captain Farinholt sent me one which I preserved as a souvenir of the fight and still have in my possession. It is a most serviceable gun, carries sixteen cartridges, has a long range and shoots accurately. I could knock off the head of a squirrel with it easily and except that the calibre is too large for ordinary game, it makes a good sporting rifle. Our military came back the day after, proud of their brief campaign and the North Carolina troops returned the same day to their station.

Among the medical staff on duty in Danville was Dr. E. Lewis Carter, an assistant surgeon, who was a native of Hanover County, and the winner of the hundred-dollar "Warren prize" for the best graduating thesis of his class. He was tall, blond and fine-looking, qualities which I suppose took the fancy of my eldest daughter, Lizzie, then in her eighteenth year. They were married August 10th, 1864, and they continued inmates of my house. The wedding was by no means an elaborate affair, though it came off with considerable eclat, and the wedding feast, though greatly enjoyed and much complimented, was devoid of many of the delicacies usually regarded indispensable on such occasions, but with rye coffee, sorghum cakes, and good beaten biscuits, the guests made merry until the small hours and the bridal couple seemed to think nothing was lacking. The ceremony was performed at the church, the Rector, Dr. G. W. Dame, officiating, from whose school the bride had just graduated.

During the summer we had a visit from Colonel John Withers, A. A. General, his wife and child. They had been living in Richmond but concluded to spend the summer in the country. He was a distant relative and a native of South Carolina. Being a West Point graduate and an old army man, he was thoroughly conversant with his duties and was a valuable officer. He married, just before the war, a lady who was of Spanish blood and I think, a resident of Mexico near San Antonio. She was a charming lady of elegant manners, highly accomplished, and a zealous member of the Romish Church. Of course, under these conditions, it was not very long before her husband withdrew from his own church, the Protestant

Episcopal, and joined the Romish. They had at that time only one child, a promising boy. We were all much pleased with the Colonel and his wife and had pleasant visits from both more than once before the close of the war.

About this time my friend, Colonel Thomas D. Claiborne, who had command of Company B of my regiment, and was subsequently transferred to the cavalry service with the rank of Lieutenant Colonel, was brought home severely wounded, his thigh bone being fractured very high up. As the surgeons deemed amputation impracticable, he was treated tentitatively, but lived only a few weeks, dying from supperrative fever, as was to have been expected. He was as gallant and brave an officer as we had in the service, one of my warmest personal friends and whose loss was keenly felt.

GOVERNOR LETCHER'S VISIT.

Governor Letcher's term had now expired and his administration had met with universal approval so far as I ever heard. The wisdom, firmness and patriotism which he exhibited in that trying time was highly appreciated. After his term as Governor came to a close, citizens through the Mayor and Common Council of Danville extended him a cordial invitation to visit Danville as a guest of the city, to which he gave a favorable response, and designated the period of his visit. Now, the Hotels of Danville during the war had achieved quite a reputation for the meagre character of their accommodation. So the Council called a meeting and after consultation appointed a committee to visit Mrs. Withers and request that she would come to the rescue and entertain the Governor at her home. They promised to provide all that was necessary in the way of refreshments, both solid and liquid, for his use. She finally agreed to receive him with the promise that she was willing to see that the food was prepared and he made as comfortable as possible during his visit. I knew nothing of this until I came home at night, when my wife told me all. I was glad to hear what had been done but demurred to the arrangement that the town should send provisions, but my wife said she would not agree to feed the guest of the town at her own expense.

At the appointed time the old Governor made his appearance and was received by the Mayor and Council and escorted to my house, where he was duly installed. Of course a supply of the best obtainable whiskey had been sent up, as it was known that the Governor was fond of that beverage. But I will here record the fact that I am satisfied public rumor did him injustice, for though he drank with every visitor who called, and they were many, I never observed any evidence of too free indulgence on his part. The explanation is simple. He took the smallest drinks of any man I ever saw and therefore could do honor to all his guests without transcending the limits of propriety.

He remained with us several days, and I have rarely enjoyed a visit more. His conversational powers were exceptionally fine, his judgment of men unsurpassed, his sense of humor delicate, and his gift as a raconteur most remarkable. Dr. Roger P. Atkinson, at that time Mayor, was himself a man of infinite humor and a fine talker, and as he was always a warm admirer and political friend of the Governor, their intimate intercourse, during his stay, was manifestly a source of much enjoyment to each. All my family, including the children, regretted when the time came for him to leave, as he had been socially a great success.

One morning early I was surprised by a visit from Mr. James Whittle, a distinguished lawyer and a brother of Bishop Whittle, who thus saluted me, "Doctor, I have driven over from home to carry you back with me and I don't mean to take any denial, you have to go."

"Why, what's up?" said I.

"My brother, Colonel Powhatan Whittle, is at my house in a very dangerous condition. He was badly wounded in the arm some weeks ago and came near dying from hemorrhage, but the artery was tied, but from some cause the hemorrhage recurred again and they tied the artery above the elbow, but that has given away and he is every moment in danger of dying from hemorrhage and the doctors say the only chance to save him is by amputation of the arm and you must go with me and do it."

"Why, Mr. Whittle," said I, "there are a dozen army and

navy surgeons here, any one of whom will perform the operation much better than I can do it and I will get one of them to go with you."

"No sir, I came after you and you have got to go. So come along and get in my buggy at once."

I tried to convince him that the operation would be more skilfully performed by the surgeons who had done so much more of this work than I, but with the pertinacity characteristic of the man and of the family, he would listen to nothing, but insisted that I should accompany him at once. So I got into his buggy and went with him home and when I reached there found Colonel Whittle really in a very critical condition, with a tourniquet around his arm and Dr. Rawley Martin in constant attendance. Recognizing the necessity for prompt action, I at once proceeded with Dr. Martin's assistance to amputate the arm, which was speedily done without any unusual complications except that it was necessary to tie many more arteries than usual, owing to the previous ligation of the brachial. I visited him once or twice afterwards and he had a speedy convalescence. He is still living in Georgia, I learn, and speaks to his friends in complimentary terms of my kindness and skill as a surgeon.

As winter approached, food became more and more scarce in the country and the people were called on more earnestly to contribute of their supplies to the sustenance of the forces in the field. Inspection of corn cribs and smokehouses all through the country by officers of the Quartermaster and Commissary Departments delegated for the purpose, and all surplus food carried off. They generally estimated the surplus at a very liberal figure and there was little meat consumed by the country householder. No one thought of eating meat more than once a day, and at my own table for some days my little girl, Virginia Secessia, ate all the meat that was cooked for dinner. This was usually boiled with blackeyed peas to give them a flavor, and sent in on top of the peas and the child consumed it. The rest ate peas and other vegetables with bread and sorghum. We had, however, plenty of sugar, and rice also, as a general thing, and did not really suffer from hunger. But with prisoners it was different, for of necessity their food supply was curtailed to such an extent that I know the sensation of hunger was rarely absent. The negroes, too, were on shorter rations than they had ever been in their lives, and as a consequence, thefts of everything to eat were constantly occurring.

Mrs. Stuart, the mother of General J. E. B. Stuart, was one of my near neighbors, and calling in one afternoon to see her I was both surprised and amused to find a large turkey gobbler tied to a very handsome rosewood bedstead. On enquiring what it meant, she said a friend from the country had sent it to her for a Christmas turkey, and she knew if she turned it out it would be stolen, therefore she kept it tied in her room. I, too, was the fortunate recipient of a fine lamb sent me by my old friend, Major George Wilson, but unfortunately did not guard it so carefully as Mrs. Stuart did her gobbler, for I had it turned out in the yard, supposing it was safe during the daytime at least. The animal did not remain long in the yard, for it cleared the palings at a bound, and ran off up the street as hard as it could go, and though speedily pursued, it could be traced no farther than the camp of reserves at the head of the street where the trail was lost completely and never recovered, much to the regret of all the family. Indeed, I scarcely know how we could have gotten along without suffering, had it not been for the kindness of friends in the country who generously ministered to our necessities. Major Wilson often aided us in this way. Mr. Crenshaw Miller, of Chalk Level, sent me at one time a present of half a dozen nice hams, and so did Mr. William Banks. Both the latter gentlemen lived more than twenty miles in the country, and you may be sure their kindness and liberality were highly appreciated.

On the thirteenth day of March, 1865, my first son was born to the great surprise of parents and sisters. The birth of ten daughters in succession had apparently demonstrated the folly of expecting any change in what seemed to be an established precedent, and no one, I suppose, had any idea that the expected stranger would prove a boy, but boy it was, and the children were all delighted that the "long lane had a turning." His mother said she was "sorry it was not another girl," but I always had my doubts of the sincerity of the declaration. For myself, I felt pleased that at last I had a son to perpetuate the name, of which there appeared good prospect, as he was a robust and healthy specimen, likely to grow and thrive. "Sece" was now almost four years old and the unprecedented interval was, in the opinion of many of our lady friends, sufficient to account for our change of luck. I suggested that it portended a long war, though I did not really see how it could be protracted much longer.

One or two circumstances in connection with military service in this war was strongly impressed on my mind. One was the backwardness in enlisting of most of those persons who so ardently championed the cause of Secession, and spoke with such contempt of the danger of war. Of all the men in Danville known as "Before breakfast Secessionists," very few entered the army except on compulsion, and the varied devices and excuses offered in explanation or apology were contemptible and disgusting. Without recording names I will cite a case. One man, young, healthy and strong, who "in season and out of season" urged the secession of the State, avowed his purpose of joining the army at once, but as he did not care to go as a private he proposed to raise a company of artillery, and for some time paraded around in the full uniform of a captain in that branch of the service, but weeks and months passed and the company failed to materialize. After the passage of the conscript laws, fearing to fall into the hands of the conscript officers, he prevailed on his grandmother, who was a wealthy lady and owned a large number of slaves, living in an adjoining county, to appoint him her manager, and secured exemption from service on that ground. As the conscription became more rigid this class of exempt was ruled out, and finding that it would no longer avail him he resorted to another device and bought out a newspaper, published in North Carolina and had his name at the head of its columns as editor in chief, though he lived fifty miles from the issuing office, and it was doubtful if he ever wrote an editorial, but under this pretext he secured exemption from service until after General Lee's surrender. Colonel George C. Cabell of the 18th Regiment was an honorable exception to the rule as he was about the only active and earnest advocate of Secession among the better class of citizens who acted up to his profession, for he went to the front with the first troops and continued until the last an officer in the field. It is not to be wondered at, that, as the war progressed and its privations, hardships and dangers constantly increased, those who had opposed Secession and had entered the army on compulsion became more and more dissatisfied with the service and larger and larger numbers were reported "absent without leave." I think there were not a great many soldiers who actually deserted to the enemy, but numbers left without leave and concealed themselves in the mountains, and remote fastnesses to avoid service. The schemes devised to escape detection and arrest were often ingenious and amusing, as reported by the squads detailed to arrest the skulkers. Some were brought in dressed in women's clothes, who had worn this costume for months, and thus escaped detection, though frequently seen by the search parties who visited the houses where they dwelt. The secret was usually disclosed by some neighbor with whom they had had a "falling out." One man lived for months in a pit dug under a stall in the stable, the stall being occupied all the time by a horse. To this cave he retired whenever a stranger was seen approaching the house. In another case a closet was constructed between the weather boarding and ceiling of a log house, by cutting out a log leaving nothing visible to mark the location. These and many similar expedients were resorted to for the purpose of eluding the search of detachments sent out to arrest and return to their command those who had no "stomach for the fight." In a few instances the parties resisted arrest, but in the majority of cases, after being found they submitted without further trouble. I recall the case of a man of good family, who came to Danville handsomely dressed in a colonel's full uniform, and who registered as such at the leading hotel, gave the number of his regiment to enquirers, and by his boldness and audacity escaped suspicion for a while. I finally received an intimation that he was no officer at all, but a deserter, and when I sent for him and asked to see his commission, and leave of absence, he was compelled to acknowledge that he had none. This man escaped punishment, as I was informed, on the plea of being insane, the charge being made by the members of his family, and accepted by the court martial which tried him.

As the winter of 1864-5 advanced, the prospects of the Confederacy became more gloomy and desperate. Indeed, after the disastrous campaign of Gettysburg, the displacement of Johnston from command at Atlanta, and the absolute destruction of the Army of Tennessee at Franklin and Nashville, the sad finale of our fight for independence and self-government was plainly foreshadowed in the minds of all thoughtful men. General Lee's army, which had so long confronted Grant, was dwindling rapidly away by the casualties of war, and the desertion of the cowardly and unpatriotic. Reinforcements became impracticable, there was no possibility of replenishing our food supply, which made it certain that the army would be compelled to withdraw from Petersburg whenever Grant chose to advance. This he did on the first of April, 1865, with Sheridan's Cavalry covering his left and constantly thwarting every effort of the Confederates to reach the Richmond & Danville Railroad at Burkeville, thus forcing Lee to retreat along the line of the South Side Railroad until Appomattox was reached, when Sheridan was interposed between his army and Lynchburg and the end came.

CHAPTER XIX.

DANVILLE THE SEAT OF GOVERNMENT.

When General Lee was compelled to leave Petersburg, the fact was communicated to President Davis and he and his cabinet hastily left Richmond and made their way to Danville. Strenuous efforts were made to find suitable quarters and accommodations for the distinguished guest. Major Sutherlin invited the President and his immediate family to his house which, being a large and commodious mansion, accommodated them comfortably. The others were quartered, some in public, some in private houses. Governor Smith and the State officials of Virginia pretty soon followed. The Governor, accompanied by one of his aids on horseback, retreated by way of the canal towpath. It was said that the old Governor filled his saddlebags with the gold from the Treasury and the weight thereof came near costing him his life, for on attempting to cross a deep stream both the Governor and his horse were in danger of being drowned, however, he ultimately reached Danville in safety.

The day after the President and his party arrived, he sent for me to learn something of our means of defense, and I accompanied him on horseback around the whole line. He found occasion to criticise the location of one redout but concluded that the place could not be made tenable against a superior force. On the same day he issued his celebrated proclamation evidently designed to neutralize the depressing effect of the surrender of the Capital of the Confederacy, by assuring the people that Richmond's loss was rather an advantage than otherwise as it gave to General Lee greater freedom in the conduct of the campaign. But I neither saw nor heard of any one who was much enthused by the assurance. We had daily reports from the army until the eighth of April, when all communication ceased. We heard nothing on the ninth and on the afternoon of that day the President called for two reliable and courageous men, who would ride across the country and bring him authentic intelligence from the army. I sent Captain Graves and Dr. E. D. Withers to report to him for this duty, as I knew that both would fully meet his requirements, and besides Dr. Withers was well acquainted with the country around Appomattox, having been born and raised in that vicinity. They started at once on their journey, but even before they left, rumors of General Lee's surrender were in circulation, but could be traced to no reliable source. The next day, however, the news was confirmed by returning soldiers and before Captain Graves and Dr. Withers returned, the fact was generally accepted. The President and his party left by train for Greensboro, North Carolina, the next morning and on the afternoon of that day General Lomax's Cavalry came into town with orders to burn the bridges across the river, and destroy all the stores accumulated in the place. From that night my special troubles began. I told General Lomax that I objected to the burning of the bridge as that would certainly involve the destruction of the town or a great portion of it, as several large buildings were immediately contiguous to that structure and would necessarily be fired by the flames from the bridge. In addition I assured him that it would be of no service as the river below was easily fordable and the burning of the bridge would not at all delay the passage of the river by either cavalry or infantry. The General contended that he had no option in the matter, and must carry out his orders. I sent a company of guards to the bridge with instructions to resist, by force if necessary, any attempt to fire the structure and notified General Lomax of my action. He contented himself by sending a detachment to destroy the bridge by cutting it down, but when they found a guard in front to protect it they returned and reported the fact. General Lomax, being a man of good sense, desisted from further effort and reported to his superiors. By this means the bridge and town were saved from burning.

A short distance in front of my dwelling was a large factory used as a storeroom for medical supplies and I called General Lomax's attention to the danger which would accompany any effort to destroy these stores by burning, and he agreed that it should not be attempted, but instructed the officers in charge to stave in the barrels of spirituous liquors, wines, etc., and to break up and otherwise destroy the other contents of the building. About midnight there was an alarm of fire and it was soon seen that this building was ablaze. I naturally thought it had been fired by General Lomax's order and being both incensed and alarmed I went straight to his room, and in set phrase denounced the act. He at once assured me that it had not been fired by his command and I saw he was telling the truth. As it turned out, among the stores were several barrels of alcohol, and when these were "staved in," the vapor became ignited by the flame of a candle or lamp, an explosion occurred which killed the Assistant Surgeon engaged in destroying the stores, and of course fired the building, which burned with great rapidity. Fortunately the night was perfectly calm and the flames were not communicated to any of the adjoining buildings.

Among General Lomax's aides was Mr. E. P. Goggin, son of John O. L. Goggin, a lawyer of distinction in Lynchburg and a personal friend of mine. Young Goggin slept at my house, breakfasted with my family and appeared to be much taken with my third daughter, Alice, then a girl of twelve or thirteen years. This passing fancy for the child was subsequently intensified when we became neighbors in Lynchburg, and it ultimately culminated in their marriage in Russell County some two years afterwards.

Colonel John Withers, A. A. G., in the War Department, came to my house after the surrender. His wife and children were on a visit to friends in Mecklenburg County on the southern border of the State. He was naturally anxious to rejoin them and waited a few days, hoping that the stragglers from Sheridan's command who were stealing and robbing in Halifax and Mecklenburg Counties would pass on, and leave the way open for him to do so. I owned at the time a fine thoroughbred mare, but supposed she would be confiscated by the Northern Army when they came along. I therefore suggested to the Colonel that he had better take my mare and by making a little detour through North Carolina he would be able to reach his family. He objected on the ground that, as it was very doubtful whether he could ever return the animal, he would rather not take her. I insisted that if he could not, it would make little difference, as I would much prefer that he should have her than the Yankees. I therefore mounted him on a fine English saddle, with my holsters and pistols, and started him off. I did not hear from him for nearly a year, when he sent me a check for the value of the mare, stating that he had ridden her all the way to San Antonio, Texas, as his family had left Mecklenburg when he reached there.

CHAPTER XX.

CHAOS.

About the thirteenth of April the town was filled with soldiers returning South after the surrender at Appomattox, the greater number of whom were in an utterly disorganized condition, with no officers in charge; and worse than this, crowds came in from the surrounding country, attracted by the reports that large quantities of Government supplies were stored in Danville which could be had for the taking, and they thronged the streets bent on plunder. The disbanded soldiers were crazy for clothing and food, and the mob of country people would point out Government store houses and tell the soldiers that they were filled with shoes and clothing or flour and meat. Crash! would go the doors at once, and the soldiers would rush in to find nothing that they cared for, but the mob would follow them and speedily carry off everything they could lay their hands on. The situation was rapidly becoming critical, so much so that a called meeting of the Council was held and the danger confronting the community was anxiously considered. The police were confessedly unable to cope with the rioters, and it was finally proposed to send a committee to me, with the request that I would take charge of matters and do what I thought best to protect the lives and property of the citizens. This proposition at first met with favor, but before final acton was taken, some one suggested that if it were done, "Colonel Withers would certainly put the town under martial law and force all the men in town to do guard duty." They finally adjourned without doing anything, except to order an additional number of policemen to be sworn in.

The next day matters were decidedly worse. In the early morning I was informed that a mob headed by a returned soldier who lived in Danville, of gigantic size and great audacity, was visiting the dwellings of prominent citizens, demanding that they should be allowed to search the house, for the purpose of getting possession of the large supplies of sugar, flour, and bacon believed to be stored therein. I called out the guard and rushed with them to the house where the mob was reported to be, found they had just left to visit another dwelling in the upper part of the town. I pushed on to this place, and met the Mayor at the head of his augmented force of policemen, who had succeeded in dispersing the mob and arresting their leader. The Mayor was James Walker, a plucky fellow, who had fired at the leader of the mob, barely missing him, and showing that he meant business, when they immediately scattered. About ten o'clock I was summoned to the railroad station, where about two thousand returning soldiers were said to be looting all the houses in the vicinity. I reached the spot as quickly as possible, and found the country people occupying the Arsenal and Armory, and carrying off everything they could lay their hands on, the buildings having been first broken open by the soldiers in the belief that they were stored with food and clothing. The soldiers said all they wanted was transportation home, but the railroad Superintendent would not start any train. I went to his office and found him pretty drunk but with sense enough to know what he was about. I asked why he did not send off a train with these soldiers, he said he had done his best but the railroad men were so demoralized that they would do nothing to aid him. He could get no one to pump the water to fill the tank of the engine, and wound up by saying they might all "Go to h-ll, both soldiers and railroad as for him." Going back to the station, I jumped on a flat and calling to the soldiers commanded "Attention!" in a loud voice, and secured it. I then explained the cause of the delay, and called for volunteers to pump water for the engine. Some men came forward and said they were willing to do this, and in fact had made the effort, but as soon as they commenced to pump the train was filled with others until no place could be found for those who had pumped the water. I told them I would put guards at the doors of every coach and would permit no one to enter until the men who had pumped the water were accommodated. By the assistance of several officers who were in the crowd, this plan was carried out and the train started.

I then made an effort to get another train off in the same

way and while standing at the tank, I was startled by a tremendous explosion near me. The Arsenal stored with cartridges, loaded shells, and similar munitions went up in smoke, but for some time there was heard the sound of exploding cartridges and occasionally of a shell, similating precisely the sound produced by a pretty brisk skirmish in which both artillery and small arms figured. As I afterwards ascertained, the impression up town was that the Yankee army had arrived and was firing on the town. The effect of this was seen in the speedy rush of all the country people from the town, which was evacuated in about five minutes.

The cause of the explosion was never definitely ascertained, as all the persons in the building were killed, I believe, but it can be easily understood that a lot of boys and young men engaged in breaking open cartridges and collecting the powder, would soon fill the floor with waste powder, which might ignite from the spark of a pipe or cigar with such consequences as ensued that day.

There were, however, some comic features mingled with the tragic scene, and I think I never witnessed a more ludicrous spectacle that that presented by an old crone from the "Mountain Hills" who ran past me on her way to the railroad bridge with her petticoats way up above her knees and carrying three guns in her hands which she had secured at the Armory. She made no pause but ran for life, clutching her plunder in tenacious grasp.

Just before the explosion, the Mayor sent me a message to come up town quickly, as the mob were in complete possession and the police could do nothing with them. Telling the messenger to return at once and tell him I would be there in a few minutes as I only awaited the starting of the train with the soldiers, but to get all his force of policemen in a body ready for action by the time I reached him. I started up town in five minutes after the explosion, but when I reached there I could see no semblance of a mob on the streets. They had vanished utterly.

The town people were by this time almost in a state of panic. The Council met at night and at once agreed to ask me to take charge of matters and do what I could to protect the lives and property of the people. I at once accepted the trust, and went to work to organize the citizens between sixteen and fifty years in squads of twenty, armed them and sent a guard to each bridge, ferry, and ford that gave access to the town, and to place pickets on every road leading into it, with orders to permit no one from the country to enter town without a pass from me.

By daylight next morning, my pickets and outposts were all on duty, and they were none too soon, as they turned back crowds on foot and horseback.and some with wagons and teams, prepared to haul away the plunder they expected to secure. Curses loud and deep were showered on me for my action, and long afterwards many countrymen in the neighborhood of Danville, in Halifax and Pittsylvania Counties, would not support me for any office because I refused them permission to enter Danville when so much desirable property could have been secured. My remedy proved effective, however, and relieved the apprehensions of the citizens.

When you recall the fact that seven or eight thousand Yankee prisoners were confined in the factories, that the guards who had been on duty had now in great numbers left for their homes, and that only a limited number of substitutes could be had to supply their places, you will admit that the people had cause for apprehension as to their safety.

The quiet that ensued was of short duration. A telegram was received from South Boston in the morning, to the effect that quite a number of Yankee bummers were on board crank and pole cars coming up the road and announcing that Danville was their destination. This was very disturbing intelligence, for we were now without any military guard, they having pretty generally left for their homes under the belief that the war was ended and they could do as they pleased. As it was known General Wright, commanding the sixth army corps of Grant's Army, was enroute for North Carolina to join Sherman, then being assailed by General Jos. E. Johnson, and would pass through Danville, I determined to make an effort to communicate with him, hoping he might be able to throw some obstacle in the way of the marauders, and prevent them from reaching Danville. I spent several hours in the effort to get into telegraphic communication with him and finally succeeded about the middle of the afternoon. I briefly described the situation at Danville, and urged him if possible, to stop these men before they reached our town. He replied by expressing his regret that he could do nothing to aid me and told me I would "have to do the best I could."

By this time the party was reported from Barksdale's Station, only twelve miles off. The situation was becoming desperate. I rushed around town, enlisted several of the officers of the post attached to the Quartermaster, Commissary and Medical Departments and we repaired to the station. The telegraph operator said the party had just left Ringold five miles below. We stationed ourselves on both sides of the railroad just at the station, and I gave the party my last instructions. We numbered between fifteen and twenty men and we had not long to wait. The first lot of the bummers came in on a crank, about twenty in number, in high glee, talking and laughing with their muskets between their knees. As soon as they halted we leveled our revolvers on them. I ordered them to throw down their guns or they would be dead men. Never was a greater change seen. They commenced to remonstrate, but I gave them no time to talk. "Throw down your arms and surrender instantly if you wish to save your lives."

They obeyed instanter. I put them in charge of a guard and sent them to the guard house. Hardly had they gotten out of sight before another contingent came rolling in on a pole car and the same performance as with the first was enacted. And so the affair proceeded until four squads, numbering in the aggregate, upwards of eighty men, were disarmed and made prisoners. After waiting a while to see if any more were coming, I went up town and to the guard house, which was pretty well filled. As soon as I entered they began to remonstrate, saying the war was over and I had no right to arrest them. I told them I did it on their own account, that they were not safe in town, and that if not under guard some of them as well as some of our citizens would certainly be killed. Observing among their number one or two men with the stripes of a sergeant, I addressed myself to the most intelligent looking one of the number and told him that I came up to make a proposal to the party. Said I, "General Wright with his army will be here tomorrow. I know you had rather see the devil himself than to be turned over to him. Now, if you will agree to remain quietly in the guard house, I will guarantee to you kind treatment, a good supper, and a release in the morning soon enough for you to get out of town and rejoin your command and thus save yourself trouble."

They readily agreed to this arrangement and I then went to various housekeepers and prevailed on them to cook a sufficiency of food to give them a full supper, which they would send around to the guard house. This was done and keeping a guard over them all night I had no trouble until morning. By daybreak they began sending messages to be let out, but I put them off until I learned that the advance guard of Wright's corps was within a mile of town when I ordered their release, and in a few minutes all had disappeared. The Sergeant to whom I first spoke, lodged a formal complaint against one of the guards in charge of his party for having as he phrased it "Gone through him." That is robbed him of every thing he had. I told him I had no doubt he had done the same for many a rebel prisoner and that he could now judge how a man felt under such circumstances. He did not appear to receive much consolation from this suggestion.

When the troops came in sight of town, Major Hutter and I took with us a "flag of truce," and met them at the Bridge and I formally surrendered the Post. We were instructed to return to our quarters, and remain quietly within doors until arrangements had been completed for the control of the Post, and parole of the officers and men. I obeyed accordingly for I felt greatly relieved by the presence of the troop, as our situation was both peculiar and dangerous, because of the crowded prison now to be thrown open.

I was sitting in my office about twelve o'clock when General Wright rode up, dismounted and entered, preceded by a large and very handsome New Foundland dog. After the first salutation he said, "I understand Colonel, you have about a hundred of my men prisoners in your Guard House."

"That's a mistake," said I, "I have no one in the Guard House now."

"Strange," said he, "I heard it as I thought from a reliable source."

"Well, General, I did have them there last night, but I turned them loose this morning."

"What the h-ll did you do that for? I should have thought that an Officer of your rank would have had no sympathy for such a lot of bummers as they were. I would have given anything in reason, to have gotten hold of them."

"I too would have been glad, as I had not the slightest desire to shield them, but I was in a tight place. You advised me to "do the best I could," and I did so. As they kept their part of the bargain I was bound to keep mine."

I then told him the whole story. After hearing it he said he supposed it was all right, but he was greatly disappointed in not getting hold of them as he wished to make an example of the rascals.

The day Wright's Corps reached Danville, we heard of Johnson's surrender to Sherman, so General Wright encamped just outside of the town, and remained there about a week I think, possibly a little longer. His Corps then numbered about twenty-six thousand men and presented a magnificent appearance. All in new uniforms, supplied with the most approved appliances known to modern warfare, and with a profusion of Quartermaster and Commissary stores. The contrast between their appearance and that of our ragged and half-starved soldiers was really humiliating, until I recalled the fact that we had always been able to hold our own with them when they did not have more than two to one against us, and the remembrance gave me considerable comfort. The last prisoners taken from the Federal troops in Virginia were doubtless those I took as described above, and this is the first and only account ever written of the occurrence.

All the Officers and men connected with the Post received their Paroles the next day. A Provost Marshal was appointed to control the affairs of the town. We speedily realized that we were indeed a conquered people. I will do the Yankees the justice to say that they generally were well-behaved, and conducted themselves properly. Indeed I was greatly surprised at the good order observed by the prisoners when liberated. I neither heard of, or saw any disorderly conduct on their part nor any indulgence in excesses of any kind, which was certainly both remarkable and creditable. Indeed, I seldom saw one at all, and think they generally betook themselves to General Wright's camp, and there remained until they secured transportation to their respective homes.

PRESIDENT LINCOLN'S DEATH.

I first heard of President Lincoln's death from Colonel Fletcher, the Provost Marshal, who announced it without preface, with a sharp enquiring scrutiny as he told the news. He admitted afterwards that he had suspected it was the outcome of a plot devised by the Confederate Government and of which he suspected most of the prominent Confederates were fully cognizant. My reception of his intelligence disarmed his suspicions so far as I was concerned, for my first exclamation was one of horror and reprobation, followed by one of deep regret. In truth, I was entirely sincere, as I felt then and ever since that his death was a greater calamity to the South than to the North. Had he lived the cruelties and abomination of Reconstruction would never have been enacted.

CHAPTER XXI.

DANVILLE UNDER A PROVOST MARSHAL.

The question of food became a subject of absorbing interest, as soon as the town was occupied by the Federal troops. We had been obliged to keep open house for several days after the departure of President Davis and his party, as a large number of officers and officials who had been connected with the Government were passing through the place *en route* to Johnson's Army. One day we fed at dinner thirty persons besides our own family; among them General J. C. Breckenridge, the Secretary of War, and a party of six, who were traveling with him. And every day and every meal we had company. This pretty well exhausted our meagre supplies, and as our Confederate script was absolutely worthless, we had not the wherewithal to buy anything in the way of food. My children's old nurse Rachel, as faithful a friend as any one ever had, was the first to solve the problem. She came to her mistress and said, "Miss Ginny, if you will give me some flour, sorghum, and dried apples I'll soon get you some money."

"How?" said her mistress.

"I will bake some turnover pies and ginger cakes and sell them to the Yankee soldiers."

She got what she called for, and in the course of an hour or two, marched off with a basket of pies and cakes, and soon sold them all out, returning with nearly two dollars in green backs. She continued to do this for several days, and thus materially aided us.

The first morning after the occupancy of the town, from my back porch, I saw two soldiers going into the kitchen in the back yard. I ordered them at once out of the yard with preemptory voice and words, on the theory that a soldier was apt to yield obedience to an order when he would pay no respect to a request. One of them gave me an impudent reply when I pretended to fall in a violent passion, and told him if he said another word I would at once report him, that I never allowed our own soldiers to come into my kitchen, and certainly would not permit them. They went off muttering some unintelligible threats. In the afternoon of the same day, I was waited on by Colonel Fletcher of a Maine Regiment who informed me that he had just been appointed Provost Marshal, and asked permission to occupy my office, which was supplied with the necessary furniture and appliances for the dispatch of business. The very fact that he asked permission to do, what he had the right to command, proved him a gentleman, and I was more than willing to grant his request, as the office was one of the front rooms of my dwelling and I knew that his presence in the house would effectually protect us against any intrusion from soldiers or others.

He at once installed himself, and entered actively on the discharge of his duties, with a strong Provost Guard at his command, insuring us quiet and safety. In a few days, getting wind I have no doubt of the trouble we had in the matter of food, he asked me to see Mrs. Withers and let him know if she would permit him to eat at our table, remarking at the same time, that he would be able to help us out by adding the rations he was entitled to draw to our own supply. Mrs. Withers agreed to the proposition, and he proved a most agreeable and pleasant inmate of the family. The day before he made the arrangement to eat at our table, I had noticed in front of a Sutler's door, who had established himself on Main Street, a large dried codfish, and had told my wife that as we all had to turn Yankees now, we had better begin the transformation by learning to eat Yankee food, and advised her to send and purchase a codfish and have it prepared for breakfast. It was very malodorous, but I told her by soaking it over night it would lessen this disagreeable smell. Neither mistress nor cook had ever before seen a codfish, and of course knew nothing of the best method of preparing it for the table. So the cook after soaking it all night cut off portions of the fish and broiled it as she would a herring. When the bell rang for breakfast, and I opened the door of the dining-room I was met by such a scent that I ordered the servant to take that codfish away and throw it into the street or somewhere else, an order speedily executed, as no one interposed the slightest objection. When we told Colonel Fletcher the result of our first attempt to live on codfish diet, he was greatly amused, and said no Yankee ever could eat a dried codfish prepared in that way. He gave my wife some instructions as to the preparation of codfish balls, mixed with Irish potatoes and other things, which he thought we would like. But at dinner when the dish was brought in though some of us tasted it, no one wanted a second mouthful. Colonel Fletcher and my wife tried various recipes to make a palatable dish but no one except the Colonel himself would eat it. For prepare it as they might "the scent of the roses would hang around it still," and at last the remaining fish was thrown out on the dung hill, and this was our first and last attempt to eat dried codfish.

Among those who came to Danville on the evacuation of Richmond were various Bank Officials to look after their specie, which I had had for some time in my custody, in the vaults of the Bank. After consultation they concluded to move on further south and the officers of the Bank of Virginia and several of its branches had their specie moved down to the station, chartered a car in which they stored it and lived in the coach night and day, ready to start whenever danger threatened. They finally moved off to Greensboro, N. C. just before President Davis and party left, and subsequently went on to Georgia, where the gold was captured by a detachment of Federal Cavalry. After considerable loss by looting, the residue was turned into the Federal Treasury as property of the Confederate Government. Long years of effort followed on the part of the assignees of the Bank for the recovery of this money, and in time they obtained permission to bring suit in the Court of Claims, which they did. I was summoned as a witness in the case, when the fact transpired that I was then, the only person living who was personally cognizant of the facts in the case as connected with the custody and removal of the specie from the vaults of the Bank of Virginia, at Danville.

But to return to affairs in Danville under Federal administration. Orders were issued prohibiting the wearing of Confederate uniforms, which was subsequently modified to the requirement that the buttons should be cut off or covered. My old comrade and friend, Colonel Robert Preston, came to my house in Danville after the surrender of Johnson's army and there heard of the order for the first time. He said to a friend afterwards "it took all the buttons on my coat to give each of Colonel Bob Withers' daughters one." He remained with me two days and then left for home in a very despondent mood. I did not see him again for some years, when we met at an Agricultural Fair in Richmond, where he made his appearance in great form, clad in black broad cloth from head to foot and with his magnificent beard falling to his waist as white as snow, his genial countenance and florid face, he certainly presented a striking appearance. A race was on and we walked out to the first hurdle to see how the horses would clear it, while on our way, wishing to smoke, he pulled out a cigar, but neither of us could raise a match to light it. Turning to a lot of negroes standing near, he said, "Boys can't one of you give me a match?"

"Certainly sir," answered a young man nicely dressed, as he advanced and with a polite bow tendered the article in question. It was received by the Colonel with marked courtesy, and thanks returned in the most courtly style. As the negro walked away the Colonel said, "Colonel Bob Withers, I certainly do love a nigger as a nigger, but when they set up for white folks I've no use for them at all."

And this I think correctly describes the feelings of most gentlemen towards their former slaves.

Colonel Fletcher, the Provost Marshal, was waited on by crowds of negroes of both sexes, who every morning thronged his office with requests and petitions for all imaginable things. Having been bred in Maine, he had probably never seen a negro until he came south, and of course was entirely ignorant of their peculiar characteristics. It was not long before he asked me to aid him by advising what was best for him to do in any difficult case. I always did this cheerfully and no doubt, often was of real service to him.

I witnessed one morning an interview between him and a very intelligent negro of my acquaintance, who had been the foreman of a wealthy planter living on the river below Danville. I noticed this man, and spoke to him, but he did not disclose the object of his call, but sat patiently until the crowd had dispersed, when Colonel Fletcher turned to him and said, "Well, my man what can I do for you this morning?"

"I came sir," was the reply, "to ask you to lot me my land. They tell me the niggers is all free now and has to look out for theirselves. I've got a wife and seven children, it's now late in April and time corn was in the ground, and I want you to lot me my land so I can get to plowing."

The Colonel looked surprised, but at once replied, "Why, I have no land to give you, your former master's land still belongs to him, and so with all the other land. It still belongs to its owners, and the Government does not own an acre of it." The negro looked at him in evident surprise, but said, "Didn't you all set all Master's niggers free?"

"Yes," said the Colonel, "but we had no right to take his land." I never saw disgust and contempt more plainly expressed on the human face than they were on that of this negro. He said, "If you had the right to take Master's niggers you had the right to take Master's land too. And what good will freedom do the niggers if they get no land to work to make their bread?" This was evidently a poser and the Colonel could only reiterate his assurance that the Government owned no land that could be distributed to the negroes just set free. After he left I said, "Well Colonel, I think Jack's logic was too much for you."

"It certainly was," said he, "and I don't see what the poor creatures can do."

The whole incident was evidently an object lesson to which he frequently recurred in subsequent conversations, but he was never able to solve the problem to his own satisfaction.

My wife was forced to employ a wet nurse for her boy as his appetite speedily demanded more food than she could supply, and she engaged the services of a strong healthy woman named Maria, and I engaged her husband Sam, as house servant. They were genuine Africans, black as the ace of spades and both of excellent character, having been slaves of Dr. Welford of Fredericksburg, who had been refugeeing with them in Danville for two years or more. Colonel Fletcher was greatly pleased with Sam, and the liking appeared to be mutual. They speedily came to an agreement that Sam, his wife and children should accompany the Colonel to Maine when he should return. I heard nothing of this arrangement until a short time before the period fixed for their departure, and when my wife heard of it she was instantly up in arms, and going at once to the office of the Colonel she asked him if it was true that he proposed to carry off her baby's wet nurse. It appeared that he had not thought at all of this complication, but he earnestly disclaimed any purpose of interfering with the baby's comfort. After some consideration it was agreed that Sam should go with Colonel Fletcher, taking his oldest child with him, leaving Maria and the other children with us until the fall of the year when he would return for them. And this arrangement was carried out. Sam wrote pretty regularly to his wife by proxy of course, and professed to be greatly pleased with his prospects in his new home. When he came in the fall for Maria and the children he had many wonderful tales to tell, but nothing seemed to have aroused his wonder so much as the fact that he was permitted to sit down at the table with the white folks. He admitted that he had never "got used to it," and would have much preferred eating by himself. He occasionally wrote to us after they left and I always replied to his letters, but finally all correspondence ceased for twenty-five years or more. But when in the winter of 1896 we celebrated the fiftieth anniversary of our marriage, among the many letters of congratulation I was surprised to receive one from Sam, enclosing a photograph of himself and two of his daughters.

We were made glad this year by the return of Major Ellison and his family from South America, where he had been engaged for several years in the construction of the Don Pedro Railroad in Brazil, and from whom we had received no communication during the war. Being a Northern man, of course his sympathies were with the winning side, but he was very reticent and never alluded to the war if he could avoid it. He carried away a wife and one child. He returned, bringing with him a wife, three sons and a daughter, but he also communicated the sad intelligence of the death of Sydnor Royall, my wife's youngest brother, who had gone out with him, a boy about eighteen. He had died more than a year before their return. He had worked as a sub-contractor under Messrs. Harrah & Company, who admitted an indebtedness to him of eight thousand dollars, but Major Ellison said they owed him a good deal more than that, but he had no evidence of the fact and I saw no prospect of recovering more by litigation. As Sydnor left no will, his mother being heir-at-law, inherited whatever estate he had, and at her request I went on to Philadelphia, where Mr. Harrah lived, to settle the matter. After one or two interviews with him and his partner, I accepted their statement of account and settled on that basis, by which settlement Mrs. Royall received a little more than eight thousand dollars, which was a great relief to her, and she was able to live comfortably the remainder of her life.

When in Philadelphia, attending to this matter, I was detained over Sunday, and attended service at an Episcopal Church located in the neighborhood of the Continental Hotel, where I was stopping. I was greatly surprised and offended by the sermon delivered that day by the officiating minister, whose name I have forgotten, as he dwelt a good deal on the war and denounced the cruelties perpetrated by the rebels on the wounded soldiers of the Union Army and the indignities inflicted on the dead. When I returned to the hotel, I wrote this man quite a long letter, giving him my name and address, in which I stated some unpalatable truths. I told him I was a member of his Church, that I had never heard during the war from a minister of our Church, a single political sermon, nor a word of denunciation against the Union Army. That I had served through the war, and after the first battle of Manassas, had given up my tent to a wounded Colonel of the Northern Army, his orderly and surgeon, feeding them all from my mess, and caring for him as I would have done for one of our own men, and ended by giving the name and address of Colonel Wood, of the Brooklyn Zouave Regiment, to whom he could refer if he thought proper. It is hardly necessary to say that to this communication no response was made.

In the month of December of this year, my second daughter, Sue Dabney, was married to Mr. Henry S. Williams, a native of Mecklenburg County, Virginia, but when the war began, a resident of Norfolk, engaged in merchandizing. He joined the "Richmond Howitzers," was made 1st Lieutenant and served during the war. Having been sent to Danville on some detail duty, he met Sue Dabney, then a bright young girl, fell in love with her and though she was very young, insisted on marrying that fall. The wedding came off with the usual concomitants of a large crowd, a big supper and a gay dance. Shortly after which he took his young bride home to Mecklenburg County.

CHAPTER XXII.

I TURN OVER A NEW LEAF.

After the departure of the Federal troops when we were left again to our own devices my mind was considerably exercised, as to the best mode of providing for the wants of a large family, as I was so crippled up by wounds that I was physically disqualified from following my old profession. I could neither walk nor ride any distance, and the town of Danville was then too small to justify the expectation of securing an office practice sufficiently large to furnish a support. As this was before the Congress of the United States had entered upon their odious reconstruction policy, the people of the South took it for granted that they could at once resume their former status with Representatives in both Houses of Congress, and as there was an election to be held for members of Congress that year, some of my friends suggested that I should offer myself for election. Others contended that as I could not take the iron clad oath, it was useless to undertake the labor and expense of a canvass. After due consideration I came to the conclusion that as there were no persons in the South who could truthfully take that oath, it was folly to suppose that it would be required of them. I therefore announced myself a candidate and entered at once on a canvass of the district. This was my first experience as a candidate for any office in the gift of the people, and I entered upon it with considerable zeal. Several other gentlemen who were ambitious of being elected to the same position, declared their candidacy and entered on the canvass. Mr. J. Foote Johnson of Bedford County, Dr. Stovall of Halifax, for many years Treasurer of the State of Virginia, Rev. B. A. Davis of Patrick County and Mr. Thomas Grasty of Danville, were all on the track. I was of course compelled to do my traveling on wheels, as I could ride only a short distance without suffering severely. We had a good many discussions, all of which were conducted with courtesy. After a few weeks

Mr. Foote Johnson withdrew, but the rest held on to the day of election. I had received one or two messages from parties in Henry and Patrick Counties, saying it would be unsafe for me to visit that section, as the deserters and their friends would hold me to account for my active efforts to secure their arrest. Before starting I applied to the officer in command at Danville for permission to carry arms, which had been forbidden by military order, and after telling him the circumstances, he readily gave me the permit requested. I had no idea that anyone would molest me, but thought it best to be prepared. I attended Henry County Court and through a friend applied to the presiding magistrate for permission to speak in the courthouse. This dignitary, who had been appointed by military authorities because of his avowed Republican principles, refused to grant the permission with scant courtesy, coupled with the intimation that I had better not attempt to make a public speech that day. I then recalled the fact that his brother had after much trouble been arrested as a deserter and returned to his command. And, as the detail making the arrest reported that his brother had aided in concealing him, I, of course, understood at once the cause of his hostility.

I addressed a large crowd from the porch of the hotel immediately in front of the court-house, and commenced my speech by referring to the warning I had received and the discourteous refusal by the presiding magistrate of the use of the courthouse. I announced my purpose to canvass the county and stated that I had no apologies to make for my conduct in connection with the deserters or their friends and asked no favors at their hands. This bold defiance elicited great applause and I concluded my speech without being interfered with or interrupted by any one.

The Rev. Beverly A. Davis was quite a clever man, a good speaker and very astute. He was the first man to inaugurate the practice in his electioneering tours of speaking all the week and preaching every Sunday, and as, in every neighborhood, some soldier had died or been killed in the war, he advertised in advance that he would preach the funeral sermon of Tom, Dick, or Harry, as the case might be, on Sunday at the neighborhood church. This device stood him in good stead, and it was subsequently adopted with equally good results in the various canvasses in which "Parson Massie" engaged. I wound up my canvass at Patrick Court-House, on the day of election, where I received a heavy vote, very nearly equal to that of Mr. Davis, though he resided in the county near the Court-House. The result was, however, that the Parson received the highest vote, and was declared elected, but was never permitted to take his seat.

When I returned home from my canvass, I found that Dr. E. D. Withers had just returned from a trip to Southwest Virginia, had traveled through several counties in quest of a good grass farm which he could lease or rent, and had finally succeeded in renting the farm of Colonel Henry Bowen, located on the Maiden Spring Fork of Clinch River in Tazewell County, and proposed to move his family there the same year. He gave such a favorable account of the country and people, and so urged me to follow his example, that I concluded to pay a visit to the same section and take a look at some of the farms he had recommended. I had at this time no property except a house and lot in Danville, and I thought that if I found a place that suited me and which I could lease on favorable terms for a series of years, I might embark in the same business. I argued that we might live on the products of the farm as I could certainly make bread and meat enough to feed us, and the question of food for my large family was now the dominant one.

As I was passing through Lynchburg, I stopped over to visit Mrs. Royall, my wife's mother, and when I again started on my way to the station I met on the street a friend whom I had known from boyhood, Mr. Edward D. Christian, at that time a prominent and prosperous member of the Lynchburg bar, who appeared very glad to see me, and in the course of our conversation, as we walked on together, he said,

"Bob, I have a notion of starting a daily paper here. What do you think of it?"

"I don't think it will pay," said I. "Already there are two long-established daily papers here, which are as many as this place can support."

He insisted, however, that his plan was feasible, said that

Mr. Waddle, who had been foreman in the *Virginian* office for more than twenty years, was anxious to join in the venture, and would attend to all the practical work of the office, and he could secure the advertising of all the lawyers in the contiguous counties and a large subscription list, and it ought to succeed. Believing that neither he nor Mr. Waddle could edit the paper, I asked,

"Who is to be your editor?"

"I don't know yet," said he, "we are thinking of Mr.—" mentioning a young man of my acquaintance. "How do you think he would do?"

"Very well," said I, "if it is to be a literary paper, but if you propose publishing a political paper, he has had no experience in, and I suppose little knowledge of, political questions."

By this time we had reached the street leading to the station, and telling him I had to make the train, I bade him good-bye. As I started off he said,

"Look here, I would rather have you to edit the paper than any one I know."

Without pausing in my walk I said, "Well, you can get me very easily if you pay me enough to support my family."

"What is your price?" he said.

"Twenty-five hundred dollars a year," I called back, still without stopping.

"I'll see Waddle," he said, "and let you know."

We parted at that. I took the train for the Southwest and started on my quest for a good grass farm, which could be leased.

I have often reflected on the incidents narrated, the apparently accidental meeting on the streets of a city through which I was merely passing, the casual conversation and the manifestly impulsive proposition of my old friend, were all trivial matters, yet they sufficed to alter all my plans of life and lead to conditions and results momentous in their influence on my after life. Truly,

> "There's a Divinity that shapes our ends,
> Rough hew them as we may."

I do not remember that my mind reverted once to my conversation with Mr. Christian during the time I was engaged in looking for an eligible farm. I finally selected a large farm in the county of Russell, about thirty miles north of Abingdon, belonging to a gentleman named Lampkin, who had left it the second year of the war, removed to Lynchburg with his family, and was then engaged in merchandising. The farm, though a good one, and of large extent, was in very bad condition. The fences were in a great measure destroyed, the meadows grown up in bushes and briers, and everything in a dilapidated condition. The dwelling house was large, located on the turnpike extending from Lebanon, the county seat of Russell, to Tazewell Court-House. I leased the premises with the exception of a store house and garden attached, for eight years at an annual rental of eight hundred dollars in gold, or its equivalent. I had no experience in farming, for though reared in the country on a large plantation, I had never taken any interest in farming operations, and knew absolutely nothing of the business of grazing cattle. I was fully conscious of the risks attending so radical a departure from my previous habits of life, but was confident of my ability to master the principles of my new calling in a reasonable time. So, with a cheerful heart, I prepared to embark on my new business. I sold my house and lot in Danville for a good price, and this constituted my sole capital. When I reached home I was greeted by two telegrams and a letter from my friend Christian, informing me that after consultation with Mr. Waddle, they had determined to accept my offer, and as they wished to get out the new paper by the first of January, 1866, desired me to come at once to Lynchburg. This was rather startling, as I could not well back down from my own proposition, but it looked as if I would have an elephant of rather large proportions on my hands in the shape of a lease for eight years of a farm in Russell County. It was now nearly the middle of December, and it would certainly keep me busy to close up my affairs in Danville, move my family to Lynchburg, and arrange for the farming operations in Russell in the two weeks intervening before the first of January. My wife and I had a long conference that night and she suggested that Dr. Carter and Lizzie, with their young child, should go to the farm in Russell to look after my interests there, and at the same time practice his profession, while we could go to the city of Lynchburg, where I was to take charge of the paper. And this was done. I sold out in Danville, settled up my business as far as practicable, and with my family, accompanied by Dr. Carter, his wife and child, removed to Lynchburg, which we reached the day before Christmas, at once rented a house, hired servants, bought furniture, and went to housekeeping. I also hired three negro men for the Russell farm and had the contracts drawn up and executed before the Freedmen's Bureau, as required by the reconstruction laws. The first number of the *Lynchburg Daily and Semi-Weekly News* made its appearance on the fifteenth of January, 1866. Messrs. Christian and Waddle, proprietors, Robert E. Withers, editor, John Perry, local and news editor. We started out with a very respectable list of subscribers, to which additions were daily made, and in a very short time we were in the van of the city papers. Soon after the Christmas holidays, Dr. Carter and his family, with the three negro men hired for the farm, started by rail for Abingdon and from thence made their way by wagon to "Oak Forest," as the Lampkin farm was called. The store house was occupied by Mr. John Lampkin and his wife, he being the oldest son of the owner of the property. He and Dr. Carter were made joint managers and arrangements were at once made to stock the place and clear up and fence the farm. I made a flying trip to the place early in the year, directed what fields were to be put in cultivation, laid off the fences, rented land to tenants, bought stock cattle, and returned to my editorial duties in Lynchburg. Dr. Carter and his wife took Willie Clare, one of the children, with them, and James Royall, my wife's oldest brother, was also of the party. They were all comfortably installed and had fair prospects. There were several families living near them of nice and cultivated people, but the mountain population were an unending source of wonder and amusement. In the early spring I paid a visit to my old friend, David McGavock, of Pulaski, and selected from his herd of thoroughbred short-horns, a lot of yearlings, and purchased from Mr. Robert Crockett, of Wythe, some full-blooded Cotswold sheep and sent them to the farm.

When summer came, my wife concluded to pay a visit to Russell, and I accompanied her and the children. I had purchased an army ambulance and sent it out to be used in transporting family and visitors to and from the farm, and had written for it to meet us in Abingdon. We went on the night train and took berths on the sleeper for the party. It was my wife's first experience on a sleeping car. She stood it very well until the curtains were closed, then but a few minutes elapsed before she complained that she was smothering and would die unless the curtains were opened. No argument or remonstrance prevailed, those curtains were bound to be opened, and they were.

When we reached Abingdon in the morning, we found James Royall with the ambulance in waiting. He had gone out with Dr. Carter as he wished to go to the country and was so pleased that he lived with us until we left the county. Our whole party was stored in the ambulance, and with two good horses we made the trip without accident, arriving a little after dark, and of course, had a joyous welcome from Dr. Carter, Lizzie and the rest. I left all my family when I returned to Lynchburg a few days later and they spent a pleasant summer. Mr. Henry Smith, one of our near neighbors, had married a Richmond lady, a sister of Dr. W. W. Parker, of that city, who had friends and relatives spending the summer with her, and Mrs. Dr. Smith, a widow with one son, was also a near neighbor and a lady of culture, who usually had summer visitors also, and with the young lawyers and others from Lebanon, we usually had a merry time during the warm season.

When I first announced my purpose of settling in Russell County, some of my friends remonstrated because of the troubles which had broken out after the war between the returned soldiers and the horde of deserters and Union men occupying a section of country known as the "Doubles," lying between the farm I had leased and the Clinch River. In truth, there had been a great deal of trouble in that particular locality. The Union men, as they called themselves, only claimed this name as an excuse for keeping out of the service. After the surrender they became very aggressive, and, relying on the support of the army detachments quartered in every county, they sought to wreak their vengeance on the loyal Confederates, who had raided their fastnesses during the war and arrested them as deserters or robbers as the case might be.

Scarcely a Sunday passed without a collision, generally precipitated by an attack on some obnoxious Confederate officer or soldier, several of whom were shot and severely wounded. Finally they assaulted a returned Confederate officer named Fuller, belonging to an influential family in the county, and shot him dangerously one Sunday at church. An impromptu meeting was held and some one proposed to organize a party and clean out the "Doubles." No definite action was taken, however, but on the next day placards were put up in public places, signed by the ring leader of the union party, saying that such an expedition was in contemplation and defiantly inviting them to come on, as they were ready to receive them. Two mornings afterwards, as he came out from his cabin into a road running around my field fence and leading into a public road, he dismounted to let down a pair of draw-bars, and as he was leading his horse through, the crack of a dozen guns was heard, and he fell dead in his tracks. The party who inflicted this summary punishment rode directly to his house to call out his father, who had also been very conspicuous in the attacks made on the returned Confederates, but as they approached he fired on them, wounding one of the party seriously. The rest dashed into the house, after breaking down the door, but could find no one but women in the cabin, who alleged that the old man had escaped by the back door. This story was not accepted, and they began a systematic search of the premises, finally pulling up a plank from the floor which was loose, and there he was found. He was ordered to come out, and as his head appeared at the opening, one of the party blew his brains out.

They then went to the house of a magistrate near by, believed by all to be the chief fomenter of the strife, but too great a coward to take an active part personally, and gave him unmistakable warning, that if he dared to issue any warrant or legal process designed to procure the arrest of any of the party, his life would not be worth an hour's purchase. The men then returned home, but complaint was soon made to the officer in command of the military at Abingdon, requesting his interference. He detailed a squad of men, under command of a lieutenant, and sent them over to Russell, with orders to investigate and report the facts. This officer, fortunately, was a man of good sense and sound judgment, and after hearing th[e] testimony, returned to Abingdon and reported that the tw[o] Hubbards had certainly been killed in defiance of law, bu[t] that they richly deserved the fate meted out to them. The onl[y] wonder was that the community had so long submitted to th[e] outrages and violences committed by these men and their asso[-] ciates. This heroic remedy proved effective and put a stop t[o] further violence.

I rented land to some of these very men after I came int[o] possession of the farm, and never had any trouble or difficult[y] with any of them.

Soon after the establishment of the *News*, the "Consolida[-] tion Railroad War" was inaugurated. General William Ma[-] hone, soon after the close of the war, was elected president o[f] the Norfolk & Petersburg Railroad, and subsequently of th[e] Southside Railroad, between Petersburg and Lynchburg. Col[-] onel Robert L. Owen was at that time president of the Virgini[a] & Tennessee Railroad, running from the city of Lynchburg t[o] Bristol on the Tennesse line. Lynchburg was about equi-distan[t] from Norfolk and Bristol, and General Mahone was desirou[s] of effecting the consolidation of the three roads, and securin[g] his election to the presidency of the consolidated line. He wa[s] ably seconded in his efforts by the leading stockholders of th[e] Norfolk & Petersburg and the Southside Road, the stock o[f] which was practically worthless. The contest was long an[d] bitter. At the annual meeting of the stockholders of the Vir[-] ginia & Tennessee Road, the conflicting parties were repre[-] sented by some of the ablest lawyers in Virginia, and the di[s-] cussions were very interesting.

The people and press of Lynchburg opposed the consolida[-] tion and the first meeting of stockholders was unfavorable t[o] the proposed consolidation. Learning wisdom by experience[,] however, the astute managers of this raid on the Virginia [&] Tennessee Railroad corrected some errors in their first cam[-] paign and materially improved their chances by adopting th[e] policy of dividing up the holdings of the large stockholder[s] among parties friendly to their policy and thus avoiding th[e] scaling of their votes, which was necessary at the first fight[.] There were not as many large stockholders of Virginia [&]

Tennessee as of Southside and Norfolk & Petersburg Railroads, but the victory was finally secured by inducing the Governor to change the State Proxy, who had opposed consolidation, and putting in his place a gentleman known to be favorable to that policy.

The News had persistently opposed the scheme, and I as its editor, incurred thenceforth the undying hatred of General Mahone. When the final fight came off, Colonel Owen resorted to the desperate expedient of thwarting the wishes of the stockholders by securing the intervention of the Federal officer in command of the Lynchburg post. I thought this unwise and unwarranted, and when a Federal officer marched into the meeting and announced that by order of the General commanding no further steps could be taken in the matter, the announcement caused some cheering on the part of Colonel Owen's friends, but it excited great indignation on the part of General Mahone's party, in which I fully sympathized, as I regarded it as an outrage on the rights of the stockholders, and I offered a resolution for the appointment of a committee, charged with the duty of framing a protest against the action of the commanding General, coupled with the request to be informed at what time the corporation would be permitted to complete the business before it. This proposal was opposed by some because they regarded it likely to give offense. It was finally passed in a modified form. The reply, however, was in conciliatory language to the effect that he would request specific instructions on the subject from the general in command of Military District No. 1, and communicate the reply as soon as received. Subsequently the inhibition was withdrawn and General Mahone was elected president and a board of directors favorable to his views were placed in control. They voted him a salary of twenty-five thousand dollars per annum, and he became "Monarch of all he surveyed." The name of the road was changed and it became the Atlantic, Mississippi & Ohio Road. Mrs. Mahone's given name was Otelia, and some wag, familiar with the policy which marked its administration, gave to the initials A. M. & O. a new translation—"All Mine and Otelia's." The subsequent history of the road may be briefly told. A million and a half of State bonds were issued by authority of the

Legislature for the purpose of constructing a branch from Bristol to the Ohio, which was never built, and in a few years the road was bankrupt and passed into the hands of a receiver.

In 1867 I purchased a house and lot in Lynchburg, it was a comfortable and commodious building with fine garden and fruit, but there was found to be a flaw in the title, and I declined to take it, but paid rent for the year. While we occupied this house our twelfth child was born and named Mary, for her mother. She was petite and beautiful, and a great pet with all.

CHAPTER XXIII.

POLITICAL LIFE.

The News had by his time assumed considerable prominence among the public journals of the State. Its policy was aggressive and outspoken. No one had any difficulty in understanding its position on any important matter of public interest. It criticised with unsparing severity, the revolutionary and tyrannical features of the reconstruction policy of the Republican party, protested boldly against the arbitrary rule of the military authorities and was among the first to advocate a coalition of all the conservative elements of society to resist the usurpations and encroachments of the Radicals, who now proposed to direct the affairs of the State.

By order of the general commanding District No. 1, a Convention had been called for the purpose of framing a constitution, and an overwhelming majority of those elected to membership were either ignorant negroes, just emancipated from slavery, carpet-baggers from the North, or a class of Virginians known as scalawags, men without political or personal standing in the community. The proportion of gentlemen of probity and honor who were elected constituted but a small and helpless minority. This Convention met December 3d, 1867, and selected as its presiding officer John C. Underwood, who had come from the North to Virginia a few years before as a school teacher. And having secured a sufficient number of scholars, opened a school in the upper part of Fauquier County, where he married a Miss Gibson, of a good Virginia family. He soon made himself so obnoxious to the people of Fauquier County by his anti-slavery sentiments that he was forced to leave the State, but returned after the close of the war and was elected a member of the Convention of 1867.

In pursuance of a call through the public press, delegates were sent to Richmond for the purpose of devising some plan to resist the radical constitutional changes proposed. It met in Richmond and was largely attended by the most prominent and representative citizens of the State, who, after some deliberation, determined to organize a new political party, to be known as the "Conservative Party of Virginia," embracing in its membership all persons, without regard to previous political affiliations, who were willing to dedicate their most earnest efforts to the conservation of those principles of civil liberty now so seriously threatened.

Prior to the period when Virginia had been degraded from the position of a "Sovereign State" to that of Military District No. 1, Governor Pierpoint had been sent down as Governor, and still continued nominally to act as such, although General Scofield really exercised the supreme power. And here I wish to bear my testimony to the conservatism which almost always characterized his administration of the supreme powers confided to him, but for which the condition of the people of Virginia would have been much more intolerable than it was.

The Underwood Convention or as it was commonly called, "The Black and Tan Convention," continued its labors until the middle of April, 1868, when, having exhausted every dollar of the amount appropriated for its expenses, it was starved into adjournment.

A schedule attached to the Constitution required the military commandant to submit the Constitution to a vote of the people on the second day of June, 1868, and at the same date to hold an election for members of Congress and of the General Assembly of Virginia. By the provisions of this Constitution no person was permitted to vote or hold any office whatever who had held office of any kind under the State or United States Government and subsequently rendered any aid, countenance or encouragement to the Confederate Government, or to any person engaged in its service. A man who had given a drink of water or a meal's victuals to any starved or wearied soldier was by that act prohibited from voting or holding any office. Of course such a sweeping disfranchisement left the absolute control of the State, and of every county or corporation in it, to the recently emancipated slaves and the carpet baggers who had thronged into the State like hungry cormorants intent only on plunder.

The dangers which threatened us were patent, and the necessity for prompt and united action to counteract them was apparent. Measures were taken accordingly. As soon as the Convention adjourned, a State Convention of the Conservative Party was summoned to meet in Richmond. I was among the delegates appointed from Lynchburg and made preparations to attend. As a meeting of the Scottish Rite Masons of the Southern Jurisdiction of the United States, of which General Albert Pike, of Arkansas, was the head, was to assemble in the city of Charleston, South Carolina, a few days prior to the Richmond Convention, and I had been delegated to attend it as the representative of the Grand Consistory of Virginia, I went first to Charleston, remained there three days and left in time to reach Richmond the night before the State Convention was to meet. But from defective railroad connections and other causes I was delayed, and did not reach Richmond until nearly twelve o'clock on the day of meeting. Without delay I rushed from the station to the Exchange Hotel and found the Convention in session and dispatching its business with rapidity. They had agreed to nominate a full State ticket and put them into the field at once to contest every inch of ground until the day of election. The candidates would be expected to devote their whole energies to secure an adverse vote on the adoption of the Underwood Constitution.

As I entered the hall I encountered an acquaintance and asked for information as to what had been done. He gave me in brief the facts above stated and said the Convention was about to nominate a candidate for Governor. I asked who was likely to be selected for the high honor. He replied that several names had been presented, but, said he, "I think you stand the best chance." Supposing he was jesting, as I had never heard my name mentioned in connection with the place, I rather impatiently replied, "Oh, I am not joking, I really want to know."

"I'm not joking, either," said he. "Your name has been presented and was received with many indications of popular favor."

The balloting commenced very soon after, and to my great surprise, I received the nomination on the first ballot. General

James A. Walker, of Pulaski, was put on the ticket as Lieutenant Governor, and my old university friend, John L. Marye, of Fredericksburg, was nominated for Attorney General. The ticket seemed to command the confidence of the people throughout the State. A strong executive committee was selected by the Convention, and this committee invited me to meet them the same night for conference, as it was desirable that the canvass should begin at once, as hardly a month intervened before the day fixed by the ordinance for submitting the constitution to the ordeal of a popular vote.

Various views were expressed in the conference as to the best policy to pursue in regard to the negro vote. Some gentlemen of large experience and good judgment thought by pursuing a conciliatory course and appealing to their loyalty to their former masters, many of them could be induced to support the ticket. I insisted that the only chance for a successful fight lay in making the race issue. It was a well-known fact that through all the Southwest and in the mountain counties a strong Union element had been demonstrated to exist to such an extent that it dominated almost every county in the section named, which added to the immense negro vote in the East, would surely defeat us. As to the negro vote, it had been clearly demonstrated in the election of delegates to the Constitutional Convention that they would vote solidly, as they were instructed by the carpet baggers. These views were combated by some of the committee, until I took the ground that as the burden of the fight would rest on me, I thought I should be allowed to select the lines of my assault on the work of the Convention. This view was accepted, and we then proceeded to arrange for public meetings through the State. For the Eastern section, mass meetings were called at central and accessible points where the citizens of several contiguous counties could readily meet and local speakers were appointed to aid me. For the counties west of the Blue Ridge, and especially those in Southwest Virginia, appointments were made for almost every county.

The first public meeting was at Petersburg, and as only a brief notice was practicable, I did not expect a large attendance. The place of meeting was the "Poplar Lawn Park," and when I reached it I found several thousand persons present, at least fifteen hundred of whom were negroes. Before starting out I had consulted some legal friends of high repute as to the law points likely to arise in the discussion of the provisions of the constitution, and thus prepared, I felt confident of my ability to sustain myself before the people.

General H. H. Wells, of Michigan, recently registered a citizen of Virginia, was nominated for Governor by the Radical party, but I really do not now remember who were his associates on the ticket. We had, in our conference determined that joint discussions were not desirable, and so I thought the Petersburg meeting afforded a suitable occasion for raising the flag of the white race in face of the large crowd of negroes present. I took, therefore, an early opportunity to declare that in my canvass I did not propose to ask, nor did I expect to receive the vote of any negro, that however honest they might be in their purposes, they neither possessed information or intelligence sufficient to enable them to decide matters of State craft, and for this I did not hold them accountable. I said that Virginia had always been governed by the white men, and I was determined to use my best efforts to perpetuate their rule. This declaration was received with many growls of dissent from the blacks in the audience, but was vociferously cheered by the white men. But as I do not propose to recapitulate the arguments and appeals addressed to the white people of Virginia, I make no attempt to reproduce them. I merely wish to record some of my personal experiences in prosecuting this laborious canvass of the State from the seaboard to its western borders. As a sample of the difficulties encountered and overcome, I will relate in detail my experiences in my first round of appointments.

Orange Court-House I visited two days after Petersburg. I was met there by a large audience, embracing several hundred negroes. My next appointment was in the old town of Fredericksburg, reached, of course, without difficulty, by rail. I was met by J. L. Marye, one of my colleagues, who took me to his house, where I spent the night very pleasantly. The itinerary arranged for me by the executive committee assumed that at Fredericksburg I would meet a Baltimore steamer, which would convey me to a wharf in the vicinity of old "Farnham

Church," in Richmond County, where the meeting for the Northern Neck was called for the next day but one after Fredericksburg. When I told Marye this, he said it would not be possible to meet the appointment, as the committee was misinformed as to the time of leaving of the Baltimore steamer, which left the morning of that day, and would not be back for two days. I was much put out, and told him it would never do for me to fail to meet my engagements, and asked him the distance to old Farnham Church. He computed it to be a little more than ninety miles. Then said I, "If you will secure for me a pair of good horses, a driver, and a light vehicle, I think I can reach the place in time."

"You can't possibly make it," said he.

"Yes," said I, "it can be done in this way. Tomorrow I will speak first, and as soon as I finish will come here and get a snack, have the vehicle in waiting, and I can drive twenty miles or more that afternoon. And by starting early the next morning can spend the night at some point which will enable me to reach the place of meeting the next day."

After thinking a while, he admitted that it might be done, but thought that I would not feel much like speaking when I got there. He said by going to Mrs. Mason's in King George County, in the afternoon, which was about twenty miles, I would receive a hearty welcome and secure an early start in the morning, which was all important.

We had a good crowd the next day, but the meeting did not open until twelve o'clock and I spoke only an hour and a half, when I left the other speakers to entertain the audience, got my snack, and started by two o'clock. I found the roads good and had a good team. So we progressed finely, reaching Mrs. Mason's a little after sunset. I found General Field here, who had married a daughter of Mrs. Mason, and spent a very pleasant evening. Mrs. Mason was a typical Virginia matron, and a model housekeeper. She had my breakfast ready next morning by sunrise, horses and driver fed and everything arranged to meet my wishes. I had proposed to dine in Westmoreland County with my old Almshouse friend, Dr. William Wirt, and reached his door about two o'clock, just in time to avoid a hard thunder shower. Dr. Wirt, however, was not at home, and I thus missed an anticipated pleasure. His wife, however, gave me a most hospitable welcome, and an excellent dinner, somewhat delayed, however, by my late arrival. When we started again, I found that the road was quite muddy from the shower and I had only proceeded five or six miles, before the axle of the vehicle broke and let me down in the road. I walked until I reached a house, and learned that there was a blacksmith's shop at "Oak Grove," a small village about a mile farther on. The blacksmith said he could not mend the axle until midday the next day, and I found it impossible to hire or borrow a buggy in the village. But the blacksmith thought that if I sent a note to Mr. Henry Wirt, a brother of the doctor, he would let me have his buggy. I sent the note at once by the driver, stating who I was and how desirous I was of meeting my engagement of the next day, and in about half an hour the driver returned with the vehicle, and we again started, and reached Westmoreland Court-House after nine o'clock. I had supper, and got to bed as speedily as practicable. Next morning I was up by light and without waiting for breakfast, drove to Warsaw, the county seat of Richmond County, there I stopped for breakfast and to have the horses fed. I was now within five or six miles of the place of meeting, which I reached by eleven o'clock. There was a large gathering here and, for a wonder, all the gentlemen appointed to aid me in the meeting were in attendance. Ex-Senator Hunter, Hon. Willoughby Newton, and the Rev. W. W. Walker, all delivered able addresses. The ladies were out in large numbers with a most bountiful basket dinner and fully sustained the reputation of the people of the Northern Neck for unbounded hospitality and high living. According to arrangements, Mr. Greshan, of Lancaster Court-House, took me to his home that evening, but said he did not think it possible for me to reach my next appointment, which was at Bellhaven on the Eastern Shore, two days after. Said I, "Mr. Greshan, if I had listened to the Fredericksburg people I should never have been here today, now if you know of any one who has a good sail boat or oyster pungy, which can be hired to take me across the Bay, and will procure it for me, it can be done."

"Well," he said, "I expect Jack Tancel has a good boat we

could get and I will drive you down there early in the morning."

He was as good as his word and we drove down to the Bay, and I saw for the first time a large body of salt water. Tancel's house was on a creek or estuary, only a short distance from the Bay, and I found him a jolly old fellow and an ardent Democrat. He said that I could get his boat, which was then in the creek, and that his son would soon clean it up for the voyage across. He called to one of his other boys "to run down to the 'crik' and pick out a few good oysters for the Colonel, and to come by the net and he might find a 'shipshead.'" He was only gone a few minutes before he returned with three beautiful sheepshead and some nice oysters, of which I made a hearty meal. The old oysterman was hospitality personified and I was delighted to make his acquaintance. The wind by this time had freshened up considerably, and the old man asked me "if I had ever been much on the water?" I told him "I had never seen before any body of water larger than a mill pond." He laughed heartily and said, "Well, the Bay is middling rough and I wouldn't be surprised if it made you a little seasick."

I replied that "I had no doubt that he was right in his surmises, but I was obliged to go, sick or no sick."

We went down to the "crik," and I found his son a strong, active young fellow, on board the pungy, and an old darkey named Jack, who was the pilot of the expedition, as few persons on this side of the Bay are familiar with the harbors of the Eastern Shore. Old Uncle Jack, however, professed to know them all and their bearings. I told him to shape his course for Pungoteague, and we started on our voyage. While in the creek everything went on very smoothly, but ere long we emerged into the waters of the Bay, which is here about thirty miles wide, and of course on so large an expanse of water the wind has much greater power, which was shown by the "white caps" which adorned the crests of all the waves. I took my seat without a word on the deck near the companionway and we soon felt the force of the strong northwest wind blowing down the Bay. The little sloop began to pitch and toss in the most lively manner, and the waves dashed against her sides with a great splash and noise, sending showers of spray over the deck.

The young captain of the craft presently said, "This is middling rough, Colonel, and maybe you had rather turn back?"

Said I, "I know nothing at all about it, but if you think it too dangerous to go on, then turn back."

"Oh," said he, "there is no danger, but it will be rough."

"You must decide these matters yourself," said I. "If you are afraid to go on, then I am also, but if you are not afraid, neither am I."

"Oh," said he, "we can go on."

Old Uncle Jack had said nothing, but I thought he cast his eyes to windward very often. We had not gone much farther before a wave broke over the deck, giving us a good wetting, and this elicited a big grunt from old Uncle Jack, but he still said nothing. In about two minutes a much larger wave struck us, swept across the deck, and carried off not only a stool, but the covering which closed the companionway, and they went floating off to leeward. Old Jack now spoke out, "Umph, umph!" he said, "neber get across in de face of dis win, I tell you sho."

"Then go back," said I. And go back we did.

We ran into another creek near a handsome house with a good farm attached, where a Baltimore Brig was lying, taking on a load of grain. On landing I walked up to the house, and was kindly greeted by the owner, whose name I can not now recall. Of course I told him who I was and the business upon which I was engaged, being then on my way to the Eastern Shore to fill an appointment to speak. He insisted on my taking supper with him, as he knew the fare on the pungy would be pretty rough, and I willingly accepted his invitation and was rewarded by a bounteous meal. I again went aboard and we ran out of the mouth of the creek and took an observation with no encouraging results, as the wind was still strong from the northwest. Uncle Jack said there was nothing to be done except to anchor, and spend the night, or until the wind changed, which he thought it might do about midnight. They surrendered the little cabin to me, and I went down and got into the bunk, hoping to get a good night's rest. Before I got to sleep, however, I found that certain homesteaders were very active in asserting their preëmption right to that territory. I speedily retreated to the deck, and as I emerged from the companionway Uncle Jack chuckled softly to himself and presently said, "Did the bugs bother you, boss?"

"They certainly did," said I, "they are too many for me."

"Dey is mighty bad down dar certain. I've been telling Marse John we would have to sink her a while to get rid of em." I climbed to the boom on which the main sail was lying in loose folds and crawling between these, tried to sleep, but 't was a hopeless effort. As Uncle Jack had predicted, soon after midnight I found the wind was changing and waked up Uncle Jack and asked if we couldn't get under way at once. He looked all around and aloft, and finally agreed that it was practicable, and he and the captain set about hoisting sails, a work which was speedily accomplished, and we started across the Bay with a good breeze. Before we got under way, however, the captain took the boat and visited a fish net not far off, and returned with a large flounder and a small sheepshead, which he said would make us a good breakfast. I asked him if it was Chesapeake Bay law to take what he wanted without leave. He laughed and said it was custom if it wasn't law, and my doubts and scruples vanished with the odors of the frying fish at breakfast time. For two or three hours we made fine progress, but about sun up the breeze began to die down, and though then in sight of Pungoteague, I feared we would never reach there in time to make the trip to Bellhaven, as we seemed to be merely drifting with the tide. We finally passed through a fleet of fishing boats and I asked the fisherman in the nearest boat if he knew of any conveyance which I could hire to take me right away to Bellhaven. He pointed to a boat not far off and said, "There is a man who can take you, I think."

I hailed him and asked if he could drive me over to Bellhaven at once. He "allowed he could." I asked him what would be the charge. He said, "About a dollar and a half."

I asked how far it was to his house. He pointed to a cabin on the beach only a short distance away. Telling him to bring his boat alongside, I took my satchel, and, having settled with the captain for my fare, and tipped Uncle Jack liberally, I got into the fisherman's boat and he rowed it as near shore as he could, jumped into the water about knee deep, took me on his back and waded ashore. We walked to his cabin and I said, "Now hitch up as soon as you can, for I am in a great hurry."

He replied, "I'll soon be ready for you," and went out for a few minutes. He returned and, picking up a gray blanket and folding it into a small compass, said he was ready. I went out to get into a buggy, as I supposed, but was astounded to find nothing but the wheels and axle-tree of a cart, to which a small bay mare was hitched. He laid the folded blanket along the axle of the cart, got on it, took the reins, and invited me to a seat by his side. I mounted, but being a pretty tall man, my feet were in dangerous proximity to the ground, and I expressed a fear lest they should be struck by the rocks in the road.

"No danger," said the driver, "there are no rocks."

I took my cane, which had a crook on the head, and reaching forward, hooked on to the cross piece between the shafts and gripping it with both hands, told him to go ahead. The little bay mare astonished me by her fine action and spirit.

I said, "How long will it take the mare to make the twelve miles to Bellhaven?"

"About an hour and a half, but she can make it in an hour if pushed."

"Well, if you will make it in an hour, I'll pay you an extra dollar."

"Good," said he, "I'll do it."

He spoke to the mare and she at once responded and started off at a racing gait. As he had said, the road was perfectly smooth and level as the floor, and we spun over it in fine style, never drawing rein until we reached the little village of Bellhaven. I looked at my watch and found that we had made the trip with three minutes to spare. While en route, I asked my driver if there was not a political meeting at Bellhaven that day. He thought he had heard "some talk about it." I thought the uncertainty indicated by his answer argued unfavorably for a good attendance, but my friend spoke up and said, "May be you are going there to speak today?"

I told him that was just what I proposed doing, adding that I was Colonel Withers, who was running for Governor of the State and aiming to prevent the adoption of the Underwood Constitution, stating briefly some of the objections to it. He then said he believed he would go to the stand and listen to my speech as soon as he had attended to his horse. When we reached the place, I no longer felt any anxiety about the attendance, as the large number of horses and vehicles of all kinds there assembled indicated the presence of an immense crowd. I saw an hundred or two of vehicles such as I had just traveled on scattered around. The inhabitants call it "shaft and wheels," and it is much used by the common people. Besides these, there were spring wagons, buggies and carriages in large numbers.

I started towards the speaking stand and met a gentleman of whom I inquired the way. He politely instructed me, but then remarked that they were greatly disappointed at the non-arrival of the speakers. They expected Colonel Withers, Mr. John Goode, and Robert L. Montague, but none of them had come.

"Yes," said I, "one of them is here—Colonel Withers."

"Are you Colonel Withers?"

"Yes, sir, that's my name, and I had a pretty hard time of it trying to reach here."

He expressed great gratification and led the way to the stand, at that time occupied by the State Senator from the district, who had been pressed into service to fill the gap made by the absence of the expected foreign speakers.

When I left Fredericksburg I told Jack Marye that I could recall only one acquaintance I possessed on the Eastern Shore, and that was Dr. John Wise, of Accomac, who had been stationed at one of the hospitals in Danville during the war. Now, as luck would have it, we had gone but a few steps through the crowd before I met Wise face to face. After a hearty handshake, he took me by the arm, saying, "Come right along to the stand and let our people see you."

"Oh, don't interrupt the speaker," said I, "wait until he gets through."

But he would not hear of it and rushed me on the stand, interrupting the speaker, who, I think, was Judge Pitts, of Accomac, and at once presented me to the audience. Never had any one a warmer welcome. I saw before me not less than two thousand people, a great number of whom were ladies, and such a hurrah as they gave me, was enough to make me forget fatigue and arouse me to make my best effort. I asked for a glass of water, and was handed almost every fluid except water. As water straight did not seem to be available, I compromised on lemonade, and proceeded to discuss the Underwood Constitution in a speech of more than two hours, which was well received by the audience. An adjournment for dinner was then announced, and we had a most bountiful repast. Amongst many others I was introduced to Colonel Hamilton Neal, who said he lived at "Cherry Stone," and had come up to take me to his house for supper, and then would drive me to the harbor, where a vessel had been engaged to take me across the Bay to Old Point, whence I could take the morning steamer for Portsmouth, my next appointment. This was in every way a pleasant arrangement, and as "Cherry Stone" was about twenty miles distant we started as soon as dinner was over. The Colonel had a fine horse and buggy and we traveled rapidly. I noticed many evidences of prosperity and thrift and some very good farms as we drove along and was generally informed that this farm is now owned by Mr. So & So from some Northern State. Being desirous of learning whether the new settlers had prospered in their operations and I asked the question if they had introduced many improved methods in agriculture and were accumulating money rapidly. The Colonel was silent for a moment, and then replied laughing, "I was not long since investigating that very matter said he and was struck with the fact, that however readily many Virginians may surrender their ancient customs and traditions, the soil of the old State is still true to itself, for I'll be d—d if it has not broken every one of them."

We soon passed through the village of Eastville, the county seat of Northampton, where we stopped for a few minutes to ascertain if the sail boat bespoken for my use was ready to start that night, and being told it was all right we continued our drive and reached Colonel Neal's residence a little after dark. His family were not at home but we soon had a good supper and started for "Cherry Stone" about six miles distant, which we reached about ten o'clock and I was soon aboard. I found my navigators father and son were Massachusetts men who seemed to know their business and thought they would reach

Old Point before day if the wind continued fair. As I had slept none the night before and had been either traveling or speaking all day I went into the cabin for rest, after assuring myself by inquiry that I was not likely to be disturbed by any preëmption claimants. I suppose I had been asleep about an hour when I was awakened by the creaking caused by the swinging of the boom, and the noise of the waves striking the sides of the vessel. These sounds were repeated at intervals of about five minutes preventing any possibility of sleep, so I got up and went on deck, finding as I expected that the wind had shifted to the west and was blowing a gale, requiring us to tack every five or ten minutes to make any headway at all. The gale increased in violence and the most watchful care was required to avoid being swamped by the force of the squalls that struck us. The Captain, however, was very watchful, and as soon as a hard blow came would throw the boat up into the wind and hold her there, till the force of the gale was abated, when he would resume his effort to beat across the Bay. We finally sighted a light which was thought to mark the entrance to Back River, but when after long effort we reached it, found it to be the light ship anchored on the Frying Pan Shoals about fifteen miles farther north than we should have been. The force of the wind and tide had driven us that distance up the Bay. There was nothing to be done but change our course and in the face of this head wind beat our way to Old Point. This was a tedious and tiresome process and we did not reach the wharf at Old Point until after ten o'clock, the steamer having long since passed and gone on to Norfolk. I had therefore to wait for the evening boat to take me to Portsmouth, where the meeting had been called for 8 o'clock p. m. I paid and discharged my Yankee crew and being thoroughly tired out, I made my way to the hotel, and entering inquired if I could get some breakfast and a private room. I met a surly response, "No sir, you can get neither, this hotel is closed."

I attempted to plead my case stating briefly my fatigue and want of sleep, but before I finished he interrupted me by saying, "I told you this hotel was closed. It's a private house." This of course closed the interview, and as there was no other public house in the place, I thought my chance for a meal was pretty slim, but as I walked along one of the streets I passed a shanty, in the porch of which was a fat, good natured black woman, who appeared to possess all the requisites for a good cook according to Dr. George Bagby's standard. I accosted her and asked if she could give me a cup of coffee and something to eat as I had had nothing since the day before. "Certainly sir," she said, "walk in and I will get you up a meal in a few minutes."

She was as good as her word for it was not half an hour before I sat down to a very good meal of coffee, biscuits and fried ham and eggs, nicely cooked. I enjoyed it greatly. The little village was full of negroes who had congregated there during the war. My hostess told me the hotel had been closed because of a row between the commanding officer of Fortress Monroe and the hotel Proprietor, growing out of a sale of liquor to some of his soldiers. Though I watched the wharf closely, there was no steamer or other vessel by which I could reach Norfolk or Portsmouth until the regular Baltimore Steamer called about sunset. I boarded her and landed in Portsmouth after eight o'clock feeling as thoroughly "done up" as I ever was in my life. I thought it was not possible for me to fill my appointment that evening. It was soon known that I was at the Hotel and a committee waited on me to escort me to the place of meeting, saying there was a large crowd out. I asked for a cup of strong coffee and a bath. These were soon obtained and I started with the committee, telling them I could only make an apology to the audience as I felt that there was no speech in me. When we left the hotel, however, we were enlivened by a fine Band belonging, I think, to a Man-of-War in the harbor, which greeted me with the inspiring strains of Dixie so magnificently rendered that it stirred my stagnant blood and the enthusiastic greeting of the large crowd assembled at the Park supplemented the music and aroused me to such a degree that I surprised myself with the animation and vigor of my address which occupied fully two hours. Mr. John Y. Leigh, who had married my niece, had come over from Norfolk and he took me to his home, where I was put into a good bed and speedily lapsed into forgetfulness. The next day being Sunday, I rested quietly in the house all day and by Monday was ready to enter again on my canvass.

I have thus sketched my experience for one week in the very beginning of my campaign. I will not attempt to describe in further detail the particulars of my canvass, but it is worthy of note that the whole people of the State were aroused to a degree unprecedented in my experience. The dangers by which they were confronted were recognized fully, hence the crowds which were in attendance at almost every appointment. Race antagonism for some reason appeals more strongly to the common people than to the better class commonly so called. Hence the ready response when the appeals to race fealty were presented.

When in my canvass, I reached those counties where opposition to the Secession movement had been most pronounced, I always showed my audience that the necessary effect of the adoption of the Constitution was to turn over the political control of the State to the negroes and their Carpet Bag allies. And I told them I cared not a jot whether they were Whigs or Democrats, Unionists or Secessionists, all I asked of them was to show by their votes that they were white men, willing to stand with white men in driving back the horde of blacks and their Carpet Bag allies who wished to rule Virginia. The response to this appeal was always prompt, enthusiastic and decided. It will be remembered that the Convention passed an ordinance that the new Constitution should be submitted to a vote on the second day of June, 1868, being very little more than a month after the adjournment of that historic body. This was done evidently for the purpose of preventing any effective effort to explain to the people the abominations embodied in the proposed organic law, but fortunately for Virginia, General Scofield, at that time commanding Military District No. 1, was a fair-minded and conservative man and refused or omitted to issue the order, necessary to carry out the ordinance of the Convention, hence ample time was allowed for a canvass of the whole State. When I reached Staunton I met General Walker our candidate for Lieutenant Governor, and was pleased to have his assistance in the canvass. We had a good meeting in Staunton, and in order to get to our appointment at Lexington the next day, it was necessary for us to cover at least half of the distance the day of the Staunton meeting. The General and I occupied a carriage, which took us to the Hotel that evening kept by a German, usually known as Johnny Blouth. He was a character in his way. We got there after dark and retired soon after supper. Rising early the next morning, we went into the basement barroom where the General partook of a julep which he seemed to enjoy. While casting my eyes around my attention was attracted by a printed placard hanging on the wall to this effect, "No one permitted to have more than two drinks before breakfast except John Letcher, or a man from Amherst County."

This was something unique and I made bold to ask an explanation. "Well," said he, "at first the only exception to the rule was Shon Letcher, for everybody knows he can drink many times and not hurt him, but some time ago two men stopped here from Amherst County and in the morning called for a drink. I gave it to them and pretty soon they say, "Landlord we want another drink." "They got it and joost before breakfast they want another. I say no, look at the sign."

They say, "What of that, do we look like drunk men."

"No," says I, "I can't say you do."

Den dey say, "An Amherst County man can drink as much as Shon Letcher or any man." And I believes them and so I add to the sign "or a man from Amherst County."

In the light of recent events (1903) it would appear that even as early as 1868, Amherst County had established a reputation in the drinking line which still sticks to her.

After reaching the mountains I had to travel by private conveyance mostly and as I had appointments almost every day and sometimes twice a day I was kept very busy. I spoke in almost every county west of the Blue Ridge including the valley counties. I have since made several canvasses of the State but have never seen anything like such interest displayed as was in that canvass of 1868. After speaking in Wytheville my next appointments were in Grayson, Carroll and Floyd. All without railroad communication. When I started from Wytheville Colonel Joe Graham, the State Senator from that District, joined me on horseback and accompanied me to each of these appointments, introducing me to every man we met no matter of what political party and taking the deepest interest in the discussions. I had never seen the man before in my life and his kindness involved a ride on horseback of at least one hundred and fifty miles and almost or quite a week's absence from his home and business. General James A. Walker, accompanied me in this round, which included also the Counties of Montgomery and Pulaski.

From Russell County I was furnished a spring wagon and a pair of mules and a young man Soule Fannin by name, volunteered to drive me to the appointments in Scott, Lee, Wise and Buchanan. On this trip I visited the remarkable curiosity known as the Natural Tunnel over Stock Creek in the County of Scott, then but little known, but now daily traversed by the trains of the Virginia & Southwest Railroad. At the county seat of Lee, in the extreme Southwestern corner of the State, I met for the first time General Peter Johnston an older brother of General Joseph E. Johnston and found him a man very entertaining in conversation and possessed of a large fund of information on scientific, geographical and geological subjects. That section of the State, I found to be much more fertile than I had expected, and I made a remark to this effect, in conversation with General Johnston, "Why sir," said he, "you haven't seen anything yet. I can carry you to a section of country a few miles hence where in walking over the land you will find yourself involuntarilly looking down at your shoes to see if they are not greasy, the soil is so fat."

When I spoke in Henry County, an old fashioned barbecue had been arranged and as usual attracted a very large crowd. Among them was an old man of great influence in that and some of the adjoining counties. This was "Father Minter," as he was called by every one. He belonged to the Primitive Baptist Church, which had a large membership in that portion of the State. They are a very peculiar people, plain in dress, honest in their transactions; they never go to law with each other, and in fact are very worthy and highly esteemed citizens.

"Father Minter" was accomodated with a seat on the stand and no one was apparently more interested in the speaking. After I concluded he arose, as he said, to make a few remarks. "I have listened carefully," said he, "to the speech of the young brother who has just set down, and I want to say that I don't see how any Christian man can vote for such a Constitution as that. I don't believe any honest man can do it. And I say more than that, I can't fellowship any man who will vote for it, and I want to give notice while I am up that there will be a Sacrament meeting on next Sunday week at— and no man that means to put such a Constitution as that on the people need come to that Sacrament for I won't fellowship him." I have always regarded this as the most effective stump speech I ever listened to.

This reminds me of a very good story that the Hon. Thomas S. Bocock told in connection with this same Father Minter. Mr. Bocock represented the district for several years in the Congress of the United States, and of course had made the acquaintance of Father Minter and was fully aware of the influence he wielded. On one occasion the old preacher was on his way to the City of Baltimore, and as he had to pass through Washington, Congress being in session, thought he would call on his friend Colonel Bocock. He wended his way to the Capitol and sent in his name to Mr. Bocock by one of the pages. The Honorable Member as soon as he received the card rushed out with a cordial greeting for a constituent so highly respected, and after offering to serve him in any matter was informed that he did not ask for anything and merely called to pay his respects as he was passing through on his way to Baltimore. Mr. Bocock thinking to confer a pleasure offered to give him a letter of introduction to Rev. Dr. Fuller a celebrated Baptist Minister in that city, which the old preacher accepted with thanks and after reaching Baltimore delivered in person at Dr. Fuller's study. After the usual civilities were exchanged, and Dr. Fuller ascertained that he would remain in the city over Sunday, he invited him to fill his pulpit on that day. Father Minter at once agreed to do so and appeared at the Church in due time. Dr. Fuller met him and took him in charge installing him with great dignity at the sacred desk. After the usual preliminary services the old gentleman got up, announced his text and began his sermon. After half an hour his audience became restless, after three quarters had passed a good many left the Church, an hour was consumed and still larger numbers quietly withdrew until when he closed after nearly two hours had elapsed, very few were in the building except the two preachers. Father Minter looked at Dr. Fuller and said, "Brother Fuller, I am afraid your people can't stand strong doctrine."

I closed my canvass at Halifax Court-House I think on the fifth of August by which time the hostility of the people towards the Constitution proposed was so pronounced that no fear was felt as to the result of a vote should one be ordered.

I returned to Lynchburg after my arduous labors and resumed my position as editor of the News, but later in the season resigned the position that I might rejoin my wife and children who had gone to Russell, as soon as I left Lynchburg for my speaking tour over the State. When the State Convention met to appoint delegates to the Convention for nominating a President they virtually instructed them to support Horace Greely. General James L. Kemper and I were appointed Electors for the State at large, and in the performance of the duties incident to my position I delivered several speeches in different sections of the State though I can't claim that I was enthusiastic in my support of the ticket, but thinking it was good politics, discharged my duty as Elector at large. For some time his prospects for election were very fine, and many of the Republicans conceded it. Had the election taken place a month before the time fixed there is no doubt such would have been the result, but by a concerted and most enthusiastic effort on the part of the Republicans he was defeated. The very negroes who had before idolized him, at the bidding of their leaders went back on him, and the old fellow was so mortified at his defeat that he died a few months after.

CHAPTER XXIV.

LIFE ON A FARM.

I joined my family in Russell in the early fall of 1868, glad of the opportunity to rest and look after my interests on the farm, which now had attained a certain degree of importance. I soon became deeply interested in my farming operations and as birds were fairly plentiful and Clinch River only a short distance away, with its fine supply of Black Bass, I did not lack for sport to fill my leisure hours. The house was filled with visitors that summer and fall, and as Mr. Lampkin had moved back from Lynchburg, and occupied the storehouse with his large family of boys, the young folks had a gay time. They could get up a dance any day on short notice, as there were two or three fiddlers on the place, who with the piano to aid them, furnished a pretty good article of dance music. The piano itself was a great source of wonder and admiration to the girls and boys from the mountains, who were frequent visitors to see for themselves if half what they heard about it was true. When my wife moved over to Russell while I was occupied in my canvass she took the piano and most of her furniture including the library with her, also, the cook Nancy who had been reared by her mother, and her husband Sam, who was a pretty good carpenter and two grown sons who worked on the farm. So we were pretty comfortably fixed. I had a blacksmith hired, who rented a cabin on the farm, a good shop and tools where all the farm work and horse shoeing was done. Had a saw mill put up to furnish lumber for fencing and building purposes, to which a grist mill was this year added and a miller employed, who with his family lived on the place. The blacksmith was named Abednago Harris, and was himself an unending source of amusement to me. He was very shrewd, and had a fine sense of humor. We lived here in regular country style, grew our own wool for the manufacture of men's clothes, which was spun and woven on the farm, raised our own beef, mutton, and pork, cured our own bacon, grew our own bread stuffs, in short, except for the purchase of groceries and clothing our family expenses were small. I found by experience that it was better to hire only two or three men to work regularly and when a larger number were required, to hire them for a day or two at a time. For such work as planting corn, harvesting grain, shucking corn, and making hay, I could always get from the mountains from five to ten men and complete these jobs in a day or two. Feeding cattle during the winter is probably the hardest work on a grass farm, and in cold and stormy weather requires the personal supervision of the owner, otherwise the cattle are liable to suffer. When the winters are unusually long and severe the food supply is liable to run short in the early spring, then if no food can be bought the grazier has to divide his cattle into small lots, and board them out around the neighborhood. In former days, I have been told, it was not unusual when food gave out entirely to turn the cattle out in the woods, accompanied by axe men to cut down lynn trees, the smaller limbs of which are soft and contain a good deal of nutritive matter, which the half starved animals will speedily devour. I have never seen this done myself, but am credibly informed improvident cattle men in former days had to resort to this expedient not unfrequently, and it was a unique but pitiful spectacle to see the cattle lowing and running after any man they saw with an axe on his shoulder.

There were several sugar camps on the place, and after my family came over Mrs. Withers and the children were all very anxious to go into the sugar making business, and I was nothing loath as I had never witnessed the operation. Accordingly "Uncle Sam" was directed to prepare a number of "sap troughs," and "spiles" during the early winter, ready for the "run" which usually begins in February. The fluid which runs from the trees, though called "sap," is really not sap at all, for when the spring has sufficiently advanced to start the sap proper, sugar making has to stop as the water which runs from the trees if mixed with sap will no longer crystallize into sugar no matter how long it may be boiled. The "troughs" are small trays made by hollowing out blocks of wood, each capable of holding from a quart to a half gallon. The "spiles" are tubes usually made of elder with the pith forced out. The "tapping" of the trees is done with an auger with which a hole is bored in the body of the tree an inch or two in depth, and the spiles inserted into holes. Under each spile a trough is fixed to receive the dripping water. The amount of this varies greatly with the weather, if cloudy and warm, the flow is small, if the nights are clear and frosty followed by a bright sunny day the flow is much greater.

Preparation for sugar making begins with the construction of a Camp. From four to six large iron or copper kettles are fixed over a flue constructed of stones, their bottoms being exposed to the heat of the fires lighted in the flues. A shed is built over this to protect them from the weather and a supply of dry wood provided to keep up a regular moderate fire. Persons provided with ordinary water buckets visit the trees as often as may be necessary to empty the troughs into the buckets, and when they are filled and they are taken to the camp and emptied into barrels. This water is clear and possesses a sweet and pleasant flavor. The percentage of sugar it holds in solution is small, as it is usually estimated that it takes eight bushels or sixty four gallons to yield a pound of crystallized sugar. The whole process consists in evaporating the water by slow boiling until it is reduced to a syrup of proper consistence to be determined by the expert manager. During the boiling process the water is constantly dipped from the first kettle always the largest into the next in size, until it is ready to be "stirred off." This is the most critical part of the process, if not carefully conducted, the syrup is liable to burn, which of course spoils the product. If the boiling is stopped too soon the syrup will not granulate into sugar and is then only "tree molasses." During the whole procedure, it must be constantly stirred with a wooden paddle prepared for the purpose and is frequently "tried" by dropping a little into water and as soon as the proper degree of concentration is reached it is dipped out into cups, bowls, pans or other receptacles, and left to granulate, which completes the process of manufacture. It is necessary that the boiling should be continuous to secure the best results, hence some hands have to be up most of the night and this novel experience was always attractive to the children and I have even known their mother to remain at the Camp until long after midnight. Sugar making is the great festival of the mountain people, it beats hog killing, harvest or corn shucking and is greatly enjoyed by the young people of both sexes who at camp during the boiling process enjoy a favorable opportunity to arrange their love affairs in a satisfactory way, usually ending in marriage soon after. I have thus described in detail the various steps of this industry as it has almost become a lost art now. The sugar orchards on the farm I occupied and which were the source of so much pleasure and enjoyment to the children, have long since disappeared under the axe of the scientific farmer, who stands ready to prove by figures which can't lie, that the ground dedicated to sugar orchards will yield a much larger revenue if well set in blue grass and that the operatives who make "tree sugar" could at other employment earn wages sufficient to purchase ten times the quantity of "standard granulated." My children who were with me during these years, though most of them are now grandmothers never cease to recall the pleasant memories connected with the days they spent in Russell, and all agree that never before or since have they enjoyed life more.

That fall I could not get a satisfactory offer for my cattle, some of which were not first-class, and I concluded to join with Mr. Higginbotham, a wealthy grazier of Tazewell County, and drive our cattle to Baltimore. Dr. Carter was very anxious to make the trip, so I put him in charge, as Mr. Higginbotham who was an experienced dealer, proposed to accompany the drove himself. They started about the middle of October and drove through the Shenandoah Valley of Virginia, where they disposed of the "top cattle" to Mr. John G. Meem, of the "Mount Airy" Farm, at a satisfactory price, carried the residue of the cattle to Baltimore and sold out there. The result on the whole was a moderate profit, but the expense and loss of weight of the cattle was greater than when shipped by rail.

Mrs. Withers had an attack of illness that winter which seriously threatened her life and for a while alarmed us all greatly. Dr. Carter was absent on a business trip to Tazewell, and my wife's condition was so critical that I thought it necessary to send a special messenger for him, and James Lampkin kindly offered to go. I have never ceased to appreciate the kindness of heart which prompted this offer, and have always regarded it rather as a tribute to my wife's good qualities than to personal friendship to me. The night was very cold, it was snowing like lint, and there was a ride of sixteen miles before him. My wife always believed that snow storm was sent as a special providence for her benefit, and attributed to it her recovery. She was parched with fever, and an intolerable thirst, which water did not quench, but when she heard it was snowing she eagerly asked for some and I gave her as much as she demanded and evidently with good effect. When Dr. Carter reached home about daybreak, she was in better condition than when the messenger left. I don't know whether I ought to tell what follows, but I will venture to do so that I may record the opportunity offered me of reciprocating James Lampkin's kindness to me and mine. He would at times take too much liquor, and on the occasion in question, partly, I think, in fun, and with the object of alarming his family, got hold of a vial of strychnine, and dipping out a considerable dose on his knife blade, swallowed it in the presence of his father and brothers, who had no idea he was in earnest when he threatened to take it. The two houses were not more than one hundred yards apart, and one of the boys ran up for me, telling what had occurred. I ran down at once and by the prompt use of emetics and stimulants, in the course of a few hours relieved him. He had, however, several severe spasms, and was greatly alarmed. But for the prompt treatment he received, the dose would probably have proven fatal.

My wife continued feeble, nervous, and low-spirited for some weeks after her attack. She said that the cook didn't prepare food to suit her, and as her diet consisted mainly of mush and milk, I told her I knew that I could make cornmeal mush as well as any cook in christendom, so I had a skillet brought in her room and prepared it before her eyes, and, fortunately, it met with her approval, and I continued to perform this service for several days. When her appetite improved, I went out and killed a good lot of partridges, which I hung up in the porch, and cooked one for her every day by hanging it before an open wood fire by a string, and basting it while cooking with fresh butter and pepper. For more than two weeks she ate nothing except what I cooked for her. So the experience acquired by the camp fires in my hunting and fishing excursions stood me in good stead. Hers was the only case of serious illness we had in the family during our residence in Russell County, and during the whole of it Mrs. Lampkin was as unwearied in kindness and attention as if she had been her sister. She was indeed a most excellent woman.

Hospitality to strangers is not one of the crowning virtues of the people of Southwest Virginia, at least of those living on or near the public roads. It is difficult for a stranger, traveling over the roads which traverse that section to obtain accommodations for the night, as there are few or no houses of public entertainment outside the towns and larger villages. I lived on a road much traveled, namely the turnpike from Lebanon in Russell County, to Jeffersonville in Tazewell, a distance of thirty-five miles and there was no house of entertainment between the two points except at Liberty Hall, about twelve miles from my residence. As a consequence, we were frequently asked to take in sojourners for a night and occasionally for a midday meal. We never refused any one, and consequently had a good many amusing experiences with these casual visitors. Amongst the many odd people who thus visited us, as I now recall them, I am disposed to award the palm to an elderly visitor who rode in one afternoon about sunset, and walking up to the door, asked if "I would give shelter for the night to a poor preacher." I answered jestingly, "I suppose so, as I am not in the habit of refusing a night's lodging to any traveler, and I reckon a preacher isn't much worse than other men." He looked at me curiously for a moment, and I added, "Come in, the servant will be here in a few moments to take your horse to the stable."

"Oh," said he, "I wouldn't put you to that trouble, but will attend to him myself."

"As you please," said I, interpreting his offer as a desire to see for himself that his horse was properly fed. "Go through that gate and you will see the stable and as you pass the corn house, take what you wish for him and you will find hay in the stable."

He thanked me, and took his horse to the stable. When I went in my wife asked who the visitor was. I replied, "By his own account a poor preacher."

She said, "I would suppose he was, judging from his looks."

He was very dirty and travel-stained, and his face evidently had not seen water for some time. In a short time he returned to the house, and I invited him into the sitting room where there was a fire, the evening being cool. I asked to what place he was journeying.

"Oh, to no particular place," he said, "I'm one of the two witnesses mentioned in the eleventh chapter of Revelations."

"Then," said I, "you have a long journey before you."

"Yes," said he, "and as I am a blacksmith, as I journey I shoe a few horses when I can, and preach the Gospel."

I thought to myself that this might account for his disreputable appearance, as the "two witnesses" are described as being clad in sackcloth, but I said no more on the subject. Supper was soon announced, and as we reached the table, without any suggestion from me, he pronounced a very long grace in a very loud voice which surprised the children a good deal. Returning to the sitting room, after talking on commonplace matters for a while, he turned to me and asked if I had any objection to his holding "family duty."

"None whatever," said I, "it is my custom to have family prayer both night and morning."

"Then," said he, "you are a professor, I suppose, what church do you belong to?"

"To the Episcopal Church," said I.

"To what?" said he in apparent surprise.

"The Protestant Episcopal," I repeated.

"What's them?" said he, "I never heard of 'em before. I have seen Baptists and Methodists and a few Presbyterians, but I never hearn of any sich church as yourn."

"There are few members of my Church in this county," said I. "I think I and my family are the only ones."

I told some of the children to bring him a Bible, but he declined it (I think it doubtful if he could read), but shutting his eyes and throwing his head back he broke out into a wonderful hymn entirely unknown to me and sang several verses,

Then kneeled down and prayed in such stentorian tones that he might have been heard a mile, emphasizing it, moreover, pretty regularly with loud clapping of his horny hands, and the turmoil so alarmed my little girl, Mary, that she commenced crying and had to be taken out of the room. The negroes from the kitchen came running to the door to find out what was the matter, and take it all in all, it was the most remarkable season of "family duty" I had ever known. Some of the larger girls, after prayers were over, asked him to sing again, which he did at once, not only singing hymns, but a long and puzzling ditty on worldly matters, of which I can remember only the chorus to this effect,

> "When you go up to Con-ge-rus
> To make the laws for you and us—"

The children remembered a good deal more of it for a long while, but all is now forgotten. He left after breakfast the next morning, after thanking me for his entertainment, and I never heard of him again.

Early the next year, having a pretty good number of cattle on hand, I rented from Mr. Aaron Hendricks, the "Rich Mountain," a fine grass farm on the summit of Rich Mountain, for which I agreed to pay five hundred dollars, and "thereby hangs a tale," which I had as well tell now as at any time, though I will have to ignore chronology to some extent. Mr. Alexander Stuart, of Saltville, later in the year purchased Mr. Hendricks' farm on Cedar Creek and also the Rich Mountain, and as he was a creditor of Mr. Hendricks', wished to secure to himself the payment of my rent bond when due. Other creditors were also pressing to do the same thing. I was served with several notices of garnishment and summoned to court to answer questions. I appeared accordingly, and when questioned admitted my indebtedness, and avowed my readiness to pay into court, or to the party entitled under the decree of the court the amount of the bond as soon as it matured. Litigation continued, and finally the court decided that Mr. Stuart had the best right to the rent, and instructed me to pay it to him, which I did, taking his receipt therefor. Of course I considered that this payment ended the matter, but some two or three years after this, I was astonished by having the sheriff present an execution sent to him for collection from Russell Court, with instructions to levy at once and make the five hundred dollars with costs and interest from 1869. I could not understand what it meant, but got out an injunction to stay the execution until the matter could be investigated. I wrote at once to Mr. Stuart and he promptly replied that I need give myself no uneasiness as he would attend to it. As was subsequently ascertained, a certain Judge Burns was one of the counsel employed by one of the other claimants for this rent and noting that Mr. Stuart's counsel after obtaining the decree had neglected to have the cause stricken from the docket, took advantage of the oversight, and called up the case after I left the county, and in due process of law obtained judgment, there being no defense, had the execution issued and sent over to Wythe to be collected. I always thought this man should have been disbarred for his attempted swindle, for he knew personally that the money had been paid for the rent, and that not one cent was due and the Court of Appeals so determined without a moment's hesitation.

Mr. Alexander Stuart invested largely in some of the finest farm land in Russell County during this year. In addition to the Hendricks farm he purchased of my near neighbor, Mr. Henry Smith, his farm of twenty-five hundred acres, also of Mr. Lampkin the farm on which I lived, of about three thousand acres, including the Doubles Place, and two other farms of smaller area. Messrs. Lampkin and Smith concluded to move to California the next year. Mr. Stuart, of course, after his purchase, being entitled to the annual rental, soon proposed to buy out my lease, but I declined to sell, as I had no other business to which I could turn for the support of my family.

THE DEATH OF GENERAL LEE.

The whole country was startled and the South greatly shocked by the announcement of General Lee's death in October, 1870. It occurred just before the Annual meeting and Fair of the Virginia Agricultural Society in Richmond of which my friend Major W. T. Sutherland was at that time President. In consequence of this great calamity there was some talk of postponing the meeting but this was deemed inexpedient and the President in his opening address made feeling and appropriate reference to the sad event. This meeting of the Society was made memorable by the presence of the President of the late Confederacy, Mr. Jefferson Davis who had been freed from Fortress Monroe and the cruel atrocities of General Miles only a few days before. I have rarely had my feelings more stirred than when I unexpectedly met with him on the stand. Mr. Davis in his palmy days had never been a prime favorite of mine and certainly I had no special cause to admire him, but the indescribable cruelties to which he had been obliged to submit while a prisoner at Fortress Monroe as the vicarious representative of the Confederates had appealed so strongly to the sympathies and sense of justice of the Southern people as to disarm entirely the prejudices which many felt towards him and to condone all his faults. I felt this to the full and never hear his name mentioned now that these memories do not recur to my mind.

At that time it was arranged to hold Memorial Services in honor of General Lee at a subsequent date, and the committee of arrangements did me the honor of selecting me as one of the speakers on that occasion. When the day came the speakers were confronted by a most distinguished audience embracing not only the chief dignitaries of the State but almost every surviving officer of high rank in the Confederate Service. President Davis' tribute to General Lee was exceedingly touching and appropriate. Indeed all the speakers seemed to vie with each other in doing honor to the great Chieftain, whose name stands today throughout the civilized world as the synonym of all that is great and good in humanity.

It was at this meeting that I met General Dabney H. Maury, for the first time since we parted at the University of Virginia almost thirty years before. I recognized him while I was speaking and as soon as I was through, went to him and gave and received a hearty greeting. I saw him frequently afterwards and we served together, for years on the Executive Committee of the Society of the Army of Northern Virginia in which organization he always took deep interest. He paid me more than one visit at my home at "Hedgefield" where he was a great favorite with every member of the family. I do not now remember a more charming talker or a better raconteur and his varied experience on the plains in Indian warfare and in the War with Mexico furnished inexhaustible stores of anecdote and incident. He received a Diplomatic appointment as Minister to Venezuela or some of the Central American Republics. After his return he spent some time in Richmond, but died a few years since at the residence of his son Dabney H. Maury, Jr., in Illinois. A most genial and delightful companion he was, and there are few like him left.

Parties had been very quiet during the winter in Virginia. Nothing was said about the Constitution or the reconstruction of the State. Subsequently it was developed that a self constituted "Committee of Nine" had undertaken to negotiate an arrangement with General Grant, intended to secure the admission of Virginia into the Union, which General Grant was greatly desirous of effecting before his term of office expired. I was not consulted at all in the matter as I think I should have been in view of the fact that I was the nominee of the people of Virginia for the office of Governor. But the movement was kept quiet until all preliminary arrangements were perfected. The "Committee of Nine," or one of them rather, told me that General Grant advised that the ticket which I headed should be withdrawn, and that a ticket should be put forward of "Liberal Republicans" pledged to oppose the arbitrary policy of the Radical Party and if that were done he would use his influence with Congress to secure the passage of a law authorizing a separate vote on two or three of the most objectionable features of the Underwood Constitution, and also a vote on the adoption of the residue, of that instrument.

Mr. Gilbert C. Walker, of New York, but now a resident of Norfolk, was selected to head this ticket, Mr. John F. Lewis as Lieutenant Governor, and Colonel Taylor of Christiansburg, as Attorney General. When the scheme was first made public there was much excitement, and a decided division of sentiment. I received many letters on the subject, some begging me to withdraw and leave the field to Walker, others insisting that I should stand my ground, and some of these were from the foremost men in the State. I came to the conclusion after mature and careful deliberation, that as I had been nominated by a Convention of the people it would be a betrayal of the trust imposed on me, and a desertion of my post to withdraw, unless requested so to do by a State Convention. The men who manipulated this scheme opposed the call of the Convention at first, but ultimately gave in as the only way of harmonizing the party, and a Convention was called to meet in the city of Richmond. A good many able speeches were made on both sides of the question, but from what I saw I was satisfied that Walker would be run at all hazards, in which event it was clear that General Wells, the Radical candidate, would be elected, if I continued in the field, and as both my colleagues on the ticket favored withdrawal, I also consented.

I returned to my home in Russell pretty well disgusted with politics, and devoted myself more closely to my farm. I had now a large quantity of meadow, and I cut every foot of it myself with one pair of mules. I was much fascinated with hay making, of which I had known little in Eastern Virginia. When stacking season came on, a fine stacker, who had agreed to aid in putting up the hay, failed to appear. I had an idle hand, the one who came to throw up the hay, and I asked him if he couldn't stack.

"Oh, yes," said he, "I have put up a good many stacks but don't call myself a number one hand at it."

"Well," said I, "take your fork and I'll throw up to you."

"Did you ever try throwing up hay?" said, he, looking at me rather quizzically.

"No," said I, "but I know I can do it."

"Well," he said, "you'll find it middling hard work."

We commenced the stack, and for some time I got on pretty well, not finding it as hard work as I expected, but after a while when the stack got much higher than my head, it became more and more difficult to raise a large fork full of hay to the stacker, and before the stack was finished I was as tired as any man ought to be. When we got ready for the next stack, I had come to the conclusion that it would be much better for me to learn to stack than to throw up. I told my helper that I would put up the next stack, and he could throw up. He laughed and said he was not surprised, as he thought I would get tired of throwing up. My first stack was not a very symmetrical one, but the next was a decided improvement and I stuck to it until I became as good a stacker as any one. Indeed, the next season I put up the largest and most beautiful stack of hay in the county, containing nearly two hundred large hay cocks. It was not a rick but a pyramidal stack.

The election came on in the fall and the clauses of the Constitution on which a separate vote was allowed were stricken out by a vote, if I remember aright, of about one hundred and twenty-five thousand against about eighty-five thousand for retaining them. The rest of the Constitution was adopted by a vote approaching unanimity, though I voted to strike out all I could and then against the residue. It was not a great while after this that the County Government was reorganized and supervisors elected. The gentlemen who arranged the four districts of the county were able to so run the lines of division as to throw nearly all the negro vote and that of the white Republicans into the Rose Dale District, in which I resided. As there was a Republican majority of at least three to one in the district, I had no idea that any Conservative would be brought out, and consequently was surprised to hear that there had been a meeting held and it had been determined that I should be voted for. A gentleman named Smith, a Republican, was a candidate and actively canvassed the district, boasting how badly he would beat the "Governor," as he called me. I positively refused to accept the nomination and told all inquirers that I was not a candidate and did not want that or any other office. When the day of election came, I did not go to the voting place and was informed that night that I had been elected Supervisor by a large majority. I expressed my astonishment, and was told that "Old Sam," a negro who lived near me and whose influence over the negroes of the neighborhood was supreme, had told them all to vote for Colonel Withers, that he was the only large land holder in the county who would let a negro have pasturage for his cow, and as some leading white Republicans were also living on my place as tenants, they actively exerted themselves in my behalf, with the result I have mentioned. Though I had always truly said I did not want the office, I did not feel that it would be right, under the circumstances, to refuse to serve the people who had voted for me, so I accepted and attended every meeting of the Board as long as I lived in the county. I learned on inquiry at the first meeting of the Board, that the court-house and other county buildings were not insured. I made every effort to induce the Board to insure them, but did not then succeed. I brought the matter up at every meeting and finally attained my object and secured a policy of insurance for twenty thousand dollars on the buildings. Three years had not elapsed before the court-house and all were burned, and but for the insurance the county would have been unable for years to replace them.

Mr. Charles Smith, the largest grazier, and the best judge of cattle in the county, lived about eight miles above me on a farm of seven thousand acres of fine grass land. He was an old bachelor, a brother of Mrs. Dale Carter. He generally got the highest price for his cattle, usually a little more than the other graziers of the county, but this year, for some cause, did not sell and concluded to carry his stock over another year. One day he came to see me and surprised me by offering to purchase for me as many young cattle as I wished, as he had none to buy for himself. I highly appreciated and gratefully accepted his offer, as he was admittedly superior in judgment of cattle to any one in that whole section. When I recall the very great expenditure of labor and of time required to purchase a lot of two year old cattle, I can not sufficiently appreciate the kindness which involved an examination of numerous herds, not only in Russell, but in several adjoining counties. In due time he started out, and in a few weeks reported that he had bought the number I wanted, most of them in the county of Washington, and that all were to be delivered a certain day in October at the farm of Mr. Robert Preston, near Abingdon. I had always been told that Charles Smith knew by sight every individual head of stock on his place, and could tell without counting when one or more were missing, but I had not believed it possible. I was given proof of the fact in connection with these same cattle that he purchased for me. When I went to Washington County with my hands to receive the young cattle, there was one in low condition, though evidently of high grade. I feared it would not be strong enough to stand the drive across the Clinch Mountain, so I struck up a trade with Mr. Preston for one of his, which was in better condition, but not so well bred. We got our cattle safely home the second day, and just before reaching there met Mr. Smith on the road. He passed through the herd of about seventy-five yearlings without any pause, and apparently with little notice, and when we met, said, "Well, Colonel, I see you are getting your cattle in."

"Yes," said I, "and I want to thank you again for the trouble you have taken in buying them."

"Oh, that's all right, but there is one in the lot that I never bought."

"Why, which one is that?" said I, pretending surprise.

"I never bought that white yearling with one black ear," said he.

And this was the very one I had traded for, and he recognized it as a stranger the moment his eyes fell upon it. I concluded he fully deserved the reputation he enjoyed.

The power of accurately estimating the weight of an animal on the hoof is, of course, only attainable after close observation and study of all the elements that enter into the matter. But assiduous study will bring the knowledge to a person of ordinary capacity. I sold my cattle this year to a dealer from Washington County named Grey, who had been in the business for many years, and was a good judge of cattle. They were to be delivered in October. I had them in lots as there was considerable difference in weight. They were sold by weight. As the time of delivery drew near, I found that I would be obliged to leave home for a few days on a trip to the East, but knowing that Grey might come for the cattle, I left with James Royall written instructions to weigh the cattle, unless Grey would accept the estimates I had made. I gave him in writing the lowest average weight of each lot which I was willing to take. When I returned home I pretty soon inquired if Mr. Grey had been for the cattle.

"Yes," said James Royall, "he came the day after you left."

"Did you guess the weights or have to go to the scales?"

"Well," said he laughing, "it was the strangest thing I ever knew. As you supposed, he proposed to agree on the weight if we could, and mentioned what he thought would be about right.

I told him he would have to do better than that, and we chaffered a while, until I told him that you had left with me the estimate you had made, with instructions to weigh them if he would not agree to it, and handed him the paper. He looked at them and said, 'Of course we will weigh them. I don't know what the Colonel could have been thinking about, they will not weigh anything like his estimate.' So after dinner we drove them down to the cattle scales, and would you believe it? The large lot weighed an average of three-quarters of a pound less than your estimate, and the small ones a pound and a quarter more. That certainly beat any guessing I ever heard of, and I had a good laugh at Grey, who said he could not understand it."

CHAPTER XXV.

ON THE WATERS OF SANDY.—FUN ON SANDY.

I think I have talked enough about cattle and farming, so I will relieve the monotony by giving an account of a trip I made to the waters of the Big Sandy on a fishing and hunting trip in company with two of my neighbors, Major John Smith and Ira Reynolds, the last an old man of sixty-six years, and an enthusiastic fisherman. Major John Smith was also fond of the sport and was well acquainted with a man living on the Pound fork of Sandy, named Willis, who had invited him over to hunt and fish. According to agreement, I started after an early dinner with fishing tackle, gun, some ground coffee, sugar, and a coffee pot. I was joined in Lebanon by Ira Reynolds and with little delay we rode on to Major Smith's home, on Clinch River, near the mouth of Dump's Creek, which we reached by sunset. He lived with his wife's mother, who did not give us a very hearty welcome, I thought, but afterwards concluded it was only her accustomed manner, as she was one of those lugubrious natures, always pessimistic, and mourning over present or anticipated troubles. She gave us, however, a good supper and before bed time got out her Bible and asked if either of us was a professor. Old Ira spoke up at once, and answered, "Yes ma'am, the Colonel is."

She handed the Bible to me and asked me to have prayers. I tried to excuse myself by saying that I had prayers in my own house, but not in the houses of others, and added that as evidently she was accustomed to the duty she should as usual hold prayers herself. But no! she said it was true she "had it to do," but it was always a great cross and she avoided it when she could. I thought this a curious conception of the duty, but to save further discussion, took the Bible, read a chapter, and prayed. She was evidently conciliated by the act, and gave us an early and good breakfast in the morning. John Smith put a large chunk of fat bacon in one end of a sack, and half a bushel of salt in the other end, swung it across his saddle, and we started off in good shape for Willis'. We crossed the Clinch River, followed up Dump Creek to its head, and across the mountain, descending on the Buchanan side, thence down Russell's Fork to a place called the "Sand Licks," where we stopped to get dinner with a man named Jim Colly, who knew both Smith and Reynolds, and treated us with hospitable kindness. He took pay for our horse feed, but would accept nothing for our dinner. He was the son of Dave Colly, a celebrated bear hunter in his day, of whom Ira Reynolds told this story as we traveled on:

"Dave Colly," said he, "often boasted that he could whip a bear in a fair fight, and on one occasion, when a party was out hunting, the dogs brought a bear to bay. When the hunters came up, one of them rallied Dave Colly on his oft-repeated boast that he could whip a bear, and told him here was a fine chance to prove it. Dave had had a drink or two, and unwilling to stand the chaffing of the party, said he could do it and would show them he could. So the dogs were held and Dave grappled the bear with no weapon whatever. He had on a pair of heavy cow-skin boots, and trusted to blows with his fist, choking and kicking with his heavy boots. After a long struggle he succeeded in killing the animal, but when the fight was ended he had on nothing except his boots, and was marked all over with wounds from the teeth and claws of the bear."

With stories such as these we beguiled the tedium of the way until about sunset, as we passed a cabin, we stopped to enquire the distance and the road to Am Willis'. The man told us it was about five miles, and said, "When you get to a cabin in an old field half a mile further on, take the path to the left leading down the hollow and it will carry you there."

Said I, "Is there any other road that may put us out, for it will soon be dark."

"None," said he, "if you turn down the hollow to the left as I told you, you can't go anywhere else."

We found it even so, for after entering the hollow, which led to a small stream, we could do nothing but follow that stream, until we reached a road near the place of our destination.

It was now after dark, and as we rode up we were greeted

by a chorus of dogs and children, who thronged the door. To the question if Am Willis lived there, a woman's voice answered, "Yes, light, and the boys will show you where to put your horses."

We dismounted, unsaddled our horses, and guided by some boys, led them to a pen where they were fed with corn and fodder. We had asked the lady of the house if Mr. Willis was at home and had an affirmative reply, with the remark, "He has just stepped out a piece, but will be back presently. Come right in." We walked in, and the good woman instantly began to prepare our supper, a meal which the family had already dispatched. The house was a good-sized cabin with one room on the ground floor, and another above. There were at least seven or eight children, one daughter grown, and another almost as large. Mrs. Willis soon had biscuits baked, coffee made, and some venison stewed. We did full justice to our supper. After supper, wondering why Mr. Willis did not appear, I asked where he had gone.

She replied, "Well, one of the neighbor women died today, and as they had nothing to shroud her, Am stepped over to the store to get some cloth. He'll be back twixt midnight and day."

"Why, how far is the store?" said I.

"About fifteen miles," was the reply.

Pretty soon preparations were made for sleeping, which was a less difficult matter than usual, as there was a loft, and the visitors were quartered there in large feather beds, of which there were three in the room. We slept the sleep of the just, but I heard some stir below, caused by the return of our host "twixt midnight and day," from his "step of fifteen miles."

When we came down in the morning Am Willis gave us a hearty welcome, said he was very glad to see us, and proffered his services for any sport we fancied. He was a small man and noticeably lame, evidently from a badly adjusted fracture of the thigh, but stepped about very quickly, arranging for our fishing excursion. By his advice we left our horses at his house and started on foot for the river, which was not far off. When we reached it the term river seemed a misnomer, as there was no appearance of water in it. The bed of the stream was nothing but a bed of rocks and stones through which the water could be heard percolating below, but it was not visible. In the fall after summer droughts and evaporation the stream is an alternation of shallows and deep pools, hence the reputation it has acquired as a fine stream for fishing. All the fish in it are concentrated in the deep pools and of course overstocking the water, and they soon devour the small fish and minnows, and then, ravenously hungry, they make a dash for the bait when it strikes the water, which is as clear as crystal. And the fisherman can see the streaks made in the water by the various game fish converging from all directions to the bait. There are no trout in the stream but an abundance of black bass, pike, salmon, so called, but properly salmon trout, perch, some gar and blue cats. One difficulty was met with everywhere, that of procuring live minnows for bait, but Am Willis soon had lots of boys and men industriously engaged in dragging the branches for them, and thus we were kept pretty well supplied. We had fairly good sport, caught our fish, cooked and ate them with relish, and returned to Willis' at night. I will here remark that this house was considered "headquarters" during our whole trip, though sometimes we were not there for several days together, but when we came, our welcome was always cordial, our host as ready to take any trouble for our accommodation or pleasure as if we were the dearest friends, or nearest relatives he had in the world.

We had agreed to try the "Breaks" the next day, and thence to cross the Cumberland Mountain and descend on the Kentucky side until we struck the river, not far this side of Piketon, and then fish back to the foot of the breaks again. A little more preparation was required, so Mr. Willis by breakfast time had several men in waiting to accompany us, carry our baggage, catch bait, or do anything else needed. It was the special province of one selected for his trustiness and reliability to carry the jug of liquor, which they regarded as an indispensable requisite, and as long as any whiskey remained in it they would all follow. When the supply was exhausted, the bearer would report the jug empty, and we would hand him a dollar for the purpose of getting it replenished. He would at once look around and if he saw no smoke he would trot up the side of the mountain until he could get a good outlook, and then start for the nearest smoke, for smoke indicated a distillery, and it would not be long before he would be back with a jug full, hot from the still. Revenue officers in that country were then unknown, and it was a long time after before they ventured to molest the people of Sandy. I will state right here before I forget it, that Am Willis' was the only house at which we ate that furnished us bread made of flour or meal *ground in a mill*. The month being September, the corn was too hard for roasting ears, but not sufficiently hard for grinding, hence it was manufactured into what was universally known as "gritted" bread, a corruption of grated, as it is made by grating the corn on a large tin grater by drawing the ear rapidly back and forth until all the grain is scraped off the cob, then collecting the product and making it into a pone. When hot and freshly baked, and a man is really hungry, it can be enjoyed, but when in the early morning it is offered you cold, it is not a tempting morsel. No one, however, could criticise, when the best they had was offered with such free-hearted hospitality. The people are typical mountaineers, peculiar in many respects, but kind-hearted and hospitable to those they like and who understand their ways. Frank and entirely unaffected, full of fun, and with a fine sense of humor they greatly entertained and amused me around our camp fire at night, while narrating hunting adventures, and unconsciously bringing out the multifarious superstitions with which they are imbued. I saw among them men of fair education and more than ordinary intelligence, but none doubted the power of certain persons to place a "spell" on a rifle so that its owner could not possibly strike a deer, bear or other game, until the "spell" was removed by some one possessing occult powers greater than those of the man who had laid the spell. The idea was phrased in this way—"There's nine ways of casting a spell, but ten ways of taking it off." When I laughed and ridiculed the idea, they looked at me with genuine pity in their eyes, that any man of common sense could doubt a fact so well established by the experience of every man.

"Well," said I, "I will give you leave to employ your most skilful spell-binder to spell my gun, provided only that he shall keep his hands off it, and if I don't kill the first deer that gives me a fair shot, I'll treat the crowd."

They only smiled in pity at my ignorance and folly. Not a man of them would on any account throw a bone or a hoof or any part of a deer in the water while butchering it.

"THE BREAKS."

"The Breaks," so called, is a long, deep canyon where the Pound fork of Sandy River breaks through the Cumberland Mountains, and is really a great curiosity, though entirely unknown at the time of my visit to any except the people in the immediate vicinity. When I returned from this trip, I wrote an account of the "Breaks," which was published, and from which Mr. Edward Pollard in the "Virginia Tourist," quotes the following passage, with this prefatory paragraph:

"This scene from the bed of the stream has been thus described by one who, like ourselves—and even beyond those routes which we have considered accessible to the ordinary traveler and which, therefore, limit this work—has sought out the beauties of Virginia scenery.

" 'Bold and perpendicular walls of sandstone rise in naked majesty hundreds of feet above, while the waters which chafe and madden at their base are filled and choked by the shattered fragments which have been riven from their summit. Here and there the hand of nature, the great restorer, has softened the asperities of the scene and clothed in verdure and beauty both beetling cliff and precipitous ravine. Here the spruce towers in somber majesty, there the laurel and ivy throw their dark mantle over the spectral rocks and anon the bramble and muscadine mingle foliage and fruit in wild and graceful beauty crowning with tender tendrils and purple berries some tempest-riven or lightning-blasted trunk. For several miles this wild and savage scene stretches in unbroken continuity. Soon the majestic outline of the colossal "Chimney" arrests our gaze, as it lifts its savage head hundreds of feet into the deep blue sky above the gigantic rocks, the falling cliffs and shattered arches of antediluvian architecture.

" 'He who attempts to tread the mazes of this wondrous canyon will find it no child's play, and even with the aid of experienced guides we found it a laborious task, though relieved by frequent pauses to fish in inviting pools whose deep blue waters seemed to claim a "cast," and rarely was the cast in vain. And many a fine bass thus added to our basket gave assurance of a good meal when the outlet should be reached.'"

I omitted to say that as a necessary prelude to entering the Breaks, we were advised by our host, Willis, to ride as far up the mountain as "Pound Sol Mullins'" who would take care of our horses until we could get back. His house, we found to be the last dwelling on the trail leading across the mountain, which was nothing but a foot-path at best, and beyond Mullins' was scarcely distinguishable. Am Willis accompanied us thus far to introduce us to "Pound Sol," and invoke for us his kindly offices. These were promptly pledged when thus vouched for, and he readily promised that his son, "Pres" should see to the watering and feeding of our horses. His two daughters gave us some dinner and "Pound Sol" himself volunteered to accompany us through the Breaks and aid us with our baggage. Evidently incited thereto by the jug which constituted, as usual, an important part of our outfit. He was a nephew of Jim Mullins, who was in his time a man of note, as he was the maker of the "Sandy River dollars," which fifty years before constituted an important article of traffic. He was a blacksmith by trade and with the help of a negro man he manufactured and put into circulation dollars and half dollars so artistically made that it was exceedingly difficult to distinguish them from the genuine coin from the government mint. I have heard that their only defect was too great brittleness, as they could be broken by a blow with a hammer. But in weight, appearance, and resonance they were identical with the genuine and it was always believed that Mullins made them of silver or some of its amalgams, which he procured somewhere in the mountains near him. He sold them at from fifty to seventy-five cents in the dollar, and drove a brisk trade, as merchants and traders of good repute made him annual visits, bringing back saddle-bags well weighted with Sandy River dollars. "Pound Sol" told us that he and many others had explored the mountains in every direction, vainly searching for Jim Mullins' mine. "Pound Sol" himself was a mine of traditional lore, ballads of local origin, descriptive generally of neighborhood feuds and battles growing out of them were often recited or sung by him at the camp fires, some of which I transcribed and preserved for a while, but regret that they are now lost. The passage through the Breaks was reckoned dangerous for any one to attempt without a guide. The natives said that if a deer was run into the Breaks he could never get out, as the walls were so high and steep that they could be scaled at no point, either by man or beast. The whole bed of the river from cliff to cliff was filled with rocks from the size of a barrel to that of a house, concealing the water, which ran in gurgling streams twenty feet or more below. Progress was made by alternately climbing up and scrambling or sliding down these rocks, at times varying the exercise by jumping across crevices from four to eight feet wide where the swift sluices could be seen as well as heard. Occasionally a pool of deep, still water could be seen, and in such places we always found fish. At times a drift log would span the space between two rocks, thus furnishing a bridge to the wayfarer. Before we got through "Pound Sol" had become decidedly hilarious, and once, being attracted by his voice raised in song, I turned and saw him dancing and singing on the middle of a log we had just crossed with great care and circumspection, which was at least twenty feet above a deep crevice, a tumble into which was death pure and simple. But there was Sol, loaded down with saddle-bags, cooking utensils and blankets, dancing a breakdown to his own music and it was some time before we could prevail on him to leave his dangerous perch. Our party finally emerged from the "Breaks of Sandy" about dusk and camped at the mouth of "Grassy Creek," sufficiently tired to ensure a good night's rest, after the preliminary treat of the usual camp stories. Among others we heard one of which our host, Am Willis, was the hero. He was not with us, but those present knew him and vouched for its accuracy. He was out with a party on a bear hunt, and after a long chase, the bear took refuge in a cave on the side of the mountain which had not been explored. Persistent efforts were made to induce the dogs to go in and force him out, but in vain. Finally, Willis volunteered to go in and shoot the bear, if any of the party would carry the torch to give light enough to enable him to shoot. A young man of the party agreed to perform this service, and a good lightwood torch was speedily arranged and the pair entered the cave. After proceeding some distance without seeing the game, they reached a ledge of rock about three feet in height which ran across the cave. The torch bearer held up the light in the endeavor to ascertain what was beyond the barrier, and finally held the torch over and beyond the ledge, when, like a flash, the bear at one blow knocked the torch out of the man's hand, leaving all in total darkness. The adventurous hunters were in a quandary indeed, not knowing which way to turn, expecting a grip or a blow from the paw of the bear every moment and out of the reach of aid, they could only halloo to their friends, and guided by the sound of their voices grope their way out. They finally emerged in safety, and held another consultation as to the best means of effecting the capture of their game. They finally determined to build a frame or barrier of white oak saplings, which could be pushed before them along the narrow passage, which it filled, and thus reached the lurking place of the bear and speedily dispatched him with their guns and knives. They then dragged him out and bore him in triumph home. I asked Willis when we got back to his house if the story were true and he answered that the bear did knock the light out, and that they finally killed it, which was all he would tell. He, himself, told us another bear story, which amused us. He said he was on one side of a ravine standing on a bench of the mountain which gave him a good outlook, watching for a bear which the dogs were running and on the other side of the ravine was another man standing in a path which had been cleared through laurel and ivy bushes, leaving many projecting limbs. Pursued by the dogs the bear came along this path and the huntsman waited until he came very near that he might make a sure shot, but when he pulled the trigger the gun failed to fire, and as the bear was only a few feet off and coming directly towards him, he was obliged to turn and run for his life. The bear only followed him a few steps before he turned into the laurels, but the huntsman, not knowing this, continued his flight, expecting the bear to grab him every minute and as he ran the stubs of the cut bushes would now and again catch into his hunting shirt and almost jerk him back. Thinking this was the bear he would knock back and yelling,

"Scat, you bitch, scat." He ran nearly a quarter of a mile, all the other men of the party nearly dying with laughter.

But to return from this digression. The next day we fished down stream until we reached a point opposite "Pound Sol's" house, who invited us up to take dinner with him. After dinner we set out across the Cumberland Mountains. A short distance before reaching the top we passed the remains of a fire easily distinguished, which we were told marked the place where a party of deserters from both armies had burned their accoutrements during the war before entering on the soil of Kentucky, as they had determined to fight on neither side. The descent of the mountain was very trying, and I was surprised to find it more fatiguing than the ascent. After going a mile or two the muscles of the thigh became so wearied by the unaccustomed exercise that it became positively painful for me to proceed, and I was obliged to rest frequently before reaching the bottom. Near the foot we found a splendid spring where we luxuriated in copious draughts of the cooling water, and took a good rest. Our attendants set out to forage for bread but came back without any, bringing in, however, some very good sweet potatoes as a substitute. This was the first time we had been absolutely without bread. We camped on the river bank on a sand bar which furnished a luxurious bed which we all enjoyed. After passing the mountains the river makes a considerable curve but still preserves its peculiar characteristics of deep pools alternating with long stretches where no water is visible. We arose early as we had to catch our breakfast before we broke our fast. We got some fresh baked "gritted" bread for breakfast and with fish and coffee fared well. Our baggage men seemed as if they would never get enough coffee. I always made it myself, and as I used a liberal quantity of fine Java and Mocha mixed, I knew they had never tasted such coffee before, which they were ever ready to admit. We were two or three days getting back to "Pound Sol's," where we had left our horses. Passing each day pretty much like the preceding, wherever night caught us we would build a fire, take off our shoes, and wrapping a blanket around our wet clothes, feet to the fire, and sleep the sleep of the just. None of us took the slightest cold or suffered from any sickness.

We got back to our horses, to my great delight I admit, and "Jemima" appeared as glad to see me as I was to see her. We paid Pres' Mullins in greenbacks for caring for our horses, but at first he demurred, as he did not think anything but specie was money, but being at last convinced, took it greedily. Without any further stop we made for Am Willis', and that night around the fire had a council. Uncle Ira Reynolds was fagged out and wanted to go home, but I insisted that we should not return without having a hunt. John Smith agreed to stay longer but Uncle Ira stuck to it that he must go. Am Willis was in for a hunt, and sent word that night to a young man who kept his hounds to bring them over the next morning for a drive. This he did, and after breakfast we started out. We were placed on the stands and it was not long before the dogs started a deer which did not run by any of our stands but made for "Crane's Nest Creek," where he was killed by the driver. We were again placed upon stands and the dogs got up another deer, which was killed by a man not in the hunt, but Am Wilson soon found out who killed him, rode over at once and got his portion of venison. As it had by this time commenced raining, we all left for home. I was much disappointed that I failed to get a shot, but hoped for better luck next day, but, alas! the next day it was raining "cats and dogs," as it was about the time of the autumnal Equinox, we concluded to break up and go home. Mr. Willis would not hear of any payment for his hospitable entertainment, and would only accept some hocks and snoods, and a few pounds of duck shot which I had with me. He owned a shot gun but had no shot suitable for ducks. He insisted upon my taking the haunches of a young deer as a treat to the home folks. We started on our return trip through the rain and carried with us enough memories of the Sandy River country and its hospitable people to furnish topics of conversation for a long time. I reached home without any mishap on the night of the second day, wet and tired, for the rain had never ceased, but received a warm welcome from the family, no doubt intensified by the treat of fresh venison, which was a rarity. Thus ended my last camping out tramp, though I did not then expect it to be the last.

By this time I had the farm in good shape, well fenced, a hundred and twenty-five acres in meadow and the fields not in cultivation, in grass and clover. The house was filled with visitors, among them my son-in-law, Henry Williams, and his wife and child. My third daughter, Alice, was married this fall to Mr. E. P. Goggin, a rising young lawyer of Lynchburg, a bright, agreeable and attractive gentleman.

One afternoon of the next fall, as I sat in the front porch, a stranger rode up to the gate, halted, and at my invitation, dismounted and came in. He asked if I could give him accommodations for the night. Supposing him to be alone, I told him he could stay and he then said he had a drove of cattle coming on and two or three hands with them, had tried every house for several miles back and no one would agree to receive them, but all had told him if he could come on as far as Colonel Withers' he could "get to stay." I told him the trouble would be the cattle, as I had no grass to spare and did not see how I could let him have pasturage. He appeared distressed and worried, and said he didn't know what to do, that every one told him there was no place he could go in after he passed my house until he reached Mr. White's, six or seven miles further. It was now after sunset and it would be impossible for his cattle to travel so far. I finally asked him where he was from. He replied, "I live on Sandy." I felt that I could not with decency refuse shelter and accommodations to any man hailing from the Sandy country, but I inquired on what fork he lived. "At Sand Licks," he said, "on Russell Fork."

"Why," said I, "I have been there, and taken dinner at the house of a man named Jim Colly. Do you know him?"

"Well," said he, "that's my name, I'm Jim Colly."

I surrendered at once, told him I would take him and his cattle in and do the best I could for them, as I had been so kindly treated by every one on the Sandy during my stay among them. I also told him to tell the people over there that any of them could "get to stay" at my house whenever they wished. He was greatly relieved and when his cattle came up I had them turned on the best grass I had and gave his party supper, lodging and breakfast.

CHAPTER XXVI.

A NEW ROLE.

The summer of 1870 passed without any incident of special importance, and I looked forward to a quiet country life for the remaining three years of my lease. Whenever I met Mr. Stuart he proposed to purchase my lease and stock, but I had always declined to sell. One Sunday morning in the month of September after getting breakfast, I walked up to the sheep pasture on Priest's Mountain to see if the flock had been disturbed and returned to the house about eleven o'clock. When I came in my wife handed me a letter, covering a telegram, which had been sent to Abingdon and forwarded thence by mail. It was from my friend Major W. T. Sutherlin, sent from New York, and this was the message: "Meet me Tuesday morning in Richmond, business of importance to yourself."

I puzzled over it in silence, at a loss to know what it could mean, until my wife asked, "What do you make of it?"

I answered, "I have not the slightest idea, but if I am to get to Richmond by Tuesday morning, it is necessary to start at once."

"Why," she said, "you surely are not thinking of going to Richmond on such a vague message as that?"

"Certainly," was my reply. "Major Sutherlin is a business man and would never send such a message unless it were really of importance. So let me have a snack before the regular dinner."

I ordered my horse to be saddled and when the boy brought her he said, "Colonel, Nellie has a shoe off."

"Then run over to 'Bednegoes and tell him to come to the shop and nail a shoe on her as soon as he can, Sunday or no Sunday."

He soon returned with the news that the blacksmith's house was locked up and he gone away.

"Then take the mare to the shop," said I, "and I'll put on the shoe myself."

This made my wife laugh and she said, "You know you can't do that. Did you ever try to put a shoe on a horse in your life ?"

"No," said I, "I never did, but as the mare can not travel without a shoe, I must nail it on."

So I went to the shop, found an old shoe, and as I had the nails ready made, I nailed it on without any great difficulty, then ate my snack and started to the railroad, which I reached an hour before train time and arrived in Richmond early Tuesday morning. As soon as I reached the hotel I inquired for Major Sutherlin's room, and found him dressing. He laughed when he saw me and said, "Well, I know I have put you to wondering. haven't I ?"

"That is certainly so," said I, "but what's up ?"

He then told me that when in New York he had met with the General Manager of the University Publishing Company, who have a series of school books prepared by Southern authors, which they are desirous of introducing into the public schools just being organized in Virginia. He said the company was anxious to secure the services of an efficient agent in Virginia, and asked the Major if he knew of any one whom he could recommend for the place. He answered, "Yes, I know the very man you want, but you'll have to pay him a good salary."

This they said they were willing to do. He then told them that Colonel Withers was probably more extensively acquainted in Virginia than any man within its borders, having only a short time before made a thorough canvass of the whole State and was then living on a farm in Southwest Virginia. They at once authorized him to wire me and offer a liberal salary and all my expenses if I would accept the position, and asked that I would come at once to New York for conference and instructions. The Major asked me what I thought of it. I told him I thought there was enough in it to justify a trip to New York. On inquiry I learned that a steamer of the Old Dominion Line would leave for New York at ten thirty, that morning. I breakfasted, procured the address of the publishing house and at once went aboard the steamer. We made the trip without accident or mishap, and I at once sought an interview with Mr. Richardson, the General Manager of the company, and some of the Directors, informed myself fully of their plans and purposes, and contracted in writing to accept their agency and do my best to secure the introduction of their publication, as well as to secure additional subscriptions to the capital stock of the company. I left New York next day for home and as I passed Glade Spring station left a note for Mr. Stuart at Saltville, telling him that if he was still desirous of buying out my interest in the Lampkin place he must come over at once as I was in the humor for trading. I had my mare brought out, mounted her and rode home, and the shoe I had put on lasted her until we got back.

Mr. Stuart came over the next day and I sold him the unexpired lease at a good premium, sold him all the stock on the place of every kind, all the crops, plantation tools and the greater portion of my household and kitchen furniture, agreeing to give him possession of all in a week. We had little trouble in trading, there being only two or three matters on which we differed. These were the price of corn and the quantity of hay on the place, and we agreed to leave these questions to the decision of one of the neighbors. He decided that corn was worth what I asked for it, but his estimate of the quantity of hay was very little more than half what I knew it to be, so Mr. Stuart got the laugh on me. When we came to price the milk cows, of which there were about thirty, I told him they were worth on an average about forty dollars apiece. He thought the price too high, and this was the first difference of opinion between us as to value of stock. I told him I would have the cows driven up and he might price each one separately, and after dinner we went down to the cow pen, I asked him to put a value on each animal, of which I made a record. One cow I asked him to allow a rise of five dollars on the price to which he consented, and when we had gotten through the list he asked me to average the lot, which I did and found the average to be exactly forty dollars, the value I had originally fixed on them.

"Well," said he, "we have lost an hour to no purpose."

It was certainly a little remarkable that the outcome should have been the exact amount of my valuation, but it shows how nearly men accustomed to it, will agree in judging as to the value of cattle.

The next day I set out to seek a home, which must of necessity be on or near the railroad. I visited places in Washington County, in Abingdon, Smyth and Wythe, and finally bargained for a place near Wytheville. I paid a little more than I thought it was worth, but being obliged to have a place without delay could not afford to wait. When I reached home I moved all my furniture which I had retained, to the railroad at Saltville, where I chartered a car and loaded it, spent the night with my family at Mr. Stuart's, and the next day reached Wytheville, went at once into the house which I had purchased, located immediately on the railroad, and in two weeks from the day I received Major Sutherlin's telegram, was ready to embark in my new business, which I thought pretty good work.

When the Legislature of Virginia organized the public school system of the State, they required that the books used in the schools should be uniform, without prescribing who should be invested with the power of selection. They placed at the head of the system a "Superintendent of Public Instruction," who with the Governor and Attorney General should constitute the School Board, which was clothed with plenary power to determine all matters connected with the schools. The Rev. William H. Ruffner, D. D., of Lexington was made Superintendent of Public Instruction, and I made it my first business to interview him on the subject of text-books. After telling him that I had accepted the agency of the University Publishing Company, I asked him who would decide upon the text-books for use in the schools. He promptly answered, "the County Superintendent in each County." I indicated my belief that University Series would be generally adopted through the State, as books written by such Southern scholars as Maury, Venable, Holmes, etc., would be preferred to those of Northern production. I saw at once that he did not favor the idea though he said little. After procuring a list of the County Superintendents I visited or corresponded with each and I am sure that four fifths of the number avowed themselves in favor of adopting the series I represented. Judge, then my surprise when on my next visit to Richmond I was informed by Dr. Ruffner, that the County Superintendents would not select the text-books, but the matter would be left to the School Trustees of each county. Under this ruling it became necessary to visit each county in the State as far as practicable, and endeavor to secure from the Board of Trustees the adoption for use in the public schools of the books of the Company I represented. Several old publishers of school books when the question of adoption became a practical one in Virginia, formed a combination against the University Publishing Company and employed as their agent Major Jed Hotchkiss of Staunton, an astute, energetic and talented man, who had served during the war on the staff of General "Stonewall" Jackson, had a large acquaintance and was personally popular. In canvassing the merits of the books we respectively represented before the different County Boards the Major and I had quite a lively time. I had, however, no cause to complain of the result, for in nearly every county where we appeared together before the Board of Trustees I secured the adoption of the University Series. He carried a good many counties where I did not appear and favored as he undoubtedly was by the Superintendent of Public Instruction, it was a wonder that I came out as well as I did. I do not mean to charge that Dr. Ruffner was not an efficient public officer, or that he failed to meet the important duties incident to his position. This was shown by the success which attended his efforts to put the public school system of the State on a high plane, and to him the State is mainly indebted for their present efficiency. He certainly showed no favors to me or to the University Publishing Company. He construed the constitutional requirement of uniformity in text-books to mean uniformity in each school district, insisting that it was a technical term and always so construed by educational officials. I believed that it was designed to compel the use of the same books in all the public schools of the State. But the State Board agreed to accept Dr. Ruffner's construction. The canvass of the counties occupied the greater part of the summer of 1871, and I was consequently absent from home a great deal during that period. Major Hotchkiss and I had some pretty sharp contests at times before the different Boards, relieved, however, by some amusing incidents, but our personal relations were never effected.

At the close of my first year's service with the University

Publishing Company, I accepted the place of "General Agent;" charged with the supervision of their interests over all the Southern States. As this involved the necessity of being almost constantly from home I thought it best to rent out "Green Meadows" and remove my family to the City of Richmond, being more central and accessible. This arrangement I carried out, securing a commodious house at the corner of Twelfth and Marshall Streets. Soon after this change of residence, my fourth daughter Janet Ann was married to Mr. Henry Cook, a druggist from Alexandria, Va. The occasion was as usual, celebrated by a large entertainment, a bountiful wedding supper, and a lively dancing party.

My work as General Agent of the University Pulishing Company, required me to look after local agents, aid in the introduction of the books into new territories, supervise the settlements of the various book depositories and select others when necessary. I was kept pretty constantly on the road, visiting in succession different counties and towns in North and South Carolina, Tennessee, Kentucky, Georgia, Alabama, Mississippi, Louisiana, Missouri and Arkansas. On one trip through Georgia, being at Atlanta I paid a visit to General J. B. Gordon, who was warmly interest in the success of the Company and was one of its Vice-Presidents. When I left there for Macon, I felt as well as usual, but the next morning I found myself absolutely helpless from a sudden attack of rheumatism and could not turn in bed without assistance. I was kept in Macon several days before I was able to take a step, the disease having located itself at the seat of my old pelvic wound. After settling my business in Macon, it was necessary for me to visit Brunswick in the Southern border of the State near the Florida line where my presence was required. I had myself carried to the train on a litter and was placed on the cars enroute for Brunswick. As had occurred to me more than once, the concussion of the railroad travel instead of increasing the pain seemed to give relief and when I reached Brunswick I was able to hobble along a little by the aid of two canes. The business which carried me to Brunswick was less troublesome than I expected to find it, and was soon completed. About sunset, as I was sitting in the Hotel porch, a man drove up in a spring wagon and delivered two large fish, such as I had never before seen, each weighing fifty or sixty pounds. I had one of them brought to me and examined it with much interest. The man who brought them said they were "Red Drum," and had been caught with hook and line in St. Simon's Sound near Cumberland Island. I was seized with a strong desire to attempt the capture of such noble fish myself, and inquired of the vendor how I could reach Cumberland Island. He offered to take me there in his sail boat the next day. The distance he said was about twenty-five miles and he said that no danger attended the voyage as it would not be necessary to go out on the ocean at all. He also informed me that I could find comfortable quarters at a good hotel on the Island, which was resorted to by many invalids during the summer months. I bargained with him for the trip there and back, and agreed to start by daylight next morning. A little son of the landlord, a lad of about twelve years sat by an eager listener to this conversation, and he at once put in a plea that I would take him with me. As he had been very kind and obliging during my stay, going for my mail and on any errand I wished I was glad to gratify him and said, "All right, ask your father when he comes in, and if he has no objection I'll take you along willingly."

"Oh no," he said, "he won't let me go if I ask him but if you'll ask him he will."

I agreed to make the effort, and when his father came in lost no time in proffering the request. He at first refused, saying, "Jimmy was too young to go on such a trip," but as I insisted there would be no danger and promised to look after him, he finally said, "Well Colonel, if you really want him to go he can do so, for I am not afraid to trust him with you, and I suppose he can save you some running about."

Jimmie was the happiest boy in Brunswick that night, and talked of nothing but that trip until bed time. I cautioned him that we must wake up early to get to the wharf in time, and he promised to be punctual and after supper his mother fixed us an abundant snack for our trip. He was at my door long before light and we reached the wharf before our fisherman was moving, and as he was at anchor out in the harbor we had to wait some time before he made his appearance. I found getting into the boat, crippled as I was, was quite an arduous undertaking, yet with his aid I finally succeeded, and we were off a little before sunrise. We ran down the coast, through various sounds and estuaries, favored by a pleasant breeze and reached Cumberland Island before midday. I had only a vague recollection that this Island had been donated by the State of Georgia to General Nathaniel Green, in acknowledgment of his patriotic services during the War of the Revolution. "Dungeness" the old mansion house was destroyed by fire some years before. The Island itself is of considerable extent mostly rich alluvial soil. It had on it a good deal of game, some deer and a bear will pay an occasional visit by swimming over from the main land. The waters of the Sound team with fish of many varieties and various species of water fowl frequent its shores and waters. In the fall it is said to be a very paradise for sport and in spring and summer it is much frequented by fisher folks, who catch sea turtle and find great store of their eggs which are highly prized by epicures. For a few years past it has been a resort for invalids, who in the pure air and with abundant store of appetizing food find their waning strength restored, and enfeebled vital powers reinvigorated. The hotel where I stopped crowns a bluff near the shore, and has quite a pretensious appearance, but the accomodations were rather primitive.

My skipper rowed me till the water shoaled to such a degree that the boat grounded, and he then got me on his back and waded to the shore, and with his aid and Jimmy's we ascended the hill to the hotel. I went to my room and sent for the landlord who was at the time absent. In a short while he came into the room where I was lying on the bed, and with very solemn face and lugubrious voice inquired what he could do for me.

"Well," said I, "my wants are easily told. I came down here for no purpose in the world except to catch a Drum fish, and the sooner you can put me in the way of doing that, the better pleased I will be."

I think I have never seen a more sudden change come over a man's countenance. He broke out in a loud laugh, "Good

Lord," said he, "when I saw them two fellows helping you up the hill I thought to myself, there comes an old fellow now, who has come here to die, and now I find you want to go fishing. There'll be no trouble about that. I'll have a man and boat ready with hooks and bait for the flood tide this evening. Drum bite only on the flood, and that will be near sunset this evening."

Glad to find "mine host" appreciated the emergency so fully, I gave myself no uneasiness, and quietly awaited the coming of the flood tide. I was duly notified when the boat was ready, and after almost an hour's rowing we came to anchor at the spot selected by him, as he informed me over an oyster bed, on which the Drum feed. They are not a game fish in the proper sense of the word, feeding on oysters, crabs and other crustacea. The mouth and upper throat are lined with boney plates by aid of which they can crush the shells of oysters or other mollusks, before swallowing them. After we got out our hooks, which were almost as large as a small pipe stem, baited with half a crab, and with a heavy sinker, I inquired of my attendant as to their habits of feeding, the character of their "bite" and other particulars, and he readily furnished all the information asked. They bite very gently, and as soon as a steady draw is felt, you give a sharp jerk, as it requires considerable force to drive the large hook far enough to bury the barb in the fish's mouth. The name is derived from the drumlike sound emitted while feeding and of which I soon had an opportunity of judging. Soon my attendant said, "I've got a bite," and presently gave a hard jerk which evidently hooked the fish as it ran off at once rapidly taking line, I watched the proceedings with interest, when I was asked if I would like to take the line to which I readily assented, and for a while was kept busy in playing the fish. When my attendant called out, "Oh by jings you've cotch 'em before."

"You are mistaken," said I, "for until last night I never saw one."

"Well you know more about it than any 'wire grass fellow' I ever seed down here."

I afterwards learned that it was considered a capital joke to put the line in the hands of a novice when the fish was hooked and to see his fingers cut and burned by the line in the vain attempt to pull in the fish by main strength. Of course I was too old a fisherman to furnish a subject for this amusing performance, evidently to the chagrin of my companion, and after some ten or fifteen minutes, the fight was over and the fish hauled in hand over hand. It weighed about sixty-five pounds. Some half hour after I felt a steady pull on my line and obeying instructions drove the hook in by a strong jerk, and was soon busy with a much heavier fish than the first. It was finally landed after a long tussle and proved to be the largest I saw during my excursion, weighing eighty-four pounds. With the exception of some shark, this was the largest fish I have ever taken. Some time after dark I hooked and caught another much smaller, but the capture was attended by a beautiful phenomenon. The water was highly phosphorescent and the fiery sparkles which lighted up the whole surface of the disturbed water, and gave to the line the appearance of fire itself was a treat to see that I can never forget. It was the very poetry of fishing. We returned to supper and I retired to a good night's rest on a hard couch, but greatly pleased with my effort for Drum fish. I remained the next day, fishing, both on the early and late tide. In the last outing my boatman furnished me some amusement, I had baited my hook and thrown it out when it was seized before it reached the bottom, and as the pull on the line was very strong I gave a hard and quick jerk, which at once added to the strain, the fish darting through the water at a rapid rate, it was as much as I could do to turn it and as I succeeded I remarked to my boatman, "Well, I've got the king of all the Drum hooked now."

"Yes, by George," said he, "he is a whale."

When I checked strongly as he made another rush, he sprang out of the water, full length and we saw it was a large shark. My man cried out, "It's a shark! It's a shark! and will bite off my hook, pull him in quick."

"That's easier said than done," was my reply.

But at that moment the fish changed his tactics and made right for the boat so rapidly that it was difficult to take in the line fast enough to keep it taut. Seeing his course would bring him very near the boat my man got up and as the line passed near him, he reached out and caught it not more than three or four feet above the fish, and putting his foot on the gunwale depressed the edge of the boat sufficiently to enable him by a dextrous pull to land the fish in the bottom of the boat. As it was still full of fight, matters between him and the fish soon became interesting. He had on a pair of very heavy fisherman's boots and tried to stamp the fish, and the shark was snapping at his legs like a bull dog. One of the oars and the paddle were knocked out of the boat and the contest was kept up for some time to my great amusement, as I was in the bow at a safe distance from the combatants. He finally got his foot on the shark's neck and with the bailer which he had caught up, stunned it sufficiently to enable him to cut its throat. It was a lively scene while it lasted. This was a specimen of the "Shovel Nose," was nine and a half feet long and weighed one hundred and twelve pounds. The next morning we returned to Brunswick with my catch of seven Drum fish. My whole bill for two days board for self and Jimmy, hire of boat and boatman was only two dollars and a half. I wrote back to my wife that I had found a place where a man can live in luxury and plenty without work, as everything necessary for one's wants except bread, was furnished from the water, and was to be had for the taking. I fully made up my mind to go back in the fall of the next year, but "Man proposes, God disposes." I have never seen Cumberland Island since.

Perhaps another record of my experience may be of interest. When in Nashville I had a letter from the House in New York instructing me to go at once to the county seat of ———————County, Tenn. to look after a business matter. On inquiry I found that the county in question was in the southern part of the State in a mountainous section accessible only by steamers on the Tennessee River. I travelled by rail to Johnson City, where the steamers could be taken, which would land me at a point about twelve miles from the Court-House. I started and in due time reached Johnson City, and after some hours' waiting the small stern wheeler came along, and I got aboard with my satchel. The river was rather low and the boat frequently grounded, and at times delayed us considerably. One of my travelling companions was a Doctor who could certainly eat more morphine without any sensible effect, than anyone I ever met. He kept a vial in his vest pocket and about every fifteen or twenty minutes would take it out and with the point of his knife take out all it would hold and put it in his mouth. We fell into conversation and I found him sensible and well informed. He got off some hours before I did. When I reached the landing it was about sunset Sunday night, and as the place consisted of only two or three small dwellings I secured accommodations at one with the promise of a horse to ride the next day to the Court-House, it being Court day. After a breakfast of black coffee, and fried bacon and eggs, I asked for my horse to be brought out, and when he appeared, lo, it was a mule caparisoned with an old Army saddle and a blind bridle; as nothing more pretentious could be had I was perforce compelled to take the mule or walk, so I mounted and reached the Court-House in good time. Soon found the parties I wished to see and settled my business with less trouble than I expected. The steamer Captain had promised that he would call for me on his return trip, when he would pass that landing soon after midnight. Accordingly after my return from the Court-House, I told the agent at the landing that I wished the boat to stop so that I could get aboard and he promised to attend to it without fail. After supper I laid down for an hour or two sleep as the prospect was bad for sleeping on the boat. I was awakened from a sound nap by hearing the whistle of the steamer, so rising at once as I had not taken off my clothes, I seized my satchel and ran to the landing a few hundred yards away and had the pleasure of seeing the steamer pass down the river, without making any stop, though the agent had a fire burning as a signal and hailed the boat repeatedly. I have rarely been more angry, but as the fault was not with the agent, there was no one on whom I could wreak my vengeance. As it would be at least forty-eight hours before there would be another boat the out look was not pleasant. I went back to bed, and was up by light in the morning inquiring if there would be any chance to hire a skiff or row boat to take me to Johnson City that day. Soon a rough, stalwart young fellow presented himself and offered to take me to Johnson City for five dollars. I closed with him at once and directed him to get off as soon as possible. I got some bread and meat from my host, and in about half an hour my boatman made his appearance in a small skiff about twelve feet long and two and a half feet wide. I stepped aboard, to my seat in the bow and we started down the river for Johnson City about fifty miles below. My boatman took leisurely strokes, but as we were going with the current I thought we were making fair progress. It was my first voyage in so diminutive a craft, and it was not long before the cramped position became quite disagreeable. We had made perhaps twenty miles, when as we were passing the landing at which the morphine eating Doctor had gotten off on our trip up, I was hailed from the shore, and it was the Doctor who had recognized me as we approached. He begged me to land for a few moments and I did so, suspecting that he also had missed the down boat, and wished to get a passage. This was pretty nearly the truth, but not the whole truth, he had escorted a lady to the landing that morning who wished to take the down boat but it had passed before they reached the landing, and he now besought me to let her take passage with me on my chartered skiff. I referred the request to the boatman, supposing he would object, but he was anxious to add to his earnings and agreed to take her, so I had to submit silently though I knew it would add to the discomfort of the voyage. When I told the Doctor to escort her down, he went off and returned not only with the lady but accompanied also by a big Saratoga trunk, which literally filled the boat. Placing it amidship it effectually barred the passage way from one end of the boat to the other, and the added weight of its mistress made us pretty deeply laden. There was no help for it now, and we pursued our voyage without further loss of time. Whenever the current was pretty strong our rower rested from his labor, only to resume the oars when there was little current perceptible. Dark overtook us before we were anywhere near Johnson City, but as the train did not pass the bridge until nine o'clock, I still hoped to make it, but we heard the whistle and rumble of the wheels as they crossed the bridge while we were yet two or three miles away. I was so tired and cramped when the skiff reached our destination, that it was some time before I could get out of the boat. I went to a hotel, got a room and thoroughly fagged and worn out speedily fell asleep. I heard a freight coming in about two o'clock, dressed and negotiated a passage on it for my next objective point, about twenty miles distant which I reached in safety. In journeyings and experience such as these the year of 1872 was passed, and except for the frequent and prolonged absence from my family, not unpleasantly. I have always been fond of traveling, and visiting new scenes and associating with new people caused the days to pass with rapidity.

CHAPTER XXVII.

"COFFEE AND PISTOLS FOR TWO."

An incident which occurred just before this, and which at the time caused considerable excitement amongst some of the officers and men of the Confederate Army was much discussed, but the details were known to but few persons, all of whom except myself, have now passed away, is I think worth narrating, as none of the accounts which I have read are correct. I refer to the personal difficulty between General Jubal Early and General William Mahone, which had its origin in an article published in the "Historical Magazine of which General Du Peister was the author, highly eulogistic of General Mahone, and containing severe strictures on other Confederate officers of high rank especially General Early. As the article was palpably based on information furnished by General Mahone, General Early at once addressed him a note inquiring if he assumed responsibility for the publication. To this note an evasive reply was made, and the correspondence culminated in a note from General Early so offensive in its terms that no alternative other than a hostile meeting seemed possible. I had been informed of these facts by General Early, but mentioned them to no one. On a visit to Richmond about that time, I was called on by Mr. James McDonald, then Secretary of the Commonwealth, a friend and relative, who informed me that unless the friends of General Early and General Mahone promptly interferred there certainly would be a hostile meeting between these two gentlemen, with probably fatal results. He asked me to see General Early and try to induce him to withdraw his last communication to General Mahone, and he added that it must be done that day or it would be too late. He professed to be acting on his own volition as a friend of both parties. I promptly declined to interfere in a matter that did not concern me particularly, adding that General Early was not a man who would brook any interference in his private affairs. He admitted the fact, but continued to urge me to interpose in the matter, stating that General Bradley Johnson had consented to act with me if I agreed to undertake it, I persisted in my refusal, and he then said it would be a source of undying regret if a hostile meeting should occur between two distinguished Confederate Generals with probable fatal results, when by friendly intervention the whole matter could be settled. I suggested a doubt as to the probability of such settlement, and he assured me that if Geeneral Early would withdraw his last letter General Mahone would make any explanation or withdrawal of the offensive article in the "Historical Magazine," which was the original cause of the offense to General Early, and which he charged had been written or inspired by General Mahone. I expressed a doubt of the possibility of such action, he insisted that he knew positively that it could be done. I then said, bring me a written statement from General Mahone or some one authorized to act for him, pledging such retraction on his part, and I will do what I can to influence General Early to do what you ask. He left me and after a time returned and showed me this note addressed to himself by Mr. Alexander Mosely, Editor of the Richmond Whig and endorsed by Captain Ham Chamberlaine, acting for General Mahone.

"JAMES MCDONALD, Esq.

"*My Dear Sirs*—In reply to your inquiry I feel authorized to say from my knowledge of the matter that if all the correspondence except General Early's first letter is withdrawn, General Mahone will make a reply to that letter expressing regret for the injustice done to him (General Early) and others by the publication in the "Historical Magazine" and with an explanation of the measures taken by General Mahone (when he heard that a publication was intended) to prevent the incorporation in it of expressions and strictures reflecting upon the conduct and capacity of Confederate officers.

Yours truly,
"(Signed) A. Moseley.

"I concur in the above.

"(Signed) Hampden Chamberlaine."

When I read this letter which was placed in my hands by Mr. McDonald, I took it to General Bradley Johnson and we came to the conclusion that it would furnish sufficient basis for an effort at adjustment. We accordingly started to find General Early, who was then in Richmond. On our way to his room, General Johnson said to me:

"Look here Colonel, you must tackle old Jube on this business; I tell you I am afraid to do it, he is such a cantankerous old fellow, and you know him better than I do."

We had reached the door of his room by this time, and in answer to our knock were bidden to enter. As soon as General Early saw us, I was satisfied he suspected the object of our meeting, for he drew himself at once into his shell, and stood on the defensive. Seeing this I thought the best policy was to approach the subject at once which I proceeded to do, at the same time explaining our action in the matter and our refusal to interfere, until we read the letter of Mr. Moseley endorsed by Captain Chamberlaine. The old General was obdurate, he refused positively to withdraw his letter, said he had Mahone right where he wanted him, and would on no account "Let him up" as he phrased it. We insisted that it would never do for him to force matters to an extremity in the face of Mr. Moseley's letter, and that public sentiment would not sustain him in forcing a fight under the circumstances. Colonel Lewis Harvey, of Amelia by chance called, while we were debating the matter, and as he was a personal friend of General Early and had considerable experience in such affairs we told him the object of our call, making known to him all the steps which had been taken. He agreed with us fully and added such additional reasons as occurred to him, but General Early still refused to follow the advice we proffered. As the talk progressed, however, I thought I could see some evidence of yielding, and I proposed to General Johnson that we take the responsibility of withdrawing the correspondence ourselves, and if General Early was not satisfied with the response of General Mahone he could repudiate our actions. To this General Johnson agreed, and we left General Early growling.

We then sent Captain Chamberlaine the following note:

CAPTAIN H. CHAMBERLAINE,

Captain:—The undersigned desire to procure an adjustment of the pending difficulty between Generals Mahone and Early. Our regard for the Confederate service in which these gentlemen filled such prominent places, prompts us to make this effort. We therefore assume the responsibility of requesting you to consider the entire correspondence as withdrawn except the first letter of inquiry from General Early to General Mahone as indicated by the note of Mr. Moseley to J. M. McDonald, Esq., endorsed by you and handed to us by Mr. McDonald, with the understanding that if our efforts fail our entire interference is to be treated as if it had never been made, and all letters and correspondence growing out of it be returned and destroyed. In the same view we request you to forward us General Mahone's reply which we have been induced to believe will be of a satisfactory character.

Very Respectfully,
(Signed) Bradley T. Johnson
(Signed) R. E. Withers.

The above note was written by General Johnson, and to it the following reply was received:

RICHMOND, July 4th, 1871.

"GENTLEMEN:—Your note of this date suggesting a withdrawal of the entire correspondence between Generals Early and Mahone except that from General Early of the twenty-first of March, 1871, is duly received. Concurring fully in your suggestions, I have to inform you that as soon as the time necessary to communicate with General Mahone will allow, he will address to General Early an answer to the letter of the twenty-first of March, in accordance with the note of this date written by Mr. A. Moseley and endorsed by me.

Very respectfully, your obedient servant,
(Signed) HAMPDEN CHAMBERLAINE."

A few days after this letter was received, General Mahone's reply to the letter of the twenty-first of March was handed us, read and given to General Early with the assurance of our belief that it ought to be regarded as satisfactory. To this General Early ultimately acceded, and so expressed himself in a note to General Mahone. The matter was now considered closed, but some years afterwards, General Early was so exasperated by publications in the *Richmond Whig* and *National Republican* of an insulting character which he believed inspired by General Mahone, especially an intimation in the last named paper, that General Early had had an opportunity of meeting General Mahone on the field, of which he did not avail himself, that he denounced General Mahone, in a speech delivered at a public meeting in Richmond, and soon after published the whole correspondence in pamphlet form, as he said, to protect himself from further misrepresentation. The only response to this publication, so far as I know, was a paragraph in the *Whig* stating in substance, that General Early's age and infirmities made further notice by General Mahone improper.

Whether the steps taken by the friends of General Early and General Mahone to adjust the difficulties between them alone prevented a hostile meeting, may be a mooted question, but there is no doubt that such was the conviction of Mr. James McDonald, to whose untiring and persistent efforts to bring about a solution of the difficulty that result was almost wholly due.

During Governor Walker's term of office the Legislature was struggling with the State Debt question. Many conflicting schemes were proposed as a basis of compromise with the Bond holders, ranging from full payment of principal and interest, to virtual repudiation of the whole debt. There were some who with plausibility argued that as the State of Virginia had been wiped out of existence by the Government of the United States, and her territory relegated to "Military District No. 1," the creditors of the State should look to that government for the payment of both Bonds and interest. After mature consideration and full discussion, what was known as "The Funding Act" was passed by the Legislature in 1873. One-third of the State debt was apportioned to West Virginia, and new bonds issued by the State to its creditors bearing six per cent. interest. This settlement was effected during the last month of Governor Walker's administration, and he was much gratified that the difficult problem was solved during his term of office. I did not myself approve all the features of the "Funding Bill," notably the provision for the payment of the interest accruing during the war, but as a settlement of the whole debt question, hoped it would meet with general acquiescence. I have no doubt that such would have been the result but for the disappointed political aspirations of one man—but I will not anticipate.

During the Fall of this year, Commodore Maury and I were appointed by the Governor to represent Virginia at a meeting of the National Agricultural Association, to be held in the city of St. Louis, Missouri. Two organizations of similar character were in existence, in one of which membership was restricted to citizens of the Southern States, the other was designed to embrace the whole of the United States. After a few years of independent existence, a consolidation of the two societies was proposed, and the meeting at St. Louis was designed to consummate this purpose. A simultaneous meeting of both bodies was arranged, with the understanding that the gentlemen who at the previous meeting of each society had been designated to deliver addresses, should alternately read their papers to deliver their addresses, and thereafter the Southern organization should be merged into the National Society.

Commodore Maury and I started from Washington, and journeyed pleasantly together until we reached our destination. Up to the time of this trip, my acquaintance with Commodore Maury had been slight, having met him casually on two or three occasions, but I soon found him to be quite sociable and companionable, and I was much impressed by his simple, genial manners, his intimate knowledge of almost all scientific subjects, and his familiarity with the incidents of current events. We stopped at the Southern Hotel and Commodore Maury was the recipient of many social attentions from leading citizens. General and Governor Marmaduke was amongst the first callers and engaged us to dine at the Executive Mansion where we met a distinguished company, and were handsomely entertained. We regularly attended the joint sessions, before whom the Commodore delivered an able and instructive address, and we heard several essays read and reports, some of which were of much interest. I met there for the first time,

General William H. Jackson, or "Red" Jackson, as he was called, the noted Cavalry leader, who after General Forest's promotion to Lieutenant-General, succeeded him in command of the Division. He was a very frank and pleasant gentlemen, who had married a daughter of General Thomas Harding, who resided on the celebrated "Bellmeade Farm" near Nashville, where I was often entertained in subsequent years. The old General was a high-toned gentleman of the old school, a noted breeder of fine stock of all kinds, notably thoroughbred horses, of which he imported several, from the best English stables. He was in one respect peculiar. He was fond of racing, many of his horses were trained and successful on the turf, and his hall was filled with purses, plates, and other trophies, won by his stable, but he was never known to bet a cent on the race beyond the entrance money required. His charming daughter, Miss Mary, at that time single, was subsequently married to Judge Jackson, who was afterwards in the United States Senate, and resigned his seat when appointed a Judge of the United States Court for Tennessee. After the adjournment of the Agricultural Society I bade adieu to Commodore Maury, for the purpose of paying a visit to my wife's brother, John William Royall, who resided at Cottleville, a small town in the neighborhood of St. Charles, Missouri, where I spent a week and then returned East.

I attended the State Convention of the Conservative Party of Virginia to select delegates to the National Democratic Convention of 1872. Mr. Horace Greely was favored by the Convention, but the proposition to instruct the delegates for Mr. Greely failed. General Kemper and I were chosen Electors at Large, and each took an active part in the canvass. This selection of General Kemper for this place plainly foreshadowed that he had been chosen by those who opposed my Gubernatorial aspirations, to contest with me the nomination for Governor.

General Mahone was at this time owner of the leading newspaper of Virginia, The *Richmond Whig,* and with the command of unlimited capital, had greatly extended its circulation and influence throughout the State. My friends as well as I, knew that this portended no good to my political aspirations, and that fact was soon made patent.

General Kemper of Madison County received the support of the *Whig* and its corps of correspondents all over the State as their candidate for Governor. He and I had been warm personal and political friends for many years, and I am happy to say that the fierce fight waged by our respective friends did not at all affect our personal relations. When the Convention met to select a candidate for Governor, I was by no means sanguine of success, though many of my friends were very confident, but I knew the whole power of the *Whig* Newspaper, and of the Atlantic, Mississippi & Ohio Railroad, extending through the heart of the State from Norfolk to Bristol, would be exerted in behalf of General Kemper, not for any special fondness for him, but from hostility to me. No communication favorable to my nomination, no paragraph in my praise, was permitted to appear in the columns of the *Whig,* and when the Convention met, every delegate opposed to me was granted a free pass over the road, and every one favorable to me required to pay full fare. I was in Richmond when the convention met, and was not surprised that General Kemper secured the nomination, by a small majority. I was mortified I admit, but submitted without a word. When the convention met again after dinner, I was greatly surprised by a visit from a Committee of that body commissioned to tender me the second place on the ticket. I promptly declined with thanks the proffered honor, and the Committee after using their best efforts to alter my decision, returned to make their report to the Convention. It was not very long before I was again visited by another Committee of my warmest personal and political friends, who sought to induce me to yield to the wishes of the Convention. I expressed my surprise that they should suppose I would accept the nomination for Lieutenant-Governor, and their reply was "Go back with us and announce your decision to the convention yourself." I at first declined to do this, but finally yielded to their wishes, with the remark, I will go with you as you so insist upon it, but will not accept the place. I entered the carriage with them, and the whole way they were urging me to accept the place for the sake of party harmony. As I descended from the carriage I noticed my old friend General Early waiting, and said to those with me, "here is a man that won't say that I ought to accept the place." To my great surprise he said in his drawling way "Well Colonel, I don't know about that, thar's a very curious state of things in that Hall and you must remember that a good soldier will fight wherever he is ordered, whether he is armed with sword or musket." I was slightly impressed by the earnestness of his manner, but ascended the steps leading to the Hall fully determined as I thought, not to recede from my position. As soon as I made my appearance on the stage I was received with the greatest conceivable enthusiasm. The applause, stamping, clapping, and shouting, continued for fully fifteen minutes, and was absolutely deafening. When order was partially restored, the President of the Convention addressed me personally, said he "Colonel Withers, the Conservative Party of Virginia in Convention assembled has unanimously selected you as their choice for Lieutenant-Governor of the State, and I sincerely trust that you will yield to their wishes and accept the position." Pandemonium again broke loose, and the shouts and cheers continued even longer than at first, every man was on his feet, and as the floors, gallery, and stage were packed and crowded to their uttermost capacity, and every one yelling at the top of his voice, the effect was startling. I do not know to this day how or when my mind underwent a change, but it must have had its origin in that peculiar magnetic feeling which swayed the thousands who were present, and was transmitted from them to me. I surrendered at discretion and in a few words, said that I was willing for the sake of the cause, to take any position they might assign me. The Editor of one of the Richmond daily papers, some years afterwards, in recalling this scene, wrote as follows:—"Never can Virginia forget that when he (Colonel Withers) was commanded to throw up his commission as candidate for Governor, he obeyed and fought on, how when again struck down he still fought on. Whoever on the occasion of his second defeat saw him yield to the overwhelming demand of his party and take the second place on the ticket, can never forget the ovation that he received. Pressing his hand on his heart he prayed in the presence of the Convention, and the vast assemblage gathered in the theater, that God might make him worthy of the great demonstration then occurring in his honor."

I have been told that General Mahone was greatly chagrined

at my acceptance of the office of Lieutenant-Governor, and is credited with having said, that he would rather have seen me made Governor. If this be true it is only susceptible of one explanation. The Lieutenant-Governor as President of the Senate of Virginia, has the privilege of appointing the various Committees of that body, and as the General was deeply interested in Railway projects, and other enterprises of similar nature, the formation of the various committees of the Senate was a matter of vital moment.

CHAPTER XXVIII.

ELECTED TO THE SENATE OF THE UNITED STATES.

The harmony of the party being now assured, the canvass was soon opened with every prospect of a triumphant issue. The Republicans put up the following ticket:

For Governor: Colonel Robert Hughes, of Norfolk; for Lieutenant-Governor: C. P. Ramsdell, of Surrey County; for Attorney-General: Mr. David Fultz, of Augusta County.

There were few joint discussion, but I have a distinct recollection of the first. It was in Warrenton, Fauquier County. General Kemper and I represented the Conservative Party, Colonel Hughes and Mr. Chandler, the Republican side. The crowd, of course, was overwhelmingly with us, and so well were our opponents satisfied that nothing was to be made by a joint debate, that few were afterwards held. I can not recall any other, except one in Harrisonburg, Rockingham County, where I met Mr. Ramsdell and Mr. Fultz both, and I was abundantly satisfied with the outcome. When the election came on in November, the Conservative ticket was elected by twenty-five or thirty thousand majority. On the first of January, 1874, we took the oaths of office, and I took my seat as President of the Senate of Virginia. Upon the Legislature then in session, devolved the election of a Senator of the United States to fill the vacancy occasioned by the expiration of the term of the Honorable J. F. Lewis. To secure this coveted prize, the friends of every man prominent in political life in Virginia were using their best endeavors. The Legislative caucus was in session some weeks, and I think seventy or eighty ballots were taken before a choice was made. It was not at first supposed that the friends of ex-Senator R. M. T. Hunter would present his name to the caucus, but they finally determined to do so, and this deprived me of the aid of some influential gentlemen who had without solicitation on my part, volunteered their support. Among these was Colonel Frank Ruffin, always a power in

Virginia politics. The Colonel wrote to me offering his support and influence, for which, of course, I expressed my acknowledgments, but subsequently I received another letter, asking to be relieved of his pledge, as Mr. Hunter was his life-long personal and political friend, and he could not antagonize him. Of course I gave him the desired relief, the more cheerfully, as I knew the relations existing between them, and that Senator Hunter was mainly indebted to Colonel Ruffin and his father-in-law, Colonel Lewis Harvey, for his first election to the Senate of the United States. Lieutenant-Governor R. L. Montague had also promised me his support, but for similar reason, fell into the ranks of the Hunter contingent. For two weeks the caucus met once or twice daily, before it was willing to bring the fight to an issue by adopting a resolution to drop the lowest candidate on every ballot, and permit only one renomination. The passage of this resolution was at last secured by a combination of the Hunter and Withers supporters, aided by individual votes from the friends of others in the field. Mr. Hunter's friends were now confident of his election, relying on the usage of defeated aspirants to support an incumbent or an old official in preference to any new man. When the balloting commenced under this rule, there were, I think, fully a dozen names and possibly more, placed in nomination. As the struggle progressed, first one and then another was retired, until only three were left, from whom the choice was to be made at the next meeting of the caucus. So great was the interest felt, that both branches of the Legislature adjourned without doing any business as soon as they met, and went into caucus. The three names were those of Mr. Hunter, Mr. John Goode, and myself, and I had the highest vote. Soon after the doors were closed on the caucus, my friend, Colonel Ruffin, came to me and said, very gleefully, I thought, "Well, Colonel, Mr. Hunter is going to beat you, but you ought to be proud of the run you have made."

Said I, "Colonel, my judgment differs from yours, as matters now stand, I consider Mr. Hunter's defeat certain."

"Upon what grounds do you base your opinion?" said he.

"Because," was my reply, "the fight is now between the old politicians and the new ones. I do not know whether Mr.

Goode or I will be nominated, but I am sure that the friends of the candidate dropped on this ballot, whether it be Goode or I, will rally to the support of the new man as against the "old fogies," as they call them."

"You will find yourself mistaken," said he. Almost with the concluding sentence, a gentleman rushed up with the news that Mr. Goode's name had been dropped, and they were balloting between Hunter and Withers. There was a great crowd in the lobby, and it was not long before a shout was heard in the chamber, and General Early, who was near me, said, "Colonel, by G-d you have won, that was the Rebel yell."

And he was right. Out rushed the crowd, at the head of which was Major John W. Daniel, who, lame as he was, grabbed me, and as others picked me up bodily and bore me into the Hall, he followed closely, yelling at the top of his voice. Of course I had to return thanks as soon as the Chairman of the Caucus announced to me my nomination, and the next half hour was given to congratulations. As soon as I could, I started to my home on Lee Street to let my wife know the result, but when I reached there, I found about a dozen friends, most of them members of the Legislature, who had gotten ahead of me, and the house was in an uproar. My boy, Robert, then eight years old, came in soon after I did, greatly excited, as he had heard the news on the street, whither his mother had sent him on an errand, and at the first pause told his mother with serious face, that he had dropped and broken the jug of molasses for which he had been sent. Said "he dropped it to holler," and it broke. "Yes," said Major Daniel, "if you had not smashed that jug, you ought to have been thrashed," which assurance gave the boy much comfort.

I enjoyed the victory greatly, because I had the proud consciousness of never having mentioned the election to any member of the Legislature unless the matter was broached first by him, that I had never solicited a vote or the influence of any man, nor had I ever expended a cent directly or indirectly to influence a vote. I was, and am still, sure that the result was a protest by the people through their Legislature against the unfair machinations by which I had been defeated in the Gubernatorial Convention. I know quite well that but for this feeling in my favor, I could not have triumphed over men intellectually my superiors, and endowed with much larger measure of political experience.

And while speaking of money expenditure in connection with Senatorial elections, I had an opportunity of contrasting the conditions in Virginia with those prevailing in some other states, very much to the advantage of our State, from my point of view. One day in Committee room, the subject of expenses came up in connection with the very recent re-election of one of the Senators present, who was commenting on the greatly-increased expenditure of money as compared with his first election, and remarked in the most matter-of-fact way, that his expenses first and last were not much short of ten thousand dollars. I was so surprised that almost involuntarily I said, "I can not imagine how it is possible to spend such a sum." "Why," said he, "did you not find it necessary to spend a good deal in connection with your own election?" I replied, "If my election to the Senate cost me five cents, I never knew it."

All present expressed surprise, and some were evidently incredulous, which was not surprising, as I learned that the expenses of some others had been not less than twenty thousand dollars, and now it is asserted that from half a million to a million has been expended in recent years to secure a seat in that august body.

I did not resign my office of Lieutenant-Governor of Virginia until the next year, but held my position and discharged my duties as President of the Senate of Virginia until about a month before the commencement of my term as Senator of the United States. I then resigned, and the Senate of Virginia elected Judge Thomas, of Fairfax County, as President of that body.

CHAPTER XXIX.

SENATOR OF THE UNITED STATES.

An extra session of the United States Senate was convened on the fifth of March, 1875, by proclamation of President Grant, for the purpose of acting on nominations requiring the approval of the Senate, and to transact other executive business. I was, of course, in attendance and took the oath binding me to support the Constitution of the United States and the laws made in pursuance thereof. I was impressed by one feature of this ceremony of "swearing in new members." Those from the Northern States are required not only to take an oath to support the Consitution of the United States, but in addition that "Iron-Clad Oath," as it is called, while the Southern members only swear to support the Constitution. I, of course, felt some awkwardness on first taking my seat as a member of so august a body as the Senate of the United States, for it must be remembered that I had never before served as a member of any Legislative body, and but for the experience gained as President of the Senate of Virginia, I would have been entirely ignorant of the methods of procedure, but I had fortunately acquired a fair knowledge of Parliamentary Law by my service in that capacity. I was assigned to three committees, two of them important ones, viz: on Appropriations and on Pensions, the other involved only nominal duties, viz: That on Engrossed Bills, as I never knew it to have a meeting. Subsequently I was also made a member of the Committee on the District of Columbia. The hardest-worked Committee of the Senate, with the possible exception of that on Claims, is the Committee on Pensions, of which Mr. John J. Ingalls, of Kansas, was then Chairman. Mr. Ingalls was a Republican of the most pronounced type, but a very bright, intelligent and cultured gentleman. He seemed greatly pleased when informed that I was by education and many years' practice a member of the medical profession, for he said that he and the Committee were often at a loss for want of competent knowledge on medical points, so often involved in pension cases. I served either as a member, or as Chairman of this Committee during my whole term as Senator. I can hardly describe, in appropriate terms, the amount of fraud, rascality, and perjury connected with the prosecution of claims for pensions. A pension claim once filed is immortal, there is no possibility of killing it. An adverse decision by the Commissioner of Pensions only brings back the claim in an amended form, until the Pension Agent becomes satisfied that the Commissioner will not grant it, then it comes to the Senate or House in the form of a petition or bill and is referred to the proper Committee. If reported adversely, the Member from the state or district where the applicant resides will have the bill recommitted, and this will be done again and again, until the close of the session. The next session it reappears again, and the process is repeated. When I left the Senate, applications were on file, which had been rejected time and again, every year during the six of my service. I can say with truth, that I never failed to use my best efforts to secure a pension for a deserving applicant, nor did I ever consent to the passage of a pension bill which I believed fraudulent or undeserved. On one occasion in the Senate, when resisting an effort made to reverse the adverse action of the Committee on a case, in which one of his constituents was the applicant, I charged that the papers in the case were redolent of fraud, that the certificates were forgeries as was apparent on inspection; and that were the Senate to reverse the conclusions of the Committee, they would perpetrate a great wrong, not only on the Pension Committee, but the whole country, by encouraging other fraudulent claims. To my surprise Senator Zachariah Chandler, of Michigan, perhaps the most extreme and intolerant Republican in the Chamber, arose and sustained my position heartily. He said that he had served as Secretary of the Interior during the Grant Administration, and the Pension Bureau was under his control, and he testified that he had not the slightest doubt, that at least three-fourths of the pension bills passed by Congress were steeped in fraud, that the Commissioner of Pensions would surely approve all valid claims, and when he rejected them, it was because they possessed no merit, and then they came before Congress. Thanks to this backing, the report of the Committee in this particular case was sustained, but this was by no means uniformly the case. Some of the most earnest and persistent advocates of all pension claims were Democratic Senators and Southern men.

The Committee on Appropriation have comparatively little work until towards the close of the session, then they are kept constantly busy, and often have to sit night and day, even during the sessions of the Senate. Divergent views of the House and Senate, especially if the two bodies are of different political complection, necessitate Committees of Conference, to adjust the differences between the two Houses, and this is generally a very difficult problem. And after an agreement is reached by the Conference Committee, it is still a doubtful question if either or both Houses will accept their conclusion. Should this be the case, it is necessary to appoint another Committee to go over the whole matter again.

Extra sessions of the Senate convened for the consideration of executive business are usually of short duration, but in 1875, in addition to the usual executive business, the Senate had to struggle with the vexed question of Louisiana politics, which for some time had been troubling the Administration and the country. Senator Morton introduced a resolution, as soon as the Senate was organized, declaring P. B. S. Pinchback entitled to a seat in the United States Senate, as a Senator from Louisiana, to which he claimed to have been elected by the Legislature of that State and held the certificate of Governor Kellogg to that effect. This resolution was opposed by the Democrats and a few Republicans, notably by Senator Edmonds, of Vermont, and was finally postponed until the regular session in December. Then I supposed we would adjourn, as we had completed the executive business, but the Republicans called a caucus, and the result was seen in the presentation of a resolution by Senator Frelinghuysen, approving the course of the President, in sustaining by military power the Kellogg Government, an action which had been much criticised by the Democrats. After debate extending over several days, Senator Anthony, of Rhode Island, Chairman of the Caucus, offered the following resolution: "Resolved, That the action of the President in protecting the Government of Louisiana, of which W. P. Kellogg is the Executive, and the people of that State against domestic violence, and in enforcing the laws of the United States in that State, is approved."

As the resolution embraced in effect the same questions which had been occupying the attention of the Senate while considering the claims of Pinchback to the Senatorship, there was really not much necessity of protracted debate, but a round of speeches from Democratic Senators followed on the condition of affairs in Louisiana.

As for myself, the novelty of my position, the want of familiarity with the methods of Senatorial procedure, and of intimate acquaintance with the details of the Louisiana embroglio, combined to interest me greatly in the debate on this question. I had been much impressed by the vigor, boldness and strength as a debater of Senator Morton, of Indiana, while undoubtedly most bitter and uncompromising in his hostility to slavery and the South, he challenged my admiration by the audacity of his assaults on Democratic men and measures. He was a man of little culture, but of vigorous intellect and a born fighter. Before the debate closed, many of the newly-elected Senators took part, and I among others, as I thought my constituents would expect it. During the progress of my speech, which was not written out, I took occasion to compliment Senator Morton for his ability in debate, and especially for the severe castigation he had given the Republican Senators who had differed with him on the question of the admission of Pinchback. He must have been pleased with the compliment, for a day or two afterwards, before the Senate was called to order, and while I was at my desk writing, he hobbled over to my seat, stopped, and introduced himself, and after a pleasant conversation for ten minutes, returned to his own seat. This incident was the prelude to subsequent interchanges of courteous communications, which continued until his death, not very long after. He was a martyr to spinal disease, producing paraplegia, or paralysis of the lower extremities, compelling him during the latter portion of his service to address the Senate from his chair, being unable to stand on his feet.

CHAPTER XXX.

PEN AND INK SKETCHES.

I will here record my estimate of some of the more prominent Senators of each political party, as they figured in the debates of the Forty-fourth Congress. Senator Thurman, of Ohio, was, by general consent, awarded the first place among the Democratic Senators. He was a native of Virginia, having been born in Lynchburg, but his family moved to Ohio while he was yet a youth. Without being an orator, he was a very effective speaker, and in debate, one of the most formidable men that I have ever heard, being, according to my judgment, more than a match for Conkling, Edmunds, or Morton, usually reckoned the ablest debaters on the Republican side. Next to Thurman on the Democratic side I should place Bayard, of Delaware. He was a man of unusually fine physique, polished, courteous and fluent, and took prominent part in all debates during his long Senatorial career. Senator Stephenson, of Kentucky, also a Virginian by birth, was a man of decided ability, and an influential member of the body. Senator McCreery, his colleague, was remarkable for the beauty and polish of his utterances, and the gracefulness of his diction. He never spoke without preparation, and yet he never put pen to paper. He possessed the extraordinary faculty of being able to think out, not only the general line of what he proposed to say, but to make careful selection of every word and phrase of every sentence. He was a large and rather heavy-looking man, but with fine eyes and the blackest hair I think that I have ever seen, with the slow action and deliberate utterance, so often seen to accompany men of large frame. His speeches were veritable poems, yet their effectiveness was impaired by their very beauty. The hearer was less impressed by the matter than by the grace of the diction in which it was clothed.

The Georgia Senators were Norwood and Gordon. Norwood was a man of good sense, and possessed an inexhaustible fund of humor, but was rather indolent, and averse to Committee work. He attained notoriety by the delivery of a very amusing and satirical speech in the Senate, descriptive of the genus, "Carpet Bagger," as seen in the Southern States. This speech was widely circulated and gave him considerable reputation. General John B. Gordon had won great renown by his military career in the armies of the Confederacy, which was unsurpassed by any officer of the service, for personal gallantry, undaunted courage, and untiring energy. He was the idol of his men, and a great favorite throughout the army. After the close of the war, he entered public life, was an unsuccessful candidate for Governor of Georgia, but was soon after elected to the United States Senate, where he served with distinction. He was a fluent and ready speaker, and was personally popular with both Democratic and Republican Senators. Jones, of Florida, was a new member of more than ordinary ability. He was Irish by birth, and came to America when a small boy. He had no educational advantages, was a stone-mason and worked at that trade for several years, and was never ashamed of it. During intervals of labor, he studied hard and became a lawyer and politician, and was finally elected to the Senate of the United States. He was a logical and effective speaker, but unfortunately his light went out in the intellectual darkness of insanity before the close of his term as Senator. Wallace, of Pennsylvania, and Whyte, of Maryland, were clever lawyers and good speakers while Morgan, of Alabama, a new member, soon gave evidence of that wonderful faculty of giving expression to his thoughts in a flow of words, as spontaneous and unremitting as Tennyson's Brook, which has, through a long term of service in the Senate, been his most noted characteristic.

On the Republican side, after Morton, Conkling, and Edmunds, came Ingalls, of Kansas, Allison, of Iowa, Windom, of Minnesota, Sherman of Ohio, Sergeant of California, Logan of Illinois, and Frelinghuysen, of New Jersey, all men of more than ordinary ability, good business capacity, and able to take care of themselves in the debates of the Senate Chamber. Mr. Conkling, of New York, was probably the ablest man on the Republican side, but was by no means the most influential. Several causes combined to produce this result. In the first place, he was inordinately vain—vain of his personal appearance, vain of his physical powers, being a trained athlete, vain of his accomplishments, mental and physical, and undoubtedly a gentleman of more than ordinary culture. His manner was rather supercilious, fond of sarcasm, which was one of his favorite weapons in debate, and haughty and dictatorial to an offensive degree. These attributes, of course, did not add to his popularity on either side of the Chamber, therefore he wielded less influence than many Senators, who, in intellectual power, and readiness and skill in debate, were greatly his inferiors.

I will here introduce an anecdote of Mr. Conkling which was going the rounds when I first came to Washington. Senator Chandler, of Michigan, was a man considerably above the average height and weight, and when a young man, was said to have been fond of sparring, but as he grew older abandoned the exercise. On one occasion he had dined with Senator Conkling, and after the wine and cigars, his host proposed that they should put on the gloves for a little exercise. Mr. Chandler rather reluctantly consented, but Mr. Conkling soon proved himself so immeasurably his superior in "the noble art of self-defense," that Mr. Chandler could hardly get in a blow, while he was himself most unmercifully pummelled by the New York Senator. He took his punishment like a man; never uttering a word of complaint, but set his wits to work, devising some scheme by which he could get even. Inquiry among his friends resulted in securing the name and address of a pugilist in the city who had attained considerable reputation as a prize fighter. The Michigan Senator secured an interview, and giving him an inkling of his purpose, came to an agreement that he should hold himself in readiness to come to his call whenever summoned. Some days after, the Senators again met at dinner, and Chandler having sent word for his prize fighter to come in his best toggery, introduced him to Mr. Conkling as an acquaintance just arrived from Michigan. The stranger was very quiet during dinner, and took little part in the conversation. After dinner as before, Mr. Conkling proposed some exercise with the gloves, but Mr. Chandler excused himself on some pretext, but remarked casually, that possibly his friend might be able to furnish the New York Senator with the exercise he sought. Mr. Conkling at once inquired if he could use the gloves, and he modestly confessed that he sparred a little sometimes. The gloves were soon donned, and very much to Mr. Conkling's surprise and disgust, he found himself unable to cope with the stranger, who in pursuance of Mr. Chandler's instruction, punished, and banged him about, most unmercifully, bunging up his eyes to such a degree that he was not in a presentable condition for several days. "Old Zac" told the joke in confidence to a few friends, but of course it soon leaked out, and it was a long time before the intimate relations formerly existing between the two Senators were completely restored, but Mr. Conkling never afterwards proposed to spar with the Michigander.

Senator Morton, of Indiana, possessed none of the graces of oratory, but with directness of purpose and plainness of speech struck sledge-hammer blows in debate, and was always formidable. Mr. Edmunds, of Vermont, possessed an acute, analytical mind, metaphysical in its operation, and disposed to dwell on minutiæ, oftentimes to the neglect of the more vital and important aspects of the subject matter under discussion. One of his own party in speaking of this peculiarity, illustrated it thus. "Edmunds," said he, "can see a fly on a barn door further than any man in the Senate, but he sometimes fails to see the door." He was, however, an adroit debater and socially a very pleasant and entertaining conversationalist. I liked him much and our personal relations were always pleasant. Allison, of Iowa, was one of the most useful men in the Senate, uniformly courteous and respectful to all, a good speaker, of fine business capacity, industrious and energetic, he wielded a good deal of influence. And these characteristics continue to adorn his career in the Senate, now of almost thirty years duration. He has several times been supported for the Presidential nomination by a respectable vote in the Conventions of his party, and there is little doubt that he would fill the place with ability should he ever reach it.

Mr. Ingalls, of Kansas, was a bright and cultured man, of decided literary taste, and I always thought was more fond of Belle Lettres than politics. He was a Massachusetts man by birth and education, but having removed to Kansas, and edited a paper there for several years, and thus embarked on a political career, which subsequently landed him in the United States Senate, where he served two terms, and when his party was in power, was always Chairman of the Committee on Pensions. He and I had a "general pair" on all political questions during the greater part of my service in the Senate. He was socially a very pleasant and genial gentleman, and when I was closely confined to my room on one occasion for several weeks, from trouble with my eyes, Mr. Ingalls visited me several times, and evinced the greatest interest in my case. I deeply regretted his death a few years after the close of his Senatorial career.

When I entered the Senate, General Cameron was the Senior Senator from Pennsylvania. He was then about seventy-five years of age, but hale and hearty. He was Lincoln's first Secretary of War, and under his direction, the armies of the Union were organized. He had served in the Senate off and on since 1845, and had also been Minister to Russia, and wielded much influence in the councils of his party. He was a bitter and uncompromising Republican, but was not devoid of kindly feeling, of which I had a demonstration during the latter days of the Grant Administration.

After the Presidential election of 1876, when every one except a few astute and unscrupulous politicians admitted the election of Mr. Tilden, Mrs. Long, the wife of General Long, of the Confederate Army, having a large family of children on her hands, in addition to a husband totally blind, was advised by some of her friends, particularly by Colonel Charles Venable, of the University of Virginia, to make application for appointment as Postmaster at Charlottesville, where she lived, but after getting up her recommendations, the Electoral Commission decided that General Hayes had been elected, and her chances for the position seemed desperate. She came on to Washington, however, with letters to myself and others, urging us to use our best efforts in her behalf. When I went out to the Marble room in response to her card, and listened to what was really "a tale of woe," my sympathies were greatly enlisted in her behalf, but I could see little to encourage her hopes. I told her frankly that my influence was nil with the Grant Administration, and I knew of no Democratic Senator able to furnish efficient aid. I asked if she could think of no Republican Senator upon whom she might have a claim, she reflected a moment and shook her head hopelessly, saying there was not one with whom she had any acquaintance, or on whom she had the slightest claim. "I used to know General Cameron when I was a child," she said, "and often visited his daughters, who were my schoolmates, but he has doubtless forgotten all about me." Mrs. Long was a daughter of General Sumpter, of the United States Army, and knowing this, I felt a little encouraged by what she had said, and replied, "Mrs. Long, there is not a Senator who can aid you as much as General Cameron, if you can enlist him earnestly in your cause. It will be hard to get an interview with him, because he never pays any attention to the cards of strangers, but you remain here, and I will go in and try my best to get him to come out, and if he does come, you tell him exactly the story you have told me, and I do not think that he can refuse to aid you." She retained her seat and I returned to the Senate Chamber. While not intimate with General Cameron, our personal relations were of rather a pleasant character (as I will illustrate with another anecdote presently), and I went at once to his seat, and after a friendly greeting, opened the conversation by telling him that I had been greatly interested in an interview that I had just had with a lady who was an acquaintance of his, and a schoolmate of his daughters. "Who is she?" he asked. "Mrs. Long, who is a daughter of General Sumpter, and says that she went to school with your daughters." "Yes," he replied, "I recollect her very well, and she was a very nice girl." "Well, she is now in the Marble room," says I, "anxious to see you, and I will esteem it a personal favor if you will see her for a few minutes." "Certainly I will," he said, and went out at once. I watched the door very anxiously, as I thought the length of the interview would furnish a pretty good augury of the result. He was absent at least half an hour, and on re-entering the Chamber came at once to my seat. His first words were: "Why Senator, that poor woman is in a h - ll of a fix." "She certainly is," was my reply, "and you are the man to get her out of it." Said he, "I will do anything that I can for her." "Then," I said, "go at once and see General Grant, and ask him to appoint her post-master at Charlottesville, and I am sure that he will do it." "Well," said he, "I will try it." "Then I know you will succeed," said I. I went out and cautioned Mrs. Long not to mention a word of what had passed to any one whatever. And she, of course, promised silence.

Two days afterwards, General Cameron came to me with the gratifying intelligence that she had been appointed, and though the Virginia Republicans aided by several Republican Senators, made desperate efforts to induce General Grant to withdraw the appointment, they failed utterly, and she was speedily in possession of the place.

This incident secured for the old General a high place in my regard, which was subsequently shared by his son, Don Cameron, who succeeded his father in the Senate, and by his earnest efforts four years after prevented Mrs. Long's removal from the office after her first term expired. This occurred about the close of my term in the Senate, and as soon as I heard of the scheme, I went to Senator Don Cameron and told him that as Mrs. Long had been appointed at the request, and upon the recommendation of his father, he must see to it that she was not turned out. He at once pledged his best efforts to retain her in position, and succeeded in so doing.

Not very long after I entered the Senate, General Cameron came to my seat and invited me to his Committee room to take a glass of champagne with some friends. I excused myself on the ground that I never drank champagne. "Oh, well," he said, "I can give you some good old whiskey if you prefer it." "But I don't drink whiskey either," said I, "and I hope you will excuse me." "Oh, certainly," said he. A few days after, as he was passing near my seat, he stopped and said, "Senator Withers, I wish you would give me a chew of good old Virginia tobacco." "I am very sorry," said I, "that I am unable to accommodate you, but as I never use tobacco, I have none." "Good G - d," said he with manifest feeling, "A Senator from Virginia, who neither drinks whiskey, nor chews tobacco! Why, what's the world coming to?"

Whether rightfully or wrongfully, General Cameron was generally recognized as the first "Boss" in Pennsylvania politics, and the system organized by him has been elaborated and improved by his successors until it has attained its present state of perfection. General Cameron's axiom was never to attempt to control the choice or election of members of the Legislature, but afterwards to secure the support of a majority of that body, which he averred was less troublesome and much less expensive.

Thomas W. Ferry and Isaac P. Christiancy were the Senators from Michigan, when I entered that body. The first was elected President *pro tem.* of the Senate, and was selected for that honorable service whenever his party was in the majority, during the whole of my term. He was a gentleman of good appearance, courteous and polite, a fair presiding officer, and well versed in Parliamentary law. He did not often participate in the debates of that body, and his speeches were generally prepared carefully.

Judge Christiancy had just supplanted Senator Zac Chandler as Senator, much to the gratification of the moderate Republicans and of course of the Democrats. He had for years filled the place of Chief Justice of Michigan, and had a high reputation as a jurist, but his political experience was limited. I do not think his service in the Senate of the United States added much to his reputation. He was a widower, sixty-six years of age and by no means handsome, but he fell in love with a beautiful young girl who was employed in one of the departments, and who boarded, I think, at the same house, and despite the opposition and against the advice of his family and friends, married her with little loss of time. Few persons were aware of the intended marriage, and the morning it came off, he was, of course, absent from his seat. The roll was called on some question before the Senate, and when his name was called, his colleague gravely announced that Senator Christiancy was absent, but was *paired that morning,* the witticism, of course, being greeted with a laugh. As was to have been expected, the marriage was not a happy one. The stalwarts of the party being desirous of securing the return of Chandler to the Senate effected an arrangement by which Judge Christiancy was nominated and confirmed as Minister to Chile, accepted the appointment, resigned his seat, and departed with his young wife on his mission, and Chandler was elected to succeed him. Judge

Christiancy and his wife, after giving occasion to considerable gossip and scandal, separated and were subsequently divorced.

One of the Senators from Mississippi when I entered that body was Blanch K. Bruce, who enjoyed the distinction of being the only negro who up to that time had ever served in the Senate of the United States. He was a native of Prince Edward County, Virginia, was born a slave, and I knew his master personally. After the close of the war he went to Mississippi, and being a man of good sense, acquired some property, and was in Reconstruction days appointed Sheriff of his county and filled the place creditably and profitably to himself. He was made a member of the Levee Board, and Tax Collector of his county, and elected in 1875 to the Senate of the United States. Bruce was conservative in his views, and a good representative of his race, for though a pronounced Republican, he would, not unfrequently, when he believed the interests of the colored people demanded, break loose from his party associates and act with his Section. I rarely failed to secure his vote on any measure in which the South was interested, which was not purely of a political character. I think both he and his colleague, Governor Alcorn, had a pretty correct conception of the estimate put by Northern Republicans on the race issue, for I heard each of them avow the belief that the lynching of negroes and other cruelties inflicted on them in the South were really welcomed by the Northern Republicans, as they furnished the material for firing the Northern heart and were potent political factors in elections. Bruce's speech avowing this belief was, it is true, made at a night session, after he had been dining out, and was another illustration of the truth of the old Latin axiom, "*In vino veritas.*" He was greatly interested in the affairs of the "Freedman's Bank," and submitted a resolution providing for a special committee to investigate its management, which passed the Senate by unanimous vote. He was made chairman, and allowed to select the members of his committee, and to the surprise of many of his political friends, selected Garland, Brown, and myself as three of them. We all agreed to serve, and made an earnest and protracted effort to ferret out the parties responsible for the catastrophe which ended in the loss of some millions of money deposited by the credulous colored people of the South. The rogues who engineered the scheme were sharp enough to cover up their peculations so effectually as to elude conviction. With the exception of Senator Cameron of Wisconsin, the Republican members of the committee evinced little interest in the proceedings and rarely attended the sessions.

Among others examined as witnesses was Frederick Douglas, the somewhat noted fugitive slave, who was President of the bank at the time of its suspension, and as he was reputed to be an unusually clever and astute individual, many thought him responsible for the failure and a beneficiary by that catastrophe. His examination before the committee satisfied every member that this suspicion was unfounded, and that he had played the role of dupe throughout. The artless way in which he detailed the circumstances by which he was inveigled into giving his individual check for $10,000.00 to meet an overdue draft, "Just until tomorrow, as a draft we expected today failed to come," was conclusive on this point. "I thought it was all right," said he, "but that draft has never come yet, so far as I know, nor have I ever seen anything of my $10,000.00."

Boutwell and Daws were the Senators from Massachusetts in the forty-fourth Congress. Each had been long in political life. Of course they were Republicans of the most pronounced type, but there was a great difference between them. Senator Daws was courteous, and always observed the proprieties of debate, but Senator Boutwell was, without an exception, the most bitter, malignant, and offensive radical Republican in the whole body. He really seemed to entertain feelings of personal hatred towards every Southern man, and rarely spoke without exhibiting these traits. He was a man of ability, and had filled many honorable positions in the public service, had been Governor of Massachusetts, and a member of General Grant's Cabinet in 1869, but in 1873 resigned after his election to the Senate to succeed Vice-President Henry Wilson. I have in my experiences met with many bitter partisans of all political parties, but Senator Boutwell went a bow-shot beyond them all. He appeared not only to dislike the South as a section, but to feel a personal animosity towards every man from that locality. On one occasion during a debate in the Senate with Mr. Bayard, he declared his belief "that all men reared under the influence of slavery, when they professed loyalty to the Union, were liars and hypocrites," with a good deal more of the same vituperative character. Senator Bayard, General Maxey, of Texas, and I, myself, commented on these utterances with such severity, that he revised his remarks before they were printed in permanent form in the Congressional Record, and modified the coarseness of his language in some degree, but it was still bad enough. This debate was published by the Democrats as a campaign document in the canvass of 1876.

James G. Blaine was appointed to fill the vacancy occasioned by the resignation of Senator Lot M. Morrell, of Maine. when he accepted a seat in President Hayes' Cabinet. The rather unique incidents connected with this appointment caused a good deal of gossip at the time.

While a member of the House of Representatives some years before, Mr. Blaine was charged with certain corrupt acts in connection with the Little Rock & Fort Smith Railway Company, and a committee of investigation was appointed to examine into the matter, and make report of the results of their inquiry. Of this committee, my old friend and comrade, General Eppa Hunton, was made Chairman. This committee in the discharge of its duties, elicited some damaging testimony, and the friends of Mr. Blaine were anxious and apprehensive as to the result. I ought to add that the House which originated these proceedings, and appointed this committee was a Democratic one, and of course a majority of the committee were connected with that political party. They formally demanded of Mr. Blaine, the production of a somewhat famous correspondence, known as the "Mulligan Letters," which it was supposed would throw much light on the matter under investigation. Mr. Blaine refused to produce them. The next day, the public was startled by the intelligence that Mr. Blaine had been suddenly stricken down by a sun-stroke, or, as his friends feared, by apoplexy. When the committee met on Monday to continue their investigation, they had to adjourn for two weeks on account of Mr. Blaine's extreme illness. Two days after this the Republican Convention met in Cincinnati to select a candidate for the Presidency, and General Hayes was nominated for that office on Friday, the sixteenth of June. The Monday afterwards, Mr. Blaine addressed a large crowd of Republicans in front of his residence. Senator Morrill, of Maine, was appointed Secretary of the Treasury, and accepted the position after a few days' consideration, and of course resigned his position in the Senate. The Governor of Maine at once appointed Mr. Blaine to fill the vacancy, and he lost no time in resigning his seat in the House of Representatives, and on the twelfth of July was sworn in as a member of the Senate, which removed him from the jurisdiction of the House of Representatives, and, of course, put an end to the pending investigation.

Entering the Senate with these antecedents, Mr. Blaine was undoubtedly and seriously handicapped. Indeed, I may safely say, that his brilliant forensic powers and wonderful rhetorical gifts, were better adapted to the arena of the House than to the Senate. He was by no means "*Persona Grata*" to many of the leaders of his party, and they rather "gave him the cold shoulder." Senator Conkling and he were scarcely on speaking terms, in consequence of some very sharp passages which had occurred between them while members of the House, in which sparring, it was generally conceded, that the distinguished New Yorker came out second best. When Mr. Blaine came into the Senate, he was, with the exception always of Senator Boutwell, my pet aversion. His fiery denunciations of the South and her people, his extravagant laudation of the Republican party and its policy, the charges of venality and corruption everywhere rife, had generated in my mind a strong prejudice against him, which I made no effort to overcome. He was placed on the Committee of Appropriations, and there I, of course, met him frequently. He was always markedly polite to the Democratic members of the committee, and evidently strove to secure the personal good will of those who differed from him politically. As well as I can remember, the first change of my sentiments towards him had its origin in an occurrence which transpired in committee during the consideration of the "*Sundry Civil Bill.*" When the war broke out, considerable amounts were due Southern Mail Contractors. These claims were, of course, hung up when the war begun, but the Accounting Officers of the Treasury Department had audited and adjusted these claims, and ascertained the balances due each contractor, which was placed to their credit on the books of that department, but the Republican Congress persistently refused to appropriate any money for their payment. As more than ten years had now passed since the close of the war, and the Treasury books showed that the balances were justly due for services actually rendered, I moved in committee to amend the bill by inserting an item of an amount sufficient to pay these claims. There was little discussion, as the Chairman remarked, "I suppose we had as well vote on the amendment at once, as all of us understand the question. And to my disgust and indignation, the amendment was defeated by a party vote. Though not entirely unprepared for the result, the manifest injustice of the procedure aroused my indignation, and I did not hesitate to give expression to my feelings, and arising from my seat at the table, walked the floor in high dudgeon. I had taken but few turns, when Mr. Blaine joined me, saying as he did so, "You are mad now because we refused to vote for your amendment." "Yes," said I, "I am. You will all admit that the claims are just, that they have never been paid, and these balances stand to the credit of these men on the books of the Treasury Department, and I can not understand how any honest or honorable man can refuse to pay them." He put his arm through mine and continued the walk, saying: "I have been a great deal longer in political life than you have, and will therefore venture a suggestion: Had we adopted your amendment, and incorporated it into the bill, as soon as it was read in the Senate, don't you know that Conkling, Boutwell, and men of that stripe would jump right on it, and on the committee which reported it, set up a howl and crack the party lash, thus insuring its defeat." I saw, of course, the force of his suggestion, but replied, "You mean to say, then, that as long as your party is in power, these men can never hope to receive what is justly their dues?" "You do this," said he. "Wait until the bill gets into the Senate and when amendments are in order, watch your opportunity, and quietly move your amendment without making any remarks at all, and I and several others on the committee will vote with you if no fight is made on it, and it may pass." I saw at once that he was right and thanked him for his suggestion. This plan was successfully carried out, and thus the long-deferred payment was made. This is only one instance of many which showed a kindly desire to render me a service and I could not refuse to recognize the friendly interest which prompted them. Personally, Mr. Blaine was one of the most genial and pleasant men that I have ever met, socially, one of the brightest and most attractive, possessing to a remarkable degree those qualities usually characterized as "magnetic." His standard of political ethics, however, was far different from ours. In politics he believed that the end justified the means, and to secure results, everything was fair. He could not, therefore, be called a sincere man, and hence arose those bitter and vindictive utterances, in which he was from time to time wont to indulge, in his speeches and writings. On one occasion after an exhibition of this kind, I met him in the corridor of the Senate, when he addressed me in a friendly way, and I told him plainly, that "I could not respect a man who really felt towards the people of my section such bitterness and hatred as were embodied in the speech which he had just made." "Oh," said he, throwing his arm over my shoulder, "my dear sir, can't you understand that a man is bound to make some speeches for *home consumption?*" And he evidently regarded this as ample explanation of the bitter denunciations in which he had been indulging. It frequently happened that I was called on to serve with Senator Blaine on a sub-committee, to which was entrusted the duty of preparing the regular appropriation bills, and the intimate and free intercourse thus engendered afforded me ample opportunity to study his character, and to observe his peculiar traits. The result was, that while I hoped that my principles were not at all impaired, my prejudices entirely disappeared under the molifying influences of his geniality, his kindness of heart, and winning personality.

Senators Howe and Angus Cameron, of Wisconsin, were both men of ability. The first was serving his third term in the Senate having been elected from the Supreme Court bench of Wisconsin. He was in appearance and characteristics a typical New Englander and an ardent Republican, inclined to humor; but the humor was rather of a grim than genial character. Senator Cameron was elected to succeed Zack Chandler by a combination of liberal Republicans and Democrats. He proved a competent and useful member of the body, but stuck to his party on all political questions.

Senator Harris, of Tennessee, was placed in the Senate as successor to Henry Cooper. He had served more than one term as the Governor of Tennessee, was devoted to the cause of the Confederacy, served on the staff of General Albert Sidney Johnston, and was by his side when he received his fatal wound at the battle of Shiloh. He was quick and fiery in temperament, of undaunted courage, and possessed of much more than ordinary ability. I was very partial to him, and always regarded him as a high type of Southern gentleman. As illustrative of his quick temper, I recall an occasion, when a Conference Committee of the two Houses were laboring to reach an agreement on the divergent views of the Senate and House on one of the regular appropriation bills, the gentleman representing the views of the House maintained their position with great persistency, and one of them, a giant in size, from one of the Northwestern States, was doing most of the talking, and with scant courtesy and in very objectionable tones, characterized a statement made by Senator Harris, as unwarranted by the facts of the case, and added that the members of the committee from the Senate were manifestly uninformed as to the merits of the question at issue, instantly Harris sprang from his seat, and with fiery tones and flashing eyes, told him that he was a "d - - d liar." There was instant silence, and I fully expected the Honorable Member to resent the insult by a blow, but he opened not his mouth. I quickly interjected some observation on the matter in controversy, to tide over the unpleasantness, other gentlemen of the committee chimed in with the same object in view, and the affair passed off at that. As soon as the conference ended, Harris took me aside, and asked if I thought he had said anything improper, and I replied that "I thought he was more savage than the circumstances demanded." "Oh, well," said he, "if that is all you object to, I am satisfied. I thought perhaps that I had not repelled the offensive language with sufficient vigor."

The Senators from North Carolina were General Mat. Ransom and Judge Merrimon. The first was a gentleman of handsome person, very polite and affable, cordial and pleasing in manner. He seldom spoke, but always spoke well, and was personally popular with the Senators of both parties. His colleague, Judge Merrimon, had been elected by a coalition between a faction of the Democratic party and the Republican members of the North Carolina Legislature. As General Vance had been the caucus nominee of the Democratic party, the election of Judge Merrimon placed him in bad odor with the Democratic party of his State. He was, however, an active and efficient member, attentive to his duties, fond of debate, and being generally well informed, sustained himself fairly well.

From South Carolina, the cradle of Secession, came Thomas J. Robertson, a Republican, and what was remarkable, a native of the State. He had always been an outspoken Union man, and an old line Whig. He was a man of large means, amiable, indolent, rarely ever spoke, and cultivated the friendship of Democrats, rather than Republicans, and voted with them on most questions. His seat was just in front of mine, and we had frequently interchanges of friendly chat and banter. When the prospects of obtaining a Democratic majority in the State became bright, and the result was plainly foreshadowed, I said to him one day, "Well, Senator, I see that the prospects for our party in your State are very good. The change in public sentiment seems to be going on rapidly, and what will become of you then?" "By Gracious," said he, "if the people think that they can change any quicker than I can, I would like to see them try it!"

These pen and ink sketches of the more noted members of the Senate have been sufficiently extended, and I will now refer to some of the most interesting questions which came before that body for consideration. The first of these was the Louisiana Question, to which I have already referred. Rival State Governments had struggled for supremacy in that locality for years. Fraud and bribery, perjury and forgery, were charged against the Carpet Bag interlopers, who by these means, aided by a solid negro vote, strove to perpetuate their rule. And as all the Returning Boards in the State were composed of the adherents of that party, they had no difficulty in supplying their candidates with certificates of election in due form of law. The process was simple. If the Conservatives obtained a majority of hundreds or thousands in any parish or district, the Returning Board would simply throw out a sufficient number of precincts on the plea of intimidation to leave the Republican candidates in the majority, and would give them the certificate of election. Violence and intimidation were charged against the Democrats no doubt in many cases truly. Each side claimed recognition by Congress and the Executive as the legitimate State government. Armed collisions between the supporters of each party were of frequent occurrence, and the City of New Orleans was the principal theater, upon which these scenes were enacted. The Senate of the United States, under the leadership of Senator Morton, Logan, Boutwell, and others of that stripe, appointed a committee, largely Republican of course, with instructions to visit Louisiana during the recess, examine into the condition of affairs, take testimony, and make report to the Senate. This committee subsequently reported that the State was without legal government, that neither the Kellogg nor McEnery State Government was a legal one, and recommended that Congress should order an election to be held in accordance with law, and thus to make final settlement of the question. The Senate, however, refused to sanction this procedure. There were some Republicans who still believed that the State only could take such action, and their votes together with those of the Democratic members of the Senate, defeated the recommendation of the committee. Subsequently the President issued a proclamation, recognizing the Kellogg Government, and ordered a military force to be stationed in Louisiana, for the purpose of sustaining that government, and enforcing the decrees of the Court, which supported Kellogg. This Kellogg Legislature had elected Pinchback as Senator of the United States, and he had ever since been clamoring for admission. But the Committee on Elections, to which his credentials had been referred, reported that the Legislature which elected him was unconstitutionally created, and therefore all its acts were illegal, consequently Mr. Pinchback was still hung up between earth and heaven.

At the extra session of the forty-fourth Congress, Mr. Mora resolution, declaring Pinchback entitled to his seat in the Senate, and on this motion a protracted debate was precipitated which lasted for two weeks or more. Senator Edmunds of Vermont led the debate in antagonism to Morton's resolution. And the Democratic Senators, with a few Republican members, sustained his views. A caucus was finally called by the Republicans, and they ascertained that if the resolution was forced to a vote they would be beaten, so the next day, on motion of Pinchback's friends, the whole matter was postponed until the regular session of Congress in December. By this refusal to recognize the legality of the Kellogg Legislature, the Senate, in effect, administered a rebuke to the Grant Administration, which had not only given such recognition by Presidential proclamation, but had ordered troops to New Orleans to sustain it by force of arms if necessary. To relieve the faithful from this implied censure, after caucus consideration, a resolution was introduced into the Senate by Mr. Freelinghuyser, of New Jersey, specifically approving the course of the President, and urging a continuance of this policy. This resolution was opposed by the Democrats, but they had no assistance from the Republican members. They illogically, as it seemed to me, approved the recognition of the Kellogg Legislature and Government, although claiming it an unconstitutional body, and its acts null and void. The only excuse offered was, that by this action of the President, the State was saved from the domestic violence and lawlessness which would otherwise have ensued. In the course of the debate, however, that feature of the resolution recommending an indefinite extension of the interference by the Federal Government with the domestic affairs of the State was so severely criticised, that Senator Anthony, of Rhode Island, proposed an amendment to the original resolution, omitting that clause, which was finally adopted by a party vote. That I may close the Pinchback episode, I will state that when his case was taken up in December, after a repetition of the arguments, pro and con, which had been ventilated during the special session, a vote was finally reached, and Senator Morton's resolution was defeated. Pinchback was quite a handsome and shrewd Quadroon, the reputed son of a noted gamester of New Orleans, and was born in slavery.

CHAPTER XXXI.

IMPEACHMENT OF GENERAL W. W. BELKNAP.

The forty-sixth Congress was noted for the fierce antagonism between the two Houses of Congress on the appropriation bills. The House of Representatives was largely Democratic, and under the leadership of the Hon. Samuel Randall, of Philadelphia, Speaker of the House, made a determined effort to curtail the extravagance and reckless expenditure of money which they charged had marked the Republican Administration. As all of the appropriation bills are required by the Constitution to originate in the House of Representatives, the committees of that body presented bills largely reducing the amounts appropriated for the support of the Public Service. When their bills came to the Senate, they were amended by a large increase in all the items. In these the House, of course, refused to concur, hence many Committees of Conference were necessary before they could come to an agreement. While in full sympathy with my party friends in their effort to reduce the expenditures, I thought in some cases they went too far. For example, many of the officers and employes of the Government were in receipt of salaries fixed by law, the pay of the soldiers and sailors was also a fixed sum, and I could see no valid cause for refusing to make an appropriation of the money required to make these payments, yet in many such cases, the House bills did not provide the means of doing this. The Senate amendments increased the amount appropriated to enable these employes to receive what the law allowed them. I thought that the proper thing to do, and so voted to the dissatisfaction of some of my party friends, who seemed to think it good politics to be able to show a great saving in public expenditure, though admitting the necessity of providing subsequently in a deficiency bill for the shortage in these salaries. I adhered to my own opinion, however, nor has subsequent reflection taught me that I erred in my conclusion. On many of these appropriation bills the fight was very bitter and protracted, notably on the "Army Bill," and each House adhered with such tenacity to its own views that no committee of conference (and there were many) could reconcile their conflicting views, and the bill failed to pass in consequence, thus necessitating an extra session of Congress.

Another matter which occupied a good deal of the time and attention of the Senate was the impeachment and trial of General William W. Belknap, Secretary of War. The House presented articles of impeachment against him, charging the corrupt sale of Post Traderships, accompanied by proofs designed to sustain the charge. The affair created a great scandal, and as developments disclosed testimony going to sustain the charge, General Belknap resigned his place in the Cabinet and in the Army, early on the morning of the second of March, 1876, and the President at once accepted his resignation. His friends and counsel claimed that after his resignation was accepted, he was no longer amenable to prosecution or impeachment. The Senate as a Court of Impeachment, after much discussion by the counsel on each side, refused to sustain this view, and the trial proceeded. The House had appointed a committee of seven of its members to conduct the impeachment before the Senate. These were Messrs. Knott, of Kentucky, Lord, of New York, Lynde, of Wisconsin, McMahon, of Ohio, Jenks, of Pennsylvania, Lapham, of New York, and Hoar, of Massachusetts. Messrs. Jere Black, Montgomery, Blair, and Matt Carpenter acted as counsel for the accused, all lawyers of great ability and national reputation. I was much impressed by the dignity and solemnity of the proceedings during this trial, as it was the first time I had ever witnessed anything of the kind. The Chief Justice of the Supreme Court of the United States presided, as President of the Court of Impeachment, and the utmost decorum marked all the deliberations. After the question of jurisdiction was decided there was little time lost in discussing methods of procedure. Carpenter was the most aggressive of the counsel for the accused, and McMahon of the managers, and these two had some lively passages at arms. Each day the Senate transacted its usual morning business, and at the hour fixed, resolved itself into a Court of

Impeachment and proceeded with the trial. The proof of the charges was conclusive and unassailable, and the arguments of the managers and counsel were able and interesting. The chief point in the defence was that General Belknap having resigned and his resignation having been accepted by the President, he was no longer amenable to impeachment. When these were concluded, the vote was taken on the different articles of impeachment, the verdict of thirty-six Senators was "Guilty," and of twenty-five "Not guilty," and in nearly every case where the vote was in the negative, the Senator so voting alleged that his vote was so cast because of "Want of Jurisdiction." As well as I remember, only two or three Senators expressed the opinion that the proof offered did not sustain the charges beyond a doubt. As a two-thirds vote is required to convict, the accused was declared acquitted.

The Centennial Exposition came off at the City of Philadelphia in 1876, and the bill making an appropriation to assist in meeting the expenses of the Mammoth Show, gave rise to a protracted struggle, both in the Senate and House. Many of the old-time Democrats believed that Congress had no power under the Constitution to vote money to a private corporation for the purpose of aiding them in their enterprise, and called on the advocates of the bill to point out the clause of the Constitution authorizing it, which, of course, they could not do, but claimed the right under the shadowy inferential powers deducible from that instrument. It was also claimed, and with some plausibility, that as our Government had announced its purpose of holding this Exposition, and invited other nations to attend, they were bound to provide the means for receiving and entertaining the invited guests who might accept the invitation. The appropriation qualified by certain conditions was finally voted in each House, and both Houses of Congress were invited by the managers to be present at the opening ceremonies in May. Many Senators and Representatives attended, the Senate having taken a recess of a week to enable them to do so. I was not of the party, as I proposed attending with some of my family in the fall after the adjournment of Congress, when the weather would be more pleasant. I carried out my purpose in the month of October, when, accompanied by my wife and son, Robert, then eleven years of age, with my brother-in-law, Dr. Robert T. Lemmon, and his wife, and my son-in-law, E. P. Goggin, and his wife, we made the trip. When we reached Philadelphia and were driven to the Hotel at which I had engaged board some time before, we found we could get no rooms and as the city was greatly crowded, we had much difficulty in securing accommodations, which we did finally at a private boarding-house. We remained a week "doing the Exposition," but there was so much to see, so many things claiming and deserving attention, that one's mind became so crowded by different images and impressions, that it was difficult to retain a distinct recollection of anything. I believe I spent more time in inspecting and enjoying the painting and statuary in the Art Building, than any other part of the Exhibition. The State of Virginia had made no appropriation for the construction of a building to receive the exhibits of her citizens, and provide room for their accommodation, but this neglect was partially remedied by the liberality of one of her public-spirited citizens, Mr. E. G. Booth, who was at that time a resident of Philadelphia, where he had married. He caused a building to be erected on the grounds at his own expense, furnished it, and each day provided refreshments to which all Virginians were invited, and with generous hospitality contributed to the comfort of all comers. My wife and I spent a day in Burlington, New Jersey, at the home of Major Ellison, who had married my wife's only sister, who had died a few years before, but her children were still living. He resided in a beautiful estate with magnificent house and grounds, about a mile outside of the town of Burlington. On our return we stopped a while in Baltimore to visit some friends, especially that I might consult Dr. Chisholm, the oculist, in regard to my right eye, which had been causing me a good deal of trouble as well as suffering for some months. He examined, prescribed and treated the diseased spot on the cornea, which had recently appeared, and thought it susceptible of cure. I visited him at stated intervals for many months, and underwent various minor operations, and other methods of treatment, but without permanent benefit. Subsequently, I placed myself under the care of Doctor Marmion, an oculist of Washington City, who soon decided that I would have to submit to a severe operation, involving the division of the cornea and the removal of the iris, which was done at my residence in Alexandria in 1877. I took no chloroform and he did the work with rapidity and efficiency. I had to submit to several weeks' confinement in a dark room, with eyes closely bandaged, which was anything but a pleasant experience. All, however, proved in vain, as useful vision was never restored. One of the most regretable results of this trouble was, that it put an end to my hunting and fishing. Having lost the use of my "shooting eye," I concluded it was useless at my time of life to learn to shoot from the left shoulder, so I gave it up altogether, which was a great privation. Fishing with one eye only, a person can not judge distance accurately, and in bass and trout fishing this is indispensable, for without this faculty your fly is liable to land almost anywhere in making a cast.

During the first session of the Forty-fourth Congress, Hon. Allen T. Caperton, Senator from West Virginia, died rather unexpectedly. He was a sufferer from that painful and distressing form of heart trouble known as *Angina Pectoris,* and in July had a severe paroxysm, which for a while threatened his life, but the remedies administered gave apparent relief, but before he was able to leave his bed another and more violent attack supervened, under which he speedily sank and died on the twenty-sixth of July. He was a gentleman of Old School, a native of Monroe County, universally esteemed and respected by a large circle of friends and relatives. Of the strictest integrity, undaunted courage, polished and graceful manners, a fine lawyer, and a man of wealth, his death was a great loss, not only to his family and friends, but to the whole State of which he was in part the representative in the Senate. I was requested by his colleague, Senator Davis, to deliver an address on the occasion of his Memorial Services, which were held on the twenty-first of December, 1876, and consented to do so, as we had been warm personal as well as political friends. This was my first experience in the discharge of this peculiar and mournful duty. Among other participants in this Memorial Service was Senator Edmunds, of Vermont, whose remarks made a lasting impression on my memory, because of the virtual admission of the truth of the claim so constantly asserted by leading Democrats, that the provisions of the Federal Constitution were violated when West Virginia was made a state in 1863. True, he did not distinctly admit that such was the case, but no other conclusion could be drawn from the language used by this distinguished leader of the Republican Party. "The character of the political body," says he, "that as the Legislature of Virginia assented to the dismemberment of the State was not the clearest as being the Constitutional Legislature of the old State," followed by this: "It is not one of the least evils flowing from powerful assaults upon lawful government, that the Government itself is often forced to extreme measures, and to the verge of its authority to preserve and protect itself, and thus it sometimes transmits to later times unsatisfactory precedents and examples that many less emergencies are too apt to resort to as the justification or excuse to other steps dangerous to the Commonwealth." I have made this quotation that my readers may know how the steps taken by a reckless Republican Congress to wrest from the old State so large a portion of her territory were regarded by some of the participants in this political rape. Indeed, more than one of the prominent actors in the legislation of the Reconstruction days have admitted to me that many of the measures adopted were of more than doubtful constitutionality and only excusable on the ground of political necessity.

In December we heard of the death of John W. Royall, my wife's favorite brother, in Cattleville, Missouri, leaving a family of six children, their mother had been dead for two years or more. As James Royall, my wife's oldest brother, had also died in July, 1876, and as they had no near relatives living in Missouri, after conferring with Mrs. Royall, we concluded to have the children come to Virginia, where we could look after them. The oldest, a boy named Brumfield, then twelve or thirteen years of age, brought them to Virginia, and Jennie and I met them at the station in Washington and took them to Alexandria, and subsequently to Lynchburg. We took Brumfield to Wytheville with us, and Carrie, the youngest but one, of the children. Brumfield was an uncommonly steady business boy and got a place in Captain Gibboney's store, the largest mercantile establishment in the place, and gave entire satisfaction. Mrs. Royall took the other girls to her home and there they were educated and lived until her death, except that Lizzie, the oldest, went to live with my daughter, Mrs. John Reed, and remained with her until her marriage. Returning from this digression on family matters, I turn to public events.

CHAPTER XXXII.

THE ELECTORAL COMMISSION.

When the Presidential election came off, it was claimed and believed by all Democrats, and I think, by most Republicans that Mr. Tilden was elected by a safe majority, and the claim put forward by William E. Chandler, of New Hampshire, that the states of South Carolina, Florida and Louisiana had been cast for Hayes, electing him by one vote, was regarded as a mere piece of bravado to soften the sting of defeat, for the fact was notorious, that each of these states had been carried by the Democratic candidate by several thousand majority. But as time passed and the claim was persistently urged, the people began to recall the audacious acts of Republican Returning Boards, especially in Louisiana, thoughtful men began to realize that the situation was not devoid of danger, and that the Democrats might be called on to defend their Constitutional rights by every means at their command. The Government was practically in the hands of the Republicans, for though the House of Representatives was Democratic, that body, under the provisions of the Constitution, played but a small part in the determination of the results of a Presidential election. Anxious researches were made among the old records to determine precisely the relative powers of the Vice-President, the Senate, the House, and the joint Convention of the two Houses before whom the vote was to be counted. It was then seen that the mode of procedure had varied considerably in counting the vote cast at the election for President. The Constitution directs that the Electors in each state shall meet and vote by ballot for President and Vice-President, and shall make distinct lists of all persons voted for, and the number of votes each received which list they shall sign and certify and transmit, under seal to the seat of Government of the United States, directed to the President of the Senate. "The President of the Senate shall in the presence of the Senate and House of Representatives, open all the certificates, and the votes shall then be counted." Ordinarily a very simple procedure, as there are usually only one set of returns transmitted to the Vice-President, but the case is very different when there are conflicting returns forwarded to the President of the Senate, as was the case after this election. From several states two sets of returns were sent in, and from one three returns, or papers claiming to be returns, were in the hands of the President of the Senate. Now, the Constitution does not indicate the authority which shall determine which are the legal returns when more than one set of papers are sent to the President of the Senate, and this, therefore, became the controverted point, which elicited much debate both in the Senate and House. Some argued that the power was placed by implication in the hands of the President of the Senate, as he was alone authorized to receive and open the returns, and of course, when more than one set of papers were sent him, should decide which were the legal and proper papers. To this it was answered that under the Constitution the President of the Senate was a mere Administrative Officer, vested with no judicial power to determine between antagonistic returns, but that the decision rested with the two Houses of Congress acting separately. To this it was answered that the two Houses acted as mere spectators, and had no power to decide on the validity of the returns when opened by the President, but could only see that the votes cast were correctly counted. Others contended that when the question arose as to the papers returned, it should be determined by the Judges of the Supreme Court, who alone can authoritatively construe the Constitution. Now, the President of the Senate was a Republican, the majority of the Senators were Republican, the same was the case with the majority of the Supreme Court, but the House was Democratic, and among other suggestions, one was made proposing that the House voting by States should determine which was the valid return. As it seemed impossible for the Senate to unite in any action looking to a decision of the vexed question, a bill was prepared providing for an Electoral Commission, to whom the decision of all disputed matters in connection with counting the vote should be referred. This Commission was to be composed of five members of the Senate, five members of the House of Representatives (to be selected by viva voce vote), and five associate Judges of the Supreme Court of the United States, viz: those assigned respectively to the First, Third, Eighth and Ninth Circuits, who were empowered to select a fifth Circuit Judge in such manner as a majority of them might determine. These were the Commissioners so appointed:

Hon. Nathan Clifford, Associate Justice of the Supreme Court; Hon. William Strong, Associate Justice of the Supreme Court; Hon. Samuel F. Miller, Associate Justice of the Supreme Court; Hon. Stephen J. Field, Associate Justice of the Supreme Court; Hon. Joseph Bradley, Associate Justice of the Supreme Court; Hon. George F. Edmunds, United States Senator; Hon. Frederick T. Frelinghuysen, United States Senator; Hon. O. P. Morton, United States Senator; Hon. Thomas F. Bayard, United States Senator; Hon. Allen G. Thurman, United States Senator; Hon. Henry B. Payne, United States Representative; Hon. Eppa Hunton, United States Representative; Hon. Josiah Abbott, United States Representative; Hon. James A. Garfield, United States Representative; Hon. George F. Hoar, United States Representative.

On the twenty-fifth of February, 1877, Mr. Thurman was taken sick and could serve no longer, and in his place, Hon. Francis Kernan, United States Senator from New York, was appointed. Of the members of the Supreme Court, first appointed, two were Republicans and two Democrats. Of the Senators, three were Republicans and two Democrats, of the Representatives, three were Democrats and two were Republicans. Hon. Joseph Bradley was selected as the fifth associate Justice, who was a Republican of liberal sentiments, as was supposed, and had expressed opinions unfavorable to the Carpet-Bag Government of some of the Southern States. When the personnel of the Committee was first considered during the winter of 1876, it was conceded that the fifth associate Justice would be Hon. David Davis, noted for his fairness and freedom from political prejudice, but unfortunately for the Democrats and for the country, he was that winter elected a member of the

Senate of the United States in place of General John A. Logan, of Illinois, and thus rendered ineligible. The bill creating the Electoral Commission was reported from the Committee on Privileges and Elections, of which Senator Morton was Chairman, and subsequently the duty devolved on him to present and defend it in the Senate, and he proved equal to the occasion, impressing me more than ever with his ability as a debater, and displaying less of the partisanship of the politician than he had ever before exhibited. The debate was earnest, able and protracted, and during its progress all of the different phases of the question to which I have alluded and several others also, were presented and urged with more or less force and efficiency. Many amendments were proposed to the bill as reported, but few of any importance were ingrafted on it. The Senate was not divided on the question exactly by party lines, but as a general thing the Republicans stood by the bill as reported and the Democrats sought to amend it, so that all the votes of all the states cast in the Presidential election should be counted, and that where fraud could be proven, it should vitiate the returns secured by such agency. And here I take occasion to remark that no supporter of the bill ever to my knowledge denied the power of the Commission to go behind the returns for the purpose of showing frauds committed, though it was not distinctly proclaimed that they were invested with such power. Frauds were alleged to have been committed in the states of Florida, South Carolina, Louisiana, and Oregon. The sixth section of the act creating the Electoral Commission as it was finally passed, is as follows:

"Sec. 6th. That nothing in this act shall be held to impair or affect any right now existing under the Constitution and laws in question, by proceedings in the Judicial Courts of the United States, the right or title of the person who shall be declared elected or who shall claim to be the President or Vice-President of the United States, if any such right exists."

The last five words of this section constituted the barb of the hook upon which the Democrats were caught. That such a right existed was generally conceded, though not by all. Believing that fraudulent acts could thus be rendered nugatory, many members of the Senate and House were induced to give their support to the Electoral Commission Act. Others were influenced by a desire to secure a peaceable solution of a question fraught with danger to the public peace. It is an open secret that the Republican Administration had arranged for the concentration of a number of troops, both infantry and artillery, in and around the City of Washington, prepared to use force if necessary to prevent the seating of Mr. Tilden, and many Democrats believed that a resort to physical force was justifiable to prevent the successful consummation of the conspiracy to steal the Presidency. It was even rumored that Mr. Tilden had been consulted as to the advisability of such a procedure, but had at once declared it inadvisable, as it would produce a financial crisis, ruinous in its effects on the business interests of the country. I do not know what truth was in the rumor, but it was believed by many, and was in keeping with his conservative character. Southern men, as a rule, took little part in these schemes. They had made their fight for Constitutional rights and lost, and now left the initiative to Northern Democrats. All these disturbing rumors, however, were quieted by the passage of the bill. Debate on it lasted until the last of January, 1877, when it was brought to a vote in the Senate, and was passed by a vote of forty-seven ayes and seventeen noes, and ten absent or not voting. Of the affirmative votes, twenty-six were Democrats and twenty-one Republicans, and of the negative there were sixteen Republicans and one Democrat. Most of the absentees were Republicans. The Commission, constituted as I have described, met in the Supreme Court Room in the Capitol on the thirty-first of January, organized and at once commenced their labors. The people of the whole country were aroused to a pitch of the highest interest and excitement, and watched the proceedings with great anxiety. The first contested case taken up was Florida. Three papers had been filed with the President of the Senate, Mr. Ferry, two of them purporting to be returns of the electoral vote, and one signed by Senator Jones, of Florida, and others denying the eligibility of one of the Electors on the Hayes ticket, because he was, at the time, the incumbent of a Federal office, and consequently disqualified to act as an Elector. Proof positive of palpable fraud was introduced to discredit the Electors on the Hayes ticket, but as the Governor of Florida, who was a Carpet Bag Republican, had signed the certificate, it was claimed that proof of fraud was inadmissable as the returns were in due form, thus constituting a *prima facie* case of regularity, and the Commission had no authority to "go behind the returns." This was the pivotal point in the case and it was argued with great ability on each side by the objectors and the distinguished counsel on each side composed of the ablest lawyers in the United States. It was understood from the first that the key of the situation was held by Mr. Justice Bradley, the fifth member of the Supreme Court. On the preliminary questions, he had voted sometimes with the Republicans and sometimes with the Democrats, but the impression had gone abroad that he was disposed to take the Democratic view of the question as to the right of the Commission to "go behind the returns." As the time for voting approached the greatest excitement prevailed about the Capitol and all sorts of stories were started, denied, and others took their places. When it was known certainly that Justice Bradley had voted with the Republicans to accept as legally elected the Hayes Electors, the jubilation among the Republicans was extreme, of course accompanied by corresponding depression among the Democrats. Individually I did not fully share the pessimistic views of my party friends, for to my unsophisticated mind, it appeared incontrovertible that whether the decision of he Commission was in favor of "going behind the returns" or against it, the Democrats ought to win, for as the frauds in Florida were patent, if they had the power to go behind the returns, they would certainly reject the Hayes Electors, so if it were determined that they could not do this, then the Oregon vote on the same principle would have to be counted for the Democrats, as one of the Tilden Electors had the returns from that State. The Republicans, it is true, claimed this to be fraudulent, but if they acted on the principle which controlled the Florida case, they could not consider this. In all this "I reckoned without my host," as was soon demonstrated. By eight to seven the same result was declared in South Carolina and Louisiana, but when Oregon was reached, *presto change,* by eight to seven, the Commission threw out the returns as fraudulent, and counted in the Hayes Electors there, too, thus electing General Hayes to the Presidency by a majority of one vote.

The result of this struggle taught me and others the lesson which was never forgotten, viz: that political conviction and party interests wield as potent sway over the minds of men in the most exalted judicial positions, as on those of lower station in life; that Judges and Senators are men of like passion with ourselves, and that it is folly to expect disinterested decisions from any bench when party advantage is to be weighed in the balance of judicial determination. The great question being thus settled and the theft of Presidency consummated, in due time President Hayes was inaugurated and assumed the duties of his high office. The fourth of March proved dark, rainy, and disagreeable, and the crowd in attendance was not as large as usually greets the advent of a new President. No incident of special interest marked the occasion. He had an able Cabinet to aid him. Evarts was Secretary of State, in recognition, I suppose, of his services of leading counsel before the Commission, Sherman was Secretary of Treasury. and Carl Shurtz, Secretary of the Interior, all men of national reputation. The Secretary of Navy was R. W. Thompson, a native of Culpeper County, Virginia, but long a resident of Indiana. He was an old man by this time, and in the palmy days of the old Whig Party attained considerable prominence in the political arena. I called on him soon after the Senate confirmed his nomination, and found him to be genial, pleasant and conciliatory to a remarkable degree. As soon as I was introduced, he asked me from what portion of the State I hailed. I answered from the Southwest, and added, "But my family are from the County of Fauquier." "Then," said he, "I expect you are a relative of my old friend, Martin Withers, of Culpeper." Said I, "It is quite probable that I am, I have heard of him from my father. Wasn't he a blacksmith?" "Yes, he was a blacksmith, but one of the most upright, honorable, and highly-esteemed men in the county." He then told in detail the circumstances connected with a journey on horseback when he was a young man, made by himself, Martin Withers, and another, whose name I have forgotten, from Culpeper to Indiana, and the difficulties encountered. He said that in those days the business of counterfeiting money was carried on more largely than in modern times, and to protect themselves against the danger, when they started, they procured from the bank all of the money they needed in new, crisp bank-notes. When they reached some small town in what is now West Virginia and spent the night, on paying their bill in the morning, the landlord declared that the note tendered in payment was counterfeit. Naturally indignant, they offered other notes, but as they were all similar to the first, this fact only intensified the belief of the landlord that they were counterfeiters. They were all arrested as suspicious characters, and on being searched, all of the money of the party consisted of notes similar to the one first offered. They with difficulty escaped the walls of the jail as a gang of counterfeiters. Martin Withers, he said, was the most indignant man he ever saw, and offered to whip then and there the landlord or any other man who brought such an accusation against him. Finally, I think, one of the notes was sent to a bank in a large town not a great distance away, and when the decision of the cashier was received pronouncing the notes good, they were permitted to proceed on their journey, having lost two or three days' time. Martin Withers' parting admonition to the landlord was, "You just wait, I am coming back this way, and mean to give you the worst whipping that you ever had." "I remained in the West some months after Martin Withers returned," said the Secretary, "and when I got back the first time I met him, he said as soon as he had shaken my hand, "Well, I did whip that rascal when I came back, and gave him a good one too."

This reminiscence seemed to give the old Secretary a good start, and for at least half an hour I listened to various incidents and recollections of his old life in Virginia.

President Hayes always appeared to me as if he was burdened by the consciousness of the fact that he had never been elected by the people and was occupying a false position. He was an upright, honorable gentleman, desirous of doing his duty and promoting the best interests of the whole people. He was kind-hearted and conciliatory to a fault, for to the appeals of office-seekers he always listened with patience and never rebuffed an applicant by a decided rejection. The appointment of a few Democrats to official positions of importance, notably that of Senator Key to a seat in the Cabinet as Postmaster General, was the direct cause of a very large increase in the number and pertinacity of office-seekers, adding to the Republican applicants many Democrats, especially those of Whig antecedent, for whom it was thought he had a special regard. He was more accessible than men in his position usually are, and gave personal audience to an unusually large number of applicants, every one of whom left his presence charmed by his urbanity, and encouraged to believe that his application would be favorably acted on.

The stalwarts among the Republican Senators looked with an evil eye on the liberal policy thus inaugurated, while there was not any active hostility at first, and no special fight was made against the confirmation of his nominees, until the Augean Stable of the New York Custom House was touched. These fat places had always been jealously guarded by Senator Conkling as the most valuable of his political preserves, and his indignation knew no bounds when the effort was made to investigate the many charges of corruption made against the occupants of these places, with the result that the Collector of the Port, Mr. Chester A. Arthur, was removed, and another name sent to the Senate for the coveted place. The storm then broke, and Senator Conkling exerted his really great powers to the utmost, to prevent the confirmation of the nominee. Knowing that this could not be accomplished without the aid of the Democrats, he at once became conciliatory and companionable towards many of those who previously received from him only the most formal recognition, or supercilious greeting when casually meeting. Strange to say, he succeeded beyond my expectation in enlisting Democratic Senators in his crusade, and for a time, I believe, he had strong hope of playing his game successfully. Whether the charges of crookedness in the administration of the Custom House were well founded was doubted by many, and it was thought by some that the whole thing was gotten up by the Blaine interest to break down Conkling and destroy his influence with the Administration. Be that as it may, after delaying action as long as possible on the nomination before the committee to which it was referred, it was reported favorably to the Senate, and was confirmed by a decided majority of the Senators on each side of the Chamber. From this time Mr. Conkling arrayed himself openly against the Hayes Administration, and he lost no opportunity of ventilating his views on the floor of the Senate Chamber. The most contemptuous scorn, the most biting irony, the most disdainful *invective*, hurled against the President and his policy, fell from the lips of the leading Republican in the Senate, and demonstrated the truth of the charge often uttered, that the Senator from New York was a good hater.

CHAPTER XXXIII.

NEW SENATORS IN THE FORTY-FIFTH CONGRESS.

The day preceding the Presidential election, General Grant had ordered a detachment of United States Army to proceed to the City of Petersburg and remain there during the day, ostensibly to preserve the peace, really to stimulate the attendance of the negro, and discourage that of the Democratic voters. This is in direct violation of the Constitution, as no application either by the Legislature of Virginia or the Governor of the State had been made for the presence of the military. I presented in December a resolution of inquiry addressed to the President, asking information as to the authority and the cause for the presence of the soldiers in Petersburg on the day of the election. After some debate the resolution passed the Senate, but some days, perhaps weeks, elapsed before the response was sent. It was accompanied by a printed copy of a communication from prominent Republicans requesting that troops should be sent as they feared that the Republican voters would be driven from the polls unless United States troops were present to protect them. Prominently among the gentlemen thus urging was Mr. L. L. Lewis, at that time District Attorney of the United States, since occupying a prominent position in the State, having for several years been President of the Court of Appeals of Virginia, and subsequently again appointed District Attorney of the United States.

Governor Kemper was greatly exercised by this invasion of United States troops, and by proclamation protested against it, but urged the citizens of Petersburg to submit quietly to the conditions, and to give no pretext of justification for the outrage. A few days after the reply of the President was received, Senator Johnson and I delivered speeches in the Senate protesting against the act, as an insult and outrage without valid reason or excuse. Several Senators took part in the debate which ensued, and two or three days after Senator Morton replied in an elaborate defense of the course of the Administration, contending that the Constitutional provision was modified by the revised statute, which authorized their presence "to keep peace at the polls." The speech I made was one of the few written speeches I delivered during my term of service, and many copies were distributed through the State, eliciting numerous letters of approval from the recipients. The discussion ended finally by the adoption of the resolution offered by myself requesting the Judiciary Committee to examine and report whether the construction placed on the clause of the Revised Statutes of the United States by the Attorney General was correct. This was referred to the committee on the Judiciary, and as far as my recollection serves, was never heard from again.

Several new Senators appeared at the opening of the forty-fifth Congress, some of whom were men of ability and of national reputation. Augustus H. Garland took the place of Powell Clayton, of Arkansas. Garland was a lawyer of high repute, having gained his suit before the Supreme Court of the United States in the celebrated case establishing the right of a lawyer to practice in the courts of the United States without taking the test oath. He was also prominent in the politics of his State, having been Governor and afterwards elected without opposition to a seat in the Senate of the United States. His ability both as a lawyer and a debater was soon recognized and when Mr. Cleveland was elected President he gave Senator Garland a place in his Cabinet as Attorney General of the United States, a position which he filled with distinguished ability. Henry M. Teller, of Colorado, made his first appearance as a Senator in December, 1876. Prior to his election as Senator, he had never held a political office, but he speedily vindicated the wisdom of his constituents in selecting him for the distinguished position, and took rank among the best debaters of the body after an unusually brief probation. He was a pronounced Republican, but an enthusiastic advocate of silver, as was to be expected from a Colorado Senator. He also was elevated subsequently to a Cabinet position, having been selected by Mr. Garfield for the place of Secretary of the Interior. At the close of his service in the Cabinet, he was again elected to the Senate, and in the fierce fight to degrade silver made by the Republicans, he, no doubt to his own surprise found himself on the other side of the political fence, voting and arguing as a Democrat. But his people stood by him, and he was again elected to the Senate last year (1902) as a Democrat. The most desperate and unscrupulous efforts were made to defeat him by one branch of the Legislature, controlled by the Republicans, even proposing to unseat the delegates representing fifteen of the counties of the State, but he finally won out. Benjamin H. Hill took his seat as a Senator from Georgia in the forty-fifth Congress, having previously served in the House of Representatives for one or two terms, where he distinguished himself as a speaker and debater of more than ordinary force. He had served as a Senator from Georgia in the Confederate Congress, had opposed the secession of his State, but after the passage of the ordinance, accepted the decision, and served the Confederacy with zeal and ability. He speedily took a high position as a defender of the principles of his party, and commanded the respect of the Republicans as well as the Democrats. Unfortunately, he fell a victim to an incurable disease of the throat, which carried him off before the close of his first term in the Senate, and in the midst of his usefulness. As I have already mentioned incidentally, Illinois sent a new Senator to this Congress, in the person of Judge David Davis, formerly an Associate Justice of the Supreme Court of the United States, who supplanted General John A Logan, by a combination of Democrats and moderate Republicans. He was a native of Maryland, and though a pronounced Republican, was thoroughly conservative in his views and actions on all political questions. His long service on the bench not only in Illinois, but as a member of the highest Judicial Tribunal of the United States, somewhat marred his efficiency as a politician, as he regarded all contested questions from purely judicial standpoint. The Republicans of the Senate were so much incensed at the defeat of General Logan that in the organization of the Senate committees they made no assignment of Judge Davis, though nominally a Republican, and it was left to the Democrats to make provision for him in this respect and they placed him at the head of the Judiciary Committee of the Senate on the list of Democrats. A high compliment, indeed. He was also given a place on the Pension Committee, but I have no recollection of his having ever attended its meetings. During his term of service he took no prominent part in debate, indeed, seldom addressed the Senate unless on business matters affecting the interests of his constituents. On the whole, I can say of him as I did of Judge Christiancy, that his reputation was not greatly enhanced by his services as Senator of the United States. He was a very corpulent man, kind-hearted, genial, and of the utmost probity. From Iowa, Samuel J. Kirkwood had been elected in the place of Senator Wright. He also was a Marylander by birth and education, but had long been a resident of Iowa, had been twice or three times Governor of the State, and once before, served as Senator of the United States. In appearance, dress and bearing he reminded one of a plain, unsophisticated country farmer. He was not a violent partisan, but generally voted with his party, but he was honest, upright, sincere and amiable. He was a member of the Committee on Pensions most of the time, and I became quite intimate with and very fond of him. He did not often occupy the floor of the Senate, and when he did, spoke plainly and forcibly to the point at issue without any attempt at oratory, and employing no rhetorical ornamentation. Preston B. Plumb succeeded Senator Harvey as Senator from Kansas. He was a journalist by profession, afterwards served through the war in the 11th Kansas Infantry, became a banker, served one or more terms in the Kansas Legislature, and was elected to the Senate in 1877. While not as brilliant a speaker as his colleague, J. J. Ingalls, he was a man of good sense, spoke always sensibly and well, was genial and kindly in his personal bearing and was liked by the Democrats as well as Republicans. This Congress also witnessed the advent of James B. Beck into the United States Senate, in the place of John W. Stevenson. Mr. Beck was by birth a Scotchman, but came to the United States when quite young. He had served three or four terms in the House of Representatives, where he had established a reputation as a fearless and able debater, perhaps second to none. Making no pretension to the gifts of the orator, he was exceedingly strong in debate, where his vigorous intellect, and ready command of forcible phrases rendered him formidable on the floor. He was very aggressive, and a hard hitter, and could "give and take" with the best men of the Senate. He had a long and honorable career in the Senate and finally died in the harness from a diseased heart. He dropped dead without a word at the railroad station on Sixth Street on May 3d, 1890, having just gotten off the train after a run from New York. Senator Beck was a member of the Committee of Appropriations and served there with me for some years, and I knew him well and esteemed him highly. A man of stalwart frame, industrious, never afraid of work, he was one of the most laborious and reliable members of the Committee, always able and willing to repel all attacks, and with unflinching courage maintained his convictions. In all that goes to make an efficient Representative, Senator Beck was fully equipped. I think every Democrat in the Senate and a large majority of Republicans, were much gratified when George F. Hoar succeeded George S. Boutwell as a Senator from Massachusetts. Mr. Hoar had served with distinction in the House of Representatives for eight years or more, and was recognized by men of all parties as a cultured, able and eloquent speaker, and an adroit and forcible debater. He had been selected as one of the conductors, on the part of the House, of the impeachment trial of General Belknap, and proved himself one of the ablest of the number. He had also served on the Electoral Commission with dignity and efficiency. With such antecedents, his advent into the Senate Chamber was hailed with pleasure by his Republican associates as a strong reinforcement to their numbers and strength. Courteous and gentlemanly in his bearing, dignified and urbane in his social intercourse with all, he claimed and was accorded the respect and personal esteem of his political opponents, and the confidence and admiration of his political confreres. That he was the "right man in the right place" is proven by the fact that he still (1903) holds the seat which he assumed in 1877. He has not always followed the lead of his party during this long career, but on more than one important question has asserted his individual right of opinion, and criticised the policy of the Administration with caustic and effective denunciation, but alas, has not always by his vote sustained the views he enunciated in his arguments, thus demonstrating that his political sympathies were stronger than his intelletual convictions. The lapse of time appears to have softened Mr. Hoar's political and sectional prejudices, as is but natural in all persons of philosophic temperament, as his recent public addresses furnish incontrovertible evidence. He is now more than ever disposed to "put himself in our place," and view conditions from that standpoint, a position which few Northern Republicans are able or willing to occupy. An address delivered by Senator Hoar a few years since, before the Virginia Bar Association, was very favorably regarded by his auditors, and received flattering encomiums from Southern men generally. Another brilliant and able Senator was added to the Democratic contingent of this year, in the person of Lucius Q. C. Lamar, of Mississippi, elected in the place of Senator Alcorn. He was, I think, a Georgian by birth, but having removed to Mississippi, was elected to Congress, and served one or two terms in ante-bellum days. After his resignation, he was a member of the Secession Convention of Mississippi, and served for a time in the Army of the Confederacy. After the war he held a professorship in the State University, and served two or more terms in the Congress of the United States. It was while serving as a Representative in Congress, that I first made his acquaintance under rather peculiar circumstances. He was suddenly seized with vertigo on the floor of the House, which caused great alarm to his friends and produced quite a commotion in the House. For some cause the attendance of a physician could not be readily secured, and some of his friends knowing that I had for years been a practitioner, ran over to the Senate Chamber and asked me to go over and see him, which of course I did at once. By the time I reached him, reaction was beginning, and with the aid of restoratives he soon regained consciousness, and no after ill effects were developed. Mr. Lamar was an exceedingly clever man, but diffident and modest to a degree. He was a good speaker but never satisfied with his utterances. After a speech in the Senate of more than ordinary force, I one day congratulated him on his effort as he sat near me, and was surprised by his response. "It is very kind of you to say so," said he, "but I know I made an ass of myself," and such was his conception of all his oratorical efforts. His sensitiveness was morbid in its intensity. He rarely spoke without preparation, but the speech which gave him most reputation, was strictly impromptu, very brief, but it was to the point. I allude to the reply he made to Senator Conkling, of New York, in the controversy which made Lamar famous, the particulars of which I will narrate in the proper sequence of events. Senator Lamar was also honored by a Cabinet appointment, being made Secretary of the Interior by President Cleveland in 1881. The circumstances leading to this event were rather curious. The friends of Senator Money, of Mississippi, being anxious to secure his appointment as a member of Mr. Cleveland's Cabinet, delegated Senator Lamar to interview the President on this subject. In performing this service Mr. Lamar urged the policy of giving to the South recognition by placing in the Cabinet a gentleman so well recognized that his selection would meet the approval of all Southern Democrats. Mr. Cleveland was so much impressed by the able arguments of Mr. Lamar that he avowed his preference for him as a representative Southerner, and offered him a place in his Cabinet. Senator Lamar was much embarrassed by the offer, and at first declined to consider it, as he was representing Mr. Money and deemed it improper under the circumstances for him to serve, and it was only after repeated and urgent requests from his friends that he changed his mind. Mr. J. R. McPherson, Democrat, succeeded F. P. Frelinghuysen as Senator from New Jersey. He had been engaged in business matters most of his life, in which he had met with financial success, but had served one or more terms in the Legislature of New Jersey, before his election to the Senate. He had the reputation of being a good political organizer, but did not often appear on the floor of the Senate. Stanley Mathews, of Ohio, was elected Senator to fill the vacancy occasioned by the resignation of Senator Sherman, when he accepted the Treasury Portfolio at the request of President Hayes. He was a man of parts, had served in the Army of the United States, and had been Judge of the Supreme Court of Ohio, and was Presidential Elector.

He only remained two years in the Senate, and did not take a very prominent part in its deliberations. His best speeches were in favor of the bill for remonetizing silver. General M. C. Butler had been elected a Senator from South Carolina, but his credentials were referred to the Committee of Elections and his admittance stubbornly fought by Morton and the stalwarts on account of his alleged connection with what they called the Hamburg massacre. General Butler lost his leg at the great cavalry battle at Brandy Station. After the war he engaged in politics, was a member of the Legislature of South Carolina, and was elected to the United States Senate in 1876. As well as I can recollect, Mr. William Pitt Kellogg's credentials as a Senator from Louisiana were also presented and referred, his recognition being resisted by the Democrats, which resulted in a sort of compromise by which both Butler and Kellogg were admitted at the same time. General Butler's desk was immediately on my left and I had many occasions for interchange of views. He was a most genial and attractive personage to me, and his record of undaunted valor and unselfish generosity on the battle-field should endear him to all generous natures. By the shell which carried off his leg, another brave officer, Captain Farley, was mortally wounded, and when the surgeon hurried up to see to their injuries, Butler refused to be examined until the hurts of Captain Farley should be looked after, as he thought him more seriously injured than himself. This proved to be true, as he died in an hour or two afterwards. From Texas, Richard Coke was sent as Senator in place of Hamilton, Republican. Coke was born in Williamsburg, Virginia, a lawyer by profession, moved to Texas and held several prominent positions, served in the Confederate Army during the war, twice elected and served as Governor of Texas, and was finally sent to the Senate in 1877. He was a man almost gigantic in size, and with a voice of corresponding volume. When aroused or excited in debate, his voice could easily be heard reverberating through all the corridors of the Senate wing and in the Chamber itself was almost deafening. It was not mere *brutum fulmen*, either, for he was a man of strong mind, as well as body, and his speeches were usually powerfully argumentative without much effort at oratory.

From what I have said of the personnel of the Senators just entering on their careers in the forty-fifth Congress, it may be assumed that each party had gained strength. But the gain was greater on the Democratic than on the Republican side. This preponderance was increased soon after by the unexpected death of Senator Bogy of Missouri, whose place was filled by Mr. George Vest, one of the brightest and ablest debaters in the Senate. The second session of the Congress witnessed further and important changes in the personnel of the Senate. Senator Morton, of Indiana, died rather unexpectedly and was succeeded by "Dan Voorhees," the noted orator, generally known by the soubriquet of the "Tall Sycamore of the Wabash." He was of splendid physique, over six feet in height and magnificently proportioned. A natural orator with unlimited command of choicest English, a charming rhetorician, as well as logician. On the floor he was a tower of strength to our party. The death of Morton was an irretrievable loss to his party and his place was never supplied. The State of Louisiana had now two Senators on the floor for the first time since the forty-third Congress. These were John B. Eustis, Democrat, and William Pitt Kellogg, Republican. Eustis was a man of culture and ability, as well as considerable political experience, while Kellogg was a smart Carpet Bagger who had served in the Union Army and was appointed Collector of the Port of New Orleans immediately after the war closed, subsequently elected Governor, and United States Senator. He was from one of the New England States, and a pretty shrewd but utterly unreliable politician. But with all of these changes the Republicans dominated the Senate, by a very small majority, it was true, but it enabled them to control Legislation through the agency of the party caucus which was frequently called into requisition and from the dicta few were bold enough to dissent. The remonetization of silver was one of the most important measures which was considered and consummated by the forty-fifth Congress, and it was not then regarded or discussed as a party question. The Senate after long debate passed the bill which also passed the House, was signed by the President, and became a law. The "Double Standard" thus received the indorsation of both political parties, being favored by the Democratic House, the Republican Senate, and received the approval of the Republican President. More than twenty years afterwards it became the test in the election of a President of the United States in two successive contests, in which the friends of the double standard were beaten. The "Chinese Exclusion Act," became a law. It was not treated as a party question. Members of each House from the Pacific States stood as a unit in its favor, and exerted all their powers to secure the passage of the Act. Their arguments appealed to me very feebly, for they were based mainly on the fact that the Chinese would work for half the wages paid to other laborers, that they were economical and saved their earnings, that they spent nothing in drinking houses or restaurants, but carried all their gains back to China. To my mind these traits were rather to be commended than condemned. Economy, sobriety, and industry are usually regarded as commendable, and emigrants who possess these traits are preferable to those of opposite characteristics. I, therefore, had opposed the passage of the Act. While it was pending, however, I was greatly interested in a movement looking to a reduction of the revenue tax on tobacco, then burdened with a tax of twenty-four cents per pound. I had introduced a bill proposing a reduction to sixteen cents, which was referred to the Finance Committee, the first session, but not reported back until the second session, and though the friends of the measure succeeded in getting a favorable report from the Committee, it was strongly opposed by the Chairman, Mr. Morrill, and also by the Secretary of the Treasury, Mr. Sherman. The short session was rapidly passing and the chances for getting any measure through the Senate, except the Appropriation Bills, was lessening every day. I had by industrious canvassing secured the promise of most of the Carpet Bag Senators, from the Southern States, to vote for it, and felt confident of passing it if we could succeed in getting a vote. The "Chinese Exclusion Act" was also in the same state of uncertainty, except that it was understood that the Steering Committee of the Republican Caucus had decreed that it might be taken up and voted on, but its fate was doubtful, as on a test vote they could not show a majority in favor of it. Under these circumstances, I was approached one morning by Senator Sergeant, of California, with whom I had become quite friendly as we had been on the subcommittee, to which several of the regular Appropriation Bills had been referred, and I had found him an unusually intelligent and industrious worker. He told me confidentially that the caucus had decided not to allow the Internal Revenue Bill, containing the provision for the reduction of tax on tobacco, to be taken up by the Senate at that session. I was greatly worried, as I knew no way of over-riding the decision of the caucus, and feared that all the efforts of the friends of the measure would come to naught. He waited a time sufficient for me to take in the full significance of the news, and then said, "Your people are not specially interested in the Chinese matter, are they?" "No," said I, "Not specially. I oppose it because I think the principle is wrong on which it is based." Said he, "I will make this proposition to you, if when the Chinese Exclusion Act comes to a vote, you will retire to the Cloak Room and not vote at all on the question, I will promise you the votes of a sufficient number of Republican Senators to call up the Tobacco Tax Bill and to enable you to get a vote of the Senate on its passage. Mind, I don't promise to vote for it, but only to aid you in bringing it to a vote." "Wait half an hour," said I, "and I will give you an answer."

I at once sought Mr. Bayard, whose opinion on such matters I held in the highest respect, and told him the whole proposition, asking what he thought I should do.

"Take him up by all means," said he, "there will be nothing wrong in it." Thurman gave the same advice, and so did Senator Johnston, my colleague, so I returned and notified Sergeant that I accepted his proposal. This was the first and last "bargain," if it may be so called, in which I was a participant, during my whole term of service. When I notified my friends to be on hand when the time came for action, some suspected the California Senator of a purpose to secure the passage of his bill, and then leave me in the lurch, but I felt no fear or anxiety in this regard.

A few days after the test came. The Chinese Exclusion Act

was passed by a close vote. I did not vote, of course, and as soon as the subject was disposed of, one of the Post-Office Committee proposed to take up the Post-Office Appropriation Bill, which had been reported a week before. Mr. Bayard antagonized it with the Internal Revenue Bill, and when the vote was taken *viva voce*, a majority had voted to favor Mr. Bayard's proposition. The Republicans were evidently surprised, and called for the Ayes and Noes, and many of them commenced an active canvass to induce the Republicans who had voted with us to change their vote when the roll was called. I saw two or three of the Republican Senators make a rush for Bruce, the negro Senator from Mississippi, and I made a bee line for his rescue. As I approached I heard one of them say in an excited tone, "Why, surely you are not going back on the caucus of your party." Without giving him time to reply, I rudely cut in, "No! He is not going back on the caucus, but he is not going back on his own race, every one of whom are interested in reducing the tax on tobacco." I saw that he was embarrassed, so I stood by him and fought off his party friends until the roll call was finished, and the Revenue Bill was laid before the Senate. It was a very long bill and many amendments of the Committee were to be acted on before the Tobacco Tax was reached. Repeated efforts were made to reconsider, to postpone, to lay it aside informally, all of which were successfully resisted, and at last, the amendment reporting in favor of reducing the tax was reached and the fight began on its merits. It was debated two or three days, as well as I remember, and was passed by a decided majority, as the discussion on the merits of the proposition gained us friends. Senator Morrill, Chairman of the Finance Committee, was most determined in his opposition, but we won out, and this is the secret history of the arrangement by which the victory was achieved.

CHAPTER XXXIV.

DEATH AND OBSEQUIES OF PROFESSOR HENRY.
REMONETIZATION OF SILVER.

During this session, I was honored by being elected by the Senate one of the Board of Regents of the Smithsonian Institution, to fill the place formerly held by Senator John W. Stevenson, of Kentucky. I was both surprised and gratified by the selection, as the subject had never been mentioned to me until I was notified of my appointment, and I have never to this day known to whose kind offices I was indebted for the honor. I certainly appreciated it highly, and during my continuance in office rarely ever failed to be present at the meetings of the Board. I admired and esteemed Professor Henry very highly, and it was my custom when the Board met at night and remained in session so late that the last trains for Alexandria had left, to spend the night at his hospitable home. Dr. McCosh, President of Princeton University, was also a member of the Board, and also occasionally spent the night there. He was a charming old Scotch Presbyterian Divine, uncommonly bright, and a fine conversationalist. Chief Justice Waite was *ex-officio* Chancellor of the Smithsonian Institution, and rarely failed to be present at the meetings of the Board. Another distinguished member of the body was General William T. Sherman, who always took great interest in the Institution, and was very agreeable socially. He differed much from his brother, John Sherman, being genial, pleasant, and rather jolly, while the Secretary of the Treasury was cold, phlegmatic, and unsympathetic to a degree. Ex-Vice-President Hamlin was also an active and efficient member of the Board, taking great interest in its affairs. Vice-President Wilson, General James A. Garfield, afterwards President of the United States, Senator Sergeant, of California, Hon. Heister Clymer, Member of Congress from Pennsylvania, Professor Asa Gray, of Harvard, Hon. Peter Parker, and President Noah Porter were other members of this distinguished Board. In the spring of 1878 the Smithsonian Institution and the whole scientific world was shocked by the death of its distinguished Secretary, Professor Joseph Henry, who died after a brief illness, on the thirteenth day of May. He was selected as the first Secretary of the Smithsonian, and had for more than thirty years controlled the affairs of the Institution, directed its policy, and guided its affairs. Under his wise administration the success of the organization, at first deemed problematic by many, was assured. In the world of science, he was widely known as the real discoverer of the principle from which was eliminated the electric telegraph. He was an active and honored member of most of the scientific associations in this country and in Europe. The death of such a man in the opinion of the Board of Regents demanded much more than casual recognition. A called meeting of the Board was held as soon as the announcement of his death was made, and a committee appointed to report such measures as might be deemed judicious to secure a national observance of the sad event. Accordingly a public funeral was determined on, to be followed as soon as circumstances would admit by funeral obsequies to be held in the Capitol Building, at which the highest dignitaries of the land should be asked to participate. The Committee of Arrangements consisted of General William T. Sherman, Dr. Peter Parker and Spencer F. Baird, who had been selected to succeed Professor Henry as Secretary of the Smithsonian. The interment took place from the New York Avenue Presbyterian Church, of which Professor Henry had been a member for many years. I quote as follows from the "Memorial Volume":

"The leading officials in every branch of Government, men eminent in science, in literature, in diplomacy, and in professional and business life, assembled at the Church. Among them was the President of the United States, the Vice-President of the United States, Secretary of State, Secretary of Treasury, Secretary of War, Secretary of Navy, Secretary of Interior, Post-Master General, Chief Justice and Associate Justices of the Supreme Court of the United States, the General of the Army, the Admiral of the Navy, the Senate and House of Representatives of the United States, the Regents of Smithsonian

Institution, Officers of the Army and Navy, the Clergy of the District, the National Academy of Sciences, represented by its Officers and others, the Philosophical Society of Washington, the Alumni of the College of New Jersey, the Trustees of the Corcoran Art Gallery, the Washington National Monument Society, the Examining Corps of the Patent Office, the Superintendent and Trustees of the Public Schools, and the Telegraphic Operators Association of Washington City. Only a small portion of the crowd could obtain access to the church. The funeral sermon was preached by Rev. Mr. Mitchell, Pastor of the Church, and was a most appropriate and feeling tribute to his life, character, and public services." His text was "Know ye not that there is a prince and great man fallen this day in Israel." The opening prayer was made by the venerable Charles Hoge, D. D., of Princeton, New Jersey, and who followed Professor Henry to the grave within a month after his participation in these ceremonies. The solemnity of the funeral discourse was somewhat marred by an involuntary ebullition on the part of Senator and Ex-Vice-President Hamlin, who sat by me. The speaker was alluding to some incident in the life of the deceased Secretary, and in his description made a statement not in accord with Mr. Hamlin's recollection, and evidently without thinking of time, place or circumstance, he corrected him in a voice audible to all around, "That's a mistake," said he, but as the speaker paused not, he turned to me, "Why the man is all wrong, that is not correct at all." Now, in the Senate debates, with all the much-vaunted "Senatorial Courtesy," such interruptions are not unusual, when any statement is made not in accordance with the facts, as they may be understood by any hearer, and the old Senator on this occasion was only oblivious of his surroundings, and imagined himself in the Senate Chamber. While I am on the subject of Professor Henry's death and the high honors accorded to his memory, I had as well conclude the account with a report of the final ceremonial, which did not take place until the beginning of the next year. The crowded business of a closing session would not permit the elaborate preparation necessary for carrying out the wishes of the Regents, and the resolutions of both Houses of

Congress, so after consultation it was agreed to postpone the national tribute until the next session. These exercises were held in the Hall of the House of Delegates on the evening of the sixteenth of January, 1879. The Vice-President of the United States presided, supported by the Speaker of the House, Hon. Samuel J. Randall, and the following was the order of procedure:

1. Opening Prayer, by Rev. Dr. James McCosh, President of Princeton College.
2. Address by Hon. Hannibal Hamlin, of the United States Senate, one of the Board of Regents.
3. Address by Hon. Robert E. Withers, of the United States Senate, one of the Board of Regents.
4. Address by Professor Asa Gray, of Harvard University, one of the Board of Regents.
5. Address by Professor William B. Rogers, of Boston.
6. Address by Hon. James A. Garfield, of the House of Representatives, one of the Board of Regents.
7. Address by Hon. Samuel S. Cox, of the House of Representatives.
8. Address by General William T. Sherman, one of the Board of Regents.
9. Concluding Prayer by Rev. Byron Sunderland, Chaplain of the Senate.

This program was carried out fully. The gathering on that evening was the most august and distinguished assemblage on which my eyes have ever looked. The President of the United States, all the members of the Cabinet, the Chief Justice and the Associate Justices of the Supreme Court, the members of the Senate and House of Representatives, distinguished officers of the Army and Navy, the members of the Diplomatic Corps in official costume, the Board of Regents of the Smithsonian Institution, delegations from all the Scientific Organizations in the United States, Alumni of Princeton College, etc., etc., all crowded the Hall of the House of Delegates and its galleries to their utmost capacity. Senator Hamlin was unavoidably absent, having been appointed one of the Joint Committee of the two Houses to accompany the remains of the Hon. Gustave

Schleicher, member of the House from Texas, recently deceased. His address was read by the Vice-President. Mine was the next in order, and I must mention a little incident which impressed me as an evidence of a friendly desire on the part of one of my Senatorial colleagues that I should credibly perform my share of the ceremonial. Senator Edmunds who was sitting near, leaned forward and cautioned me to remember that the Hall was much larger than the Senate Chamber in which I was accustomed to speak, and I must raise my voice correspondingly in order to be heard. I felt much gratified by this evidence of his friendly interest and did not fail to act on the suggestion. My address was the shortest one delivered, with the exception of General Sherman's. Some were entirely too long. Professor Asa Gray's was a biographical sketch and necessarily long, Professor William B. Rogers, then upward of eighty years old, delivered an address as remarkable for its vigor as its volume, while "Sunset Cox" consumed nearly, if not quite, three-quarters of an hour. All the addresses, proceedings, and other memorial addresses on the same theme delivered elsewhere, were published in a handsome memorial volume, which was printed by order of both Houses of Congress and largely distributed.

CHAPTER XXXV.

THE RISE, MATURITY AND COLLAPSE OF READJUSTERS.

I must go back to the year 1877 to describe the rise and progress of the Readjuster Party, as they styled themselves in Virginia politics. I have previously referred to the settlement of the State Debt by the passage of the McCulloch Act a year or two before. There was violent opposition on the part of many members of the Legislature to the Act, and they believed that some of its provisions did great injustice to the people of Virginia, notably, that portion which decreed that the State should pay interest on the bonds for the period covered by the war. I myself thought this portion of the Act exceedingly objectionable, but after some grumbling by the opponents of the Act, there seemed to be a disposition on the part of the people to accept its provisions in good faith, and the refunding of the debt of the State in accordance with the requirements of the bill was proceeding in a satisfactory manner. But in 1877 a Governor was to be elected, and a Convention was called to meet in Richmond to nominate a State ticket. Several names were brought forward as aspirants for Gubernatorial honors, but it was soon evident that the three most prominent candidates were General William Mahone, of Petersburg, Major John W. Daniel, of Lynchburg, and Colonel F. W. Holliday, of Winchester, each having a large and enthusiastic following. My son-in-law, E. P. Goggin, was Major Daniel's law partner, had the direction of his canvass, and was very sanguine of his success. General Mahone's friends were equally or more confident, while the many friends of Colonel Holliday were hopeful if not boastful. When the Convention met, much speaking was indulged in, and no nomination was made the first day. When the Convention adjourned, General Mahone was the foremost candidate with Daniel a good second, and Holliday behind. As the Convention had agreed to drop the hindmost candidate on each ballot, Daniel's friends were very sure of his selection, as it was an open secret that when Colonel Holliday should be dropped on the next ballot, a large majority of his supporters would vote for Daniel as against Mahone. The antagonism between the supporters of Mahone and Daniel was very pronounced, and was intensified by the occurrences of the first day.

When the Convention again met, to the surprise of all, not in the confidence of the Mahone men, General Mahone's name was withdrawn, thus leaving the vote between Daniel and Holliday. Such a procedure was unprecedented in the history of political Conventions in Virginia, and the effect of the announcement was electrical. When the roll of delegates was called, the County of Accomac was the first on the list, and John S. Wise of that county called out in a loud voice, "Friends of Mahone follow the lead of Accomac," and cast the vote of that county for Holliday, as had doubtless been arranged in previous conference. A large majority of the Mahone men followed this lead, and thus Colonel Holliday secured the nomination. Though greatly disappointed and chagrined, the friends of Major Daniel submitted with good grace, as the nominee was universally recognized as a high-toned gentleman of culture, intelligence, and probity. His election by a large majority followed in due course.

The result, however, sounded the death knell of General Mahone's aspirations to secure the Governorship of Virginia at the hands of the Democratic party. His astute mind speedily devised a scheme, however, by means of which he hoped to attain the position so much coveted. In a short time he published an article advocating the re-opening of "the State debt question" and the readjustment of the debt, on lines more favorable to the State. This at once secured the adhesion of all those who had opposed the McCulloch Bill, and such men as C. T. O'Ferrill (afterwards Governor), Harry Riddleberger, John Paul, Frank Blair, Parson Massie, and many others flocked to his standard. The regular Democrats did not at first attach much importance to the movement, but soon realized the danger which confronted them. The Republicans saw at once a chance to rend asunder the party which had hitherto dominated the State, and they, almost to a man, joined the ranks of the Readjusters. As the canvas progressed, it was soon seen that the campaign was directed by one who was master of the art. The new party was thoroughly and speedily organized in every county and precinct of the State, and a State Convention met in Richmond on the thirteenth of July, when an active and aggressive campaign was at once inaugurated. Realizing their danger, the Democrats called out their strongest speakers also, but were met on every hustings by the ablest speakers of the new party, who, by adroit appeals to the "pocket nerve," hoped to carry the crowd with them. Thus originated the noted and significant phrase, "Honor won't buy a breakfast," being the response of one of their ablest men to the State was bound in honor to meet the obligations incurred.

Doubtless the greater number of those Democrats who united themselves with the Readjusters were only desirous of securing from the creditors of the State a settlement more advantageous than that provided by the Legislature, but it is equally certain that General Mahone contemplated a far more insidious and far-reaching policy. He proposed to use Readjustment as a bridge over which he could lead the Readjusters into the Republican camp. This was repeatedly charged during the canvas, but always indignantly denied.

After Congress closed its sessions, I returned to Virginia and at once took an active part in the fight, meeting on the stump most of the leading speakers of that party.

The result was favorable to the new party, as they elected a majority of the members of the Legislature. The Coalition was triumphant and the Republicans were greatly elated. They knew very well what the program was, and were confident that the Democrats would never again control the State of Virginia. Whatever else may be thought of General Mahone, there can be no doubt that his plan of campaign to capture and control the Legislature of Virginia and dominate its action was both sagacious and able. Never before in the history of the State had such a thing been attempted. No one except Mahone would have believed such a policy to be practicable. No one would have supposed that Virginians possessing sufficient character and intelligence to aspire to a seat in the Legislature to enact laws for the people, would tamely and without a word of protest or remonstrance agree in advance even of their election, to surrender absolutely their freedom of action, and independence of judgment to the keeping of another, and to subordinate their duty to their constituents to the dictation of a "Boss." And yet there is no doubt this was done by at least three-fourths of the Readjuster members of the Legislature. This fact was brought to light by Judge Lybrook of Patrick County, who was one of the "Big Four" who saved Virginia from the mad and ruinous measures which General Mahone proposed to inflict on the State. He published a copy of the circular sent to the candidates of the Readjuster Party throughout the State, and the letter of the Republican Collector of Internal Revenue who was made the medium of its transmission. The following is a copy of these remarkable documents:

UNITED STATES INTERNAL REVENUE OFFICE,
DANVILLE, VA., September 14th.

Dear Judge:

I send you herewith two pledges, to sign one, and have the party nominee for your county to sign the other one, and return to me, and I will forward them to General Mahone, *who directs me to do this.* Of course it is nothing for an honest man to do, and signed his hand to his faith. Please attend to this matter promptly, etc.

FERNALD.*

THE PLEDGE.

PATRICK COUNTY, VA.
.... Date.

"I hereby pledge myself to stand by the Readjuster party and platform, and to go into Caucus with the Readjuster members of the Legislature and vote for all measures, nominees, and candidates to be elected by the Legislature, that meets in Richmond as the Caucus may agree upon.

·Given under my hand this ——— day of ——— etc.
(Signed)

---

*Fernald was a Republican office holder in the Internal Revenue Department of the United States.

Judge Lybrook did not "sign this pledge and return it" as requested by Mr. Fernald, that it might be sent to General Mahone. On the contrary he preserved both letters, but, as I said, at least three-fourths of the candidates did sign and return the pledge to General Mahone, who thus fastened his collar on the neck of every one of them, and virtually assumed in his own person all the power, privileges, and responsibilities of the State Legislature. Though not a member of the body, he remained in Richmond during the whole Legislative session, and from his rooms in the "Whig" Office, dictated every measure, selected every candidate, and determined on every appointee. His edicts for some time remained unchallenged and unquestioned. But the possession of this unlimited power over the Legislation of the State produced the natural effect. His ambition and arrogance grew constantly by what it fed on, and in the end brought disaster in its train. But I am anticipating.

When the Readjusters began their fight it was generally supposed that General Mahone's objective point was the Governorship of the State, as his aspirations to that office were well known. As his power increased he concluded it would be better to wait for the expiration of my term in the Senate of the United States, and secure, through the votes of his subservient followers, this coveted honor. As the readjustment of the State Debt was purely a local question, it was a little difficult to see how it could be made an issue in national politics, but that constituted but a small difficulty. At first I was inclined to hope that the election of a Readjuster Legislature did not necessarily involve the loss of my seat in the Senate, especially as I had received the personal assurance of several of the candidates of that party, that they would support me for re-election, as they had no complaint to make against me, and I gave full credence to these promises, but I was not aware that the men making them had themselves forfeited all power to exercise their right of individual choice, by affixing their names to the "Pledge." Rev. Mr. Massie was unquestionably the most efficient, active and formidable of all the champions of the Readjuster party during their canvass. He was fluent, versatile, and well informed, and to him more than any other speaker was due their success, and it was generally agreed that he was to receive the support of the party for Governor at the close of Governor Holliday's term. Paul, of Rockingham, was booked for District Judge of the United States Court, Mahone to take my place in the Senate, and H. H. Riddleberger to succeed Senator Johnston in the same body. But when the time came for making nominations, General Mahone concluded to substitute Captain William E. Cameron for Massie, as Gubernatorial candidate, and put the latter in the comparatively unimportant place of Auditor. And this change of program brought to my remembrance an incident of the canvass which I will narrate if for nothing else to break the tedium of so much political narrative.

On the occasion in question, I had an appointment in company with Major Daniel to meet Mahone and Massie in a discussion at Pearisburg, the county seat of Giles County, and Major Hoge Tyler of Pulaski, afterwards Governor, had promised to meet us at Dublin with a conveyance to take us to Pearisburg, as there was at that time no public conveyance or railroad connection with that place. When Major Daniel and I reached Dublin, Parson Massie also got off the train expecting to meet a conveyance to take him to the place of meeting, but Mr. Frank Blair came, in a single buggy, and took General Mahone with him, leaving Mr. Massie without any means of getting to Pearisburg, as no conveyance could be had at Dublin. When we got into the spring jersey with Major Tyler, some one remarked on the dilemma in which Mr. Massie had been placed, and Major Tyler, with that innate sense of politeness inherent in a Virginia gentleman, suggested that as there was a vacant seat in our vehicle, he would, if agreeable to Major Daniel and myself, invite the Parson to occupy it. Of course we made no objection, and thus, greatly to his relief, Mr. Massie was enabled to make the trip. During our long drive of course we had lots to talk about, and finally, after some chaffing to the canvass and its probable results, Massie predicted an overwhelming victory for his party and the consequent fruits of that victory would inure to the benefit of its champions.

"Well, Mr. Massie," said I, "if your predictions should

realized, you need not expect any rich plums to fall to your share, as General Mahone will have the distribution of them and has no idea of conferring any of the important ones on you." He laughed good-naturedly, and replied, "I guess if we succeed these questions will not be left to General Mahone's decision, but will be determined by a Convention of the party." "Well, remember this conversation, will you, and mark the result."

I had heard an intimation from one whom I knew to be in Mahone's confidence that Cameron was slated for Governor, and as the seats in the Senate were pledged to Mahone and Riddleberger, and Frank Blair was fixed on as Attorney General, and Paul for District Judge of the United States Court, I knew no important office would be left for Massie.

During the year 1878, hoping to be able to bring about a settlement of the State Debt question, and thus take it out of politics, I made three trips to New York, Philadelphia, and other cities, twice in company of my colleague and Major Borst of the Immigration Bureau, and had interviews with the leading bankers and brokers representing the holders of a large amount of the bonds of the State, notably, Mr. Belmont, of New York, at that time the agent of the Rothchilds, who held a large block of the bonds, and for a while was quite sanguine of success, as all these gentlemen evinced a very liberal and accommodating disposition, and Governor Holliday, with whom I had several conferences on the subject, was equally hopeful, but as soon as the Legislature met, it was seen that they had no idea of anything but carrying out their own program, which was represented by the "Riddleberger Bill," as it was called, which proposed to assign one-third of the debt to the State of West Virginia, to eliminate the war and reconstruction interest, and assume the payment of what was found due the creditors after this was done with a low rate of interest, and to submit this settlement to a vote of the people for ratification. When the "Pledge" Legislature met they changed the program, and the bill as passed did *not* eliminate the war and reconstruction interest, and *did not* provide for any vote of the people upon the subject. Before the time fixed for the election of a Senator,

Major Daniel and Governor Holliday both wrote to me suggesting that I withdraw from a hopeless contest, as it was manifest that I stood no earthly chance of election. I replied that I preferred to be beaten rather than retire without a fight. When the time came I was nominated in the Senate by Major Daniel and in the House by Mr. Ellis, of Montgomery, and received the votes of every conservative member except one who voted for Major Daniel. I was beaten by about twenty-five votes, if I recollect aright. The only comfort that I could derive from the affair was that not one word of criticism or censure for the manner in which I had performed my duties as Senator was uttered either in the House or Senate by Readjuster or Republican, white or colored. Indeed, when Senator Daniel, after eulogizing highly the record I had made as a Senator, placed my name before them for re-election, Riddleberger followed in a speech nominating General Mahone for the same place, and said, "He had not a word to say against Senator Withers, and agreed to all Major Daniel had said of him, and he was glad that no Senator here today who would cast his vote for General Mahone had cast any reflection on the political or private course of Colonel Withers." Mr. William Wirt Henry, a grandson of Patrick Henry, seconded my nomination in highly complimentary terms, but the fiat had gone forth, and I was beaten as I have described.

The history of that pledged Legislature is a foul blot on the records of our State. The Court of Appeals was substituted by a Court of Readjuster Justices, some of the old Court whose term of office had not expired were removed all the same, and if a rebellion had not broken out in the ranks of the Readjusters, no Circuit or County Judge would have escaped. This was to be done by a re-arrangement of the Judicial Districts, and new elections of the Judges thereof. Another of his schemes was to appoint a Commissioner of Sales in each county, who was to have the exclusive right to sell all the lands sold by order of Court, and to have the charge of all property in litigation to be executor of every man's estate, if in any way it should come under control of Court, to act as a guardian of all infants and litigants were to be forbidden to settle their difficulties themselves unless with the approval of the Commissioner of Sales. A Mahone newspaper was to be set up in each county to be run by this Commissioner, and no order of Court, or notice would be valid unless published in this paper, thus compelling the public to support it. Furthermore it was proposed to require all laws to be published in his organ, the *Richmond Whig,* involving an immense tax on the people of the State for the support of his "Organ." Fortunately for the State, four members of the Senate, elected as Readjusters, finding that the ruin of the State would be inevitable unless a stop were put to these high-handed measures, determined to resist the proposed legislation and prevent it at all hazards. They were fully conscious of the odium they would incur, and the abuse and denunciation of which they would be the recipients at the hands of Mahone and his adherents, but regardless of all this they carried out their purpose, and their names should be held in perpetual reverence by the people of Virginia. These men were Judge Lybrook, of Patrick, General Samuel Newberry, of Bland, Major Peyton Hale, of Grayson, all former supporters and personal friends of mine, to whom should be added the name of a debt-paying Republican from Chesterfield and Powhatan, Mr. Walker.

The uncompromising resistance of these four men effectually prevented the consummation of the nefarious measures proposed, and "scotched the snake," but did not kill it. When the Presidential election of 1880 was to come off, the Democrats as usual held a Convention and appointed delegates to the nominating Convention and selected an electoral ticket. In these movements the Readjusters took no part. They called a meeting of their own party, put forward an electoral ticket, but this ticket was not pledged to support Hancock and English. More than half the meeting which selected and put forth the electoral ticket were negroes. Their organ, the *Richmond Whig,* in advance of their action, proclaimed that "the July Convention will be neither Republican nor Democratic, nor will its Electors be Republican or Democratic." And again, "We are not standing on any national Democratic platform. We are not parading (falsely) under the national Democratic name or banner.

We are not supporting the Democratic nominees or the Cincinnati nominees. No! We are the Readjuster party of Virginia." Their chosen orators, such as John S. Wise and Mr. Massie, proclaimed in their speeches their readiness to support Garfield and Arthur, if thereby they could secure the success of the Readjusters.

An earnest effort was made by General Mahone and his chief supporters to prevent the formation of a distinctively Republican organization in Virginia, hoping to secure the support of that party for their unpledged ticket, but this scheme signally failed, as the Republicans called a Convention to meet at Staunton, and put forth there a regular Republican ticket pledged to support Garfield and Arthur. After this was done, no avowal of their policy was made so far as the action of their Electors was concerned, in the event they could carry the State, of which they professed to be confident.

Events, however, demonstrated that the purpose of General Mahone was to aid in the election of Garfield and Arthur, though an avowal of that purpose was impolitic and therefore not made, as he knew he would drive off those Democratic members of his party who were bitterly hostile to the Republican party. That such was General Mahone's purpose, however, is shown by the following significant facts. In 1879 General Simon Cameron, Senator from Pennsylvania, made a trip South, ostensibly for health and recreation, visited Richmond, and had an interview with General Mahone, at which time, if Republican testimony can be believed, a compact was agreed on by which the "Solid South" should be broken, and Virginia at least enrolled in the Republican column. General Cameron was one of the most astute men of his party, and best skilled in party strategy. He soon after resigned his seat in the Senate, to which his son, Don Cameron, was elected, and he ran down to consult with General Mahone. I knew him well and liked him personally. Having received intelligence of his quiet visit to my home, after he got back, I charged him with having gone on a political mission and rather taunted him with having formed a coalition with the Readjuster party. His reply was significant. "Oh," said he. "Withers, anything is right which will beat you d—— Democrats." But in further proof, the Chairman of the Republican party in Pennsylvania, Mr. Cooper, from his position became cognizant of the facts I have cited, and in a book entitled "American Politics," published soon after the occurrences, says:

"In the Presidential campaign of 1880, the Readjusters supported General Hancock but on a separate electoral ticket, while the Republicans supported Garfield on an electoral ticket of their own selection. This division *was pursuant to an understanding,* and at the time thought advisable by General Mahone, who, if his Electors won, would go for Hancock or not as circumstances might suggest, while if he failed the Republicans might profit by the separation. The Readjuster movement at first had no other than local designs, but about the time of its organization there was a great desire on the part of the leading Republicans to break the Solid South, and every possible expedient to that end was suggested. It was solid for the Democratic party and standing thus, could with the aid of New York, Indiana and New Jersey (then all Democratic States) assure the election of a Democratic President." He goes on to say that President Hayes had tried to break it by conciliatory speeches, and then by putting a Southern Democrat (Mr. Key) into his Cabinet, but it proved a failure. Mr. Cooper then adds:

"The next and most quiet and effectual effort was made by General Simon Cameron. He started on a brief Southern tour ostensibly for rest and enjoyment, but really to meet General Mahone and his leading Readjuster friends, and the leading Republicans. Conferences were held and the union of the two forces was made to embrace national objects. This was in the fall of 1878. Not long thereafter, General Mahone consulted with General Don Cameron, who was, of course, familiar with his father's movements, and he actually devised and carried out schemes to aid the new combination by which the solid South should be broken."

From "American Politics," page 263.

One of the schemes "to aid the new combination" was to redistrict the State, by adding negro counties to the large white districts, whereby General Mahone expected to make eight at least of the Congressional Districts Republican. This "scheme" failed because of the opposition of the "Big Four," consequently General Mahone was never able to "deliver the goods" to the Republicans, and the South remained "Solid." After reading the proofs I have cited, showing conclusively the existence of "an understanding" between General Mahone and the Republicans, it is almost incredible, but certainly true, that General Mahone sought recognition at the hands of the National Executive Committee of the Democratic party as the true representative of the Democrative party of Virginia in the Presidential contest of 1880. I attended by invitation a meeting of that Committee held in New York when the matter was up for consideration. That they should have given serious consideration to such a claim passes my comprehension. None of the Readjusters had taken part in any of the Conventions of the Democratic party in Virginia, no delegates had been sent to the nominating Convention in Chicago, no recognition had ever been asked by the Readjusters as part of the Democratic party of Virginia, and when these facts were cited to the Committee, and the only counter claim was the demand of the General that they receive recognition, it did not take long for the Committee to come to a decision. The claim was made solely for the purpose of quieting such members of the party as were unwilling to be transferred to the Republican ranks, and after the formal recognition by the Committee of the regularity of the Democratic organization in Virginia, most of the men I have described left the Readjuster ranks and ranged themselves with the Democrats. As a consequence, when the election came off the Mahone contingent was found to be far behind both the Democratic and Republican tickets. This election was practically the end of the Readjuster party. General Mahone went to the Senate, affiliated at once with the Republican party, but they profited by his accession only to the extent of *his vote.* Harry Riddleberger, as he was familiarly called, succeeded Judge Johnston and also acted with the Republicans. He was personally much better liked than his colleague, as he was goodhearted, genial and generous, clever and fluent, but convivial in his tastes to a degree, and the temptations of Washington life proved speedily destructive to his influence. All the Readjusters who were elevated to office by Mahone followed him into the ranks of the Republican party, with the exception of Governor Cameron and Parson Massie, who returned to the Democratic ranks. In their brief career the Readjusters proved themselves more intolerant and proscriptive than any party ever before known. It might have been supposed that one who had played so prominent a part in the service of the Confederacy would have felt some sympathy for his old comrades in arms, but General Mahone turned out of office every Confederate soldier, who adhered to the Democratic party, however maimed, dependent and faithful, and gave their places to his own satellites. The negroes received small favors at his hands, though they stood by him almost to a man. One of unsavory reputation was made door-keeper of the House of Delegates in the place of Sullivan, a one-legged Confederate, who had long held the place, and one other position of small importance was given another colored man, and I think these were all the "loaves and fishes" which fell to the lot of the negroes in the distribution of the spoils. I have thus sketched as impartially as I could this remarkable episode in the political history of Virginia, and will now resume my narrative of Senatorial experiences, which will render it necessary for me to return in point of time to the year 1878, that I may narrate one or two events of interest to me and I hope to some at least of my readers.

CHAPTER XXXVI.

LEE'S RECUMBENT STATUE.

In the month of December, 1878, during the Christmas recess, Major Benjamin B. Douglas, representing the first Congressional District of Virginia, died suddenly in Washington from an apoplectic attack. His colleagues of the House requested me to introduce the usual resolutions of respect in the Senate, which of course I did. As this was a short session and Congress was much pressed with business, eulogies were fewer in number and less extended in scope than were usual on similar occasions. I received a beautiful letter from his daughter thanking me for the memorial remarks I submitted on that occasion, which I appreciated highly.

During this session Colonel Mosby was nominated as Consul at Hong Kong, and the nomination was referred to the Committee, which I supposed would have no difficulty in reaching a favorable conclusion, as the Colonel's character and qualification for the position I regarded unassailable. I was, therefore, surprised to find a decided disinclination on the part of several of the Senators on each side to vote for his confirmation. Prominent Republicans, especially from the New England States, had not forgotten his war record and were unwilling to forgive his "guerilla" exploits, while many Democrats were equally reluctant to condone his affiliation with the Republican party. I had always liked Colonel Mosby, and as his admiration and respect for General Grant had been, as I thought, the natural consequence of the active and decided stand taken by General Grant in Colonel Mosby's behalf at the close of the war, I felt that they deserved recognition. It must be remembered that Colonel Mosby had been outlawed during the war and a price set on his head, and after General Lee's surrender, the Federal authorities refused to recognize the parole which he, in common with all other Confederates, had given. This placed him in a very dangerous and exceptional situation, which he and his friends fully recognized. His wife, as I was told, went herself to the City of Washington to see Stanton, the Secretary of War, on his behalf, and if public rumor is to be credited, met with a very harsh and cruel rebuff at the hands of that official. She left his office in tears, and knew not which way to turn for relief. As it happened she learned that General Grant had just reached Washington, and she at once sought him out, and laid the whole facts before him. General Grant was astonished that the Secretary of War refused to recognize the parole which under the terms of his agreement with General Lee at Appomattox was to be given to all officers and soldiers under his command. He went at once to the War Office, saw the Secretary, and demanded an explanation. As usual, the Secretary was obstinate, and refused at first to accede to the General's demand, until told that unless he did so the resignation of the General commanding the Army would be placed in his hands. Confronted with this alternative, the Secretary had to yield, and Mrs. Mosby left Washington with a safe conduct for her husband under General Grant's own hand. Such was the account current at the time, and never to my knowledge contradicted, and I think, if true, no one could fail to see in it sufficient apology for and explanation of Colonel Mosby's personal regard for General Grant. This friendly feeling was fully reciprocated by General Grant, and it is a well-known fact that during his administration few men exercised a greater influence over the President than Colonel Mosby. He always declined to accept an appointment, himself, but secured many for those who had fought under his command. When President Hayes came in, Colonel Mosby was offered this lucrative Consulship and accepted it. As I said, the opposition to him was decided and the appointment was hung up several days. I finally succeeded in securing a favorable report from the Committee and ultimately the confirmation. Two of the Republican Senators told me that they would vote favorably from personal regard to me, and another said that he would not vote at all for the same reason, and it was thus the favorable result was secured. I was much gratified, and when I informed Colonel Mosby he was evidently relieved and greatly pleased.

The Mayor of Alexandria during Hayes' Administration was a young man belonging to a prominent family of that city, Mr. Courtland Smith. Washington's Birthday was generally observed in Alexandria, and on this occasion the Mayor and Council determined to invite President Hayes to participate in the observance by paying the city a visit, delivering an address, receiving a public ovation, etc., and partaking of a lunch at the residence of Mrs. Smith, the mother of the Mayor, afterwards attending the banquet at night. Accordingly, an invitation was duly sent, signed by the Mayor and Common Council, which was accepted by the President, who expressed his earnest desire to do honor to the memory of the great Virginian. I, of course, as a resident of Alexandria and a Senator from Virginia, was also invited to take part in the proceedings. On the day appointed, all the preparations having been completed, a suitable stand for speaking having been erected and numerous guests invited, the President came over from Washington on the steamer, accompanied by his Secretary and a few officials, and was met at the wharf by the Mayor, Council, and Committee of Arrangements, a procession formed led by a band of music, which traversed the principal streets of the city and escorted "His Excellency" to the stand. General Fitz Lee presided, and the Mayor delivered an appropriate address of welcome, to which the President made appropriate response, and several other addresses followed. I was of the number who spoke, and General Fitz Lee was another, and there were probably others. All passed off well except that the stand, being much crowded and constructed hurriedly, gave way and all occupying it fell to the ground during the President's address. Fortunately, it was only four or five feet high, and no one was seriously hurt. In the melee the President and I were thrown in a pile together, but he was perfectly cool and collected, and as soon as it was ascertained that no one was injured, he resumed and concluded his address from a lower plane, however, and the rest of the program was carried out fully. We had a delightful lunch at Mrs. Smith's, and the President returned to Washington late in the afternoon. As I remember them, General Fitz Lee's speech was the best one made. I was myself surprised at its effectiveness, for the General at that time was not accustomed to filling that role, but very soon thereafter demonstrated his ability to please and entertain a crowd as well or better than many accustomed to public speaking for years. He was always personally popular, not only in Virginia, but everywhere he was known.

After the death of General R. E. Lee, his friends and admirers in Lexington and elsewhere, desirous of giving expression to those sentiments of love, veneration, and gratitude so widespread, and I might say universal in the States of the Confederacy, finally agreed on a memorial in the form of a Mortuary Chapel to be built, on the College Green at Lexington, and adorned with a marble recumbent statue of the immortal chieftain. Valentine, of Richmond, was entrusted with the production of this work of art, and knowing that success would send his name "sounding down the ages," he was deeply interested and sought information from all available sources of the details of General Lee's form, pose and general appearance. As I lived opposite his studio while he was engaged in modeling from clay, he almost daily called me over to give him my impressions of the work. The statue in marble was now approaching completion, and the construction of the Mortuary Chapel was begun. A public ceremonial was decreed by the Committee at the laying of the cornerstone with addresses and other exercises. As one of the Senators from Virginia, and a Confederate soldier also, I was honored by being selected to deliver the address, and General Joseph E. Johnston, then a Member of Congress from the Richmond District, was also to speak. The twenty-eighth of November was fixed for the laying of the cornerstone. We started on the twenty-sixth, hoping to reach Goshen that night, where we had to take the stage for Lexington, as there was no railroad connection at that time. We were delayed from some cause, and did not reach Staunton in time to make connection with the train for Goshen and had to remain there until two oclock the next day. It rained steadily and at times heavily all day. We reached our destination about five o'clock, expecting to go right on to Lexington, but found a telegram awaiting us requesting that we lay over till the next day, as all the streams were impassable, and the ceremony would have to be postponed until the twenty-ninth. As this delay did not suit the engagements either of General Johnston or myself, we replied insisting that the original program should be carried out, as we would make an early start, and reach Lexington in time for the ceremonial. We supposed as the weather had now cleared, the mountain streams would run down to a fordable point by next morning.

We spent a very pleasant evening at the hotel, no other guests being present, and chatted until late. I had never seen General Johnston as talkative and sociable. He entertained me by relating several anecdotes and incidents in his life while a cadet at West Point. I was much interested in his reminiscences of an affair between General Jubal Early and General Joseph Hooker, both being cadets at the same time General Johnston was. We were discussing the peculiarities which distinguished the people of each section, and especially the standard recognized in each for the adjustment of personal difficulties. He illustrated it by the following incident: "One night," said he, "at a meeting of a literary or debating club, Joseph Hooker and Jubal Early were discussing some matter, and Joe Hooker gave Early the lie. Early at once walked across the Hall to where Joe Hooker stood, and without a word, commenced booting him in fine style. Hooker made no resistance except to protest earnestly against such rude treatment, when, as he said, he had given no provocation whatever.

"The Southern cadets all supposed a hostile meeting inevitable after such an occurrence, but when several days had passed without any action by Hooker, most of the corps tabooed him, and he had few associates thereafter. The Florida War came on soon after, and both Early and Hooker were in the army sent to subdue the Seminoles. According to General Johnston's opinion a more miserable, dangerous, and utterly abominable campaign was never fought. Said he, "We were in almost impenetrable swamps, where nothing could be seen ten steps, but any movement was speedily greeted by the crack of the rifle from invisible foes, and the death or wounding of an officer or soldier. It required the finest kind of pluck to stand square up to your work, and to my surprise I found that

Hooker, who had been ostracised as a coward at West Point, exhibited as much or even greater indifference to danger than many of those who had "cut him." The consequence was that he was at once restored to his proper standing and from that time no suspicion of want of courage was ever whispered. Indeed, the soubriquet of "Fighting Joe Hooker," which he fairly won in the Indian Wars, was the best possible voucher for his nerve."

In narrating such incidents as these the time passed quickly until we were compelled to retire, in order to prepare for our proposed early start. We got up at five o'clock, and without awaiting breakfast, started promptly on our journey of twenty miles. When we reached Bratton's Run, the driver pronounced it unfordable, and said there was no alternative except to go by the Rockbridge Alum Springs, which increased the distance considerably. We made the best speed practicable, and drove into Lexington about eleven o'clock. Professor White and General Pendleton met us, the first taking charge of General Johnston, the latter of myself. We had breakfast speedily served and were ready to carry out our part of the program in ample time. Everything seemed to pass off smoothly, though some of the audience complained that the speeches were too short, rather an unusual source of dissatisfaction, according to my observation and experience. Mr. Randolph Tucker made, of course, a very pleasant introductory address, I followed him in a speech of about fifteen or twenty minutes, I suppose, and General Johnston's was, if anything, shorter. They were all well received by quite a large audience. Among other friends, I met with Mr. James Southall and his charming wife, who was Miss Sharpe, of Norfolk, with whom I had spent many pleasant hours, in their rooms at the Exchange Hotel when he was editing the *Richmond Enquirer,* and I was as Lieutenant Governor presiding over the Senate of Virginia.

Mrs. Southall took the first opportunity to compliment my speech, which she said her husband pronounced "First-rate and in every way appropriate." and she said "I know he is a judge." I dined with a large company at Professor White's, took tea with my old friend, Governor Letcher, and returned to General Pendleton's about eleven o'clock, having had a busy and very pleasant day. We returned the next morning to Goshen.

In August of this year, I purchased of Mr. John Henry Ewald the "Old Mathews Place," as it was called, about one mile east of Wytheville. The place had been purchased by an Englishman named Topham, where he had lived for some years, but had never finished paying for it, and it was sold under the deed of trust executed at the time of his purchase. At the sale, it was bought by Mr. Ewald, but his wife was not willing to reside there from some unexplained cause, and he came over and offered it to me for less than I had bid on it at the sale. I agreed to take it, as it was so near town, the farm of two hundred and twenty-five acres in fine condition, and the house an old-fashioned country home, commodious and comfortable, with a splendid spring near the house, and the most beautiful spring-house of cut limestone I ever saw. Most of the outside enclosures were hedges of Osage Orange, and we promptly named it "Hedgefield." I took possession at once, removed my family from "Green Meadows," and immediately began plowing for wheat, hiring several teams, by which means I was able to seed in time between fifty and sixty acres of wheat. I will here mention that I sold "Green Meadows," the next year, to my brother, Austin C. Withers, of Suffolk, and his brother-in-law, Mr. John Riddick, losing five hundred dollars by the sale. Being fond of farming and raising stock, I now had an opportunity of indulging my taste to a limited extent at least, and I and my family passed seven pleasant years of country life at "Hedgefield." As several of my daughters were by this time married, the enlarged accommodations now at our command enabled us to entertain them and their little ones during the summer months with little inconvenience, and nearly all of them eagerly availed themselves of the opportunity. The large and excellent orchard on the place was a source of much comfort and enjoyment as the fruit of all kinds was of first-class quality and abundant in quantity, and there was usually a surplus which could readily be sold. The last owner had constructed a dam for an ice pond, but it had been broken by a freshet, but as soon as practicable I repaired it and had a large pond which I utilized for fish as well as ice. The advantages of fish culture were about this time urged upon the public, and the enlarged food supply furnished by the newly introduced German carp was much dwelt on by the Fish Commissioner and others. I availed myself of my position to secure a supply of the fry from the first batch ready for distribution, and thus stocked my pond. These soon grew and multiplied, so that in two or three years the pond was so well stocked that it furnished us with quite a number for table use. I was, however, disappointed in the quality of the carp, as a table fish, for it is really not quite so good as the ordinary sucker, but in size greatly exceeds it, for we often caught them of eight or ten pounds weight. As Mrs. Withers and many of the children were very fond of fishing, we spent many a pleasant hour on the banks of the pond engaging in the pleasing pastime. In the spring and fall it was frequented by many wild ducks, which fell an easy prey to our guns and made a delicious addition to our bill of fare. In the winter it gave us opportunity for the healthful and invigorating exercise of skating, and in the summer a cool bath was always easily attainable. Taking it all in all, I think a large pond of pure spring water well stocked with fish contributes as much to the comfort and enjoyment of a family as any other one thing.

The farm on the north of the Pepper's Ferry Road, originally a part of the "Hedgefield" place, was owned by my friend, David S. Pierce, a bright, clever lawyer, a nephew of General J. E. B. Stuart. As he lived alone at the time, he spent most of his evenings at my house, and being very well informed and a sparkling and agreeable conversationalist, we were always glad to welcome him. When December came I returned to Alexandria, but Mrs. Withers concluded she and the family had best remain at "Hedgefield." Henry Cook and his wife accompanied me to Alexandria, and we arranged to board with Mrs. Bryant, a widow lady of our acquaintance, where we were comfortably quartered and fed. I, of course, returned to "Hedgefield" for the Christmas holidays, which were, as usual, much enjoyed by the children and by the grown ones as well, had company from town almost every night, with dancing and feasting according to our usual custom.

CHAPTER XXXVII.

DEMOCRATIC CONGRESS.

The first session of the forty-sixth Congress was convened on the eighteenth day of March, 1879, in extra session, by proclamation of President Hayes. The event had been impatiently awaited by the Democratic party everywhere, as it marked the return of that party to the control of the Senate for the first time since the beginning of the war. The extra session was rendered necessary by the failure of two of the important Appropriation Bills because of irreconcilable differences of opinion between the two Houses of Congress. These two bills were for providing the means required for the support of the Army, and for the Legislative, Executive and Judicial Expenses of the Government.

The Democratic majority in the Senate was about twelve, counting Judge Davis, of Illinois, who usually voted with us. The roll call showed the presence of several new Senators, some of them men of national reputation. I will briefly sketch the more prominent. Matthew Carpenter, of Wisconsin, filled the seat of Timothy Howe, and both sides of the Chamber agreed in their estimate of his ability and efficiency. He had once before served a term in the Senate, and his old acquaintances hailed his reappearance with pleasure. As I have mentioned, he was a noted lawyer of high attainments and national reputation. He was one of the counsel for the defense in the impeachment of General Belknap, Secretary of War, and also appeared as counsel for the Hayes Electors before the "Electoral Commission," and in each case acquitted himself well and added to his celebrity. His service in the Senate did not, I think, enhance his reputation, as he was evidently more of a lawyer than a politician. General John A. Logan had also reappeared as a Senator from Illinois, and was warmly welcomed by the stalwarts of his party. He was aggressive as usual, but not wanting in a certain rugged force which made him effective on the floor. Henry W. Blair, of New Hampshire, who was elected in place of Wadleigh, was a courtly gentleman of pleasing manners and ready flow of words, but possessed little strength as a debater. He came to Virginia during a stumping tour in behalf of the Garfield ticket, and was met at Bristol by "Cyclone" Jim Marshall, of Craig, and hearers of that debate without distinction of party characterized it as the most striking illustration of the complete demolition of a Senator of the United States by the keen wit and sharp thrusts of his mountain competitor. Few men indeed could get the better of Marshall in a debate before a crowd.

Mr. O. H. Platt, of Connecticut, also made his first appearance in the Senate, and though he did not at that time take a prominent part in debate, he impressed us all favorably by his gentlemanly deportment and his fair-minded consideration of the questions submitted to the adjudication of that body. He is still (1903) an influential member of the Senate, and one whose judgment is much relied on by his colleagues in all doubtful matters.

On the Democratic side we were re-enforced by George H. Pendleton, of Ohio, who succeeded Stanley Mathews. He had attained prominence by several years' service in the House of Representatives, and had been supported by the Virginia delegation, as well as those from several other states, for the place of Vice-President on one of the national tickets, and was the nominee of his party for Governor of Ohio in 1869. He was a man of fine appearance, courtly manners, a perfect "Turvey drop" in deportment, personally liked by all, and well deserved the soubriquet of "Gentleman George," by which he was familiarly known. He was noted as being the father of the "Civil Service Law," enacted during this Congress. Merrimon, of North Carolina, was succeeded by Zebulon B. Vance, noted for his efficient administration of the Gubernatorial office during the war. He was elected thrice to this position, and had served also in the Army of the Confederacy, reaching the rank of Colonel, and would doubtless have received higher promotion had he not left the army in 1862 to serve his people as Governor. He wisely assumed the task of supplying the North Carolina troops with necessary food, clothing, and equipments, by importing these supplies directly, when the Confederate Government was confessedly unable to furnish them, and thus the troops from that State were enabled to do more efficient service than would otherwise have been possible. He was genial and pleasant in manner, possessed a quick sense of humor, and was socially a great favorite. Another gentleman of high distinction made his debut in the Senate this session from South Carolina. This was General Wade Hampton, the noted Confederate Cavalry leader. The first time that I ever saw him was at the first battle of Manassas. He was a member of the South Carolina Legislature when the State seceded and at once resigned and raised a mixed command of Cavalry and Infantry, known as the "Hampton Legion." He served through the war with great gallantry and distinction, and his name was a household word throughout the Confederate States. He was twice elected Governor of his State, and it was under his leadership that South Carolina was redeemed from Carpet Bag and negro domination. He was moderate and conservative in his political views, and enjoyed the esteem and confidence of Senators on both sides of the Chamber. It was noted as a singular circumstance, that the two Senators from South Carolina had only two legs between them. General Hampton's, however, was not lost in battle, but by his horse falling in the hunting field. Another warrior of distinction appeared in the forty-sixth Congress, as Senator from Kentucky—General John L. Williams, commonly known as "Cerro Gordo Williams," an appellation given him for his distinguished gallantry at the battle of "Cerro Gordo" during the Mexican War, for he was the hero of two wars. In the Mexican War he attained the rank of Colonel, and in the Confederate Army was a Brigadier General. He served through the war and surrendered with General Joseph Johnston. He succeeded Senator McCreery. He claimed to be a farmer by occupation, was not often on his feet, and made no pretension to oratory, but expressed his views when he did speak, with clearness and brevity. He was popular personally with all his brother Senators. A new Senator appeared from

Florida in the person of Wilkinson Call, elected in place of Conover, the Carpet Bagger. He was fond of speaking, and to some extent impaired his efficiency by the frequency of his appearance on the floor of the Senate. His people, however, seemed satisfied with his services, and he was repeatedly re-elected. R. F. Jonas, a new member from Louisiana, in place of Eustis, also presented himself. He was a native, I believe, of Kentucky or Illinois, but removed to Louisiana in early life, served through the war as a private or non-commissioned officer, became a lawyer, and took an active part in the Reconstruction measures which ultimately brought the State back into the Union. He was a member of the National Democratic Committee, and was actively instrumental in securing the recognition by the Committee of the regular Democratic Organization of Virginia, as against the Readjuster faction in the Presidential election of 1880. It will be seen that the elections had, with the exception of Kellogg, of Louisiana, eliminated the whole Carpet Bag gang of Senators, and it was not long before the latter followed the procession. Of course as soon after the Senate met as possible there was a reorganization of the committees and a change in the personnel of the officers of that body. I was made Chairman of the Committee on Pensions, was second on the Committee on Appropriations, also was one of the Committee on the District of Columbia, and on Engrossed Bills, and a member of the Select Committee to investigate the Freedman's Savings and Trust Company. Three of these committees have a large amount of work to perform, and as I have always endeavored to attend to all duties properly devolving on me, it will be seen that I was of necessity kept very busy. The loss of that absolute control of the Senate which for nearly two decades they had enjoyed, appeared to affect injuriously the tone and temper of most of the Republican Senators, particularly those accustomed to play the "Leading parts." They became more irritable, and showed their bad temper on the slightest provocation. This was not unnatural under the circumstances, but it added a zest to the enjoyment of their political opponents, who had thus by a turn of fortune's wheel attained control of the highest Legislative body of the world. The consequence was that we had an unusual amount of fervid partisan oratory, in the course of which all the old issues were again reviewed and the old straw of sectional hate was again and again threshed over. Much of this was developed in the debate on the Army Appropriation Bill, which happened to fall under my charge. It will be remembered that the failure to pass this bill, and one other, necessitated the extra session. The House Bill of the last Congress was reported by the Senate Committee, but one of the sections had a clause added for the purpose of repealing that provision of the Revised Statutes which permitted the use of the Army for the purpose of "keeping peace at the polls," which, under the construction of the Attorney General, had been made the pretext for interfering in elections as was the case in Petersburg in 1876. This was denounced as revolutionary and outrageous, as it was incorporating general Legislative provisions, on an Appropriation Bill, and all the changes were rung upon it. The Democrats cited repeated instances in which this had been done by the Republicans when in power, but they refused to admit that they were committed to the principle. There was much bad feeling displayed, and I was occasionally in danger of losing my own temper, but was fortunately able to retain my self-control and to observe the amenities of debate. After some weeks of effort, we reached a vote and passed the bill as reported by a strict party vote. This was about the last of April. When the bill went to the President, it was vetoed, and of course our majority in either House was not large enough to pass it over the veto, consequently a new bill was passed by the House differing in no essential particular from the first, except that the sixth section which forbade the use of the Army at the polls for the purpose of keeping the peace was left out and in lieu thereof, a clause was inserted prohibiting the use of any of the money appropriated for the pay of the Army when employed "as a police force." When the bill came to the Senate it was reported back from the Committee on Appropriations as it came from the House, and I was again placed in charge by the Committee.

The debate was even more sharp and acrimonious than on the preceding bill. Mr. Conkling was, if possible, more offensive, contemptuous, and arrogant than before, and hence became involved in a bitter passage of arms with Senator Lamar, of Mississippi, which not only attracted the attention of the Senate, but aroused the interest of the public to a degree almost unprecedented in the history of the Senate.

The discussion had extended over several days, and I finally gave notice that on the next day but one, I proposed to ask the Senate to continue the consideration of the bill until a vote should be reached. When the day came, in the morning hour Mr. Lamar called up a bill providing for the appointment of the "Mississippi Commission," which was discussed until the expiration of the "morning hour." Mr. Lamar then asked unanimous consent to continue consideration of the bill, as he thought it could be passed in a few minutes more. I objected, unless a vote could be had at once, as I had given notice of my purpose of getting a vote on the Army Bill that day, if the Senate would sustain me in my effort. Mr. Conkling asked, "Are we to understand that notwithstanding this unanimous consent, if it is given, the Senator from Virginia will insist on a vote today on the other bill?" I replied, "That is precisely my purpose, I shall ask the Senate to dispose of the Army Bill before adjournment." Mr. Conkling in his blandest manner urged that I would not really expedite the passage of the bill by insisting on a vote that day, for reasons which he assigned. I repeated my purpose of getting a vote if possible before adjournment. The President *pro tem.* asked if there was unanimous consent to proceed further with the consideration of the Mississippi Commission Bill, and asked "Is there objection?" Mr. Conkling said, "For one Senator I will give my consent, and will trust to the courtesy of the other side of the Chamber, when we reach an ordinary hour of adjournment, and if any Senator wishes to be heard, that he shall not be cut off or pushed into the night." I replied, "The Senator must not trust to my courtesy in the matter, if he alludes to me."

With consummate sarcasm in voice and manner, Mr. Conkling interrupted me by saying, "I did not indicate the Senator from Virginia as one to whose courtesy I could trust."

I answered, "As I am on the other side of the Chamber,

and as the bill is under my charge, I supposed perhaps I was alluded to."

He repeated, "I did not select the Senator from Virginia as the Senator to whose courtesy I intended to trust."

Assurance was given that not more than twenty minutes would be asked to complete the bill and this being granted, the bill was passed within the time, and the Army Bill was taken up. Senators Beck, of Kentucky, Blaine, of Maine, and Voorhees, of Indiana, continued the debate, the first and last at considerable length. In the course of the discussion, and the running debate constantly interjected in it, little was said on the bill under consideration, but almost every other conceivable matter of a sectional and exciting nature was brought in. At six o'clock Mr. Carpenter took the floor, but at Mr. Conkling's request gave way for a motion to adjourn. I demanded the yeas and nays, and the vote was ayes 22 and nays 25, Senator Eaton, of Connecticut, Voorhees, of Indiana, and Davis, of Illinois, voting with the Republicans.

I had stated my willingness to adjourn provided an agreement were made to fix an hour when the vote should be taken the next day. Mr. Conkling said he would not agree to fix an hour, but expressed the belief that the vote could be had the next day. When the Senate refused to adjourn, he was greatly disappointed and evidently very angry, and he, Carpenter and Blaine, backed by their party, commenced a series of filibustering motions, which under the rules of the Senate they could easily keep up indefinitely, as we had not a quorum of Democrats in the Chamber, and found it impossible on account of pairs and absentees to procure one, we were powerless to force a vote, but the effect of the fight was to arouse a feeling of indignation on both sides of the Chamber which culminated about two o'clock in the morning, when Mr. Conkling undertook to recapitulate the occurrences which resulted in the dead lock. He dwelt on the fact that at the request of the Senator from Mississippi (Mr. Lamar) he had consented to continue consideration of the Mississippi Bill after the morning hour, expressed his regret that he had done so, and averred that when he had expressed the hope that under the circumstances an adjournment would be had, he had received an affirmative nod from five Democratic Senators. He continued thus, "The Senator from Virginia rose with such a disclaimer as he had a right to make, in order that he might keep within the bounds of his instructions from the Committee, but when I heard every Democratic Senator vote to commit such an outrage as that upon the minority of this body, and upon the Senator from Wisconsin, I do not deny that I felt my full share of indignation; and during this evening, Mr. President, I wish to assume all my own responsibilities, and so much more as any Republican Senator feels irksome to him, for what has taken place. I have endeavored to show this proud and domineering majority, determined apparently to ride rough-shod over the rights of the minority, that they can not, and should not do it. But I am ready to be deemed responsible in advance for the assurance that while I remain a member of this body, at all events until we have a previous question, no minority shall be gagged down, or throttled or insulted by such a proceeding as this. I say, Mr. President (and I measure my expression), that it was an act not only insulting, but an act of bad faith, I mean that." He proceeded in the same strain for ten minutes longer, when he sat down and Lamar took the floor. After alluding to the incidents of the morning hour, he continued:

"With reference to the charge of bad faith, that the Senator from New York has intimated toward those of us who have been engaged in opposing these motions to adjourn, I have only to say that if I am not superior to such attacks from such a source, I have lived in vain. It is not my habit to indulge in personalities; but I desire to say here to the Senator, that in intimating anything inconsistent, as he has done, with perfect good faith, I pronounce his statement a falsehood, which I repel with all the unmitigated contempt I feel for the author of it." Mr. Conkling's face paled perceptibly, but he rose and said, "Mr. President, I was diverted during the commencement of a remark the culmination of which I heard, from the member from Mississippi. If I understood him aright, he intended to impute and did in plain and unparliamentary language impute to me an intentional misstatement. The Senator does not dis-claim that." Mr. Lamar said, "I will state what I intended—" The presiding officer asked if the Senator from New York yielded to the Senator from Mississippi? Mr. Conkling said, "I am willing to respond to the chair. I shall respond in due time. Whether I am willing to respond to the member from Mississippi depends on what that member intends to say, and what he did say. For the time being I do not choose to hold any communication with him. The chair understands me now, I will proceed. I understand the Senator from Mississippi to state in plain and unparliamentary language that the statement of mine to which he has referred was a falsehood if I caught the word aright. Mr. President, this not being the place to measure with any man the capacity to violate decency, to violate the rules of the Senate, or to commit any of the improprieties of life, I have only to say that if the Senator, the Member from Mississippi, did impute, or intend to impute to me a falsehood, nothing except the fact that this is the Senate would prevent my denouncing him as a blackguard and a coward." (There was some applause in the galleries which was rebuked by the Chair). Mr. Conkling continued, "Let me be more specific, Mr. President, should the Member from Mississippi except in the presence of the Senate, charge me by intimation or otherwise, with falsehood, I would denounce him a blackguard, a coward and a liar, and understanding what he has said as I have, the rules and proprieties of the Senate are the only restraint on me. I do not think I need to say anything else, Mr. President." Lamar replied at once, "Mr. President, I have only to say that the Senator from New York understood me correctly. I did mean to say just precisely the words and all they imported. I beg pardon of the Senate for the unparliamentary language. It was very harsh, it was very severe, it was such as no good man would deserve and no brave man would wear." Then there was applause on the floor and on the galleries, promptly rebuked by the presiding officer, and there the incident ended.

Many persons anticipated more serious results from this encounter, as it was generally understood that the Senator from New York was not only a first-class athlete who kept in good training, but that he recognized "the Code" as a gentlemanly mode of adjusting personal grievances, and as he had been so pointed in avowing his personal responsibility for what he had done or said, it was natural to anticipate some more strenuous effort to repel a deadly insult than this, which amounted only to the proverbial "You are a liar again." Lamar's seat was near mine and I cautioned him to keep an eye on the New York Senator, and not to permit him to approach sufficiently near to take him at a disadvantage. Lamar was quite cool and self-possessed, and his only reply was, "If he can take me at a disadvantage, he will have to be d--d quick about it." I watched Conkling closely, and he soon passed over among his political associates, and I noticed the persons he appeared to consult, and drew my own inferences. These were that he had no intention to prosecute the matter further, which proved to be the case.

The affair, however, produced marked results. Senator Conkling seemed to feel a consciousness that he had gained no credit by the encounter, and his arrogance and superciliousness of bearing were noticeably less, during the whole period of my service.

The extra session closed on July 1st, 1880, and the three and a half months it was in session were consumed mainly in a struggle to correct some of the vicious legislation or abuses which had grown up under long continued Republican rule.

Returning home at the close of the extra session, I busied myself with farm work until the opening of the campaign of 1880. General Garfield had been selected by the Republican Convention, as a compromise candidate and to conciliate the New York Republicans, who, under the lead of Mr. Conkling, had fought hard to nominate Grant for the third term and had been defeated, the Convention in effect gave the stalwarts the privilege of naming the Vice-Presidential candidate. Mr. Conkling saw his opportunity of giving the Hayes and Blaine wing of the party a dig in the ribs, by putting up Mr. Arthur for the Vice-Presidency, the same man who had been removed by the Hayes Administration from the control of the New York Custom House for allged malfeasance and corruption.

It was doubtless a bitter pill for them to swallow, but they had no alternative. General Hancock was the nominee of the Democrats and Mr. English, of Indiana, was his running mate. The canvass was spirited and active from the start, and I took a prominent part in it, speaking at many places in Virginia and elsewhere. I was invited to speak in New York City by the Tammany Society and with others addressed an immense meeting at night on Union Square. The meeting was kept up until long after midnight, but I left at 11:30, and Senator Morgan was in swing at that hour.

In October, in company with Mr. William B. Isaacs and his wife, and Mr. Peyton Coles and his daughter, I attended the meeting of the Grand Encampment of the Knights Templar at Chicago. There was a large gathering of the order from all parts of the United States, and an immense procession, but the intense heat of the weather marred the enjoyment of all, and many casualties from sun-stroke and heat exhaustion marked the occasion. Mr. Benjamin Dean, of Boston, was made Grand Master, and I was elected D. G. Master by a very flattering vote. The same fall I attended the meeting of the General Convention of the Episcopal Church held in St. George's Church, New York City, which remained in session about three weeks. While here I accepted an invitation from Senator and ex-Governor Randolph, of New Jersey, to visit him at his home in Morristown. I greatly enjoyed the graceful hospitality of the Governor and Mrs. Randolph and regretted that I could not remain longer with them. I also called on General Hancock, in company with Judge Parker, of Winchester. He was stationed at Governor Island, which is located in New York Harbor. He received us with great cordiality, and though the unfavorable result of the October election in Indiana was well calculated to depress him, he seemed cheerful, and even hopeful of the result in November. General Hancock was a man of fine face and figure, quite a striking personage, and we were charmed by his genial address and affable deportment. Another General called on me while in New York and I was much pleased with his modest and quiet manner. I had formed a high estimate of his professional attainments, and strategic ability from the gallantry and bravery which always characterized the troops under his command, whenever we had met them during "the late unpleasantness." This was General Fitz. John Porter, whose Division made such a stubborn fight at Gaines' Mill. He was subsequently made the scape-goat for General Pope's disastrous campaign and by sentence of Court Martial been found guilty of cowardice and neglect of duty at second Manassas, and cashiered. The rankling of such a wound might well account for the shade of melancholy which was then the marked characteristic of his features when in repose.

His friends, among whom was General Grant, believing him innocent of the charges brought against him, were at this time laboring earnestly to secure a reopening of his case, believing that this would result in his complete vindication. A bill or resolution was introduced into the Senate having this end in view. It was fiercely fought by General Logan, who spoke several days in opposition to its passage, but it was finally passed by a decided majority, many of the Republicans voting against it, or refusing to vote at all. The result fully vindicated the wisdom of his friends, as the testimony of all the prominent Confederate Generals who had taken part in that fight, and which was now for the first time available, fully sustained the truth of his contention at the first trial, and the result was his complete vindication. The debate testimony and proceedings in full were published by order of Congress making several volumes, which were in great demand among Army men and those interested in military matters. The year 1881 marked the close of my political career as on the fourth day of March I ceased to be a Senator.

The election of General Garfield was a great disappointment to the Democrats, for until the loss of Indiana in October, they had confidently anticipated the election of General Hancock. The short session commenced in December and I recollect no incident of special importance that would be of interest to my readers. Indeed, I doubt not the large majority of those who have followed my narrative to this point have had enough and to spare of political incidents and occurrences, and I willingly close the chapter, with one or two reflections.

Senators may be roughly divided into two classes. The

speakers and the workers. Few are capable of filling both roles. To make a long political speech worthy the attention of the Senate and of the country demands preparation, and a good deal of it. This militates greatly against the attendance of committee meetings and the preparation of bills and reports, consequently, as a rule, the best speakers and debaters are the most careless in attendance at committee meetings, and most negligent of matters outside of political issues. I elected to join the workers, first because I knew that without careful preparation I could not hope to make any reputation as a debater, and even with all preparation, I was far inferior to many of my colleagues, but I felt myself capable of doing efficient work in committee, and able to acquit myself decently in a running debate on the provisions of a bill. I, therefore, delivered few prepared speeches, but I rarely ever missed a meeting of my committees, and never neglected the interest of any constituent confided to me, visiting the departments and the different bureaus whenever this was necessary. I always made it a point to answer all letters on business with promptitude, and as a consequence never heard any complaint of want of interest or neglect of any business entrusted to my care. I never found time hanging heavily on my hands, as I was occupied all day, of every legislative day, in attending to my duties as a Senator. The most disagreeable experience in the life of a Senator arises from the importunities of those seeking office and this really constitutes a grievance. Almost every applicant believes, or seems to believe, that nothing is required to secure success but effort on the part of his Senator or Representative, and the success of one applicant is made at once the incentive for half a dozen others, who urge that "You got A. B. a place, and I don't see why you can't get me one if you only try in earnest!" My patience was often tried by their importunities, but the dispensations of a wise Providence in a short time enabled me to "Put myself in their place," as I was under the necessity of playing the same role myself.

CHAPTER XXXVIII.

DRIFTING.

The close of my term as Senator threw me at once on my own resources for a livelihood, and being now in the sixtieth year of my age and fully entered on the down grade of life, the maintenance of myself and family constituted a problem not so easy of solution as when I was in full possession of all my mental and physical powers. True, I had a home and a small farm, but the income from the farm would be entirely inadequate to meet our necessities. Various expedients were suggested, considered and abandoned, but soon after the meeting of the forty-seventh Congress, the Senate lost its Secretary, whose death left a vacancy to be filled by election. As I deemed myself qualified for the position, and supposed that my personal acquaintance with a large proportion of the members would aid in securing the position, I wrote to each Senator on the Democratic side soliciting his support. I ought to have mentioned that the Democratic majority in the Senate was almost extinguished by the result of the elections in 1880, and the control of that body was held by a very narrow margin.

I soon found that Mr. L. Q. Washington, who had for years held the position of correspondent for several leading Democratic Journals, and who was extensively acquainted with the members, was also a candidate, and being on the ground had interviewed all the Senators and secured pledges of support from quite a number. Consequently when I reached Washington and commenced a personal canvass I found many already committed to Mr. Washington. But worse than all, my former colleague, Judge Johnston, who was still in the Senate, threw cold water on my candidacy, for some cause unknown to me, and for which I have never heard an explanation suggested, failed to support me. This, of course, destroyed all hope of success and a majority of the caucus agreed to support Mr. Washington for the place. But they were never able to elect him, as one or two Senators refused to support him. Senator Davis, of Illinois, who, as I have said, occupied an independent position, though generally voting with the Democrats, alleged his willingness to vote for me, and had the Democratic Senators supported me, Davis' vote would have given me the place, but so far from aiding me, Senator Davis' position was construed into an effort to dictate to the caucus, and I was more damaged than helped by his advocacy of my claims. The result was, that no Secretary was ever elected, and the Chief Clerk of the Senate discharged the duties of the office during the whole session. I was not only surprised, but astonished by Senator Johnston's action, as we had always been on the most friendly and cordial terms, as I supposed, and certainly had no falling out or disagreement of any kind in our lives. The thing is still a mystery to me. Thus ended my quest for office.

Mr. Garfield's administration was not a success in harmonizing the discordant factions of the Republican party, and Mr. Conkling soon resented the refusal of the administration to permit him to control absolutely the patronage of New York City and State. The breach rapidly widened and the feud was a matter of public notoriety. It was the exciting cause of a lamentable catastrophe, for on the second day of July, when the President, accompanied by Mr. Blaine, was passing through the rooms of the Pennsylvania Railroad Station at the foot of Sixth Street to take the train, he was shot by a cracked-brained fool, and received a mortal wound. He lingered for more than two months, but finally succumbed in the month of September. His assassin was tried, convicted, and executed for the crime. His avowed reason for the perpetration of the act was a desire to remove the President as an obstacle to the progress of the Republican policy, so that Mr. Arthur, the Vice-President, could succeed him. The man, Guiteau by name, was no doubt crazy, but there was "too much method in his madness" to permit him to escape the penalty of his crime.

I ought to mention here a gracious act on the part of Mr. Blaine, Secretary of State, which took me completely by surprise, and though I could not profit by his kindness, it greatly impressed me as evidence of his confidence and personal regard.

He, without any suggestion on my part, offered me any position I would accept under the Department which he controlled.

I expressed my high appreciation of his offer, but replied, "You know, Mr. Blaine, that I could not accept office under a Republican Administration." "Why not?" said he. "There are many offices which you could fill, involving no sacrifice of your political principles." I, however, persisted in my refusal, but feel satisfied that he was entirely sincere in his proposal, though some of my political friends think differently, and are of the opinion that he made the offer because he knew I would not entertain it.

Shortly after my return from Washington, I was urged by my friends in Danville, Virginia, to return to that place and establish a daily political paper, which they were of opinion could be made a success. The town was rapidly growing, and had only two weekly papers, and all the business men desired to see a daily paper established. As there was some plausibility in the suggestion, I made a visit to the place, and was warmly welcomed by many old friends, but after carefully examining the conditions, concluded the experiment was too risky for a man without considerable cash capital, as my experience in the editorial department of the *News* taught me how great was the expense connected with the publication of a daily paper. I, therefore, abandoned the project and returned to Wytheville.

The nineteenth day of October, 1881, was the Centennial Anniversary of the surrender of Cornwallis at Yorktown, and the Government decreed that it should be observed by public addresses and laying of the corner-stone of a monument to commemorate the event. The ceremony of laying the corner-stone was, of course, entrusted to the Grand Lodge of Masons of the State of Virginia, of which body Mr. Peyton S. Coles was at that time Grand Master, and under his direction elaborate preparations were made for an imposing ceremonial by the Masonic Fraternity, including a procession of Masons headed by the Grand Lodge and its officers, escorted by the Grand Commandery of Knights Templars of the State of Virginia, and an oration by Past Grand Master Beverley R. Welford. I was appointed Grand Marshal, aided by several prominent Masons as assistants, and directed and controlled the parade and procession. The civil part of the celebration comprised an address from Governor Holliday, of Virginia, with incidental remarks from President Arthur, who with some of his Cabinet were present and a delegation of Senators and Representatives, in considerable numbers, with the special Envoys sent by the French Government to represent that nationality, with officers of the Army and Navy. Grand Master Coles had in August arranged all the details of the Masonic ceremonial at a conference held at his hospitable home in Albemarle County, which was attended by the Grand Secretary, William B. Isaacs, James Scott, myself, and other officers and past officers of the Grand Lodge of Virginia. We were in session several days, and arranged all the details of our part of the ceremonial. Many distinguished members of the Masonic Fraternity from all parts of the United States were in attendance, and of course an immense crowd. As Grand Marshal I was anxious to secure a handsome horse for the parade, and fortunately succeeded through the kindness of my friend, Dr. Clopton, of the Eastern Asylum at Williamsburg, who sent me a magnificent stallion with splendid accoutrements, silver-mounted Texan saddle and bridle, which showed to great advantage. The Doctor had been stationed in Danville during the war at one of the Hospitals, where we became acquainted, and to this acquaintance I was doubtless indebted for his kind offices in securing such a handsome mount for me. Unfortunately the day proved to be disagreeable because of the prevalence of a strong gale from the Northwest, which as the season was dry, filled the air with dust, and which became at times almost stifling. The corner-stone ceremonial and the addresses were delivered under a large awning which somewhat lessened the annoyance from dust, but both Governor Holliday and Judge Welford fell into the common error of elaborating their views at such length, that the audience exhibited unmistakable signs of impatience before they concluded, and to make matters worse the delay brought the hour for the steamers from Washington to return and their impatient signals for departure broke up the crowd in a hurry, and there was anything but an orderly dispersal of the audience. This was the cause of an awkward incident. The crowd in leaving the stand rushed between the President and his party, and he was left with only one or two attendants, and found it impossible to rejoin his escort. The confusion and disorder was momentarily increasing, and I saw, or thought I saw, on the face of the President, who was near me, an expression not only of annoyance, but of apprehension. Fortunately my escort of Templars was unbroken, and putting myself at their head, and drawing my sword, gave orders to close ranks and made a push for his Excellency, placed him and the friends with him in a hollow square of Templars, and escorted them through the crowd and to the company of his escort. He expressed his thanks for the service in tones of genuine feeling, which his countenance more than emphasized.

The weather before night became quite cool, and as we were quartered in tents provided only with cots and blankets for sleeping, and had no fire or fuel, our rest was considerably disturbed. This, however, was favorable for a prompt and early departure, so after a hurried breakfast, the camp was struck, and the Grand Lodge and its subordinates returned to Richmond, and I continued my journey without delay to Lynchburg.

CHAPTER XXXIX.

IN PRIVATE LIFE.

This year of 1881 was in many respects a sad and trying one. I not only lost my Senatorial position, but, what was much worse, I had to suffer great family bereavements. My elder sister, Mrs. Jennet Lemmon, died after a brief illness early in the year, from no specific disease, but mainly from mental depression and grief caused by the death in New Orleans of her youngest daughter, Flora, who had married a son of Major Robert Saunders, a young lawyer, who settled in New Orleans and started his professional career with every prospect of success, which, by the way, was subsequently realized, but within a year his wife died in childbed, and her mother never recovered from the shock. She and I were raised together, went to school together, played together, and all our lives were devoted and affectionate, sharing each others' joys and griefs. She was indeed most lovely and lovable. She had taken my father and mother when they became old to live with her, and waited on them night and day with the most affectionate solicitude. Of course her death greatly disturbed and distressed them, as no one except Dr. Lemmon was left in the house. I attended the burial in Lynchburg, and my wife met me there, and we went down the next day to see my father and mother and consult as to what arrangement would be best for their comfort. My sister, Sue Massie, and I both wished to take them to our homes, but Dr. Lemmon thought the best arrangement would be for my brother William and his wife, who lived near, to come over and live in his house and let everything remain as before, and this was the arrangement finally made. The health of my father was becoming a source of anxiety to us, as his strength was manifestly failing day by day, and his great age, eighty-seven years, forbade the hope of any permanent improvement. This necessitated frequent visits from me during the summer and fall, and on each visit I saw with distress the gradual decadence of his physical and mental powers. He sank gradually and died quietly on the twenty-third of October, 1881. I was not present at the time, owing to the failure of the railroad connection at Lynchburg, and had to wait over for the next day. We buried him in the churchyard of Old St. John's, surrounded by his children and grand-children, to wait the joyous resurrection of a Virginia Gentleman of the Old School, who had well discharged all the duties of husband, father, and citizen, with Christian fidelity and unswerving probity. Many of his old neighbors and servants attended his burial, and attested by their presence the respect anad esteem with which he was universally regarded by those who knew him. My mother bore her great affliction with wonderful composure, merely remarking that the separation would not be for long, for she would soon follow him. This belief was prophetic, for in less than four months we placed her by the side of him with whom she had passed more than sixty-two years of married life. Rarely indeed can a parallel to this be found.

My sister, Mrs. George D. Sanders, of Buckingham County, who was present at the death and burial of my father, persuaded my mother to return with her for a visit, prior to taking up her residence with her youngest daughter, Mrs. P. C. Massie, in the County of Nelson. She stood the trip well, and seemed about as well in health as usual, until the middle of February, when she had a slight attack of indigestion, and on being raised to a sitting posture to take her cup of tea, suddenly said, "I am gone, children," and dropped back dead from heart failure. She was in her eighty-fourth year at the time of her death. She was the proud mother of eleven children, seven sons and four daughters, and all lived to mature age except one, Edward, who died at the age of sixteen from organic disease of the heart, following an attack of acute rheumatism.

This large family demanded and received from her the most untiring care, the most devoted affection, the most careful instruction in all the duties of life, coupled with a careful religious training as was usual in those days in the families of country gentlemen of the South. I was left, by my father's will, executor of his estate. There was little trouble in settling it, as he had himself divided his lands among his children some years before his death. There was considerable delay before I could dispose of the bonds of the City of Baltimore, in which most of his estate was invested, owing to the laws of the State and of the City of Baltimore, but finally all the red tapery was satisfied, and the money collected for the bonds and distributed according to the provisions of the will. There were no debts except the burial expenses of my father and mother.

I was much gratified this summer of 1881 by a visit from an old and highly-esteemed friend, General Dabney H. Maury. He spent a week or ten days with me at "Hedgefield," and his visit was enjoyed by every member of the family. Indeed, I can not now recall any one who possessed in a higher degree than General Maury the charm of brilliant and entertaining conversational talent. As a raconteur he was unsurpassed. His great fondness for field sports, the unusual opportunities which his long service on the plains and frontiers had offered for indulgence in this pastime, his wonderful memory and vivid power of description, gave to his varied narrative a degree of interest almost unsurpassed. He was preëminently what Professor Van Dyke called a *talkable* man as contra-distinguished from a *talkative* one. He did not lecture, he did not harangue, he did not monopolize the conversation, but was full of narrative and incident, with a fine sense of humor, and always had a crowd of listeners, old and young, hanging on his words with almost breathless interest.

The General and I were associated as members of the Executive Committee of the Army of Northern Virginia, and also of the Southern Historical Society ever since the organization of these bodies, and this intercourse seemed to renew the friendship and intimacy which began at the University of Virginia in 1840. As well as I remember, it was to confer with me upon some matter connected with one or the other of those associations that prompted his visit on this occasion, and being gratified at his reception and entertainment, protracted his sojourn with us for nearly a fortnight. He might have remained much longer without wearing out his welcome.

I had a visit about or just before this time, from another old friend, Dr. George Bagby, which I much enjoyed. He came to Wytheville on a lecturing tour, and as we were friends since our boyhood, he came out to "Hedgefield," to pay us a visit. He was a Lynchburger, and a gentleman of literary taste and culture. He studied and graduated in medicine but never did much practice, as all his leanings were in the direction of literature. He was connected with the Editorial Department of several Virginia Journals, was devoted to the interests of his State, a Virginian of Virginians, and as a humorist was, in my judgment, the peer of any. As an essayist and lecturer, he ranked high. He first obtained recognition as an humorist by the publication of a series of letters under the *nom de plume* of "Mozis Addums," a name which stuck to him through life. Many of his essays and lectures possessed unusual merit. That called the "Old Virginia Gentleman" was a particularly fine description of country life in Old Virginia before the war. "Bacon and Greens" was a deservedly popular lecture, which he repeated all over Virginia and in many parts of the South, while his description of a Piano Concert by Rubenstein has always been a favorite exercise for elocutionists since its first appearance. He succeeded John R. Thompson as editor of the *Southern Literary Messenger,* not a great while before the war began, and continued it under all the adverse conditions growing out of the constantly increasing privations and impecuniosities of the ill-fated Confederacy, the scarcity of paper, the worthlessness of the currency, the want of skilled labor and intelligent aid, and the burthen of a large and increasing family, until almost the close of the struggle. After his death, his life-long friend, Mr. James McDonald, Secretary of the Commonwealth, and Adjutant General of Virginia, collected and edited two volumes of his papers, for the benefit of his family. Bagby wrote a humorous report of his visit to "Hedgefield," which appeared in the columns of the *Journal,* with which he was then connected, an extract from which I will give:

"I spent an evening at Senator Withers' home a mile out of town. I could write a whole letter about it. The noble spring, the spring house just below, the most beautiful piece of stone work that I ever saw; the grand old cherry trees, the garden filled with luscious fruits and berries, and every variety of vegetables, etc., etc., well deserve a letter. I found the patriarch, for such he is, surrounded by children, grand-children, adopted children, friends, guests, relatives, dogs, puppies, little negroes, babies and pet foxes—about a million of them. He was suffering with rheumatism from his old wounds, but happy with all, as the king of the jolliest household in Christendom ought to be. A Northern Senator's house would have every luxury, and even splendor, but here in this plain Virginia Farmer's home was found every comfort and the best of cheer. Long may this Roman simplicity obtain. He told me two good ones which I shan't forget. The first of a man so lazy that he spent his days in summer lying under the shade of a tree on a cow skin with the tail attached, with a negro to keep off the flies and whose additional duty it was to drag the cow skin by the tail around the tree as the shade moved, so that he was never out of the cooling shadow. The other story was of a debtor whose impudence was so colossal that he could without blushing review a regiment of his creditors in a borrowed uniform."

I spent the first part of the year 1882 in an effort to raise a joint stock company for the purpose of engaging in the production of iron on a large scale and with all the "up-to-date" appliances. The County of Wythe had been for years a producer of valuable pig-iron smelted from the rich and easily-reduced brown hematite ores, in charcoal furnaces of primitive construction and of limited capacity. The opening of the Pocahontas coal veins in Tazewell, and in West Virginia, the construction of the New River Branch of the Norfolk & Western Railroad, and the superior quality of the coke made from this coal, all suggested that the time had come for the production of iron on a much larger scale than had ever been attempted by the old furnace men. There was, immediately on New River, seven or eight miles above the railroad crossing at Radford, a body of land known as "Rich Hill," on which large deposits of brown hematite ores were known to exist. The United States Government had made appropriations for opening the navigation of New River from the Lead Mines to Radford, and a channel of three to three and a half feet deep had been thus secured. Major John T. Hamlett, formerly connected with the Internal Revenue Department, an ardent mineralogist, proposed that I should make an effort to secure stock subscriptions sufficient to build a two-hundred-ton coke furnace at New River or Radford, which would be the nearest point at which the iron ores of Wythe and Pulaski could make connection with the coke of the Pocahontas mines. The plan we agreed upon was to buy the "Rich Hill" property and ship the ores from it on barges down New River say for eight miles to the railroad crossing, where the furnace would be reached. The ore could have been loaded on the barges by a shute from the bluff of the ore that overhung the river. The project seemed feasible, so we got an option for ninety days on the property after as thorough an examination of its minerals as was practicable, and agreed to make the effort to secure subscriptions to the amount of $500,000.00, which we deemed sufficient to carry out the project. I visited Richmond, Lynchburg, Norfolk and Petersburg, and afterwards extended my efforts to Baltimore, New York, Harrisburg, Philadelphia and Boston. I interviewed many capitalists, Furnace men, and others, but though almost without exception the persons approached deemed the proposed enterprise feasible, yet few were willing to make large subscriptions of stock. The Virginians were generally not at that time able to command large sums, and the Northern Iron Masters, while admitting the probable success of the scheme, declined to embark in it, as they could not afford to abandon their extensive and costly plants then in operation. After some months spent in the effort, I was only able to secure subscriptions aggregating less than half the amount required, and part of this was hampered with conditions. We were forced reluctantly to abandon the effort and suffer our option on the "Rich Hill" property to lapse. I regretted the failure, for I believed then as now, that the enterprise would have been profitable could we have raised the capital necessary. I was just about twenty years in advance of public sentiment, as at this time (1903) Northern capital has come into the same region and several large coke furnaces have been erected and are in full tide of successful operation, and the owner of the very property on which we held an option is now in receipt of a large income from the royalties received on the ores taken from the "Rich Hill" mines, he having wisely refused to sell, but permitted the mining of the ores on a royalty.

My visit to the "Hub" was made in the month of February, and as it was the first opportunity I had ever enjoyed of seeing this noted city, it was a source of much pleasure. I had letters which put me in communication with many prominent people, and I never met with greater courtesy anywhere. The Governor of Massachusetts was particularly kind and courteous, and I found him very agreeable and well informed. Mr. Cooledge, a gentleman largely engaged in the manufacture of shoes and boots, having visited my house in Alexandria at the time of the marriage of my daughter, Ellie, to Mr. Stephen Putney, was especially kind and cordial. He had not long been married himself, and was keeping house on one of the principal streets in the fashionable quarter of the city, and he insisted on my leaving the Parker House where I had stopped, and making my home with him while in the city. Indeed, he would take no denial, and in the afternoon Mrs. Cooledge called in her carriage and took me to her house, where I was, of course, treated with the greatest hospitality. I remained with them about a week, and was taken around to see all the noted places and buildings in the city. A public meeting was called during this time for the purpose of celebrating jointly the birthdays of George Washington and Abraham Lincoln, and I was greatly surprised one evening by a call from the Chairman of the Committee of Arrangements, accompanied by several members of the committee and invited to address the meeting. I tried to excuse myself on the ground that I had been an avowed rebel, and was an officer of the Confederate Army during the whole war, but they still insisted, and as my host, Mr. Cooledge, added his voice to those of the committee, I yielded, mainly because my host had, I was sure, brought about the call and invitation. So I attended on the evening fixed and faced a larger audience than I expected. Of course there were several speakers, the principal address being made by the President of

Harvard University. When my time came I discoursed mainly of Mr. Lincoln's great kindness of heart, his earnest desire to secure the restoration of the Union, and more especially did I emphasize my own deep regret and the horror and distress of the Southern people at the great crime which ended his life. I avowed my belief (and I was sincere in the avowal), that the greatest calamity which could have befallen us after Lee's surrender was the death of President Lincoln. Had he lived, I said, the South would never have been called on to pass through the furnace of Reconstruction, which caused us more suffering, humiliation and unhappiness than anything which occurred during the war. My speech was very well received, and the whole affair passed off more pleasantly than I anticipated, but it was rather a startling and unexpected event, that I should ever have been asked to deliver an address in the City of Boston, commemorative of the birthday of Abraham Lincoln.

CHAPTER XL.

AGAIN AN EDITOR.

With the failure of my furnace scheme, I abandoned further effort to originate any scheme of business on a large scale, and devoted myself to affairs of more modest proportions. My farming operations were fairly successful, but the proceeds from a small farm required to be supplemented by income from other sources to meet the wants of so large a household as was gathered at "Hedgefield."

I sent my son Robert to the Virginia Military Institute this year to continue his education, and of course this entailed additional expenses, but he was very prudent and spent as little as was consistent with this position. Mr. Frank Terry, a son of General William Terry, of Wytheville, who had been employed as salesman in a mercantile establishment, did not fancy that line of business, but thought he would prefer journalism as a future career, and as he knew I had experience in that line, proposed to unite with me in the purchase of the *Enterprise*, a semi-weekly Democratic newspaper then owned by Mr. John Caldwell and Mr. Brady. As he was a young man of good sense and good habits, I agreed to join him provided the paper could be bought at a fair price, which I indicated. He saw the owners and made the offer, but they asked more. We declined to advance our offer, and the matter was dropped. About this time Mrs. Withers desired to pay a visit to our daughters, Mrs. H. L. Williams and Mrs. John T. Reed, residing in Martinsville, Virginia, and we visited that place, and spent some weeks there very pleasantly. We were recalled by a telegram from Mr. Frank Terry saying that the owners of the *Enterprise* had agreed to accept our offer. When I reached Wytheville and saw the parties I was surprised to learn that they had reconsidered the matter and declined to sell. As I was a little worried at their vacillation, I went to see the owner of the *Dispatch,* a weekly Republican paper, and soon bargained with him for the material and good will of the paper, and Frank Terry and I at once took possession and promptly commenced the publication of a Democratic weekly paper. Of course I had for a time almost all the work to do, but it was not long before my young partner got the hang of it, and as our subscription and advertising lists rapidly grew, we were satisfied with our investment, and by close attention to business and square dealing with all, soon had it on a paying basis. The paper and my farm now gave me all the occupation I wanted, and as during the summer months the house was always filled to overflowing with the families of my visiting children and friends as well as summer boarders, we managed to get along comfortably.

The Grand Encampment of Knights Templars met in San Francisco in September, 1883, and as I held the office of Deputy Grand Master, I felt it my duty to attend, though I could ill spare the time or money for so long a journey. My friend, Peyton S. Coles, Grand Commander of Virginia Knights, agreed to accompany me, and William B. Isaacs, J. Thompson Brown, and several Knights from Richmond and other places proposed going, but no organized Commandery attended from the Virginia Jurisdiction. We went by way of St. Louis, Kansas City, and Denver, and as neither of us had ever been over the line or visited the Pacific coast, we were of course much interested. From Kansas City to Denver there was little to attract attention. The prairies were less impressive and beautiful than I had expected and the Rocky Mountains as we approached them much less imposing. Though the tops of the higher peaks were white with snow, it was difficult to realize their actual height. This is because there is a gradual and almost imperceptible ascent of five or six thousand feet to Denver, and this causes a peak of ten or twelve thousand feet to appear only half as high as it really is. There were some impressive points of view in passing through the Rockies, but on the whole I was disappointed in the views. When we reached Ogden, we found we would have to stop over for a night. Sir Knight Coles, Yates of Warrenton, and myself were together, and when we reached the principal hotel we found there was no possibility of securing rooms. In fact, as we proceeded West the trains were more numerous and much more crowded by Grand and Subordinate Commanderies en route to San Francisco. We tramped around from hotel to hotel in vain quest of sleeping quarters, next tried boarding-houses with no better luck, and it really seemed as if we would have to "camp out." As we were on our return to the station we passed a restaurant with a sign out offering "Lodging." So we walked in and asked if we could get rooms. The reply being in the affirmative, we asked to see the rooms. The first into which we were shown was just back of the bar-room, and as the furniture in it was new, I at once said I would take it, and Coles and Yates were escorted upstairs. I was soon in bed, but did not put out the lamp, as I feared there might be other and prior occupants, and I soon learned that my fears were well founded, but before I made this discovery I had a hurried visit from Coles and Yates, who reported with hushed and bated breath that we ought to leave the house, for there was in the room next to theirs *the corpse of a woman.* "Well," said I, "are you sure it is a corpse?" "No doubt of that," said Coles. "Then," said I, "there is not the slightest danger, for I will guarantee she won't disturb you." They reluctantly went back. My pillow and person were soon spotted with the alert and hungry forms of the ravenous insects whose preëmpted territory I had invaded. I arose quickly and shook off the intruders, dressed and took my seat in the rocker, got a book out of my satchel and spent the night in the chair alternately reading and dozing. Soon after daylight I went up to see how my friends had fared, and in all my life I have never seen such a spectacle as their couches presented. They had not slept at all, but had spent the night in an active campaign against the invaders, and as they had no lamp, but instead a tallow dip, they had used the flame of the candle as an implement of destruction, and had applied it remorselessly to the body of every bug they could reach. Of course the grease and smut from the wick invariably left their mark on sheet and pillow-case, you may imagine, if you can, the appearances presented. We paid our bill for lodging without a word of complaint, and went to the station where we boarded the first train for the West. The arid plains of Utah and Nevada are, of all lands I have ever seen, the most woebegone and desolate. Literally nothing but sage bushes and sand, alternating with white alkaline wastes where the platforms of the coaches are covered with crystals of borax or some kindred salt, and the eyes of the traveler are smarting from the finer particles which penetrate the whole interior of the coach, sifting in through every crack and crevice.

When we reached San Francisco we stopped at the Palace Hotel where our rooms had been engaged. The boasted climate did not appear to me to be worthy of the commendation bestowed on it by the Californians. The mornings were foggy, damp, and raw, making an overcoat pleasant if not necessary, and by mid-day this is succeeded by a strong breeze carrying at that time clouds of sand from the dunes which surround the city. This nuisance is now abated if not neutralized by the growth of the place, and the planting of trees and shrubbery in all the suburban lots and parks which surround the city. We had a large attendance and a harmonious session of the Grand Encampment. Sir Benjamin Dean, of Boston, was Grand Master, and came over escorted by a large delegation of Templars from that city, who kept open quarters at the Palace Hotel for the entertainment and refreshment of all callers, during the whole meeting. The hospitality of the California Knights and the citizens was on a magnificent scale, culminating in a splendid banquet over which the Grand Commander of California, ex-Governor George Perkins, presided. He is now, and has been for some years, one of California's representatives in the United States Senate. In the election of officers, I was honored by an almost unanimous selection as Grand Master of the Order, a distinction which was emphasized by the fact that I was the first man of Southern birth and residence who had ever been elected to this high office. On Virginia was conferred the additional compliment of having Past Grand Commander William B. Isaacs, of Richmond, selected as Grand Recorder, a position he ably filled until his death some years afterwards. In San Francisco I enjoyed meeting some near relatives, the

Mansons, sons and daughters of my first cousin, R. Emmett Manson, who are now residents of that city, the eldest son, Marsden, holding a high position in the City Government. On our return trip, we traveled over the Denver and Rio Grande Railroad. Stopping a day in Salt Lake City, and two or three in Denver, visiting Leadville, the noted mining city, ten thousand feet above the sea level, where we met some Virginia acquaintances, notably Mr. James Langhorne, formerly of Roanoke County, who had been very successful in his mining operations and accumulated a handsome fortune. We were received with the greatest kindness and hospitality and enjoyed our whole return trip greatly. The scenery on the Denver & Rio Grande Road far excels in beauty and grandeur that on the Union & Central Pacific lines. I have perhaps dwelt unduly on this California pilgrimage, but so much occurred of interest, and so much observed of novelty, beauty and grandeur, that the impressions left are distinct and durable.

When in 1884 Grover Cleveland was nominated by the Democratic Convention at Chicago, and an active canvass commenced in his behalf, I was appointed one of the State Canvassers by the Executive Committee, and urged to devote my whole time to this duty. I could not consent to do this as other business would demand attention, but I agreed to do my part, and delivered many speeches and engaged in several discussions in different sections of the State, and continued my canvass up to the day of the election. Cleveland carried my county by a small majority, the State by several thousand, New York by thirteen thousand, which elected him. Mr. Conelly Trigg was elected to Congress from the Ninth District. Nothing of special importance occurred after the election and I remained at home attending to my paper and farm during the winter and spring.

When Mr. Cleveland was inaugurated, he made Mr. Bayard, of Delaware, his Secretary of State, and I hoped to be able through his influence to secure some appointment under the Administration. Accordingly, about the tenth of March, I went to Washington to make an effort in this direction. I interviewed many of the Cabinet officers, most of whom were old acquaintances, and also saw the President, who impressed me as a man of strong intellect, but with little geniality or "personal magnetism," as it is now called. Senator Harris, of Tennessee, introduced me and gave me a warm recommendation to his Excellency, who of course dealt only in generalities. I found it difficult to see either Senator Daniel or Barbour, and did not much wonder at it, as the city was full of their constituents, every one anxious to get an office and to secure the aid of their Senator and Congressman. I was one of the number and confess to a conscious feeling of humiliation at occupying such a position. But I could only say with the man in the play, "'Tis not my will, but poverty consents."

Mr. Bayard was polite and dignified as usual, expressed his willingness to aid me, and advised me to file a written application for some specific place. Mr. Lamar was equally courteous, and "would be glad to see me in a good office." The Attorney General, however, Mr. Garland, was more frank, outspoken and cordial than any of the Cabinet. True, he had no place in his department that I could fill, and I had already written him in behalf of Mr. John Goode as Solicitor General, a position, by the way, which he secured and ably filled during Mr. Cleveland's first term. Mr. Garland said he would gladly endorse favorably any application I would make for he knew I would apply for no place which I did not feel that I could fill.

I found that the Congressmen elected from Virginia had agreed to meet in Washington on the seventeenth of March to consider the matter of appointments. Colonel Cabell and General Hunton thought I ought to apply for appointment as Commissioner of Agriculture, though Colonel Robert Beverley's name had been mentioned for the place, but it was thought doubtful if he would accept it, as he was a gentleman of large wealth with important interests demanding his constant attention. My own Congressman, Mr. Trigg. was if possible, more reticent and non-committal than any of the delegation. I sent in an application for the place of "Commissioner of Agriculture," with strong endorsements, but when the papers went to the President he said he proposed to confer that position on some gentleman from Missouri.

I then made application to the Virginia Congressmen for the place of Marshall for the Western District of Virginia, and returned home. The Congressmen met, distributed the offices among themselves, and Mr. Trigg gave the place of Marshall to a gentleman from Buchanan County. I visited Washington once or twice afterwards, but was not much encouraged by the prospect. In the latter part of April I had to pay a visit to the Grand Commandery of Maryland, which met in Baltimore, and on my return stopped over in Washington and saw Mr. Bayard, who told me the best thing at his disposal was the Consulship at Hong Kong, as the Department had decided to remove Colonel Mosby, and I could have the place if I would accept it, expressing at the same time his regret that it would involve my departure from the United States. I asked him to hold the matter open until I could consult my wife and family, which he agreed to do. On consultation, we agreed that as the salary was a good one, and the position one of importance, I should accept it, and a few days after the appointment was announced in the Washington papers. I soon received official notice of the fact and was instructed to execute a bond for a large amount with security, the sufficiency of which was to be certified by a member of Congress or other responsible person, all of which was promptly done, and preparations were made for my speedy departure. I proposed to my wife that I should go out first, examine the conditions existing at Hong Kong, and if I thought the outlook favorable, she and the family could follow. But she would not agree to this, saying that she was not willing to remain behind, and if I could live there comfortably, she could also.

Fortunately about this time a gentleman came to the neighborhood from England, who was anxious to rent or purchase a farm. He was brought to my house by Mr. Crowgey, an Englishman who had been living in the neighborhood of Wytheville some years, and was much pleased with the country and people. It did not require any great while for Mr. Williams and myself to came to an agreement by which he leased the place for five years, with the option of purchasing at a stated price at any time during the pendency of the lease. He also took all my stock, crops, farming utensils, etc., exclusive of household and kitchen furniture, all of which I priced very low as an inducement and in this way I speedily arranged all my affairs. I sold Mr. Frank Terry my interest in the *Dispatch* at far less than its value for the same reason, and perfected all my arrangements for starting on our long journey on the fifth day of June, 1885. Our house was at that time full of visiting children, grandchildren, and friends, so it was decided that my daughter, Mrs. G. W. Smith, should take charge of the place and keep it open until the fall, with her sisters, Willie and Sece to aid her, who could come to Hong Kong in the following spring, and Carrie and Robert should accompany my wife and myself to our destination. In order to carry out this program, I wrote to General Smith of the Virginia Military Institute, requesting that my son Robert might have permission to anticipate the time for the regular final examinations, so that he could go with us. This was readily agreed to by the authorities of the V. M. I., and he reached home about the first of June, having passed all of his examinations for graduation.

And now I was surprised and much gratified by the reception of a communication from a committee composed of some of the leading citizens of the town and county, tendering me the compliment of a banquet at the principal hotel on the evening of the second of June in testimony of the friendship and good wishes of the community. Of course this was accepted with the highest appreciation of the kindly feeling which prompted it, and on the evening fixed, there was a large attendance of the first citizens of the town and surrounding county at the Fourth Avenue Hotel, where a splendid banquet was served in handsome style, with the accompaniment of complimentary toasts and responses, which was not brought to a close until after midnight.

I had arranged to leave San Francisco by the "City of Tokio," of the Pacific Mail Line, the Captain of which was a relative of Commodore Maury and of the same name, and I had a letter of introduction to him from Mr. Maury, the Assistant of the Attorney General. But I was not able to get off in time to take that steamer, and it was a fortunate thing that I did not, for she was wrecked on that voyage, on the coast of Japan, near the entrance of the harbor of Yokohama, and though there was no loss of life, the vessel was a total loss. Much of the cargo was saved by the efforts of the Japanese officials, who had the wreck guarded until the salvage was completed.

I had written to my old friend, General Roome, of New York, asking him to see the officials of the Pacific Mail Steamship Company, asking special rates for my family and myself, and in return received free tickets for us all, which saved us considerable expense. A similar application to Mr. Huntingdon, of the Southern Pacific Line, procured me half-rate tickets over the Chesapeake & Ohio to New Orleans and thence by Southern Pacific to San Francisco, thus effecting another saving.

We left Richmond at 7:20 p. m. on the evening of the fourth of June, traveled by a circuitous route via Chesapeake & Ohio Railway to Louisville, thence to New Orleans, which we reached on Sunday morning, the tenth, and found we would be detained until 7:30 p. m. So we spent a hot and disagreeable day in the "Crescent City." Robert took advantage of the delay to pay a visit to Mayor Shakespeare's family, who had spent several summers in Wytheville, and the Mayor, his wife and daughters called to see us off in the evening. Our journey through Texas was slow and uneventful. Much of the country we passed after leaving Houston was thin and covered with chaparral, but a good deal was evidently fertile, with black alluvial soil, and every indication of thrift and prosperity. This section appeared to be settled by Germans mainly. West of El Paso through New Mexico and Arizona the country is uninviting and barren. Rocks, sand and sage bushes the dominant characteristics. At one point we passed for two or three hundred miles through a depressed, hot and arid country three or four hundred feet below the level of the sea. I was not before aware that there was such an anomaly in the geography of the country. The heat and dust continued until we reached San Bernardino in Southern California, when a magical change in the appearance of the country and people was apparent. The country around Los Angeles is highly cultivated and very beautiful, oranges, apricots, etc., abundant, fresh and fine. We laid in a stock of each sufficient to last until we reached San Francisco. Across the Mojave Desert we saw immense cacti covering the surface, interspersed with the inevitable sage bushes, and everywhere sand. After passing this we found a fertile country again. The San José Valley is very beautiful, covered with orchards and vineyards in a high state of cultivation. We reached Oakwood at 10 a. m., on the twelfth of June, and by eleven were landed at the Ferry House in San Francisco. We took up quarters at the "Occidental," enjoyed a bath and a good dinner, and had many callers in the afternoon and evening. George Lemmon, of Baltimore, who fought through the war, and is still unreconstructed, Marsden Manson and his wife, Nat Manson, his brother, and Mr. Bea, the Chinese Consul, Mr. Coleman, the leading merchant of San Francisco, who was also the leader of the Regulators who rescued the city from the rule of the gamblers and roughs who had dominated it for years, Judge Thornton, who was at the University of Virginia with me in 1840-41, Major and Mrs. Maynard, who had known us in Russell, and Mrs. Lampkin, whose husband had died since they came to California in 1870. Ex-Senator Sergeant seemed glad to meet me and we had a long talk of our experiences in the Senate.

CHAPTER XLI.

CROSSING THE PACIFIC.

The next morning I visited the office of the Pacific Mail Company to procure tickets, was introduced to Captain Searle, the Commander of the "City of New York," on which we proposed to make the voyage. He advised me to be on board by 1 p. m., as he would sail in the afternoon. We had dinner and went aboard before 2 o'clock. Mr. Coleman sent us a box with a dozen bottls of wine of different kinds, confectioneries, cigars, etc. We loosed from the pier and started at 2:15 p. m., on what was to all of us except myself, the first sea voyage, with the prospect of seeing no land till we reached Yokohama about the Fourth of July. This being the thirteenth day of the month was regarded by some of our friends as an inauspicious time to leave, but we were not much impressed by the superstition. We had not crossed the bar before Mrs. Withers and Carrie both had to seek their state-rooms from sea-sickness. We were gratified by seeing near the Faralone Islands a school of whales, fifteen or twenty in number. They were not a great way from us and in plain view, my first sight of these monsters of the deep. Captain Searle said he had never seen so many at one time. I felt no ill effects from the motion of the vessel, as the sea was not rough. Robert was up for breakfast the next morning, but soon after yielded to the *"mal de mere,"* by which nearly all the passengers seemed affected, as very few were visible for some days. There were not many first-class passengers. Besides ourselves, there was a Mr. Zeigler, a silk merchant of Yokohama, and his bride. These were Germans. A young medical missionary named McCandless, sent out by the Presbyterian Church to their mission in Shanghai, a fine-looking Chinaman, who spoke English fluently, having been for four years Secretary of Legation at Washington and Havana, a Mr. Sulzer and his son, Germans who could speak English, and one or two young men, completed the list. A large number of Chinamen were in the steerage, and a good many second-cabin passengers. McCandless showed me the first copy I had seen of the Revised Version of the Old Testament, which I examined with a good deal of interest. I had myself a copy of the New Testament, which, while showing internal evidence of being a more literal and accurate translation of the original, is far inferior in euphony and diction to the King James Version. Robert and Carrie, after the first few days, had no more trouble from sea-sickness, but my wife was a great sufferer. Indeed, she was so sick that she could neither eat nor sleep to do much good. I think she went only once to the dinner table and did not eat as much the whole voyage as would suffice for a single square meal. As a consequence, she became so weak and debilitated that I became really uneasy on her account. I gave her iced champagne, and all the usual remedies in vogue, but nothing seemed to be of much service. She became, for the first time in her life, low-spirited and depressed, and lost all the cheerful optimism which had always been one of her marked characteristics. I fared better than any of our party, as I found several of the passengers were chess players, and as I had my chess men and board along, I was enabled to beguile the tedium of the voyage by games with one or another of them. None were very good players, however, and victory usually perched on my banner. We had a rubber of whist usually at night when the wind and water favored, and Robert found in the Purser's Clerk a young fellow of congenial tastes, fond of music, and with a good bass voice, so that the two occasionally favored us with a concert on violin and guitar or banjo. I think Carrie summoned courage to try the piano in the Saloon only once or twice during the voyage. The days passed in monotonous uniformity. The vessel making an average of about ten knots hourly, but when we had head winds and rough seas, less. When we passed the one hundred and eightieth degree of longitude we had to lose a day from the calendar, a necessity which all my efforts failed to explain to the satisfaction of my wife. I told her when she came back she would "pick up the dropped day," but this only made matters worse. She pronounced the whole thing utter folly and nonsense, this talking of having no Wednesday going West, and two Wednesdays going East. We did not see a single vessel during the whole voyage until the day we sighted the Japanese Coast, when we saw a few junks. When we had been out a little more than two weeks, the engineer told me he had seen a large turtle that morning, which showed that we were in the "Black Stream," as it is called, which flows up the Eastern coast of Japan, and is, for the Pacific, what the Gulf Stream is for the Atlantic, a warm current parallel to the coast line. The water appears darker in color, hence its name.

On the thirtieth day of June we experienced a severe gale, which much increased the suffering of Mrs. Withers. As night approached, the force of the wind increased, until it seemed to me that it lacked nothing of being a first-class storm. Captain Searle, however, said it was only the "tail end" of a typhoon which had passed up the coast. Tail end or head end, it was sufficient to prevent sleep, and greatly to intensify the seasickness of Mrs. Withers, and most of the passengers. I escaped, unless a severe headache which came on about this time was an effect of the same cause. None of us slept at all during the night, as all my time was spent in trying to lessen the sufferings and cheer the spirits of my wife. The next day, I think it was, the Captain called us early to have our first look on Asiatic land. The early sunbeams were brightly reflected from the snowy crest of "Fusiama," the sacred mountain of Japan. It was indeed a splendid sight. Its outline was a regular and well-defined cone, piercing the sky and all the upper portion white and glittering in the early sunlight. My attention was soon diverted, to ask an explanation from the Captain of the immense number of paper slips floating around the ship in the air, or on the water. "Those," said he, "are the prayers and thanksgiving of the Chinese and Japanese to the God of the Sea, for his kindness in bringing them safely across the Great Water." I was much impressed by the act, and thought the intelligent and enlightened Christians might well emulate the heathen in their public acknowledgment to the "God of the Sea" for His beneficent kindness.

The Captain estimated our distance from "Fusiama" to be nearly a hundred miles, as the storm of the third had driven us far to the north of our course. We ran all day almost parallel to the coast line, and on the morning of the third of July I was awakened about daylight by the jabbering of hundreds of voices, and on looking out of my window found the ship anchored in the harbor of Yokohama, surrounded by innumerable small boats of novel construction, manned by men almost, and some altogether, naked. As soon as we got breakfast, we went ashore, and to the hotel, where we engaged rooms, and by the afternoon Mrs. Withers had rallied sufficiently to enjoy a carriage drive through the city and into the country contiguous. We found the scenery very bright and attractive, and the land fertile and cultivated like a garden, producing fine crops of cereals, rice and cane, and when we got back at sunset, my wife was as bright and cheerful as usual, greatly to my relief. We heard full particulars of the wreck of "The City of Tokio" from the American Consul, and subsequently from Captain Maury himself, who appeared greatly concerned at the loss of his fine steamer, as well he might be. He thought the vessel might have been gotten off the rocks after the removal of the cargo, as she appeared not to have been seriously injured, but the "tail end" of the typhoon which we had felt on the third, was the full-grown article at Yokohama and it only took a few hours to smash the stranded steamer into a hopeless wreck. The next morning we were awakened early by the booming of cannon, and the popping of large and small fire crackers, this being the Fourth of July and observed with great noise and hilarity by Americans and many sympathizers of all conceivable nationalities. We had an extra dinner at the hotel with patriotic toasts, etc., and had a stream of visitors, official and otherwise, during the whole afternoon and evening. We sent letters home by the "Arabic," which sailed the Fourth, and Carrie and Robert returned to the "New York" to participate in the festivities there. The vessel was decorated with gay flags and a general observance of all the customs with which the day is honored in America.

Mrs. Withers declined to go on the vessel as long as she could stay on shore, and I, of course, remained with her. I returned the visit of the Consul, Mr. Green, and found him sensible and pleasant. The next day was Sunday, and as the "City of New York" would not sail until Monday, we concluded to remain on shore and attend divine service at the Union Church, used by all denominations. The sermon was by a Methodist minister, and was a very fair one. Robert, however, concluded to have a sight of the Capital City, Tokio, which is only thirty miles distant, and a railroad to travel on. He spent the day, and got back about 5 p. m., reported he had seen many strange sights, but met with no one who could speak or understand English. We went on board Monday morning, and at 4:20 o'clock started for Hong-Kong. The voyage was uneventful, but we enjoyed the beautiful scenery along the Japanese coast, and through various groups of islands, several of them having volcanic peaks, from which smoke in the day, and fire at night were plainly visible. Scientists, I believe, are agreed that this portion of the world is the center of seismic disturbance. Most of the earthquakes have their origin here, and their intimate connection with volcanic action seems to be thoroughly established. When active volcanos become quiet, and remain so for any length of time, an earthquake is almost sure to follow, and these shakes are so frequent that they excite less fear and apprehension here than in any other portion of the globe. Mrs. Withers' sea-sickness followed her during the whole voyage, one or two days of which were rendered particularly uncomfortable from the intense heat, unrelieved by the slightest breeze. This was followed by a succession of thunder showers, which gave us relief by cooling the atmosphere. When the weather was calm, and the sea smooth, we saw great numbers of flying fish, which were much smaller than I had expected to see them. They reminded me of grasshoppers flying over a green meadow. On the thirteenth of July, we entered the outer harbor of Hong-Kong, and at 8:30 p. m., cast anchor, as the entrance to the harbor proper is very narrow and difficult at night, thus our voyage began and ended on the thirteenth of the month. I was up by 5 o'clock the next morning, as I was anxious to see the city and harbor, as I had heard they were strikingly beautiful. The channel leading to the inner harbor is very narrow, and appears strongly fortified. A man might throw a stone across it. As the inner harbor and the City of Hong-Kong opened upon our view, a cannon shot was heard from the signal station on the summit of "Victoria Peak," the highest point in the Island, and simultaneously the Stars and Stripes were run up to the top of the flag-staff, which announced to all the arrival of an American Mail Steamer. As we slowly threaded our way through the harbor, crowded with vessels of all nationalities, and of every description, Men of War, Steamers, Sailing Vessels of all sizes and descriptions, and Chinese Junks and innumerable small boats, the City itself impressed me by the picturesque beauty of its location. It was built in terraces rising up the steep side of a mountain, tier over tier, adorned with handsome public and private buildings, interspersed with beautiful shade trees, and tropical shrubs of unfamiliar appearance, all sparkling in the bright rays of the tropical sun, and I thought my eyes had never looked on a fairer picture. Robert and Carrie were equally impressed by the beauty of the scene, but my poor wife was unable to participate in our pleasure as she was still a martyr to her sickness, which held her with tenacious grip. Indeed, when she left the ship for the deck of the hotel launch, she did not surrender the possession of her constant companion, a small tin bucket, to which she still clung. I looked in vain among the varied craft which surrounded our vessel for a boat carrying the United States flag, as I supposed the boat belonging to the Consulate would be sent to take us in, but seeing nothing of such a craft, I took all our party on the steam launch belonging to the "Hong-Kong Hotel," and was safely landed at the pier in the immediate neighborhood of that noted public house. Our host, Greely, soon had us comfortably quartered in a nice suite of rooms, where my wife luxuriated in a spacious and luxurious bed, and after taking a refreshing nap of nearly three hours, awoke greatly refreshed.

CHAPTER XLII.

LIFE IN HONG-KONG.

I remained indoors most of the morning, only presenting myself at the counter of the "Bank of India, Australia, and China," where I was introduced by Mr. Greely, and presented a draft from the Bank of California, for the money deposited there. This was duly honored and I returned to the Hotel. In the afternoon Colonel Mosby called, and said he had been expecting me at the Consulate all the morning, as it was customary for all Americans to call there. I excused my failure by pleading Mrs. Withers' indisposition, but told him I would be up the next day. I had also a visit from Captain Harrington, commanding the United States Sloop of War, "Junietta," accompanied by several of his officers, who invited me to come aboard his vessel Thursday morning, as he had orders to sail the afternoon of that day, and he particularly desired to have the pleasure of firing the first salute in my honor as Consul of the United States at Hong-Kong.

The next morning, accompanied by Robert, I went up to the Consulate, which I found to be a large and handsome building, standing some distance back from the street, with abundant trees, shrubbery and flowers around it. Indeed it was one of the most imposing and beautiful places in the city. Colonel Mosby was more cordial than at his short visit yesterday. I found at his office the Captains of several American vessels in port, also made the acquaintance of Chue Asine, the Interpreter, and Choi the Shroff, Chinamen who had filled these positions for several years, and Franco, a clerk in the office, who was a Portuguese. Colonel Mosby informed me that he had advertised a sale of his effects for Tuesday, the twenty-first, on which day he would turn over the office to me. This, of course, was entirely satisfactory to me. He also advised that I should at once see the owner of the building occupied as the Consulate, as the lease would expire on the first of August. He had been paying a rental of one hundred dollars per month, but did not know if the lease could be renewed on the same terms. He gave me the address of the owner, and I went the next day to see him and renewed the lease on the same terms. In accordance with official etiquette, I called, accompanied by Colonel Mosby, and left cards at the Government House, and also at Head Quarter House. The Governor, Sir George Bowen, was at this time in Japan, and General Cameron was acting in his place, who was the ranking military officer at the Post. His family, consisting of wife and three grown daughters, were summering at the "Peak," a mile or two above the town on the Victoria Peak, where the temperature at this season is more agreeable than in the city itself. The Chief Justice, Sir George Phillipo, and his wife, were also in Japan for the summer. Mrs. Withers speedily rallied after getting on shore, and took a walk with me through some of the principal streets of the city. Those which run parallel to the water front are level, but all intersecting streets are very steep. Few vehicles drawn by horses are to be seen, the Sedan Chair borne by coolies, and the "Jinrickshaw," propelled by coolies, are the vehicles ordinarily used, and are pleasant conveyances. The principal objection I had to them was a purely sentimental one, as it violated my sense of propriety to see human beings taking the place of beasts of burden, but this feeling gradually wore off. On Thursday afternoon I visited the "Junietta," and for the first time was received by the officers and crew of a "Man of War" with all the honors due my position as Consul of the United States, including the salute of artillery. I was pleased with the neat appearance of the vessel, the thorough discipline of the crew, the polite and courteous bearing of the Captain and officers of the vessel. Robert and Franco commenced and completed an inventory of the property belonging to the Government in possession of the Consul, and I receipted for the same. When the sale of Colonel Mosby's effects came off, I, of course, purchased largely, not only his household goods, but of his curios, of which he had a large collection, many of them being of more than ordinary value. I did not feel able to buy these as they were too expensive, and the Colonel appeared disappointed that I did not. My credentials having been delivered to the acting Governor, I received official recognition as the Consul of the United States, and at once took charge of the office and business. Was soon visited by the leading merchants of the place, most of whom were Chinese, and took my first lessons in "Pidgin English," the hybrid language universally used throughout the East. It is a strange compound of words from various languages inextricably mingled, many belonging to no known tongue.

Mrs. Withers was very busy for some days in getting together furniture, and other housekeeping appliances, and being initiated into the mysteries of a new menage. It has many peculiarities. The head servant is known as "the boy," no matter what his age may be. On him devolves the duty of employing all the servants and he is responsible for their honesty and good behavior. A much greater number of servants are required than in America, what with cooks, and assistants, gardners, housa coolies, and chair coolies, ahmas and tailors, there is quite an array of domestics. To the "Boy" is entrusted the duty of making purchase of all household supplies of every kind, groceries, provisions, fuel, butcher meat, poultry, game, etc. It is his duty to see that none of these traders wrong, cheat or defraud you, and he is usually faithful to his trust, as he himself monopolizes these privileges. His expense accounts are usually settled monthly, and he invariably adds a small percentage to the cost of every article brought into the house. For example, if eggs cost ten cents, he will put the price at ten and one-half cents, beef or mutton one-half to one cent more than the cost, and so with everything else. The theory seems to be that the employer will either fail to detect the cheat, or will regard it as so trivial a matter that it is not worth while to take notice of it. If this proves to be the case, the next months' settlement shows a still further rise in the price, and this will continue until the employer "kicks" and refuses to pay the prices charged. The "Boy," with smiling face and perfect equanimity, will, without a word, listen to his protest, and accept what his employer believes to be a fair charge, and then begin the same process anew, and this they will keep up indefinitely. They call it "a squeeze," and it is universally practised throughout the colony, indeed throughout the East.

As he always collects a percentage from the tradesman with whom he deals, his earnings are considerable. I speedily caught on to the dodge and determined that I would not submit to the "squeeze," but would only pay actual cost of purchases, but one of my neighbors, a "Canny Scot," who was president of one of the banks, told me his experience in a similar effort to correct the evil. He called up his boy, told him he had an invincible objection to being cheated, but did not mind paying him a commission, provided he abandoned the practice of "squeezing." "Now," said he, "tell me how much you make each month by your present practice, and I will pay it to you, provided in your bills you charge no more than the actual cost of every article." "The Boy" demurred for some time, denying that there was any "squeeze," but Mr. Whitehead stuck to his purpose, and finally made the "Boy" name a sum which he said represented the increased charge. "Now," said Whitehead, "remember I will pay you this every month, as long as you give me a true return of the cost of your purchases." "All lite," was the reply. It was not two months before Whitehead detected him at his old trick, and charged with it, reminding him of his agreement. The "Boy" impatiently exclaimed, "No, can help, old custom, no, can help." Mr. Whitehead gave up the struggle, and afterwards adopted the practice I followed.

Though we were forced to employ so many domestics, yet the cost was not much greater than we were accustomed to, because labor is so abundant, that the price is correspondingly low. All foreigners, however, have to pay more than double the hire a Chinese employer would pay. But the Chinese make the most satisfactory "help" of any class of servants I have ever had in my employment. They require less looking after. Teach them how any given thing is to be done, and they will go on each day doing the same thing in the same way, for an indefinite period. During the four years of our residence in Hong-Kong, we had no trouble at all with servants, a novel and very pleasing experience. The Chinaman who is accustomed to the duties of a house servant, is an expert in all that pertains to his calling. His hands are delicate and soft as a woman's, he deftly handles all glass and chinaware, rarely breaking any article in washing, wiping, or putting in place the utensils used. Quick and alert in his movements, he is a very satisfactory waiter and house cleaner, never noisy or impertinent, in short, they are first-class domestics.

A curious custom prevails in Hong-Kong that, so far as my observation enables me to judge, is unknown elsewhere. When a large dinner party is given, especially if gentlemen only are invited, each of the guests carries his "Boy," who stands behind his master at the meal and waits on him during the whole function. He then aids the "Boy" of the host in putting everything in order, washing and wiping the china and glass ware, and in this way little labor or trouble devolves on the domestics of the host, as each of the "Boys" is an expert in this service.

We had, of course, many callers as soon as we were fairly settled in our new quarters. General Cameron within a few days invited us to dine at the Government House on the Peak, where we made the acquaintance of Mrs. Cameron and her daughters, as well as several other officials and the ladies of their families, and this was the beginning of numerous entertainments of similar character, and as the social circle in Hong Kong is not a very large one, we soon knew every one worth knowing. The Military and Naval Officers and their families, the Governor, Chief Justice and members of the Legislative Council, the leading merchants, lawyers, and doctors, with their respective families constitute "society" at Hong-Kong. These are all cultured and refined people, there being of course a large preponderance of gentlemen, ladies, married or single, never lack for attention, and wall-flowers are unknown.

Only one American mercantile firm is located here, the large and long-established house of "Russell and Company," with branches in most of the large cities of India and China. Mr. Forbes was at that time the head of the firm, and he resided with his accomplished wife only a short distance from the Consulate. They had no children. Another American was Mr. Harman, the Agent of the Pacific Mail Company, with an American wife and no children, and these two, with my own, were the only American families in the city. There was a Virginian here, however, from Petersburg, but he had no family with him. Doctor Locher had resided here many years. He was rather eccentric, but had plenty of sense, and was very well informed and an enthusiastic Mason. He was employed by the captains of most of the trading vessels which wintered in Hong-Kong, to look after the health of their crews and families, and as there were always several such vessels in harbor, he managed to make a comfortable living.

Of the one hundred and fifty thousand population, less than five thousand were Europeans or Americans. The great bulk of the people were Chinese, but there were to be found here representatives of almost every nationality known. It is indeed a most cosmopolitan city. The throngs which fill the streets present, therefore, a most picturesque appearance, as nearly all were robed in their national costumes. With the exception of the North American Indian, of whom I saw no representative, I think individuals of all other races, tribes, and peoples were to be found in Hong-Kong. Though an English Colony, Englishmen are comparatively rare. Most of the English were Scotchmen, if the Hibernicism be permissible, and equally paradoxical is the fact that of the men composing the Regiment of "Scotch Highlanders" at the Port, a large proportion were *Irish*. The Police Force is composed of Sikhs and Chinamen in about equal numbers. It would be difficult to imagine a stronger contrast than they present in appearance and characteristics. The first are tall, straight, active and silent men, with a decided military bearing, to which their voluminous red turbans give an imposing air. They are thought to be the finest Police Force known, as they are sober, brave and incorruptible. The Chinamen of Hong-Kong are diminutive in size, slouching in their walk, with garments more resembling those of a woman than a man, and generally purchasable. The two nationalities hate each other cordially and the Chinese population stand in great fear of the Sikhs, and not without cause. It is stated as a fact, that when gas lights were first introduced for lighting the streets of Hong-Kong, the duty of lighting and turning off the gas was assigned to the Chinese employes of the Gas Company, but a Sikh policeman, seeing a Chinaman climb up the gas post about daylight, and observing the simultaneous extinction of the light, fired his rifle at the supposed offender with fatal effect. He reported to his Chief that he had shot a Chinaman who had climbed up, *and was stealing the lights.*

The Colony of Hong-Kong embraces only a small area of land consisting of the Island, about nine miles in length and five in breadth, being entirely mountainous, and the Peninsula of Kowloon, lying directly across the harbor from the city. The harbor itself is about one and a half miles across, and the peninsula is of small extent. England, being desirous of acquiring a coaling station near the Chinese coast, secured this Island as indemnity from the Chinese Empire for her expenditures in money and men growing out of the "Opium War," as it was called, and after forcing the cession from the Emperor, at once took possession, and commenced a system of scientific fortification, which was steadily prosecuted and elaborated until it is now a place of great strength. Governor Bowen was always fond of describing it as "The Gibraltar of the East." It is now a place of great commercial importance, ranking third of all the seaports of the British Empire in the number of vessels arriving and departing annually. It is the rendezvous of the Asiatic Fleet, their many "Men of War" arriving and departing at short intervals. We had generally a British Admiral in port and always a Commodore; and I have sat at the dinner table with a British, a Russian, a French, and an American Admiral.

The climate I found less oppressive in summer than I expected. The heat is not excessive, the thermometer rarely registers over ninety degrees, but there is great humidity which increases the discomfort, and for seven or eight months the heat ranges from eighty-five to ninety degrees. This long-continued and uniformly high temperature is no doubt debilitating, especially to those who have passed middle age. The rains and heat begin about the first of May and continue till November is well advanced, but the remaining months are simply delightful. The weather is bright and bracing, though ice and snow and frost are unknown, but an average temperature of about forty degrees makes fires pleasant, and the cool exhilarating breezes constantly invite to out-of-door sports, and all sorts of amusements. I suppose no city is more gay than Hong-Kong during this period. The gaiety of the year seems to be concentrated in these three or four months. Balls, dances, and parties, with theater, operas, races, etc., occupy the time of both young and old.

Race Week constitutes the festival of the year. During that week the city is almost deserted, and the population migrates to the race track, a mile or two out of town. Here bamboo sheds and other temporary structures of considerable size are erected by leading merchants, officials of the Government, and wealthy citizens. These front on the track with amphitheatrical seats, to give all guests an opportunity of witnessing the race, and in the rear is a large room where refreshments are constantly served to guests and visitors who, in the intervals between the several events, make the circuit of these booths calling on friends and booking bets on every event. Every one bets; men, women, children, church members, chaplains, and preachers alike book wagers on their favorites. These are not usually for large amounts, but just enough "to add interest to the race," as the common phrase expresses it. I did not follow the fashion myself, but my wife and daughters did, and I was told by the Governor, on one occasion when he proposed a wager which I declined to accept, with the explanation that I never bet, "Well, I venture to say that you are the only man on the ground who does not bet." Thoroughbreds are not permitted to enter the lists, entries are restricted to Chinese horses, these are usually brought from Amoy and other places north of Hong-Kong, the sporting men buying up fifty and sometimes a hundred of these Chinese ponies early in the fall. They are not high priced, and are muscular and game, running heats of from one to two miles, and repeating until the winner is known. The trainers take the herd of untried ponies and test their speed and endurance until the best can be determined, and three or four of these, rarely more, put through a course of training. Most of the mounts are gentlemen riders, from the Subalterns of the Army, or clerks and salesmen from the "Shops," and success, as a rule, depends as much on the skill and judgment of the rider, as on the speed and bottom of the pony.

During the summer the "Ladies' Recreation Grounds" are much frequented, where talk, tennis and tea constitute the attractions. These grounds are beautifully kept, and the devotees of tennis, both male and female, have abundant opportunity of indulging in the pastime, as there are eight or ten courts, some of sod others of "Chunam," or cement. While the young ladies and gentlemen are playing, the more staid and dignified matrons drink endless cups of the beverage "which cheers but not inebriates," and discuss current events, the latest scandal, and other subjects of interest to feminine minds. "Cricket" is, of course, a favorite game of the gentlemen, and it was on the grounds of the Garrison Club that I for the first time witnessed this sport so dear to the Englishman. I can't say that I much enjoyed it as a spectator, but Robert joined the Club and appeared to take pleasure in it. Considerable attention is paid to music, and concerts, vocal and instrumental, are of frequent occurrence and largely patronized. Amateur operas are performed during the winter months, and very creditably, those of a comic character being preferred. Every Sunday afternoon, when the weather permitted, there was a public concert by the professionals at the "Public Garden," which was always well attended and appeared to be much enjoyed.

Hong-Kong is fairly supplied with churches. The "Cathedral" is about the first building to attract attention as one enters the harbor. Its commanding position and architectural pretension makes it a noticeable structure. This is, of course, frequented by most of the officials, and also the English inhabitants. A Bishop makes his residence in Hong-Kong, but does not often officiate in the Cathedral. He is a "Missionary Bishop," and the Cathedral is not under his jurisdiction. Besides this, the services there are higher than he approves, though they can not be called Ritualistic, but Bishop Burdon is of the Evangelical School. He was a man of culture, and by odds the best preacher I heard while sojourning in the Colony. There are two or three Romish Churches, an Episcopal Chapel for sailors, one or two Methodist and Presbyterian Chapels, a German Lutheran Church, a Mahometan Mosque, a Parsee Temple and several Joss Houses, and Buddhist Temples in the Chinese Quarter. Two large convents, one of Italian and the other of Portuguese Romanists, were near the Consulate, doing good service and caring for the foundlings which are numerous in all Chinese towns. These infants are, of course, very young when left or found, and though carefully nursed and cared for, the mortality among them is very heavy, but those which survive are carefully reared and educated. The Italian Convent was separated only by the width of a street from the Consulate, and we had opportunities for learning what a good work they were doing.

Two daily English papers are published in the city, well edited at the time I speak of, and keeping abreast with the general news and the local incidents of the Colony. I was made acquainted with a fact in connection with their publication which struck me with surprise. It was stated that most of the typesetting was done by Chinamen who were ignorant of the English language, and could not read the article they had set up when printed. This statement I refused to credit, until I was forced to believe it by the testimony of disinterested parties with full opportunity of knowing whereof they spoke.

CHAPTER XLIII.

A VISIT TO CANTON.

I will return to my personal narrative from which I have perhaps too long digressed. I retained Colonel Mosby's clerk, Franco, for a month, and then reluctantly dispensed with his services, and installed my son as Vice and Deputy Consul, Chue A Sine, the Interpreter, acting as bookkeeper, as he had been long accustomed to do, and was thoroughly conversant with the duties of the position. My Exequatur was sent promptly from Her Majesty's Government, recognizing me as Consul of the United States at Hong-Kong, and directing that I should be respected accordingly.

I found that the fees for certifying invoices was always required to be paid in gold coin, and of course the Government would be the loser of counterfeit coin, or those of light weight were received. When first informed of this, I feared we would be often victimized, as I was by no means an expert in coin, but Chue told me that I need feel no uneasiness, as "Choi," the Shroff, was from long practice the best judge of gold coin in the city, and would never receive one of light weight or of spurious character. And this proved true, for during the four years I served as Consul nothing was ever lost from either of these causes. Ah Choi was to all appearance very stupid, and outside of his peculiar duties, I think, did not belie his looks, but no one could ever fool him into acceptance of a much-worn, or spurious gold coin.

The Governor, Sir George Bowen, returned from Japan in August, and assumed, of course, the duties of his position. I found him a genial, jolly Irishman, who had served in the same position in the Barbadoes, Canada, Mauritius, and other colonies of Great Britain. He had visited the United States a few years before, and was fond of recalling his experiences while in New York and Washington City. He was evidently pleased with the country and people. He paid a visit to Mount

Vernon with a large party from Washington, amongst whom was Mr. Evarts, with whom he appeared to have been charmed, and quoted a witticism of his relative to the legend that General Washington had thrown a dollar across the Potomac at Mount Vernon, where the river is almost a mile broad; after narrating the mythical story, Mr. Evarts concluded by saying, "But you know, Sir George, that in General Washington's time a dollar would go much farther than it will now." This "Old Chestnut" received its due meed of applause, as a matter of course.

The Governor returned my call promptly, and was introduced to my wife and Carrie Royall, who at that time wore short dresses, and had not been permitted to "go out" with "grown people." In course of the conversation he told us there would be a ball at the Government House the next week, to which we would receive invitations and urged that we should all attend. My wife hesitated a little, and finally said she would not know what to do about Carrie, as she knew of no one with whom she could leave her. "Oh," said the Governor, "that's easily arranged, just lengthen her petticoats and bring her along, I know she can dance, and she will have a fine time." Sir George was recalled the next year, and was succeeded by Sir William Marsh, who was married, and we found Lady Marsh very agreeable and sociably inclined, and having no children, she was a frequent visitor at the Consulate. Sir George Bowen had no family.

A public dinner was tendered him before he left, which was attended by all the high officials, the French and English Admirals, General Cameron and the Officers of the Garrison. I was selected by the Consular Body to respond to the toast in their honor, which I did to their satisfaction. The French Admiral also made quite a long speech, of which I understood very little, and the whole was concluded by a dance kept up until the "wee small hours anont the twelve," thus sending the old fellow off in a blaze of glory, which he highly appreciated. He was made a Privy Councillor when he reached London.

During the fall most of us had an attack of malarial fever of more or less severity. Mrs. Withers' was mild, mine more severe, lasting three weeks, and even after I was apparently free from disease I did not regain my strength. Dr. Manson advised me to take a trip to Canton for a change of air, and as I wished to see that populous and typical Chinese city, I took passage with Mrs. Withers on the Canton boat the next day. Canton is nearly a hundred miles from Hong-Kong, and our Consul there was Mr. Charles Seymour, who was appointed from Wisconsin by General Grant, and proving efficient and popular, was still retained in office. I had met him during a visit he made to Hong-Kong and liked him very much. The boat had few first-class passengers, but the steerage was crowded with Chinamen. I observed in my stateroom an army rifle and a cutlass hanging by the cot, and observing a sentinel standing at the head of the stairway leading to the lower deck, with a cutlass drawn, asked the Captain what these warlike tokens indicated. "Protection against river pirates," was the reply. "Last year a steamer was seized by them, the officers and most of the crew murdered, and the vessel run off, but it was subsequently recaptured, and the actors lost their heads." This narrative was not particularly reassuring, but no *emeute* among the denizens of the steerage occurred during my trip. Whampoa is really the shipping port of Canton, and is about thirty miles below that city. Vessels of deep draught can go no higher. It is noted for the handsome Pagoda near the banks of the river, which attracts the eye of all who pass up or down the stream. It is still an unsettled question to determine what purpose the Pagodas were designed to subserve. They are found in various portions of the Empire, are from five to ten stories in height, handsomely proportioned, durably constructed, beautiful in appearance, and usually unoccupied. They are certainly very striking features of the landscape, being visible for many miles in every direction. The generally-received opinion that they were simply temples designed for the worship of idols is doubted by many well-informed writers, for in a majority of cases no idols or priests are to be found in them. Night overtook us between Whampoa and Canton, and to my surprise we came to anchor, and did not reach the city until the next morning.

The first object which impresses a visitor in approaching Canton is the "City of Boats." Thousands and tens of thousands of boats are moored in the stream side by side with regular streets and alleys left open, along which boats can be rowed, making communication easy. These boats constitute the homes of the people. Many are born, live and die on them, and the number thus spending their lives is estimated at between two hundred and three hundred thousand. The main channel of the river is left open for the passage of vessels, but the rest of the stream is covered with boats permanently moored. Passing through these we at length reached our wharf, where Mr. Seymour met us, and we were speedily conveyed in chairs to the Consulate, located in what is called the "Shameen," (I am not certain as to the orthography). The name is bestowed on that portion of the city lying between the canal and the river. It is, in fact, an island, the buildings on it are generally occupied by foreigners of various nationalities, especially the Consuls and officials of friendly powers who have Diplomatic Representatives here. These constitute a social circle, banded together not only for society's sake but for safety as well. The populace of all Chinese cities are proverbially turbulent and disorderly, with strong antipathies against "Foreign Devils," as they call all white persons. Mobs are of common occurrence, and always hard to suppress. Whatever may have been the original cause of an *emeute,* it rapidly degenerates into a howling pack of plunderers, intent only upon looting every house into which entrance can be had. A single bridge spans the canal and gives access to the city, and here a guard is kept night and day, but it appeared a useless precaution to me, as the canal itself is usually so crowded with boats that a passage across it can easily be effected by stepping from one boat to another.

Mr. Seymour treated us with great kindness and hospitality. He had not brought his family out at this time, and was the only white man at the Consulate. His Interpreter was a young Chinaman who had been educated in the United States, and was a graduate of a Northern College, a sensible and obliging young fellow, who piloted me through the city and was of much service. The Province of Kwantung, in which the City of Canton is located, furnishes at least ninety-nine hundredths of the emigrants from China to other countries. They are more adventurous, energetic, and ambitious than the residents of the other provinces. They are small of stature, quick in their movements, delicately rather than robustly formed, and are said to be representatives of the original Chinese population, before the country was overrun and conquered by the Mongolians, who now constitute the ruling race of the Empire.

Canton is a typical Chinese city. The old city is surrounded by a high stone wall, with embrasures in which cannon are mounted, and along which sentinels are stationed night and day. Such artillery I had read of, but never before seen. I suppose the guns were centuries old, such as were used when the science of gunnery was in its infancy, jingals, falconets, sackers, and such antiquated ordinance, and I should judge from their appearance, more dangerous to the artillerist than to the enemy. The modern city surrounds the old walled city, which can be entered only by certain gates opened in the morning and closed at night, and when once closed, it is said that it requires uncommon effort and influence to cause them to be again opened. The streets, particularly in the old town, are exceedingly narrow. Many of them so constructed that two chairs can not pass each other, unless the occupants alight and permit the chair coolies to turn the vehicles on their sides, an operation to which I was subjected more than once in my peregrinations.

The skill and dexterity of the handicraftsmen in China and Japan is something wonderful. In silk embroidery the Chinese excel all others, so also in ivory carving they bear the palm. Porcelains are produced in great perfection. We visited many houses engaged in each of these lines of business, and wondered at the perfection attained in each. Inquiry, however, accounted in some degree for this excellence. In China all these, and many other pursuits, are hereditary. The father educates his son in the calling he pursues, thus bequeathing to him the accumulated knowledge and discoveries of many generations. Their patience and industry are something wonderful, which will be well illustrated by the following incident.

At the shop of a dealer in ivory carvings, I saw many beautiful specimens of the art, but was especially impressed by the intricacy, ingenuity and delicacy of the work shown in the carving of an elephant's tusk, whereon three different layers of carved figures of men, houses, trees and birds were shown, and it was hard to imagine how they could have been executed. I asked the proprietor, through the interpreter, where the work had been done. His reply was "top side," pointing upwards, from which I understood that it had been done upstairs on the premises. To the further inquiry if any one was then engaged in similar work, his answer was in the affirmative, and when I asked to be permitted to see the work in progress, to my surprise he gave a prompt assent, and I at once followed him up two flights of stairs and into a small room where a man of middle age was at work carving a piece of ivory in a fashion similar to the tusk I had seen below. I watched him for some time with great interest. On the bench before him were a large number of slender steel implements resembling more those seen in the work-room of a dentist than anything else, with variously-shaped points and cutting edges. Selecting one suited to his purpose, he passed it through the interstices of the outer layer already outlined and using the thumb of his left hand as a fulcrum, scratched off an infinitesimal scale of ivory, so minute as scarcely to be perceptible, and this process he repeated, *ad infinitum,* changing his implement as occasion required, and gradually evolving from the ivory surface the outline of the object he proposed to portray. The slow progress made indicated how long must be the time required to complete such a work, and when I asked how long the workman was engaged in completing the carving of the tusk I had seen below, his reply was "about three years." The price asked for the completed work was three hundred dollars, so I suppose he regarded one hundred dollars per annum a fair equivalent for the time and labor required to produce it. The effect of this life-long work was plainly visible in the extraordinary development of the left thumb of the workman, which was fully twice as broad as the right one, and the nail on the edge of which his implement rested was more than double the thickness of an ordinary thumb nail. We bought a goodly number of specimens of carvings, embroideries, and similar works of art, including two paintings by a native artist, ordered dinner and breakfast sets of porcelain to be ornamented according to the design selected, and bought a lovely black-wood cabinet for the display of curios, which I had already begun to collect. This craze for collecting curios is one likely to attack most foreigners who visit the East, and once formed, the habit very speedily becomes incurable. There is, of course, no satisfying such a greed. One purchase leads to another, the temptation is irresistible to buy any beautiful and rare piece of work of which you do not possess a specimen, whenever you see it, and many dollars have I thus squandered, simply for the gratification of this taste.

An export duty is levied at Canton on all articles shipped from that port, so in arranging for the transportation of our purchases to Hong-Kong, I proposed leaving with Mr. Seymour an amount sufficient to meet this expense, but he refused to receive it, saying he would himself see the Custom Officer and he would doubtless permit my goods to be shipped without charge as I was in the Consular service. This he did, and I was thus saved a considerable expense.

Consul Seymour was evidently highly esteemed in Canton, not only by the whole Consular Body, and by the Officials of the Chinese Government, but by the merchants and tradesmen of the city, and was apparently well known to the people generally. I asked him how he managed to extend his personal acquaintance so largely among the people. His answer was that any one who saw him once would never forget him, as he was the only person in the city *who wore a plug hat.* This conspicuous piece of head gear served to identify him everywhere as the "Melican Consul."

The criminal code of the Chinese Empire must be decidedly Draconic in its character, as the death penalty is inflicted on those convicted not only of murder, but of theft, robbery, arson and many other offences. The Criminal Court must be in daily session, as on almost any morning decapitations may be witnessed by any one who chooses to visit in the early morning the location selected for this operation. Having no desire myself to witness this bloody spectacle, I declined an invitation to be present, but I have seen several whose sensibilities were less acute than their curiosity, and who have been eye-witnesses to this punishment. They describe as wonderful the Stoicism of all the parties concerned, even the criminals, who with perfect composure kneel at the word of command, their "pig tail" is seized by an assistant and held out of the way and the executioner with a heavy sword wielded by both hands, at one blow severs the head from the body. From two to a dozen thus suffer almost daily. Offences not capital, are punished by the bastinado, or blows on the soles of the feet by a heavy bamboo, or the "Cangue," a terrible contrivance by which life is made so miserable that drowning, or other mode of suicide is often resorted to by the victim, to free him from the torture. It consists in fixing closely around the neck a horizontal platform of boards extending about two or three feet on every side and this is securely fastened so that it can not be dislodged. Its effect is to make the condemned one almost entirely helpless. He can't reach his face with his hands for any purpose; to eat or drink is impossible without the aid of a third party, lying down to sleep is impracticable, and in many cases this neck gear is worn for weeks or months. One feature of Chinese jurisprudence is peculiar, as, so far as I can learn, it can be found nowhere else. This is the liberty of substitution. The law demands a victim to expiate crime, but should the condemned be a person of large means he may, and sometimes does, hire a substitute to suffer in his stead, and this vicarious punishment satisfies all the requirements of the law. Incredible as it may appear, such substitute may be found willing to suffer decapitation in lieu of the principal. When I was first informed of this wonderful feature of criminal jurisprudence, I was utterly incredulous, and refused to believe that any one could be found who would, for hire, suffer his head to be stricken from his shoulders, but careful inquiry satisfied me that the story was true. The explanation is to be found in their devotion to their ancestry. This feeling more nearly approximates a religious sentiment than anything of which Chinese character seems capable. Every Chinaman, from the Emperor to the lowest coolie, at least once a year, repairs to the spot where his ancestors' bones repose, and there engages in worship for two or three weeks, burning incense, and offering prayers. The highest ambition of a Chinaman is to be able to construct a shrine or temple to the memory of his ancestors, and make provision for this annual ancestral worship. By appealing to this sentiment of filial reverence a man may occasionally be found who will sell his life for a sum sufficient to enable him to erect a temple at his ancestral tombs, and secure a perpetuity of prayers, and incense, and burning tapers in honor of the departed. So this self-sacrifice has its inspiration in a most ennobling sentiment—filial affection.

I took advantage of this trip to pay a visit to the mission stations of the various American Churches established in Canton. The Presbyterians, the Baptists, and the Methodists have what they call flourishing missions in Canton, each with a Hospital attached, which appears to be the principal attraction to the Chinese population. The spectacle of frequent cures of severe injuries, ailments and diseases, which in the hands of the native doctors are irremediable, has proved educational in the highest sense. This is particularly the case with surgical diseases and the treatment of wounds and injuries. The native doctors never make use of any operative interference in cases of injury. A dislocated joint or a fractured bone, and a wound of the soft parts involving lesions of blood vessels whether arterial or venous, is left to the unaided efforts of nature. Though intelligent and intellectual they submit to be duped and bamboozled by the ignorant pretenders who claim to cure all the ills that flesh is heir to. Incantations, witchcraft, and innumerable superstitions play always an important part in their treatment of disease. The result is, of course, *nil*, and when they see similar affections entirely relieved by the appliances of modern surgery in the Hospitals of the Missions, they are obliged to admit that the "foreign devils" are better skilled in the treatment of disease or injuries than any of their native doctors.

Dr. Kerr was, at the time of my visit, the head of this Presbyterian Mission, and Dr. Graves of the Baptist. I do not recall the name of the leading man at the Methodist Mission. The Episcopal Church had no mission in Canton, but some flourishing ones further North, especially in Shanghai, where a Theological School was in successful operation, now known as "St. John's College," under the fostering care of Bishop Booth. The mission of the Romish Church at Canton, however, is the largest, oldest, and apparently most successful of all.

American interests at Canton were at this time guarded

effectively by the large United States Gunboat, "Monocacy," with full complement of officers and men, always riding at anchor in mid stream opposite the "Shameen," with the Stars and Stripes imposingly displayed.

After spending almost a week at Canton, we returned to Hong-Kong, much improved in health and vigor.

CHAPTER XLIV.

CHINA NEW YEAR.

China New Year in 1886 fell on the fourth of February (for the date depends on certain conditions of the moon, I believe), but it is almost always about the first week in February. Some of the customs connected with its observance are so peculiar as to merit special mention. To begin: every trade, business or calling among the Chinese is managed and controlled by a "Guild," whose edicts and decisions, if not law, have the force and potency of law. One of these unwritten laws is that every man engaged in business, must pay up all he owes at New Year. If he fail to do this, he must close his shop or store and go out of business. This inexorable rule might be followed with advantage by other nationalities calling themselves more enlightened. Its effect is to confine the loss of an unsuccessful business enterprise or venture to the principal, and the sum total of his indebtedness will not reach a large amount as a general thing. By industry and economy he may hope to work out of his difficulties and restore his credit, and thus his friends and endorsers are not ruined by suretyship. With us, however, a man situated as above described, keeps on in business, borrows more and more, until after a few years when the crash can no longer be postponed, the debtor drags with him to hopeless financial ruin, a large number of his friends, with results most disastrous to themselves and families.

The practical working of this law or custom is demonstrated on the approach of each New Year by a greatly-increased anxiety to sell, if the party is engaged in merchandising, or if a shop keeper, mechanic or professional man, by urgent offers of service or labor at exceedingly low rates. As the day draws near, the shop keepers and merchants offer their wares at greatly reduced rates. Cost plays no part in fixing value. It soon becomes hazardous to make an offer to buy at any price, unless you are prepared to have your offer accepted. Goods, wares, and merchandise are moved out on the sidewalks, or even in the street, and the proprietors solicit passing purchasers in the most seductive tones, evincing the greatest anxiety to effect sales at any price. The night before New Year the streets are filled with crowds of pedestrians. The noise is deafening, men and women looking, chaffering, bargaining, and buying until the day is almost breaking. With the rising of the sun, the busy scene comes to an end. The die is cast, the last effort made, and the merchant either manages to meet his liabilities or sinks into bankruptcy. The spectacle presented in the streets of any Chinese city or in the Chinese quarter of any Eastern city, is really a wonderful one, and the student of human nature finds much to engage his thoughts or arouse his sympathies. He may not understand a word spoken by any of the chattering crowd around him, but the pantomime is so eloquent and significant, that he translates it without any difficulty. Among the well-to-do Chinese, this is the season for exchanging gifts, or as they term them "Cumshaws." Your grocer will send you a box of choice tea, your butcher a quarter of fine mutton, your poulterer a brace of fat fowls, your dry goods merchant a box of silk handkerchiefs, and so on *ad infinitum,* but you feel obliged to respond to the kindness.

I wish to put on record my high appreciation of the honor and honesty of Chinese merchants. I have had dealings, personal and official, with this class of men belonging to many nationalities, Asiatic, European, and American, and can truly testify that in all that constitutes commercial honor, strict integrity, and unswerving honesty, none excel the Chinese. I never had one to deceive or attempt to deceive, nor to fail in any particular to redeem any pledge or promise made me. In all their transactions they seem scrupulously fair and just, and I will say frankly that I had formed a different opinion of them before I went to the East. I think this characteristic of strict probity has a good deal to do with their success in business. In this connection I recall a conversation I had with Governor Holliday, who paid me a visit during one of his tours, after the expiration of his term as Governor of Virginia. I was criticising the features of the Chinese Exclusion Act, and argued that the very characteristics urged as an objection

to Chinese as emigrants constituted usually a recommend
Their industry, their sobriety, their frugality and thrift,
to make them good citizens. He differed with me and cont
that sound policy justified their exclusion, because, said
permitted to settle in the United States, in a few yea:
whole trade of the country would be under their control
said he had traveled the world over, and found Chinese
most every city of the East he had visited, and he said
the single exception of Saigon in Tonquin, they control
and business in every locality, and would soon do the sa
America. He admitted that the Chinese merchants as a
enjoyed the reputation for honesty and probity I accorc
them in Hong-Kong. I suggested that the Jews would
ably be able to hold their own in a trade contest with Chin
but he said no. Wherever they had been thrown in compe
the Jew had been forced to the wall. "Then," said I, "the
conclusion, it seems to me, is that they are intellectually :
ior to other nationalities." "I am not prepared to say tha
is not the case," said he in conclusion.

We had been notified by their letters that our daug
Willie and Sece, would come over by the "City of New \
(the same vessel on which we came), and on the thirteent
of March she arrived in safety. Robert and Carrie went (
meet the steamer, and soon returned with the girls, accomp
by Mr. Harnett, the Purser, and Doctor Seymour, Sur
They were received with great joy, and we all felt so tha
for their safety. They reported a rough voyage, as was to
been expected at this season, but had no severe storm, and
were delighted with the polite attention of Captain Searl
all of his officers. They made the journey from Virgir
Hong-Kong without a male escort and without the sli;
difficulty or inconvenience. This exploit was the sour
many wondering comments on the part of our English fri
who seemed unable to comprehend the self-confidence and
lessness of the young ladies of America. Of course they
greatly interested in the many new scenes and people by ·
they were surrounded, and had many callers, both ladie;
gentlemen. There are few places where young ladies can
a "better time" than in Hong-Kong. The large numb

educated and intelligent young men, officers of ships and garrisons, make a gay company, and as the season for social festivities was not passed, they enjoyed a full benefit. I had been laid up sick myself from an attack of erysipelas of the scalp, which disabled me for three weeks, but was now relieved, but Dr. Manson again advised a change of air, and I concluded to visit Macao, which was the first spot occupied by Europeans in this section of the world, having been settled by the Portuguese at a time when that people were the first of all European nations in maritime ventures and discoveries.

CHAPTER XLV.

MACAO.

This Island is quite a small one, only three miles long, and averaging one and a half in width. It was ceded by the Chinese Government to the Portuguese and the town was built in 1585. It is at, or nearly opposite, the mouth of the Canton River, and once enjoyed a lucrative trade, but now it amounts to little. At least three-fourths of the inhabitants are Chinese, who monopolize all the trade, the Portuguese holding themselves above such sordid pursuits. The most noted of Portuguese poets, Camoens, resided here when he wrote the "Lusiad," and his garden and tomb are objects of interest to all visitors. Mrs. Withers again accompanied me on my visit, and as the distance is short, the steamer made the trip in three hours. The Captain of the steamer surprised me by stating that he was a Georgian and a nephew of General Benning of that State, whom I had known during the war. We had a good deal of pleasant conversation, reaching the wharf before sunset. We took up our quarters at the only hotel in the place, kept by a Chinaman, but it proved a well-kept and comfortable inn, with clean beds and good fare.

The next morning we hired chairs and made a tour of the place, visiting all the objects of interest. There are two or three monasteries and a convent, the monks and nuns being Portuguese almost exclusively. There is also a Protestant Chapel and cemetery, and two Romish churches, one of them bearing marks of great antiquity, but all presenting a very dilapidated appearance. The streets have a deserted look, and the shops present few attractions to purchasers. Camoen's Garden is kept in pretty fair condition, and is the most attractive spot we visited. The Portuguese garrison and the defenses of the place are weak and inconsiderable. The Island itself is bare, rugged and uninviting. We only remained two days and were glad to get back to Hong-Kong.

I received two cable messages, before the arrival of the "City of New York," one from the Chief of Police of San Francisco, the other from the State Department, requesting the arrest of a Chinaman named Ang Tai Duck, who had committed a murder in Oregon or California, fled and had taken passage for Hong-Kong on that steamer. I at once notified the authorities, and he was arrested as soon as the vessel came into port, and lodged in prison to await the arrival of extradition papers. These were, from some cause, delayed, and before they were received Mr. Ang Tai Duck relieved us of further trouble by committing suicide, having hanged himself in his cell with a small cord of green silk, which he wore as a girdle. I was notified of the occurrence and attended the inquest held. The cord was no larger than an ordinary piece of twine, but it proved strong enough "to answer the purpose."

The identity of the body was established, and death by his own act the verdict of the jury. Authenticated copies of all the proceedings had in connection with the matter were prepared and forwarded to the State Department, and copies furnished the authorities at San Francisco. About a fortnight or more after all was completed, I was surprised by the arrival of two police officers from San Francisco, who came to take charge of the accused and carry him to America for trial. They said no notice of the suicide had been communicated to the police, which I always thought strange.

I had some bother with another criminal about the same time. The Steward of an American vessel in port called the "Saint Davids," in an affray, or as a sequel to the affray, shot and killed the second mate of the vessel. He was arrested, imprisoned, tried, and sentenced to penal servitude for life, and of course all these proceedings required my personal presence, and the forwarding of authenticated reports of every step taken in the trial.

Ho Amei, a wealthy, educated, and traveled Chinaman, who had spent some years in the United States, and in Europe, being impressed with the importance of pushing his country forward in the march of progress, determined to embark in mining operations on the main land not far from Hong-Kong, where minerals were known to exist apparently in considerable quantity. He had an American employed as Mining Engineer, under whose direction extensive preparation had been made to open the mines on a given date, and to celebrate the occasion in a manner commensurate with its importance. He had accordingly chartered a steamer, and invited a number of prominent citizens of Hong-Kong, officials, merchants, and scientific men, to take part in the excursion. Quite a number accepted his invitation, among them Robert and myself. We started early, and in due time disembarked at a point marked by flags and banners at the foot of a slope of mountain extending to the sea coast. The Mandarin in charge of that section of the Province was present in great state, accompanied by his guard of honor, and bearing all the insignia of his rank. After some enigmatical ceremonies which I did not understand, we all repaired to the locality selected, where many holes had been drilled in the ledges of rock, and charged with dynamite cartridges, which the Engineer fired by electricity very successfully. A large quantity of stone was blown out showing the presence of metal, and in considerable quantity. I secured several handsome specimens of "galena," and all the indications pointed to a successful result.

This was followed by a banquet where all the luxuries of the season were served, with beer, wine, and "brandy and soda" in lavish profusion, followed by toasts and speeches according to established usage. I was honored by selection, as the person to propose the health of our host, Ho Amei, to which he responded in English in good, set phrase. I will add, in conclusion, the characteristic outcome of this mining venture. It was forbidden by the Emperor, in consideration of the intense hostility of the people of the neighborhood, who believed by thus penetrating into the bowels of the earth, and removing such quantities of stone and mineral, the equilibrium of the globe might be destroyed, and the earth turned over, placing them at the bottom.

This will serve to illustrate a peculiar feature of the Chinese Government. Though nominally an absolutism, it is in reality almost a pure democracy, as the government never persists in any enterprise to which the people seriously object. They fear a popular uprising and will yield almost any point, rather than risk such an occurrence. At one time the Government began to improve the navigation of the Hoangho River, so that steamers could penetrate thousands of miles into the interior, but the work was stopped, because of the opposition on the part of many thousands of boatmen and Sampanmen, who made a living by navigating the stream with their small craft.

I received a letter in the spring of 1886 from Colonel Charles Denby, the United States Minister to China, stating his purpose of paying a visit to the various treaty ports of the Empire, for the purpose, among other things, of inspecting and familiarizing himself with the operations of the Consular Service. I was, of course, not under his control or supervision, and consequently felt only a general interest in his mission, except that he was to pay a visit to Hong-Kong during his tour, which was to be made on a Man of War detailed for that duty. He came in the latter part of April and was accorded the honors due his rank and position by the Governor and authorities of the Colony. He was dined by the Governor, where he met all the officials of the Colony, with many others, I and my son, wife and daughters being of the number. We also gave him a large dinner party at the Consulate, and the short period of his stay was pretty well engrossed by these festivities. Colonel Denby was a friend whom I had met on one of my visits to my daughter in Evansville, Indiana, where he then resided. He was an able, intelligent, and attractive man, and his services as Minister to China were very beneficial to this country. He was very popular with the Chinese Officials who formally requested that he should not be removed when the election of General Harrison involved a change in the Officials of our Government. President Harrison permitted him to continue in office during his term, a graceful concession to the Chinese Government, and a cordial recognition of his distinguished services.

He went from Hong-Kong to Canton, but I did not accompany him, as I had proposed, being prevented by the press of official business. While in our city, Mrs. Withers aided him in selecting handsome embroideries, carvings and porcelains to take home with him. We had a pleasant call from him as he returned to Pekin, and were much amused by his report of his experiences in Canton, particularly his visit to a wealthy and influential Mandarin who gave him a dinner and introduced him to his mother and other female members of his family, a thing almost unprecedented in China, where the females of the higher classes are usually excluded carefully from the sight of foreigners.

The United States Man of War "Trenton," Captain Phythian, bearing Mr. Child, United States Minister to Siam, reached Hong-Kong in May. Among her officers was Lieutenant Lee Holcombe, whose father was first cousin to my wife. We were, of course, glad to welcome him, and he seemed to enjoy meeting us. Several of his younger brothers had visited and spent some time with us when we lived at Green Meadows, but we had not known Lee. He seemed bright, gentlemanly and well informed, making a favorable impression on us all. The girls gave the Officers of the "Trenton" a german after the American style, which was very largely attended. The music was furnished by the band of the "Trenton." That there might be no lack of room, the dining-room was converted into a ballroom, being very spacious, my office converted into a dining-room, and the outer office into a reception room; thus necessitating an upheaval of all the lower floor of the building, as a complete change of furniture was necessary. The "Boy" got some extra help, and with the house coolies made all the preparations required, and the ladies had no trouble about it. We had all the big men of the Colony, and their families, and the fun was fast and furious, the dancing kept up until two o'clock, and when the company left, we at once retired to bed, thoroughly fagged. When we awakened the next morning, perhaps a little later than usual, my wife remarked, "Well, I dread the trouble of getting everything back in place." "Yes," was my reply, "But with all the girls to help, and the boy and coolies it won't take very long."

We had hardly gotten on our clothes before the breakfast bell rang at the regular hour, and much surprised, we went down and found the breakfast table set in the dining-room as usual, all the furniture in every room in place, including both offices, every dish, plate, glass and spoon washed and in their proper places, and wonderful to relate, not a piece of china or glass broken. And all this by nine o'clock in the morning. This will serve to illustrate the excellent service rendered by Chinese domestics, and to our minds demonstrated their superiority to all others.

CHAPTER XLVI.

CAUGHT IN A TYPHOON.

The Triennial Conclave of the Grand Encampment of Knights Templars was to assemble in the City of St. Louis in September, and it was necessary that I, the Grand Master of the Order, should prepare my report to be laid before the Grand Encampment.

As I was so widely separated from all my official papers and documents, the preparation of this report was a difficult undertaking, as I had to trust to an unaided memory for the important matters to be reported, as well as the sequence of events up to the time I had transferred the supreme authority to the Deputy Grand Master, General Roome, of New York.

I had to put in a good many hours of anxious thought, as well as physical labor to prepare my manuscript, and when completed, the question of having it printed was a serious one, as there was no English job printing office in Hong-Kong. Chinese compositors, most of whom could neither write nor speak English, got up the English newspapers, however, and I concluded they could also print my report of about two hundred printed pages, and this they did in good style and clear print, with fewer typographical errors to be corrected by the proof reader than I had been accustomed to in American printing offices. This work kept me busy in my spare hours, until the time came for me to start to St. Louis.

Having some time before applied for and obtained leave of absence, I left Hong-Kong on the tenth day of August on the steamer "City of Rio De Janiero," Captain Cobb, about four o'clock p. m. We had a good many passengers, and the Captain expected large additions at Yokohama. The first day out we passed the wreck of a large steamer, which had not long before gone ashore in Formosa Channel. The bow was on the sandy beach, and the stern submerged, masts still standing and a lot of sampans and small junks breaking up and carrying off all things portable. The next day was calm, and the water as smooth as a mirror, the temperature high and causing much discomfort. The day after there was no breeze, but a long swell, causing the steamer to roll a good deal. The Captain did not much like this, as he said it showed that there had been a heavy storm, which we might run into, and his prediction proved true, as by dark we had a heavy gale, which increased during the night, and by the next morning we were evidently in the midst of a first-class "Typhoon." Now, I had seen what Captain Searle called "the tail end of a typhoon" on my first voyage across the Pacific, and found its switchings enough to satisfy the aspirations of any one anxious for a new sensation, and had fondly thought I had little to learn in that connection, but I soon found my mistake.

I might attempt a description of the commingling of wind and wave, of air and water, of howling and shrieking squalls, and deluges of rain, but language is not capable of giving expression to the horror and sublimity which characterizes a first-class "Typhoon." We were in the midst of the China Sea, the birth-place and habitat of these destructive cyclonic storms. The waves at first were simply appalling in their magnitude, and driven by winds of resistless force. They far over-topped the decks of the vessel, and occasionally broke over us with a sound louder than the thunder which accompanied them, and a shock which caused the staunch vessel to quiver and tremble like some leviathan in its last agony. One of our life boats securely lashed on the upper deck, was burst into splinters and carried away by the force of one of these gigantic waves, that swept the ship from bow to stern. Hatches were all securely fastened, however, and little water found its way below. But as the wind increased in violence the danger from the mountains of water was lessened, because the force of the wind was then so great that the waves could not mount to such a height. Their tops were all swept off as by a blast of powder, and drifted away in scud and spray. The whole atmosphere was filled with it, and you could not see an object fifty yards from the ship. Had not the bow of the steamer been kept steadily pointed into the very eye of the wind, she would have been blown over like a board fence. As it was, the sharp bow split the winds and waves and their force was thus minimized. Captain Cobb was cool, alert and watchful; was on the bridge night and day while the storm lasted, and vindicated his reputation as a brave and skilful sailor. Little cooking or eating could be done while the storm lasted, and every passenger and all the crew were anxious and uneasy. The blow continued nearly three days before there was much indication of abatement, and then the rain began to pour from the clouds in sheets that fairly darkened the air. Even then, we were told that it was possible for us to have a recurrence of the trouble, as these typhoons have a nasty habit of recurring, and again passing over the same area in an obverse direction. Fortunately for us, however, we escaped this, and the fourth day the sun was bright and clear, the wind and sea calmed down, and we went on our way rejoicing. We passed near and in full view of "Smoky Jack," as the seamen call an active volcanic peak, which was spouting smoke and flame in fine style, presenting an appearance at once fascinating and terrible. We reached Yokohama on the eighteenth and were glad to come to anchor in a safe harbor after our dangerous experiences. I had suffered a good deal from an attack of acute dysentery coming on a few days after leaving Hong-Kong, and was not relieved when we reached Yokohama. Dr. Lubbock, the ship's Surgeon, had kept the disease in check, but was not able to arrest it. Consequently I was not able to get out much. I called at the Consulate to pay my respects to Mr. Greathouse, who had been appointed in place of Consul Green, removed for cause. I found him a bright and pleasant gentleman. He had been editor of the leading Democratic paper in San Francisco, had no family, and his mother, a very sensible lady, was the head of his household. I met there also Admiral Shumate of the Navy, an officer of considerable repute, and evidently a man of brains. I received a visit from the Rev. Mr. Thompson the same day we entered port, bearing the card of his wife, who was Miss Ruth Withers McCown, a native of Danville and named for me. Her father was a Baptist preacher, and I had been his family physician before the war. This young lady had been educated by the Church as a Medical Missionary, and after graduation set out for her station in China. On the same vessel was a Presbyterian minister who had been sent to Corea as missionary, and agent for the Bible Society. He became enamoured of Miss McCown and by the time they reached Yokohama, they had agreed to unite their fate and fortunes, so were married on short notice, and were then preparing to go to Corea. I returned Mr. Thompson's visit as soon as I was able, and spent a pleasant morning with them.

I said to her, "Ruth, I am surprised that your father's daughter and my namesake should have so swindled the Baptist Brethren as to desert their service after they had spent so much money on your education."

Her face flushed, and she quickly responded, "Oh, that's all right. Mr. Thompson's paid back every dollar that had been expended on my education. I did not feel exactly right about it, but I was obliged to marry Mr. Thompson." They seemed a very loving and happy pair, and their future was to them bright with promise. I have never heard from them since.

We left Yokohama on the twenty-first of August, with large additions to our passenger list. Rev. Mr. Royall, a Methodist Missionary at Shanghai, and his family returning to Virginia after six years absence, is probably a relative of my wife, though he and I were not able to trace the relationship definitely. He was very kind and attentive to me during the voyage home, and when my sickness increased to such a degree that I was confined to my bed all the time, he was untiring in his good offices. Mr. Happer, a son of Dr. Happer, of the Presbyterian Mission at Canton, and his widowed sister, Mrs. Glover, clever, and agreeable, an English "my Lord," Lord Kesterven, and two traveling companions, were among the new passengers. Mr. Happer was a good chess player, and of course we soon ascertained our mutual interest in the "game of games," and had daily contests, as long as I was able to sit up, with pretty equal fortunes, but slightly in my favor. I had to give up the game, however, as my doctor kept me full of opium in some form or other which affected my brain considerably. Mr. Happer contended, however, that the effect of the drug corroborated what he had always heard, that it increased one's mental acumen, as I beat him oftener towards the last sittings than at first. He learned me the game as played by the Chinese, but I did not like it as well as our game.

I had a good deal of conversation with Lord Kesterven and found him well informed and companionable after the crust of his British reserve was broken. He does not at all admire "the Grand Old Man," Gladstone, being a strong Tory. We crossed the one hundred and eightieth degree of longitude on Sunday, consequently had two Sundays in the week. I had grown steadily worse since we left Yokohama, and as the doctor appeared to have exhausted his resources, I commenced using a remedy proposed by Captain Cobb, which, he said, was never known to fail in similar cases. As the two active ingredients were paregoric and pulverized charcoal, I thought it might do good, and dropping all else, confined myself to this for several days. At first I thought myself improving, but not for long. The pain became so severe that I was forced to use morphia or chloral before I could get even a little sleep. For a week before reaching San Francisco, I was confined to my bed, indeed could sit up only for a short time. I thought the outlook unfavorable, but was anxious to reach port, which we did on the eighth of September before midnight.

My cousin, Marsden Manson, and his wife met me at the wharf, and took me to their home in a carriage, sent for his physician, who thought quiet and rest would soon put me on rising ground. His treatment varied little from what I had received from Dr. Lubbock, of the "Rio De Janeiro."

By a strange freak of fortune I read in the morning paper the day after my arrival an article copied from the *"Washington Critic,"* charging me by name, on the authority of an officer of the Navy, with having been guilty of all sorts of offences, defrauding seamen of their wages, systematically conniving with boarding-house keepers to rob and plunder them, and stating that the same thing had been done by my predecessor, Colonel Mosby. In addition it was alleged that I was an habitual drunkard, and guilty of the grossest immoralities. To say that I was astonished feebly describes my sensation on reading this tissue of foul accusation, but the very grossness of the offences charged lessened my indignation. I was only concerned to ascertain what officer of the Navy could have manufactured such slander out of whole cloth, and what motive could have prompted him. One of the statements was that an English seaman had appealed to the British Consul at Hong-Kong and secured redress of his grievances through him. Now, any one possessing a particle of knowledge would know that this stated a falsehood on its face, as there could be no British Consul in a British Port, but all the same, there it was in a newspaper paragraph scattered, no doubt, over the whole country. Sick as I was, I got Marsden Manson to see the news editor of the paper in which the article appeared, and ask him to come up and give me an opportunity of correcting the slander. He came promptly, expressed his regret at the publication, but excused it as an item of news found in one of the Washington Dailies. He readily agreed to publish in the next morning's paper any statement that I desired, and then, at my dictation, wrote an authoritative denial of all the charges, and also exonerating Colonel Mosby as well, and avowing my purpose of exposing the author as a liar and slanderer.

This appeared in the next day's paper, and I also dictated a letter to the *"Washington Critic,"* denying the statement published and demanding the name and address of his informant. I received an answer in due time and wrote to the Lieutenant of the "Alert," whose name was Clement, upon whose authority the charge was based, and he indignantly denied ever mentioning my name, or having made any statement as to the discharge of seamen. It was evidently a sensational story manufactured out of whole cloth, by the reporter of the *"Critic,"* who excused it by saying he made a mistake, and that what he described had not taken place in Hong-Kong, but in Yokohama. He and the editor apologized fully, and I concluded to let the matter drop, only requiring the Washington papers to publish the correspondence, which was of course done. Several of my legal friends wrote offering their services to prosecute for libel the newspaper which published the scandal, free of all expense to me, but I refused to seek redress in the Courts. Indeed, the publication elicited from almost every newspaper in Virginia, and in many other localities, such prompt denial, and such indignant protest, coupled with most complimentary comments on my character and standing, that it was almost worth the publication of the calumny to have elicited so many and such flattering expressions of public confidence and esteem. It may be imagined that all this did not materially aid my convalescence, as it had, of necessity, a depressing effect. This was partly neutralized by the visits of numerous influential friends in San Francisco, who called to see me. My old University friend, Judge Thornton, and his son were among the first but I will not attempt to enumerate them. The Grand Commander of Knights Templars in California at this time was Reuben H. Lloyd, a lawyer of high standing and influence. A resident of San Francisco, he came to see me for the purpose of urging my acceptance of an invitation sent me by the Grand Commandery of California to make the journey to St. Louis as their guest, and proffering their escort. They had chartered a train and proposed to start on Tuesday, the fourteenth of September. I told Mr. Lloyd that I was doubtful of my ability to travel such a distance, but he assured me that I would not be required to exert myself in the least, that he would have reserved for me the best section on the best Pullman sleeper, and he himself would look after my welfare during the journey. Though Marsden Manson and Judge Thornton both protested that it was imprudent to start so soon, I agreed to make the effort, as I was anxious to reach St. Louis in time for the meeting of the Grand Encampment. Accordingly, on the afternoon of the fourteenth, Grand Commander Lloyd came for me in a carriage, stating their train was ready and only awaited my coming to start. We got off soon after I reached the station, and no monarch was ever waited on more royally than I was by the Grand Commander and his fellow Knights of the Grand Commandery. Night or day, if I needed anything, I had only to raise my hand and a Templar was at my side to know my wishes. I have very vague recollections of the incidents of that journey. I know we had no accidents or disasters, that I occupied my berth on the sleeper all the time, that I had the advice of two able and distinguished physicians, and that we reached St. Louis in time for the meeting. I do recall, however, that when we reached Kansas City I was both surprised and gratified by the entrance of my old and valued friends, Peyton Coles, Grand Commander of Virginia, and William B. Isaacs, Past

Grand Commander of Virginia, and several other Virginia Knights, who escorted us to St. Louis. I was driven to the Southern Hotel, assigned splendid quarters, which had been engaged in advance, and made as comfortable as was possible under the circumstances. I completed my sixty-fifth year the day before.

CHAPTER XLVII.

REVISIT VIRGINIA.

Many visitors called, but after Dr. Edward Saunders came and examined me, he interdicted all visitors. Dr. Saunders is a son of my boyhood's friend, Major Robert Saunders of Campbell County, and his brother married my niece, Flora Lemmon. He was very kind and attentive, and though I rebelled against one of his orders, he did not take offence. I was very desirous of appearing in the procession, and also of attending the second day's session, when the officers were to be elected. He forbade both. I acquiesced reluctantly in regard to the procession, as my old comrade and adjutant, Robert McCulloch, who was Captain General of the Local Commandery, and was in charge of all the arrangements, was anxious for me to appear in parade. I gave it up, however, but the next day after the doctor's visit in the morning, I told Coles and Isaacs I must go to the meeting of the Grand Commandery if I only remained a short time. I had a carriage brought around, dressed myself and was driven to the Masonic Temple, where the Grand Encampment met. The cause of my anxiety to be present at the election of officers was because my old and tried friend, General Roome, was next in succession, being Deputy Grand Master, and was then acting as Grand Master, and I had heard that an effort would be made to prevent his election by the Sir Knights of one or two of the largest Grand Commanderies, because of dissatisfaction with some of his rulings. As these were really my rulings which he carried out when he succeeded me, I felt a deep interest in his elevation to supreme authority, and had done all I could to secure that result. As it turned out, there was no special cause for uneasiness, as he was elected by a large majority. I was also desirous of seeing Grand Commander Lloyd elected Senior Deacon, instead of United States Senator George F. Perkins, who had been made Junior Deacon in San Francisco, but who evidently took no interest in the matter, as he was not in attendance at the Conclave, nor did he send any letter of regret or explanation. Under such circumstances it is not the custom of the Grand Encampment to promote an incumbent, and as I thought California was entitled to the place, I wished Sir Knight Lloyd to be substituted for Sir Perkins.

So it turned out, and what was equally gratifying, Virginia was complimented by the selection of William B. Isaacs of Richmond, Grand Recorder of Virginia, to the high position of Grand Recorder of the Grand Encampment of the United States, a place he filled with great ability until the close of his life several years thereafter. I was able to install the Grand Master elect, General Roome, and then returned to my hotel, and never again left my bed until I started for Virginia after the close of the Conclave. As I purposed to go to Lynchburg from St. Louis, I left that city under the care of Sir Knight and Past Grand Commander Robert Craighill, of Lynchburg, who gave me every care and attention possible until we reached our destination on the morning of the twenty-seventh of September, and was met by G. W. Smith and Kate, taken to their home, put to bed, and there remained many days under the care of Dr. Otway Owen and Dr. Dick Lemmon, the last my nephew and the first my life-long friend.

It is useless to dwell on the days of sickness and suffering which followed. My daughters, Mrs. Putney, from Richmond, and Mrs. Read and Mrs. Williams, from Martinsville, came, and Mrs. Goggin, from Bedford, aided Kate in nursing, and I lacked for nothing. There was little improvement in my condition for some weeks, but when I did commence to get better I was myself surprised at the rapidity of my convalescence.

On the twenty-sixth of October I sat up for the first time, on the twenty-seventh my nephew, Sam Withers, drove me out in the afternoon for a short distance, and on the twenty-ninth I started on my return journey, going first to Washington, where I spent a day attending to business in the State and Treasury Departments, and then left for Evansville, Indiana, where I stopped over two days to visit my daughter, Lizzie, and Dr. Carter and their children. They were delighted to see me, as they had not heard of my improvement and were very anxious about me. They begged me to remain with them until I regained my strength, but I was anxious to take passage by the steamer "San Pablo," booked to sail on the ninth of November, and I thought I would do as well in the sleeper as sitting about in the house. I found Lizzie's boys growing finely and Robert and Edward learning well at school, but Sydnor, the second son, had the greatest possible aversion to school or study. He was a very strong, athletic fellow, inheriting my own fondness for hunting, a fine shot, and the first among his companions in all athletic sports, but he plays truant almost every school day, and the only way he can be gotten to school is when led by the collar by his father to the door, for if he lets him loose a moment, he is off like a shot, and as he easily outruns Dr. Carter, he is seen no more till night. Thrashing does no good whatever, he says he does not want to learn and seriously asked a friend of the family who was urging the importance of education, "If there was not some way of making a living without knowing the multiplication table."

He persisted in this course, would learn nothing more than to read and write, procured work in an Iron Foundry, served his time as a moulder, and thus supported himself, but when I was in Evansville he was the best, bravest and most adventurous fireman on the force, always volunteering for the most dangerous work, where his great strength and utter fearlessness many times stood him in good stead, until he became the Chief of the Fire Department in Evansville. He was also the finest wing shot in that section, and the winner of many prizes at shooting clubs.

Edwin, the third son, who had lived with us until he was six or seven years of age, was a lover of books and a fine student, who entered Roanoke College, afterwards the Theological Seminary at Alexandria, was ordained a Deacon and Priest and is now a successful and devoted Rector.

I left Evansville on the second of December, and made no further stop, passing over the Central & Union Pacific Railroads to San Francisco without accident or mishap, reaching that city on the eighth of December at 4 o'clock p. m. Went at once to the shipping office and secured my ticket and berth, and then to Marsden Manson's where I spent the night, enjoying the pleasant converse of himself and wife. As the San Pablo did not leave until one o'clock, I had opportunity to call on several friends before starting, and executing some commissions for my wife and daughters. The passenger accommodations on this vessel were very limited. A French nobleman and his traveling companion, a merchant from Yokohama, and I were the only first-class passengers. The Baron Meron de Meruil and his companion, Leopold Ussile, were both young men. The Baron speaks English imperfectly and seems to be a musical enthusiast, as he spent most of his time composing an opera. His friend was more companionable, and as he was a pretty fair chess player, we had many games together before we reached Yokohama. We had fairly good weather, with the exception of a Northeast storm of considerable violence one night, when the waves broke over us, and invaded the precincts of my state-room to the depth of a foot or more. I had to keep my trunk on top of my bunk for twenty-four hours to save its contents from damage. The "San Pablo" rolls much worse than the larger steamers of the line, but is faster. The Captain did not take the usual course, running North as high as forty-five degrees, but bore South, and crossed in Latitude twenty-seven degrees, giving us a more equable and pleasant temperature, but a longer voyage.

We dropped Sunday when we passed the one hundred and eightieth degree of Longitude.

On Thanksgiving Day we had a big dinner, with regular New England dishes, the Mate being a typical Maine man. We reached Yokohama the evening of the twenty-ninth of November, where we parted with the Frenchmen, who proposed touring Japan, before going to China. The "City of New York" came in the next morning straight from Hong-Kong, and I went aboard and saw Captain Searle and Mr. Harnett, who reported all my people well when they left. I called and took tea at the Consulate with Mr. Greathouse and his mother, and went aboard about ten o'clock and started the next morning for Hong-Kong. We reached Hong-Kong on the sixth of December, and took my family by surprise, as they were not expecting me. I found all in fine health and spirits, in the midst of the gaieties of the winter season. Robert said he had no trouble about getting up his quarterly report and everything was going on smoothly. He was then training for the boat races, and Sece practicing for an Oratorio which came off on the fourteenth, and her solos received much applause.

The "City of Pekin" having collided with a French steamer, was detained beyond her regular day by legal proceedings, to fix the responsibility, but eventually got off three days late.

Mr. Seymour wrote, inviting us to spend Christmas in Canton, and Mrs. Withers and the girls agreed to visit him on the twenty-eighth, which they did and had a pleasant time. The Regatta came off on the sixteenth of December, and Robert's crew won two races, and came within a length of winning the "International," beating five other boats. He was much elated, and received many compliments, ranking as the best of all the new oarsmen. The season was, if possible, more gay than usual. Balls, parties, dinners, amateur operas and theatricals, fetes, and all sorts of entertainments filled up the time. Mrs. Withers projected a large ball in honor of the forty-first anniversary of our marriage. A large number of guests were invited and few regrets received. The Garrison Band furnished the music. All the chief people of the Colony were present and all appeared to enjoy themselves. The eating was especially good. Dancing kept up until 2 o'clock a. m., and all the household were by that time pretty well used up.

At an *"al fresco fete"* in the Public Gardens, gotten up to purchase a new organ for the Cathedral, fancy costumes were very much in evidence, some of which were very fine. Mrs. Dr. Manson, a handsome lady with dark skin and very black hair, proposed to Sece to open a booth as Gypsy Fortune Tellers, and as Sece was an expert in fortune telling with cards, having been taught by Mrs. Coates, from Shanghai, she readily agreed. With the aid of bright costumes, a black wig, and plenty of rouge, she made a very passable Gypsy, and the Gypsy booth had a fine run of custom for the two nights the fete lasted, realizing six hundred and four dollars and twenty two cents, and the whole amount taken in was about two thousand dollars clear of expenses.

We formed the acquaintance of Mrs. Knapp of Portland Oregon, this winter. She was the wife of a very wealthy citi zen of that place, who had come to Hong-Kong to spend the winter by the advice of her physician, as she was threatened with pulmonary trouble. She was bright and clever, and took a great fancy to the ladies of the Consulate, especially to Sece, whom she wished to keep with her all the time. She was much improved in health and came back every winter as long as we were in Hong-Kong.

The "Monocacy" was ordered to leave Canton and go to Yokohama, her place to be supplied by the "Palos." The Captain kindly offered Robert a passage on her, and as he wished to visit Japan, I gave him leave of absence and he left on the twenty-third of March. He came back about the middle of June having traveled over the greater portion of the Island, and was perfectly delighted with the country and people. He says the Northern part is very much like Southwest Virginia in appearance and climate, being mountainous and fertile, with a dense population. He brought back many souvenirs for us all, had good health all the time and made many pleasant acquaintances. He was disappointed in not meeting an American steamer in Kobe, and returned by the "Peninsular" an Oriental boat.

I applied for permission to erect a mat shed on Stone Cutlers Island to serve for bathing purposes, and after some delay received permission to do so, provided I would remove it when notified so to do by the officer in charge of the fortifications, as the Government was then engaged in erecting defensive works on that Island. I took a contractor over, selected a location near the sheds of General Cameron, and agreed to pay twenty-five dollars for the work. It was completed in a day or two, and thenceforward we could enjoy sea bathing at our pleasure. It only required about twenty minutes to make the run from the wharf on the Steam Launch, and the bathing was not only a source of pleasure and enjoyment, but I think conducive to health. Robert, who was a fine swimmer, taught the girls to swim, Carrie proving the most apt scholar. The ladies went out about three times a week generally accompanied by several friends, and five o'clock tea was served on the boat after the bath.

CHAPTER XLVIII.

"THE KING OF THE CANNIBAL ISLANDS."

Captain O'Keefe, of the brig "Swan," hailing from the Island of "Yap," one of the Cannibal group, came into port in April, and reported at the Consulate. He is known here as "The King of the Cannibal Islands," and is evidently a man of parts, with fine administrative capacity. It is said that he was one of the crew of an American vessel which was wrecked on one of these Islands, when all hands except himself perished. Being the first white man the Islanders had ever seen, instead of eating him they treated him with great distinction, and finally made him their king. He came from South Carolina, as he informed me, and was engaged in trading among the ports of India and China. He was able to solve a problem which had puzzled me and many others, relative to the fate of Captain Crayton P. Holcomb, who some two or three years before sailed for these Islands in a small trading vessel, of whom nothing had since been heard. I had received several letters from his sister in Connecticut, and also from a legal firm in Glasgow, Scotland, invoking my best efforts to ascertain his whereabouts or learn his fate. I had made every effort to meet their wishes but in vain, no authentic information was obtainable. As soon as Captain O'Keefe gave his residence as the Island of "Yap," it recalled Captain Holcomb, and I asked him if he had ever known a man by that name. "Certainly," said he, "I knew him very well, but he was killed by the natives in 1885." "Do you know that fact?" was my next question. "I know it as well as I know anything of which I was not an eye witness." "Are you willing to sign an affidavit to that effect?" "Certainly I will, if it is a matter of any importance," was his reply. I showed him the letters I had on file from his sister, and also from the Glasgow lawyers, and while he was reading them, drew up a deposition reciting the time and manner of his death which he signed under oath, and a copy of which I sent to Glasgow and one to his sister.

In speaking of the matter he told me he had seen and conversed with some of the party who had killed Captain Holcomb and his companions, who said they had first fired on the natives and before they could reload, they had been "rushed" and killed with the wooden spears used by the natives. He sent me up the next day quite a large collection of these spears, models of boats, samples of cloth, ornaments made from cocoanut, and sea shells, beads, and many similar curiosities, among others a set of dishes and spoons made of tortoise shell by the natives. I prized all these curios highly, and brought most of them home when I returned. He also sent a lot of fresh cocoanuts, the first we had ever seen, which are much more delicious than the dried nuts we are accustomed to eat. We planted two of these in the yard of the Consulate, and when we left they had grown to the height of a man. I have seen within the last few months (1903) a notice of the death of Captain O'Keefe, and a statement that he left a fortune of $1,500,000.00, most of which will be inherited by his wife and family in South Carolina, none of whom had seen him for twenty years.

The whole Colony celebrated with great *eclat* the Queen's Jubilee, in the month of June, 1887. A salute of fifty guns was fired in the early morning, and every war vessel in the harbor followed suit, and the din was deafening. Business was suspended in the city, Jubilee Services were held in the Cathedral, which all of us attended, and the building was crowded. Music on the new organ just put up, attracted favorable comment and the singing of the choir aided by many amateurs of the best vocalists in the city, was of unusual excellence. At night there was a general illumination and fire works, the harbor presenting a beautiful appearance, as we returned from our bathing expedition, accompanied by several friends. In Chinatown the consumption of fire crackers was enormous. I walked through some of the principal streets in that quarter accompanied by "Trip," who was frightened greatly at the noise, and no wonder. On each side of the narrow streets strings of fire crackers of all sizes were suspended from the third story to the ground, and as they were fired from the bottom, the popping and cracking of the small ones alternating with the deafening detonations of the large ones was stunning. "Trip" with his tail tucked, kept between or under my feet, until at last in pity I took him into my arms, and carried him until we reached a more quiet quarter.

And now that I have mentioned his name it will be as good an occasion as any to introduce our household pets. "Triptolemus" or "Trip" was a "Dandy Dinmot," Terrier, given to my wife when a pup by Mrs. Seth, the wife of Mr. Orathoon Seth, who was Secretary to the Colonial Council. They, by the way, were Armenians, and very good people. "Trip" was quite a pet of my wife until he was almost grown. She was teaching him to "fetch" and he soon learned, but one day tired of running after the ball he refused to bring it; she tried to make him, and all other means failing, took a switch and gave him several cuts. He never forgave her for it, and at once attached himself to me, following wherever I went, lying in a chair by my desk while I was busy, and always sleeping at night by my bedside. I took no special pains with him, but noticed him enough to satisfy myself that he possessed unusual sagacity.

Our second summer was marked with a white stone, because of the advent of "Dot." Robert came in one day, and laid him on my wife's lap without a word. Every one exclaimed, "Why what is this? Not a dog surely." He was the first of his race any of us had ever seen, nor have I met since with another specimen. He was a "Mongolian Pug," and a great curiosity. He was only six or eight inches high, with a Pug's head, and beautiful, bright eyes, with fore legs bowed to an extraordinary degree. He at once showed his familiarity with ladies, and curled contentedly in my wife's lap, who chanced to be wearing a satin dress, for which he had the greatest admiration. He preferred silk velvet to satin, however, and never failed to select a velvet trail to lie on, and next to that a satin one, if attainable. Pugs I had always thought stupid, but "Dot" had great sagacity, and was altogether so cute and lovable that he soon became a pet of the first water, and was spoiled accordingly by all the family. "Trip" at once constituted himself special friend and body guard of "Dot," and in our evening walks never left him under any circumstances, would fight for him in a second, never resented any insult offered him by "Dot," would not even growl at him, no matter how great the provocation. "Dot" attracted the greatest attention among the ladies, and many efforts were made by different persons to procure one of the same stock, but no one succeeded in doing so. Robert never told how he got him, or what he paid for him, and to this day is silent on the subject.

"Jocqualine" was a small monkey that had been given to my wife, who had a great fondness for those bright and mischievous little animals, but like Trip, Jocqualine soon selected me as her master and seemed to care little for any one else. I have seen many monkeys, and all are proverbially mischievous and smart, but this particular specimen was a bow shot beyond any I had ever observed. Of course we had to keep her tied most of the time, at least we tried to do so, but it appeared almost a hopeless effort. She could untie in a few seconds the most complicated knot ever reeved by a sailor, and if chained, and the chain fastened with a lock, would pick the lock and undo it in a few minutes. If there was a flaw in the chain she would find it and with her teeth open the link and loose herself in a very short time. She and the gardener were at perpetual feud, for her first aim when loosed was to get to the flowers, and she always selected the most rare and choice for destruction. Two large camelias were on pedestals each side of the flight of stone steps leading up to the front door, and we were all looking forward to the time when their flowers would adorn, and fragrance perfume the entrance to our home, when one day while sitting at the dinner table I heard the greatest row in the front yard, the coolies laughing and chattering, and the voice of some other Chinaman obviously in great wrath. I told the boy to go to the door and see what it all meant, when Jocqualine ran in, jumped on my shoulder chattering in great excitement, the gardener following in hot haste with a stick, saying something in a most excited tone, of which I could understand nothing but the words, "Kill um." I had the monkey in my lap by this time where she knew she was safe, and when the "Boy" was able to interpret the gardener's grievance, I found she had pulled the buds off the camelias. I examined her mouth and found both cheeks puffed out like a child with mumps, and opening her mouth by force, extracted from her pouches fifty-two camelia buds, which she had safely stowed away. On Christmas day we were at the table and the monkey running around the room, and when the traditional egg-nog was served, my wife sipping hers attracted the attention of Jocqualine, who jumped into her lap, seized the glass with both hands, put it to her mouth and tasted it with evidence of decided approval. My wife tried in vain to wrest the glass from her, but before she succeeded, nearly all the enticing fluid had disappeared down her throat. My wife was afraid it would kill her, and I was not myself certain but it might. While we were discussing the probabilities the potent spirit began to tell on her, and soon the whole family were convulsed with laughter at the wild vagaries she committed. She tried to stand on her head, turn fair summersaults, jumped up and down in a frantic dance, and performed a thousand and one antics. This was kept up until dark, when she was put to bed in her house and securely fastened. The next morning her appearance was pitiable, and appealed to every one's sympathy. She was evidently a martyr to the "headache and repentance" incident to excessive potations. She put her little hands to her head, and moaned in the most piteous manner conceivable, she would eat nothing, and evidently felt as if "a sicker monkey you never saw," would express her sentiments precisely. But mark the difference between men and monkeys. No pursuasion could ever induce her afterwards to taste liquor in any form. She never forgot her first lesson.

We had also a large and beautiful black Retriever, called "Rover," who had been given us when a puppy by Lady Phillippo and who grew to be one of the handsomest dogs that I have ever seen. He always went with the chairs when the ladies rode out, and was a great pet with the coolies. He was a great fighter though not quarrelsome, but could thrash the biggest "Chow Dog" in a few seconds.

CHAPTER XLIX.

LIFE AT THE CONSULATE.

I had a visit in July from Professor Steene, of the University of Michigan, who with three associates were *en route* to the Philippines to prosecute scientific researches in the domain of Natural History and kindred sciences. They appeared to feel no apprehension as to their personal safety, when I suggested that they might find it a dangerous undertaking. They were, of course, intelligent and educated gentlemen, and I was glad to make their acquaintance. I had them up to dine at the Consulate before they left for Manila. They expected to be gone about two months, and after that lapse of time, I frequently thought of them, as I saw no notice of, or allusion to them in any of the public journals. One day I was surprised by seeing a most woebegone, ragged and dirty skeleton enter the door with languid step and almost hopeless expression, who in tremulous tone held out his hand and asked if I did not remember him. Of course I had to admit that I had no idea who he was. He then recalled his party to my recollection, and gave a harrowing account of their sufferings and privations, while wandering through the unexplored jungles of this little-known group. One of the party had died from fever and exposure, the Professor had in some way gotten separated from him, and he did not know whether he was alive or not. He himself was near death's door for a long time, but had finally made his way to the coast and eventually to Hong-Kong. I, of course, did everything I could to aid him, arranged for him to procure board and clothing, and when he was able, advanced money to take him home, which, unlike some others similarly befriended, he promptly returned. I never knew whether Professor Steene lived to reach home or not.

A portly Chinaman accompanied by a respectably dressed white woman came in one day and surprised me by saying in good English, "Good mornin, Consul, I am Charlie Winn, have lived long time in New York, where I married. This is my wife, and we came to ask you to help us." "Very good," said I, "in what way can I be of service?" He told me he now lived in Canton, and had come to Hong-Kong to collect moneys due him, and had gone to a gambling house and lost every cent he had, amounting to more than three thousand dollars. Of course, he charged that he was cheated, and thought if I would threaten to have the proprietor of the house arrested he would refund at least a portion of the money. His wife then spoke up, and I saw she was a German woman. She said if they would give them back half the money they would be satisfied, which he assented to. I told him I had no authority to interfere, that neither he nor his wife were American citizens, and advised him to consult a lawyer who would be more likely to be of service. He insisted that if I would try he knew I could help them. I told him to come the next day, and I would at least give him a note to a law firm, and they left. I sent Chue that evening to make inquiry at the place he named and ascertain the facts. He reported the story true, and said the proprietor of the house would give the wife five hundred dollars for her and the children. When Winn came in the morning I sent him to Mr. Deacon, a lawyer, who said the best thing he could do was to compromise on the best terms he could obtain. I sent word to the party that he must pay back one thousand dollars. He refused, but finally agreed to pay the wife seven hundred and fifty dollars. Which, I think, was the basis on which a settlement was effected.

I expressed my surprise to Chue that the gamester should have disgorged so much. "Oh," said he, "he was feared the woman and children would come and sit down at his door." He then told me it was not uncommon when a person had wronged or defrauded another and refused to make restitution, for the wife of the victim, accompanied by her children, if she had any, to go and sit in the street, in front of the place of business of the man who had committed the wrong, and sit there day after day, for weeks or longer, telling her tale to all who entered or passed by, until the offender was obliged to pay to get rid of her. "Oh," said he, "Chinaman rather see the devil than women come and sit down at his door." This gave me a new idea of Chinese methods. I ought to add that Charlie Winn came a few days afterwards, and offered to pay me for the trouble I had taken. I, of course, declined to make any charge, and the next morning his little son brought a handsome gold-headed ebony cane, which his father had sent with his compliments. I have it still.

One of the most noted and intelligent Chinamen in the Colony was a young man known generally as Dr. Ho Kai. He had been educated in England, afterwards studied law and passed his examination, then studied medicine and obtained his degree in that profession also.

Being possessed of large wealth he married an English lady and brought her to Hong-Kong, but did not long enjoy his marital happiness as she died very soon after. Those who knew her formed a high estimate of her character and intelligence, and he was apparently devoted to her.

As a fitting testimonial to her memory, he proposed to build and endow a Public Hospital for the care of the sick of all nationality who might apply, and called it for her, "The Alice Memorial Hospital." It was to be an up-to-date Hospital, with the most approved appliances for the treatment of all medical and surgical cases. He then asked aid of the citizens in the work of providing all necessary furnishings, etc., and the community promptly responded. The Government Officials, the merchants of all nationalities, the officers and soldiers of the garrison, Parsees, Hindoos, Malays, Greeks, Turks, Syrians, Armenians, Protestants, Mahometans, Buddhists, Sintos, Confucians, and Infidels, joined in the charitable work. The Chinese were especially enthusiastic and liberal, both in donations and purchases, at the "Bazaar," which was held for three days, at the Botanic Gardens, many of the prominent ladies of the city took charge of booths for the sale of every kind of refreshments and every other thing imaginable, and during the three days tens of thousands crowded the grounds. Mrs. Withers and all the girls worked with the foremost. I have never known so successful a Bazaar held anywhere, the whole sales realizing about $12,000.00. The enterprise promised to be a great success and a public blessing.

Young Chinamen were admitted as Students, and the leading Physicians of the City lectured gratuitously to the classes, on all branches of the profession. Doctor Manson, who stood at the head of the profession not only in Hong-Kong, but in all that section of the East, was elected Dean of the Hospital and as long as I remained there did most efficient service.

I recall with much pleasure my intercourse with all the members of the Medical profession in Hong-Kong. As soon as it became known that I had for many years been a practitioner of Medicine and Surgery, I was invited to all the meetings of the Medical Society, made an Honorary member, and invited to visit any case of surgery or medicine presenting features of more than ordinary interest. Dr. Manson was my intimate friend as long as he remained in Hong-Kong. Dr. Cantlie his partner, was a very bright clever Scotchman, also an excellent physician, Dr. Hartigan had the largest practice amongst the English, and was a near neighbor. Each of these were always prompt to respond to any call for aid or advice in my family, and none would accept any remuneration for their services. Dr. Manson was my regular family physician, and I was a frequent visitor at his office. On one occasion I had called in to consult him about some matter, and found a Chinaman in his room evidently in conference, but who, as soon as I came in withdrew into the next room, at a sign from Dr. Manson. After I had concluded my talk the Doctor called in the Chinaman, and asked me to look at his hands and give him my opinion as to the nature of the eruption. I took hold of the man's hand, examined it carefully and finally said, "I have never seen anything like this Doctor, and don't know what it is." He smiled slightly and said, "There is one feature you have not noticed I think," and picking up an exploring needle lying on the table, he took the man's hand and ran the needle through a fold of skin in two or three places without eliciting any complaint or indication of pain. In fact there seemed to be perfectly insensibility. This gave me a clue, as I had heard that in one disease prevailing in China this symptom was persistent, but with the thought a very disagreeable sensation came over me, and I exclaimed in horror, "You don't mean to say that this man has leprosy?" That's exactly what it is," said he, as if it was a most trivial matter. Said I, "Well is there not danger of contracting the disease from handling the man's hand as we both have been doing?" "No," said he, "It is contagious to a slight degree only. A little soap and water will remove all danger." I can't say that I felt at all satisfied with his assurance, and used in addition to the soap and water, some more potent disinfectants before I felt at all comfortable.

He then said that in this man the symptoms had very recently made their appearance and he was trying to see if he could not arrest it, but he never succeeded in doing so. Dr. Manson is now the foremost man in his profession in London, and noted for having first demonstrated the fact, that Intermittent fever was caused by the bite of mosquitoes.

After many false rumors the new Governor of the Colony reached our City in the fall to fill the office vacated by Sir William Marsh in the summer, the place having been temporarily filled in the interim by General Cameron, the Commander in Chief of the Military Post. I was invited with other gentlemen holding official positions to meet him at the wharf when he landed and escort him to the Government House, an invitation which both Robert and I accepted. Quite a large crowd was in attendance and the landing was accompanied by salutes fired from all the Men of War in the Harbor whether English or Foreign, and from the heavy guns in the Battery. Speeches of welcome and responses were made as soon as the Government House was reached, and wines and refreshments served to the company. His Excellency rejoiced in the name of Sir George William des Veaux, and he must have been of French extraction. He was a tall, graceful gentleman of fine manners and appearance, and evidently desirous of making a good impression. He had no family with him, and we all agreed that the Government House would not be so popular a resort as it had been when occupied by Sir William and Lady Marsh, or General and Mrs. Cameron, with all of whom my family had most pleasant relations socially, and were on terms of intimate friendship.

The first Ball given by the new Governor came off within a short time after his arrival, and tickets were sent to myself, Mrs. Withers and Willie, but none to Sece, Carrie or Robert. Mrs. Withers at once sent our regrets, as she said she would not submit to such discrimination, so we missed the first function altogether, but her action produced its effect, for at the next entertainment we were all invited by name, and this continued to be the practice until we left the Colony. The English are great sticklers for precedence, and though I cared little about such things, my wife was different and was never backward in asserting her rights. She did this as she said by the advice of Mrs. General Cameron, who told her when she first came, that it was all important, and she ever after acted on the theory.

Our City was honored about this time by a visit from Prince Devawongse of the Siam, the eldest son of the King, and heir apparent to the throne. He was received with great eclat. The thunders of the salutes deafened us for an hour or two. He was entertained at dinner by the Governor in high style, and I was one of the company invited to dine with him. I found him a very diminutive specimen of the *genus home,* scarcely five feet in height, but with an excellent face, good manners, dressed in the height of the English style, and spoke English fluently and correctly. He conversed very pleasantly, and seemed to be generally well informed. My neighbor, Captain Hopkins, a retired sea Captain, was Consul for Siam at Hong-Kong, and he also entertained the Prince at dinner, and I there met him again, and had a good deal of pleasant conversation, which literally bore fruit, as not long after the Prince's return to Siam, Captain Hopkins sent around to the Consulate with the compliments of Prince Devawongse, a crate of beautiful Mangostenes, the most delicate and delicious of tropical fruits in my estimation, and which grow to the greatest perfection in the Kingdom of Siam. They were highly appreciated and greatly enjoyed. My nearest neighbor in Hong-Kong who resided immediately opposite, was Mr. Belilios, said to be the most wealthy citizen of that Colony. His wife was a very small black-eyed woman, a native of Bagdad. They were Jews, and possessed many of the characteristics of that people. They were fond of show, entertained largely, owned a fine house magnificently furnished, and were liberal and charitable. Their oldest child was a very handsome boy about eight or nine years old, who was very fond of my wife and she of him. His name was Raphael, and he soon became very intimate and spent much of his time at the

Consulate. His mother encouraged him in this, as she was anxious for him to learn to speak English correctly, she herself could hardly speak it intelligibly. He had many animal pets, as he was never denied anything, and he gave my wife the first monkey we had, which was much more gentle and tractable than Jocqueline, but the poor fellow accidently hung himself, to the great grief of Mrs. Withers as well as the rest of us.

Just above Mr. Belilios lived Count Minami, the Japanese Consul, whose wife was quite a pretty and pleasant little woman, who soon became a frequent visitor also, as she had no children or other tie to keep her at home. Count Minami himself was able to read and speak English fairly well, and was anxious to inform himself on all matters American, as he had great admiration for the Country and people. He informed me that he was thinking of becoming a Christian, but he had apparently no conception of the essentials of Christianity, but seemed to regard it in pretty much the same light as an American would regard a change in political affiliation. I tried to explain to him the leading points in our religion, but doubt if he realized my meaning. He evidently thought well of me, for he never failed at any Conference of the Consular representative in Hong-Kong to consider matters of common interest, to put my name forward as leader and principal spokesman for the fraternity.

Mr. Seymour, Consul at Canton, came by in the fall en route to Yokohama to meet his wife and daughter, who had at last consented to come out and join him. He told me he had been urging them to do so for two or three years, but they would not agree to become residents of Canton, where there were so few white ladies. They came, however, in November and we gave them a dinner, and promised to pay them a visit in the winter. The daughter was evidently the ruling spirit in the family, and was really a very sensible and well informed woman. A subsequent visit found them snugly domiciled in the "Shawmeen," and after we left, I had an invitation to the marriage of Miss Mary, to an attache of the English Legation.

Not long after the Seymours left, I was awakened one morning by a most tremendous cannonade which lasted for a great while. On going out to see what occasioned so great a waste of powder, I found that the Chinese "War Fleet" under Admiral Lang, had entered the harbor. There were four brand new Men of War, two of which had been built in England and two in Germany. They were on their first cruise after being fitted out, as each vessel had saluted the flag, and also the other Men of War in the harbor, of course each had to respond, and the aggregate consumption of powder was enormous. I was invited to dine with the Admiral at the Government House, and found him able to converse in English with tolerable fluency, and having subsequently called on him on his Flag ship with Robert in company, we were handsomely received and entertained. I found one or two English officers in each of the vessels, (one had three,) but the Admiral made no secret of the purpose of the Chinese Government to retain them in service no longer than might be required to train their own naval officers sufficiently to enable them to fill the places of the foreigners. They remained in our port less than a week, and proceeded on their cruise with a repetition of the saluting ceremonies.

We were visited in the fall by two Typhoons, one of considrable force, but not to be compared with the one we encountered on the "City of Rio de Janeiro." It wrecked a good many Boats and Sampans, and drowned a few hundred Chinamen, but no serious damage was done in the city. It destroyed utterly our bamboo Pier at the bathing place on Stone-Cutters Island, so that we had to take a small boat to reach shore from the Launch, until the Pier was rebuilt. On these bathing excursions we usually took Dot and Trip with us, and I amused myself by teaching Trip to swim in and bring sticks or chips thrown into the water, but Dot had no use for the water, and would never willingly enter it.

There was a Chinese Village on the hill not far from the Mat Sheds, and the Chow-dogs would sometimes come down to the beach and bark at us, but no one paid any attention to them, but one one occasion I was walking near them, the dogs with me, and when I turned to walk back towards the Sheds while the ladies were dressing, I did not observe that Dot did not follow me as Trip did, but he ran off to make acquaintance with the Chow-dogs, and I had gotten some fifty yards from the place when I heard a snarling and growling among them and looked back saw the whole pack were worrying poor little Dot and bent on killing him. I ran to his rescue as fast as I could go, storming at them at the top of my voice, and throwing my cane at them, but they never retreated until I got almost to them when the cowardly rascals ran and I pursued them, throwing rocks, as I could do nothing else. When I picked up the little dog he was almost buried in the sand, and I thought he was killed outright. He was very nearly "done for," being badly bitten through the breast, and with one or more ribs broken, one of his eyes apparently out, and he could neither stand nor walk. I know I had not been so mad for twenty years, and had I been possessed of a gun I would have exterminated every cur in the village. My wife and the girls were greatly distressed, and cried over their pet as if he had been a child. It was a long time before he recovered, but he eventually did. Whenever we visited the place afterwards I took with me either a small rifle or a large Colt Revolver to get my revenge on the Chow-dogs, but strange to say they never again came down on the beach when we were there. The "Chow" dog is a peculiar species, resembling in appearance the Esquimaux dog, except in size. They are very numerous in all the towns and villages of China, and derive their name doubtless from the fact that they furnish food to the people in time of scarcity, "Chow" being the Chinese word for food. They are heavily built, with long hair not curled and either black or tawny in color, with upright ears and black tongues. This last is a distinctive feature of the species.

There was almost an epidemic of Smallpox in Hong-Kong in the winter of 1887-88. It prevailed every winter more or less, but on this occasion assumed the proportions of an epidemic. Smallpox in the winter, and Cholera in the summer is what the people expect, and they are not often disappointed. Since I left they have been visited once or twice by a still more dreaded disease, the Bubonic Plague, which was much more fatal among the Chinese than either Smallpox or Cholera. Dr. Manson called one morning and advised me to have all the family vaccinated as a protective measure, as the disease he said was all over town. There were more than a dozen cases at the Italian Convent, separated from us only by the width of a street, but as the younger members of the family had all been revaccinated since we came to Hong-Kong I did not think it necessary to repeat the operation. Within a few days the "City of New York" came in, and the Purser, Mr. Harnett, came to dine with us as he usually did, being interested in Willie's paintings. I was busy in the office and did not go up until the bell rang. Shaking hands with Mr. Harnett I said, "Harnett your face is much flushed, and you have a high fever." "Yes," he said, "I've the worst headache I ever had in my life." He continued at the table until dinner was over, and soon after left to consult a Doctor, and I remarked to the family that he was evidently about to have a sharp attack of some kind. Judge then my alarm when I heard next day that Mr. Harnett had been sent to the Hospital with a bad case of confluent Smallpox. I at once sent for Dr. Manson to come and vaccinate us. He came very promptly, and after operating on the younger members of the family, said he thought both I and my wife should be vaccinated. I replied that each of us had been repeatedly vaccinated without effect, and I hardly thought it necessary, but as the operation was a very trivial one, I would submit to it, and took off my coat and he vaccinated me. My wife at first refused, but we persuaded her to do the same, and he put the virus in four places on her fore-arm. To my astonishment every one produced a vescicle, and the constitutional symptoms were so severe that she was in bed for two weeks or more, and the Doctor visiting her daily. Indeed she never again enjoyed as good health as before, while she remained in the Colony. We all escaped Smallpox, however, but Mr. Harnett came near dying, and did not get out of the Hospital for six weeks or two months, and was badly disfigured for life.

This year, 1887, had in many respects brought troubles in its train. My daughter Mrs. John T. Reed, who had been for years a martyr to a diseased knee joint, was obliged by her sufferings and rapidly waning strength, to seek relief, and entered Dr. Hunter McGuire's Hospital (St. Lukes) in Richmond, where it was found that nothing but amputation of the limb offered any chance for saving her life. This was done and though the outcome in the end was satisfactory, her life for two months was held by a thread. For eight weeks she was not turned over in bed. I suppose under God's providence nothing but the untiring and watchful attention of her sister Mrs. Stephen Putney and her cousin Mrs. John Spotts, won her back to life under the skillful treatment of Dr. McGuire. We, in Hong-Kong were kept long in anxiety and suspense, but we never knew until we returned, the extremity of danger through which she passed. Dr. McGuire told me he had little hope of saving her when he operated, but he knew it was the only chance, and so long as he lived he spoke of her case as one of the most remarkable recoveries he had ever witnessed. He attributed it to what he designated "the magnificent Withers pluck which eventually pulled her through." The year also witnessed the death of Mr. Peyton S. Coles of Albemarle, one of the truest and staunchest friends I ever had, who died after a few days illness. My nephew, Dr. Richard Lemmon, who had waited on me so untiringly during my long illness the year before, died of heart disease in the summer of 1887, a young man of great skill and high promise in his profession.

CHAPTER L.

VISIT FROM ADMIRAL CHANDLER.

We commenced the year 1888, with a large entertainment, ball and supper, which was numerously attended of course. Mrs. Withers suggested that I should make a big bowl of egg-nog, as the beverage was not known in the city. At first the visitors were a little shy about partaking, but as soon as they got a taste of it, there was a great run, and I had to warn the young officers that it was a more potent beverage than they reckoned on, and this alone saved some of them from excess. Among our guests was a tall and portly Chinaman, Tan Kin Cho, who had been Secretary of Legislation at Washington and Havanna. He was returning to his home in Manchuria after four years absence. As he spoke English fluently and well, I had a good deal of conversation with him, while the dancing was going on, and he surprised me greatly by expressing a desire to take a few turns himself, if I could "persuade any of the ladies to favor him so much."

I called up "Sece" and introduced her, and she at my intimation accepted him as a partner. His appearance on the ball room floor, among the waltzers was a genuine surprise as none of the company had ever before seen a Chinaman waltzing. He knew what he was about, too, and Sece said he acquitted himself very creditably. Some of the company insisted that he was not a Chinaman at all, but some American we had dressed up in Chinese costume to hoax the company, but he stood the test of the closest scrutiny. He appeared to enjoy the exercise, and the novelty of dancing with a Chinaman, secured him partners without difficulty.

The dancing ended about 2 o'clock, and every one seemed to enjoy it. Tan Kin Cho left the next day, but sent me a "Cumshan" before he took his departure, which on opening proved to be a beautiful set of gold fruit knives for my wife.

We concluded from the expensive character of his gift that he must be a man of wealth.

On February 1st, "The Brooklyn," "Admiral Chandler's Flag Ship," came in and the next day I went out to call on him and the Captain and off·cers of the ship. I found the Admiral to be a tall, stout man, with a strong face, who seemed unaffected and sociably inclined. I gave him and the officers an invitation to the entertainment we proposed to give on our wedding anniversary the next evening, which was promptly accepted. I accompanied him and his officers to the Government House to introduce them, and subsequently dined with them at the same place.

We had quite a distinguished company on the third of February. The Governor, and the General Commanding the Post, The English, French, and American Admirals, and their respective suits, Commodore Morant, and all the first people of the place. There was, however, an awkward but amusing *contre temps* in connection with the high dignitaries. We had the Head Quarter Band, to furnish music for the occasion, and the leader had been instructed to play "God save the Queen," as soon as the Governor and General entered, and "The Star Spangled Banner" when Admiral Chandler came in. It so happened that the Admiral was first to arrive, but he was followed almost immediately by the Governor and General Cameron. As soon as the Admiral entered the Band struck up "The Star Spangled Banner," but before many bars had been played the Governor and General came, and entered the room to the strains of the American National music. Of course it was changed to "God save the Queen" as soon as practicable, but the imposing entrance was spoiled.

Arrangements had been in progress for some time among the music lovers for presenting the Opera of "The Sorcerer," in which Sece was to take the part of the leading Soprano, Willie and Robert led the Chorus, in which Carrie also took part, so we at the Consulate felt very much interested in its success. The time fixed for the first appearance was on the tenth of February, and I invited Admiral Chandler and his Flag officer to dine with us that day informally, and accompany us to the Opera. He accepted gladly as he expressed it;

and the programme was carried out. The house was packed
and jammed, and while I felt confident that Sece's vocal powers would carry her through, I doubted if she possessed sufficient histrionic acquirements to make a success of the part. I
was agreeably disappointed. I never witnessed a more successful amateur performance. Everything went off with great
eclat. The Chorus was wonderfully effective. The house
shouted itself hoarse. And when the curtain fell after the two
hours exhibition I have rarely heard more applause. It was
repeated by special request the next night, but one, and was
equally well patronized, and the Governor a few days after
wrote a note to the Choral Society requesting as a personal favor
that another performance might be given on the 25th. Sece,
and several others were very reluctant to comply with the
request, but felt it would not do to refuse, so it was repeated,
and many thought the last performance the best. I did not see
it, for the impressions of the first rendition were so pleasing
that I felt unwilling to mar them by witnessing one of inferior
merit. The universal verdict of the public was that it was
the best Opera ever seen in Hong-Kong.

Mrs. Knapp the lady from Portland, Oregon, again spent
the winter and was at my house the greater part of the time,
though she retained her rooms at the Hotel. We were all
delighted at the improvement of her health. Sece was her
special pet on account of her voice, and after the success of
the Opera Mrs. Knapp gave Sece a rich satin dress, and sent my
wife a handsome set of pearls on her wedding anniversary. The
Captain of the "Brooklyn" and the Ward room Officers invited
Robert to accompany them on their voyage to Singapore, Batavia, etc., provided the Admiral would permit, and he, so far
from objecting seconded the invitation warmly, and I urged
him to go, as I knew the voyage would be a source of great
pleasure and improvement, as he would see a portion of the
world rarely visited by Europeans or Americans, and under
peculiarly favorable auspices. So he hurried up his preparations and on the afternoon of the 12th, the Flag Ship steamed
slowly out of the Harbor by the Lynemoon Pass bound for Singapore. I had letters from him when he reached that place,
and also from Batavia, Spice Islands, Manila and other Ports,

describing the novel sights and queer people he had met in those out of way places. One thing struck me as peculiar, I had instructed him when he reached Batavia, the principal shipping port for Java Coffee, to buy and ship me a bag, but he was unable to purchase a single sack, as all the coffee was sold and bought in cargo lots, and none could be had by retail. He reached Hong-Kong about the middle of April, by way of Naygasaki, as the "Brooklyn" went to that place from Manila. He brought home a great number of curiosities, of various kinds with many photographs of places and people he had seen, and a beautiful Lory, a small species of Parrot, bright scarlet in color, which spoke, however, only Malay, which none of us could understand. He was very gentle and affectionate but lived only a few days after reaching us. He died suddenly to our surprise and sorrow, having given no evidence of sickness until he dropped dead from his perch. I sent the body to a taxidermist and had it mounted, and it still adorns the top shelf of our Curio Cabinet at Wytheville.

The Governor left Hong-Kong in the spring to meet his wife, at Singapore, who was on her way to join him, and they returned in due time, and were met at the Pier by a large deputation of Officers and citizens with the usual accompaniment of salutes, addresses, etc. They landed so late, however, that the latter part of the ceremonial was necessarily abbreviated. As soon as they were fairly domiciled they had many callers who were, however, considerably surprised by being informed that visitors were expected to register their names and leave their cards at the Guard House. This was a novelty to all, caused much unfavorable comment, and many declined to call in consequence. I suppose this feeling became known to his Excellency in a short time, as the edict was not long observed. Their first regular reception was largely attended, and the impression made upon the greater number of visitors was favorable to the new leader of Colonial Society, as she was of pleasing appearance, gracious manners, but very like a Jewess in physiognomy.

About this time a strike occurred among the Cargo-Boat men, caused by an order emanating from the Government, directing that all should be photographed. Now the lower class of Chinese, and many of the better class, have an invincible repugnance to being photographed. They have some superstitious idea, that the likeness is part of themselves, and are not willing for any one to possess a portion of their individuality. The day the order was promulgated, there was great commotion among the boating population and after consultation every man of them left the harbor and rowed their boats into Chinese Waters, beyond the jurisdiction of the Colonial Officials. The Ocean Steamers were greatly inconvenienced as they could get no other boats to deliver cargo. The "City of New York" endeavored to load at the wharf, but it was a tedious and difficult job. These boat coolies soon brought pressure to bear on the Coal Heavers, coolie laborers, and chair and Rickshaw men through their respective Guilds, but the Government refused to yield an inch, it became a square trial of strength. Intimidation was resorted to, and the Rickshaw men were by force compelled by the strikers to cease their carrying even on the most public streets of the City, the Police, to my surprise, not interfering. The next day, however, there was a grand parade and review of all the Police force, accompanied by a volunteer Company of Artillery, I suppose for the purpose of over-awing the strikers, at any rate no subsequent violence was offered. This state of affairs lasted two or three weeks, when the Cargo Boats gave in, and returned to work without any concessions from the Government as it was stated. After quiet was restored the Governor intimated that if they had any real grievance he would give fair consideration to a respectful petition setting forth their complaint, but I heard nothing further from them, and was never able to ascertain whether the Boat Coolies were photographed or not. My wife was anxious to get a photograph of her Night Chair borne by four coolies, but the coolies would not consent to be taken, even refusing a bribe of a dollar each.

We received intelligence in April of the death of Mr. Thomas Holcombe Royall, my wife's brother, being the last of the family, my wife only excepted. My wife was of course greatly distressed and as her state of health was low, the depression produced by this sad news, had a bad effect. She had some symptoms of heart failure, that caused me to send for Dr. Cantlie, who came and gave her some fluid extract of Digitalis with good effect. Holcombe, as he was always called, died in Lynchburg at his mother's in the same room in which he was born fifty-three years before. He was sick about three weeks, but I do not know of what disease he died. He had lived with us, off and on, for many years, and was a favorite with all the children. He had been living in Richmond for some years as one of the leading salesmen in one of the largest Dry Good Houses of that City, being a No. 1 salesman of ladies' goods especially.

The Steamer "San Pablo," Captain Reed was wrecked in Formosa Channel, and though no lives were lost and Cargo saved, the vessel was a total loss. She was one of the finest vessels of the line, having recently been altered, enlarged and put in thorough repair. Captain Reed was deservedly reckoned one of the best and most careful navigators in the employment of the company. He was greatly grieved at his mishap. The crew and cargo were sent to Shanghai, and subsequently to Hong-Kong to be discharged.

I had made the voyage from San Francisco to Hong-Kong with Captain Reed in 1886, and esteemed him highly. At first it was thought that the vessel could be gotten off, and the Counsel at Shanghai wired me to have a powerful tug or tugs sent to her relief, which I did, but when they reached there it was found that the damage was irremediable and she soon commenced to break up. This is the third large American Steamer lost on this coast since I have been here. I had a visit from Mr. Davis of San Francisco, with whom I had a slight acquaintance formed in Washington when he was a member of the lower House of Congress. He was extensively engaged in milling and exporting flour, and sold a large quantity in Hong-Kong, which is the distributing point for all goods and merchandise seeking a market in Middle or Southern China. The Chinese Commission Merchant to whom Mr. Davis consigned his flour, being a man of wealth and anxious to show attention to one of his best patrons, proposed to entertain him at a large dinner party. He accordingly issued invitations to many of his Chinese and European friends, among others to Robert and myself. I had declined in the past, more than one similar invitation, as I could not speak or understand Chinese, but Robert wished to go, to gratify his curiosity, and as I felt somewhat desirous of witnessing the ceremonial of a typical dinner party among the Celestials, I told him to send an acceptance. We were invited for 7 o'clock p. m., and appeared promptly on time. Several of the guests both Whites and Chinese were already assembled, and it was not long before we were ushered into the Dining-Room.

The first thing that attracted my attention was the crash of Chinese music, in which the gong plays the most important part, assisted by many squeaking and ear splitting instruments, but to my unaccustomed ears there was an utter absence of melody.

In a Gallery overlooking the large Dining-Room, there was a dramatic performance going on, with full compliment of Actors in splendid costumes, who ceased not during the whole evening to shriek out in falsetto notes, their respective parts of the play. The dinner table was long and seats provided for the guests. Mr. Davis was of course the guest of honor. I was on his right, and the balance of the company were ranged on each side of the table in regular order. After we had taken our seats Samshu, the Chinese wine, was served hot in tiny cups not much larger than a thimble, and then we commenced to discuss an elaborate menu composed entirely of Chinese dishes, served in Chinese style, and eaten with "chop sticks," the Chinese substitute for knives and forks. I can't begin to recollect the dishes, having to my regret lost the copy of the menu with which each guest was provided. I know we had Shark fins, Snails, and Bird nests, all of which are palatable, the last particularly so. Of course I could not make much head way with chop sticks, being my first attempt to use the novel contrivance, and none of the Europeans or Americans present seemed able to do much better. I determined to taste every dish offered, and as the result showed there were sixteen full courses of these viands. The waiters, I should have mentioned were the second and third wives of our host and his Chinese guests. These were without exception young and good looking girls, except for the disfiguring quantity of *rouge* with which their cheeks were covered. When we had eaten through the sixteen courses, we rose from our seats, cigars were handed around, and most of the company indulged in a smoke, but no one left the room. The table was cleared and reset with plates and dishes, knives and forks, goblets and wine glasses, in European or American style, and we were invited to resume our seats at the table, when a regular European *Menu* was laid beside each plate, and soup, fish, roast beef, and mutton, ham and the usual side dishes were presented, sixteen courses more, accompanied by claret, champagne, port, and sherry. Of course the capacity of our stomachs was unequal to this additional demand upon them, and the guests partook sparingly of the different courses. Then healths were drank but no speeches made, and last scene of all some of the ladies passed around the table inviting each guest in turn to drink healths in lisping voice, and with seductive smiles. By this time (2 a. m.), I felt as if my head would split, as the abominable music of the interminable dramatic performance had never for one moment ceased, during the whole evening. We took leave of our host and of each other a little after two o'clock and Robert and I reached the Consulate about half an hour later, as we had to walk home. This was my first and last experience of Chinese hospitality, which I found in some respects oppressive, to say the least.

CHAPTER LI.

FAREWELL TO HONG-KONG.

The condition of my wife's health had become so precarious that it was deemed advisable to send her from Hong-Kong and this decision was accelerated by the prevalence of Cholera in the city to an extent which almost reached the proportions of an epidemic. Many Europeans and other foreigners died from it, after a few hours' illness. I had every precaution taken to prevent an invasion of the Consulate by the dread disease. The whole premises were thoroughly cleaned and disinfected, and great caution exercised in the use of fruits and vegetables. In a family council it was decided that Mrs. Withers, Willie and Carrie should go to Japan by the first steamer, and after spending a few weeks there should go on to America. Sece agreed to remain and look after our housekeeping. As only four days would elapse before a steamer would leave for Yokohama, they had to hurry greatly to get off, but as they had the assistance of many friends they managed to leave on the "Belgic" on the twenty-first of June. The steamer was to go first to Macao to get a consignment of opium, so Robert and Sece accompanied them to that place, where they spent the night on board, and returned the next day, the "Belgic" going on to Yokohama. My wife dreaded a repetition of the sea sickness from which she had suffered so terribly on her voyage to Hong-Kong, but fortunately she suffered very little from that cause. They reached Yokohama in safety where Mrs. Greathouse, the mother of the United States Consul, took them to the Consulate, and treated them with the greatest kindness and hospitality. They had a pleasant sojourn in Japan for about three weeks, visiting Tokio and many other points of interest, and took passage on "City of Pekin" about the middle of July for San Francisco, which they reached after a pleasant passage with little suffering from sea sickness. After spending a few days pleasantly with Marsden Manson, they took the train for the East, and without mishap reached Virginia in due time. As it may be supposed their departure left a great hiatus in our family circle, and I felt especially for Sece, as I feared she would be lonely, but Captain Hopkins' only daughter, Florrie, a young and very pretty girl of whom we were all very fond, came almost every day to visit Sece, and with other numerous friends, and her musical engagements, comic operas, etc., she never appeared to suffer from *ennui*.

Our neighbor, Mr. Belilios, some time last year paid a visit to the United States, and being especially desirous of visiting Virginia, of which State he had heard so much, I gave him letters of introduction to the Governor, General Fitz Lee, and several others, including my son-in-law, Mr. Putney. As I also gave him letters to several high officials in Washington City, he was given the opportunity of making his tour under very favorable conditions, and returned greatly pleased with the country and people, and was never tired of assuring me that he was indebted to my letters for the greater part of his enjoyment. He had a handsome home on Victoria Peak, with large grounds, and this summer of 1888, projected a series of weekly fetes, where games or "sports," as the English call them, were to be indulged in, and scores kept of the weekly contests, until the series should be completed, when very handsome prizes were to be awarded the victors. They had Tennis, Archery, Rifle shooting (for lady contestants), throwing at a mark, throwing heavy hammer, etc. After the first meeting Sece was expressing her regret that her sister Willie was not present to contest for the prize for rifle shooting, as she knew she could beat any of the others at that sport. I asked her why she did not enter the contest, but she said she had never shot a rifle in her life. I told her she could soon learn, and if she could borrow a parlor rifle (which was the weapon used), I could soon teach her to shoot it.

The next day she procured the rifle, and I gave her daily lessons in its use. She soon became interested, and her score at the games constantly improved, and finally she won the prize, a very large and handsome silver cup. Robert also won a handsome cup at "Aunt Sallie," a game the object of which is to strike a lay figure of an old woman with a pipe in her mouth, with missiles of short sticks thrown from a distance of twenty-five or thirty steps. Mrs. Belilios seemed greatly pleased at Sece's triumph, as she was very fond of us all. When Mrs. Withers left Hong-Kong, Mrs. Belilios was greatly distressed, and wept bitterly when she bade her farewell. She brought over and put on her wrists a beautiful pair of bangles of twenty-two caret gold, which she had made to order in Bagdad, especially for the purpose, also a silver gilt puff-box, a very handsome affair. All of us had pretty sharp febrile attacks in the fall Sece's being especially so, and for some days I was very uneasy about her. I employed as a nurse an American widow, who had lost her husband a few months before, and who did good service, being attentive and intelligent. Robert also was under the weather for some time, and Chue, my right hand man, was also unable to do his work, and had to lay off several days at a time. As for me, after an attack of erysipelas, I was for nearly six weeks down with my old enemy, rheumatism. I had supposed in that warm climate I should be free from it, but this was the worst attack I have ever had. Mrs. Manson took Sece to stay with her on the Peak, and she was benefited by the change, but later I sent both her and Robert to Shanghai for two weeks or more. As neither had ever been there, they enjoyed their visit, and returned much benefitted. I, of course, had rather a lonely time during their absence, being the only white inmate of the Consulate, but having plenty of work to occupy me during the day, and plenty of reading at night, got on fairly well.

I was shocked by receiving intelligence from Wytheville of the death of one of my oldest friends in that place, General William Terry, who returning from Grayson Circuit Court with Mr. J. W. Caldwell in a buggy, was drowned in crossing Reed Creek within a mile of his home. The water was high, but as they met a wagon not more than half a mile from the creek, which had just crossed, they drove at once into the stream and were swept away. Both horses and General Terry were drowned and Mr. Caldwell was washed down the stream some distance but finally got hold of a bush and with this support was enabled to reach the bank. General Terry had served with distinction in the Stonewall Brigade during the whole war, part of the time commanding it, was a Past Grand Master of

Masons, and served two or more terms in Congress. We had known each other for many years, being natives of adjoining counties in Eastern Virginia.

Colonel Denby, our Minister to China, paid us another visit in the fall, and I took him to inspect the "Titam Water Works," then nearing completion. The water supply of Hong-Kong was meagre and of inferior quality, and during the dry season there was really a water famine in the Chinese part of the city. At the Consulate we were supplied by a never-failing well in the yard, and supplied many of our neighbors. Being disturbed several nights by the noise and talk in the street as I supposed, I got up one morning about two o'clock to see the cause, and found the yard around the well crowded with Chinamen, and on investigation learned that my gardener who lived in the Porter's Lodge at the gate, was driving a brisk trade in well water, which he sold to the Chinese Water Carriers at one or two cents per bucket, and was getting rich fast. I, of course, put a stop to the traffic, and gave the water to all who needed. The public necessities demanded a more liberal supply for the city, and the authorities had for a year or more been engaged in damming some small streams on the opposite side of the mountain, which it was estimated would, when completed, give twenty-five to thirty gallons per day to each person in the city. To do this it was necessary to construct a dam one hundred and twenty-five feet at the base and ninety feet at the top, one hundred feet in height, of granite blocks, and to tunnel the mountain for two thousand feet. The work was completed about the time I left the Colony. I was much impressed by the substantial and permanent character of the public works constructed in and around Hong-Kong. They are, as a rule, much more durable and substantial than those in the United States, and remind one of the similar achievements of the old Romans, whose roads built in England and Europe during the period of their occupancy, are still in serviceable condition.

The result of the Presidential election in 1888, while not a surprise, was to me somewhat disconcerting, as it necessitated the surrender of the position I held, but as I began to realize that the climatic conditions would in any event render it necessary for me to do so, I was the less disturbed. To avoid the discomfort of being removed from office, I tendered my resignation, to take effect the fourth of March ensuing, but Mr. Cleveland declined to accept it, on the ground that it would be doing injustice to the incoming Administration to permit the Government Officials in foreign countries, to vacate their offices, and thus leave the Government without officers of experience, whereby the interests of the country might suffer. Recognizing the soundness of this reasoning, I remained quietly at my post of duty.

The 58th Regiment which had been on duty here, were ordered to change their Post in accordance with usage, and their place was to be taken by the 91st, a Highland Regiment. We had formed so many pleasant acquaintances among the officers of the 58th that it was really a grievance to part from them. Their departure was proceeded by a large dinner and dance at Regimental Headquarters, which was a splendid affair, and greatly enjoyed by the young people. Governor and Lady Des Vaux and their daughter recently arrived, were of course the guests of honor. General and Mrs. Cameron expected to be ordered away in the spring, and a great change in our social relations seemed impending. Before the Regiment was relieved the Opera "Tolanthe" was rendered, for which Sece and Robert had been long rehearsing. It was a decided success and was repeated two or three times.

General Cameron having ordered that the Military should exercise themselves on the sixteen of January by an attack and defense of "Mountain Lodge" on the Peak, a great many persons went out to witness the maneuvers. Major Provost of the 91st Highlanders in command of one of the attacking columns was so exhausted by his efforts to scale the steep mountain side, that he fell and died almost instantly, no doubt from heart failure. It was a sad ending of the day, as he left a wife and two young children. Bishop Burdon officiated at his burial which was largely attended by the military and civilians.

In January I commenced packing my goods and chattels for shipment to the United States. It proved a bigger job than I expected as it took thirty-two large boxes, and the packing alone proved quite expensive. The goods were shipped on the Steamship "Ridgeway" for New York on the twenty-sixth of

January; and left a sad hiatus in the appearance of the Consulate which looked very naked afterwards. On the eighth of February the "Marion" flying the flag of Admiral Chandler, came into Port, and after the usual salutes were ended I went to call on him, and found Admiral and Lady Salmon and their daughters, and several others present. The Admiral and Mrs. Chandler with their daughters took rooms at the Hotel, where Robert and Sece called on them and their call was promptly returned. On the eleventh, Admiral Chandler, his Flag Officer, and Captain Dyer of the "Marion" paid a visit to the Governor, and as I was returning from the Post-Office I met them on their return near the Hotel and was instantly struck by the peculiar position of the Admiral in his Chair and at once divined the cause, and followed the chairs to the Hotel, and found, as I feared, that he had been stricken with paralysis while at the Government House. There was great commotion among the Naval Officers indeed among all the Government Officials. The Governor sent frequent messages of inquiry, and proffers of aid. I remained at the Hotel most of the day, but soon saw the case was hopeless, as there was a steady and progressive increase in the gravity of his symptoms. He died soon after 9 o'clock that evening, never having regained consciousness. Sece went down and did all she could for Mrs. and the Misses Chandler. I prepared and distributed a circular to each of the Consuls in the Colony announcing his death, and inviting their attendance at the burial on the 14th. At Captain Dyer's request I asked and obtained from the Government leave for a party of Marines to land under arms, for the purpose of acting as escort at the funeral and as a firing party. I acted as one of the Pall Bearers. The funeral was the largest and most imposing every seen in Hong-Kong, and all honors were paid the deceased, all the business houses were closed, traffic everywhere suspended, and the greater part of the foreign population marched in the procession to the "Happy Valley" Cemetery where the burial took place. Sece, at Miss Chandler's request took charge of all arrangements for the family, procuring mourning dresses for Mrs. Chandler and her daughters, and her discharge of these duties was highly appreciated by them. Colonel and Mrs. Seymour came from Canton to attend the funeral, and remained over a day, and I took them in the launch to call on the two English Admirals on their respective Flag Ships, and they returned the next day to Canton.

I was amused by the receipt of a note from the Editor of the "Daily Telegraph" on the twenty-second of February, asking what was the meaning of the salutes fired by the American Men of War at 12 o'clock and the dressing of all the American vessels in Port. The fame of the Great George did not appear to have reached this remote region. I sent my resignation to President Harrison early in February and asked for a leave of absence which was granted, and we soon after commenced really to prepare for leaving the Colony. Two young married ladies, wives of Naval Officers whose acquaintance Sece had formed in Shanghai, came down and spent some time with her at the Consulate, and being bright and pleasant, made the time pass rapidly. One was the wife of Captain Smith, a Pay Master in the Navy, the other, Mrs. Hogg, was the wife of Lieutenant Hogg of the "Essex." After they left Sece concluded she would go to Yokohama, and spend a week or so, and join me at that place on my voyage homeward. Accordingly she took "Dot" with her and left Hong-Kong by the Steamer "Oceanic" on the 24th. The day preceding she had a great many callers, both ladies and gentlemen. The Chairs of visitors filled the walk from the house to the street, and many were in the street. Expressions of regret were heard on all sides at our proposed departure, which was of course regarded by us as evidence that we were liked in the social circle of the City. Miss Florrie Hopkins was so much distressed that she had to abandon her purpose of going with Sece to the steamer, and went back in tears to her home.

After Sece left us, the Consulate was lonely indeed, and I felt truly sorry that the outlook for Robert, after I should leave would be so gloomy. He wrote for "Franco" our old clerk who was at Macao, offering to give him employment again as clerk, and also to arrange with Dr. Lockhead to come up and stay with him at the Consulate. Poor "Trip" was very disconsolate after "Dot" left and spent his spare time looking for him everywhere he was in the habit of going.

Several married ladies of our acquaintance came over and took tea with us before I left, and Mrs. Belilios surprised me by presenting a very heavy and expensive watch chain and locket attached, which she said was intended for a photograph or miniature of my wife. Her wish was subsequently carried out, and I have worn the chain ever since. General Cameron and his family took their departure from the Colony at the same time I did, on the thirty-first of March 1889. The General, Mrs. Cameron, three Misses Camerons, and his aide-de-camp Captain Sommerville made up the party. Dr. and Mrs. Manson and two children also were passengers, so we did not lack for acquaintances. No incident of importance marked our voyage to Yokohama, which we reached on the fifth of April. When I went ashore I found that Sece was in "Tokio" at the house of Mr. Ballagh, the President of the College attached to the Presbyterian Mission. I went to Tokio, and first paid my respects to Governor Hubbard, our Minister, who was very hospitably inclined, and when I started he had his carriage in waiting to take me to Professor Ballaghs, which was at the opposite side of the city, at least five miles distant. When I reached there I had an explanation of Sece's sojourn with him of whom I had never heard. I found that his wife was Miss Bettie Falls, of Alexandria, a friend of our family with whom we were quite intimate when we lived in that city. I spent two days very pleasantly with them and then we returned to Yokohama, and took the Steamer "Rio de Janerio" for San Francisco on the morning of the ninth of April. Having pleasant company, a good Captain, and staunch ship, we had on the whole a pleasant voyage, only marred by the rough water, which caused some of our passengers much suffering from Sea Sickness. Miss Cameron was especially unfortunate in this regard, as I do not think she appeared at the table more than once or twice during the voyage. Sece was also a sufferer but not to the same extent. We amused ourselves with games as is usually the case on a sea voyage. Whist, chess, checkers and reading filled our time, and we reached San Francisco in safety, on the twenty-fifth of April. Sece's birthday came on the twenty-third of April, and the cook sent up a fine iced and ornamented cake at dinner, and General Cameron treated the company to champagne in honor of the occasion. Marsden Manson met us at the wharf, and took Sece and Dot to his house, and I went to the "Occidental" and wired to my wife at once to relieve her anxiety.

CHAPTER LII.

"CARRY ME BACK TO OLD VIRGINNY."

We left San Francisco on the twenty-seventh of April, reached Chicago on the second of May, where Sece wished to stop a few days with Mrs. Rosa Bemis, a cousin of her mother, whose husband was proprietor of "The Richielue," one of the finest hotels I ever saw. Here we were entertained in princely style for several days. Learning from Mrs. Bemis that Willie was at Evansville, Indiana on a visit to her sister Mrs. Carter, I wired her to come to Chicago and join us, as we proposed to return by the Michigan Central, to have a look at the Falls of Niagara, which none of us had seen. She came the next day, and there was a joyful greeting of course, but I told her she showed more pleasure at meeting "Dot" than she did to greet either Sece or myself. We had a pleasant trip to Buffalo, stopping to see the Falls on the Canadian side. The first view was rather disappointing, and did not greatly impress me. The morning being cloudy there was no rainbow spanning the Cataract, to our regret. The longer it is viewed, however, the more it grows upon you, and it is not a great while before you feel a satisfying sense of its grandeur.

We stopped over a day or two in New York where we met several Hong-Kong friends, Mrs. Smith, wife of the Pay Master, and Lieutenant Rodman, who had been with us a good deal. The girls begged hard to stay longer, but I was impatient to get home, and we left on the night train, reached Lynchburg in due time where Mrs. Withers and Carrie were staying. I need not say it was a joyful reunion, for during our whole married life we had never been so long separated.

I had purchased in Hong-Kong five Mandarin ducks, most beautiful birds, the drakes especially marked in a very peculiar and lovely manner. The expense of bringing them over was much greater than I expected. I had expressed them from San Francisco to Lynchburg, and found on my arrival that they had preceded me, and G. W. Smith my son-in-law, had them in a woven wire enclosure and was giving them every attention. It was alleged by the vendor that they were domesticated, but this was clearly an error. Mr. Smith kept them some months feeding and caring for them himself, but they never became gentle, and at last they were donated to the "Druid Hill Park" Baltimore. I returned to Washington a day or two after reaching Lynchburg, where I placed in General Hunton's hands my claim for compensation for extra official fees, which the Court of Claims and the Supreme Court of the United States had decided to be due Colonel Mosby for similar services. I also paid a visit to the State Department of which Mr. Blaine was Secretary, and had a very pleasant interview with him. He urged me to return to Hong-Kong, saying I could remain as long as I wished. I told him I had already done that, but suggested that as my son was discharging the duties, as Deputy Consul, and I knew him to be thoroughly competent, I hoped he would be in no hurry to appoint a successor. He laughed at this, but did really make no appointment for six months I think, and then my successor reappointed my son Vice and Deputy Consul, and he remained with him until he was recalled to Virginia by the extreme illness of his mother and subsequently of myself. When he left Hong-Kong the Chinese Merchants presented him with a "Testimonial" which was really a work of art. It was several yards in length and about two in width of heavy scarlet satin, richly embroidered, with a long inscription in Chinese characters embroidered in gold, being a tribute to his honesty, ability and fidelity as an officer, and his virtues as a man, expressing their regret at his departure, and good wishes for his health, happiness and prosperity. Altogether it is a tribute of which any official would be proud, and he no doubt prizes it very highly.

I returned to Wytheville and as my tenant, Mr. Williams' lease would not expire until September, I rented and occupied "Loretta," the residence of Mr. A. A. Campbell, who proposed to attend the Law School of the University of Virginia.

Returning to Lynchburg, I made all arrangements for taking my family to Wytheville, which I did during the month. My boxes having by this time reached Richmond I had them shipped by rail to Wytheville, no duty being charged, as they were household goods mainly, and all had been in use for more than a year, which entitles them to free entry. I chartered a car to take my goods to Lynchburg and thence they were transported to Wytheville by the Norfolk & Western Railway. My wife and I left Lynchburg on the twelfth of June, and at Wytheville Mr. Logan met us and took us to his house, where we remained two days until Mr. Campbell moved out of "Loretta," when we at once took possession, and our scattered family soon reassembled at our new home.

Behold me again out of business, and with little prospect of securing anything which promised a support. I had no inclination to embark again in public life, though some of my friends urged that I should. But I was now nearing the three score and ten land mark, and felt an invincible repugnance to embark in another tour of office seeking, and looked forward to the time when I could resume possession of "Hedgefield," and take up again the life of a farmer. But it was not so to be. A Banking and Insurance Company had been organized at Wytheville some two or three years before, at the head of which was Mr. H. G. Wadley, who had recently settled in Wytheville. He was reputed a man of wealth, and had married a grand daughter of Mr. Isaac Leftwich, also a capitalist and President of the "Farmers Bank of Southwest Virginia," who was a large stockholder in the new concern. Mr. Wadley was President and General Manager of the Insurance Company, which was said to be in a prosperous condition, and had declared an annual dividend of six per cent. on last years operations.

I received a communication from the Board of Directors of this company offering me the Presidency at a salary sufficient to support me, and I accepted this position, and at once entered upon the duties. I was surprised to find that so far from being in a prosperous condition it had actually lost money the previous year, and the dividend had not been earned. I concluded, however, to change the policy which had been pursued, and make an effort to recuperate its losses, and devoted my whole time thenceforward to this object, visiting the different Agents, appointing others, investigating losses, and adjusting claims. I declined to issue Policies on most of the applications from

Insurance Brokers as I found they only sent us extra risks, or those in which the moral risks would not justify insurance at any premium, and of course this necessarily involved a curtailment of receipts, but I felt sure the losses would diminish in more than a corresponding ratio.

At the expiration of six months the Annual Meeting of stockholders came on, and my report showed the actual condition of the company, the losses were about the same as when I assumed control, but I felt that the course I had pursued would result in benefit to the Company. Mr. Wadley who owned a controlling interest in the stock, asked me if I thought the condition of the Company would justify the payment of a salary of $2,000.00 per annum. I told him I did not think it could afford to do so. I was then asked if I would act as President without a salary as Mr. Wadley had done. I declined to do that, as I was not willing to assume such a responsibility without remuneration. I only owned a few shares of the stock, while Mr. Wadley owned or controlled more than half. The upshot of the meeting, was that Mr. Wadley resumed the position as President, put in as Directors a number of non-residents, and ran the whole business himself, never consulting the Directors or having them meet. As soon as his policy was developed I went to him and sold out my stock at 75 per cent. of its par value, and considered myself fortunate in getting off with 25 per cent. loss. In a few years the company went into the hands of a Receiver, and most of the stockholders lost all of their investment.

Mr. Williams, my tenant at "Hedgefield" notified me a short time before the expiration of his option, that he would take the place at the price fixed by me, and thus I was again without a home.

I consulted my wife as to her wishes, telling her we "had the world before us where to choose," and I was willing for her to to decide where we should buy a home. After some reflection, she said, "Well, I don't know any place in the world offering greater inducements than here, except that I had rather be in town than in the country where it is so hard to get servants in the winter months."

I fully concurred in her views as I thought Wytheville as

desirable a place of residence as any of which I had any knowledge. There is good society, good schools, with Churches of all Denominations, and above all the most salubrious and delightful climate during the summer months that can be found anywhere. In addition the country around is most beautiful, picturesque, fertile and accessible. Several places were offered us as soon as it was known that "Hedgefield" was sold and after examination and consultation my wife selected the house owned and built by Mr. J. W. Caldwell, which I bought with five or six acres of land around it, with orchard and garden large enough to meet our wants. To this place we removed the last day of September, 1889. As most of my children were spending the summer with us at "Loretta" they helped in the removal of our household goods, and in family council fixed on "Ingleside" as the name by which it should be known. The house was large and commodious, and had been built only about fifteen years, and by repairing and building a kitchen will furnish ample accommodations for the children, grand children, great grand children and friends on their annual summer visitations.

In October, 1889 I attended the Triennial Conclave of the Knights Templars, which was held in Washington City. There was large attendance of members and visiting knights. Grand Master Roome of New York was present and presided, but his health was manifestly failing, and he survived the meeting only a few months. The procession and review was a magnificent spectacle. By actual enumeration twenty-three thousand Sir Knights passed the Reviewing Stand, and the Banquet and receptions were crowded. Our business was harmoniously and promptly dispatched, and it was generally conceded that few more delightful reunions had been held. Denver, Colorado was selected as the next place of meeting, and General Gobin of Pennsylvania, was elected Grand Master, and other officers advanced one grade with little opposition to any.

Late in the fall I was called to Newbern, North Carolina, to examine into a claim for loss by fire, and met on the train General Robert Ransom, who was a resident of that city. He was a brother to General Mat Ransom with whom I had served six years in the Senate. He invited me to his house to stay during my sojourn, an invitation which I declined, but dined with him and his young wife the next day. She was a young, attractive and handsome woman, and in addition quite agreeable. She gave us an excellent and enjoyable dinner, handsomely served. I had the good fortune to meet here in the person of the wife of our lawyer's, a daughter of an old Danville friend, Tom Doe, and also a daughter of Colonel Buford, who was former President of the Richmond & Danville Railroad, and had been Sergeant Major of my Regiment during the War. These old acquaintances contributed greatly to my enjoyment during my stay in Newbern. I finally settled my case by a compromise, as I was satisfied our agent who issued the policy would go back on us in his testimony if the case went to trial. I was taken sick as I was returning home, and though I thought the affair a trivial one, found to my sorrow that it was but the beginning of a long and dangerous illness.

In the Gubernatorial election of that year Mr. Philip McKinney, of Farmville, who was the Democratic candidate beat General Mahone the Republican Nominee upwards of 20,000 votes, which pretty effectually crushed the General's political aspirations, though he continued to boss his party in Virginia as long as he lived.

Major Hoge Tyler, of Pulaski, was elected Lieutenant Governor, and Scott of Fauquier, Attorney General, all of whom served faithfully and acceptably until the expiration of their respective terms. The year 1890 will long be remembered as the "Boom Year."

It had its beginning a year or two previous when the Norfolk & Western Railway constructed the Shenandoah Valley Road, and located the Shops and Offices of the Company at a point in the County of Roanoke, then known as "Big Lick Station." The place was incorporated as a city under the name of Roanoke, and the rush of purchasers for lots and building sites began. Speculators vied with bona fide investors, and soon the madness for speculation became a craze. Lots changed hands several times a day at constantly increasing prices, until they reached values comparable only to those on the main thoroughfares of large cities. Salem, a small town eight miles from Roanoke and the County Seat, soon felt the influence, and their town lots were thrown on the market and speedily found sale at enhanced prices. Some of the oldest citizens of that town recalled a time in the history of the place, when in the earlier part of the century, a similar craze had broken out, at the time the Roanoke and Staunton River was made navigable for batteaux as high as Salem, where being the terminus of the works of the "Roanoke Navigation Company," it was confidently predicted that the place would speedily attain the proportions of a city, and its real estate rapidly appreciated in value. In a few short years the bubble burst and property resumed its normal value. Untaught by this experience, however, people again rushed into speculation, and lots were sold and purchased all over and outside the State.

From this commencement the craze rapidly invaded every railway station from Roanoke to Bristol. Wytheville not to be out done entered the arena, and under the name of the "Wytheville Improvement Company," a Joint Stock Company was formed, which soon held options on all the land around the little town, and on many of its houses and lots at prices far in advance of their actual values. These lands were surveyed, streets located, lots laid out, many of which were sold at public auction by the "Promoters" at prices which would have proved highly remunerative had the deferred payments ever been made. But in a large majority of instances when the twelve months given on the deferred payments expired, no money was forthcoming on the bonds executed, and the promoting companies were obliged to purchase back the lots at nominal prices.

Connected with the speculations in real estate, many joint stock companies were formed for various manufacturing enterprises. An Ice Factory, a Woolen Mill, a Plaining Mill, and Wood Working Plant, a Mammouth Stove Factory, a Foundry, and various other projects were put under way. In no single instance did they prove successful ventures. Most of them were wrecked on the same rock, viz., the payment to the General Manager of salaries much more liberal than the amount of capital or business transacted would justify. This and the sale of bonds to raise the money necessary to meet operating expenses swamped them all. I was a small stockholder in most of these companies and of course suffered the total loss of the money invested. But 'tis useless to dwell longer on the "Boom" and its consequences, which were most disastrous not only in respect to the heavy pecuniary loss inflicted on individuals, but from the demoralization necessarily resulting from the wild craze for speculation pervading all classes of the community, and the disreputable shifts to which many resorted to avoid meeting the financial obligations they had incurred, and more than all in the impairment and unsettling of values, from which the country has not yet recovered. Not only were the "Boom" prices annihilated, but the value of real estate (in Wytheville, at least,) is not much over half what it was before the craze began.

CHAPTER LIII.

RELEGATED TO PRIVATE LIFE.

My life for the next few years passed without any incident of moment. I lived quietly at home taking little part in political or other public matters, attended the Annual Councils of the Diocese of Southern Virginia, in the organization of which I took an active part, being one of the Committee appointed for that purpose, and also for preparing and reporting the Constitution and Canon Laws of the new Diocese. I also attended the sessions of the Triennial General Convention of the Church which met in Baltimore in 1892, and in Minneapolis in 1895. At this meeting, being the first ever held in the Northwest, contrary to the predictions of many there was a large attendance of both clerical and lay deputies, and I have never seen a more harmonious gathering. I was obliged to leave before the close of the Convention in consequence of a severe cold caused by a sudden change of temperature. Among the lay deputies to this Convention was my old friend Ex-United States Senator George E. Edmunds, of Vermont.

The year 1894, witnessed the close of the life of General Jubal A. Early of the C. S. Army. He was in some respects one of the most remarkable of that group of distinguished soldiers who shed such lustre on the Confederate cause. He was a native of Franklin County, Virginia, a graduate of West Point Military Academy, and served as Major in the War with Mexico. He afterwards practiced law with profit and distinction in the Courts of the Commonwealth. He was a member of the Convention of 1860-61, and noted for his intense hostility to Secession. He was recognized as one of the ablest and most determined opponents of that measure, and his views were shared by a decided majority of the members of that body. Lincoln's call for 75,000 troops to aid in crushing the Rebellion, as if by magic changed the whole complexion of the Convention, and in no less degree of the State of Virginia.

This was shown by the prompt passage of the Ordinance of Secession on the seventeenth of April, 1861. General Early's signature with that of many other Union members of the Convention, was appended to the Ordinance, and as soon as the Convention adjourned he addressed himself to the task of raising troops for the defense of the State. He was made Colonel of the 24th Virginia Regiment, and appeared with it at Manassas Junction in May. At the first battle of Manassas he contributed largely to the success of the movement, which turned back the advancing columns of the Union Army by outflanking them with his command, and pursued the retreating enemy by Sudley Mills to the crossing of Cub Run, on the Warrenton Pike. At the Battle of Williamsburg he commanded the Brigade, and led the charge of the 24th Virginia and the 5th North Carolina Regiments on the Artillery of Porter's Division, with a gallantry which elicited the highest encomiums from both armies. But I do not propose to enter on a narrative of his military career; I will content myself with citing the fact, that after the death of General Jackson, General Lee selected General Early to command the army of Shenandoah Valley, where, with a force never exceeding 20,000 men he threatened the approaches to Washington so persistently and boldly, as to require a force double and treble his own, to keep him in check, and until the very last, he retained his hold on this fertile and important section of the Confederacy.

After the War closed he devoted his time mainly to the defense of the Confederate cause, and constituted himself Censor of the Press, and whoever ventured into print with a statement of any transaction of the War, unless it were absolutely and entirely in accordance with the facts, as he understood them, might count surely on being held to account by "Old Jube." He was of the "unreconstructed" to the day of his death. He never took the oath of allegiance to the United States Government, nor ever ceased to censure those quondam Confederates who, to use his own phrase "deserted after the war."

Associated with General Beauregard, he was employed by the managers of the Louisiana Lottery Company, at a large salary, to supervise the drawings of their Lotteries, and this supervision was by everyone accepted as a perfect guarantee of the fairness with which the drawings were conducted, and doubtless contributed not a little to the pecuniary success of what, in latter days is generally regarded as an illegitimate method of raising money. The salary he received from this company enabled him to give aid and comfort to many impoverished and destitute soldiers, and no applicant with a good record of service faithfully rendered, was ever turned away with wants unsatisfied. He never married, and by his will left a considerable legacy to his relatives. He always wore a suit of Confederate gray, and being a chronic sufferer from lumbago, following severe attacks of rheumatism contracted during his service in Mexico, was never able to walk without stooping, and his bent form, gray clothing, piercing black eyes, and intellectual face made him a noted man in any company into which he was thrown. He had his weaknesses and foibles, it is true, but for strict veracity, unswerving honesty, undaunted courage, unflinching fidelity, and perfect sincerity, he had few equals. Peace to his ashes.

On the third of February, in 1896, an event occurred of no particular interest to the public it is true, but regarded as important by my family and friends. On that day the 50th anniversary of my marriage, was observed by the celebration of our "Golden Wedding." To add additional interest to the occasion, the marriage of my youngest daughter Virginia Secessia was fixed for the same date. The bridegroom was Mr. John Y. Terry, the third son of General William Terry, who claimed to be the last Commander of the Stonewall Brigade, with which he had served since its first organization. After graduating at the Virginia Military Institute, he had sought and obtained employment as Civil Engineer under General Rosser of Confederate Cavalry fame, then engaged in the construction of the Northern Pacific Railroad. He and Sece had been fond of each other as children, but after he secured employment on the Northern Pacific Railway, he appeared no more in Wytheville for fourteen years. He then returned for a short visit to his mother and family, and was warmly welcomed by the whole community. To my surprise the fire of the old flame was rekindled, and a marriage was speedily agreed on between him and Sece. Hurried preparations were made for its celebration on our wedding anniversary, for which elaborate arrangements had been in progress by the children and grandchildren, who had collected from widely separated homes, pretty well filling our roomy residence. One of the parlors was decorated with yellow chrysanthemums and golden hangings, the other with white. A large "Marriage Bell" was suspended from the center of each ceiling, one covered with yellow flowers, the other with white. Sece was married at church at 6 p. m., and all the family and friends were present, the church having been beautifully decorated for the occasion. Rev. Dr. Logan performed the ceremony, and soon after its conclusion the company returned to "Ingleside," where a reception was held, preceded by a short "Thanksgiving Service" conducted by Dr. Logan, during which a series of complimentary Resolutions passed by the Vestry and Wardens of the Parish, were presented to me by the Rector. I briefly responded to the unexpected compliment, and then read a copy of verses of a reminiscent character, briefly sketching our matrimonial experiences for half a century. This was listened to with interest and amusement and all were taken by surprise, as not even my wife was privy to my purpose of reading it. We were the recipients of many handsome presents, and numerous congratulatory letters and telegrams from friends unable to attend in person. One of the most beautiful and highly prized came from the Venerable Bishop Whittle of the Virginia Diocese, a gentleman of intimate friendship and association in the Councils of the Church as well as in social life.

True we had not always been in accord, in our views of Church Polity, but each gave to the other full credit for sincerity and an earnest desire to promote the best interest of our mother Church, and our pleasant personal relations remained unimpaired until his death in 1901.

As the train in which the newly married couple proposed to start on their long journey to their future home in Seattle, was scheduled to leave soon after 9 p. m., they were rather hurried to meet it, but got off in time, and the company left behind had a merry time, until a late or rather early hour on the fourth of February.

The Diocese of Virginia was divided in 1891, by separating the Counties lying south of James River, adding to them the Peninsula and the Eastern Shore, which constituted the "Diocese of Southern Virginia." Bishop Whittle having elected to remain Bishop of Virginia, his Assistant Bishop, A. M. Randolph became Bishop of the new Diocese, which embraced a much larger area, and more Parishes than the old. There were, however, in the Southwestern portion of the territory many counties where there were not only no organized Parishes or churches but no single Communicant of the Episcopal Church, so far as was known. At the time it was hoped and designed that as the Church increased in strength and extended its area, a further division would be made. The large section extending from Lynchburg to the Tennessee line, was generally known as Southwest Virginia, and it was hoped that the Episcopal Church would find in this territory soil adapted to its growth. Being rich in minerals, it was attracting the attention of wealthy capitalists of the North, who were organizing Coal & Iron companies, all through this area, and emigrants were flocking to it from all quarters. Many of these were communicants of the Church, and of course anxious to secure for themselves and families the privilege of attending on its ministrations. Pioneer Missionary Churches and Chapels were built, and the committee on Diocesan Missions labored zealously to secure for them a firm footing in the new territory.

The first Diocesan Council ever held in Virginia, west of Lynchburg, met in the little town of Wytheville in June, 1896. It was an occasion of great interest to the friends of the Church throughout the Diocese; and especially so to the Rector and Communicants of St. John's Church, Wytheville.

This was the first Episcopal Church organized west of the Blue Ridge. Its first Rector, was the Rev. Mr. Goodwin, who was a native of New England, and married Miss Archer, of Richmond. They came to Wytheville in 1857, and for nearly twenty years he had charge of that Church and Parish. He may truly be called the Father of the Church, in Southwest Virginia. Two of his sons, and a grand-son of the name are now successfully filling their places as Rectors of Churches, two in Richmond and one in the old City of Williamsburg; and three other grandsons are also Episcopal Ministers. Rev. Mercer P. Logan, D. D., was in 1896, Rector of St. John's to which place he was called in 1882. He has proved most efficient and acceptable in the discharge of his duties, and the Church has grown and prospered under his ministration. But as the time drew near for the Council to meet, some apprehension was felt lest the Church might not be able comfortably to accommodate the members of the Council. The anxiety was needless, however, for though the attendance of both clerical and lay delegates was larger than usual, the Committee of Arrangements had no difficulty in finding nice quarters for all, as the citizens of all denominations proffered aid in the work, and demonstrated the hospitality and good feeling of the people of that lovely little town. The Bishop and many others of both orders found homes at "Ingleside," and we entertained from twenty to thirty at every meal. The weather was cool even for Wytheville, and expressions of surprise at the low temperature of the place were frequently heard from the delegates from Tide Water, who found overcoats indispensable to their comfort. All the visitors were loud in their laudations of the place and people, and I have never known a more enjoyable meeting of the Council than was held in Wytheville.

In September, 1898, the General Convention of the Church met in triennial session in Washington, D. C., and in October of the same year, the Triennial Conclave of the Grand Encampment of Knights Templars of the United States, met in Pittsburg, Pennsylvania. My wife and I concluded to attend the meetings of each of these National organizations. I accordingly secured rooms at the Ebbitt House in Washington, and as most of the clerical and lay Deputies from our Diocese were also quartered at the same place accompanied by their wives, we had a charming circle of friends. Mrs. Beverly Tucker, and Mrs. W. W. Old, of Norfolk, and Mrs. Charles Blackford, of Lynchburg, were all old acquaintances of my wife, and they had what ladies characterize as a "good time" during their stay in Washington, of two weeks or more. President McKinley tendered a Reception at the White House to the members of the General Convention, and their families, and the ladies of our party decided to attend. I protested, and argued with them to show how exceedingly trying and uncomfortable they would find it, as the crowd would be great, and the labor of passing through the rooms exhaustive to persons much younger and more vigorous than they, adding by way of a clincher, that during my whole term in the Senate, I had never attended a Reception at the White House. Quick as a flash came the retort, "then you can not know anything about it, and we will risk it all." This of course ended the discussion, and when the hour arrived the whole party set out for the President's Mansion. My grandson, Edwin Carter, was at the time a student at the Theological Seminary, and I took the precaution, as he was young and active, to wire for him to come over and accompany us.

An immense crowd was assembled, which filled the halls and anterooms, and the procession moved at a snail's pace through the apartments to the Reception Room. It took us an hour and a half to make our way through the room next to where the reception was held. We soon found it necessary to place the ladies together and form a cordon of gentlemen around them to protect them from the pressure of the surging crowd. As Rev. Dr. Tucker was quite a stout gentleman, I was myself no chicken, while Captain Blackford, and Mr. Old and Edwin Carter were all pretty robust, we managed to safeguard our charges until we reached "the Presence." As we passed on towards the door of entrance, we were separated from Mr. and Mrs. McKinley only by the wall of the room in which, however, was a open window which gave us a full view of the President and his wife. Mrs. Withers having studied her face a moment said, "That's a good woman, and I would be glad to know her, and I mean to have some talk with her anyway." "That," said I, "You can not do, for you will have no time to talk." When we were finally introduced by the Master of Ceremonies, my wife preceded me, and after shaking hands with Mrs. McKinley, sure enough commenced a conversation, which was kept up until the President said, "My dear, Colonel Withers is waiting to speak to you." This of course ended the talk, but brief though it was, it confirmed my wife's first impressions, and she declared her purpose of calling on her, if she could possibly find the opportunity. This opportunity did not offer itself, much to her regret, as we left Washington a few days later, but there is no doubt her intuitions were correct as regards Mrs. McKinley; indeed she rarely failed to interpret correctly the character of all strangers she met, a faculty more frequently found among women than men, according to the tenor of my observations.

After leaving the Reception Room we passed into a Withdrawing Room, where refreshments were served, and here we had a somewhat novel experience. Having procured a chair for my wife, who confessed by this time to a feeling of fatigue, I sat by her, but soon observed the entrance of a lady very handsomely dressed, with very black hair and rather dark complexion, whom we both recognized at once as a Japanese. As chairs were now generally occupied, this lady was standing near us, and I offered her my chair, which she hesitatingly accepted.

It was not long before I heard a conversation going on with some animation between Mrs. Withers and the Japanese lady, who spoke and understood English. It turned out that she had been sent by the Empress of Japan as her representative to a Convention of Women interested in matters connected with the education of females, and she was an intimate friend, and I believe a relative of Count Minami, the Japanese Consul at Hong-Kong during our sojourn in that City, who lived almost immediately opposite our Consulate, and with whom we were quite intimate. The discovery of this fact, of course furnished them a fruitful subject for conversation.

CHAPTER LIV.

VISIT TO PITTSBURG.

My son Robert, had for some years been living with his family in Pittsburg or its vicinity, and was now a resident of New Kensington, a suburban village in the neighborhood of that prosperous City, where the works of the Pittsburg Reduction Company are located, in which he held a responsible position. As the Grand Encampment of Knights Templars was to be held in Pittsburg, my wife and I prepared to pay a visit to our son Robert, when I could also attend the Triennial Conclave of the Templars.

We reached our destination in safety after a rather fatiguing journey, and were met at the station by Mr. M. J. Alexander, a native of Pulaski County, Virginia, and a distant relative. He has prospered and is now a wealthy citizen of Pittsburg, connected with the Plate Glass and other manufacturing enterprises of that city. He took us to his handsome residence on Lilac Avenue, where we were warmly welcomed by his wife and daughter. We remained here during the session of the Conclave, and Robert and his wife came the morning after our arrival and spent the day with us. Mr. Alexander entertained us with much hospitality during the time the Grand Encampment was in session. I met of course many old friends and acquaintances at the Grand Encampment. Grand Master LaRue Thomas, was at this time presiding, and P. G. M. General Gobin, of Pennsylvania and Judge McCurdy, of Michigan also a Past Grand Master, were present at this meeting, as was also P. G. M. J. H. Hopkins, formerly a Pittsburg man. At the election of officers my esteemed friend Reuben H. Lloyd, of San Francisco was elevated to the highest place in the Order, to my great gratification, as he had much endeared himself to me by his unwearied attentions during my long journey from San Francisco to St. Louis, in 1886, while I was so extremely ill that I hardly expected to live. After the Grand Encampment was closed we went to New Kensington, and spent some time with my son Robert and his family. He had taken my grandson, Royal Reed, a year or two before to New Kensington, and he was now running an Electric Crane for the White Lead Company, and making his own living. Subsequently he entered the Westinghouse Company and served a regular apprenticeship in Mechanical and Electrical Engineering and is now erecting a large Electric Plant on the Sierra Nevada Mountains in California. I was much interested in the operations of the Pittsburg Reduction Company. They were at that time operating at New Kensington, but now have several additional plants, located at other points. They really have a monoply of the production and manufacture of that curious metal Aluminum. I had often seen specimens of Aluminum, and knew that it was extracted from clay, but was not aware that a mineral known as Beauxite (Bo-site), was the source of nearly all the Aluminum of commerce. The preparation of this ore, if it may be so called, and the extraction of the metallic base, was at the time of which I speak, carried on at the New Kensington Works, but this part of the business has since been transferred to Niagara Falls, as the Electric Power generated by the Falls, furnishes a cheaper and more expeditious method of reduction than steam. Various domestic and culinary vessels made of Aluminum are now coming into general use, as the lightness, cleanliness, and strength of these utensils will insure their introduction and use in the kitchens of the country. It is now also rapidly superseding copper wire as an electrical conductor—being almost but not quite equal to it in conductivity, and being so much lighter is esteemed a great advantage. The obstacle to the extended use of this metal for domestic utensils and household articles is, that no process of soldering has yet been discovered, whereby broken, injured, or worn out pieces can be repaired or again made useful. Much time and money has been expended by the Company in the effort to devise some scheme by which this difficulty may be obviated, but so far without success. After a pleasant sojourn of nearly four weeks we returned to Wytheville.

Our winter was enlivened by a visit from our youngest daughter Sece, who with a little girl baby of six weeks, reached home about the last of November. Her husband finding it necessary to visit Minneapolis on business, told her if she could manage to get ready she could accompany him to Minneapolis, and thence go to Wytheville if she was willing to travel alone. She jumped at the chance, as it had been nearly four years since she left home, and she was crazy to see her mother. She made the trip without difficulty, and when one afternoon about 4 o'clock a telegram came asking me to send to the station that evening to meet her, you may imagine what a commotion it caused. We had no intimation of the contemplated visit, and were taken by surprise. Her mother laughed till she cried, and then cried till she laughed. The telephone was kept constantly going. A stove was put in her room, and a fire made as quickly as possible, a cradle for the baby was prepared and put in place, curtains and carpet arranged, and when the carriage brought her at 8 o'clock everything was prepared and joy reigned supreme at "Ingleside." She did not leave us until the following May, by which time the little Virginia had greatly grown, and endeared herself to us all, as she was very pretty and bright, and possessed of many winning ways. Very little more than a year passed and when her beauty, intelligence and attractiveness had rapidly developed, she died in her mother's arms almost without warning. She had never been really sick in her life, but for some slight indisposition the doctor who saw her administered some simple remedy, and assured her mother there was nothing serious the matter with her. She asked her mother soon after, to sing her a song which she liked, and before it was concluded she passed away without a struggle. "Heart failure" was the explanation of the doctor, which had as well been explained by diagnosing "breath failure."

The year 1900, passed with little in my life which would interest the public. Some of the stock companies formed during the boom days wound up their business, others were wound up by their creditors. One or two new ones were organized with the purpose of saving something out of the wreck of the old companies, by purchasing their property and assets when brought to the hammer. On the whole the result was rather beneficial. I had been offered in 1896, and accepted the office of Examiner of Records for the 15th Judicial Circuit, and each spring saw me busy for three months or more in the discharge of the duties of the office. My oldest daughter Mrs. E. L. Carter was anxious that her mother and I should spend the winter in Evansville, where her youngest son, Rev. Edwin R. Carter was Rector of the Church of Holy Innocents, with a large and comfortable Rectory attached, and as my daughter, Mrs. Josephine Read was anxious to pay a visit to her son Royall and her brother Robert E. Withers, Jr., in or near Pittsburg, Mrs. Withers concluded to go to Evansville, Indiana for the winter, Willie proposing to spend the winter in Richmond, in attendance on the Art School, as was her custom. We left Wytheville on the morning of the ninth of November, weather cold, and ground covered with snow. We reached Evansville the afternoon of the next day, and were heartily welcomed by Lizzie and her children. For the first time in my life I was about to cast my lot with those who were domiciled north of Mason and Dixon's line, and separated only by the width of the Ohio River from Southern soil. I was prepared to expect radical differences in the habits, appearance, modes of living, and social customs of the people. Nor in this was I disappointed. During my first month's residence I was four times accosted on the street by persons I had never seen before to my knowledge, with this inquiry, "Mr. you don't belong in this town do you?" or, "Stranger, what place might you hail from, I know you don't belong here." A polite response on my part to the query confirming their impression was always accepted with an air of gratified pride, as evidence of their shrewdness and the acuteness of their faculty of observation. The last interview of the kind was with the keeper of a Saloon at the corner near where I was living. I had observed him several times watching me closely from his door as I was passing, until at length his curiosity got the better of him, and he asked, "Mr. why do you walk with such a long cane?" alluding to a handsome staff which for some years had been my constant companion. "Because," said I "sometimes it is hard for me to walk at all because of a bad wound, and then a long staff furnishes me more help than a short cane." "Then you were in the war," said he. "Yes from the first to the last," said I. "Were you wounded more than once?" "Yes five times," said I. "Gracious," said he, "I guess you get a good Pension, don't you?" "Not a cent," said I. He appeared greatly surprised, and said, "I was in the war for a while and got a wound too, but not a very bad one, but I get a Pension, and all the men about here, who were in the army get Pensions, and I don't know why you don't. May be though, you are rich and don't need it." "No," said I, "I am not rich but poor." "Then I can't understand it," said he. "Did you never apply for a pension." "No," said I, "never." "But why don't you?" "Because it would be useless," said I. "I fought on the Rebel side." His countenance changed and he relieved his feelings by a prolonged "O——h."

My attention was attracted soon after reaching the City by a notice of a meeting of the Medical Association, which all members of the profession were invited to attend, as lectures were to be delivered on several important subjects by distinguished members of the Faculties of noted schools in Chicago, St. Louis, Indianapolis, and other places. Though long withdrawn from the practice of medicine I still felt an interest in the profession, and believing that the meetings would prove a source of pleasure, determined to attend. On the evening of the meeting, I walked down to the Hall, and found the Secretary in place recording the names of those in attendance, and in my turn reported Dr. R. E. Withers, Virginia. After entering the name, the Secretary struck, no doubt, by my rather venerable appearance, asked how long since I graduated. I answered, in 1841, just sixty years before. He introduced me at once to several by-standers, and as I retained my position near his table, continued at intervals to make me known to others as they presented themselves for registration. Observing the approach of a middle aged gentleman, plainly dressed and possessing all the ear marks of a country doctor, I mentally catalogued him as such. After registering, he was introduced to me as Dr. Rucker, and he began at once to relate the particulars of an accident of which he had been the victim a few days before, resulting in a dislocated shoulder, from the effects of which he still suffered. He next inquired what part of Virginia I hailed from, and I responded, Wytheville in the southwestern part of the State. Said he, "I am a Virginian also, but have been out here several years." "Ah," said I, "From what section of the State?" "From near Lynchburg," was the reply. "Why, I was born in Campbell County and married in Lynchburg," said I. "You must be related to George and Ambrose Rucker, both of whom as merchants of that city, I knew well." "Yes," said he, "I am." And then his face lighted up and he said with animation, "Why Doctor, you are Colonel R. E. Withers, who was United States Senator, are you not?" I had to acknowledge my identity, and he gave me another very cordial hand grasp, with the declaration, "I rather see you than any man in the world, and have long desired to do so." Of course my *incognito* could no longer be preserved, but I none the less enjoyed the meeting before which several very interesting and able papers were read, and discussed in a manner attesting not only the great interest in the scientific subjects reviewed, but demonstrating the fact that the medical men of that City and State were fully abreast with the rapid advances made in their profession during the last few years. My personal acquaintance in the city was rapidly extended, and I was honored by many calls from prominent citizens. Among these were Colonel Charles Denby and his wife. He had for many years ably represented his country as Minister to China, and had only recently been recalled, much to the regret of the Chinese Government. He had visited my house on more than one occasion while I held the place of Consul at Hong-Kong, and was always a welcome and entertaining guest.

In January, I was surprised by the receipt of a letter from a Committee of the Chapter of the "Daughters of the Confederacy," inviting me to attend a meeting of their Chapter, on the nineteenth of that month, to do honor to the birthday of General R. E. Lee, by appropriate exercises. On inquiry, I learned that there was quite a flourishing organization of the "Daughters" in the City, numbering between thirty and forty members, of whom were my daughter, Mrs. Carter and her daughter Alice. Of course, I could not decline their invitation, and on the evening named attended the gathering held in the parlors of one of the prominent ladies of the city. The rooms were quite filled with ladies, comparatively few gentlemen being in attendance. Of course I had to give them a "talk," for it could not be called an address, consisting mainly of reminiscences of our late Chieftain, and unpublished anecdotes illustrative of his high character and patriotic principles. These were received with more demonstrations of approval than their merit deserved, and were followed by readings, recitations, music, and Confederate Camp Fire and other songs, and all culminating in a delicious Banquet, which embraced all the delicacies of the season. I have been present at the meetings of many of the Chapters of this organization, but never at one in which more devotion to the "Lost Cause," was shown, or more endearing memories of those who "wore the gray," and sacrificed their lives on the altar of Constitutional Liberty. Of course the membership was confined mainly to the natives of Kentucky, Virginia, and other States of the late Confederacy, then living in Evansville. Speaking of anecdotes and incidents in the life of General Lee characteristic of the man, I make no apology for introducing one which has recently come to my knowledge, and which has never appeared in print. It will serve to illustrate the deep interest in the comfort and welfare of the private soldier, for which he was so noted. This incident I learned from Major Stephen Putney, a Quartermaster of General Lee's Army, who was personally cognizant of every detail given.

The Major had up to the commencement of hostilities been constantly engaged in the shoe trade, and from the expert knowledge thus acquired, was selected to organize and conduct a Factory for making and supplying shoes to the Army. This was located in Richmond, and quite a number of skilled workmen were detailed from the army and assigned to duty in this Factory. In addition to these, on his recommendation, he was authorized to employ several hundred Yankee prisoners skilled in the work, who were not only willing but anxious to be thus employed, as they not only thus escaped the confinement of the prison, but secured better and more abundant food, and it should be noted that they proved competent and efficient workmen. General Lee took great interest in this shop, and not unfrequently consulted with Major Putney as to the best means of increasing the product and improving the quality of the shoes. He was in the habit, when opportunity offered, of visiting the Factory in person, and on the occasion described had during a visit to Richmond called and expressed his gratification at the excellent quality of the shoes then made, as well as the increased output. Major Putney had just received from England through the Blockade Runners, a supply of the finest calf skins, sole leather, and other material for making fine boots, and observing that the General's foot gear appeared worn, suggested that he have his measure taken for a pair of fine boots. Admitting his need, the General consented, and Major Putney called a man named McCrosky, detailed from a Mississippi Regiment, and the best boot maker in the shop, and directed him to attend to it. McCrosky feeling highly honored by the Commission, carefully took the necessary measures, and promised the best job of his life. When General Lee turned to leave the room every workman spontaneously rose and gave him three rousing cheers, in which Yankees and Confederates alike participated. This unexpected outburst seemed to move General Lee very much, as he bowed his acknowledgments, but turning to Major Putney, he asked, "Major! What is the man who took my measure now doing?" "Making shoes for the Army," was the reply. *"Then let him keep at it,* for if making those boots for me will cause a single soldier to go barefooted an hour longer, I don't wish them made. Let the whole thing drop. Shoes for the men are of more importance then boots for me."

CHAPTER LV.

FIFTY-FIFTH WEDDING ANNIVERSARY.

On the third of February, 1901, we celebrated the 55th Anniversary of our marriage by partaking of an excellent family dinner, no invitations to outsiders having been sent out. We received with pleasure the congratulations and good wishes of children, grand-children, and great grand-children, and entered on the 56th year of our married life with every prospect of continued health and happiness. But alas! These proved fallacious, for within a short time my wife, sprained her ankle by falling down a few steps of stairway, and to lessen the pain and swelling bathed the joint for some time in cold water. This caused her to take cold, which subsequently developed into bronchitis, and though she had the constant attendance of some of the most prominent and skilful physicians of the City, she steadily grew worse until the end came on the second day of March. It would be useless for me to attempt to describe my feelings at this crushing blow, and I shall make no effort to do so. For more than half a century she had held the first place in my thoughts, my esteem, and my affection. She was literally the maker of my home and few men have had a more pleasant one. On her devolved not only the ordinary obligations of domestic life, but the far more important and responsible duties of rearing, training, and leading her children in the paths of virtue, morality and religion, and faithfully and efficiently did she discharge them. She was to me a "help meet" in all my trials, a safe counsellor in all difficulties, a loving solace in all sorrows. Her disposition was bright and cheerful. Always optimistic she never yielded to despondency, but however dark the horizon, could discover the rift in the cloud through which the sun would soon brightly shine. She enjoyed life as much as anyone I ever knew. In proof of this, I now recall with much gratification, an incident which occurred not more than a month before her fatal illness. The company were discussing that much debated question, whether if permitted again to pass through this earthly pilgrimage, they would pursue the same course, or make radical changes in their conduct; and she with much earnestness said, "Well! If I could live my life over again I do not know that I would wish it materially different from what it has been." It was some time before I rallied before the stunning, crushing, weight of this great calamity, which was mitigated, however, by the tender love and affection of my children, and the many friends with whom I have been blessed through a long life.

We bore her remains to her home in Wytheville, and laid it by the side of "Little Mary," her youngest child, nearly all her children being present, and a large concourse of her friends and neighbors. My widowed daughter, Josey Read and Willie, my only unmarried daughter and myself now constituted the family at "Ingleside," but with the returning summer the house was as usual filled with children, grand-children, friends and visitors. Willie took charge of the housekeeping after the first of June, soon after which time every room in the house was filled. I had at first concluded to resign the place of Examiner of Records for the 15th Circuit, but subsequently reconsidered the matter, as I believed the discharge of the duties incident to the position would give me something to think about besides my own trouble, and was very glad of the enforced diversion of my mind to other matters. There is nothing like employment to cause forgetfulness of self.

The Triennnial Conclave of the Grand Encampment of Knights Templars, was held in the city of Louisville, Kentucky in August, 1901, and although I had not intended going, yet as the time approached, and I found that several Sir Knights from my town proposed attending, and urged me to accompany them, as the distance not being great I changed my mind, and agreed to make one of the company. I was the more inclined to do this as I desired to witness the closing hours of the administration of my friend, Grand Master Reuben H. Lloyd, who had proved himself the best administrative officer in my judgment, of all who had held that high position. I also desired to aid in the election to the Grand Mastership, of Deputy Grand Master Henry B. Stoddard, of Texas, as he was a Southern Templar and well worthy the distinction.

As I had not engaged quarters in advance I felt some apprehension lest I might have trouble, as I heard all the rooms at the Galt House, which was selected as Headquarters for the Grand Encampment Officers, had been long engaged, but on arrival I drove to that Hotel and was told there was no vacant room, as I had expected. Asking to be shown to the rooms of the Grand Master, I was received most cordially by that official, who when I stated my dilemma, at once sent for the Grand Recorder, whose official duty required that he provide accommodation for the officers of the Grand Body, and instructed him to see to it that I had a room at once. This order met with ready obedience, and I was soon shown to my quarters, and was able to take in two of my traveling companions, much to my gratification, as they had been very attentive to my comfort during our journey. I was warmly greeted by many old friends among the members of the order, and though the weather was uncomfortably hot, was able to attend all the sessions of the Grand Encampment, and to participate actively in the dispatch of business and the settlement of some important questions which had caused much controversy and discussion. The hospitality of the Templars of Louisville and indeed, of all the citizens of that noted Kentucky City, was unstinted and cordial, to a wonderful degree. After the close of the Conclave we returned to Wytheville without mishap, delighted with our experiences, and fully conscious that we "had a good time."

The Triennial session of the General Convention of the Episcopal Church came off in October, 1901, at San Francisco, and as I was among the Lay Deputies elected, after some consideration I determined to attend its sessions. My granddaughter, Josephine Putney, having just completed her education, was very anxious to accompany me on this trip, as she had been little from home, and desired to see as much as she could of the different sections of the country and its people. In addition to this my daughter Sece, was living in Seattle on the Pacific Coast, and with little additional expenditure of time or money it was in my power to pay her a visit en route. I therefore purchased tickets by way of Chicago, St. Paul, and thence by the Great Northern Railway to Seattle, by Northern Pacific to Portland, Oregon, and by Southern Pacific to San

Francisco, and return tickets by the same road to New Orleans and thence to Virginia. This line of travel afforded us the opportunity of seeing almost the whole line of the Pacific Coast from the Dominion of Canada to Mexico. I had never been over the line of the Great Northern Road, which at some points almost touches the Canadian line, being further north than any of the roads of the West, and hence made choice of that line. And here I think it my duty as well as pleasure, to place on record my high appreciation of the kindness of Mr. William Bevill, the General Passenger Agent of the Norfolk & Western Railway, to whose kind offices I am indebted for having arranged my tickets, including sleeping berths, for the whole route, both going and returning, thus insuring a most pleasant and satisfactory trip over about 8,000 miles of railway.

We started from Wytheville, on the afternoon of the nineteenth of September, and without accident or delay completed our journey to Seattle, in a little more than four days, said by our friends in that City, to be a shorter time than they had ever known such a trip made. John Terry and Sece met us at the train, and with great delight escorted us to their home on 30th Avenue.

The appointments of the Great Northern Railway I found first class in every respect, not only comfortable but luxurious, the officials uniformly polite and accommodating. The scenery, however, for the greater portion of the route is tame or rather monotonous. Through the immense elevated plains of Northern Dakota and Montana, there is little to attract attention. The agricultural interests seem centered almost wholly on the production of wheat, which was being threshed from the stack or shock over hundreds of miles. We noted several conflagrations of wheat or straw, or both, which had evidently been fired by sparks from the engines of the steam threshers at work. Indians in varied costumes, were to be seen at almost every station, a listless stolid looking people, appearing to take little interest in their surroundings, occasionally some of the squaws would offer articles for sale, but I saw none of artistic value. The Rocky Mountain range so prominent a feature on the other Trans Continental lines appears to have dwindled away to a few rather insignificant ranges, and it was only when we reached the magnificently bold profiles of the Cascade Range, that we could revel in the imposing grandeur of the incomparable mountain scenery.

Spokane, on the Columbia River, is quite a considerable City, though our opportunities of viewing it were limited. We reached the City about light, and only tarried about an hour to change engines and attend to other matters of railroad detail. The river here is quite a bold and very beautiful stream, the water clear as crystal, but filled for miles with immense rafts of saw logs, moored to the banks. We had some acquaintances here but the unseasonable hour of our arrival, and the limited time at our disposal combined to prevent us from seeing them. The course of the river here is a little west of north, and when we crossed it again about one hundred and twenty-five miles from Spokane, it was apparently little augmented in size. The greater portion of country lying between these crossings is altogether the most desolate and uninviting I have ever seen. The soil appears to be little more than a layer of scoriæ, producing a little seedy grass wherever a stream of water runs, with no forests or even bushes to give variety to the land-scape. The whole outline of the Cascade Range soon became visible in the west, looming up in indescribable grandeur. The higher peaks covered with snow, the lower ranges and foot hills clothed in magnificent garments of hemlock, firs, pine, spruce, and other evergreens, while Mount Rainier in the south, and Mount Baker in the north appeared to stand as sentinels guarding the approaches to the Great Pacific, the everlasting snows which covered their summits glittering in the sunlight, and forming a crown of glory on their crests, towering 16,000 feet above the level of the sea.

Josephine had proven herself an ideal traveling companion, always bright, cheerful, and good humored, companionable and affable to others, minimizing all troubles, and difficulties of the road, and prompt to save me all unnecessary exertion.

We spent about a week in Seattle, and I was much struck with the evidences of the energy and enterprize, which everywhere met my eyes. New streets being opened in every direction, new houses, public and private, in process of construction everywhere, many of them on a handsome scale. I saw no place on the Pacific Slope excelling Seattle in every evidence of prosperity and rapid growth. The climate was a riddle. Though a thousand miles further north than Wytheville its winters are much milder, with little snow or intense cold. There is much dampness, however, owing I presume to the warmth of the Japanese Black Water Stream, which in its characteristics resembles the Gulf Stream of the Atlantic. The lands around the City appear fertile, and the very rapid increase of its shipping shows that in a very short time she will in this regard excel San Francisco or any other Pacific Port. This is due to the fact that it is the nearest shipping point to the sea port towns of Japan and China, with which places the trade of the United States is rapidly increasing. The City is built on a strip of land between Puget Sound on the west and Lake Washington on the east. The last is a lovely body of fresh water, clear as crystal and almost as cold as ice water, of unfathomable depth, separated from the waters of the Sound by a strip of land less than two miles broad at the narrowest part, through which a ship canal was being cut whereby vessels can pass into the lake, where iron built ships can lie free from the injurious effects produced by sea water. There is one peculiarity connected with this body of water. It never gives up its dead. The bodies of persons drowned therein never rise to the surface, and consequently are never recovered. The explanation of this phenomenon is to be found in the fact that extreme depth of the water and its very low temperature preserve the bodies from those *post mortem* changes, which usually follow death, consequently they remain indefinitely unchanged in nature's "cold storage."

I met some old friends in Seattle, among them General Gilbert S. Meem and his wife, who formerly lived on the Mount Airy Farm, in Shenandoah County, Virginia, then owned by his father Mr. John G. Meem, of Lynchburg. In former days this was reckoned equal if not superior to any grazing farm in the state. General Meem was one of my groomsmen, and as I believe, the only one of the number living. He was very kind and took great pleasure in escorting me around every day to see places of interest. He was Postmaster of the City in

Mr. Cleveland's Administration, but at the time of my visit was out of office.

We left Seattle on the last day of September, en route for San Francisco, accompanied by some pleasant acquaintances we had formed, whose destination was the same, and barring the delays and inconveniences arising from crowded trains and overburdened roads, met with no accident or incident of special interest. We reached San Francisco the morning of the second of October, the day of the meeting of the General Convention, and drove at once to the "Occidental Hotel," where rooms for the delegation from the Diocese of Southern Virginia, had been engaged some time previously. The Hotel was so crowded that I could not secure a room for Josephine at all. We would have been in an awkward fix if our traveling companion, Mrs. Ford, of Covington, Kentucky, had not come to the rescue. Hearing of our dilemma, she offered to take Josephine in with her and her daughter, Miss Augusta, a favor which we highly appreciated.

When the Convention met I found our Diocese fully represented in both orders, and as we were all quartered in contiguous suites of rooms, we found it very pleasant. The Clerical Deputies were Dr. Lloyd, of Lynchburg, Dr. Tucker, of Norfolk, Dr. McBryde, of Lexington and Dr. Grammar, of Norfolk; the Lay Deputies were Mr. Old, of Norfolk, Mr. Zimmer, of Petersburg, Major Elder, of Staunton, and myself.

I shall not attempt to narrate the proceedings of this notable body of Churchmen, or discuss the many matters of interest which came up for action.

As a Virginian, my state pride was gratified by the selection of a Virginian as the presiding officer of each of the Houses of the General Convention. Right Rev. Thomas U. Dudley, of Kentucky, a native of Richmond, Virginia, being elected President of the House of Bishops, and Rev. John L. Lindsey, of Boston, also a Virginian, was elected on the first ballot President of the House of Clerical and Lay Deputies. What made this more remarkable was that each was a graduate of the Virginia Theological Seminary, at Alexandria. The question which elicited most debate, was a proposal to amend one of the Canons and declare it unlawful for any minister of the Church to unite in marriage any person who had been divorced, regardless of the cause, during the life of the other party. After a long and able debate, the proposed amendment was agreed to by the Clerical Deputies, by a small majority, but the lay vote was decidedly in the negative, thus affording to my mind, another proof of the conservative sentiment of the laymen of the Church.

The Convention was in session just two weeks. It was probably more largely attended than any ever before held, contrary to the prediction of those who thought the remoteness of the place of meeting, and the great cost involved, would materially diminish the number in attendance. The very low rates offered by the Trans-Continental Lines of railway caused many who were not delegates to make the journey, as they could thus gratify a long felt desire to visit San Francisco and the Pacific Coast. This was especially the case with people of the New England and Atlantic States, who were present by thousands. It was estimated, by conservative and well-informed enquirers that the visitors from the New England States alone numbered between three or four thousand. The immense concourse tested the hospitality of the City to the utmost, but it proved equal to the occasion.

As both Josephine and I had friends and relatives in the City, we had a pleasant time socially, and many excursions were made to objects and places of interest not only in the immediate neighborhood of the city, but to towns and places lying at a distance, to the Big Trees, the Yosemite, the Geysers, Los Angeles, Monterey, etc. All these excursions were largely patronized. Taken as a whole the universal verdict of all who were present at this Triennial Convention, was that the experiment had proved a "Great Success." We waited a day or two after the adjournment of the Convention to avoid the rush of the departing tourists, and then boarded the sleeper of the Southern Pacific Line for New Orleans. Mrs. Langhorne, an aunt of Josephine's by marriage, accompanied us as she wished to return to Richmond for the winter. Our journey was not marked by any occurrence of special interest. Some delays but no accidents occurred, and our time was passed very pleasantly as we met many agreeable persons among the passengers, and as the country through which we were passing was entirely new to the ladies of my party, they were interested in observing its peculiarities. At El Paso, on the Mexican border, where we were required to change Pullman sleepers, we were delayed an hour or more and were given opportunity to disprove the opinion of Tim Linkenwater of blessed memory, who declared that "London was the only place in the world for coincidences."

Just before the train started, a lady hurriedly entered the door of the sleeper and inquired with some evidence of anxiety for the Conductor of the Pullman. As he was not in the coach, and she was evidently alone, I invited her to take a seat in my section which was near the door, until the Conductor should make his appearance. She expressed great anxiety to see him, explaining that she had that moment arrived from Mexico, and had no sleeping berth engaged, but finally took her seat to await the appearance of the Conductor. Soon after Mrs. Langhorne called me by name, and this evidently aroused her interest, for she remarked, "I once knew a Colonel Withers from Virginia." From what part of Virginia?" I inquired. "From Danville," she said. "I lived some years in Danville," said I, "and am probably the man you knew." She answered, "I did not know him very well, but knew his daughters." Josephine asked, "Which of his daughters did you know?" "I remember one called Ellie very well," she said, "when I was a child." "She is my mother," said Josephine. This was of course an incident which caused amusing comment, and as the lady was herself in route for Richmond, she attached herself to our party the rest of the journey. Josephine was much interested in that portion of the route lying in Southern Texas and Louisiana, as she had never before seen distinctively Southern scenery. The level alluvial lands, the swamps, the trees draped in Spanish moss, the fields of rice and sugar cane, the last of which crops was then being gathered, pleased her greatly. The Oil industry of that section, was then being rapidly developed and hundreds of derricks, boring pumps, and engines, dotted the country on each side of the railway. We made but a short stay in New Orleans, only sufficient time to change cars for the Northwestern line, which brought us by Birmingham, Chattanooga, etc., to Wytheville, where we took the family by surprise, as they were not expecting us so soon. We had been absent about six weeks and in that time had traversed portions of twenty-three States, seen nearly the whole line of our Pacific Coast, from near the border of British Columbia to Mexico, making a tour of about 8,000 miles, without any mishap, accident, or serious inconvenience, and reached home in good health to find all the home folks similarly blessed. Truly we had abundant cause for thankfulness to the kind Providence which had so favored us.

And as this session of the General Convention of the Protestant Episcopal Church is in all probability, the last meeting of a representative body, in which I shall ever participate, it appears to me an appropriate time to bring to a close these rambling and discursive notes of a long and eventful life.

I have under God's Providence, been called to perform my part in varied lines of action, and can truly say, that in each and all I endeavored to do my duty as I saw it. Doubtless many mistakes have I made, many blunders committed, but these were errors of judgment and not wilful wrong doing.

From a financial standpoint my life has not been a success, for I have never accumulated much of this world's gear, nor have I ever striven so to do. Provided I could support my family in comfort, and give them an education appropriate to their sphere in life, I was content.

My race in this life is nearly run, my mission ended. Cheered and comforted by loving and affectionate children and grandchildren, enjoying the respect and esteem of valued friends, I patiently and cheerfully await that final summons, which can not in the course of nature be much longer delayed. Hoping that "He who doeth all things well," will, when it seemeth good, call me away to rejoin in that better land the loved ones who have gone before, I await.

THE END.

www.ingramcontent.com/pod-product-compliance
Lightning Source LLC
Chambersburg PA
CBHW060908300426
44112CB00011B/1383